COMBAT SERVICE SUPPORT GUIDE

1st edition

MAJ. JOHN E. EDWARDS,
U.S. ARMY

Stackpole Books

Published by
STACKPOLE BOOKS
Cameron and Kelker Streets
P.O. Box 1831
Harrisburg, PA 17105

Cover design by Tracy Patterson.

Printed in the United States of America

10 9 8 7 6 5 4 3 2

Library of Congress Cataloging-in-Publication Data

Edwards, John E.
Combat service support guide / John E. Edwards.
p. cm.
Includes index.
ISBN 0-8117-2227-9
1. United States. Army—Supplies and stores—Handbooks, manuals, etc. I. Title.
UC32.E38 1989
355.4'15'0973—dc19 88-39972
CIP

To Edwin A. Edwards
Chief Warrant Officer, W4
United States Army

Contents

Foreword

The Army officer's role in combat service support positions from company level up has always been a complex, demanding challenge to those officers who want to provide optimum support to their units and customers. This axiom has held for two world wars, Korea, Vietnam, and lesser conflicts. It holds for all combat service support trained and branched officers who meet the challenge, doubly so for those junior combat support or combat arms officers who suddenly discover that they are their unit's motor officer, supply officer, movements officer, or executive officer responsible for the whole ball of wax.

In today's leaner Army of Excellence faced with a shortage of basic branch combat service support officers, it is not uncommon for combat support and combat arms officers to find themselves in positions such as forward/main/direct support battalion support operations, logistics operations, materiel officers, and a multitude of supporting-character logistics roles. While virtually everything they are supposed to instantly and instinctively know and do is in some Army regulation, field manual, or technical manual, the variety and volume of this collection is staggering.

What has long been needed for organizational missions, as well as self-preservation, is a handy, pocket-sized, quick and general reference to help these fledgling combat service supporters and logisticians get started on the right track and maybe learn a few of the lessons the easy way.

Maj. John Edwards recognized this need and decided that the young officer being introduced to his or her first combat service support functional role should indeed have a pocket guide similar to the invaluable, updated edition of *Combat Leader's Field Guide* now being published by Stackpole Books for small combat unit leaders. John called on his excellent experience as a direct support maintenance company commander in USAREUR's V Corps and in assignments as maintenance management officer of the 5th Infantry Division Materiel Management Center, 5th Division Support Command S4, and Forward Support Battalion executive officer, with extensive experience at the National Training Center at Fort Irwin, California, to assemble, compile, and write this *Combat Service Support Guide.*

I believe this guide is on target. Reading it refreshed my memory about a lot of fundamentals and told me where to go to find the more sophisticated details. It would behoove all junior officers, whether they are combat arms, combat support arms, or combat service support arms, and whether they are active, reserve, or National Guard, to read this primer. It would probably be wise for many to keep a copy nearby for handy reference during command post or field exercises and other such stressful and often challenging times. More senior and experienced officers, regardless of branch or component, could benefit from a perusal and should consider it a valuable addition to their professional libraries.

William H. Foy
COL ORDC
U.S. Army (Ret.)

Preface

The purpose of this book is to aid professional combat service support officers and officers of all branches who find themselves thrust into combat service support roles in the field. It presents facts, figures, formulas, and formats to help logistics officers find the solutions they need to support modern armies in war and in peace.

Modern weaponry, communications, and technology have made the entire battlefield vulnerable to attack at any time. Therefore, combat service support soldiers are no longer merely in the rear with the gear. These same factors have also forced support units to become involved in multifunctional operations, requiring combat service support officers to become broad-based logisticians rather than specialized technicians.

Combat service support officers must be able to operate on the move in a tactical environment, to operate in all areas of logistic support simultaneously, and to be successful in supporting their combat units. Transporting all the references covering the ten classes of supply, the service functions, tactical operations, and administration would require several trucks. Obviously, this method would be not only impractical but also inefficient.

This book, therefore, organizes a myriad of related and unrelated items of information into a logical sequence and grouping to assist combat service support officers in providing effective support operations under tactical conditions. This volume will not save the dullard, nor will it give point-by-point instruction to the novice. It should, however, give the logistician a fighting chance for success on the modern battlefield.

Acknowledgments

Grateful thanks go to Col. (Ret.) Peter Cofoni, U.S. Army Quartermaster Corps; Col. John R. Rudd, U.S. Army Chemical Corps; and Lt. Col. David Talbert, U.S. Army Ordnance Corps, whose support and encouragement made this book possible. Thanks also go to Brig. Gen. (Ret.) Carlton P. Weidenthal, U.S. Army; and Col. (Ret.) James R. Poole, U.S. Army Ordnance Corps, for reviewing the manuscript.

The encouragement of my wife and family in this project requires special recognition. Someone once said that God saved a special place in heaven for an Army wife, but God probably also has some exclusive consideration for Army brats, as well.

1

Combat Service Support Concepts

Providing combat service support to modern armies is a complex art and skill and requires relentless effort, professional dedication, and efficient application of logistic expertise. Arming, fueling, fixing, feeding, and clothing combat forces on the battlefield present an increasingly significant challenge. The mission of supporting and sustaining the combat power of an army is an essential element of success on the battlefield. This has always been true, but the combat service support mission is becoming even more critical as the sophistication and integration of high technology weapons systems and the speed of warfare increase.

Combat service support (CSS) officers must operate and react rapidly, effectively, and continually in the tactical environment of forward positions. They must approach their mission with the same aggressive execution as the infantrymen in the assault. Their planning must be correct and complete, and their response must be immediate and decisive. Their plans, procedures, decisions, and soldiers must also have the flexibility to adapt to rapidly changing situations. This professional application of management and leadership skills is the result of carefully employed combat service support concepts.

Logisticians cannot hipshoot. To accomplish their mission, their planning must focus on the battle four or five days from now while their support units execute the support for the battle today. The key to managing this undertaking is threefold: proper procedures, accurate data, and consistent application of valid support concepts and principles. These concepts and principles provide the framework for CSS operations at all levels of command. They integrate all classes of supply and service functions into a complete support system that can react to the needs of the combat elements and the command priorities in every battlefield situation.

Tactical logisticians must remember that they cannot deal with only one class of supply at a time because there are never enough assets to do everything at once. This limitation on resources quickly forces the realization that each support function in one way or another affects every other support function. Hence, the overall approach to support must incorporate *integrated logistics support* in every aspect of CSS. Priorities of support must be assigned, not only in regard to which unit is most important but also in regard to the most critical class of supply or service at any given time. These priorities must change with and match the tactical situation on the battlefield.

Because all classes of supply and service functions are parts of the whole, the situation on the battlefield is the driving force that justifies, directs, and assigns priorities to support operations. The battlefield situation normally falls into three categories: *offense, defense,* and *retrograde operations.* These types of tactical operations affect the support operations, such as supply, transportation, personnel, maintenance, and medical support. Despite the tactical situation, however, some general principles of support apply.

GENERAL PRINCIPLES OF SUPPORT

The following principles are basic guidance for effective combat service support. They are concepts, not detailed cookbook instructions. Thus, the operating logisticians in the field are responsible for the efficient use of this guidance. Success totally depends on their skill in applying these theories to the execution of integrated logistic support in the tactical environment.

In all cases, logisticians must function in a *push system* mode. They are negligent if they wait for and fill all requests for support submitted by the tacticians at the front. This method would be a *pull system.* In the past, the speed of warfare was slow enough for pull systems to provide effective support, but no longer. Victory on the battlefield will not come from hoarding supplies and demanding correct paperwork and proper justification before providing support. The only result of such bureaucratic inaction is dead soldiers, who received too little too late.

Tactical logisticians must anticipate the needs of supported combat formations and push the services and supplies forward to them, often even before they realize their own needs. To accomplish this task, tactical logisticians must read the battlefield much the way their supported commanders do, but logisticians must visualize it in the form of contingency loads, fuel requirements, ration break points, road networks, support areas, and so forth. Their real art is the projection of their support operations into combat power delivering decisive blows to the enemy, not today, but tomorrow or several days from now. The logisticians' combat power is not in their rifles but in their wrenches, trucks, fuel lines, and all the other tools of their support trade.

Class I (Rations) Support

Logisticians must always supply food at a *sustained rate.* Every soldier must receive enough food to maintain combat effectiveness. In a push system, logisticians do not wait for ration requests or personnel strength reports to tell them how many rations to send forward. Today's strength report is of little value in ensuring that food is on hand in sufficient quantities tomorrow and next week. Further, simply ordering enough rations for full Table of Organization and Equipment (TOE) strength could result in delivering too many rations. Such mindless supply practices waste not only rations but also transportation assets that might be critical elsewhere. But in the sustained-rate approach, logisticians continue to supply rations in the same quantities as previous issues. They push the rations forward at a sustained rate to ensure that the soldiers receive enough food without wasting rations and transportation assets.

Class II (General Supply) Support

In dealing with Class II items, logisticians must separate their stockage into two categories: *combat essential* and *not necessary to stock.* Class II items can mount up to significant tonnage to transport and store for issue to the troops. The two principles that apply to this class of supply are *high-use items—stock forward* and *coordinated forward delivery.*

The first step in planning is to identify and define *high-use* items. The *demand history* of the supported unit determines which items are high-use items. To the logistician, the items may seem obscure or insignificant, but if the supported unit uses many of them, the logistician should stock them. For example, if the supported unit is infantry, then helmet chin straps, boots, and pistol belts may have a high-use designation, but if the unit is mechanized infantry or armor, tie-down straps, tools, or grease rags could be more important. The demand histories for particular units provide the data that give logisticians their stockage guidance for forward positioning.

Selected and stocked high-use items will, however, do no good neatly piled in the rear areas. The combat soldier is not well supported if he or she must return to the rear to get a new pair of boots. His support unit should have pushed them forward to him. This delivery must be coordinated so that the right supplies get to the right place at the best time in an efficient manner.

Class III (Petroleum, Oils, and Lubricants) Support

In all situations on the battlefield, fuel tanks and fuel tankers must remain as full as possible. An empty fuel truck is a liability. But the same truck becomes an important asset when it is full. Logisticians should never allow tankers to sit empty anywhere. Keeping tankers full is the process of *maintaining stockage* at operational levels. Application of this concept moves fuel trucks constantly from the rear to the forward areas. This situation is healthy. The unhealthy situation is to have a feast-or-famine surge in which a shortage replaces a glut. The combat units need a dependable and steady flow of fuel to allow for operational planning.

Further, support units must stock petroleum products, such as grease, oil, solvents, and weapons lubricants, in reasonable quantities as far forward as possible. Because combat units can carry only a limited amount of package products, replenishment stocks must be within reach to sustain combat power.

Class IV (Barrier Materials) Support

Support units usually handle barrier materials as *throughput* from the rear directly to the site of the need. The response must be rapid, but the tonnage involved is so extensive that it is impractical to create forward stocks.

Class V (Ammunition, Explosives) Support

Brigade-sized units should have *ammunition transfer points* (ATPs). The ammunition stored in an ATP should be high-demand and high-use items. Further, these stocks should remain on trucks and trailers and should never be downloaded. ATPs must be as close as possible to the supported units. The proper operation of an ATP—empty trailers returned to the rear by the tractors that delivered the full trailers—will ensure a continued flow of ammunition to the combat troops.

Logisticians should supply ammunition on a basis of TOE strength for one *day of supply* (DOS) or *basic load* increments. Under this system, detailed ammunition requests are not necessary because logisticians will continue to deliver ammunition in basic load increments or DOS increments unless notified of a change in requirements.

Class VI (Personal Demand Items) Support

Personal demand items, such as razor blades, matches, cigarettes, soap, and so on, arrive on the battlefield in the form of *sundry packs.* Logisticians ship these packs forward as required by troop strength. Normally, logisticians distribute sundry packs through the *ration break point* in the brigade area to ease the strain on transportation assets to deliver to the forward areas.

Class VII (Major End Item) Support

A *major end item* is a piece of equipment—an entire identifiable item—that can stand alone and that does not lose its identity through use, such as vehicles or weapons systems. As much as possible, logisticians should put major end items through all the way from the rear to the using unit. The forward support elements have neither the facilities to store these items nor the capability of maintaining them. Logisticians must also ensure that major end items in storage do not become sources for required repair parts to maintain systems currently in use. Although such cannibalization is extremely difficult to control in the forward areas, logisticians must make sure that major end items are available as whole units in combat-worthy condition whenever supported troops need them.

Class VIII (Medical Supplies) Support

Coordination and distribution of forward resupply of medical supplies occurs through medical channels. The normal means of delivery is by return trips of ambulances after evacuation details. Forward medical units are not equipped to issue large quantities of medical supplies from established stocks, but they do attempt to support emergency needs from on-hand stocks.

Class IX (Repair Parts) Support

It is virtually impossible to carry every repair part that supported units may need during field operations; however, a stock of combat essential items must be available in a *combat authorized stockage list* (ASL) in the forward areas. This ASL must contain only deadlining parts that would bring a piece of equipment back up to combat readiness. Safety items and comfort items, such as headlights and seat cushions, do not fall into the category of forward stockage.

A primary candidate for forward stocks would be a quantity of major assemblies. Logisticians should use demand history, resupply turnaround, and cargo lift availability to determine which items to carry and the quantity. Further, logisticians should select the major assemblies in the forward stocks to support combat equipment. An engine for a warehouse forklift that is not present in the forward areas, for example, would be inappropriate, but an engine for the 10-kilowatt generator that powers the brigade tactical operations center could be essential.

The major concept concerning Class IX is to have the essential repair parts and major assemblies required to support the force as far forward as the supported units can tactically secure and practically use them. How far forward and what items depend on the tactical situation, the supported density of equipment, the number of trucks available, and the experience of the support personnel involved.

Maintenance Support

Like the different classes of supplies, maintenance support belongs as far forward as possible. Support units should provide repairs and services in aggressive operations as close to where the equipment must operate as tactically practical. Support units should issue replacement equipment to the supported unit and repair and return the damaged equipment to stock as soon as possible. The objective is to return the largest possible number of combat systems to the battlefield in the shortest possible time.

Medical Support

The main emphasis in medical support on the battlefield is to maintain the highest possible number of combat effective soldiers in the units. If possible, an injured, wounded, or sick soldier should not leave the sound of the guns. This concept does not mean that seriously injured men should stay in forward areas to convalesce in muddy sleeping bags. It means that those soldiers who can return to duty after a few hours should not go to the rear. It also means that those soldiers so seriously injured that they will require extended recovery time should be evacuated from the combat environment as quickly as possible. Qualified personnel in the forward medical units must decide which category a wounded soldier falls into.

Recovery and Evacuation of Materiel

Combat units should be responsible for recovery of their own damaged or inoperative equipment. They should recover this equipment to the rear to a collection point where the maintenance support units can either repair it or continue to evacuate it farther to the rear. This collection point should be secure from direct enemy action. The supporting units can assist in this recovery if they have enough assets. If the maintenance support units at the collection point cannot repair the unserviceable equipment, then the supporting units must evacuate it farther to the rear to appropriate maintenance facilities or to the nearest salvage operation.

Transportation Support

Transportation assets, such as trains, aircraft, and trucks, are the means of distributing supplies, evacuating damaged equipment, and moving personnel to wherever they belong. Truck transportation is the primary resource for transportation available to the logistician on the ground. Trucks are also the most versatile and flexible means of transportation. They are probably the most critical tool used in combat service support operations. Without adequate transportation, the successful support of combat operations is impossible.

Generally, a transportation manager centrally controls and coordinates employment of transportation assets. This manager will endeavor to make sure that transportation capabilities are not wasted and that the necessary materiel arrives at the right place on time. The transportation manager assigns priorities to all transportation requirements according to their importance to the objectives of the supported units. The transportation manager must also make every sortie accomplish more than one requirement by consolidating loads and never sending any truck or aircraft anywhere with an empty cargo area. Every truckload of supplies and equipment going forward should also represent a truckload of unserviceable equipment, wounded soldiers, or salvage coming back as *backhaul*.

Finally, the transportation manager has to read the tactical situation and judge the importance of each transportation requirement against the risk of loss of the truck or aircraft that carries it. Transportation managers do not complete their mission of sustaining the supported units if they allow nonessential missions to deplete their capabilities or if they make their assets vulnerable to direct enemy action. Transportation managers also must ensure that local combat commanders on the ground do not commandeer their vehicles and thus make them unavailable to support other units. These potential problems mean that logisticians must have the ability to identify transportation missions that they should not accept.

COMBAT SERVICE SUPPORT IN THE OFFENSE

Three words express the function of all combat service support operations and the mission of all combat service support soldiers during offensive operations: Maintain the momentum. Combat soldiers should never have to slow their attack to wait for support to catch up. Rather, the support soldiers must anticipate the combat soldiers' needs and push forward the required supplies, replacements, and materiel. Combat soldiers must have enough support to maintain the speed and ferocity of the attack until they achieve their objectives, and beyond that, the combat forces must achieve those objectives with enough combat power remaining to hold them or press on if the opportunity presents itself. Historians record many offensive operations as "the big push." One might well wonder whether any success was due to the combat arms' "pushing" the enemy or the combat service support units' "pushing" the combat arms. *Maintain the momentum.*

Class I (Rations) Support in the Offense

Ration transfer points should move well forward during offensive operations. These transfer points are not truly ration points because they normally handle only Class "C" (ready-to-eat) rations. Supported units simply don't have time or facilities to use "A" (fresh) or "B" (preserved-uncooked) rations during an offensive because they are constantly moving. Therefore, because units can handle "C"s the same way they handle any other dry cargo, these transfer points can be well forward of the battalion rear boundaries if coordinated. Supply units should establish water issue points with each ration transfer point. *Maintain the momentum.*

Class II (General Supplies) Support in the Offense

General supplies are not normally a high priority support mission during the offensive. The items required for troop support before the offensive, however, can be massive. This situation requires close coordination between the supporting and supported units to ensure that all soldiers have the best equipment and necessary supplies to sustain the force during the actual attack. There will, however, always be a great surge of requests for resupply of Class II items immediately following closure and consolidation of the objective. At this point, the combat arms will stop to regroup and reequip their forces. Logisticians must anticipate and plan for this surge of support requests by moving forward a stockage of high-use and combat essential items and delivering them forward as needed by supported units. *Maintain the momentum.*

Class III (Petroleum, Oils, and Lubricants) Support in the Offense

In offensive operations, logisticians must push petroleum, oils, and lubricants (POL), both bulk and package, as far forward as possible to coordinated *fuel points.* Whenever possible, support units must top off combat systems requiring fuel. Fuel consumption increases considerably during an attack, and logisticians must anticipate this increase. If possible, logisticians should coordinate with the supported operations officers to gain a complete understanding of the operation and its critical points. Logisticians must then assist in establishing fuel points and times to help guarantee effective combat power at decisive locations.

Logisticians should also advise tacticians if fuel shortages will interfere with the commander's concept of operations. The combat force commander is not well supported if his staff blithely allows him to adopt a course of action that will outrun the fuel quantities or fuel delivery systems available. *Maintain the momentum.*

Class IV (Barrier Materials) Support in the Offense

Normally, offensive operations do not require barrier materials.

Class V (Ammunition and Explosives) Support in the Offense

Generally, ammunition consumption decreases somewhat during offensive operations. This decrease is a function of more movement by friendly forces reducing target acquisition compared to the number of targets available in the defense. Ammunition still presents an enormous amount of dry cargo that support units must move forward to the combat units. The best method of maintaining continuous flow of ammunition forward is by leapfrogging *ammunition transfer points* (ATPs) forward as close to the combat forces as possible. Support units maintain this flow by having the supporting tractors drop their loaded trailers at a more forward position and falling back to the former ATP location to pick up the empty trailers for return to the rear areas. This method reduces rearward ATPs and deletes them by attrition, so the units will have less distance to travel for resupply. Logisticians must take care not to overstock the ATPs to avoid the necessity of offloading ammunition onto the ground. Trailers should never return to the rear with ammunition still on them. *Maintain the momentum.*

Class VI (Personal Demand Items) Support in the Offense

Class VI items are not of great concern during offensive operations. Logisticians do, however, need to think about resupply after consolidation of objectives. They should use demand history and command guidance to determine stockage levels. *Maintain the momentum.*

Class VII (Major End Items) Support in the Offense

Logisticians must put major end items through to supported units at coordinated pickup points. Major end items should arrive in a ready-to-fight configuration, that is, fueled, armed, crewed, and with all accessories mounted, properly stowed, or installed. Accomplishing this mission requires an orchestrated effort by supply, maintenance, transportation, and personnel support elements. (See chapter 12.) *Maintain the momentum.*

Class VIII (Medical Supplies) Support in the Offense

During offensive operations, medical supplies must move forward by the fastest means possible, which is normally the return trip of the ambulances after they have transported injured soldiers to rear areas. *Maintain the momentum.*

Class IX (Repair Parts) Support in the Offense

Repair parts supply is critical during offensive operations. Supply units must thrust stocks of deadlining parts forward. Quantities depend on the type of combat formation supported. If the needed parts are not available from stocks on the battlefield, then maintenance units may use *controlled substitution,* removing like parts from other deadlined equipment. Logisticians must properly control this activity, however, so that maintenance units can later repair the donor equipment. *Maintain the momentum.*

Maintenance Support in the Offense

Logisticians must aggressively attack maintenance requirements when the supported units are moving forward. The maintenance elements must fix everything as far forward as possible. Support units should dispatch *contact teams* as far forward as the battalion combat trains and should carry major assemblies forward to the location of the deadlined item. *Maintain the momentum.*

Medical Support in the Offense

Medical units should endeavor to return the maximum number of wounded or injured soldiers to their units. Maintaining troop strength ratios is critical for the combat arms to keep the advance going. Further, those casualties that cannot quickly return to combat should be evacuated as quickly as possible because the supporting medical unit must keep up with the supported formation; therefore, it must not become encumbered with a large number of litter patients. Only rapid evacuation can prevent such a situation, because generally our friendly forces will receive increased numbers of casualties during an offensive. *Maintain the momentum.*

Recovery and Evacuation of Materiel in the Offense

During offensive operations, the combat units have very limited time to recover their damaged and unserviceable equipment, creating a situation in which the collection points are very small and more numerous on the battlefield. In fact, if the units are moving very quickly, the combat units may do little more than notify the supporting unit of the location of the abandoned equipment. More commonly, however, combat units recover their equipment to areas adjacent to the *main supply route* (MSR) and leave it for the supporting unit to repair as the supporting unit moves forward. The supporting unit retains the responsibility to evacuate materiel that they cannot repair to the rear to appropriate maintenance activities. No items that could be used should be sent to the rear. Further, the logistician should take care that assets are not wasted in this backhaul operation. For example, returning supply trucks and partially disabled vehicles can assist by towing totally disabled vehicles or carrying salvaged major assemblies to the rear. *Maintain the momentum.*

Transportation Support in the Offense

Transportation will be hard pressed to keep up with demands for support during offensive operations. The logistician should carefully assign priorities to transport requirements to ensure delivery of essential items. The greatest demand for transportation forward will be in the area of carrying fuel supplies, repair parts, and major assemblies forward. The high priority for backhaul will be in the evacuation of casualties and damaged equipment. If at all possible, no truck should go forward or to the rear without a full load. *Maintain the momentum.*

COMBAT SERVICE SUPPORT IN THE DEFENSE

Defensive operations are tactics employed to deny the enemy offensive its objectives by fire and maneuver. It is no longer considered a great honor to die in place during a defense. The main objective is to keep the enemy from successfully gaining his objectives and forcing him to expend his men and materiel to no avail while maintaining our own forces in a suitable condition to regain the initiative at the first opportunity. The role of the logistician during such operations is to *sustain and increase the combat power.*

Combat service support units should make sure that they identify every need for the defense as quickly as possible and supply those needs to the combat units. In addition, they must seize and exploit every opportunity to return additional combat systems to the battlefield and to rebuild the combat effectiveness of the combat units. Fortunately, the relatively static locations of friendly units during a defense aid in this endeavor. The units do move and maneuver, but the more deliberate atmosphere enables logisticians to predict the length of time available for CSS operations before the next movement. This lead time makes a more systematic approach possible with more productive rebuild or reconstitution efforts.

In the back of their minds, logisticians should remember that tacticians will jump at an opportunity to regain the initiative from the enemy and go on the offensive. Therefore, combat service support units must maintain the flexibility and responsiveness to "shift gears" back to offensive support. Moreover, their efforts must drive toward replacing the combat units' ability to attack and defeat the enemy. Once again, logisticians must assume a stance of pushing the combat arms forward.

Class I (Rations) Support in the Defense

During a defense, support units can supply rations to the combat units most efficiently by establishing a *ration break point* and a *water point* in the *brigade support area* (BSA). The unit "trains" elements in the BSA have the ability to prepare and distribute rations through the use of daily *log packs* going forward. Battalion commanders have various ideas on the best time for this operation, so a centralized break point allows the supported battalion the flexibility to support its own troops as dictated by its own tactical situation. Further, because of the fluid nature of a *defense-in-depth* situation, the valuable assets committed to operate the break point, such as trucks, rations, and people, are much better protected within the BSA. *Sustain and increase the combat power.*

Class II (General Supplies) Support in the Defense

To sustain the combat units, forward stocks of critical Class II items should remain in the BSA. This practice not only allows for protection of these stocks but also keeps them available to the support personnel of the unit trains. They can draw the required items and ship them to the point of need by use of the daily log pack. This method gains greater use of a smaller stock of Class II items because the supported units do not have to carry Class II stocks with them in any great quantity. Replenishment of stocks in the BSA is the responsibility of the combat service support unit. *Sustain and increase the combat power.*

Class III (Petroleum, Oils, and Lubricants) Support in the Defense

Logisticians should centralize the supply of bulk and package petroleum, oils, and lubricants (POL) in the BSA with the supported units using their organic fuel trucks to transport fuel forward to combat systems. Supply units should use the daily log pack to distribute package POL as needed. Keeping the larger tanker trucks running between a fuel point in the BSA and the rear areas allows them to support the defensive operations and reduces their exposure to and chance of being lost in enemy action. These trucks should be carefully guarded because the capability to refuel the force that they represent is a critical key to regaining the offensive. Only appropriate higher level commanders should decide whether to send these larger tanker trucks forward if the tactical mission demands it. *Sustain and increase the combat power.*

Class IV (Barrier Materials) Support in the Defense

Barrier materials are very important during the defense. With the exception of ammunition, they should receive the highest priority for transport. Logisticians must coordinate delivery locations through the operations officers of the supported units to ensure that stocks go where they will provide the greatest benefit to friendly forces. Delivery should be by direct throughput from the rear areas to the point of emplacement whenever possible. Logisticians must take care, however, to ensure that the combat units understand that they cannot commandeer trucks that carry materials forward as mobile storage facilities. The materials should be delivered to the coordinated position and downloaded to release the trucks for other transport missions. Class IV items constitute a great amount of dry cargo tonnage, and the entire transportation assets of a brigade or even a division can become totally committed if the logistician does not maintain a watchful eye. *Sustain and increase the combat power.*

Class V (Ammunition and Explosives) Support in the Defense

Support units should remove ammunition stocks in the ammunition transfer points (ATPs) to positions in the area of, or slightly to the rear of, the BSA. Changing the drop point for the tractors bringing loaded trailers forward reduces the forward points by attrition. Because ammunition expenditures will increase greatly during defensive operations, support of these essential items as the highest priority requirement will strain transportation assets. The key is to have sufficient ammunition at critical points on the battlefield without risking its loss to enemy action. *Sustain and increase the combat power.*

Class VI (Personal Demand Items) Support in the Defense

Support units distribute Class VI items by tariff rate based on reported troop strength usually somewhere near the ration break point in the BSA. CSS units responsible for this support need to remember that these items are more in demand during defensive operations because of the more static situation. These items normally go forward by the daily log pack. *Sustain and increase the combat power.*

Class VII (Major End Items) Support in the Defense

Support units must put major end items through to supported units at coordinated pickup points. Major end items should arrive in a ready-to-fight configuration: fueled, armed, crewed, and with all accessories mounted, properly stowed, or installed. Accomplishing this task requires an orchestrated effort by supply, maintenance, transportation, and personnel support elements. (See Chapter 12.) *Sustain and increase the combat power.*

Class VIII (Medical Supplies) Support in the Defense

During defensive operations, medical supplies must go forward by the fastest means possible, which is normally the return trip of the ambulances after they have transported injured soldiers to rear areas. *Sustain and increase the combat power.*

Class IX (Repair Parts) Support in the Defense

The very fluid nature of current defense doctrine makes sending valuable Class IX assets to forward positions as stock items unwise. Support units must, however, maintain combat systems in fighting condition to the maximum extent possible, so logisticians should centralize repair parts stocks in the BSA, specifically issue deadlining parts, and send them where they are needed. Logisticians must exercise good judgment in deciding which repair parts to send forward. A deadlining item for a jeep, for example, may not have the same priority as that for a tank. Only the current situation will tell the logistician which is more important. *Sustain and increase the combat power.*

Maintenance Support in the Defense

During defensive operations, logisticians should more centrally control maintenance support from the BSA. The fluid situation of current defense doctrine makes it very risky to have soldiers engaged in maintenance operations too far forward. The main function of maintenance personnel during the defense is to establish repair operations in areas that will be secure for a sufficient length of time to allow for repairing weapons systems and returning them to the combat units. If maintenance units cannot repair the damaged weapons systems at the direct support level or below, the systems should be evacuated rearward as rapidly as possible. *Sustain and increase the combat power.*

Medical Support in the Defense

The concepts of medical support during defensive operations do not change significantly from those employed in the offense. The main objective is still to return the greatest possible number of combat capable soldiers back to the combat units and to evacuate the more seriously injured as rapidly as possible. Again because of the unpredictable, liquid situation of the defense, however, the evacuation process needs more priority. The forward medical units should not be encumbered by a large number of litter patients. These patients must be returned to the rear as soon as they can be safely moved. *Sustain and increase the combat power.*

Recovery and Evacuation of Materiel in the Defense

During defensive operations, combat units should recover their disabled, damaged, and unserviceable equipment to a central collection point.

This point should be in an area secure from direct enemy action. At this collection point, owning units should examine the recovered equipment. If their organizational mechanics cannot repair it, the owning units should recover the equipment to the closest supporting unit activity, which is normally colocated with the collection point. If the supporting unit cannot repair the equipment at this location, then that unit must evacuate the equipment to the rear to the appropriate maintenance activity.

The evacuation phase is very important in the defense because of the risk of capture by enemy units. Any equipment that can be brought out of danger to be repaired and later returned to battle is valuable. *Sustain and increase the combat power.*

Transportation Support in the Defense

Transportation is critical in defensive operations. The total amount of dry cargo lift required to sustain a force in a defense is staggering. Ammunition expenditures increase, and ammunition must be resupplied. Barrier materials increase the effectiveness of the defenses and belong as far forward as possible. In addition to the requirements that must go forward, the backhaul of evacuated equipment increases enormously. The backhaul of casualties is also critical in the defense. Logisticians must ensure that every vehicle is pressed into effective service—full going forward and full coming back—to provide the transportation support required by defensive operations. *Sustain and increase the combat power.*

COMBAT SERVICE SUPPORT IN THE RETROGRADE

Retrograde operations fall into three categories: *withdrawal, delaying action,* and *retreat.* To the tacticians these three terms indicate different approaches to disengaging friendly forces and leaving the battle area. There can be many reasons for retrograde operations, but they all come down to electing not to fight at this time because the outcome would not be favorable to the overall objectives. Tacticians also consider that any retrograde operation also has the implied mission of trying to regain the offensive as soon as possible. In lay terms, retrograde means getting out of a fight you can't win or can't afford to win. To the logisticians all three approaches have the same message: *Evacuate all assets and prepare to rebuild the combat power:*

Class I (Rations) Support in the Retrograde

Ration break points should continue to operate from the BSA. The whole BSA, however, will probably move farther to the rear according to the tactical situation. As this rearward movement occurs, supply units should coordinate drop points with the supported units so that, as the supported units withdraw, they can fall back on positions that contain a cache of rations. This cache should contain only "C" rations to ensure that they are consumable even if they are not used for several days. *Evacuate all assets and prepare to rebuild the combat power.*

Class II (General Supplies) Support in the Retrograde

Normally, Class II requirements should decrease during retrograde operations. Therefore, the forward stocks should be evacuated for two reasons. First, evacuating these stocks saves them so that they cannot benefit the enemy. Second, evacuated stocks remain available to the tactical forces to aid in rebuilding combat power after the completion of the operation. If, however, a supported unit makes an emergency request for a Class II item, the support unit should make every effort to obtain the item and ship it to the requesting unit as quickly as possible. *Evacuate all assets and prepare to rebuild the combat power.*

Class III (Petroleum, Oils, and Lubricants) Support in the Retrograde

The main fuel assets will withdraw from the area with the BSA, but the combat units must be refueled to allow them to fight and withdraw as the situation demands. The best way to refuel combat units during retrograde operations is to use coordinated *bulk transfer points,* established according to the security needs of the large tankers. These vehicles have primary importance in the rebuild stages of the operation, and the force cannot regain the offensive if these tankers are lost. The supported units must provide the maximum amount of information on the tactical situation to the supporting units. This information allows the logisticians to use any of their available assets to support the refueling as they see fit. This situation does not allow a cookbook approach to the completion of the fuel support mission. Although logisticians cannot expect the combat arms to operate without refueling, they must also consider the risk of losing the tankers. A carefully coordinated and properly secured transfer point is the answer. *Evacuate all assets and prepare to rebuild combat power.*

Class IV (Barrier Materials) Support in the Retrograde

Barrier materials are very important during the retrograde. They should receive high priority for transport. Logisticians must coordinate the locations of delivery through the operations officers of the supported units to ensure that stocks go to the areas where they will provide the greatest benefit to friendly forces. Delivery should be by direct throughput from the rear areas to the point of emplacement whenever possible. Logisticians must, however, take care to ensure that the combat units understand that they must not commandeer the trucks that carry materials forward as mobile storage facilities. Support units should deliver the materials to the coordinated position and download them to release the trucks for other transport missions. Class IV items constitute a great amount of dry cargo tonnage, and the entire transportation assets of a brigade or even a division can become totally committed if the tactical logistician does not maintain a watchful eye. *Evacuate all assets and prepare to rebuild the combat power.*

Class V (Ammunition and Explosives) Support in the Retrograde

Logisticians should remove ammunition stocks in the ammunition transfer points (ATPs) to positions in the area of, or slightly to the rear of, the BSA. Changing the drop point for the tractors bringing loaded trailers forward reduces the forward points by attrition. Ammunition expenditures may increase greatly during retrograde operations, so supplying these essential items will strain transportation assets. The key in this case is to have sufficient ammunition at critical points on the battlefield without risking its loss to enemy action. *Evacuate all assets and prepare to rebuild combat power.*

Class VI (Personal Demand Items) Support in the Retrograde

Retrograde operations usually do not receive Class VI support. Logisticians must, however, consider the need to rebuild men, as well as equipment. Therefore, logisticians should consider keeping a small stock of these items available within the BSA and leaving small quantities of high demand items with the ration caches mentioned under Class I in the retrograde. *Evacuate all assets and prepare to rebuild the combat power.*

Class VII (Major End Items) Support in the Retrograde

Support units should consolidate requested major end items in the rear areas and deliver them to the unit in the rest area or rear position assigned to the unit. Supply units should issue these items as ready-to-fight items. (See Chapter 12.) *Evacuate all assets and prepare to rebuild combat power.*

Class VIII (Medical Supplies) Support in the Retrograde

During retrograde operations, medical supplies must go forward by the fastest means possible, which normally is the return trip of the ambulances after they have transported injured soldiers to rear areas. *Evacuate all assets and prepare to rebuild combat power.*

Class IX (Repair Parts) Support in the Retrograde

Those repair parts necessary to recover combat equipment from the battle area should go forward by the most expeditious means. The majority of effort in the Class IX support of the tactical units during retrograde operations comes from cannibalization and salvage of unrecoverable equipment. Maintenance units could, in rare cases, establish drop points for required items. The majority of stocks should be evacuated to support reconstitution and rebuild efforts after completion of the operation. *Evacuate all assets and prepare to rebuild combat power.*

Maintenance Support in the Retrograde

The main effort of maintenance during retrograde operations is to assist in the evacuation of valuable combat systems for subsequent further repair in the rear areas. For the most part, the forward area maintenance personnel will be engaged in quick-fix or salvage-and-recovery functions. *Evacuate all assets and prepare to rebuild combat power.*

Medical Support in the Retrograde

The concepts of medical support during retrograde operations do not change significantly from those employed in the offense or the defense. The main objective is still to return the greatest possible number of combat capable soldiers to the combat units and to evacuate the more seriously injured as rapidly as possible. During retrograde operations, however, the evacuation of wounded personnel becomes the top priority. *Evacuate all assets and prepare to rebuild combat power.*

Recovery and Evacuation of Materiel in the Retrograde

Combat units should recover every possible item to the supporting units, and the supporting units must evacuate every item and every stock that they possibly can for two reasons. First, the enemy cannot use the recovered equipment and supplies. To assist this denial of use, all items that cannot be evacuated must be destroyed. The only exceptions to this rule are Class I (rations) and Class VIII (medical supplies) stocks. According to the Law of War and the Geneva Conventions, these stocks must not be destroyed. Second, every recovered item represents another item or asset that support units can repair, salvage, or use to re-equip and rebuild combat power to fight later. *Evacuate all assets and prepare to rebuild combat power.*

Transportation Support in the Retrograde

Transportation support is a valuable commodity in every operation, but especially during a retrograde operation. Logisticians must press into service every available transportation asset to evacuate the maximum number of soldiers and their equipment. Logisticians must assign priorities to the items and units to be lifted according to command guidance, the tactical situation, and their knowledge of the logistics system they are working with. In every case, the most precious commodity to evacuate is the soldiers. After that, however, the logistician on the spot must determine the priorities. *Evacuate all assets and prepare to rebuild combat power.*

COMBAT SERVICE SUPPORT IN THE AIRLAND BATTLE

The primary characteristics of the U.S. Army's *AirLand Battle* doctrine are *initiative, depth, agility, and synchronization.* This doctrine encourages commanders at all levels to operate in a flexible and active mode, grasping and exploiting every opportunity that presents itself to carry the fight to the enemy and to penetrate and destroy his forces. This doctrine also requires logisticians to develop within themselves exactly the same aggressiveness and responsiveness that commanders must develop.

Combat service support units must incorporate and actively employ the principles of responsiveness, flexibility, and initiative. Logisticians must anticipate and fill the needs and requirements of their supported units before they receive requests for support. They must also know the needs and personalities of their supported units and have a complete and thorough knowledge of their own assets and capabilities. Logisticians must study and understand the tactical plan of every operation they support and be ready to advise tactical commanders of support risks involved.

Logisticians and their supported tacticians must communicate and exchange information continuously so that both of them can exploit opportunities in combat. This exchange of information will enable logisticians to ensure that their support priorities match tactical priorities and will enable tactical commanders to know the capability of the support units to push their needs forward. Good communications will enable logisticians to maintain flows of supplies rather than stockpiles. The constantly changing atmosphere of the modern battlefield requires constant and complete coordination between the supporting and supported units.

Combat service support units must be instantly responsive to the requirements of their supported units, but the environment of modern warfare also means that they must be instantly responsive to their own security needs. What was once called rear area security operations has evolved into a concept called *the rear battle.* The support units must be able to coordinate security against enemy penetrations, enemy artillery fires, enemy air strikes, airborne insertions, electronic warfare, and nuclear, biological, and chemical warfare (NBC). In short, the combat service support soldier is as much involved in every operation as any combat soldier.

AirLand Battle doctrine requires logisticians to employ the same initiative and innovation that have been the trademark of combat service support for hundreds of years, except that they will have to do everything more rapidly. Logisticians must become as good as, if not better than, their supported tacticians at reading the battlefield. They, like the tacticians, must be able to predict the actions of the enemy, and they must be able to predict the actions of their supported tacticians to effectively support the AirLand Battle.

2

General Information

THE MILITARY DECISION-MAKING PROCESS

To accomplish their missions, logisticians must make logical decisions based on their analyses of many different kinds of information on the battlefield. This chapter explains how logisticians can use the military decision-making process to solve combat service support problems. It also defines frequently used combat terms and classes of supply that logisticians must work with to get the correct supplies and services to the right people at the right place or right time on the battlefield.

Like any other military organization, a combat service support unit must operate in a complex and changing environment. The logisticians who control and command these units must sift through an enormous amount of varied, complicated, and often contradictory information. The primary objective of their deliberations must be mission accomplishment. To reach this objective, the logisticians must use a methodical, precise, and repetitive process to figure out what actions they should take.

The military decison-making process is a systematic approach to problem solving, an orderly sequence of events that helps planners, including logisticians, apply thoroughness, clarity, judgment, logic, and professional expertise to their work. Planners can use the military decision-making process to accomplish these tasks:

- Recognize and define significant problems.
- Gather information and make assumptions necessary to determine the scope of the problem.
- Develop possible solutions for the problem.
- Analyze and compare the possible solutions.
- Select the best solution.

This decision-making process is continuous. Even though some actions must occur in sequence, others often happen simultaneously, as indicated in the accompanying diagram of the decision-making process. The amount of time available, the urgency of the situation, and the judg-

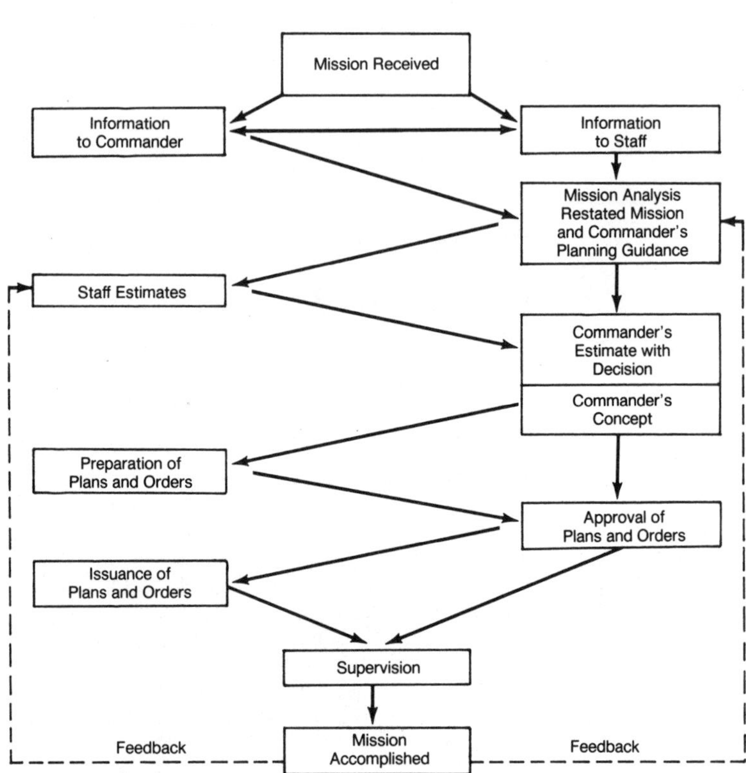

The military decision-making process.

ment of the commander all affect this approach to decision making. Of these factors, the most important is time.

Because time is the most important variable, logisticians should use this process as a guide, not an absolute, inviolate rule. Some occasions dictate bypassing or accelerating various steps of the process. This deviation is acceptable as long as the results of every decision become feedback to help refine and analyze factors and information affecting subsequent decisions. In the accompanying diagram, the dotted lines marked "Feedback" are probably the most important step of the process.

The following definitions apply to the blocks and actions depicted in the diagram:

• *Mission.* Higher headquarters or the commander himself identify and define the mission, which is the start of the problem identification steps. The commander either initiates analysis or requests and develops further information.

• *Information.* The commander and the staff exchange information required to complete the mission or problem analysis.

• *Mission analysis.* The primary objective of mission analysis is to identify every required or implied task to accomplish. The mission statement specifies some tasks, and the situation and general environment require others. In a tactical situation, the commander relates the tasks to the terrain, the enemy, and the condition and mission of the supported units.

• *Restated mission.* The restated mission is a clear, concise statement of the essential specified and implied tasks and their purposes. Usually, the restated mission does not include routine tasks or responsibilities inherent to the personnel or units involved. The restated mission becomes the basis of all staff estimates, paragraph 1 of those estimates, and paragraph 2 of any operation order or plan that results from this process.

• *Planning guidance.* The commander provides all required planning guidance to the staff and subordinate commanders. Staff officers use this guidance to prepare staff estimates and to expedite the decision making process. This planning guidance should include courses of action to examine or disregard, unusual restrictions to consider, and any other important factors.

• *Staff estimates.* The staff assists the commander in reaching a decision by providing estimates of the situation as it appears from their individual areas of responsibility. These estimates conclude with recommended possible courses of action. Staff officers may prepare and present these estimates orally or in writing. In situations driven by a shortage of time, often only the staff conclusions and recommendations go to the commander. Suggested formats for these estimates are in chapter 8.

• *Commander's estimate.* Based on the staff estimates and the commander's own knowledge of the situation, the commander issues an analysis of the situation and an estimate of the course of action to take. Both the commander and the staff constantly review and update this estimate as new information appears and the situation changes.

• *Commander's concept.* Upon reaching a decision, the commander issues his or her concept, a description of the current operation, to staff members, usually orally, but also in writing if time permits. The staff then executes the selected course of action.

• *Plans and orders.* Plans and orders are the instruments used to execute the course of action the commander has selected.

• *Feedback.* Feedback helps planners evaluate the results of the decision-making process. This information reveals whether the selected course of action has solved the problem or accomplished the mission. Feedback helps reduce doubt and provides information not previously available. Feedback may also indicate that further decisions are necessary, so the process continues.

SELECTED OPERATIONAL TERMS

Airmobile task force (AMTF)—A grouping of aviation and ground units under one commander for the purpose of carrying out a specific order.

Airspace management element (AME)—An Army element within a corps or a division tactical operations center responsible for coordinating, integrating, and regulating airspace within the organization's area of territorial responsibility. It coordinates directly with Air Force elements integrated into each operations center.

Battlefield air interdiction (BAI)—Air action against hostile ground targets that are positioned to directly affect friendly forces and that require joint allocation, planning, and coordination.

Coordinated fire line (CFL)—A line beyond which all surface-to-surface fire support means (mortar, field artillery, and naval gunfire) may fire at any time within the zone of the establishing headquarters without additional coordination. Usually established by brigade or division, but also by battalions, its purpose is to expedite attack of targets beyond the CFL.

Final coordination line (FCL)—A recognizable line close to the enemy position used to coordinate the lifting and shifting of supporting fires with the final deployment of maneuver elements.

Final protective fire (FPF)—An immediately available, planned barrier of direct and indirect fire designed to provide close protection to defensive positions and installations by impeding enemy movement into defensive areas. Normally, the brigade allocates indirect fires to maneuver battalions and further to company level. The maneuver commander of the sector where the fires are has the authority to call the fires.

Final protective line (FPL)—A line selected where interlocking fire from all available weapons is to check an enemy assault.

Fire support coordination line (FSCL)—A line beyond which any weapon system (including aircraft and special weapons) may attack all targets without endangering friendly troops or requiring additional coordination with the establishing headquarters so long as the effects of the weapon do not fall short of this line. Normally, corps or independent divisions establish the FSCL on terrain identifiable from the air to expedite the attack of targets beyond the line.

Fire support coordinator (FSCOORD)—The senior field artillery officer at each echelon above platoon level who serves as the principal advisor to the commander for coordination of all fire support within the unit's area of responsibility.

Fire support element (FSE)—The part of the tactical operations center at every echelon above company or troop that is responsible for targeting, coordinating, and integrating fires delivered on surface targets by fire support means under the control of or in support of the force.

Fire support team (FIST)—A team provided by field artillery to each maneuver company or troop commander's FSCOORD and responsible for planning and coordinating all indirect fire means available to the unit, including mortars, field artillery, close air support, and naval gunfire.

Forward area support team (FAST)—A combat service support team of the *division support command (DISCOM)* tailored to support a specific divisional combat brigade in an airborne, an airmobile, or a light infantry division. Coordinated or operationally controlled by a *forward area support coordinator (FASCO),* the elements of this team operate in the *brigade support area (BSA).*

Forward area rearm/refuel point (FARP)—Closer to the area of operation than the aviation unit's combat service area, a temporary facility organized, equipped, and deployed by an aviation unit commander to provide fuel and ammunition necessary for the employment of helicopter units in combat.

Forward edge of the battle area (FEBA)—The forward limit of the *main battle area (MBA).*

Forward line of own troops (FLOT)—A line that indicates the most forward positions of friendly forces at a specific time.

Fragmentary order (FRAGO)—An abbreviated operation order used to make changes in missions sent to units and to inform them of changes in the tactical situation.

Free fire area (FFA)—A specific, designated area into which any weapon system may fire without additional coordination from the establishing headquarters. Usually, the division or higher level commander establishes the FFA to expedite fires.

General support reinforcing (GSR)—Artillery mission requiring the unit assigned the mission to support the force as a whole and to provide reinforcing fires for another artillery unit as a second priority.

Lines of communication (LOC)—All the routes (land, water, and air) that connect an operating military force with one or more bases of operations and along which supplies and military forces move.

Line of contact (LC)—A general trace delineating the location where two opposing forces are engaged.

Line of departure (LD)—A line designated to coordinate the commitment of attacking units or scouting elements at a specified time of attack; a jumpoff line.

Main battle area (MBA)—That portion of the battlefield extending rearward from the FEBA where the decisive battle occurs. Designation of the MBA may include lateral and rear boundaries.

Main supply route (MSR)—The route or routes designated within an area of operations upon which the bulk of traffic flows in support of military operations.

Military operations on urbanized terrain (MOUT)—All military actions planned and conducted on a topographical complex and its adjacent natural terrain, where man-made construction is the dominant feature. It includes *combat-in-cities,* which is that portion of MOUT involving house-to-house and street-to-street fighting in towns and cities.

Minimum safe distance (MSD)—The minimum distance in meters from desired ground zero at which a specified degree of risk and vulnerability will not be exceeded with a 99 percent assurance.

Mission-oriented protective posture (MOPP)—A flexible system for protection against a chemical attack devised to increase the unit's ability to accomplish its mission in a toxic environment. This posture requires personnel to wear protective clothing and equipment consistent with the chemical threat, the work rate imposed by their mission, the temperature, and the humidity without excessive mission degradation.

Rear area combat operations (RACO)—Operations undertaken in the rear area to protect units, lines of communication, installations, and facilities from enemy attack, sabotage, and natural disaster, to limit damage, and to reestablish support capabilities.

Reinforcing (R)—An artillery mission requiring one artillery unit to augment the fire of another artillery unit.

Release point (RP)—A clearly defined control point on a route at which specified elements of a column of ground vehicles or of a flight of aircraft revert to their respective commanders, each element continuing its movement to its destination. In dismounted attacks, especially at night, it is that point at which a commander releases control of subordinate units to their commanders or leaders.

Required supply rate (RSR)—The amount of ammunition, expressed in rounds per weapon per day, estimated to sustain operations of a unit without restriction for a specified period.

Restrictive fire area (RFA)—An area in which units must not deliver fires that exceed specific restrictions without coordination with the establishing headquarters, usually battalion or higher. Generally, an RFA is on identifiable terrain to improve recognition from the air.

Restrictive fire line (RFL)—A line established to coordinate fires between heliborne or airborne forces and linkup forces or between friendly forces (one or both of which may be moving). An RFL prohibits fires or the effects of fires across the line without coordination with the affected force. Established by the common commander of the converging forces on identifiable terrain, the RFL replaces the fire coordination line (FCL).

Side-looking airborne radar (SLAR)—An airborne radar, viewing at right angles to the axes of the vehicle, that produces a presentation of terrain or moving targets.

Signal intelligence (SIGINT)—The product resulting from collection, analysis, integration, and interpretation of all information derived from *communication intelligence (COMINT), electronic intelligence (ELINT),* and *telemetry intelligence (TELINT).*

Signal security (SIGSEC)—Measures intended to deny or counter hostile exploitation of electronic emissions. SIGSEC includes communications security and electronic security.

Start point (SP)—A clearly defined initial control point on a route at which specified elements of a column of ground vehicles or of a flight of aircraft come under the control of the commander having responsibility for the movement.

Strongpoint (SP)—A defensive position fortified as extensively as time and materials permit. Located on a terrain feature critical to the defense or one that must be denied to the enemy, a strongpoint is essentially an antitank nest that enemy infantry can reduce only with the expenditure of much time and overwhelming forces. The force assigned to establish a strongpoint must have adequate time to build the position and to dig in all weapons with overhead cover in primary and alternate positions.

Suppression of enemy air defense (SEAD)—Any action that destroys, degrades, or obscures enemy surface air defense to increase the effectiveness of friendly operations.

Tactical air control center (TACC)—The operations center of the Air Force component headquarters. The TACC controls the activities of the *tactical air control system (TACS).*

Tactical air control party (TACP)—An Air Force team consisting of pilots, *radio-operators and drivers (ROMADS),* airborne and ground vehicles, and communications equipment required to obtain, coordinate, and control tactical air support for ground forces. Each division, brigade, and battalion have a TACP attached to ease the coordination of tactical air support operations. The TACP operates and maintains the Air Force air request net.

Tactical air coordination element (TACE)—An Air Force element that operates with a *corps tactical operations center (CTOC).* The TACE plans and controls Air Force missions in support of corps forces and assists Army planners on matters related to air operations. It replaces the corps TACP.

Tactical air support element (TASE)—An element of the U.S. Army division or corps *tactical operations center (TOC)* consisting of G2 and G3 personnel who coordinate and integrate tactical air support with current tactical ground operations.

Target reference point (TRP)—An easily recognizable point on the ground used for identifying enemy targets or controlling direct fires. Usually, company commanders or platoon leaders designate TRPs for company teams, platoons, sections, or individual weapons. They can also designate the center of an area where the commander plans to distribute or converge the fires of all his weapons rapidly. Once designated with the standard symbol and target numbers issued by the FIST or FSO, TRPs also constitute indirect fire targets.

Time on target (TOT)—The method of firing on target in which units firing various weapons time their fire to assure that all projectiles reach the target simultaneously; the time aircraft are scheduled to attack or photograph the target area; the actual time aircraft attack or photograph the target.

CLASSES OF SUPPLY AND SERVICES ON THE BATTLEFIELD

This section will define the ten classes of supply and the combat services normally found on the battlefield. In addition, it will provide the location where the class of supply or combat service usually is on the battlefield, the unit normally responsible for providing that logistic support, and the map symbol used to annotate the location on operational maps.

Class I

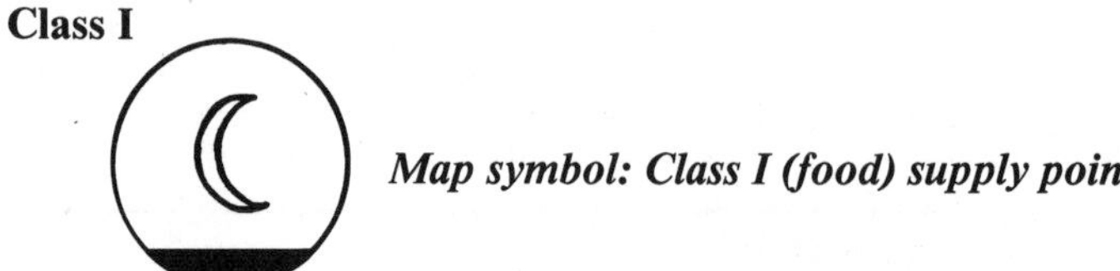

Map symbol: Class I (food) supply point

Definition: Food stuffs, subsistence, and rations.

Location on the battlefield: Class I supply points are normally in brigade support areas (BSAs), in division support areas (DSAs), and throughout the corps area.

Responsible units: The supply and service company of the forward support battalion (FSB) and the supply and service company of the main support battalion (MSB) within the division operate Class I supply points. To the rear of the division boundary, the direct support supply and service companies of the corps support command (COSCOM) operate Class I supply points.

Water Supply Point

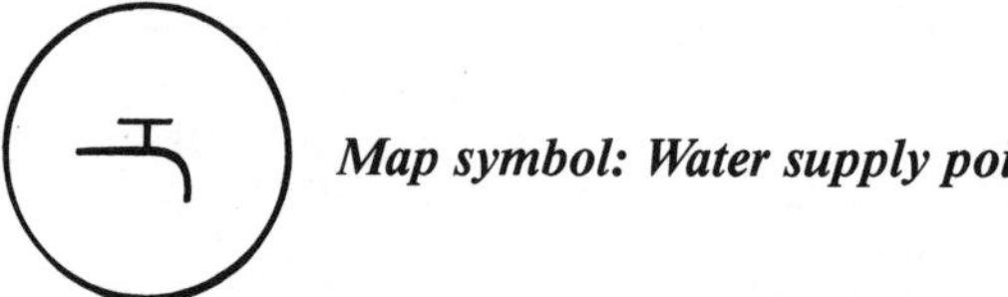

Map symbol: Water supply point

Definition: A source of potable water usually established in the vicinity of the Class I supply point.

Location on the battlefield: Same as Class I supply point.

Responsible units: Same as Class I supply point.

Class II

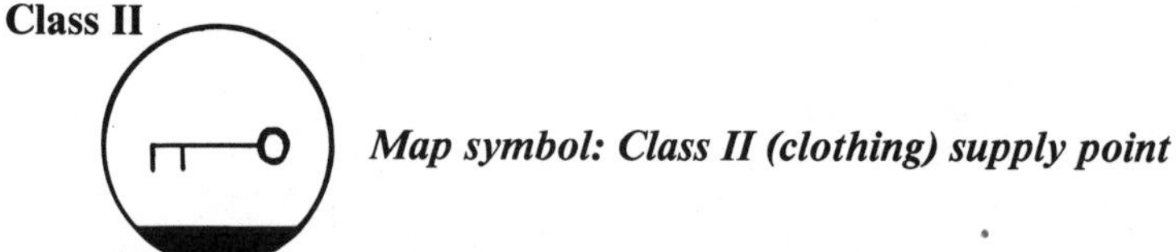

Map symbol: Class II (clothing) supply point

Definition: Clothing, tentage, tool sets, individual equipment, and all textile or leather items.

Location on the battlefield: Class II supply points are in the brigade support area (BSA), in the division support area (DSA), and in the corps areas, usually in multiclass supply points.

Responsible units: The supply and service company of the forward support battalion (FSB) and the supply and service company of the main support battalion (MSB) within the division operate Class II supply points. To the rear of the division boundary, the direct support supply and service companies of the corps support command (COSCOM) operate Class II supply points.

Clothing Exchange and Bath Point

Map symbol: Clothing exchange and bath point

Definition: Place to exchange damaged or soiled clothing for new or repaired items; shower and bath facilities.

Location on the battlefield: The clothing exchange and bath point normally is close to the Class II supply point.

Responsible units: Same as Class II supply point, although corps assets must augment bath and shower facilities.

Class III

Map symbol: Class III (petroleum) supply point

Definition: Petroleum products, including fuel, oil, and lubricants.

Location on the battlefield: Class III supply points are in the brigade support area (BSA), in the division support area (DSA), and in the corps areas.

Responsible units: The supply and service company of the forward support battalion and the supply and service company of the main support battalion within the division operate Class III supply points. At the direct support level, the direct support supply and service companies operate them, and at the general support level, the petroleum supply company in the corps area operates them.

Class IV

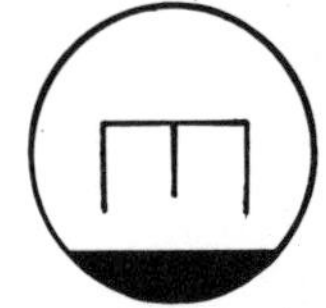

Map symbol: Class IV (barrier materials) supply point

Definition: Construction materials, barrier materials, lumber, pickets, barbed wire, concrete, bricks, and similar materials.

Location on the battlefield: The Class IV supply point is in the brigade support area (BSA), in the division support area (DSA), and in the corps areas. Often, the multifunction supply points distribute Class IV items.

Responsible units: The supply and service company in the forward support battalion (FSB) and the supply and service company in the main support battalion (MSB) within the division control Class IV items. In the corps area, Class IV support is available from nondivisional supply and service companies and the heavy material supply company at the general support level.

Class V

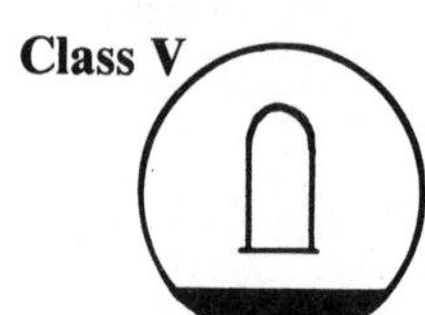

Map symbol: Class V (ammunition) supply point

Definition: All ammunition and explosives including pyrotechnics and explosive training items.

Location on the battlefield: The ammunition supply point (ASP) is in the corps area.

Responsible units: The ammunition support companies assigned to the corps support command (COSCOM) operate the ammunition supply points.

Ammunition Transfer Point

Map symbol: Ammunition transfer point

Definition: A forward position that receives and issues fast-moving items of ammunition. If possible, corps (COSCOM) tractors and trailers deliver these items. The trailers remain in place while the ammunition goes directly to the combat units' resupply trucks from them. Normally each brigade-sized element has one ammunition transfer point.

Location on the battlefield: Ammunition transfer points (ATPs) are in the brigade support area (BSA) and in the division support area (DSA).

Responsible units: The supply and service companies of the forward support battalions (FSB) and main support battalion (MSB) of the division operate ammunition transfer points.

Class VI

Map symbol: Class VI (personal demand) supply point

Definition: Personal demand items, such as chewing gum, cigarettes, soft drinks, razor blades, candy, and other items that soldiers select by personal preference.

Location on the battlefield: Usually, Class VI supply points are with Class I supply points.

Responsible units: Same as Class I.

Class VII

Map symbol: Class VII (end item) supply point

Definition: Major end items, complete pieces of equipment by themselves that don't lose their identity through use, such as trucks, tanks, guns, and power units.

Location on the battlefield: If the division support area has a Class VII supply point, it has very limited quantities on hand. Usually, the Class VII supply point is in the corps areas.

Responsible units: The supply and service company of the main support battalion (MSB) in the division support area (DSA) operates the Class VII supply point for the division. In the corps area, the direct support supply and services companies operate the Class VII supply point, and the heavy material supply companies operate it at the general support level within the corps support command (COSCOM).

Class VIII

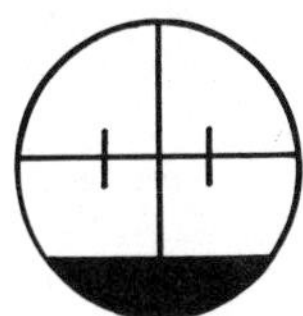

Map symbol: Class VIII (medical supplies) supply point

Definition: All medical supplies, such as medicines, medical equipment, and dressings.

Location on the battlefield: Medical resupply is available in limited quantities in the brigade support area (BSA) and the division support area (DSA). The actual Class VIII supply point is in the corps area.

Responsible units: In the division area, limited supplies are available from the medical companies of the forward support battalions (FSBs) and the main support battalion (MSB). In the corps area, direct support is available from the hospital units, and the medical supply, optical, and maintenance unit (MEDSOM) has a general support Class VIII supply point.

Class IX

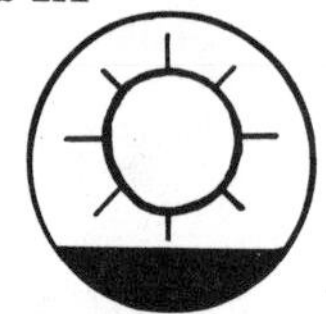

Map symbol: Class IX (repair parts) supply point

Definition: Repair parts and subcomponents used as replacement parts for other equipment, including major subassemblies, such as engines and transmissions.

Location on the battlefield: Class IX supply points are in the brigade support area (BSA), in the division support area (DSA), and in the corps area.

Responsible units: In the brigade support area (BSA), the direct support maintenance company of the forward support battalion (FSB) establishes the Class IX supply point. In the division support area (DSA), the direct support maintenance companies of the main support battalion (MSB) establish the Class IX supply point. In the corps area, the direct support maintenance companies provide direct support, and the repair parts supply company in the general support maintenance battalion provides general support.

Class X

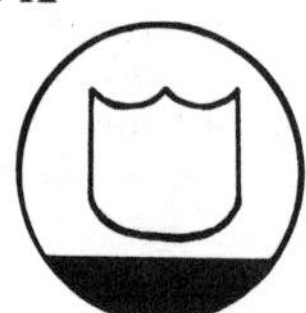

Map symbol: Class X (civil affairs items) supply point

Definition: Civil affairs items, including equipment for economic development and general civilian assistance, such as farm tractors and school supplies.

Location on the battlefield: The corps area.

Responsible units: Civil affairs units at corps level or above.

Multiclass Supply Point

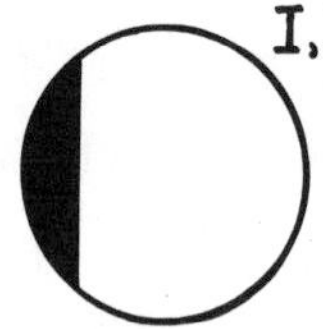

Map symbol: Multiclass supply point

Definition: A supply point that issues Classes I, II, III (packaged), IV, and VII.

Location on the battlefield: These points may be in the brigade support area (BSA), in the division support area (DSA), and in the corps areas.

Responsible units: The supply and services companies of the forward support battalions (FSB) and the main support battalion (MSB) in the division establish multiclass supply points. In the corps area, the direct support supply and service companies of the corps support command (COSCOM) establish them.

Map symbol: The upper right corner of the map symbol notes classes supplied from the point.

Medical Support

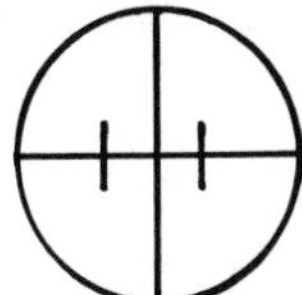

Map symbol: Medical support activity

Definition: Health services either for direct support of combat operations or for routine health care.

Location on the battlefield: Medical facilities are in the brigade support area (BSA), in the division support area (DSA), and in the corps area.

Responsible units: In the division, the medical companies of the forward support battalion (FSB) and the main support battalion (MSB) provide medical support. In the corps areas, the medical units of either a medical brigade or a medical group provide medical support.

Graves Registration (GRREG)

Map symbol: Graves registration activity

Definition: Registration service that records the death of any military personnel and provides care for and coordinates transportation of the remains to rear areas and, after appropriate preparation, coordinates transportation to their final resting place.

Location on the battlefield: Graves registration collecting points are in the brigade support area (BSA), in the division support area (DSA), and in the corps area.

Responsible units: The field service company of the corps support command (COSCOM) dispatches and provides all graves registration teams.

Maintenance Support

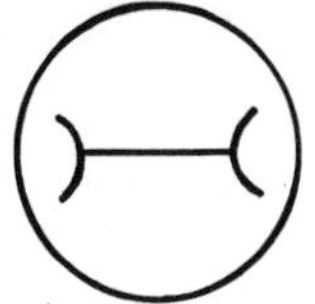

Map symbol: Maintenance support activity

Definition: All actions provided by personnel or units other than assigned operators or crew members to keep equipment in operation and ready for combat.

Location on the battlefield: Maintenance operations are in the brigade support area (BSA), in the division support area (DSA), and in the corps area.

Responsible units: The direct support maintenance company of the forward support battalion (FSB) is responsible for maintenance support in the brigade support area (BSA). The direct support maintenance companies of the main support battalion (MSB) provide maintenance support in the division support area (DSA). In the corps area, both direct support and general support maintenance companies of the corps support command (COSCOM) provide maintenance support.

Salvage Collection

Map symbol: Materiel salvage point

Definition: Collection of any piece of equipment that cannot be returned to use on the battlefield because it cannot be repaired or identified.

Location on the battlefield: Salvage points are in the brigade support area (BSA), in the division support area (DSA), and in the corps areas.

Responsible Units: The supply and service companies of the forward support battalion (FSB), the main support battalion (MSB), and the corps support command (COSCOM) provide salvage points.

SELECTED NUCLEAR, BIOLOGICAL, AND CHEMICAL INFORMATION

CONTAMINATION	PRIMARY COLOR	INSCRIPTION COLOR	28 CM
Nuclear	White	Black	ATOM 20 CM
Biological	Blue	Red	BIO
Chemical	Yellow	Red	GAS

Contaminated area markings.

Contaminated Area Markings

Because, on the battlefield, combat service support units may move into areas contaminated by nuclear, biological, or chemical warfare, one of the most important things they need to know is how to read and to establish contaminated area markers. The examples in the accompanying chart provide a quick reference for personnel who do not work with these markers as their primary duty.

Biological Effects of Nuclear Radiation

The accompanying chart provides a quick reference to the effects of radiation on soldiers.

DOSE—RADS	ONSET OF INITIAL SYMPTOMS	INCAPACITATION	HOSPITALIZATION AND DISPOSITION
0—70	Within 6 hours slight incidence of transient headache and nausea in up to 5% of personnel in the upper part of dose range.	None	Hospitalization not required. All return to duty.
70—150	Within 3 to 6 hours transient mild headache and nausea; some vomiting in up to 50% of of this group.	None to slight decrease in ability to perform duties in up to 25% of group; up to 5% may be combat ineffective.	Eventual hospitalization (20—30 days in upper part of range) of less than 5% in upper part of dose range. Return to duty; no deaths are anticipated.
150—450	Within 3 hours headaches, nausea, and fatigue; slight incidence of diarrhea; over 50% of group vomits.	Can perform routine tasks; performing combat or complex tasks may be hampered; over 5% will be combat ineffective increasing with higher doses.	Hospitalization (30—90 days) is indicated in upper range after latent period of 10—30 days. Some deaths (less than 5% to 50%) at upper end of range; return to duty questionable at higher dose.
450—800	Within 1 hour severe nausea and vomiting, diarrhea, fever early in upper part of range.	Can perform simple tasks; significant reduction in combat effectiveness in upper part of range; lasts more than 24 hours.	Hospitalization (90—120 days for those surviving) for 100% of the group; latent period 7—20 days. 50% deaths at lower and increasing toward upper end; all deaths occur within 45 days.
800—3000	Within ½ to 1 hour severe and prolonged vomiting, diarrhea and fever.	Significant reduction in combat effectiveness; in upper part of range some will undergo transient period of complete combat effectiveness followed by capability for some response until end of the latent period.	Hospitalization for 100% indicated; latent period of less than 7 days. 100% deaths within 14 days.
3000—8000	Within 5 minutes severe and prolonged vomiting, diarrhea, fever and prostration; convulsions may occur at higher doses.	Completely incapacitated within 5 minutes and remain so for 30 to 45 minutes; will then recover but will be functionally impaired until death.	Hospitalization for 100%; latent period of 1 to 2 days; 100% deaths within 5 days.
Above 8000	Within 5 minutes the same symptoms as above.	Complete, permanent incapacitation; unable to perform physically demanding tasks within 5 minutes.	Hospitalization for 100%. No latent period. 100% deaths in 15 to 48 hours.

Biological effects of nuclear radiation.

Effects of Chemical Agents

The accompanying chart provides guidance to assist in the identification of chemical contamination of personnel and immediate action required.

AGENT	DISSEMINATED	SYMPTOMS	EFFECTS	RATE OF ACTION	FIRST AID	DECONTAMINATION	PROTECTION REQUIRED
AC BLOOD	Vapor	Convulsions; Coma	Incapacitates; kills if high concentration inhaled	Rapid	None	None	Mask
G series GA GB* GD	Vapor or aerosol	Difficulty in breathing; drooling; nausea; convulsions; sometimes dimness of vision.	Incapacitates; kills if high concentration inhaled.	Delayed thru the skin; Very rapid thru inhalation.	Nerve Agent Antidote; Artificial Respiration	None required	Mask, Proctective Clothing
V series VX* VR55 GD(T) NERVE	Liquid Droplet		Incapacitates; kills if contaminated skin is not decontaminated rapidly.	Delayed thru the skin; more rapid thru the eyes.		Flush eyes with water; use M258 kit to decon skin.	
H* HN H/L L CX BLISTER	Liquid droplet; CX as a fine powder or liquid	H, HN - no early symptoms; L—searing pain in eyes, stinging of skin. CX—irritates eyes and nose.	Blisters skin; destroys lung tissue.	Delayed blisters, hours to days, eyes effected more rapidly, H/L, L and CX can be very rapid.	None	Flush eyes with water; use M258 kit on skin; wash with soap and cold water.	Mask; Protective Clothing

Chemical agents information.

Mission-Oriented Protective Posture

Mission-oriented protective posture (MOPP) is the name for the measures available to logisticians in the field to protect their troops if they end up in a chemically or biologically contaminated environment. The accompanying table provides quick reference to the five MOPP levels.

Mission-Oriented Protective Posture (MOPP) Levels

MOPP Level	*Overgarment*	*Overboots*	*Mask/Hood*	*Gloves*
0	Carried	Carried	Carried	Carried
1	Worn*	Carried	Carried	Carried
2	Worn*	Worn	Worn*	Carried
3	Worn	Worn	Worn*	Carried
4	Worn Closed	Worn	Worn Closed	Worn

*Overgarment and/or hood worn open or closed, depending on temperature.

3

Training

Logistics commanders face the responsibility for training troops and officers every day. In peacetime, they must train their soldiers to accomplish individual tasks and mold those tasks into completion of the unit's collective mission. They must also train their customers, the combat arms, in the procedures they must follow to obtain the services and supplies they need. In wartime, the constant flow of replacement personnel, both to the logistic units and to the combat units, requires continuous training programs on the battlefield. To provide adequate support, support soldiers must have the technical skills to do their jobs, the technical skills to deliver their work to the correct place as a member of a trained team, and the combat skills to survive. The purpose of this chapter is to discuss some of the obstacles that logistics commanders will encounter in conducting training and to provide an organized approach to assist them in overcoming those obstacles.

Few things are consistently true from one type of military unit to the next. Perhaps the one answer that could apply to almost every question that comes up, however, is that it depends on the situation. It is nearly always the correct response because all military plans, procedures, and objectives must be flexible and subject to adjustment. The ever-changing situation includes many obstructions that will prevent efficient operations and serve as obstacles to training. These obstacles must be overcome by logistics officers. It is their responsibility to decide what training their soldiers need to accomplish their mission and survive on the battlefield and to ensure that their soldiers receive that training regardless of the situation.

Each leader must realize that training is occurring all of the time. Training is not limited to planned situations in which soldiers are taken out of their normal duties and sent to the first aid class or the rifle range. Training also occurs spontaneously—for example, when the mechanic completes a task in the shop correctly and the supervisor praises the mechanic's work. Unfortunately, training also occurs when the same mechanic completes a job incorrectly or in a sloppy manner and the supervisor doesn't notice. The dictionary definition of training is "to make proficient by instruction, and practice as in some art, profession, or work." As this definition indicates, every action that a soldier takes is not only the result of training but also a training opportunity.

The first step in training a combat service support unit is to establish a central objective toward which the leaders of that unit can direct their training efforts. This objective should be simple, direct, and achievable. The objective should be the accomplishment of their mission through proper utilization of their resources and personnel. This is very easy to say but the word "proper" makes it hard to do. Proper utilization of resources and personnel requires the logistics officer to train his personnel not only to respond to the situation and the needs of the mission but also to respond in an organized, effective, and correctly executed manner.

The remainder of this chapter provides some methods and approaches to organizing and controlling training to accomplish the goal of effective and proper mission accomplishment.

SUGGESTIONS FOR THE FIELD TRAINING EXERCISE (FTX)

Every unit training program must include some type of field training exercise (FTX) if it is to result in complete training. Every unit must exercise the movement of its operation across the battlefield while continuing to support its mission. Units cannot simulate the difficulties of field duty in garrison; they must experience field difficulties in the field. Before leaving garrison, combat service support officers must, in the same manner as any other commanders, prepare themselves and their units to extract the maximum benefit from the FTX. The following suggestions should help in that preparation.

- Orient *everybody* early on tactical play, umpire controls, administration rules, and maneuver area restrictions.
- Establish a firm start time, but do not announce an end time. Instead of an end time, make sure that all appropriate personnel know the training objectives of the FTX. Do not return to garrison until the unit has attained those objectives. The unit should operate during the exercise as if it could remain in the field indefinitely.
- Always allow time for troop-leading procedures. Don't rush planning, reconnaissance, assembly area checks, and so forth. Avoid the hurry-up-and-wait syndrome.
- Establish procedures to discipline the FM (frequency modulation) nets. (No local codes above company level.) Use wire and messenger as much as possible. Get key messages through. Use feedback.
- Plan for total combat service support although some may be simulated. Exercise trains and reports. Have a definite plan for all classes of supply and service functions down to the lowest level.
- Make sure that attached units have received briefings and appropriate care. Exercise cross-attachment of units as required for the simulated tactical situation.

• Make sure that each unit has a firm SOP for checks and reports at march halts.

• Always use the TAC SOP, including the MOPP system.

• Conduct critiques as early as possible. (Let the junior participants speak first.)

• Remember these tips: no CPs on hilltops; no trains, POL points, or conferences at road junctions.

• Train all soldiers to keep weapons clean, lubed, and ready to fire. Always make range cards.

• Make sure that all leaders insist on personal hygiene; observe soldiers for heat and cold injuries.

• Always send hot meals out to outposts, attachments, mechanics, and so forth.

• Make sure that all personnel understand the importance of controlling vehicle speeds. All vehicles must have assistant drivers.

• Establish definite procedures to spot-check PMCS, including tire pressure, track maintenance, and generators.

• Check stowage before road marches, especially trailers.

• Make sure that packing lists include cleaning gear for weapons.

• Stop to make spot corrections at any time to avoid reinforcing bad habits.

• Plan for training during the hours of darkness. At least half of the training for unit moves should occur during periods of reduced visibility.

TRAINING MANAGEMENT

All combat service support leaders must analyze and manage their training needs and those of their soldiers. This leadership requires logisticians to study their unit missions and the different tasks that each member of their units must complete to accomplish the overall collective tasks of the unit mission. This process requires continuous evaluation and planning. The following checklists from the battalion training management system (BTMS) provide a good framework for the management and control of unit training programs.

Tips for Training Meetings

- Make the purpose(s) of the meeting clear.
- Set a time limit.
- Follow the agenda.
- Encourage participation.
- Clearly state training objectives and taskings assigned to subordinate leaders.

Company Training Meeting Agenda

The company commander, company officers, the first sergeant, platoon sergeants, and key personnel (maintenance NCO, supply NCO, and communications NCO, as needed) should discuss the following topics:

• *Last week's training.* Evaluate and critique training conducted since the last meeting. Review reasons for training planned but not conducted. Estimate the current status of training.

• *Next week's training.* Apply new guidelines from higher headquarters, especially new unscheduled requirements. Review changes to the week's schedule. Identify tasks needing training next week that are not on the training schedule. Plan use of unscheduled training time. Identify opportunities for concurrent training.

• *Future training.* Preview the training for week after next. Discuss training guidance. For the benefit of the trainers, discuss future training on the short-range plan although it is not yet scheduled. Review training recommendations from participants for training to include in future schedules. Identify key personnel losses and training needs.

Battalion Training Meeting Agenda

The battalion commander, unit commanders, the S3, the command sergeant major, and selected staff should discuss the following matters:

• *Last week's training.* Evaluate and critique training conducted since the last meeting. Review reasons for training planned but not conducted. Review training scheduled this week and next. Estimate the current status of training.

• *Short-range planning.* Discuss new guidance received from higher headquarters. Discuss items to train for the week after next, especially training objectives and resources. Issue guidance for the training schedule three weeks from now. Update the short-range plan as needed.

• *Long-range planning.* Review new guidelines from higher headquarters, resources, and chronic training deficiencies. Update long-range plan as needed.

Solving Performance Problems

Commanders should use the following method to solve performance problems in training programs.

First, identify the substandard performance.

Second, identify the causes of the substandard performance:

• Check for obstacles to performance, such as not enough time, inadequate tools and equipment, no authority, and unclear guidance.
• Check for nonmotivators, such as rewards for poor performance, punishment for good performance, and personal problems.
• Check for skill deficiencies and the need for refresher or initial training.
• Check for inability to learn.
• Look for a combination of problems.

Finally, identify solution(s).

Sample Individual Performance

Commanders should take the following steps to sample individual

performance as part of their evaluation of the effectiveness of unit training programs:
- Select a task to sample.
- Gather resources.
- Know the task.
- Select a soldier for testing.
- Conduct the performance test.
- Critique the soldier.
- Inform the trainer.
- Note the results.

On-the-Spot Corrections

When soldiers fail to perform to standard in unit training programs, the commander should use this method to make corrections on the spot:
- Explain what was wrong.
- Explain why it was wrong.
- Show how to perform it correctly.
- Always follow critique with more practice as soon as possible until soldiers perform to standard.

Critique

Commanders should use the following procedures to critique substandard performance in unit training programs:
- Get soldiers to describe what happened.
- Get soldiers to explain why their actions were unsatisfactory in terms of standards and consequences.
- Get soldiers to describe how to perform correctly.
- Always follow critique with more practice as soon as possible until soldiers perform to standard.

Performance-Oriented Training

Commanders should take the following steps before, during, and after training to improve their soldiers' performance in unit training programs:

Before training—
- Check training guidance for such information as who, what, when, where, and how.
- Find out the training objective from such sources as the soldiers' manual, ARTEP, or chain of command.
- Find references and read them.
- List resources available and everything you need to train.
- Qualify yourself to perform the task because you must be able to do the task before you can train other soldiers.
- Write the training outline.
- Gather and prepare resources to make sure everything is ready to use.

- Announce the training to the soldiers so they can be ready for training.
- Rehearse the training session until it is smooth.
- Revise the training outline by learning from mistakes that showed up in rehearsal.

During training—
- Cover the training statement. In your own words based on training objectives, state the task and how well to perform it.
- Make any necessary caution statements, such as security classification, troop safety, and care of equipment.
- Pretest the task by asking soldiers whether they are ready, preparing the conditions, stating the task, observing the standards, and critiquing the performance. Preview the what, why, and how of the training.
- Demonstrate the task.
- Walk through the task steps, hands on, and by the numbers.
- Have the soldiers practice and make on-the-spot corrections.
- Test the performance the same way as in the pretest and critique the performance after the test.

After training—
- Record results in the job book as go/no go.
- Report results to the chain of command in terms of successes and problems.

FOOTLOCKER TRAINING

General John Wickham, Jr., has captured the essence of the training responsibility of a leader: "I also believe that such 'footlocker training' should take place in the Noncommissioned Officer Corps, with the senior NCOs taking a direct hand in the professional and personal upbringing of junior NCOs." Not just the NCOs but all leaders must feel a personal commitment to their soldiers and subordinate officers. No question is too dumb to answer and no mistake is a total loss because both provide opportunities for additional training. Leaders shouldn't waste any of these opportunities to train, instruct, and nurture their subordinates.

QUESTIONS FOR THE TRAINER

The following list of questions applies to every training situation. The purpose of the list is not to check the technical accuracy of the training but to ensure that the trainer has prepared and conducted the training effectively.

- What did the soldiers know about the subject before this training?
- Why were these soldiers selected for this training?
- How did the trainer explain the training objectives to the soldiers?
- How does the training relate to SQT (skill qualification test), ARTEP (Army Training Evaluation Program), EDRE (Emergency Deployment Readiness Exercise), or contingency tasks?

• How are you using the chain of command to teach and evaluate?

• Are you keeping teams, crews, squads, and sections together?

• How are you reinforcing basic discipline and habits of respect for property in this training?

• How are you developing concern for maintenance, unit SOP knowledge, enemy tactics, and safety in your instruction?

• What are your plans for integrated and concurrent training?

• What are your plans for finding and helping the slow learners?

• What are your plans for identifying and rewarding the soldiers making the greatest effort and the greatest progress?

• What feedback on progress and shortcomings does each soldier receive before departing the training area?

• How do you measure attainment of training objectives?

• How will you critique the exercise?

• How will you pass on lessons learned today for use in future training, such as how to teach and what to train?

• How are you avoiding wasting the soldiers' time?

• How are you bringing some challenge and excitement into the exercise?

4

Intelligence

All information on the battlefield must be collected and processed rapidly and efficiently. Understanding the basic principles and methods of identifying this data is essential to the logistician in the field. This chapter addresses these basic principles and provides guidance on the handling of prisoners of war. With the current increase in infiltration and commando operations, logisticians could face the responsibility of processing prisoners and should have this information readily available.

SALUTE

The word *salute* helps soldiers, including logisticians, remember what to report if they observe any enemy activity. Logisticians should also remember that enemy soldiers try to remember and report the same information. Therefore, support soldiers need to be alert to this double-edged blade of information and try not only to gain information about the enemy but also to deny him information about friendly forces.

S = Size

Whenever soldiers see enemy activity or enemy units, they must remember and report accurately the size of the element or activity. Conversely, friendly logistic positions and units should incorporate dispersion and camouflage to mask their size as much as possible.

A = Activity

Soldiers need to identify, remember, and report exactly what sort of activity they observed, such as movement, routine garrison operations, supply activities, and so forth. By the same token, logisticians should incorporate any means they have available to cause an enemy observer to misidentify the nature of service support activities.

L = Location

Soldiers also need to remember and report exactly where the activity they observed was. Every item of information is a part of a puzzle, and knowing where the part came from helps the intelligence units fit the puzzle together. Soldiers need to report whatever they see as quickly as possible because the location part of the report loses its value rapidly as units move around the battlefield. On the other hand, combat service support units should try not to stay in fixed positions for very long to avoid identification by enemy observation.

U = Unit/Uniform

If soldiers can identify units or uniforms they observe, they should report such information to help assess enemy capabilities and weaknesses. Simultaneously, to decrease their own vulnerability, soldiers need to prevent as much as possible the identification of friendly units by enemy observers.

T = Time

Noting and reporting the time of observation helps intelligence personnel detect and trace the movement of enemy units on the battlefield. By the same theory, logisticians need to use camouflage and other deception methods to try to confuse the enemy as to the times supply and service support activities occur.

E = Equipment

Identifying and reporting enemy equipment observed can reveal a multitude of information, such as how fast the enemy can move, whether the enemy has armor in strategic locations, and how well his fuel supply and support system are holding up. Along the same lines of thinking, logisticians need to consider deception methods for masking their own equipment and its movement from the enemy.

When you observe, ask:

WHO did you see?
WHAT was he doing?
WHEN did you see it?
WHERE did it happen?

AND WHERE WERE YOU?

General observation.

OBSERVING AND REPORTING

Combat soldiers are close to the enemy and can observe him and the terrain he controls. Support soldiers also have the opportunity to gather important information by just watching and reporting what they see in their duties. For example, truck drivers and support soldiers operating refuel or supply points can report such valuable pieces of information as which way the refugees were going, how many other vehicles were on the road, how often they saw the same vehicles and people and how many civilians were around the area.

HANDLING PRISONERS OF WAR AND CAPTURED ENEMY DOCUMENTS

Usually, combat service support units do not capture prisoners, but as infiltration, sabotage, and terrorism increase, they may have to. The following pointers should help in properly handling those prisoners and the information they carry.

First, when you capture prisoners, remember the five Ss:

SEARCH – for weapons and documents immediately.

SEGREGATE – prisoners into groups: officers, NCOs, privates, deserters, civilians, females, line-crossers, and so forth.

SILENCE – *do not* allow prisoners to talk to one another.

SPEED – prisoners to the rear with personal items and documents.

SAFEGUARD – prisoners, documents, and materiel; tag and evacuate them to the rear.

Even – perhaps especially – capturing prisoners of war requires paperwork. Tag prisoners and captured enemy documents and equipment. If capture tags are not available, any piece of paper will do. The tag should include date and time of capture, place of capture (coordinates), capturing unit, and circumstances of capture.

5

Field Discipline

Survival is the essential requirement for mission accomplishment on the modern battlefield. To guarantee that survival, combat service support units must practice the same field discipline and survival skills the combat units use. This chapter presents a series of checklists and reminders to assist logisticians in ensuring that their soldiers and their combat service support units survive the dangers of operations in the combat zone.

PERIMETER DEFENSE CHECKLIST

The first and most important action a unit needs to take when it occupies a position is to establish a secure perimeter. On the battlefields of today, all units are vulnerable to enemy action regardless of their proximity to the forward line of own troops (FLOT). Thus, the following actions are just as vital to combat service support units as they are to infantry units at the FLOT.

• Establish security. Assign listening posts and observation posts (LPs/OPs), dispatch surveillance and reconnaissance patrols, and establish ambushes on avenues of approach. Local security elements should be forward of the perimeter during the entire preparation phase.

• Position crew-served weapons. Ensure that leaders physically walk the entire length of designated final protective lines (FPLs). Prepare range cards for every weapon, no matter how briefly the unit expects to be in the position. This step is especially important for the crew-served weapons, but also every rifleman should prepare a range card for his area of responsibility. Make sure that rifle positions support and protect each side of each crew-served weapon.

• Clear all fields of fire, remove objects masking observation, and determine ranges to probable targets. Do these three things for each machine gun final protective line (FPL) and primary direction of fire (PDF) and for any available mortars. In addition, riflemen should clear their individual fields of fire, and grenadiers should establish the indirect fire targets in their individual areas and record them on their range cards.

• Prepare all weapons emplacements and individual positions, including overhead cover and camouflage.

• Establish wire communications to every control element in the chain of command, to every crew-served weapon, to each listening post and observation post, and to each dismount point.

• If time permits and the materials are available, install mines, barbed wire, booby traps, and all available warning devices, including trip flares.

• Ensure that every weapon team and soldier select and prepare an alternate position and supplementary position, if space and time permit.

• Designate the personnel responsible for acting as a reaction force. Because the majority of CSS soldiers are engaged in support operations, they cannot simply man their perimeter positions. They must perform their primary mission. This forces CSS commanders to identify their reaction forces to engage security threats beyond the combat ability of any particular section of the perimeter.

PERIMETER SECTOR SKETCHES

To ensure that the defense plan is complete and coordinated, the commander should require each leader to sketch the portion of the perimeter for which each is responsible. The commander should then use these sketches as a tool to help fashion an overall sketch of the perimeter and to obtain the information to make adjustments to the individual sectors as required. Then the individual leaders use the sketches to help manage the defense of their sectors.

Squad Sector Sketch

Each squad leader should prepare a sector sketch with the following information to help plan the defense and to help control fire:

• Main terrain features in the squad leader's sector of fire and ranges to them.

• Each primary fighting position.

• Primary and secondary fire of each position.

• Type of weapon in each position.

• Observation or listening posts and squad leader's position.

• Deadspace and obstacles.

Platoon Sector Sketch

The platoon leader checks range cards and squad sector sketches. If any gaps or flaws are found in the fire plan, the platoon leader adjusts weapons or sectors as necessary. If any deadspace is found, the platoon leader takes steps to cover it with mines, grenade-launcher fire, or indirect fire. The platoon leader then makes a platoon sector sketch with the following information:

• Squad sectors of fire.

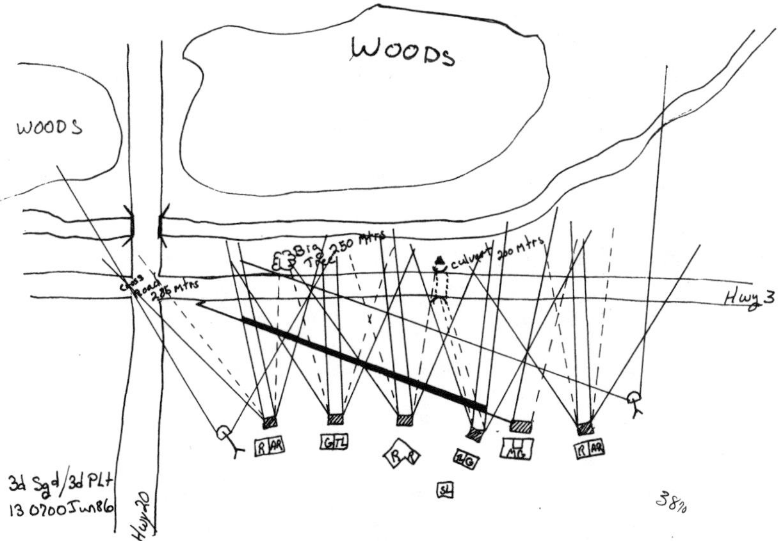

Example of a squad sector sketch.

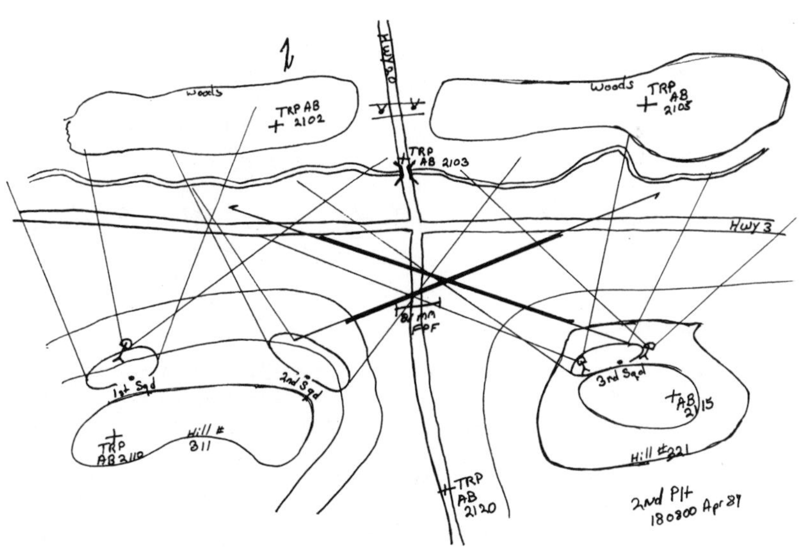

Example of a platoon sector sketch.

• Machine gun and Dragon positions, including sectors of fire, final protective lines (FPLs), and primary directions of fire (PDFs) for the machine guns and target reference points (TRPs) for the Dragons.

• Mines and obstacles.

• Indirect fire planned in the platoon sector of fire, TRPs and final protective fires (FPFs).

• Observation points, patrol routes (if any), and the platoon command post (CP).

Company Defense Plan

The company commander should review the platoon leaders' sketches. If he finds any gaps, the company commander should adjust the platoon

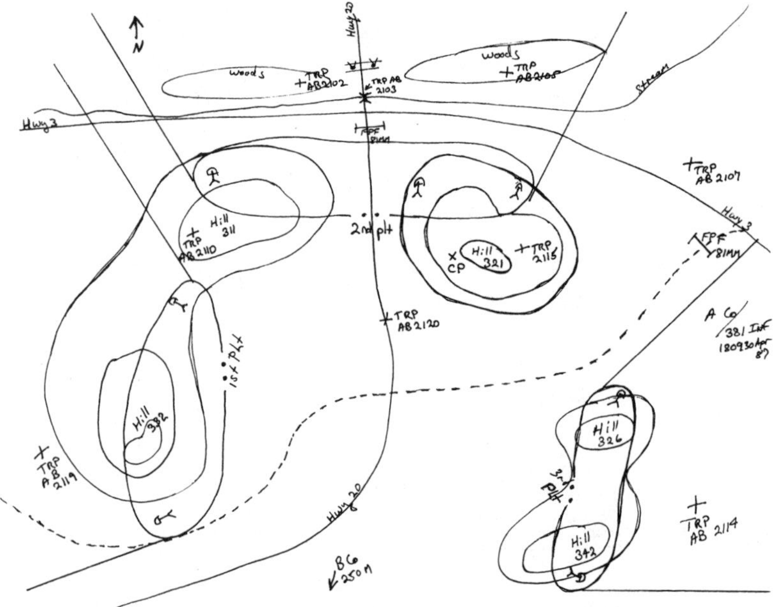

Example of a company defense plan sketch.

sectors until all avenues of approach to the unit's position are covered. Then the commander should make a sketch of the perimeter of the company, including this information:

• Platoon sectors of fire.

• Crew-served weapons and Dragon positions.

• Mines and obstacles.

• Target reference points (TRPs) and final protective fires (FPFs) for indirect fire support.

• Location of company command post (CP) and each platoon CP.

- Observation posts, listening posts, and patrol routes (if any).
- Alternate positions for each platoon.

BRIGADE SUPPORT AREA SELECTION AND DEFENSE

The location of the brigade support area (BSA) depends on the tactical situation. The BSA may be from six to thirty kilometers behind friendly forward positions. Factors to consider in the selection of the BSA site are the same as those for any other tactical operation except that the BSA is a very large area. The BSA must be forward of the brigade rear boundary and adjacent to the main supply route (MSR). It is farther forward during offensive operations, thereby reducing the number of moves the BSA must make to support the attack. Conversely, in the defense, the BSA must initially be farther to the rear to reduce the number of displacements interrupting the flow of support.

Trying to establish a rule about the size of the BSA is impractical because each situation is different. Decision makers must consider and analyze such variables as terrain, availability of usable land, type of operation, enemy capabilities, and expected support requirements to determine the right size for the BSA. Normally, the average brigade-sized unit requires from five to ten square kilometers.

One of the reasons for the large size of the BSA is the requirement for dispersion of the varied elements normally located there. The units and parts of units that usually operate in the BSA cannot secure and defend the entire area. Therefore, they spread out and establish individual secure bases or clusters of bases. They do not, however, randomly select their own positions. They are under the operational control of the unit the brigade commander has designated as the rear area command element, normally the forward support battalion (FSB).

Assigning positions in the BSA involves these considerations:

• Field trains of the combat units should be in forward positions in the BSA to reduce the traffic in the BSA itself.

• Medical units should be in the center of the BSA. They cannot defend themselves, so they are less vulnerable with friendly units around them. Further, according to the Geneva Convention rulings, no other unit can be colocated with a medical unit.

• At least one unit base should be in a position to act as a blocking force on each high-speed avenue of approach into the BSA.

• Transportation elements, especially Class III transportation assets, should be to the rear of the BSA to reduce both traffic in the BSA and vulnerability of these valuable assets.

• Units should be far enough away from one another to reduce the possibility that a single probing attack could affect more than one unit but still close enough to offer mutual tactical support.

• Units should also be in groups to ease the support effort, with related activities as close together as safely possible.

FIELD DISCIPLINE CHECKLISTS

Field discipline includes the things that soldiers and units must do regardless of the situation. Most of the items that the term field discipline normally covers are simply the soldierly skills handed down for hundreds of years. These traditions that help keep soldiers alive, effective, and fit for duty are part of the school of the soldier. Professional soldiers are very good in the practice of field discipline; amateurs are not.

Soldier Disciplines

Teach your troops these field disciplines, and make sure they practice these disciplines all the time.

- Always wear your personal equipment and wear it correctly. The pieces of equipment that you are supposed to have with you at all times are the items that can give you the ability to survive. For example, if you were outside of your position without your equipment and your weapon when your unit was attacked, you would not even be able to defend yourself. In such a case, you would certainly not be an asset to your unit, and worse, you could be killed.
- Clean your weapon at least once each day and anytime it becomes dirty. It will operate if you take care of it; it may not if you don't.
- Clean yourself. You need to stay as clean as possible to prevent sickness. Change your underwear and socks regularly, shave daily, and keep your body and hair clean.
- Rest when the opportunity presents itself. Do not stand if you can sit. Do not sit if you can lie down. Sleep if you have nothing else to do. In combat, you may have to go without rest many times.
- Practice operational security consistently and constantly. Use your challenge and password. Don't discuss your orders outside your unit. Remember the code of conduct, stay alert, and pick up your garbage.
- Practice your soldier skills. You will find them in common tasks manuals, SQT manuals, and job books. Learn to do your assigned duties correctly.
- Always camouflage your position. Do not attract fire on yourself and your unit.
- Keep your gear packed when you are not using it. You may have to move quickly.
- Practice safety. The battlefield is dangerous enough without adding recklessness to it.

Unit Disciplines

Teach your subordinate leaders these field disciplines, and make sure they include these disciplines in their unit routines.

- Keep the unit moving unless it has a defensive role. Anytime the unit is not moving, prepare defensive positions.
- Herringbone your weapons or establish a defensive perimeter at all halts. Always put out security elements.

• Always camouflage and obscure the unit. Do not allow the enemy to easily observe the outfit.

• Feed your soldiers, refuel your equipment, and rearm the unit at every opportunity. You should automatically take care of these basic needs without orders.

• Keep the unit ready to move.

• Keep the troops informed. Make sure all soldiers are aware of the current situation and understand the current operations order and frag orders.

• Send all reports to higher headquarters to arrive on time. If the headquarters has to call for information, the unit is not performing up to the required standard.

• Make sure all unit movements occur in a disciplined and organized manner. Nothing should happen haphazardly.

• Make sure maintenance is performed correctly and rapidly. Don't drag dead equipment with you; either get it fixed or replace it.

• Maintain communications links. Do not let the unit become isolated from current information.

• All unit areas, including the command post and the trains, should be operating tactically and should be properly secured.

• Make sure that your troops are trained to use operational security and communications security measures habitually and that these measures are part of the standing operating procedures in your unit.

• Be able to account for troops and sensitive items at all times. Never leave any question about where your troops and your equipment are.

DURING MOVE/TRAINING/FIGHTING CHECKLIST

Any kind of training or combat operation requires soldiers to practice soldier skills. Requiring troops to develop and practice the following soldierly habits in a professional manner helps to ensure mission accomplishment and to decrease potential losses from enemy action or accidental injury.

1. *Always camouflage.* Hide equipment, vehicles, and soldiers as much as possible to prevent enemy observation. Using face paint in all operations not only will help camouflage the soldiers but also will help protect their skin from sun- and windburn. Covering the shiny parts of equipment and vehicles with mud or any other camouflage will help prevent observation of your movements. As a logistician, you should also remember to cover your cargo, with canvas if possible, to prevent the casual observer from identifying which trucks are carrying the most important loads.

2. *Position troops correctly in vehicles.* Always make sure that all personnel are in proper and secure seats when vehicles are moving. This precaution serves two purposes. First, it helps prevent injured soldiers from falling and bumping. Second, it ensures that all soldiers are able to reach the controls of their vehicles or their weapons to take immediate action if the unit is attacked.

3. *Put air guards up and orient weapons.* No matter how short the move, ensure that soldiers are maintaining all-around security observation. Because this term includes not only 360 degrees around but also up, each vehicle should have an assigned and posted air guard. Soldiers should have their weapons oriented within the vehicle to deliver fire in any direction immediately.

4. *Keep vehicles cleaned, loaded, and maintained.* Make sure the soldiers keep vehicles free of trash and garbage and the cargo securely lashed down and properly stow all equipment in the correct locations. Make sure the vehicles receive during-operation checks at every opportunity, and report and correct deficiencies and shortcomings immediately.

5. *Conduct security and maintenance at every stop.* Have soldiers assume security positions as a matter of standing operating procedures at every stop. Drivers should perform their operational checks at every halt, and riflemen and weapons crews should prepare range cards at every halt, regardless of the duration.

6. *Maintain radio discipline.* Do not send unnecessary messages and communication checks. If you must use the radio, remember to keep all transmissions less than fifteen seconds.

7. *Conduct NBC surveillance.* Habitually practice surveillance procedures for nuclear, biological, and chemical warfare. Use the mission-oriented protective posture (MOPP) to ensure that the soldiers are protected.

8. *Brief troops properly.* Ensure that each subordinate leader understands the unit mission/destination/objective. You should also thoroughly brief them on current plans and the mission of the next higher element. Also, verify that your subordinates know the reason for the mission or the objective so that your unit can continue to pursue its objective even in your absence.

9. *Plan rest/sleep.* Give your units in the field a standard operating procedure for sleep and rest that emphasizes the tactical situation. Make sure that the sleep-and-rest SOP keeps enough soldiers awake and on duty to man all crew-served weapons and to operate the communication systems at all times. Each sleep plan should also allow equal sleep opportunity for all personnel, including commanders and leaders.

10. *Operate safely.* Conduct all actions and operations in the safest possible manner. Always use ground guides for vehicles in unit areas, and make sure that soldiers handle fires and matches properly. Teach all your subordinate leaders their responsibility to ensure that the soldiers operate safely.

AFTER MOVE/TRAINING/FIGHTING CHECKLIST

Commanders need to take the following steps immediately after a move, a training exercise, or a firefight.

1. *Always camouflage.* Hide the unit from direct observation as quickly as possible when it has moved into position. Do not allow the unit to be an easy target. Establish security within the unit area as soon as

possible. Ensure that every soldier has an assigned defensive position and has completed a range card for that position. Assign listening posts and observation posts as required.

2. *Arm, feed, and fuel.* Rearm all weapons and redistribute ammunition as required. Refuel all vehicles as soon as possible. Feed all of the soldiers as soon as possible after moving into the position.

3. *Conduct maintenance checks.* Personally emphasize that all vehicles and equipment receive complete after-operation checks and that equipment inspection sheets (DA 2404) must go to the maintenance officer.

4. *Be sure all weapons are cleaned.* The junior leaders should, however, also make sure that all weapons are not being cleaned simultaneously.

5. *See that soldiers clean all vehicles.* Loads should be rechecked for security. Vehicle commanders should ensure that all equipment not yet needed remains correctly and properly stowed on the vehicles.

6. *Account for weapons and sensitive items.* Units should reestablish and report this accountability to the commander as soon as possible after moving into a position.

7. *Make sure soldiers clean themselves.* After the unit is established and secure, the soldiers need to take the time to clean themselves and change their clothes as appropriate. Do not allow them to remain dirty if the means are available to prevent it.

8. *Get unit ready to move again.* The entire unit must remain ready to move on short notice.

COVER AND CONCEALMENT DEFINITIONS

The terms *Cover* and *Concealment* may sound alike, especially because they are most effective when used together, but they mean different things in the military.

Cover is protection from enemy fire. Anything that prevents enemy fire from reaching friendly targets is cover. Cover falls into two general categories: natural and man-made. Natural cover comes from proper use of natural terrain, such as hills, ravines, rocks, trees, and any other feature that could prevent enemy fire from hitting its target. Man-made cover includes anything people build that could stop fire, such as foxholes, trenches, buildings, walls, and berms.

Concealment is protection from enemy observation. Anything that keeps the enemy from seeing friendly units or personnel is concealment. Like cover, it can be either man-made or natural. Natural concealment could include bushes, shadows, grass, and fog. Man-made concealment could be anything from paint and nets to tarpaulin that helps keep friendly units invisible to the enemy.

Take the following measures to use cover and concealment to your best advantage.

1. *Make sure that your unit always uses all of the cover and all of the concealment that is available.* Constantly improve both cover and concealment as long as your unit is in a position. Move subordinate units to take

best advantage of the terrain. Obtain construction material and engineer support to increase your advantage.

2. *Make sure that your soldiers move only when necessary.* Movement can reveal not only the presence of the unit, but also every position within the unit.

3. *Train soldiers to keep low to the ground—prone if possible, to prevent observation of their silhouettes as they move.*

4. *Completely train all your soldiers in noise discipline, light discipline, and proper use of camouflage.* Further, sufficiently train all your subordinate leaders in camouflage techniques to hide the unit and in their responsibility to exact the highest standard of performance from their soldiers in these areas.

5. *Train soldiers to avoid hilltops and road junctions.*

CAMOUFLAGE CHECKLIST

Anything done to obscure and hide a unit or a soldier from enemy observation and to increase that concealment is camouflage. All logistics units must be very aware of their unit signature. Normally, they are noisy, dirty operations and, therefore, very hard to hide in any one location for very long. As long as the unit is in a particular location, however, its assigned personnel should continuously do everything possible to camouflage and conceal their unit. Logisticians should consider the following suggestions as minimal guidance to help camouflage their positions.

1. *Disguise the shape of things.* Because one of the distinctive and very quickly recognized objects in any unit is the helmet that every soldier should be wearing, disguise helmets with leaves, twigs, or anything else that will break up the silhouette shape. Smear them with a mixture of mud and burlap rags if nothing else is available.

2. *Change the texture of canvas equipment.* Mud can be a very big help to logisticians who have a great number of canvas-covered cargo trucks or stacks of supplies on the ground covered with canvas. Also use charcoal and paint to break up the texture and obvious shapes of canvas items.

3. *Use local foliage to break up outlines and to cover noticeable objects.* Remember to replace foliage regularly because it wilts. Also, make sure that branches and leaves used for camouflage match the surrounding terrain.

4. *Cover everything that shines.* Remember to camouflage windshields and headlights of all the vehicles, as well as all the other shiny objects on the equipment. For example, close the doors on high-voltage generator control panels to cover their operation lights, and cover the dashboards of cranes operating at night.

5. *Make things look as if they belong, not as if they are out of place.* This is the key to good camouflage. Conceal tracks. Keep boxes, cans, and other litter picked up. Check your camouflage from the enemy standpoint.

NOISE AND LIGHT DISCIPLINE

Enemy patrols, listening posts, and observation posts can hear noises, such as talking, and see a lit match or cigarette at night from great distances. Good noise and light discipline helps prevent the enemy from gaining the information he needs to find and destroy combat service support units. Bad noise and light discipline, however, provide him a road map to the most vulnerable positions. Take the following measures to deny the enemy such information.

- Exercise noise discipline by using hand and arm signals. Do not talk or whisper. Use tape to secure all items that may rattle. When the unit is getting ready to move or performing motor stables or any other operation requiring more than one vehicle, try to start all vehicle engines at the same time. Do not move vehicles unless it is essential. Conduct as much communication as possible with telephones instead of radios.
- Practice light discipline by issuing light filters for all flashlights and requiring soldiers to use them. Allow the use of matches, lighters, and cigarettes only in lightproof areas. Do not use vehicle service lights; use only blackout lights. Turn off all unneeded lights, even inside lightproof areas. If an operation requires a light, adjust the light to its dimmest setting. Ignite heating or cooking fires only in designated areas.

Noise and light discipline is very difficult to maintain in combat service support units. Quite often logisticians find themselves faced with the choice between good noise and light discipline and their support mission. It is a fact that support operations require light and produce a great deal of noise. Because he will not be able to eliminate the light and noise his unit produces, the CSS commander must identify the amount of risk he is willing to take to accomplish his mission.

6

Communications

One of the weakest areas within the operations of combat service support units is their communications procedures. They simply don't get the practice that the combat units get. This weakness coupled with their reduced speed of mobility in comparison to the combat units makes combat service support units very vulnerable not only to compromise but also to destruction through sloppy communications. This chapter will provide the logistician a quick reference for proper communication procedures.

GENERAL INSTRUCTIONS

Like all other military skills, good radio communication requires thought and practice. Soldiers cannot learn it haphazardly, and no one is a natural. Each message or transmission requires careful planning to get the most information passed with the fewest possible words in the shortest possible time. In the same manner, each transmission received requires careful listening to preclude misunderstanding or repetition. Finally, radio operators must carefully and clearly enunciate the messages to ensure clear communication. In short, follow these three general instructions:

- Plan your message.
- Listen carefully.
- Speak clearly.

PHONETICS

One of the tools used to prevent misunderstanding in military verbal communication is the phonetic alphabet. The phonetic alphabet lists carefully chosen words to stand for each letter of the alphabet. The phonetic alphabet uses words that do not sound like any of the other words on the list to reduce confusion and misinterpretation of messages.

A carefully designed list of phonetically pronounced numerals accompanies the phonetic alphabet. Again, the main purpose of the exaggerated pronunciation is to preclude misunderstanding.

Phonetic Alphabet			
A	Alpha	N	November
B	Bravo	O	Oscar
C	Charlie	P	Papa
D	Delta	Q	Quebec
E	Echo	R	Romeo
F	Foxtrot	S	Sierra
G	Golf	T	Tango
H	Hotel	U	Uniform
I	India	V	Victor
J	Juliet	W	Whiskey
K	Kilo	X	X-ray
L	Lima	Y	Yankee
M	Mike	Z	Zulu

Phonetic Pronounciation of Numerals			
0	Zero	5	Fife
1	Wun	6	Six
2	Too	7	Seven
3	Tree	8	Ait
4	Fo-wer	9	Niner

Radio operators may spell out difficult words, unusual words, or words that the receiver must understand by using the phonetic alphabet preceded by the proword "I spell." If the word is pronounceable, operators should say it immediately before the proword and immediately following the phonetic spelling of the word. For example, if transmitting the word *disentangle* over a weak radio link, an operator might send it with the following words:

". . . disentangle, I spell, Delta, India, Sierra, Echo, November, Tango, Alpha, November, Golf, Lima, Echo, disentangle. . . ."

Radio operators should transmit numbers digit by digit, except in cases of even thousands. For example, they should pronounce the number 136 as "Wun, Tree, Six," and 500 as "Fife, Zero, Zero," while 16,000 becomes "Wun, Six, Thousand."

STATION IDENTIFICATION

Identify stations by letter-number-letter call signs obtained from the communications electronics operating instructions (CEOI). Pronounce letters and numbers phonetically.

The call sign M0L07, for example, would be "Mike, Zero, Lima, Zero, Seven."

PROWORDS

Radio communications most commonly use the following list of prowords. Their use shortens transmissions and accelerates understanding and comprehension. Soldiers should memorize and use them by habit. Good military communication rests on them.

All after. The portion of the message to which I refer is all that follows ———.

All before. The portion of the message to which I refer is all that precedes ———.

Authenticate. The station called is to reply to the challenge that follows.

Break. I hereby indicate the separation of the text from other portions of the message.

Correct. You are correct, or what you have transmitted is correct.

Correction. An error has occurred in this transmission. Transmission will continue with the last word correctly transmitted, or the correct version is ———.

Disregard. This transmission is in error. (Do not use this proword to cancel any message that you have completely transmitted and for which you have received acknowledgment.)

Figures. Numerals or numbers follow.

Flash. Precedence flash (first priority).

From. The address designation immediately following indicates the originator of this message.

Groups. This message contains the number of groups indicated by the following numeral.

I authenticate. The group that follows is the reply to your challenge to authenticate.

Immediate. Precedence immediate (second priority).

I read back. The following is my response to your instruction to read back.

I say again. I am repeating transmission or portion indicated.

I spell. I shall spell the next word phonetically.

Message. A message that requires recording is about to follow in a transmission immediately after the call. (Use this proword to pass messages on tactical or reporting nets.)

Out. This is the end of my transmission to you, and no answer is required or expected.

Over. This is the end of my transmission to you, and a response is necessary. Go ahead; transmit.

Priority. Precedence priority (third priority).

Read back. Repeat this entire transmission exactly as received.

Roger. I understand your last transmission.

Routine. Precedence routine (fourth priority).

Say again. Repeat all of your last transmission. If followed by identification data, it means repeat ——— (indicate portion).

Speak slower. Your transmission is too fast. Reduce speed of transmission.

This is. This transmission is from the station whose designation immediately follows.

Time. That which immediately follows is the time or date-time group of the message.

To. The addressees immediately following should take action.

Unknown station. I do not know the identity of the station with whom I am attempting to establish communication.

Wait. I must pause for a few seconds.

Wait out. I must pause longer than a few seconds.

Wilco. I have received your signal, I understand it, and I will comply. (Only the addressee should say wilco.)

Word after. The word of the message to which I refer is that which follows ———.

Word before. The word of the message to which I refer is that which precedes ———.

Words twice. Communication is difficult. I am sending each phrase (or each code group) twice. (Use this proword for an order, a request, or information.)

Wrong. Your last transmission is incorrect. The correct version is ———.

STANDARD TRANSMISSION FORMAT

The following format is standard for all radio communications:

1. Call
2. Message
3. Time
4. From
5. To
6. Break
7. Text
8. Break
9. Ending

By using this format, each receiver immediately understands and can execute the actions indicated without the need for any further lengthy transmission. The message format tells every station in the call sign exactly whom the message is for. The proword *message* indicates that the receiver should record the material. The time tells each receiver the exact time that the originating station first sent the message. The prowords *from* and *to* identify the originating station and the specific addressee(s). The text is the point of the message, and the ending indicates that the message is complete. Consider this example:

"M0L07 This is R7G22–Message–Time 230050Z June 89–From M0L22–To All R7G Stations–Figures 6 stringers needed for all location India operations–Out."

AUTHENTICATION PROCEDURES

The only way to keep from being fooled by enemy deception over the radio is to challenge the station to authenticate. Always challenge an order to move or to change missions. Remember the rules for engagement for authentication: Authenticate when you–

- Enter a net
- Close a net
- Get instructions over the radio that tell you to do something different from what you are doing now or that tell you to give up an asset.
- Feel the station you are talking to may be phony.

Challenge and Reply

Transmit the challenge after the call up, preceded by the proword *authenticate* ———, as in "M0L07 This is R7G22–Authenticate Delta Golf–Over."

Transmit the reply similarly, preceded by the proword *I authenticate* ———, as in "This is M0L07–I Authenticate–Uniform–Over." A counter challenge may follow the reply.

TIPS ON COMMUNICATION SECURITY

Your radio can kill you! Your FM radio is as dangerous a weapon as any gun on the battlefield. Use it incorrectly and you and your unit may die. Using your radio incorrectly can give away your position, pass information to the enemy, and confuse your command. If you talk too long, the enemy can find you with radio direction finding (RDF) equipment in less than a minute. When he does, an artillery TOT will follow. If, however, he doesn't shoot you, he'll intercept you for intelligence or jam you. All these enemy responses are deadly! Use the following tips to communicate safely.

Train Yourself and Your Operator

- Conduct unit schools and net training.
- Rigidly discipline your nets in the field.
- Transmit using lowest power and shortest antenna needed. Leave antenna down unless you are talking.

Think Before You Push to Talk

- Think it out.
- Know exactly what you are going to say before you push to talk.
- Know both your call sign and your receiver's call sign.
- Think your message out or write it down.
- Use OPORD/FSOP (Operations order/field standing operating procedures) report formats.
- If the message is an order, write down your self-authentication.

Use Short Procedures

- Get rid of chitchat. Use long procedures only if you have commo problems. Transmissions must not be longer than 15 seconds with a 5- to 7-second break between them.

• Use short call signs. If you have positive commo, drop the call sign entirely.

• Cut out in-between words, such as "this is." Use them only if commo is weak.

• Use Army prowords for exactly what they mean.

• Break every 15 seconds for 5 to 7 seconds (let go of the push-to-talk button). A good message or order should take no more than one minute (3 × 15 + 10 for breaks).

• Don't use homemade codes or codewords. No matter how clever they may seem to you, they offer no trouble to enemy codebreakers and can lull you into false security.

• Use authorized operational codes and authentication tables. They're random, they constantly change, and they are as good as you can get.

Talk Short

• Eliminate needless words. Talk simply. Terminate a message when you think it is over.

• Don't ever imply seniority over the radio, or the enemy may shoot the senior person, perhaps you.

• End a transmission when it's obvious. You don't have to wait for the speaker with the higher rank to do it. If you understand what he wants you to do, give him a "Roger Out" and do it. If your boss has more traffic for you, he will call.

Talk Army

• You and all your operators must use the words that define our operations. FM 101–1–5 is the bible. Train and test on it at operator level.

• Don't confuse the net with CB (citizens band) slang.

Stay Cool

• Talk calmly. Don't shout, raise your voice, talk fast, or create air turbulence.

• Slow, calm, distinct, simple messages soothe subordinates and are easy to understand.

Format Orders and Reports

• Use report format.

• Use OPORD/FRAGO format.

• Habitually describe situation from left to right and from front to rear.

Beat Jamming

• Use low power.

• Use smallest antenna possible.

• Keep transmissions to 15 seconds.

• Set up radios out of your operations center.

• Put a hill or built-up area—even a forest—between your enemy and your radio, but not between you and the station you're talking to.

• Drop to a lower net that works.

Drop a Net

Drop a net when the enemy is jamming yours. If a battalion, for example, has traffic for a company, it can drop to the company's internal net to pass it. Using this method can help you in several ways. First, dropping a net leaves the battalion net open for traffic. Also, it may beat enemy EW/SIGINT efforts by allowing the battalion to operate on a number of different frequencies instead of only one. Second, dropping a net gives the enemy an incomplete picture. Third, while the enemy is jamming the battalion net, information can still travel.

Working Through Jamming

Even if the enemy jams your net, you can still function. First, try to work through the jamming. Sometimes it works. If not, try these steps:

• Go to high power.

• Go to a larger antenna, such as from whip to RC 292.

• Still keep your transmissions short; break them into one- or two-word groups.

• Continue the drop-a-net method to get through, but leave someone transmitting on the old frequency to lock the jammer on that frequency.

• Report the jamming to the S2 or the signal officer immediately.

• If these measures fail and you can't beat the jamming, you will have to change location or frequency.

7

Logistics Data, Formulas, and Procedures

All combat service support officers should thoroughly know their professional roles. The specific details of those functions, however, require knowing an enormous amount of information, intricate formulas, and exact procedures. This chapter provides often used, often misunderstood, or easily forgotten formulas and frequently required basic planning data. It also includes guidance on how to use this information to the best advantage.

SUPPLY CONSUMPTION FACTORS

The supply consumption factors appear in the accompanying table *(Figure 1)* as units of pounds per person per day. Use these consumption rates for general planning when more specific or current information is not available. These general factors can vary in actual situations. See the notes accompanying the table.

FORMULAS FOR ESTIMATING SUPPLY REQUIREMENTS

Supply Requirements

Note: STON = short tons; DOS = days of supply

$$\frac{\text{Strength supported} \times \text{Consumption rate} \times \text{Supply level (DOS)}}{2{,}000} = \text{STON}$$

Daily Resupply

$$\frac{\text{Average strength} \times \text{Consumption rate} \times 1 \text{ Day}}{2{,}000} = \text{STON}$$

Figure 1. Planning Factors for Supply Consumption

(Pounds per person per day)

Class of Supply	Consumption Rate	Note
I	4.03	1
II	3.67	
III	53.7	
III Packaged	0.59	2
IV	8.50	3
V	31.29	4
VI	3.20	5
VII	15.00	6
VIII	1.22	
IX	2.50	7
X	NA	8

FOOTNOTES:

[1]Consumption rate is based on ration mix of two Bs and one meal, ready-to-eat (MRE) per person per day. If the ration supplement sundries pack (RSSP) is used , an additional .41 should be used by the planner. If the female Health and Comfort Sundries pack is used, an additional .03 lb/person/day should be used by the planner. Consumption rate for the Light Infantry Division is 6.62 lb/person/day based on two Ts and one MRE.

[2]This consumption rate does not include fog oil. To calculate a consumption rate for fog oil, use 200 gallons per smoke generator per day.

[3]Per Engineer Study Center guidance (1982), consumption rate is comprised of two components: The 4.0 lb/person/day accounts for unit defensive barrier and fortification materiel. The other component is 4.5 lb/person/day which accounts for construction materiel requirements for base development in the rear combat zone. The 8.5 lb/person/day represents the complete Class IV planning factor for a theater of operations. It should be noted that for planning purposes the 4.0 figure for barrier materiel will reduce the 3.2 as the theater matures over time and less barrier materiel is required. The rate of reduction is dependent upon several variables which include the intensity of the conflict, type of battle, and the commander's initiative in the employment of Class IV (i.e., defense, offense, and highly fluid battlefield would require different quantities of Class IV for employment).

[4]The Class V consumption rate is based upon the TAA 92 P90E Study and is for a moderate level of combat.

[5]Consumption rate is comprised of the following:

Item	Lbs/Person/Day
Tobacco	.139
Food/Drink	2.375
Pers Hygiene	.168
Military Clothing	.097
Jewelry (Watch & Wallets)	.004
Stationery	.081
Civilian Clothing	.096
Gen Supplies (polish, batteries, etc)	.219
Cameras, Radio, Film, etc	.028
	3.207

In all cases, commanders have the prerogative to influence the Army and Air Force Exchange Service (AAFES) operations as they deem appropriate based on the tactical situation.

[6]Consumption rate was derived from Total Army Analysis 90 (TAA 90) and represents mean usage rate for a heavy force.

[7]Consumption rate was derived from Class IX Item Analysis Study (LOGC 1984) and represents a mean usage rate for a heavy force.

[8]Consumption rate of Class X has no meaning when based on military strength. Class X requirements should be developed based on the population, geographic location, and technological capabilities of the country involved.

Distribution of Daily Resupply

$$\frac{\text{Strength} \times \text{Consumption rate} \times 1 \text{ Day}}{2{,}000} = \text{STON}$$

Buildup of Supply Levels

$$\frac{\text{End strength} \times \text{Consumption rate} \times \text{End supply level (days)}}{2{,}000} - \frac{\text{Beginning strength} \times \text{Consumption rate} \times \text{Beginning supply level (days)}}{2{,}000} = \text{STON}$$

Storage Requirements

$$\frac{\text{End strength} \times \text{Consumption rate} \times \text{No. of days stored}}{2{,}000} = \text{STON}$$

PETROLEUM SUPPLY FORMULAS

Supply Requirements

Strength supported × Consumption rate × Supply level (DOS) = Gallons

Daily Resupply

Average strength × Consumption rate = Gallons

Distribution of Daily Resupply

Strength × Consumption rate = Gallons

Buildup of Supply Levels

[End strength × Consumption rate × End supply level (days)] − [Beginning strength × Consumption rate × Beginning supply level] = Gallons

Storage Requirements

End strength × Consumption rate × No. of days stored = Gallons

CHARACTERISTICS OF STANDARD RATIONS

The accompanying table *(Figure 2)* provides vital planning data for Class I supplies. To reduce administrative actions and to ease the handling of supplies, the Class I system uses as few levels of support as possible. Strength reports trigger the shipment of rations forward. The tactical situation, the availability of different ration types, and the desires of the supported commander will dictate the type of ration to supply.

Figure 2. Characteristics of Standard Rations

	Packaging Information				
	Contents per package or case	Gross weight per package or case (pounds)	Volume per case (cu ft)	Average wt per meal/unit including packing (lb)	Average calories per meal/unit
Meal, ready-to-eat, individual[1]	12 meals	17.6	0.83 per case	1.47	1,135 per meal
Meal, combat individual[1]	12 meals	26	0.80 per case	2.17	1,135 per meal
Food packet,long-range patrol[2]	40 packets	36	1.84 per case	0.90	1,100 per pkt
Food packet, survival, general purpose[3]	24 packets	20	0.43 per case	0.83	870 per pkt
Ration Supplement sundries pack (1 pack per 100 persons per day)[4]	1 packet	41	1.67 per case		
Ration supplement, aid station (makes 100 8-oz drinks)[5]	1 packet	16	1.01 per case		
Field Ration A[6]				2.41	
Standard B Ration[7]				1.278	
T-Ration (Tray Packs)[8]				2.575	
Female Health & Comfort Sundries Pack (1 pack per 25 females per 30 days)[9]					

FOOTNOTES:

[1]Designed for use as individual meal packets or in multiples of three for a complete ration. This packet is not to be used over extended periods.

[2]Issued to troops under combat conditions where resupply may be uncertain for as long as 10 days. Because the packet is designed for individual use, it is suitable for tactical feeding, which requires dispersion. The principal menu component is dehydrated and may be eaten as is with drinking water or may be rehydrated rapidly with hot or cold water. Eight different menus are available.

[3]Contains four food bars, sugar, instant coffee, and soup and gravy base packed in a rectangular can with a key opener taped to it. Minimal recommended issue is one-half packet per person per day in hot climates and one packet per person per day in cold climates.

[4]Composed of items necessary to the health and comfort of troops; e.g., essential toilet articles, tobacco, and confections that usually are obtained at an exchange. This packet is made available in theaters of operation for issue, pending establishment of adequate service facilities.

[5]Designed for use at forward medical aid stations to provide combat casualties with hot, stimulating beverages which alleviate shock and contribute to patient comfort.

[6]The A ration consists of both perishable and nonperishable food. It is intended for use primarily under stable conditions and during static phases of military operations when normal cooking and refrigeration are available.

[7]The B ration is composed of nonperishable food. It is used when there are kitchen facilities but no refrigeration (see SB 10-495).

[8]The T ration is a ready-to-heat and serve tray pack. It is used in the AOE divisions that do not have the inherent capability to supply themselves with A or B rations.

[9]The female health and comfort items are for female hygiene and are obtained ordinarily at an exchange. This packet is made available in theaters of operation for issue, pending establishment of adequate exchange facilities. A package weight is not available, but planners can use an estimated factor of .03 pounds per person per day based on the female health and comfort items listed in AR 700-23.

Figure 3. Water Consumption Planning Factors

(Gallons Per Person Per Day)

Uses	Climate		
	Hot	Temperate	Cold
Drinking requirements	3.0[1]	1.5[2]	2.0
Heat treatment	0.2	0.0	0.0
Personal hygiene[3]	1.7	1.7	1.7
Centralized hygiene[4]	1.0	1.0	1.0
Food preparation[5]	0.0-4.5	0.0-4.5	0.0-4.5
Laundry[6]	2.1	2.1	2.1
Divisional medical treatment[7]	0.4	0.4	0.4
Waste (10 percent)	0.8-1.3	0.7-1.1	0.7-1.2

FOOTNOTES:

[1]This figure goes up to 3.5 when personnel assume mission-oriented protection posture (MOPP) 3 to 4 levels continuously.

[2]This figure goes up to 3.0 when personnel assume MOPP 3 or 4 levels continuously.

[3]This figure includes water for shaving daily, brushing teeth three times a day, washing hands, and taking sponge baths daily. For periods of less than 7 days, the figure is 0.7 gallon; this water is used for shaving so that masks will fit.

[4]This figure provides water for one shower a week.

[5]The actual factor to use depends on the ration policy in the theater. No water is needed for meals (ready-to-eat) and meals (combat, individual). B rations require 0.5 gallon per meal per soldier for rehydration and kitchen sanitation. If individual mess equipment is used, 1.0 gallon per soldier is required to sterilize utensils and clean up.

[6]This figure allows for one clothing exchange per week.

[7]This figure is based on Total Army Analysis 88 peak hospital admission rates. All patients not expected to return to duty within 96 hours are evacuated to corps hospitals.

Figure 4. Unit Water Planning Factors (gal/day)

Environmental Region

Level of Command	Temperate (32° - 80°F)		Arctic (Less Than 32°F)		Hot Tropic (More than 80°F)		Hot-Arid (More than 80°F)	
	Sustaining[1]	Minimum	Sustaining[1]	Minimum	Sustaining[1]	Minimum	Sustaining[1]	Minimum
Company	3.8-6.8	2.4	4.4-7.4	3.0	5.7-8.7	4.3	6.0-9.0	4.6
Battalion	3.8-6.8	2.4	4.4-7.4	3.0	5.7-8.7	4.3	6.0-9.0	4.6
Brigade	4.3-7.3	2.9	4.8-7.8	3.4	6.1-9.1	4.7	9.2-12.2	6.7
Division	4.3-7.3	2.9	4.8-7.8	3.4	6.1-9.1	4.7	9.4-12.4	6.9
Above Division	4.9-7.9	3.5	5.5-8.5	4.1	7.5-10.5	6.1	15.6-18.6	10.8

FOOTNOTE:

[1]The ranges in the "Sustaining" columns are the result of differences in ration policy.

WATER CONSUMPTION FACTORS

Water is a critical combat commodity required for personal consumption, sanitation, cooking, maintenance, equipment operation, decontamination, and other purposes. Combat service support units are responsible for the water supply functions of purification, storage, distribution, and cooling. Planners can use a common planning factor of 20 gallons per person per day for gross estimates only. More accurate planning and subsequently more accurate and adequate support require breaking down the specific uses of water into requirements per person. The accompanying tables *(Figures 3 and 4)* provide the planning factors needed to plan water support on the battlefield.

BULK PETROLEUM ESTIMATES AND FORMULAS

After ammunition, fuel is the supply item that probably receives the most emphasis and concern in modern warfare. Fuel supplies and the lack thereof have been the deciding factors in several recent conflicts and will continue to greatly affect the outcome of battles. Planners can use either of these two approaches to estimate fuel requirements: computation of expected usage by type of equipment or computation of expected fuel requirements by type unit estimate.

Estimating fuel requirements by type of equipment is very useful for small units or specific tasks that require a small number of vehicles or items of equipment of known type, such as provisioning tailored task forces or specific elements of known size generally less than company strength.

The type-unit-based estimate is more commonly used when planning bulk fuel resupply. It allows the planner to build the estimate for all items in the unit simultaneously. When planning for the battalion, the brigade, or the division for major operations, this method is the one to use.

Formula for Estimating Fuel for Other than Tracked Vehicles

End item density × Consumption rate (gal/hr; gal/mi; gal/km) (Table A) × Area usage rate (hr/day; miles/day; km/day) (Table B)
= Bulk fuel requirements for 1 day.

EXAMPLE:

Truck, Cargo 2½ Ton M36A2. A computation for the multifuel consuming, 2½ ton cargo truck M36A2, LIN X40283, EI NSN 2320-00-077-1618 in CONUS with a density of 16 would look like this one:

Consumption rate for LIN X40283 = .0932 gal/km.

Daily usage rate for CONUS wheeled vehicles (WV) = 80 km/day.

Computation: 16 trucks × .0932 gal/km × 80 km/day = 119.3 gal for 1 day.

Formula for Estimating Fuel for Tracked Combat Vehicles

End item density × [(Idle consumption rate (gal/hr) (Table A) × area idle usage rate (hr/day) (Table C)) + (area cross country consumption rate (gal/hr) (Table A) × area cross country usage rate (hrs/day) (Table C)) + (secondary road consumption rate (gal/hr) (Table A) × area secondary road usage rate (hrs/day) (Table C))] = Bulk fuel requirements for 1 day.

EXAMPLE:

Tank, Combat, 105MM, M60A3. The computation for a diesel fuel-consuming, 105MM combat tank M60A3, LIN V13101, EI NSN 2350-00-148-6548 in CONUS with a density of 54 would look like this one:

Consumption rates for LIN V13101: idle = 2.00 gal/hr; cross country = 26.53 gal/hr; secondary roads = 18.79 gal/hr.

Daily usage rates for CONUS based tracked vehicles (TV), LIN V13101: idle = 4.2 hr/day; cross country = 8.5 hr/day; secondary roads = 2.9 hr/day.

Computation: 54 tanks × [(2.00 gal/hr × 4.2 hr/day) + (26.53 gal/hr × 8.5 hr/day) + (18.79 gal/hr × 2.9 hr/day)] = 15,573.38 gallons of diesel fuel for 1 day.

Formula for Estimating Fuel Requirements by Type Unit

The formula for the type unit computation is very simple. Multiply each factor listed in Bulk POL Table E by the appropriate standard usage profile from Bulk POL Table D. Then total the resulting quantities as Mogas, Diesel, and JP4. The sums obtained are the expected usage for the subject unit for one day of operations.

EXAMPLE:

Compute the total POL requirements for one tank battalion (SRC 17235J410) equipped with M60 in a heavy armored division (SRC 87000J410) (Table E) for a one-day operation for all categories of equipment, using European usage profile No. 072 (Table D).

Total MOGAS = 3.9(12) + 23.6(12) + 16.0(12) = 522 gal/day.

Total Diesel = 0.6(12) + 7.0(12) + 165.4(4.2) + 2121.9(5.7) + 1560.5(5.5) + 11.4(101) = 22,614.86 gal/day.

Consuming Equipment Codes

Bulk POL Tables D and E use the following consuming equipment codes:

CODE	CATEGORY
AB	Amphibious Equipment
CE	Construction
GN	Generators

HG	Heating Equipment
MH	Material Handling Equipment
SG	Stationary Equipment – Miscellaneous
SV	Stationary Equipment – Vehicle mounted
TI	Tracked Vehicles – Idle
CC	Tracked Vehicles – Cross Country
SR	Tracked Vehicles – Secondary Roads
WV	Wheeled Vehicles
OV	Other Vehicles
AV	Aviation

All equipment categories are based on hours of operation except the category for wheeled vehicles, which is based on kilometers.

WEIGHTS, VOLUMES, AND CONVERSION FACTORS FOR PETROLEUM PRODUCTS

Although logisticians estimate petroleum (POL) requirements in gallons, transporting them may require several different methods and all types of cargo vehicles. Therefore, the data provided *(see Figure 11)* for the various weights and volumes of the many different containers and packages used for POL allow logisticians to plan their transportation requirements regardless of the size or the type of container they use to ship POL products.

CLASS V BASIC LOAD INFORMATION

A basic load of ammunition is the quantity that is authorized and required to be on hand within a unit at all times. It normally appears as rounds per weapon or bulk measurements for other types of munitions. The size and the selection of items in a basic load should meet the anticipated initial combat needs of the unit until resupply. In wartime, the nature of the enemy, the type of mission, the intensity of combat, the availability of transport, and the availability of ammunition determine the basic load. Unit basic loads should represent comparison, consideration, and tradeoff of these factors.

At brigade level and below, the division ammunition officer, in conjunction with the operations officer (G3) and the logistics officer (G4), calculates and prescribes the actual basic load. If you need to establish an initial basic load, the data to accomplish this task are available in FM 101-10-1/2, *Staff Officer's Field Manual: Organizational, Technical, and Logistical Data Planning Factors (Volume 2).*

CLASS V EXPENDITURE DATA

Ammunition directly influences tactical operations. Therefore, tactical commanders must plan their operations and commit their forces with full awareness of the support capabilities of the ammunition supply system. Logisticians must ensure that the system anticipates and aggressively meets

Figure 5. Definition of Terms for Bulk POL Tables A, B, and C

1. LI — Line item number.

2. EI NSN — End item national stock number assigned to the item.

3. SNSN — For internal use at GMPA.

4. CMD—Command code identifying item managers. Applicable codes are:

   B, H - TSARCOM
   K - TACOM
   L - MICOM
   MK - ARRCOM
   E, J - GMPA

5. FUEL NSN — Identifies the type of fuel consumed by the end item.

   Applicable fuels are:

   Motor gasoline - 9130-00-160-1818
   Diesel Fuel Marine - 9140-00—273—2377
   JP-4—9130-00-256-8613
   Aviation gasoline - 9130-00-179-1125

6. EQUIP TYPE—Equipment Type. Applicable codes are:

   AB - Amphibious
   AV - Aviation
   CE - Construction
   GN - Generators
   HG - Heating
   MH - Material Handling
   OV - Other Vehicles
   SG - Stationary Equipment - MISC
   SV - Stationary Equipment - Vehicle mounted.
   TO - Tracked Vehicles - other
   TV - Tracked Vehicles - combat
   WV - Wheeled Vehicles

7. CONSUMP CD - Consumption Rate Code. Applicable codes are:

   H - Gallons per hour
   M - Gallons per mile
   K - Gallons per kilometer

8. CONSUMPTION RATES — IDL/AV; XCNTRY; 2NDRDS—Consumption Rates, Idle/Average; Cross-Country; Secondary Roads. Tracked vehicle fuel consumption rates are expressed by mode of operation during periods of idle time, travel cross-country, and travel on secondary roads. Rates for all other types of equipment have been expressed by an AV - average rate.

9. NOMENCLATURE — Short description of the end item.

10. MULTIFUEL—EIs with an "M" in this column are capable of burning either diesel fuel or MOGAS. In these cases, the most representative consumption rate has been provided.

Figure 6. Equipment Combat Fuel Consumption Rates—Bulk POL Table A

LI	EI NSN	SNSN CMD	FUEL NSN	EQUIP TYP	CONSUMP CD	CONSUMPTION RATES IDL/AV	XCNTRY	2NDRDS	NOMENCLATURE	MULTIFUEL
A29676	1510 01 005 5461	H	9130 00 256 8613	AV	H	130.00			APLNCGOTRANSC12A	
A29744	1510 01 070 3661	H	9130 00 256 8613	AV	H	105.00			C12C AIRPLANE CARG	
A29812	1510 01 087 9129	H	9130 00 256 8613	AV	H	105.00			C12D AIRPLANE CARG	
A30053	1510 00 929 1012	H	9130 00 179 1125	AV	H	15.50			APL FLT TRNG T-41B	
A30221	1510 00 715 9379	H	9130 00 256 8613	AV	H	225.00			APLN OBSN STOL OV-	
A30271	1510 00 715 9380	H	9130 00 256 8613	AV	H	219.60			APLN OBSN STOL OV-	
A30296	1510 00 869 3654	H	9130 00 256 8613	AV	H	252.00			APLN OBSN STOL OV-	
A30444	1510 00 368 8440	H	9130 00 256 8613	AV	H	252.00			APLN RECON PV-ID	
A30465	1510 00 945 9998	H	9130 00 179 1125	AV	H	57.00			APLN RECON UTIL RU	
A30585	1510 00 804 3641	H	9130 00 256 8613	AV	H	115.40			APLN RECON UTIL RU2	
A30586	1510 00 453 9451	H	9130 00 256 8613	AV	H	89.20			AIRPLANE RU-21E	
A30591	1510 00 394 3320	H	9130 00 256 8613	AV	H	117.10			APLN RECON UTIL RU2	
A30596	1510 00 872 7908	H	9130 00 179 1125	AV	H	39.20			APL TRNR INST T-42	
A30636	1510 00 033 6312	H	9130 00 179 1125	AV	H	20.00			APLN UTILITY U-3A	
A30637	1510 00 024 5063	H	9130 00 179 1125	AV	H	20.00			APLN UTILITY U-3B	
A30671	1510 00 508 0604	H	9130 00 256 8613	AV	H	23.80			APLN UTILITY U-6A	
A30694	1510 00 587 3375	H	9130 00 256 8613	AV	H	80.20			APLN RECONUT RU21A	
A30721	1510 00 574 7938	H	9130 00 179 1125	AV	H	57.00			APLN UTILITY U-8D	
A30762	1510 00 878 4338	H	9130 00 256 8613	AV	H	97.50			APLN RECONUT RU21B	
A30821	1510 00 701 2233	H	9130 00 179 1125	AV	H	60.50			APLN UTILITY U-8F	
A30831	1510 00 912 4084	H	9130 00 179 1125	AV	H	57.00			APLN UTILITY U-8G	
A30843	1510 00 878 4336	H	9130 00 256 8613	AV	H	97.50			APLN RECONUT RU2IC	
A30946	1510 00 933 8223	H	9130 00 256 8613	AV	H	115.40			APLN UTILITY U-21A	
A30951	1510 00 169 0295	H	9130 00 256 8613	AV	H	128.10			APLN UTILITY U-21F	
A30953	1510 00 140 1627	H	9130 00 256 8613	AV	H	115.40			APLN UTILITY U-21G	
A30971	1510 00 964 9780	H	9130 00 179 1125	AV	H	30.20			APLN UTILITY U-10A	
A30989	1510 01 011 1462	H	9130 00 256 8613	AV	H	97.50			APLN UTIL STOL UV-18A	
A93125	2350 00 140 5151	S K	9140 00 273 2377	TO	K	0.4661			M551 ARAAV 152MM	
A93125	2350 00 873 5408	S K	9140 00 273 2377	TO	K	0.4661			M551A1 ARAAV 152MM	
B01756	3820 00 201 8293	K	9130 00 160 1818	CE	H	6.00			AUGER EARTH	
B01756	3820 00 391 0514	K	9130 00 160 1818	CE	H	3.20			AUGER HDM-S	
B01756	3820 00 391 4136	K	9130 00 160 0101	CE	H	3.20			AUGER K-254	
B01756	3820 00 542 3235	K	9130 00 160 1818	CE	H	6.00			AUGER EARTH	
B01756	3820 00 931 4509	K	9130 00 160 1818	CE	H	6.00			AUGER EARTH	
B01756	3820 01 068 4078	K	9130 00 160 1818	CE	H	4.50			AUGER EARTH	
B01756	3820 01 146 7204	K	9130 00 160 1818	CE	H	4.50			AUGER EARTH 270-9	
B04441	2310 01 090 7739	K	9130 00 160 1818	WV	K	0.0373			AUTO SEDAN COMPACT	
B04715	2310 01 090 7740	K	9130 00 160 1818	WV	K	0.0435			AUTO SEDAN INTERM	
B04832	2310 01 091 1060	K	9130 00 160 1818	WV	K	0.0311			AUTO S/W COMPACT	
B12482	3815 00 017 9482	K	9140 00 273 2377	CE	H	5.00			BACKHOE CS3/4CU YD	
B12585	3815 00 618 8099	K	9140 00 273 2377	CE	H	7.00			BACKHOE 85585862/3	
B25476	1940 01 105 5728	B	9140 00 273 2377	AB	H	7.20			BOAT BRIDGE ERECT	
B31745	1935 00 375 2990	B	9140 00 273 2377	AB	H	10.00			BARGE REFR 7010	
B31745	1935 00 375 2991	B	9140 00 273 2377	AB	H	18.00			BARGE REFRIG	
B83582	1940 00 417 0526	B	9140 00 273 2377	AB	H	12.50			BOAT BR EREC DSL	
B83582	1940 00 355 4469	B	9130 00 160 1818	AB	H	15.00			BOAT T-15	
B83582	1940 00 417 0526	B	9130 00 160 1818	AB	H	12.50			BOAT BR EREC DSL E	
B83993	1940 00 268 9952	B	9140 00 273 2377	AB	H	18.00			BOAT 2001	
B84130	1940 00 267 1099	B	9140 00 273 2377	AB	H	10.00			BOAT 4003	
B84267	1940 00 268 9955	B	9140 00 273 2377	AB	H	24.20			BOAT PICKET 4002	
B84541	1940 00 554 6699	B	9140 00 273 2377	AB	H	4.00			BOAT UT 26FT WOOD	
C10908	2350 01 110 4660	K	9140 00 273 2377	TO	K	0.2796			CARR AMMO TT M992	
C12155	2350 01 085 3702	K	9140 00 273 2377	TO	K	0.2858			SUPPORT VEH XM 981	
C18481	3820 00 902 3107	K	9130 00 160 1818	WV	K	0.3107			BREAKER PAV BOM47L	
C18481	3820 01 048 8120	K	9130 00 160 1818	WV	K	0.3107			BREAKER PAV BP-50	
C36100	2590 00 649 5937	K	9130 00 160 1818	CE	H	6.50			BULLDOZER EARTH M8A1	
C36100	2590 00 801 6588	K	9130 00 160 1818	CE	H	6.50			BULLDOZER EARTH M8A2	
C36100	2590 00 838 1800	K	9130 00 160 1818	CE	H	6.50			BULLDOZER EARTH M8E1	
C36100	2590 00 944 4903	K	9130 00 160 1818	CE	H	6.50			BULLDOZER EARTH M8A3	
C36120	2590 00 708 3563	K	9140 00 273 2377	SG	H	25.00			M9 BULLDOZER MVG	
C36151	3810 01 165 0646	K	9140 00 273 2377	CE	H	7.00			CRANE 7 1/2 TON	
C36219	3810 01 165 0647	K	9140 00 273 2377	CE	H	7.00			CRANE A/A 7 1/2 TON	
C38874	3950 01 110 9224	K	9140 00 273 2377	CE	H	7.50			CRANE TRK MT 140T	
C38874	3950 01 027 9254	K	9140 00 273 2377	CE	H	7.50			CRANE MOBL 140 TON	
C38942	3950 01 027 9253	K	9140 00 273 2377	CE	H	13.20			CRANE MOBL 300 TON	
C72872	4310 01 053 3891	K	9130 00 160 1818	SG	H	10.50			COMPR AIR 750 CFM	
C39836	2310 01 090 7710	K	9140 00 273 2377	WV	K	0.4163			BUS 66 PAX	
C39836	2310 01 095 7447	K	9140 00 273 2377	WV	K	0.4163			BUS AMB CUNY	
C39977	2310 01 090 7707	K	9140 00 273 2377	WV	K	0.4163			BUS TRANSIT 28 PAX	
C39977	2310 01 090 7708	K	9140 00 273 2377	WV	K	0.4163			BUS TRANSIT 36 PAX	
C39977	2310 01 090 7709	K	9140 00 273 2377	WV	K	0.4163			BUS TRANSIT 44 PAX	
C40045	2310 01 090 7711	K	9140 00 273 2377	WV	K	0.4163			BUS AMB CONV82 PAX	
C40106	2310 01 091 0997	K	9140 00 273 2377	WV	K	0.4163			BUS MOTOR 84-90 PAX	
C43497	3810 01 144 3023	K	9140 00 273 2377	CE	H	6.00			CRANE TRK SGT YORK	
C72872	4310 01 053 3891	K	9130 00 160 1818	SG	H	10.50			COMPR AIR 750 CFM	
C74517	4310 01 015 3147	B	9140 00 273 2377	SG	H	1.00			COMPR RCP KA51GF	
C74517	4310 01 107 8006	B	9140 00 273 2377	SG	H	1.00			COMPR AIR 5 CFM	
C76335	2350 01 049 2695	S K	9140 00 273 2377	TV	H	6.40	18.00	8.60	CAV FGT VEH XM3	
C84541	8115 01 015 7039	B	9140 00 273 2377	SG	H	1.09			CONT REFRIG SC-209	
D10726	2350 00 071 0732	K	9140 00 273 2377	TV	H	1.00	8.60	10.23	M125A1 CARR 81MM	
D10726	2350 01 068 4087	K	9140 00 273 2377	TV	H	1.00	8.60	10.23	M125A2 CARR 81MM	
D10741	2350 00 076 9002	K	9140 00 273 2377	TV	H	1.00	6.20	8.90	M106A1 CARR MORTAR	
D10741	2350 01 069 6931	K	9140 00 273 2377	TV	H	1.00	6.20	8.90	M106A2 CARR MORTAR	
C82583	3610 00 598 5811	B	9130 00 160 1818	SV	H	1.00			CAMERA SECT TOPO S	
D10990	2350 00 411 2057	K	9140 00 273 2377	TO	K	0.2796			CARR CGO AMPH M116	
D11049	2350 00 078 4545	K	9140 00 273 2377	TV	H	1.00	5.90	8.50	M548 CARR CGO 6TON	
D11049	2350 01 096 9356	K	9140 00 273 2377	TV	H	1.00	11.80	16.10	M548A1CARR CGO 6TON	
D11538	2350 00 056 6808	K	9140 00 273 2377	TV	H	1.00	8.60	8.90	CARRCMD PST M577A1	
D11538	2350 01 068 4089	K	9140 00 273 2377	TV	H	1.00	8.60	8.90	CARRCMD PST M577A2	

Figure 6. Equipment Combat Fuel Consumption Rates— Bulk POL Table A (continued)

						CONSUMPTION RATES				
LI	EI NSN	SNSN CMD	FUEL NSN	EQUIP TYP	CONSUMP CD	IDL/AV	XCNTRY	2NDRDS	NOMENCLATURE	MULTIFUEL
D11621	2350 00 056 6809	K	9140 00 273 2377	TO	K	0.1491			CARR FLMTHWRM132A1	
D11621	2350 00 987 8900	K	9140 00 273 2377	TO	K	0.1491			CARR FLMTHWRM132	
D11681	1450 00 176 2697	K	9140 00 273 2377	TO	K	2.8274			CARR MISS SYS TOW	
D12087	2350 00 968 6321	K	9140 00 273 2377	TV	H	1.00	8.60	8.90	M113A1 CARRIER PER	
D12087	2350 01 068 4077	K	9140 00 273 2377	TV	H	1.00	8.60	8.90	M113A2 CARR PERS	
D14593	6675 00 526 4719	B	9140 00 273 2377	WV	K	0.1056			CARTO SECT TOPO	
D32859	4220 01 023 0246	B	9140 00 273 2377	SG	H	1.00			DIV EQ ST SPITYPEA	
E02807	2330 00 331 2307	K	9140 00 273 2377	GN	H	4.20			M200A1 CHAS TR GEN	
E32353	4940 01 017 7835	M	9140 00 273 2377	SG	H	13.00			CLEANER STEAM PRS	
E32466	4940 00 186 0027	M	9140 00 273 2377	SG	H	4.00			CLEANER STM PRESS	
E32535	4940 00 473 6218	M	9140 00 273 2377	SG	H	15.00			CLEANER STEAM	
E56578	2350 00 795 1797	K	9140 00 273 2377	TV	H	2.00	26.53	18.79	COMBT VEH ENG M728	
E56896	2350 01 045 1123	K	9140 00 273 2377	TV	H	1.00	8.60	8.90	M901 CMBT VEH ITH	
E56896	2350 01 103 5641	K	9140 00 273 2377	TV	H	1.00	8.60	8.90	VEH ANTITANK M901A1	
E61618	3895 01 024 4064	K	9130 00 160 1818	SG	H	4.00			COMPACTOR HS K300	
E69105	4310 00 049 5199	B	9130 00 160 1818	SG	H	1.00			COMPR RCP GE 321	
E69105	4310 00 208 2601	B	9130 00 160 1818	SG	H	1.00			COMPR RCP GE 3218	
E69105	4310 00 508 3361	B	9130 00 160 1818	SG	H	1.00			COMPR RCP 376 HG	
E69105	4310 00 608 1146	B	9130 00 160 1818	SG	H	1.00			COMPR RCP GE 321	
E69105	4310 00 612 1186	B	9130 00 160 1818	SG	H	1.00			COMPR PRCP IBYCH33	
E69105	4310 00 625 7622	B	9130 00 160 1818	SG	H	1.00			COMPR RCP 907AENGI	
E69105	4310 00 630 7969	B	9130 00 160 1818	SG	H	.22			COMPR RCP DEC3460E	
E69242	4310 00 075 5251	B	9130 00 160 1818	SG	H	1.00			COMPR RCP 458 ENG2	
E69242	4310 00 376 8762	B	9130 00 160 1818	SG	H	.95			COMPR RCP GE 331XA	
E69242	4310 00 620 5430	B	9130 00 160 1818	SG	H	1.00			COMPR RCP CV8969AE	
E69242	4310 00 624 3889	B	9130 00 160 1818	SG	H	1.00			COMPR RCP 458 ENG	
E69242	4310 00 678 9645	B	9130 00 160 1818	SG	H	1.00			COMPR RCP CUG 969	
E69242	4310 00 861 9818	B	9130 00 160 1818	SG	H	1.00			COMPR RCP 458 ENG1	
E69242	4310 00 880 0186	B	9130 00 160 1818	SG	H	.95			COMPR RCP HGR-8M1	
E69242	4310 00 965 1197	B	9130 00 160 1818	SG	H	.95			COMPR RCP 458 ENG3	
E69242	4310 01 128 1826	B	9130 00 160 1818	SG	H	1.00			COMPR RCP C-20X-80	
E69242	4310 01 164 5544	B	9130 00 160 1818	SG	H	1.00			COMPR RCP 50-6840	
E69379	4310 00 060 6798	B	9130 00 160 1818	SG	H	1.75			COMPR RCP 44241	
E69790	4310 00 605 2190	B	9130 00 160 1818	SG	H	1.39			COMPR RCP 60-WBO	
E69790	4310 00 810 4077	B	9130 00 160 1818	SG	H	1.54			COMPR RCP MWE60	
E70064	4310 00 079 6290	B	9130 00 160 1818	SG	H	1.00			COMPR RCP LP512EN1	
E70064	4310 00 733 2210	B	9130 00 160 1818	SG	H	.22			COMPR RCP LP512EN2	
E70064	4310 00 843 8885	B	9130 00 160 1818	SG	H	.22			COMPR RCP G3-11PC	
E70064	4310 00 861 9820	B	9130 00 160 1818	SG	H	.22			COMPR RCP LP512EN	
E70064	4310 01 055 0594	B	9130 00 160 1818	SG	H	.22			COMP RCP 20-902	
E70064	4310 01 080 5754	B	9130 00 160 1818	SG	H	.22			COMP RCP 1S-7-95-5	
E70064	4310 01 105 5794	B	9130 00 160 1818	SG	H	.22			COMP UNIT REC20-910	
E70201	4310 00 075 3311	B	9130 00 160 1818	SG	H	.45			COMPR LP823 ENG1	
E70201	4310 00 788 8969	B	9130 00 160 1818	SG	H	.45			COMPR LP823 ENG2	
E70201	4310 00 861 9822	B	9130 00 160 1818	SG	H	.45			COMPR LP823 ENG	
E70201	4310 01 079 8878	B	9130 00 160 1818	SG	H	.45			COMP RCP 20-905	
E70338	4310 00 733 2217	B	9130 00 160 1818	SV	H	.95			COMPR RCP BM452EN	
E70338	4310 00 852 1745	B	9130 00 160 1818	SG	H	.95			COMPR RCP BGR-5M-1	
E70338	4310 01 069 6935	B	9130 00 160 1818	SV	H	.95			COMP RCP KA5-54515	
E70817	4310 00 728 2030	B	9130 00 160 1818	SG	H	.35			COMPR RCP 892960	
E70817	4310 00 728 2031	B	9130 00 160 1818	SG	H	.35			COMPR RCP 3800219	
E70817	4310 00 878 7969	B	9130 00 160 1818	SG	H	.45			COMPR RCP 43040-30	
E70817	4310 00 930 0060	B	9130 00 160 1818	SG	H	1.00			COMPR RCP 3800219	
E70817	4310 00 997 6004	B	9130 00 160 1818	SG	H	.45			COMPR RCP 893811	
E70886	4310 00 231 5513	B	9130 00 160 1818	SG	H	3.35			COMPR RCP 12021A	
E70886	4310 00 402 5107	B	9130 00 160 1818	SG	H	3.35			COMPR RCP P4R15GJ	
E70886	4310 00 509 9790	B	9130 00 160 1818	SG	H	1.25			COMPR RCP SS600	
E70886	4310 00 624 3212	B	9130 00 160 1818	SG	H	3.35			COMPR RCP 15HGP5MS	
E70886	4310 00 624 3213	B	9130 00 160 1818	SG	H	3.35			COMPR RCP 15HGP9MS	
E70886	4310 01 070 5615	B	9130 00 160 1818	SV	H	3.35			COMP RCP 1-MCAA	
E70886	4310 01 087 4314	B	9130 00 160 1818	SG	H	2.54			COMPUNITRECIPROCAT	
E71023	4310 00 082 6036	B	9130 00 160 1818	SG	H	3.35			COMPRRCP415HGP3M51	
E71023	4310 00 566 8899	B	9130 00 160 1818	SG	H	3.35			COMPRRCPWK8015H1	
E71023	4310 00 679 6917	B	9130 00 160 1818	SG	H	3.35			COMPR RCP P-4	
E72393	4310 00 691 0877	B	9130 00 160 1818	SV	H	7.50			COMPR RTY	
E72393	4310 00 818 9824	B	9130 00 160 1818	SV	H	3.22			COMPR RTY	
E72393	4310 01 043 7604	B	9140 00 273 2377	SG	H	2.37			COMP ROT 6M-125	
E72598	4310 00 503 0483	K	9130 00 160 1818	SG	H	5.00			COMP RCP 250 CRM	
E72667	4310 00 797 3417	K	9130 00 160 1818	SG	H	6.00			COMPR RTY 210 CFM	
E72804	4310 00 075 7064	K	9140 00 273 2377	SG	H	6.00			COMPR RTY 250 RPV	
E72804	4310 00 078 2462	K	9140 00 273 2377	SG	H	5.75			COMPR AIR 250 RPV	
E72804	4310 00 079 4805	K	9140 00 273 2377	SG	H	5.75			COMPR RTY 18M250	
E72804	4310 00 248 3496	K	9140 00 273 2377	SG	H	5.75			COMPR RTY 9M250	
E72804	4310 00 256 9319	K	9140 00 273 2377	SG	H	5.75			COMPR RTY RTY 14M 250	
E72804	4310 00 471 3075	K	9140 00 273 2377	SG	H	6.00			COMP RTY RMS250	
E72804	4310 00 952 7142	K	9140 00 273 2377	SG	H	5.62			COMPR AIR 250 MS-1	
E72804	4310 01 079 4805	K	9140 00 273 2377	SG	H	5.75			COMPRESSOR ROTA	
E73352	4310 00 136 4369	K	9140 00 273 2377	SG	H	15.00			COMP RTY DVY DR600	
E73352	4310 00 542 2525	K	9140 00 273 2377	SG	H	6.00			COMPR RTY DR600	
E73352	4310 00 542 2526	K	9140 00 273 2377	SG	H	6.00			COMP RTY DR-600W	
E73352	4310 00 620 4056	K	9140 00 273 2377	SG	H	6.00			COMP RTY ENG 600	
E73352	4310 00 878 1905	K	9140 00 273 2377	SG	H	6.00			COMP RTY 2016	
E73489	4310 00 542 5928	K	9130 00 160 1818	SG	H	6.00			COMP RTY J21 0-FED	
E73489	4310 00 679 8696	K	9130 00 160 1818	SG	H	7.00			COMPR RTY 210GDSMS	
E73489	4310 00 679 8697	K	9130 00 160 1818	SG	H	7.00			COMPR RTY 210GD3MS	
E73626	4310 00 808 9392	B	9130 00 160 1818	SG	H	.45			COMPR RTY 3MV	
E73626	4310 00 906 8994	B	9130 00 160 1818	SG	H	.45			COMPR RTY 2MSMB	
E73626	4310 00 914 2551	B	9130 00 160 1818	SG	H	.45			COMPR RTY 4MV	
E73626	4310 00 935 5345	B	9130 00 160 1818	SG	H	.45			COMPR RTY 4MV	
E74037	4310 00 073 5431	M	9130 00 160 1818	SG	H	.25			COMPRESSOR AN-M4C	

Figure 6. Equipment Combat Fuel Consumption Rates—Bulk POL Table A (continued)

LI	EI NSN	SNSN CMD	FUEL NSN	EQUIP TYP	CONSUMP CD	CONSUMPTION RATES			NOMENCLATURE	MULTIFUEL
						IDL/AV	XCNTRY	2NDRDS		
E74037	4310 00 073 5054	M	9130 00 160 1818	SG	H	.25			COMPR AN-M4D	
E74037	4310 00 592 8560	M	9130 00 160 1818	SG	H	.25			COMPR AN M4	
E74037	4310 00 848 6075	M	9130 00 160 1818	SG	H	.25			COMPR AN M4B	
F00355	3655 00 062 7911	B	9130 00 160 1818	SG	H	.45			CARDOY DIV MDL E46	
F00355	3655 00 605 7703	B	9130 00 160 1818	SG	H	2.25			CARDOX MOL FE 3436	
F06698	3910 00 298 7088	K	9130 00 160 1818	CE	H	1.12			CONVEYOR BELT N	
F06698	3910 00 817 9170	K	9130 00 160 1818	CE	H	1.12			CONVEYOR BELT PH70	
F06835	3910 00 271 1889	K	9130 00 160 1818	CE	H	1.12			CONVEYOR BELT PBL	
F07109	3910 00 298 7176	K	9130 00 160 1818	MH	H	2.00			CONVEYOR BELT PBL	
F13075	6675 00 526 4824	B	9140 00 273 2377	SG	H	6.00			COPYSUP SECTTOP MS	
F35953	1935 00 264 6220	B	9140 00 273 2377	AB	H	46.50			CRANE 413D	
F36090	1935 00 178 8205	B	9140 00 273 2377	AB	H	45.00			CRANE 264	
F36090	1935 00 217 2302	B	9140 00 273 2377	AB	H	45.00			CRANE 250	
F36090	1935 00 264 6219	B	9140 00 273 2377	AB	H	45.00			CRANE 264B	
F36364	3810 00 701 7324	K	9140 00 273 2377	CE	H	3.40			CRANE CRLR 1125	
F36364	3810 00 728 9945	K	9140 00 273 2377	CE	H	3.40			CRANE CRLR 1125WZD	
F37460	2230 00 554 2728	B	9140 00 273 2377	OV	H	10.50			CRANE LOCO 40TFS	
F37460	2230 00 939 6649	B	9140 00 273 2377	OV	H	10.50			CRANE LOCO 840DE	
F37735	2230 00 529 9910	B	9140 00 273 2377	OV	H	7.50			CRANE LOCO DSL	
F39104	3950 00 197 4935	K	9130 00 160 1818	MH	H	1.00			CRANE TRK 10FM	
F39104	3950 00 271 1837	K	9130 00 160 1818	MH	H	1.00			CRANE TRK NC-10 QM	
F39104	3950 00 723 3294	K	9130 00 160 1818	MH	H	1.00			CRANE TRK 29690	
F39104	3950 00 723 3295	K	9130 00 160 1818	MH	H	1.00			CRANE TRK 46717	
F39172	3810 00 902 3082	K	9140 00 273 2377	CE	H	6.00			CRANE WHL M63	
F39172	3810 00 921 5055	K	9140 00 273 2377	CE	H	6.00			CRANE WHL M-65	
F39241	3810 00 948 0407	K	9140 00 273 2377	CE	H	6.00			CRANE WHL H-446	
F39378	3810 00 043 5354	K	9140 00 273 2377	CE	H	6.00			CRANE WHL 2385	
F39378	3810 00 275 1167	K	9130 00 160 1818	CE	H	2.90			CRANE WHL MTD 20T M320	
F39378	3810 00 763 7728	K	9140 00 273 2377	CE	H	6.00			CRANE WHL 2380	
F40474	3810 00 542 3048	K	9140 00 273 2377	CE	H	9.00			CRAN SHVL M855BG24	
F40474	3810 00 542 3049	K	9140 00 273 2377	CE	H	9.00			CRAN SHVL M855BG24	
F40474	3810 00 606 8569	K	9140 00 273 2377	CE	H	9.00			CRANE SHVL M855BG4	
F40474	3810 00 786 5200	K	9140 00 273 2377	CE	H	9.00			CRAN SHVL M855BG34	
F40474	3810 00 933 0588	K	9140 00 273 2377	CE	H	9.00			CRANE SHVL 855BG2	
F40474	3810 00 933 0589	K	9140 00 273 2377	CE	H	9.00			CRANE SHVL 855BG	
F40474	3810 00 933 0590	K	9140 00 273 2377	CE	H	9.00			CRANE SHVL 855BG3	
F43003	3810 00 433 7174	K	9140 00 273 2377	CE	H	8.00			CRANE SP AIR MAINT	
F43003	3810 00 144 4885	K	9140 00 273 2377	CE	H	2.00			SCAMP VEHICLE	
F43067	3810 00 859 2404	K	9140 00 273 2377	CE	H	7.00			CRANE WHL H446A	
F43077	3810 00 815 2308	K	9130 00 160 1818	CE	H	3.60			CRANE WHL GW7	
F43077	3810 00 818 3381	K	9130 00 160 1818	CE	H	3.60			CRANE WHL 155-1A	
F43364	3810 00 869 3092	K	9140 00 273 2377	CE	H	6.10			CRANE SHVL 22BM	
F43364	3810 00 937 3939	K	9140 00 273 2377	CE	H	4.50			CRANE SHVL 36M	
F43414	3810 00 087 5020	K	9130 00 160 1818	CE	H	7.00			CRANE SHVL M-22	
F43414	3810 00 151 4431	K	9130 00 160 1818	CE	H	7.00			CRANE SHOVEL M320T2	
F43414	3810 00 189 9694	K	9130 00 160 1818	CE	H	7.00			CRANE SHVL M-20-A	
F43414	3810 00 240 7502	K	9130 00 160 1818	CE	H	7.00			CRANE SHVL 34T CA	
F43414	3810 00 240 7505	K	9130 00 160 1818	CE	H	7.00			CRANE SHVL 304	
F43414	3810 00 527 8612	K	9130 00 160 1818	CE	H	7.00			CRANE SHVL M-20-B	
F43414	3810 00 527 8613	K	9130 00 160 1818	CE	H	7.00			CRANE SHVL M-20-AC	
F43414	3810 00 542 4980	K	9130 00 160 1818	CE	H	7.00			CRANE SHVL M200W	
F43414	3810 00 542 4982	K	9130 00 160 1818	CE	H	7.00			CRANE SHVL M200	
F43414	3810 00 634 8999	K	9130 00 160 1818	CE	H	7.00			CRANE SHVL M20B	
F43414	3810 00 820 0698	K	9130 00 160 1818	CE	H	7.00			CRANE SHVL M202	
F43414	3810 00 861 8088	K	9130 00 160 1818	CE	H	7.00			CRANE SHVL M320T	
F43414	3810 00 989 0505	K	9130 00 160 1818	CE	H	7.00			CRANE SHVL 2360	
F43414	3810 00 989 0506	K	9130 00 160 1818	CE	H	7.00			CRANE SHVL 2360W	
F43429	3810 00 018 2021	K	9140 00 273 2377	CE	H	7.00			CRANE TM25T M1250	
F43429	3810 01 054 9779	K	9140 00 273 2377	CE	H	7.10			CRANE 25T TMS 300-5	
F49399	3820 00 725 6462	K	9140 00 273 2377	CE	H	10.80			CRUS SCR PLT 75 TP	
F49536	3820 00 878 4285	K	9130 00 160 1818	CE	H	7.00			CRUS SCR PLT MOL2A	
F49673	3820 00 527 8577	K	9140 00 273 2377	SV	H	42.00			CRUS SCRWDE 225TPH	
F50221	3820 00 360 2475	K	9140 00 273 2377	CE	H	38.00			CRUS SCR WSH 33RTR	
F50221	3820 00 641 4971	K	9140 00 273 2377	CE	H	38.00			CRUSH SCR WSH DJ50	
F50858	3820 00 530 1184	K	9140 00 273 2377	SV	H	21.00			CRUSHER JAW 153 PAD	
F50858	3820 00 832 5168	K	9140 00 273 2377	SV	H	21.00			CRUSHER JAW 153 PRD 66	
F50995	3820 00 880 0795	K	9130 00 160 1818	CE	H	4.60			CRUS JAW 1524PAC	
F81880	4230 00 926 9488	M	9130 00 160 1818	SG	H	3.30			DECON APPR M1ZA1	
F89168	4230 00 078 5455	B	9130 00 160 1818	SG	H	.35			DELOUSER 7000	
F89168	4230 00 889 2315	B	9130 00 160 1818	SG	H	.33			DELOUSER 252QM	
F89168	4230 00 935 9361	B	9130 00 160 1818	SG	H	.33			DELOUSER CDR7000B	
G27664	3895 00 438 6857	K	9130 00 160 1818	SV	H	1.50			DISTRBTR ENTYR D52	
G27664	3895 00 459 2484	K	9130 00 160 1818	SV	H	3.00			DISTR BIT SEA 800M	
G27664	3895 00 641 5913	K	9130 00 160 1818	SV	H	3.00			DISTR BIT S-T SDC	
G27664	3895 00 641 6025	K	9130 00 160 1818	SV	H	3.00			DISTR BIT RE	
G27664	3895 00 690 8289	K	9130 00 160 1818	SV	H	3.00			DISTR BIT D-30	
G27664	3895 00 832 9337	K	9130 00 167 1818	SV	H	3.00			DSTR BIT D37	
G27664	3895 00 833 8820	K	9130 00 160 1818	SV	H	3.00			DISTR BIT 424-56CE	
G27664	3895 00 855 6248	K	9130 00 160 1818	SV	H	3.00			DISTR BIT 42456CE6	
G27664	3895 00 989 1147	K	9130 00 160 1818	SV	H	3.00			DISTR BIT MIL-D 32	
G27844	3895 00 090 0434	K	9130 00 160 1818	CE	H	7.00			DISTR BIT D60	
G27844	3895 01 028 4390	K	9140 00 273 2377	CE	H	1.20			DISTR BIT M918	
G27854	3820 01 026 1237	K	9130 00 160 1818	SV	H	3.00			DISTRIB TRK MTD	
G27859	3895 00 102 6262	K	9140 00 273 2377	CE	H	6.50			DISTR TRCTR DST CNT	
G27938	3895 00 527 8620	K	9130 00 160 1818	CE	H	7.00			DISTR BIT US3CTOD	
G27938	3895 00 641 6026	K	9130 00 160 1818	CE	H	7.00			DISTR BIT US-3C	
G27938	3895 00 767 0247	K	9130 00 160 1818	CE	H	7.00			DISTR BIT MTD	
G28212	3825 00 077 0550	K	9130 00 160 1818	SV	H	1.30			DIST WTR TNKW15A4	
G28212	3825 00 382 9001	K	9130 00 160 1818	SV	H	1.30			DISTR WTR TNK6743	
G28212	3825 00 383 7133	K	9130 00 160 1818	SV	H	4.00			DISTR WTR TNKNOE	

Figure 6. Equipment Combat Fuel Consumption Rates – Bulk POL Table A (continued)

						CONSUMPTION RATES				
LI	EI NSN	SNSN CMD	FUEL NSN	EQUIP TYP	CONSUMP CD	IDL/AV	XCNTRY	2NDRDS	NOMENCLATURE	MULTIFUEL
G28212	3825 00 403 9334	K	9130 00 160 1818	SV	H	4.50			DISTR WTR TNKGENST	
G28212	3825 00 407 0406	K	9130 00 160 1818	SV	H	4.50			DIST WTR TNK 1602	
G28212	3825 00 474 3742	K	9130 00 160 1818	SV	H	4.50			DIST WTR TNK W15B	
G28212	3825 00 527 9213	K	9130 00 160 1818	SV	H	4.50			DIST WTR TNK WD10Z	
G28212	3825 00 543 6053	K	9130 00 160 1818	SV	H	1.00			DISTR WTR TNKM73A	
G28212	3825 00 554 0079	K	9130 00 160 1818	SV	H	1.00			DISTR WTR TNKMME	
G28212	3825 00 629 5901	K	9130 00 160 1818	SV	H	1.00			DISTR WTR TNKW-1M5	
G28212	3825 00 641 5815	K	9130 00 160 1818	SV	H	1.00			DISTR WTR TNKWD100	
G28212	3825 00 774 9090	K	9130 00 160 1818	SV	H	4.50			DISTR WTR TNKW15A6	
G28212	3825 00 879 2122	K	9130 00 160 1818	SV	H	1.00			DISTR WTR TNKMSE	
G28212	3825 00 954 9033	K	9130 00 160 1818	SV	H	4.50			DISTR WTR TNKW15A	
G28250	3825 00 611 6259	K	9130 00 160 1818	SV	H	3.00			DIST WATER TRK MTD	
G28280	3825 00 431 8310	K	9130 00 160 1818	SV	H	2.50			DISTRIB WAT TK	
G29729	3825 00 438 1485	K	9130 00 160 1818	SV	H	2.50			DISTRIB WAT TK	
G29739	3825 00 616 8869	K	9130 00 160 1818	CE	H	3.00			DIST WATER TK 4200	
G29911	3805 00 457 6121	K	9130 00 160 1818	CE	H	7.00			DITCH MACH CRLR/WH	
G29945	3805 00 050 4638	K	9140 00 273 2377	CE	H	7.60			DITCH MACH 624VL	
G29945	3805 00 542 3054	K	9140 00 273 2377	CE	H	4.20			DITCH MACH 750	
G29945	3805 00 727 6719	K	9140 00 273 2377	CE	H	4.20			DITCH MACH 4262	
G36074	6115 00 260 3082	B	9140 00 273 2377	GN	H	1.50			GN ST, PU732/M	
G37273	6115 00 033 1373	B	9140 00 273 2377	GN	H	.57			GEN ST PU751/M	
G53871	6115 00 394 9581	B	9140 00 273 2377	GN	H	3.00			GEN ST 30KW PU-760	
G55186	3895 00 755 4761	K	9130 00 160 1818	CE	H	2.50			DRIER PM 415MIL	
G55186	3895 00 832 6230	K	9130 00 160 1818	CE	H	1.50			DRIER LITTLEFORD70	
G55186	3895 00 989 3243	K	9130 00 160 1818	CE	H	1.50			DRIER LITTLEFORD70	
G55186	3895 01 103 7833	K	9130 00 160 1818	CE	H	1.50			DRIER AEDGO 80M	
G55196	3895 00 591 0105	K	9130 00 160 1818	CE	H	3.00			DRIER MIXER BIT	
G58426	3820 00 554 9694	K	9130 00 160 1818	CE	H	8.56			DRILL MCH 43-SA	
G58426	3820 00 937 0489	K	9130 00 160 1818	CE	H	8.56			DRILL MCH 43SA2	
G58613	3820 00 245 7668	K	9140 00 273 2377	CE	H	16.50			DRILLMCH WELLROT T	
G58613	3820 01 075 4974	K	9140 00 273 2377	CE	H	17.90			DRILL MACH WELL RO	
G74978	3805 01 063 2012	K	9140 00 273 2377	CE	H	8.70			GRADER RD 32,000 LBS	
G96572	2350 01 089 1261	M	9140 00 273 2377	TV	H	12.20	49.50	37.70	GUN AIR DEF XM247	0
H26136	2230 00 712 7519	B	9130 00 160 1818	OV	H	1.00			EXTRACTOR SPIKE	
H26343	4520 00 287 3353	B	9130 00 160 1818	HG	H	.63			HEATER M1950 YUKON	M
H28647	1520 01 106 9519	H	9130 00 256 8613	AV	H	160.00			CPTR ATTCK AH-64A	
H30517	1520 01 088 3669	H	9130 00 256 8613	AV	H	372.80			HCPTR CH-47D	
H30616	1520 01 082 0686	H	9130 00 256 8613	AV	H	142.00			HCPTR ETRONICE H60A	
H30829	1520 01 042 9396	H	9130 00 256 8613	AV	H	86.00			HCPTR EH-1X	
H31110	1520 01 020 4216	H	9130 00 256 8613	AV	H	39.90			HCPTR OBSRV OH58C	
H31872	1520 01 043 4949	H	9130 00 256 8613	AV	H	101.67			UH1V HELICOPTER	
H55206	3895 00 410 4441	K	9130 00 160 1818	CE	H	7.50			FINISHING MACHINE	
H56391	4210 00 202 8076	B	9130 00 160 1818	SV	H	8.00			FI FHT EQ A/AC CL5	
H56391	4210 01 193 3621	B	9140 00 273 2377	SV	H	7.00			FI FHT EQ ST MULTI	
H56528	4210 00 393 0349	B	9130 00 160 1818	SV	H	8.00			FI FHT EQ ST BR CL	
H56802	4210 00 393 0353	B	9130 00 160 1818	SV	H	8.00			FI FHT EQ ST T CL5	
H79426	6230 00 179 1482	H	9130 00 160 1818	GN	H	.95			FLD LTTMGENOG42T	
H79426	6230 00 181 2498	H	9130 00 160 1818	GN	H	.95			FLD LTTMGENOG42TMA	
J30093	6115 00 559 1449	B	9140 00 273 2377	GN	H	75.00			GEN UNIT 750KWS-66	
J30093	6115 00 596 3405	B	9140 00 273 2377	GN	H	70.00			700KW DIESEL GEN	
I30492	1040 00 587 3618	M	9140 00 273 2377	GN	H	3.00			GEN SMK A1C M3A3	
J35424	6115 00 722 3760	K	9140 00 273 2377	GN	H	1.50			GEN ST PU-402/M	
J35492	6115 00 394 9577	B	9140 00 273 2377	GN	H	1.50			GEN ST, PU-405A/M	
J35492	6115 00 949 8409	B	9140 00 273 2377	GN	H	1.50			GEN ST TM PU-405/M	
J35561	6115 00 702 3347	B	9140 00 273 2377	GN	H	3.00			GEN ST TM PU-407	
J35595	6115 00 132 0488	B	9140 00 273 2377	GN	H	6.00			GEN ST TM PU-699/M	
J35595	6115 00 258 1655	B	9140 00 273 2377	GN	H	6.00			GEN ST PU 699AM	
J35629	6115 00 220 3878	B	9140 00 273 2377	GN	H	6.00			GEN ST TM PU-650AG	
J35629	6115 00 258 1622	B	9140 00 273 2377	GN	H	6.00			GEN ST TM PU-650BG	
J35663	6115 00 125 7876	B	9140 00 273 2377	GN	H	6.00			GEN ST TRK MTD PU7	
J35663	6115 00 283 9051	B	9140 00 273 2377	GN	H	6.00			GEN ST PU 700AM	
J35680	6115 00 394 9573	B	9140 00 273 2377	GN	H	6.00			GEN ST, PU707A/M	
J35680	6115 00 464 4195	B	9140 00 273 2377	GN	H	6.00			GEN ST TM PU 707/M	
J35698	6115 00 709 0469	B	9140 00 273 2377	GN	H	3.00			GEN ST TM PO-408M	
J35801	6115 00 394 9575	B	9140 00 273 2377	GN	H	10.00			GEN ST, PU-495A/G	
J35801	6115 00 823 2218	B	9140 00 273 2377	GN	H	10.00			GEN ST TM PU-495/G	
J35813	6115 00 465 1044	B	9140 00 273 2377	GN	H	.57			GEN ST DSL MEP 002	
J35825	6115 00 465 1030	B	9140 00 273 2377	GN	H	1.09			GEN ST DSL MEP 003	
J35825	6115 00 937 3523	B	9140 00 273 2377	GN	H	1.09			GEN ST LIBBY 14800	
J35835	6115 00 118 1241	B	9140 00 273 2377	GN	H	1.50			GEN ST MEP 004A	
J35869	6115 00 118 1245	B	9140 00 273 2377	GN	H	1.50			GEN ST MEP 103A	
J35869	6115 00 922 8690	B	9140 00 273 2377	GN	H	1.50			GEN ST BOGUE MOL 6	
J36006	6115 00 118 1244	B	9140 00 273 2377	GN	H	1.50			GEN ST MEP 113A	
J36040	6115 00 089 5099	B	9140 00 273 2377	GN	H	1.50			GE ST HOLGAR SPHF	
J36109	6115 00 118 1240	B	9140 00 273 2377	GN	H	3.00			GEN ST DSL	
J36304	6115 00 077 8600	B	9130 00 160 1818	GN	H	3.00			GENST HOLG CE301AC	
J36304	6115 00 118 1247	B	9130 00 160 1818	GN	H	3.00			GENST MEP-104A	
J36304	6115 00 935 5111	B	9130 00 160 1818	GN	H	3.00			GENST WESTHSESF30C	
J36383	6115 00 394 9576	B	9140 00 273 2377	GN	H	3.00			GEN ST, PU-406B/M	
J36383	6115 00 738 6342	B	9140 00 273 2377	GN	H	3.00			GEN ST TM PU-406 A	
J36725	6115 00 118 1248	B	9140 00 273 2377	GN	H	3.00			GEN ST MEP 114A	
J37205	6115 00 889 1307	K	9140 00 273 2377	GN	H	5.00			GEN ST PU-551/M	
J38301	6115 00 118 1243	B	9140 00 273 2377	GN	H	6.00			GEN ST MEP 006A	
J38301	6115 00 118 4240	B	9140 00 273 2377	GN	H	6.00			GENSTAC 3500-447237	
J38369	6115 00 118 1252	B	9140 00 273 2377	GN	H	6.00			GEN ST MEP-105A	
J38369	6115 00 937 4388	B	9140 00 273 2377	GN	H	6.00			GEN ST 60DGFH22X60	
J38506	6115 00 118 1253	B	9140 00 273 2377	GN	H	6.00			GEN ST MEP-115A	
J38506	6115 00 937 4389	B	9140 00 273 2377	GN	H	6.00			GEN ST 60DGFJ402X6	
J38547	6115 00 081 2030	B	9140 00 273 2377	GN	H	10.00			GEN ST MIL26727	
J38547	6115 00 156 4342	B	9140 00 273 2377	GN	H	10.00			GEN ST JTA D8001M	
J38712	6115 00 133 9101	B	9140 00 273 2377	GN	H	10.00			GEN ST MEP 007A	
J38712	6115 00 301 5761	B	9140 00 273 2377	GN	H	10.00			GEN ST CONS-EL4180	
J38712	6115 00 624 2767	B	9140 00 273 2377	GN	H	10.00			GEN ST JTAMD 100	

Figure 6. Equipment Combat Fuel Consumption Rates – Bulk POL Table A (continued)

LI	EI NSN	SNSN CMD	FUEL NSN	EQUIP TYP	CONSUMP CD	CONSUMPTION RATES IDL/AV	XCNTRY	2NDRDS	NOMENCLATURE	MULTIFUEL
J38712	6115 00 792 2541	B	9140 00 273 2377	GN	H	10.00			GEN ST CONSD-E4115	
J38712	6115 00 933 3498	B	9140 00 273 2377	GN	H	10.00			GEN ST HOLTEROSHB3	
J38712	6115 01 036 6374	B	9140 00 273 2377	GN	H	10.00			GEN ST MEP007B	
J38986	6115 00 133 9102	B	9140 00 273 2377	GN	H	10.00			GEN ST MEP 106A	
J38986	6115 00 798 3444	B	9140 00 273 2377	GN	H	10.00			GEN ST GMC 6910A	
J40150	6115 00 935 8729	B	9140 00 273 2377	GN	H	20.00			GEN ST MEP 108A	
J40150	6115 00 999 7901	B	9140 00 273 2377	GN	H	20.00			GEN ST ALIS CH4444	
J40158	6115 00 133 9104	B	9140 00 273 2377	GN	H	20.00			GEN ST MEO 009A	
J40158	6115 00 436 4228	B	9140 00 273 2377	GN	H	20.00			GENSTWAUKESHA E812	
J40356	6115 00 476 5878	B	9140 00 273 2377	GN	H	32.00			GEN ST MEP 011A	
J40356	6115 00 782 7099	B	9140 00 273 2377	GN	H	32.00			GENSTSTEWSTEV 5800	
J40698	6115 00 843 8501	H	9130 00 160 1818	GN	H	1.05			GN ST GAS ENG 28V	
J41041	6115 00 697 2402	B	9130 00 160 1818	GN	H	2.40			GEN ST PU253/U	
J41452	6115 00 056 8421	B	9130 00 160 1818	GN	H	2.40			GEN ST PU304C/MPQ4	
J41452	6115 00 643 4674	B	9130 00 160 1818	GH	H	2.40			GEN ST GAS EN PU30	
J41819	6115 00 753 2231	B	9130 00 160 1818	GN	H	2.40			GEN ST TM PU375A/G	
J41819	6115 00 931 6789	B	9130 00 160 1818	GN	H	2.40			GEN ST TM PU375B/G	
J41897	6115 00 702 3348	B	9130 00 160 1818	GN	H	1.40			GENSKW 60CY PU409M	
J42100	6115 00 738 6339	B	9130 00 160 1818	GN	H	2.40			GEN SE 10KW PU619/	
J42115	6115 00 127 8544	H	9140 00 273 2377	GN	H	4.20			GEN ST GAS TC-26C	
J42115	6115 01 083 7005	H	9130 00 160 1818	GN	H	3.30			GEN OV1 AIRCRAFT	
J42137	6115 00 930 9498	B	9130 00 160 1818	GN	H	.50			GEN ST HMLTE XLA	
J42137	6115 00 964 5431	B	9130 00 160 1818	GN	H	.50			GEN ST MIL-G-52368	
J42685	6115 00 436 4230	B	9130 00 160 1818	GN	H	2.40			GEN ST PU532PPS4	
J42685	6115 00 889 1212	B	9130 00 160 1818	GN	H	2.40			GEN ST PU532/PPS4	
J42856	6115 00 940 7867	B	9130 00 160 1818	GN	H	.25			GEN SET GAS ENG	
J42976	6115 00 923 4469	B	9130 00 160 1818	GN	H	.25			GEN ST MEP 014A	
J43027	6115 00 940 7862	B	9130 00 160 1818	GN	H	.25			GEN ST MEP 019A	
J43918	6115 00 591 6867	B	9130 00 160 1818	GN	H	.54			GEN ST KK15M25	
J43918	6115 00 774 9342	B	9130 00 160 1818	GN	H	.54			GEN ST WIPM153682A	
J43918	6115 00 887 8644	B	9130 00 160 1818	GN	H	.54			GEN ST HOLGAR	
J43918	6115 00 889 1446	B	9130 00 160 1818	GN	H	.54			GEN ST MEP 015A	
J44055	6115 00 017 8236	B	9130 00 160 1818	GN	H	.54			GEN ST MEP 025A	
J44055	6115 00 646 6122	B	9130 00 160 1818	GN	H	.54			GEN ST PNRGEMTRCE	
J44055	6115 00 849 2323	B	9130 00 160 1818	GN	H	.54			GENSTWIPG1528T2A01	
J45699	6115 00 017 8237	B	9130 00 160 1818	GN	H	.84			GEN ST MEP 016A	
J45836	6115 00 017 8238	B	9130 00 160 1818	GN	H	.84			GEN ST MEP 021A	
J46110	6115 00 017 8239	B	9130 00 160 1818	GN	H	.84			GEN ST MEP 026A	
J46252	6115 00 873 3915	B	9130 00 160 1818	GN	H	.84			GEN ST UM PR625/G	
J46255	6115 00 087 0972	B	9130 00 160 1818	GN	H	.84			GEN ST TM PU 626/G	
J46258	6115 00 087 0873	B	9130 00 160 1818	GN	H	.84			GEN ST TM PU 628/G	
J46265	6115 00 485 9207	B	9130 00 160 1818	GN	H	.84			GEN ST TM PU 666/G	
J46384	6115 00 738 6335	B	9130 00 160 1818	GN	H	.84			GEN ST TM PU-617M	
J46392	6115 00 937 5555	B	9130 00 160 1818	GN	H	1.40			GEN ST TM PU 629/G	
J46396	6115 00 059 5172	B	9130 00 160 1818	GN	H	1.40			GEN ST TM PU 631/G	
J46589	6115 00 857 1397	B	9130 00 160 1818	GN	H	1.05			GENERATOR SET	
J46692	6115 00 456 9792	B	9130 00 160 1818	GN	H	1.40			GEN ST MEP 027A	
J47068	6115 00 017 8240	B	9130 00 160 1818	GN	H	1.40			GEN ST MEP 017A	
J47343	6115 00 738 6338	B	9130 00 160 1818	GN	H	1.40			GEN ST TM PU 409AM	
J47480	6115 00 738 6337	B	9130 00 160 1818	GN	H	1.40			GEN SET 5KW PU-618	
J47617	6115 00 738 6340	B	9130 00 160 1818	GN	H	1.40			GEN SET TM PU-620/	
J48713	6115 00 017 8241	B	9130 00 160 1818	GN	H	1.40			GEN SET MEP-022A	
J49055	6116 00 074 6396	B	9130 00 160 1818	GN	H	2.00			GENERATOR SET	
J49055	6115 00 903 4948	B	9130 00 160 1818	GN	H	2.00			GENERATOR SET	
J49055	6115 00 926 8335	B	9130 00 160 1818	GN	H	2.00			GENERATOR SET	
J49055	6115 00 999 5935	B	9130 00 160 1818	GN	H	2.00			GENERATOR SET	
J49398	6115 00 690 8290	B	9130 00 160 1818	GN	H	1.50			GEN PAC MER PM5901	
J49398	6115 00 889 1447	B	9130 00 160 1818	GN	H	2.40			GEN ST MEP 018A	
J49466	6115 00 926 0843	B	9130 00 160 1818	GN	H	2.40			GEN ST MEP-023A	
J49809	6115 00 738 6336	B	9130 00 160 1818	GN	H	2.40			GEN ST TM PU 332AG	
J50151	6115 00 989 3296	B	9130 00 160 1818	GN	H	2.40			GEN ST TM PU 656/G	
J50185	6115 00 937 8468	B	9130 00 160 1818	GN	H	2.40			GEN ST TM PU 678/M	
J50195	6115 00 789 3656	B	9130 00 160 1818	GN	H	2.40			GEN SET PU681/TLQ	
J50220	6115 00 226 1568	B	9130 00 160 1818	GN	H	2.40			GEN SETBOGUE5380B	
J50220	6115 00 840 6577	B	9130 00 160 1818	GN	H	2.40			GEN SET GAS ENGPDI	
J50220	6115 00 972 2326	B	9130 00 160 1818	GN	H	2.40			GEN SETBOGUE5380A	
J51418	6115 00 016 2356	B	9140 00 273 2377	GN	H	4.50			GEN ST TMPU-614/M	
J51453	6115 00 778 8788	B	9130 00 256 8613	GN	H	16.60			GEN GAS TURB ENG	
J51453	6115 00 849 6030	B	9130 00 256 8613	GN	H	14.12			30 KW GAS TURB GEN	
J51480	6115 00 967 7005	B	9130 00 160 1818	GN	H	3.50			GENERATOR SET	
J51505	6115 00 758 5492	B	9130 00 160 1818	GN	H	16.60			GEN GFD 60KW 400CY	
J51547	6115 00 074 6442	B	9130 00 160 1818	GN	H	106.00			GEN ST PU697 M	
J74715	3805 00 801 4999	K	9140 00 273 2377	CE	H	3.80			GRADER 220	
J74852	3805 00 053 8448	K	9140 00 273 2377	CE	H	3.80			GRADER 12 WNTZD	
J74852	3805 00 155 7093	K	9140 00 273 2377	CE	H	5.60			GRADER F1500M	
J74852	3805 00 197 4184	K	9140 00 273 2377	CE	H	3.70			GRADER 12	
J74852	3805 00 221 1802	K	9140 00 273 2377	CE	H	4.50			GRADER 116	
J74852	3805 00 221 1803	K	9140 00 273 2377	CE	H	4.60			GRADER 4D 100	
J74852	3805 00 223 9030	K	9140 00 273 2377	CE	H	4.70			GRADER 550	
J74852	3805 00 223 9031	K	9140 00 273 2377	CE	H	2.90			GRADER 118 W/ATTCH	
J74852	3805 00 223 9037	K	9140 00 273 2377	CE	H	4.50			GRADER 402	
J74852	3805 00 542 2995	K	9140 00 273 2377	CE	H	4.30			GRADER 4D WNTZD	
J74852	3804 00 542 2996	K	9140 00 273 2377	CE	H	4.30			GRADER 4D	
J74852	3805 01 018 2866	K	9140 00 273 2377	CE	H	5.20			GRADER RD HVY	
J74852	3805 01 029 0139	K	9140 00 273 2377	CE	H	5.20			GRADER RD HVY	
J74852	3805 01 064 3878	K	9140 00 273 2377	CE	H	5.20			GRADER RD HVY	
J74886	3805 00 902 3083	K	9140 00 273 2377	CE	H	3.20			GRADER CAT MOL 112	
J74886	3805 01 029 0140	K	9140 00 273 2377	CE	H	4.20			GRADER RD SEC	
J74910	3805 00 995 4772	K	9140 00 273 2377	CE	H	5.00			GRADER RD	
J74920	3805 00 782 5290	K	9140 00 273 2377	CE	H	2.70			GRADER RD AIR DROP	

Figure 6. Equipment Combat Fuel Consumption Rates— Bulk POL Table A (continued)

LI	EI NSN	SNSN CMD	FUEL NSN	EQUIP TYP	CONSUMP CD	CONSUMPTION RATES IDL/AV	XCNTRY	2NDRDS	NOMENCLATURE	MULTIFUEL
J81750	2350 01 048 5920	S K	9140 00 273 2377	TV	H	6.40	18.00	8.60	INF FGT VEH OM2	
J95533	1425 00 937 3859	S L	9140 00 273 2377	TV	H	1.00	3.41	3.41	M48 GM STM1NCPTAER	
J96694	2350 01 017 2113	S M	9140 00 273 2377	TV	H	1.00	5.20	13.00	GUN AIRDEF M163A1	
J96820	2350 00 049 4791	S M	9130 00 160 1818	TV	H	20.7113			GUN SPET40MM M42A1	
K04697	3895 00 014 0583	K	9140 00 273 2377	CE	H	.60			HAMMER P/D CD SLE	
K04834	3895 00 443 4696	K	9140 00 273 2377	CE	H	1.10			HAMMER PLDR MKT DA	
K04834	3895 00 756 7447	K	9140 00 273 2377	CE	H	1.10			HAMMER PLDR DE30	
K04834	3895 00 854 4150	K	9140 00 273 2377	CE	H	7.00			HAMMER PILE MDL 4	
K06067	2230 00 386 3696	B	9130 00 160 1818	OV	H	1.00			HAMMER SPIKE	
K24520	3895 00 062 7912	K	9130 00 160 1818	HG	H	1.30			HEATER PSM50	
K24520	3895 00 221 1763	K	9130 00 160 1818	HG	H	6.00			HEATER DS	
K24520	3895 00 634 9215	K	9130 00 160 1818	HG	H	6.00			HEATER SG-45T	
K24520	3895 00 836 5242	K	9130 00 160 1818	HG	H	6.00			HEATER SG-52A	
K24588	3895 00 099 5242	K	9130 00 160 1818	HG	H	15.00			HEATER BIT TR MT	
K24862	4520 00 001 7726	B	9130 00 160 1818	HG	H	4.00			HEATER M1LH11049	
K24862	4520 00 086 7676	B	9130 00 160 1818	HG	H	4.00			HEATER 250	
K24862	4520 00 218 0808	B	9130 00 160 1818	HG	H	4.00			HEATER V8 3077C853	
K24862	4520 00 255 5051	B	9130 00 160 1818	HG	H	4.00			HEATER H250	
K24862	4520 00 448 0413	B	9130 00 160 1818	HG	H	4.00			HEATER V8 3077C860	
K24862	4520 00 856 5983	B	9130 00 160 1818	HG	H	4.00			HEATER VB 3077C861	
K24862	4520 00 937 6168	B	9130 00 160 1818	HG	H	4.00			HEATER VB 67-GFC3	
K24931	4520 00 223 3221	B	9130 00 160 1818	HG	H	5.00			HEATER BT400-40-1A	
K24931	4520 00 223 3221	B	9130 00 160 1818	HG	H	3.82			HEATERBT4	
K24931	4520 00 446 7314	B	9130 00 160 1818	HG	H	3.82			HEATER BT400-30	
K24931	4520 00 620 4055	B	9130 00 160 1818	HG	H	3.82			HEATER BT400-10	
K24931	4520 00 792 8257	B	9130 00 160 1818	HG	H	3.82			HTR DUCT TY400000B	
K24931	4520 00 915 7789	B	9130 00 160 1818	HG	H	3.82			HEATERBT4	
K24931	4520 00 980 3199	B	9130 00 160 1818	HG	H	3.82			HEATER PH-400	
K24931	4520 01 071 7191	B	9130 00 160 1818	HG	H	3.83			HEATER DUCT TYPE	
K25205	3895 00 066 6016	K	9140 00 273 2377	HG	H	6.00			HEATER H/0 2005	
K25342	4540 00 266 6835	B	9130 00 160 1818	HG	H	.45			HEATER IMM LQ FL	
K25342	4520 00 469 6593	B	9130 00 160 1818	HG	H	.45			HEATERM67IMMERSION	M
K25479	4550 00 266 6834	J	9140 00 273 2377	HG	H	2.00			HEATER IMM LOFL371	
K26301	4520 00 114 1055	H	9130 00 160 1818	HG	H	.75			HEATER UH68D	
K26301	4520 00 280 1830	B	9130 00 160 1818	HG	H	.75			HEATER UH68E	M
K26301	4520 00 999 8523	B	9130 00 160 1818	HG	H	2.00			HEATER UH684	M
K26301	4520 01 050 5628	B	9130 00 160 1818	HG	H	.75			HEATER UH68F	M
K26301	4520 01 068 2968	B	9130 00 160 1818	HG	H	.75			HEATER MODEL P60A	M
K26849	4410 00 542 5656	M	9140 00 273 2377	HG	H	6.00			HEATER WTR FUEL M2	
K29660	1520 00 999 9821	H	9130 00 256 8613	AV	H	106.00			HCPTR ATTACK AH-1G	
K29694	1520 00 504 9112	H	9130 00 256 8613	AV	H	123.00			HCPTR ATTACK HA-15	
K29762	1520 00 804 3635	H	9130 00 256 8613	AV	H	106.00			HCPTR ATTACK TRNTH	
K30378	1520 00 633 6836	H	9130 00 256 8613	AV	H	482.00			HCPTR CGO TRANSCH4	
K30383	1520 00 990 2941	H	9130 00 256 8613	AV	H	478.80			HCPTR CGO TRANSCH4	
K30449	1520 00 871 7308	H	9130 00 256 8613	AV	H	497.10			HCPTR MED LFT CH47	
K30515	1520 00 964 9601	H	9130 00 256 8613	AV	H	656.70			HCPTC CGO TRANSCH5	
K30516	1520 00 113 5776	H	9130 00 256 8613	AV	H	716.40			HCPTR CGO CH54B	
K30548	1520 00 368 8442	H	9130 00 256 8613	AV	H	93.00			HCPTP ECM	
K30645	1520 00 918 1523	H	9130 00 256 8613	AV	H	29.00			HCPTR OBSN CM-6A	
K31042	1520 00 169 7137	H	9130 00 256 8613	AV	H	33.70			HCPTR OBSN CH-58A	
K31153	1520 00 758 0289	H	9130 00 179 1125	AV	H	15.10			HCPTR PRIM TRNRTH5	
K31786	1520 00 859 2670	H	9130 00 256 8613	AV	H	114.50			HCPTR UTILITY UH-1	
K31795	1520 00 087 7637	H	9130 00 256 8613	AV	H	106.00			HCPTR UTILITY UH-1	
K31804	1520 00 809 2631	H	9130 00 256 8613	AV	H	106.00			HCPTR UTILITY UH-1	
K32293	1520 01 035 0266	H	9130 00 256 8613	AV	H	142.00			HCPTR UTIL UH60A	
K54707	3835 00 892 5157	B	9140 00 273 2377	SG	H	3.35			HOSELINE OUTFIT FH	
K56981	2350 01 041 4590	S M	9140 00 273 2377	TV		2.20	12.50	14.30	HOW SP 8IN M110A2	
K57667	2350 01 031 0586	S M	9140 00 273 2377	TV	H	2.20	11.80	16.10	HOW 155MM M109A2	
K57667	2350 01 031 8851	S M	9140 00 273 2377	TV	H	2.20	11.80	16.10	M109A3 HOW SP 155MM	
K90188	4940 00 077 1638	K	9130 00 160 1818	SV	H	.15			M185A3 INST REP SH	
K90188	4940 00 300 0306	K	9130 00 160 1818	SV	H	.21			M185 INST REP SH	
K90188	4940 00 973 3995	K	9130 00 160 1818	SV	H	.21			M185A1 INST REP SH	
K90188	4940 00 987 8799	K	9130 00 160 1818	SV	H	.15			M185A2 INST REP SH	
L21300	3895 00 252 1183	K	9130 00 160 1818	CE	H	4.50			KETTLE KD 750 GAL	
L21437	3895 00 051 3834	K	9120 00 160 1818	CE	H	1.25			KETTLE UPS 175-S	
L21437	3895 00 066 6015	K	9130 00 160 1818	CE	H	1.25			KETTLE US84HD3	
L21437	3895 00 247 7593	K	9130 00 160 1818	CE	H	1.25			KETTLE 7ZPSA	
L21437	3895 00 247 7594	K	9130 00 160 1818	CE	H	1.25			KETTLE 84HD3	
L21437	3895 00 351 2354	K	9130 00 160 1818	CE	H	1.25			KETTLE GS 1901	
L21437	3895 00 442 9741	K	9130 00 160 1818	CE	H	1.25			KETTLE WHITE FM 3	
L21437	3895 00 542 3260	K	9130 00 160 1818	CE	H	1.25			KETTLE 7ZPSA9	
L21437	3895 00 832 6231	K	9130 00 160 1818	CE	H	1.25			KETTLE AERIOL72PSA	
L21447	3895 00 571 6414	K	9130 00 160 1818	CE	H	6.00			KETTLE HTG 350 GAL	
L36602	1905 00 153 6695	B	9140 00 273 2377	AB	H	25.00			LCM-6	
L36739	1905 00 267 1097	B	9140 00 273 2377	AB	H	35.00			LCMB	
L36739	1905 00 935 6057	B	9140 00 273 2377	AB	H	34.16			LCM 8 MOD1	
L36876	1905 00 168 5764	B	9140 00 273 2377	AB	H	38.00			LAND CRAFT UTL 16	
L36876	1905 00 217 2293	B	9140 00 273 2377	AB	H	40.00			LCU 1466 115FT	
L36876	1905 01 009 1056	B	9140 00 273 2377	AB	H	34.00			LOADING CRAFT UTIL	
L36876	1905 01 031 6077	B	9140 00 273 2377	AB	H	34.00			LCU 1466 115FT	
L36989	1905 01 154 1191	B	9140 00 273 2377	AB	H	38.00			LAND CRAFT UTILITY	
L43390	5420 00 542 3052	K	9140 00 273 2377	TO	K	8.8798			LAUN-M48A2 CHASSIE	
L43664	5420 00 889 2020	K	9140 00 273 2377	TV	H	2.00	26.53	18.79	LAUN M60 SERIES CH	
L43664	5420 01 076 6096	K	9140 00 273 2377	TV	H	2.00	26.53	18.79	LAUN M48A5 CHASSIE	
L44644	1440 00 937 0938	L	9140 00 273 2377	TO	K	1.6343			LAUNCH GM M752	
L44894	1055 01 092 0596	L	9140 00 273 2377	TV	H	1.28	15.00	8.60	ARMR VEH LAUN M270	
L48315	3510 00 169 4735	B	9140 00 273 2377	SG	H	1.09			LAUNDRY UNIT 60LB	
L48315	3510 00 753 2895	B	9140 00 273 2377	SG	H	1.09			LAUNDRY UNIT	
L48315	3510 00 782 5294	B	9140 00 273 2377	SG	H	1.09			LAUNDRY UNIT EL191	
L66710	2305 01 061 6230	B	9130 00 256 8613	AB	H	260.00			AIRCUSH VEHLACV-30	

Figure 6. Equipment Combat Fuel Consumption Rates—Bulk POL Table A (continued)

LI	EI NSN	SNSN CMD	FUEL NSN	EQUIP TYP	CONSUMP CD	CONSUMPTION RATES IDL/AV	XCNTRY	2NDRDS	NOMENCLATURE	MULTIFUEL
L67234	1930 00 710 5728	B	9140 00 273 2377	AB	M	15.00			LIGHTER AMPH 5 TON	
L67371	1930 00 710 5729	B	9140 00 273 2377	AB	H	28.10			AMPHIBIOUS LIGHTER	
L67508	1930 00 392 2981	B	9140 00 273 2377	AB	H	33.00			LIGHTER AMPH LARC	
L67645	1930 00 705 9230	B	9140 00 273 2377	AB	H	65.00			LIGHTER MK1-D-5002	
L76282	3805 00 074 6378	K	9140 00 273 2377	CE	H	7.40			LOADED SCOOP 10.5K	
L76305	3805 00 438 1463	K	9140 00 273 2377	CE	H	3.30			LDR 1/2 TO 3 CY	
L76315	3805 00 602 5006	K	9140 00 273 2377	CE	H	5.00			LDR RK BUCH CASE17	
L76315	3805 01 052 9042	K	9140 00 273 2377	CE	H	11.00			LDR SCP DED 4-1/2CY	
K76321	3805 00 602 5013	K	9140 00 273 2377	CE	H	5.00			LDR GP BUCK CASE 1758	
L76321	3805 01 052 9043	K	9140 00 273 2377	CE	H	11.00			LDR SCP DED 5 CY	
L76328	3805 00 438 1484	K	9149 00 273 2377	CE	H	3.00			LDR 1-1/2 CY	
L76351	3805 00 679 6915	K	9140 00 273 2377	CE	H	4.00			LOADER 85A-M	
L76351	3805 00 761 1640	K	9140 00 273 2377	CE	H	4.00			LOADR DSL D 1-1/2CY	
L76488	3805 00 678 1735	K	9140 00 273 2377	CE	H	5.90			LOADER 175A-M	
L76522	3805 00 438 1464	K	9140 00 273 2377	CE	H	6.50			LDR 3-1/4 TO 5 CY	
L76556	3805 00 051 9359	K	9140 00 273 2377	CE	H	5.00			LOADER SCO 645M	
L76556	3805 00 169 4711	K	9140 00 273 2377	CE	H	5.30			LDR SCP IICASE MW2 4B	
L76556	3805 00 253 0627	K	9140 00 273 2377	CE	H	5.00			LDR SCP J I CASEMW24	
L76556	3805 00 617 7091	K	9140 00 273 2377	CE	H	5.70			LDR SCP A/C645M	
L76556	3895 01 030 2816	K	9140 00 273 2377	CE	H	5.70			LOADER SCOOP JI CMW24	
L76556	3805 01 150 4814	K	9140 00 273 2377	CE	H	7.00			LDR SCP 21/2 CU YD	
L76625	3805 00 803 2671	K	9140 00 273 2377	CE	H	5.00			LOADER H-90M	
L76625	3805 00 803 2672	K	9140 00 273 2377	CE	H	5.90			LOADER H-90M WNTRZ	
L76625	3805 00 866 3849	K	9140 00 273 2377	CE	H	5.90			LOADER 175A-M23	
L76625	3805 00 995 3236	K	9140 00 273 2377	CE	H	5.90			LOADER H-900M	
L76659	3805 00 721 9453	K	9130 00 160 1818	CE	H	1.40			LDR 3/8 CY	
L76693	3805 00 900 8546	K	9140 00 273 2377	CE	H	5.30			LDR SCP 2- 1/2 CYD	
L76693	3805 00 064 5800	K	9140 00 273 2377	CE	H	5.70			LDR A/C TL645WRROPS	
L76725	3805 00 857 3599	K	9140 00 273 2377	CE	H	3.80			LOADER SCP 1-1/2 CYD	
L76738	3805 00 438 1483	K	9140 00 273 2377	CE	H	5.40			LDR 2-1/2 CY	
L76750	1450 00 937 0939	S L	9140 00 273 2377	TV	H	1.6343			LDR TRSP GM M688A1	
L76762	1450 00 066 8873	S L	9130 00 160 1818	TV	K	0.1367			LDR TRSP GM M501A3	
L76762	1450 00 768 7046	S L	9130 00 160 1818	TV	K	0.1367			LDR TRSP GM M501A2	
L79673	2210 00 773 2510	B	9140 00 273 2377	OV	H	26.50			LOCOMOTIVE DMSITFS	
L80221	2210 00 825 5050	B	9140 00 273 2377	OV	H	6.84			LOCOMOTIVE 10T	
L80358	2210 00 112 8508	B	9140 00 273 2377	OV	H	62.85			LOCOMOTIVE 539S	
L8035S	2210 00 262 0751	B	9140 00 273 2377	OV	H	75.42			LOCOMOTIVE H1244	120T
L80358	2210 00 371 7535	B	9140 00 273 2377	OV	H	50.56			LOCOMOTIVE SWS	
L80358	2210 00 554 0785	B	9140 00 273 2377	OV	H	50.00			LOCOMOTIVE GP7L	
L80358	2210 00 819 9320	B	9140 00 273 2377	OV	H	41.48			LOCOMOTIVE ALCO	
L80495	2210 00 804 3610	B	9140 00 273 2377	OV	H	25.00			DAV BPSS D17000	
L80495	2210 00 821 1135	B	9140 00 273 2377	OV	H	25.00			45 TON GE HH1	
L80632	2210 00 819 9318	B	9140 00 273 2377	OV	H	13.42			LOCOMOTIVE RS4TC	
L80724	2210 00 804 3614	B	9140 00 273 2377	OV	H	29.60			LOCOMOTIVE NMBIS	
L80724	2210 00 804 3615	B	9140 00 273 2377	OV	H	29.60			LOCOMOTIVE 1125708	
L80724	2210 00 820 5451	B	9140 00 273 2377	OV	H	31.42			LOCOMOTIVE L1600	
L80769	2210 00 270 1354	B	9140 00 273 2377	OV	H	62.85			LOCOMOTIVE 127TN	
L80769	2210 00 554 0786	B	9140 00 273 2377	OV	H	62.85			LOCOMTV 131TN	
L80769	2210 00 814 5291	B	9140 00 273 2377	OV	H	50.00			LOCOMTV 19B238G2	
L80769	2210 00 815 3521	B	9140 00 273 2377	OV	H	50.00			LOCOMTV 19B232G1	
L80769	2210 00 819 9317	B	9140 00 273 2377	OV	H	50.00			LOCOMTV MRS1M/C729	
L80902	3805 01 066 7763	K	9140 00 273 2377	CE	H	10.00			LOADER SCOOP 3-1/2 T 60 CY	
L85283	4930 00 017 9167	B	9130 00 160 1818	SG	H	.45			LUBSVCUNIT901765-1	
L85283	4930 00 548 2766	B	9130 00 160 1818	SG	H	.45			LUB-SVC UT MT ENG	
L85283	4930 00 857 7160	B	9130 00 160 1818	SG	H	.45			LUB-SVC UNIT 251-3	
L85283	4930 00 892 5067	B	9130 00 160 1818	SG	H	.45			LUB-SVC UT 251-437	
L85283	4930 00 935 4451	B	9130 00 160 1818	SG	H	.45			LUBSVC UNIT ENG-3	
L93797	3830 00 263 2978	K	9130 00 160 1818	SV	H	1.00			MAGNETIC SWEEPER 3MAG 36	
M07888	3610 00 294 7830	K	9130 00 160 1818	WV	M	3.6538			MAP LO SEC TOPO	
M08025	6675 00 526 4788	B	9130 00 160 1818	SG	H	6.00			MAP REV SECT TOPO	
M32780	3895 00 066 6017	K	9140 00 273 2377	CE	H	26.00			MELTER ASPHALT 18BAM	
M32780	3895 00 839 5586	K	9140 00 273 2377	CE	H	26.00			MELTER ASPHALT TH 12-750	
M32780	3895 00 059 0129	K	9140 00 263 2377	CE	H	26.00			MELTER ASPHALT MT-12	
M53877	3895 00 221 1807	K	9140 00 273 2377	CE	H	6.50			MIXER BIT N/SLF LD	
M54004	3895 00 611 6258	K	9140 00 273 2377	CE	H	6.50			MIXER BIT TRK MTD	
M54076	3895 00 438 1480	K	9130 00 160 1818	CE	H	.70			MIXER CONCRETE	
M54083	3895 00 438 1479	K	9130 00 160 1818	CE	H	1.00			MIXER CONCRETE 6 CF	
M54151	3895 00 062 4628	K	9130 00 160 1818	CE	H	1.25			MXR CON JAEGER 16-S4	
M54151	3895 00 238 5093	K	9130 00 160 1818	CE	H	1.25			MXR CON KWIK MIX 16-S	
M54151	3895 00 238 5098	K	9130 00 160 1818	CE	H	1.50			MXR CON CHAIN BLT 16-S	
M54151	3895 00 444 1531	K	9130 00 160 1818	CE	H	1.25			MXR CON SMITH MOL4	
M54151	3895 00 807 7985	K	9130 00 160 1818	CE	H	1.50			MXR CON CNST MAC 16-SM	
M54151	3895 00 835 4512	K	9130 00 160 1818	CE	H	1.50			MIX CON CHN BLT HBG	
M54151	3895 00 985 5335	K	9130 00 160 1818	CE	H	1.25			MXR CON CNST MAC 16-SM	
M54630	3895 00 438 1486	K	9140 00 273 2377	WV	M	0.1243			MIXER CONCRETE 5-7CF	
M54654	3895 00 615 8814	K	9140 00 273 2377	WV	M	0.0808			MIXER CONCRETE 1-4CF	
M55384	3895 00 883 0437	K	9140 00 273 2377	CE	M	3.00			MXR FWD MDL 82-1171	
M55384	3895 00 987 5536	K	9140 00 273 2377	CE	H	2.75			MXR REX CHN BLT HD	
M57048	3895 00 936 8613	K	9140 00 273 2377	CE	H	5.00			MIXING PLT ASPH DS	
M72933	2340 01 090 7748	K	9130 00 160 1818	WV	K	0.0186			MOTORCYCLE 1E4101	
M72922	2340 01 090 7749	K	9130 00 160 1818	WV	K	0.0186			MOTORCYCLE 1E4102	
M72933	2340 01 090 7750	K	9130 00 160 1818	WV	K	0.0249			MOTORCYCLE 1E4103	
M83242	6675 00 526 4836	B	9140 00 273 2377	SV	H	6.00			MULTIPLXSCTTDPOMAP	
N34334	2805 00 294 3598	B	9130 00 160 1818	AB	H	5.00			OB MTR RDM12 25HHP	
N34334	2805 00 376 9171	B	9130 00 160 1818	AB	H	5.00			OB MTR RDM10 25HHP	
N34334	2805 00 376 9172	B	9130 00 160 1818	AB	H	5.00			OB MTR RDM11 25HHP	
N34334	2805 00 646 7987	B	9130 00 160 1818	AB	H	5.00			OB MTRG35912 25HHP	
N34334	2805 00 826 0894	B	9130 00 160 1818	AB	H	5.00			OB MTRG35691 25HHP	
N75124	3895 00 057 8715	K	9130 00 160 1818	CE	H	.75			PAVG MACH	
N75124	3895 00 281 1818	K	9130 00 160 1818	CE	H	2.75			PAVG MACH B-G 879	

Figure 6. Equipment Combat Fuel Consumption Rates– Bulk POL Table A (continued)

						CONSUMPTION RATES				
LI	EI NSN	SNSN CMD	FUEL NSN	EQUIP TYP	CONSUMP CD	IDL/AV	XCNTRY	2NDRDS	NOMENCLATURE	MULTIFUEL
N75124	3895 00 821 6951	K	9130 00 160 1818	CE	H	2.75			PAVS MACH B-G 879-A	
N75124	3895 01 063 7891	K	9130 00 160 1818	CE	H	6.00			PAVING MACHINE BIT	
N87460	6675 00 526 4631	B	9130 00 160 1818	SG	H	6.00			PHOTOMPG SEC TOPO	
N87960	3610 00 691 1707	B	9130 00 160 1818	SG	H	6.00			PHOTOMECH PRO SEC	
N91371	3895 00 254 2802	K	9130 00 160 1818	CE	H	3.50			PILEDRIVING RIG SKI	
P03804	3610 00 294 7829	B	9130 00 160 1818	SG	H	6.00			PLATE FROC SEC 10	
P11866	3820 00 950 8584	K	9140 00 273 2377	CE	H	3.53			PNEU TL COMP	
P12140	3820 00 295 9536	K	9140 00 273 2377	CE	H	10.00			PNEU TL OUTFIT 600 CFM	
P27805	6115 00 937 5046	B	9140 00 273 2377	GN	H	4.50			POWER PLT/MJQ-9	
P27819	6115 00 056 7906	B	9140 00 273 2377	SG	H	6.00			POWER PLANT	
P27819	6115 00 394 9582	B	9140 00 273 2377	GN	H	6.00			PWRPLT, AN/MIQ 10A	
P27821	6115 00 134 8485	B	9140 00 273 2377	SG	H	20.00			POWER PLNT AN/MJQ	
P27823	6115 00 257 1602	B	9140 00 273 2377	GN	H	12.00			PWRPLT, AN/MJQ12A	
P27823	6115 00 464 4194	B	9140 00 273 2377	SG	H	12.00			PWR PLANT AN-MJ012	
P28039	1450 00 005 4878	L	9140 00 273 2377	SV	H	25.00			PWR STAT GM TRANS	M
P28039	1450 00 308 5265	L	9140 00 273 2377	SV	H	25.00			PWR STAT GM TRANS	M
P28075	6115 00 400 7591	B	9140 00 273 2377	GN	H	3.00			PWR PLT AN/MJQ-15	
P28176	1450 00 541 6142	L	9130 00 160 1818	SG	H	6.00			PWR STAT GM SYS TM	
P28176	1450 00 731 8190	L	9130 00 160 1818	SG	H	6.00			PWR STAT GM TM	
P28176	1450 01 054 7197	L	9140 00 273 2377	SV	H	1.20			PWR STAT GM SYS TM	M
P41832	6115 00 033 1395	B	9140 00 273 2377	GN	H	1.14			PWR PLT AN/MJQ16	
P44377	4920 00 938 8363	H	9130 00 160 1818	SV	H	6.00			PWR UN AUX ACFT GE	
P44627	1730 01 144 1897	B	9130 00 256 8613	SG	H	12.00			AV GR POWER UNIT	
P45003	6115 00 134 0825	B	9130 00 256 8613	SG	H	35.00			POWER UNIT PPU85-4	
P45003	6115 00 937 0929	B	9130 00 256 8613	SG	H	35.00			POWER UNIT PPU85-5	
P45003	6115 00 937 0929	B	9130 00 256 8613	SG	H	35.00			POWER UNIT PPU85-5	
P50041	3610 00 204 3137	B	9130 00 160 1818	SG	H	6.00			PRESS SEC REPRO T	
P61528	3610 00 889 3262	B	9130 00 160 1818	SG	H	6.00			PRT PLT 4 COMP	
P78995	2010 00 278 0793	B	9140 00 273 2377	SG	H	10.00			PROP UB ON DLS 165	
P78995	2010 00 410 4442	B	9140 00 273 2377	SG	H	10.00			PROP UN NA165-154	
P90386	4320 00 080 2059	B	9140 00 273 2377	SG	H	4.09			PUMP CENTRE MILP52	
P90610	4320 00 150 6116	B	9130 00 160 1818	SG	H	.50			PUMP BARNES US6ACG	
P90610	4320 00 900 8544	B	9130 00 160 1818	SG	H	.50			PUMP KENCO 114MX1A	
P90934	4320 00 820 0700	B	9130 00 160 1818	SG	H	.68			PUMP BARNES MDL 10	
P91756	4320 00 752 9466	B	9130 00 160 1818	SG	H	.50			PUMP BARNES 17570	
P92030	4320 00 542 3347	B	9130 00 160 1818	SG	H	.50			PUMP CTRF GD FM125	
P92167	4320 00 082 6004	B	9130 00 160 1818	SG	H	.75			PUMP CTRF GD FM170	
P92852	4320 00 203 2546	B	9130 00 160 1818	SG	H	15.60			PUMP PEERLESS USPL	
P92852	4320 00 389 6857	B	9130 00 160 1818	SG	H	15.60			PUMP RIENER GP-75	
P92852	4320 00 542 4037	B	9130 00 160 1818	SG	H	15.60			PUMP BARNES CE4P4	
P92852	4320 00 691 0967	B	9130 00 160 1818	SG	H	4.06			PUMP CONSOL DSL 40	
P92989	4320 00 810 7310	B	9130 00 160 1818	SG	H	4.06			PUMP CARVER 4 WHIS	
P92989	4320 00 830 5344	B	9130 00 160 1818	SG	H	4.06			PUMP CARVER 4 WHIS	
P92989	4320 00 935 1618	B	9130 00 160 1818	SG	H	4.06			PUMP RURP E13-4A08	
P93263	4320 00 203 2609	B	9130 00 160 1818	SG	H	4.09			PUMP RUPP 06M260	
P93263	4320 00 409 8678	B	9130 00 160 1818	SG	H	4.09			PUMP CTRF US67-CCG	
P93263	4320 00 563 1855	B	9130 00 160 1818	SG	H	4.09			PUMP RENIER GP-57	
P93263	4320 00 595 3253	B	9130 00 160 1818	SG	H	4.09			PUMP REINER GP-58	
P93263	4320 00 630 4434	B	9130 00 160 1818	SG	H	4.09			PUMP CARVER6HJR57	
P93263	4320 00 715 7599	B	9130 00 160 1818	SG	H	4.09			PUMP KRUZ-ROOT BAL	
P93263	4320 00 929 0681	B	9130 00 160 1818	SG	H	4.09			PUMP CARVER K906MP	
P93263	4320 00 968 6264	B	9130 00 160 1818	SG	H	4.09			PUMP CARVER K906	
P93400	4320 00 063 7368	B	9130 00 160 1818	SG	H	15.60			PUMP REINER C-P 11	
P93400	4320 00 122 9642	B	9130 00 160 1818	SG	H	15.60			PUMP CENTRF IF M71	
P93400	4320 00 203 0819	B	9130 00 160 1818	SG	H	15.60			PUMP BARNES CE-6-P	
P93400	4320 00 709 2807	B	9130 00 160 1818	SG	H	15.60			PUMP A/C 501112520	
P93400	4320 00 988 1192	B	9130 00 160 1818	SG	H	15.60			PUMP EQUIP CO PR-1	
P94290	4320 00 935 1619	B	9130 00 160 1818	SG	H	2.04			SHLEYER36MSPS30116	
P94359	4320 00 440 9808	B	9130 00 160 1818	SG	H	6.08			PUMP CARVER KN6HS	
P94359	4320 00 490 1859	B	9130 00 160 1818	SG	H	6.08			PUMP BARNES	
P94359	4320 00 678 1736	B	9130 00 160 1818	SG	H	8.00			PUMP CARVER KN8L	
P94359	4320 00 812 3707	B	9130 00 160 1818	SG	H	6.08			PUMP CHNBLT REX 6L	
P94359	4320 00 878 1907	B	9130 00 160 1818	SG	H	4.00			PUMP CENTR	
P96503	4320 00 493 1861	B	9130 00 160 1818	SG	H	3.35			PUMP PEERLESS 2791	
P96503	4320 00 649 9010	B	9130 00 160 1818	SG	H	3.35			PUMP PRLS 52	
P96845	4320 00 407 2583	B	9130 00 160 1818	SG	H	2.45			BARNES MFG US36ACG	
P96845	4320 00 916 9172	B	9130 00 160 1818	SG	H	2.45			GORMAN RUP 84C154A	
P97051	4320 00 069 8494	B	9130 00 160 1818	SG	H	3.35			PUMP GR04A123MVG4D	
P97051	4320 00 195 4914	B	9130 00 160 1818	SG	H	3.35			PUMP BARNES	
P97051	4320 00 600 7590	B	9130 00 160 1818	SG	H	3.35			PUMP 04A12CMVG4D	
P97051	4320 00 691 1071	B	9130 00 160 1818	SG	H	3.35			PUMP G-R04A12 MG D	
P97119	4320 01 141 5154	B	9140 00 273 2377	SG	H	2.20			PUMP RUPP REGULATE	
P97501	4320 01 092 3551	B	9140 00 273 2377	SG	H	2.20			PUMP RUPP UNREG	
R07085	2230 00 262 0759	B	9130 00 160 1818	OV	H	2.50			RR MOTOR CAR 4 MAN	
R07633	2230 00 262 0762	B	9130 00 160 1818	OV	H	2.50			RR MOTOR CAR 4 MAN	
R14154	7360 00 082 2153	E	9130 00 160 1818	SG	H	.50			RANGE OUTFIT M 59	
R39883	5811 01 095 1875	K	9140 00 273 2377	TU	K	0.1056			TEAM PACKAGE SQ103A	
R50544	2350 00 439 6242	S M	9140 00 273 2377	TV	H	2.20	12.50	14.30	M578 RECOV VEH FT	
R50681	2350 00 122 6826	S K	9140 00 273 2377	TV	H	2.00	36.76	25.54	REC VEH FT M88A1	
R50681	2350 00 678 5772	S K	9130 00 160 1818	TV	H	2.00	36.76	25.54	M88 REV VEH FT MED	
R52776	6675 00 526 4629	B	9130 00 160 1818	SG	H	6.00			REC ROPO MAPNG SET	
R61428	4110 00 926 4251	B	9130 00 160 1818	SG	H	.95			REFRIG UNIT 1000B	
R61428	4110 01 010 5970	B	9130 00 160 1818	SG	H	1.00			REF UNIT RMPJ1-10G	
R61428	4110 01 074 5175	B	9130 00 160 1818	SG	H	1.00			REF UNIT F1000 RG2	
R65544	4110 00 026 0419	B	9130 00 160 1818	SG	H	4.50			REF UNIT KECO FSG	
R65544	4110 00 360 0157	B	9130 00 160 1818	SG	H	4.50			REF UNIT TMPMOQ15G	
R65544	4110 00 911 9208	B	9130 00 160 1818	SG	H	4.50			REF UNIT THRMO Q5G	
R65566	4110 00 933 6114	B	9130 00 150 1818	SG	H	.49			REFRIG DIXIE NORCO	
R65544	4110 01 076 1991	B	9130 00 160 1818	SG	H	1.00			REF UNIT ERU-5G	
R65681	4110 00 186 3485	B	9130 00 160 1818	SV	H	1.00			REF LEAR-SIEGLER 1	

Figure 6. Equipment Combat Fuel Consumption Rates— Bulk POL Table A (continued)

						CONSUMPTION RATES				
LI	EI NSN	SNSN CMD	FUEL NSN	EQUIP TYP	CONSUMP CD	IDL/AV	XCNTRY	2NDRDS	NOMENCLATURE	MULTIFUEL
R65681	4110 00 197 4980	B	9130 00 160 1818	SG	H	1.00			REF UNITROP9000MOD	
R65681	4110 00 588 9196	B	9130 00 160 1818	SG	H	1.00			REF UNIT THRMO Q9A	
R65681	4110 00 933 5457	B	9130 00 160 1818	SV	H	.95			REF UNIT TARMO QL9	
R65681	4110 00 935 1512	B	9130 00 160 1818	SV	H	.95			REF UNIT RDMSH RGP	
R65681	4110 00 967 9762	B	9130 00 160 1818	SG	H	1.00			REF UNIT THRMO QL9	
R65681	4110 00 987 8578	B	9130 00 160 1818	SG	H	1.00			REF UNIT DHM BUPTG	
R65681	4110 00 999 1900	B	9130 00 160 1818	SG	H	1.00			REF UNIT DHM-B	
R65818	4110 00 360 0160	B	9130 00 160 1818	SG	H	1.50			REF UNIT UNIV OEC	
R65818	4110 00 391 3207	B	9130 00 160 1818	SG	H	1.50			REF UNIT THRM CN N	
S03225	3820 00 985 2274	K	9140 00 273 2377	SG	H	12.01			ROCK DRILLING EQP	
S10682	3895 00 252 5276	K	9130 00 160 1818	CE	H	2.50			ROLLERESSIK VR55TM	
S10682	3895 00 902 3112	K	9130 00 160 1818	CE	H	2.50			RLR RROS HOL VP-4D	
S11033	3895 00 490 0560	K	9130 00 160 1818	CE	H	.15			ROLLER MOTORIZED	
S11050	3895 00 935 7909	K	9130 00 160 1818	CE	H	3.00			ROLLER MOTORIZED 2RLS	
S11050	3895 01 077 7823	K	9130 00 160 1818	CE	H	3.00			ROLLER MOTORIZED 2M	
S11054	3895 01 173 1728	K	9130 00 160 1818	CE	H	4.00			ROLLER MOTORIZED TO 21	
S11059	3895 01 151 4429	K	9130 00 160 1818	CE	H	3.50			ROLLER MOTORIZED 4T06T	
S11068	3895 00 192 7594	K	9130 00 160 1818	CE	H	3.00			RLR GST MDL 1504	
S11068	3895 00 194 8536	K	9130 00 160 1818	CE	H	3.00			RLR BFLO SPFLD KT-168	
S11068	3895 00 221 1632	K	9130 00 160 1818	CE	H	3.00			RLR GALION T5-G	
S11068	3895 00 842 5326	K	9130 00 160 1818	CE	H	3.00			RLR HUBER T58M BS	
S11068	3895 00 935 7943	K	9130 00 160 1818	CE	H	2.75			RLR HUBER T58M QXL	
S11068	3895 00 954 8181	K	9130 00 160 1818	CE	H	3.00			RLR GALION T5-8G	
S11205	3895 00 641 6414	K	9130 00 160 1818	CE	H	3.50			RLR GALION 379-G	
S11273	3895 00 917 6611	K	9130 00 160 1818	CE	H	7.20			RLR MTZDG KX25	
S11342	3895 00 194 8555	K	9130 00 160 1818	CE	H	6.80			RLR GALION CHF C G	
S11479	3895 00 194 8551	K	9130 00 160 1818	CE	H	3.50			RLR GALION CHIEF	
S11479	3895 00 223 8394	K	9130 00 160 1818	CE	H	3.60			RLR BFLO-SPFLD VM-310	
S11479	3895 00 542 4599	K	9130 00 160 1818	CE	H	3.60			RLR ROLOMATIC	
S11479	3895 00 952 5840	K	9130 00 160 1818	CE	H	3.75			RLR HUBER WRCO E1012M	
S11616	3895 00 134 8154	K	9130 00 160 1818	CE	H	5.00			RLR HUBER E1012	
S11616	3895 00 255 5054	K	9130 00 160 1818	CE	H	3.50			RLR GEN STL TANK 1503	
S11616	3895 00 902 8455	K	9130 00 160 1818	CE	H	5.00			RLR HUBER E-1012-M	
S11616	3895 00 997 6099	K	9130 00 160 1818	CE	H	3.75			RLR HUBER E1012MR	
S11650	3895 00 250 9553	K	9140 00 273 2377	CE	H	4.00			ROLL MOT PNEU TIRE	
S11684	3895 00 832 6232	K	9130 00 160 1818	CE	H	6.50			RLRMTZDBROSSP2800	
S11684	3895 00 902 3111	K	9130 00 160 1818	CE	H	6.50			RLR BROS-P-54-B	
S11701	3895 00 457 6126	K	9140 00 273 2377	SG	H	7.00			ROLL MOT PNEU TIRE	
S11711	3895 00 578 0372	K	9130 00 160 1818	CE	H	3.50			RLR MTR HYS C350BD	
S11793	3895 01 013 3630	K	9130 00 160 1818	CE	H	11.00			RLRPNEUHYSTERC530A	
S12916	3895 01 012 8875	K	9140 00 273 2377	SG	H	6.00			ROLLER VEH SELF PR	
S12916	3895 01 075 2823	K	9130 00 160 1818	CE	H	3.80			RLR VIBRATORY	
S34508	3895 01 062 6939	K	9130 00 160 1818	CE	H	1.20			SAW CLIPPER 122375	
S34508	3895 01 488 0612	K	9130 00 160 1818	CE	H	1.06			SAW GREGORY C3000	
S35741	3695 00 679 6914	E	9130 00 160 1818	SG	H	1.00			SAW CHAIN	
S37385	3220 00 837 9926	B	9130 00 160 1818	SG	H	16.00			SAW CIRCTBLSM GASD	
S40029	3210 00 115 0140	B	9140 00 273 2377	SG	H	13.00			SAWMILL MTRP0568-1	
S40029	3210 00 790 2174	B	9140 00 273 2377	SG	H	13.00			SAWMILLCIROD601NBL	
S56246	3805 01 153 1854	K	9140 00 273 2377	CE	H	7.00			SCRAPER EARTH SP	
S71613	2330 00 255 8065	B	9130 00 160 1818	SG	H	1.50			STLR BROWN GST-120	
S71613	2330 00 255 9350	B	9130 00 160 1818	SG	H	1.50			STLR ANDREWS MIL 2	
S71613	2330 00 289 6798	B	9130 00 160 1818	SG	H	1.50			STLR THOMPSON M349	
S71613	2330 00 351 9916	B	9130 00 160 1818	SG	H	1.50			STLR STEEL PROD AA	
S71613	2330 00 554 8676	B	9130 00 160 1818	SG	H	1.50			STLR FREUHAUF M349	
S71613	2330 00 892 5057	B	9130 00 160 1818	SG	H	1.50			STRL STEVENS M349A	
S71613	2330 00 973 2230	B	9130 00 160 1818	SG	H	1.50			STLR KENTUCKY M349	
S71613	2330 00 999 3591	B	9130 00 160 1818	SG	H	1.00			STLR M349A4	
S79045	1040 00 740 1152	M	9140 00 273 2377	SG	H	.17			FLAME THROWER	
T00474	4240 00 854 4144	M	9130 00 160 1818	SG	H	2.00			M51 SHELTER	
T05028	2320 01 123 2665	K	9140 00 273 2377	WV	K	0.0684			TRK UTILCUCV M1009	
T05096	2320 01 107 7153	K	9140 00 273 2377	WV	K	0.0497			WEAPONS CARRXM966	
T0543	2320 01 146 7193	K	9140 00 273 2377	WV	K	0.0435			TRK UTILITY M1037	
T10549	4940 01 006 3229	M	9140 00 273 2377	SG	H	3.50			SHOP EQUIP	
T10549	4940 00 165 4021	M	9140 00 273 2377	SG	H	3.50			S/EQ PRSM-68	
T10549	4940 00 165 4024	M	9140 00 273 2377	SG	H	3.50			S/EQ ENG-43-59	
T10549	4940 00 287 4894	M	9140 00 273 2377	SG	H	3.50			S/EQ MILS 45538	
T10549	4940 00 497 6412	M	9140 00 273 2377	SG	H	3.50			S/EQ MED-1952	
T10549	4940 00 497 6413	M	9140 00 273 2377	SG	H	3.50			S/EQ SG PRSM-61	
T13169	2350 01 061 2306	S K	9140 00 273 2377	TV	H	2.00	26.58	18.79	M60A3 TANK TTS	
T13374	2350 01 061 2445	S K	9140 00 273 2377	TV	H	10.80	56.60	44.64	M1 TNK 105MM	
T34437	2420 01 160 2754	K	9140 00 273 2377	CE	H	5.00			TRAC WHL DSL EXACV	
T38660	2310 01 123 2666	K	9140 00 273 2377	WV	K	0.0373			TRKAMB CUCV M1010	
T38707	2310 01 111 2275	K	9140 00 273 2377	WV	K	0.0497			TRK AMB M996	
T38844	2310 01 111 2274	K	9140 00 273 2377	WV	K	0.0497			TRK AMB M997	
T39518	2320 01 097 0260	K	9140 00 273 2377	WV	K	0.2672			TRK CGO TACT M977	
T39586	2320 01 100 7673	K	9140 00 273 2377	WV	K	0.2672			TRK CGO TACT	
T39654	2320 01 097 0261	K	9140 00 273 2377	WV	K	0.2672			TRK CGO TACT MB985	
T42725	3895 01 028 4391	K	9130 00 160 1818	CE	H	1.25			TRK MXR CON M919	
T48941	3930 01 082 3758	K	9140 00 273 2377	WV	K	0.2299			TRK CONT MDL 9888	
T48944	3930 01 158 0849	K	9140 00 273 2377	MH	H	5.00			TRK FL 6000 LHS R1	
T49119	3930 01 054 3833	K	9140 00 273 2377	MH	H	8.50			TRK LFT 10000 LHS	
T49255	3930 01 076 4237	K	9140 00 273 2377	MH	H	1.30			TRK LFT DSL M4K	
T53498	2320 01 044 0333	K	9130 00 160 1818	WV	K	0.0621			TRK MAINT TELEM888	
T53858	2320 00 000 0114	K	9130 00 160 1818	WV	K	0.0621			TRK MAINT TFL M876	
T58161	2320 01 097 0249	K	9140 00 273 2377	WV	K	0.2983			TRK TANK FUEL M978	
T59117	2320 01 099 6421	K	9140 00 273 2377	WV	K	0.2983			TRUCK TRAC M983	
T59278	2320 01 099 6426	K	9140 00 273 2377	WV	K	0.2983			TRK CGO TRCK M977	
T59346	2320 01 123 2671	K	9140 00 273 2377	WV	K	0.0621			TRKCG05/41 M1008A1	
T59414	2320 01 127 5077	K	9140 00 273 2377	WV	K	0.0621			SHELTER CUCV M1028	
T59482	2320 01 123 6827	K	9140 00 273 2377	WV	K	0.0373			TRK CGO CUCV M1008	

Figure 6. Equipment Combat Fuel Consumption Rates— Bulk POL Table A (continued)

LI	EI NSN	SNSN CMD	FUEL NSN	EQUIP TYP	CONSUMP CD	CONSUMPTION RATES IDL/AV	XCNTRY	2NDRDS	NOMENCLATURE	MULTIFUEL
T60353	2320 01 044 8376	K	9140 00 273 2377	WV	K	0.1305			TRUCK TRAC M878	
T60353	2320 01 121 2102	K	9140 00 273 2377	WV	K	0.1305			TRUCK TRAC M878A1	
T61035	2320 01 025 3733	K	9140 00 273 2377	WV	K	0.2051			TRK TRTR HET M911	
T61103	2320 01 028 4395	K	9140 00 273 2377	WV	K	0.2237			TRK TRTR M915	
T61103	2320 01 125 2640	K	9140 00 273 2377	WV	K	0.2486			M915A1 TRK TRTR	
T61171	2320 01 028 4397	K	9140 00 273 2377	WV	K	0.2237			TRK TRTR M920	
T61494	2320 01 107 7155	K	9140 00 273 2377	WV	K	0.0497			TRK UTILITY M998	
T61562	2320 01 107 7156	K	9140 00 273 2377	WV	K	0.0435			TRK CGO CARR M1038	
T63093	2320 01 097 0248	K	9140 00 273 2377	WV	K	0.2983			TRK WRK M984	
T87044	3825 00 153 6999	K	9130 00 160 1818	SV	H	8.00			SNW REMVL SELF-PRO	
T87243	2320 01 100 7672	K	9140 00 273 2377	WV	K	0.2983			TRK FUEL TACT M978	
T87568	3825 00 810 7074	K	9130 00 160 1818	MH	H	5.00			SNW REMVL FWRD5349	
T87602	3825 00 018 2121	K	9140 00 273 2377	MH	H	16.10			SNOW REMOVAL UNIT	
T88677	2320 01 097 0247	K	9140 00 273 2377	WV	K	0.2983			TRK TRACTOR M983	
T88745	2320 12 191 5422	K	9140 00 273 2377	WV	K	0.3107			TRK TRC M1001 W/W	
T91656	2320 01 028 4396	K	9140 00 273 2377	WV	K	0.2237			TRK TRTR M916	
T92242	2320 01 128 9551	K	9140 00 273 2377	WV	K	0.0435			TRK ARMICARR M1025	
T92310	2320 01 128 9552	K	9140 00 273 2377	WV	K	0.0435			TRK ARMTCARR M1026	
T94641	2320 12 191 5423	K	9140 00 273 2377	WV	K	0.3107			TRK TRAC M1002 W/W	
U11015	3740 00 772 0090	B	9130 00 160 1818	SG	H	.25			SPRAYER INSECT180G	
U11015	3740 00 916 6462	B	9130 00 160 1818	SG	H	.15			SPRAYER PEST 47500	
U11015	3740 00 993 4000	B	9130 00 160 1818	SG	H	.30			SPRAYER PESTCSR475	
U11426	3740 00 069 9002	B	9130 00 160 1818	SV	H	1.00			SPYR BESLER 1314E6	
U11426	3740 00 790 6188	B	9130 00 160 1818	SV	H	3.00			SPYR CRTS AUTO 400	
U11426	3740 00 930 9384	B	9130 00 160 1818	SV	H	3.00			SPYR CRTS DYN 4150	
U11426	3740 01 076 1341	B	9130 00 160 1818	SV	H	40.00			AEROSOL GEN XKA	
U58881	5420 00 491 6330	B	9140 00 273 2377	OV	H	15.00			SUPSTR TRANS T527	
U58881	5420 00 877 8679	B	9140 00 273 2377	OV	H	15.00			SUPSTR TRANS FMC	
U68809	6675 00 649 8273	B	9130 00 160 1818	SG	H	6.00			SURVEY CON SEC TRK	
U76734	3825 00 540 1437	K	9130 00 160 1818	SV	H	4.00			SWEEPER SELF-PROP	
U76734	3825 00 598 0045	K	9130 00 160 1818	SV	H	4.00			SWEEPER SELF-PROP	
U76871	3825 00 087 5019	K	9130 00 160 1818	CE	H	1.50			MUNI SUP MDL KGV 3	
U76871	3825 00 230 9690	K	9130 00 160 1818	CE	H	3.00			SWEEPER LG 100-8-1	
U76871	3825 00 377 4327	K	9130 00 160 1818	CE	H	1.50			MEILE BLUMBERG 53M	
U76871	3825 00 555 0185	K	9130 00 160 1818	CE	H	1.50			GRACE MDL MS 105E	
U76871	3825 00 633 9962	K	9130 00 160 1818	CE	H	1.50			SPENCER MDL MS-1	
U76871	3825 00 641 6398	K	9130 00 160 1818	CE	H	1.50			LITTLE GANT ES 100	
U76871	3825 00 641 6401	K	9130 00 641 6401	CE	H	1.50			LITTLE GNT ES 100A	
U76871	3825 00 832 5269	K	9130 00 160 1818	CE	H	1.50			SWEEPER MDL MP3867	
U76871	3825 00 859 7926	K	9130 00 160 1818	CE	H	1.50			IND MDL MP 38 W	
U76871	3825 01 022 7329	K	9130 00 160 1818	CE	H	2.50			SWEEPER LG ES IOOK	
V00426	1915 01 153 8801	B	9140 00 273 2377	AB	H	34.00			LOG SPT VESSEL	
V11001	3895 01 013 4328	K	9130 00 160 1818	CE	H	.50			TAMPERPISTHAMRVRII	
V11641	2230 00 294 2307	B	9130 00 160 1818	OV	H	1.00			JACK RAILWAY POWER	
V12141	4930 00 070 1181	B	9130 00 160 1818	SG	H	.45			TK PUMP UNIT	
V12141	4930 00 078 4938	B	9130 00 160 1818	SG	H	.45			TK PUMP UNIT BOW36	
V12141	4930 00 078 4939	B	9130 00 160 1818	SG	H	.45			TK PUMP UNIT MD 29	
V12141	4930 00 426 9960	B	9130 00 160 1818	SG	H	.45			TANK-PUMP UNIT	
V12141	4930 00 542 2800	B	9130 00 160 1818	SG	H	.45			TK PUMP UNIT MD 11	
V12141	4930 00 877 8678	B	9130 00 160 1818	SG	H	.45			TK PUMP UNIT HLND2	
V12141	4930 00 926 3581	B	9130 00 160 1818	SG	H	.45			TK PUMP UNIT ALTEC	
V12141	4930 00 926 3692	B	9130 00 160 1818	SG	H	.45			TK PUMP UNIT ORRBL	
V12141	4930 00 987 8576	B	9130 00 160 1818	SG	H	.45			TK PUMP UNIT ENG 2	
V13101	2350 00 116 9765	S K	9140 00 273 2377	TV	H	2.00	26.53	18.79	M60A1 TNK105MMRISE	
V13101	2350 00 148 6548	S K	9140 00 273 2377	TV	H	2.00	26.53	18.79	M60A3 TNK CBT105MM	
V13101	2350 00 582 5595	S K	9140 00 273 2377	TV	H	2.00	26.53	18.79	M48A5 TNK CBT105MM	
V13101	2350 00 678 5773	S K	9140 00 273 2377	TV	H	2.00	26.53	18.79	M60 TNK CMBT 105MM	
V13101	2350 00 756 8497	S K	9140 00 273 2377	TV	H	2.00	26.53	18.79	M60A1 TNK CBT105MM	
V13101	2350 01 058 9487	S K	9140 00 273 2377	TV	H	2.00	26.53	18.79	M60A1 TNK 105MMAOS	
V13101	2350 01 059 1503	S K	9140 00 273 2377	TV	H	2.00	26.53	18.79	M60A1 TNK RISEPASS	
V13101	2350 01 059 1504	S K	9140 00 273 2377	TV	H	2.00	26.53	18.79	M48A5 TNK LOW PROF	
W48391	3431 01 090 1231	M	9140 00 273 2377	SG	H	2.00			WLD SHOP M6270100	
W76268	2410 00 142 5283	K	9140 00 273 2377	CE	H	3.10			TRCTR D5	
W76268	2410 00 230 2767	K	9140 00 273 2377	CE	H	3.10			TRCTR D5A ELE STAR	
W76268	2410 00 828 6865	K	9140 00 273 2377	CE	H	3.10			TRCTR D5A GAS STAR	
W76268	2410 00 900 8539	K	9140 00 273 2377	CE	H	3.20			CAT D6S	
W76285	2410 00 024 4065	K	9140 00 273 2377	CE	H	7.00			TRACTOR CASE 1150W	
W76302	2400 00 434 5309	K	9140 00 273 2377	CE	H	1.40			TRCTR CASE M 480 CK	
W76302	2400 00 900 8538	K	9140 00 273 2377	CE	H	1.40			TRCTR W/BKH AND LD	
W76336	2410 00 935 0714	K	9140 00 273 2377	CE	H	6.00			TRCTR CASE MDLM450	
W76473	2350 00 808 7100	S K	9140 00 273 2377	TV	H	1.42	12.35	9.26	TRCTRFTHIGH SPD M9	
W76816	2410 00 078 6483	K	9140 00 273 2377	CE	H	6.00			TRCTR FT A/C HO-16	
W76816	2410 00 177 7284	K	9140 00 273 2377	CE	H	6.00			TRCT FT CAT DF7 DV29	
W76816	2410 00 185 9792	K	9140 00 273 2377	CE	H	6.00			TRCTR FT D7F W/ROP	
W76816	2410 00 300 6664	K	9140 00 273 2377	CE	H	6.00			TRCTR FT D7F WNTRZ	
W76816	2410 00 782 1130	K	9140 00 273 2377	CE	H	6.00			TRCTR FT HYD CAT D7E	
W76816	2410 00 901 1950	K	9140 00 273 2377	CE	H	6.00			TRCTR FT A/C HO-16M	
W76816	2410 01 050 9628	K	9140 00 273 2377	CE	H	6.00			D7E TRCT FT W/BDZR	
W77364	2410 00 542 2338	K	9140 00 273 2377	CE	H	9.50			TRCTR FT LS TD24-2	
W77364	2410 00 542 4882	K	9140 00 273 2377	CE	H	6.10			TRCTR FT LS CAT D8	
W77638	2410 00 542 2337	K	9140 00 273 2377	CE	H	6.00			TRCTR FT LS CAT D8	
W77638	2410 00 542 4881	K	9140 00 273 2377	CE	H	6.00			TRCTR FT LSW/AD-8	
W80104	2410 00 843 6374	K	9140 00 273 2377	CE	H	6.00			TRACTOR FULL TR	
W80378	2410 00 926 0910	K	9140 00 273 2377	CE	H	3.10			TRCTR FL LS DED AIR	
W80515	2410 00 542 4206	K	9140 00 273 2377	CE	H	3.10			CAT MDL D-6	
W80515	2410 00 837 4224	K	9140 00 273 2377	CE	H	1.90			CAT MDL D-4	
W80515	2410 00 983 8024	K	9140 00 273 2377	CE	H	1.90			AC MDL MD6M	
W80652	3805 00 131 4620	K	9140 00 273 2377	CE	H	2.20			LDR JI CASE 450 MDL	
W80652	3805 00 542 3402	K	9140 00 273 2377	CE	H	2.20			LDR INT TD6 ICY	
W80652	3805 00 555 1756	K	9140 00 273 2377	CE	H	2.40			LDR CAT 933 ICY	

Figure 6. Equipment Combat Fuel Consumption Rates— Bulk POL Table A (continued)

						CONSUMPTION RATES				
LI	EI NSN	SNSN CMD	FUEL NSN	EQUIP TYP	CONSUMP CD	IDL/AV	XCNTRY	2NDRDS	NOMENCLATURE	MULTIFUEL
W80652	3805 00 621 1392	K	9140 00 273 2377	CE	H	2.20			LDR JI CASE 450 L ROPS	
W80789	2410 00 541 7655	K	9140 00 273 2377	CE	H	5.80			TRCTR FT IHC TD18	
W80789	2410 00 542 2498	K	9140 00 273 2377	CE	H	5.80			TRCT FT IHC TD20-2	
W83255	2410 00 541 7654	K	9140 00 273 2377	CE	H	5.10			TRCT FT IHC TD18-1	
W83255	2410 00 542 2499	K	9140 00 273 2377	CE	H	5.40			TRCT FT IHC TD20-2	
W83255	2410 00 828 3083	K	9140 00 273 2377	CE	H	5.40			TRCT FT IHC TD20-2	
W83529	2410 00 078 6484	K	9140 00 273 2377	CE	H	6.00			TRCT FT LC DD HD16	
W83529	2410 00 177 7283	K	9140 00 273 2377	CE	H	6.00			TRCT FT CAT DF7 DV	
W83529	2410 00 185 9794	K	9140 00 273 2377	CE	H	6.00			TRCTR FT D7F W/ROP	
W83529	2410 00 300 6665	K	9140 00 273 2377	CE	H	6.00			TRCTR FT D7F WNTRZ	
W83529	2410 00 926 3697	K	9140 00 273 2377	CE	H	6.00			TRCTR LS DD CAT D7	
W83529	2410 01 050 9629	K	9140 00 273 2377	CE	H	6.00			D7EROPS TRCT W/BDZ	
E88493	2410 00 451 1003	K	9140 00 273 2377	CE	H	10.00			TRACTOR FULL TR	
W88509	2410 00 137 9194	K	9140 00 273 2377	CE	H	20.00			TRACTOR FULL TR	
W88525	2410 00 177 7091	K	9140 00 273 2377	CE	H	5.00			TRACTOR FULL TR	M
W88575	2410 00 574 7597	K	9140 00 273 2377	CE	H	6.00			TRCTR FT CAT D8K8A	
W88699	2410 00 574 7598	K	9140 00 273 2377	CE	H	6.00			TRCTR FT CAT D8K85	
W88758	2420 00 177 6861	K	9140 00 273 2377	CE	H	1.10			TRCTR AGRIC	
W88781	2420 00 177 6863	K	9140 00 273 2377	CE	H	1.30			TRCTR AGRIC	
W88786	2420 00 177 6865	K	9140 00 273 2377	CE	H	2.10			TRCTR AGRIC	
W88791	2420 00 177 6867	K	9140 00 273 2377	CE	H	3.20			TRCTR AGRIC	
W88796	2420 00 177 6869	K	9140 00 273 2377	CE	H	3.30			TRCTR AGRIC	
W88803	1740 00 134 1053	H	9130 00 160 1818	SV	H	6.00			TR WHLD ACFT TOW	
W88803	1740 00 865 9705	H	9130 00 160 1818	SV	H	6.00			TR WHLD ACFT690-1B	
W89557	3930 00 038 3166	K	9130 00 160 1818	CE	H	6.00			TRCTR WHL GAS J217	
W89557	3920 00 064 6563	K	9130 00 160 1818	CE	H	6.00			TRCTR WHL GAS MT40	
W89557	3930 00 181 3217	K	9130 00 160 1818	CE	H	6.00			TRCTR WHL WHSE GPC	
W89557	3930 00 265 6864	K	9130 00 160 1818	CE	H	6.00			TRCTR WH GAS A4525	
W89557	3930 00 347 6173	K	9130 00 160 1818	CE	H	6.00			TRCTR WHL GASCTA40	
W89557	3930 00 678 9914	K	9130 00 160 1818	CE	H	6.00			TRCTR WHL GASCTA40	
W89557	3920 00 679 4823	K	9130 00 160 1818	CE	H	6.00			TRCTR WHL GAS 2TT4	
W89557	3920 00 724 3471	K	9130 00 160 1818	CE	H	6.00			TRCTR WHL GAS MT40	
W89557	3920 00 724 8146	K	9130 00 160 1818	CE	H	6.00			TRCTR WHL GAS 2TG4	
W89557	3930 00 926 1066	K	9130 00 160 1818	CE	H	6.00			TRCTR WHL GAS JG40	
W89557	3930 00 953 4890	K	9130 00 160 1818	CE	H	6.00			TRCTR WHL GAS 2TON	
W89604	2420 00 177 6862	K	9140 00 273 2377	CE	H	1.30			TRCTR IND 4199DB	
W89607	2420 00 177 6864	K	9140 00 273 2377	CE	H	2.10			TRCTR IND 5699DB	
W89610	2420 00 177 6866	K	9140 00 273 2377	CE	H	3.20			TRCTR IND 7299DB	
W89613	2420 00 177 6868	K	9140 00 273 2377	CE	H	3.30			TRCTR IND 7300DB	
W90447	2420 00 902 3084	K	9140 00 273 2377	CE	H	4.60			TRCT WHL IND DLS M	
W90790	2420 00 088 9384	K	9140 00 273 2377	CE	H	12.80			TRCTR WHL DSL 290M	
W90790	2420 00 104 1896	K	9140 00 273 2377	CE	H	12.90			TRCT WHL DSL 830MB	
W90790	2420 00 930 5999	K	9140 00 273 2377	CE	H	11.40			TRCTR CAT 830MB	
W90790	2420 01 006 4946	K	9140 00 273 2377	CE	H	15.20			TRCTR WHL830MDROPS	
W90790	2420 01 028 4936	K	9140 00 273 2377	CE	H	11.40			TR CAT830MB ROPS	
W90790	2420 01 059 0090	K	9140 00 273 2377	CE	H	15.20			290M TRCT WHLD	
W90927	2420 00 415 6132	K	9140 00 273 2377	CE	H	4.60			TRCTR MDL 100 4x4	
W90927	2420 00 792 6163	K	9140 00 273 2377	CE	H	4.60			TRCTR WHL IND DS L	
W91064	2420 00 806 0031	K	9140 00 237 2377	CE	H	10.70			TRCT WHL DDLGT830M	
W91074	2420 00 567 0135	K	9130 00 160 1818	WV	M	0.3107			TRCTR WHL INDJD410	
W91201	2420 00 267 0136	K	9130 00 160 1818	CE	H	4.00			TRACTOR WHLD 3000	
W91201	2420 00 267 6887	K	9130 00 160 1818	CE	H	4.00			TRACTOR WHLD 3725	
W91201	2420 00 269 0802	K	9130 00 160 1818	CE	H	4.00			TRACTOR WHLD 3000	
W92160	2420 00 267 0115	K	9130 00 160 1818	CE	H	4.00			TRACTOR WHLD 3725	
W92160	2420 00 277 7495	K	9130 00 160 1818	CE	H	4.00			TRACTOR WHLD 3725	
W92160	2420 00 541 6689	K	9130 00 160 1818	CE	H	4.00			TRACTOR WHLD GED	
W92160	2420 00 542 3340	K	9130 00 160 1818	CE	H	4.00			TRACTOR WHLD 3725	
W92708	2420 00 580 7019	K	9130 00 160 1818	CE	H	4.00			TRACTOR WHLD 5200	
W92708	2420 00 856 2412	K	9130 00 160 1818	CE	H	4.00			TRACTOR WHLD 5200	
X05621	5420 00 267 0034	B	9130 00 160 1818	SG	H	2.26			TRANWAY ST AER GD	
X23277	5420 00 071 5321	B	9140 00 273 2377	WV	K	0.1554			TRANS PT BRIDG FLT	
X38172	4210 01 006 1534	B	9140 00 273 2377	WV	K	0.1243			AERIAL LADDER 50FT	
X30562	2310 00 125 5679	K	9130 00 160 1818	WV	K	0.0746			M893 TRK AMB 4x2	
X38592	2310 00 579 9078	K	9130 00 160 1818	WV	K	0.0621			M886 TRK AMB 4x4	
X38639	2310 00 177 9256	K	9130 00 160 1818	WV	K	0.0373			M718A1 TRK AMB	
X38639	2310 00 782 6056	K	9130 00 160 1818	WV	K	0.0373			M718 TRK AMB 1/4 T	
X38639	2310 00 835 8686	K	9130 00 160 1818	WV	K	0.0373			M170 TRK AMB 1/4 T	
X38776	2310 00 542 4634	K	9130 00 160 1818	WV	K	0.0621			M43B1 TRK AMB 3/4T	
X38776	2310 00 835 8516	K	9130 00 160 1818	WV	K	0.0621			M43 TRK AMB 3/4 T	
X38951	2310 00 921 6369	K	9130 00 160 1818	WV	K	0.0746			M725 TRK AMB 1-1/4	
X38961	2310 00 832 9907	K	9140 00 273 2377	WV	K	0.0621			M792 TRK AMB 1-1/4	
X39050	2320 00 277 3016	K	9130 00 160 1818	WV	K	0.0994			M45 TRK BLSTR CHAS	
X39050	2320 00 542 4490	K	9130 00 160 1818	WV	K	0.0994			M44 TRK BLSTR CHAS	
X39050	2320 00 937 0840	K	9130 00 160 1818	WV	K	0.0994			M751A1 TRK BLSTR	
X39187	2320 00 050 8927	K	9140 00 273 2377	WV	K	0.1119			M815 TRK BOLSTER5T	
X39187	2320 00 880 4615	K	9140 00 273 2377	WV	K	0.1119			M748A1 TRK BLSTR5T	
X39426	4210 00 484 5729	B	9140 00 273 2377	WV	H	9.30			TRK FIRE PROL EQ	
X39429	2320 00 579 8991	K	9130 00 160 1818	WV	K	0.0621			M890 TRK CGO1-1/4T	
X39432	2320 00 579 8942	K	9130 00 160 1818	WV	K	0.0621			M890 TRK CGO1-1/4T	
X39435	2320 00 579 9052	K	9130 00 160 1818	WV	K	0.0621			M892 TRK CGO1-1/4T	
X39438	2320 00 579 9046	K	9130 00 160 1818	WV	K	0.0621			M891 TRK CGO1-1/4T	
X39441	2320 00 579 8989	K	9130 00 160 1818	WV	K	0.0621			M885 TRK CGO1-1/4T	
X39444	2320 00 579 8943	K	9130 00 160 1818	WV	K	0.0621			M881 TRK CGO1-1/4T	
X39447	2320 00 579 8957	K	9130 00 160 1818	WV	K	0.0621			M882 TRK CGO1-1/4T	
X39450	2320 00 579 8959	K	9130 00 160 1818	WV	K	0.0621			M883 TRK CGO1-1/4T	
X39453	2320 00 579 8985	K	9130 00 160 1818	WV	K	0.0621			M884 TRK CGO1-1/4T	
X39461	2320 01 090 7889	K	9130 00 160 1818	WV	K	0.0621			TRK CGO FC1/4T 4x4	
X39461	2320 01 090 7890	K	9130 00 160 1818	WV	K	0.0621			TRK CGO 1/4T 4x4	
X39598	2320 01 090 7881	K	9130 00 160 1818	WV	K	0.0559			TRKCGO1/2T 4500GVW	
X39598	2320 01 090 7882	K	9130 00 160 1818	WV	K	0.0621			TRKCGO1/2T 4800GVW	

Figure 6. Equipment Combat Fuel Consumption Rates – Bulk POL Table A (continued)

						CONSUMPTION RATES				
LI	EI NSN	SNSN CMD	FUEL NSN	EQUIP TYP	CONSUMP CD	IDL/AV	XCNTRY	2NDRDS	NOMENCLATURE	MULTIFUEL
X39598	2320 01 090 7883	K	9130 00 160 1818	WV	K	0.0684			TRKCGO3/4T 5800GVW	
X39598	2320 01 090 7885	K	9130 00 160 1818	WV	K	0.0621			TRKCGO1/2T 5800GVW	
X39598	2320 01 091 7880	K	9130 00 160 1818	WV	K	0.0621			TRK CARGO 1/4 TON	
X39735	2320 00 542 4636	K	9130 00 160 1818	WV	K	0.0621			M37B1 TRK CGO 3/4T	
X39735	2320 00 835 8322	K	9130 00 160 1818	WV	K	0.0621			M37 TRK CGO 3/4T	
X39872	2320 00 542 4632	K	9130 00 160 1818	WV	K	0.0621			M37B1 TRK CGO 3/4T	
X39872	2330 00 835 8323	K	9130 00 160 1818	WV	K	0.0621			M37TRK CGO 3/4T	
X39883	2320 00 921 6365	K	9130 00 160 1818	WV	K	0.0746			M715 TRK CGO 1-1/4	
X39893	2320 01 090 7891	K	9130 00 160 1818	WV	K	0.0746			TRKCGOFC IT 6000 1/2	
X39893	2320 01 090 7892	K	9130 00 160 1818	WV	K	0.0746			TRKCGO 3/4T 6600 GVW	
X39893	2320 01 090 7893	K	9130 00 160 1818	WV	K	0.0746			TRKCGO IT 8510 GVW	
X39893	2320 01 090 7894	K	9130 00 160 1818	WV	K	0.0746			TRKCGO IT 10000 GVW	
X39893	2320 01 090 7895	K	9130 00 160 1818	WV	K	0.0746			TRKCGO 3/4T 8000 GVW	
X39893	2320 01 090 7896	K	9130 00 160 1818	WV	K	0.0746			TRKCGO IT 10000 GVW	
X39906	2320 00 921 6366	K	9130 00 160 1818	WV	K	0.0746			M715 TRK CGO 1-1/4	
X39940	2320 00 873 5407	K	9140 00 273 2377	WV	K	0.0808			M561 TRK CGO 1-1/4	
X40009	2320 00 077 1616	K	9140 00 273 2377	WV	K	0.1305			M35A2 TRKCGO 2-1/2	M
X40009	2320 00 542 5633	K	9140 00 273 2377	WV	K	0.0870			M35A1 TRKCGO 2-1/2	M
X40009	2320 00 739 7565	K	9130 00 160 1818	WV	K	0.0932			M34 TRK CGO	
X40009	2320 00 834 4507	K	9130 00 160 1818	WV	K	0.1554			M2111TRK CGO 2-1/2	
X40009	2320 00 835 8351	K	9130 00 160 1818	WV	K	0.1305			M135 TRKCGO 2-1/2	
X40009	2320 00 835 8463	K	9130 00 160 1818	WV	K	0.1802			M35 TRK CGO 2-1/2T	
X40077	2320 00 926 0873	K	9140 00 273 2377	WV	K	0.1243			M35A2C TRK CGO P/S	M
X40146	2320 00 077 1617	K	9140 00 273 2377	WV	K	0.1305			M35A2 TRKCGO 2-1/2	M
X40146	2320 00 542 5634	K	9140 00 273 2377	WV	K	0.0932			M35A1 TRKCGO 2-1/2	M
X40146	2320 00 834 4508	K	9130 00 160 1818	WV	K	0.1056			M211 TRK CGO 2-1/2	
X40146	2320 00 835 8352	K	9130 00 160 1818	WV	K	0.0932			M135 TRK CGO	
X40146	2320 00 835 8464	K	9130 00 160 1818	WV	K	0.1305			M35 TRK CGO 2-1/2T	
X40146	2320 00 835 8536	K	9130 00 160 1818	WV	K	0.0932			M34 TRK CGO	
X40214	2320 00 926 0875	K	9140 00 273 2377	WV	K	0.1243			M35A2C TRKCGO D/S	M
X40283	2320 00 077 1618	K	9140 00 273 2377	WV	K	0.0932			M36A2 TRKCGO 2-1/2	M
X40283	2320 00 391 0569	K	9130 00 160 1818	WV	K	0.1305			M36 TRK CGO 2-1/2T	
X40420	2320 00 077 1619	K	9140 00 273 2377	WV	K	0.0932			M36A2 TRKCGO 2-1/2	M
X40420	2320 00 647 0505	K	9130 00 160 1818	WV	K	0.1305			M36WW TRKCGO 2-1/2	
X40557	2320 00 200 1368	K	9130 00 160 1818	WV	K	0.1305			M36W/ATT TRK CGO	
X40694	2320 00 200 1369	K	9130 00 160 1818	WV	K	0.1243			M36C WATTW TRK CGO	
X40794	2320 00 050 8913	K	9140 00 273 2377	WV	K	0.1243			M813A1 TRK CGO D/S	
X40794	2320 00 761 2854	K	9140 00 283 2377	WV	K	0.1554			M54A2C TRKCGO D/S	M
X40794	2320 00 880 4614	K	9140 00 273 2377	WV	K	0.1243			M54A1C TRKCGO D/S	
X40794	2320 01 050 2084	K	9140 00 283 2377	WV	K	0.1616			M923 TRK CGO 5T	
X40831	2320 00 050 8902	K	9140 00 273 2377	WV	K	0.1243			M813 TRK CGO 5T	
X40831	2320 00 055 9266	K	9140 00 273 2377	WV	K	0.1243			M54A2 TRK CGO 5T	M
X40831	2320 00 086 7481	K	9140 00 283 2377	WV	K	0.1243			M54A1 TRK CGO 5T	
X40831	2320 00 835 8348	K	9130 00 160 1818	WV	K	0.2921			M54 TRK CGO 5T	
X40831	2320 01 047 8773	K	9140 00 273 2377	WV	K	0.1616			M924 TRK CGO 5T	
X40931	2320 00 050 8905	K	9140 00 273 2377	WV	K	0.1243			M813A1 TRKCGO D/SW	
X40931	2320 00 880 4612	K	9140 00 273 2377	WV	K	0.1243			M54A1C TRKCGO D/S	
X40931	2320 00 926 0874	K	9140 00 273 2377	WV	K	0.1243			M54A2C TRKCGO D/S	M
X40931	2320 01 047 8769	K	9140 00 273 2377	WV	K	0.1616			M925 TRK CGO 5T	
X40968	2320 00 050 8890	K	9140 00 273 2377	WV	K	0.1554			M813 TRKCGO LWB WW	
X40968	2320 00 055 9265	K	9140 00 273 2377	WV	K	0.1243			M54A2 TRK CGO 5T	M
X40968	2320 00 086 7482	K	9140 00 273 2377	WV	K	0.1243			M54A1 TRKCGO LWBWW	
X40968	2320 00 835 8335	K	9130 00 160 1818	WV	K	0.2237			M54 TRKCGO LWB W/W	
X40968	2320 01 047 8772	K	9140 00 273 2377	WV	K	0.1616			M926 TRK CGO 5T	
X41105	2320 00 050 8988	K	9140 00 273 2377	WV	K	0.1243			M814 TRKCGO 5TXLWB	
X41105	2320 01 047 8771	K	9140 00 273 2377	WV	K	0.1616			M927 TRK CGO 5T	
X41242	2320 00 050 8787	K	9140 00 273 2377	WV	K	0.1243			M814 TRKCGO 5TXLWB	
X41242	2320 00 055 9259	K	9140 00 273 2377	WV	K	0.1429			M55A2 TRKCGO 5TWWN	M
X41242	2320 00 391 0570	K	9130 00 160 1818	WV	K	0.2237			M55 TRKCGO 5T W/WN	
X41242	2320 00 880 4634	K	9140 00 273 2377	WV	K	0.1429			M55A1 TRK CGO	
X41242	2320 01 047 8770	K	9140 00 273 2377	WV	K	0.1616			M926 TRK CGO 5T WW	
X41310	2320 00 903 0883	K	9140 00 273 2377	WV	K	0.1802			M656 TRK CGO 5T8X8	M
X41327	2320 00 999 8418	K	9140 00 273 2377	WV	K	0.1678			M656WW TRKCGO 5T	M
X41615	2320 00 191 8310	K	9140 00 273 2377	WV	K	0.2734			M520 TRKCGO 8T 4x4	
X41633	2320 01 010 4957	K	9140 00 273 2377	WV	K	0.3791			TRUCK CARGO M877	
X41635	2320 01 010 4956	K	9140 00 273 2377	WV	K	0.3791			TRUCK CARGO 8 TON	
X41635	2320 00 873 5422	K	9140 00 273 2377	WV	K	0.2423			M520 TRKCGO 8T WW	
X42064	2320 01 090 7831	K	9130 00 160 1818	WV	K	0.0435			TRK CA 1/2T 4500GV	
X42064	2320 01 090 7832	K	9130 00 160 1818	WV	K	0.0435			TRK CA 3/4T 6000GV	
X42064	2320 01 090 7833	K	9130 00 160 1818	WV	K	0.0435			TRK CA 1T 7400 GVW	
X42064	2320 01 090 7834	K	9130 00 160 1818	WV	K	0.0435			TRK CA 1/2T 8500GV	
X42201	2320 01 090 7835	K	9130 00 160 1818	WV	K	0.0435			TRK CA 1/2T 6000GV	
X42201	2320 01 090 7836	K	9130 00 160 1818	WV	K	0.0435			TRK CA 1/4T 8550GV	
X42479	2320 01 695 6380	K	9140 00 273 2377	WV	K	0.1305			TRUCK CONT MAIN	
X43228	2320 01 911 5071	K	9130 00 160 1818	WV	K	0.0684			M708 TRK DUMP 3/4T	
X43228	2320 01 911 5078	K	9140 00 273 2377	WV	K	0.0684			M708A1 TRKDMP 3/4T	
X43228	2320 01 926 7154	K	9130 00 160 1818	WV	K	0.0684			M708WWTRKDMP 3/4T	
X43297	2320 00 077 1643	K	9140 00 273 2377	WV	K	0.1056			M342A2 TRK DUMP	
X43297	2320 00 834 4509	K	9130 00 160 1818	WV	K	0.1305			M215 TRK DUMP	
X43297	2320 00 835 8339	K	9130 00 160 1818	WV	K	0.1305			M471 TRK DUMP	
X43297	2320 00 835 8595	K	9130 00 160 1818	WV	K	0.1305			M59 TRK DUMP	
X43434	2320 00 077 1644	K	9130 00 273 2377	WV	K	0.1056			M342A2 TRK DUMP	
X43434	2320 00 834 4510	K	9130 00 160 1818	WV	K	0.1305			M215 TRK DUMP W/WN	
X43434	2320 00 835 8340	K	9130 00 160 1818	WV	K	0.1305			M47 TRK DUMP	
X43434	2320 00 835 8597	K	9130 00 160 1818	WV	K	0.1305			M59 TRK DUMP W/W	
X43565	2320 01 091 1681	K	9140 00 273 2377	WV	K	0.1243			TRK DUMP 3.5 CU YD	
X43571	2320 01 090 7815	K	9140 00 273 2377	WV	K	0.1305			TRK DUMP 19M GVW	
X43589	2320 01 090 7816	K	9140 00 273 2377	WV	K	0.1554			TRK D 8T 24M GVW 4	
X43589	2320 01 090 7817	K	9140 00 273 2377	WV	K	0.1554			TRK D 8T 2800 GVW	
X43589	2320 01 090 7819	K	9140 00 273 2377	WV	K	0.1554			TRK D 8T 24M GVW 6	

Figure 6. Equipment Combat Fuel Consumption Rates – Bulk POL Table A (continued)

LI	EI NSN	SNSN CMD	FUEL NSN	EQUIP TYP	CONSUMP CD	CONSUMPTION RATES			NOMENCLATURE	MULTIFUEL
						IDL/AV	XCNTRY	2NDRDS		
X43708	2320 00 045 7131	K	9140 00 273 2377	WV	K	0.1243			M51A1 TRK DUMP	
X43708	2320 00 050 8970	K	1940 00 273 2377	WV	K	0.1243			M817 TRK DUMP	
X43708	2320 00 055 9262	K	9140 00 273 2377	WV	K	0.1429			M51A2 TRK DUMP	M
X43708	2320 00 835 8336	K	9130 00 160 1818	WV	K	0.1429			M51 TRK DUMP	
X43708	2320 01 047 8756	K	9140 00 273 2377	WV	K	0.1616			M929 TRK DMP 5T	
X43845	2320 00 045 7132	K	9140 00 273 2377	WV	K	0.1243			M51A1 TRK DUMP W/W	
X43845	2320 00 051 0589	K	9140 00 273 2377	WV	K	0.1243			M817 TRK DUMP W/W	
X43845	2320 00 055 9263	K	9140 00 273 2377	WV	K	0.1737			M51A2 TRK DUMP W/W	M
X43845	2320 00 835 8337	K	9130 00 160 1818	WV	K	0.2237			M51 TRK DUMP W/W	
X43845	2330 01 047 8755	K	9140 00 273 2377	WV	K	0.1616			M930 TRK DUMP 5T	
X44393	3805 00 368 2845	K	9140 00 273 2377	WV	K	0.3977			TRK DUMP15TMDL2-FD	
X44393	3805 00 368 2847	K	9140 00 273 2377	WV	K	0.3977			TRKDUMP15TMDL5-FD	
X44393	3805 00 368 2848	K	9140 00 273 2377	WV	K	0.3977			TRKDUMP15T127-FDG	
X44393	3805 00 368 2850	K	9140 00 273 2377	WV	K	0.3977			TRKDUMP15T MDL-LR	
X44403	3805 00 192 7249	K	9140 00 273 2377	WV	K	0.4661			TRK DUMP 2QT F5070	
X44403	3805 01 028 4389	K	9140 00 273 2377	WV	K	0.4661			TRK DUMP	
X44701	4210 00 577 7656	B	9140 00 273 2377	WV	H	8.00			TRK FIRE FIGHTING	
X44701	4210 01 025 4976	B	9140 00 273 2377	WV	H	8.00			1000 GPM PUMPER	
X44718	4210 00 965 1254	B	9140 00 273 2377	WV	H	8.00			AERIAL LADDER 85FT	
X44733	4210 01 026 2567	B	9130 00 160 1818	WV	M	10.00			MIN PUMPER	
X44735	4210 00 236 6260	B	9140 00 273 2377	SV	H	8.00			TRK FF750M1LT11407	
X44804	4210 00 542 2113	B	9130 00 160 1818	WV	H	10.50			TRK FF 500 GPM HC26	
X44804	4210 00 542 2195	B	9130 00 160 1818	WV	H	10.50			TRK FF 500 GPM 530RA	
X44804	4210 00 542 2196	B	9130 00 160 1818	WV	H	10.50			TRK FF 500 GPM 530HAW	
X44804	4210 00 620 0106	B	9130 00 160 1818	WV	H	10.50			TRK FF 500 GPM WNTZ	
X44941	4210 00 225 9127	B	9140 00 273 2377	SV	H	8.00			TRKFF500GPM M44WLF	M
X44941	4210 00 449 0431	B	9140 00 273 2377	SV	H	8.00			TRKFAM A FILM454A2	M
X44941	4210 00 928 3515	B	9140 00 273 2377	SV	H	8.00			TRK FF WLF M45A2	M
X45095	4210 00 184 6415	B	9140 00 273 2377	WV	H	10.50			A/S32-P4	
X45095	4210 00 897 6190	B	9140 00 273 2377	WV	H	12.50			TRK FIRE FIGHTING	
X45187	2320 01 463 4584	K	9140 00 273 2377	WV	K	0.1305			TRUCK REFUSE 51000	
X45317	1450 00 878 9024	K	9130 00 160 1818	WV	K	0.0808			TRUCK GM 10296963	
X45549	1450 00 176 2712	K	9130 00 160 1818	WV	K	0.0808			TRUCK GM EQUIP	
X48792	2320 01 273 4426	K	9130 00 160 1818	WV	K	0.0621			TRUCK HOPPER COAL	
X48799	2320 00 463 4561	K	9140 00 273 2377	WV	K	0.1305			TRUCK HOPPER COAL	
X48904	3930 00 503 0340	K	9130 00 160 1818	MH	H	1.30			TRUCK, LIFT FORK MDL H5208	
X48914	3930 00 327 1575	K	9140 00 273 2377	MH	H	6.00			TRK LF MLT6-2	
X48914	3930 00 419 5744	K	9140 00 273 2377	MH	H	5.00			TRK LF DD MOL T6	
X45914	3930 00 903 0900	K	9140 00 273 2377	MH	H	5.00			TRK LF DD MDL	
X48914	3930 00 926 3835	K	9140 00 273 2377	MH	H	5.00			TRK LF DD MDL-6W	
X48914	3930 00 937 0220	K	9140 00 273 2377	MH	H	5.00			TRK LF MDL MLT6CH	
X48914	3930 01 053 4823	K	9140 00 273 2377	MH	H	5.00			TRK FL MLT 6CHROPS	
X48914	3930 01 054 3830	K	9140 00 273 2377	MH	H	5.00			TRK FL MLD ARTFT 6	
X48914	3930 01 054 3831	K	9140 00 273 2377	MH	H	5.00			TRK FL MLT 6ROPS	
X49051	3930 00 465 5869	K	9140 00 273 2377	MH	H	6.50			TRK LF PET B BTL10	
X49051	3930 00 903 0899	K	1940 00 273 2377	MH	H	6.50			TRK LF DD A-3520	
X51106	3930 00 271 1449	K	9130 00 160 1818	MH	H	1.50			TRK FL 2000LBRS-53	
X51106	3930 00 271 1833	K	9130 00 160 1818	MH	H	1.50			TRK 2000LB FB20-24	
X51106	3930 00 271 1834	K	9130 00 160 1818	MH	H	1.50			TRK FL FB-20-24-RS	
X51106	3930 00 273 8204	K	9130 00 160 1818	MH	H	1.50			TRK 2000LB CE20240	
X51106	3930 00 273 8223	K	9130 00 160 1818	MH	H	1.50			TRK FL KG-51T20HRS	
X51106	3930 00 273 8226	K	9130 00 160 1818	MH	H	1.50			TRK FL KG-51T-20H	
X51106	3930 00 315 9699	K	9130 00 160 1818	MH	H	1.50			TRK FL CLARK C500-	
X51106	3930 00 436 1413	K	9130 00 160 1818	MH	H	1.50			TRK FL C20B1756421	
X51106	3930 00 781 3858	K	9130 00 160 1818	MH	H	1.00			TRKFLC20B1632033RS	
X51106	3930 00 958 3683	K	9130 00 160 1818	MH	H	1.00			TRK FL FT2024PS127	
X51243	3930 00 436 1411	K	9130 00 160 1818	MH	H	1.00			TRK FL C20B1756240	
X51243	3930 00 531 6031	K	9130 00 160 1818	MH	H	1.00			TRK 2000LB KG51T20	
X51243	3930 00 781 3857	K	9130 00 160 1818	MH	H	1.00			TRK FLGAS CLARKMOL	
X51243	3930 00 958 3682	K	9130 00 160 1818	MH	H	1.00			TRK FLFT20-24PS100	
X51311	3930 00 926 3807	K	9130 00 160 1818	MH	H	1.00			TRK FL502PG4024100	
X51380	3930 00 064 5868	K	9130 00 160 1818	MH	H	1.00			TRK FL 144LHMY40MB	
X51380	3930 00 073 8676	K	9130 00 160 1818	MH	H	1.00			TRK FL 144LMFJF040	
X51380	3930 00 073 9222	K	9130 00 160 1818	MH	H	1.00			TRK FL502PG4C24144	
X51380	3930 00 151 4428	K	9130 00 160 1818	MH	H	1.00			TRK FLFJF040W/FS162	
X51380	3930 00 257 4868	K	9130 00 160 1818	MH	H	1.00			TRK FL 144 LHMDL40	
X51380	3930 00 678 9913	K	9130 00 160 1818	MH	H	.75			TRK FL144G5P4-4024	
X51380	3930 00 724 3568	K	9130 00 160 1818	MH	H	1.00			TRK FL 144 LHMON02	
X51380	3930 00 724 3570	K	9130 00 160 1818	MH	H	1.00			TRK FL 144 LHMON02	
X51380	3930 00 935 7963	K	9130 00 160 1818	MH	H	1.50			TRK FL FJF-040-M02	
X51517	3930 00 165 4102	K	9130 00 160 1818	MH	H	1.30			TRKFLACF40-24-PS	
X51517	3930 00 224 8685	K	9130 00 160 1818	MH	H	1.30			TRKFL CLARKCL1081N	
X51517	3930 00 266 8959	K	9130 00 160 1818	MH	H	1.30			TRKFL CLARK CL4024	
X51517	3930 00 542 2175	K	9130 00 160 1818	MH	H	1.30			TRKFL CLARK CL4024	
X51517	3930 00 590 7814	K	9130 00 160 1818	MH	H	1.30			TRK LF ACC 40PS100	
X51517	3930 00 678 9917	K	9130 00 160 1818	MH	H	1.30			TRKLF TOWMOTOR 461	
X51517	3930 00 781 3856	K	9130 00 160 1818	MH	H	1.30			TRKLFTMTR462EG4024	
X51517	3930 00 935 7866	K	9130 00 160 1818	MH	H	1.30			TRKLF S40CP-100	
X51517	3930 00 954 9311	K	9130 00 160 1818	MH	H	1.30			TRKLFCLC40B1615158	
X51517	3930 01 039 8291	K	9130 00 160 1818	MH	H	1.25			TRK LF ACC 40PS144	
X51517	3930 01 075 4937	K	9130 00 160 1818	MH	H	1.25			TRK LF ACC 45PS144	
X51585	3930 00 419 5738	K	9130 00 160 1818	MH	H	1.30			TRKLF 4000LB 144LH	
X51585	3930 01 040 4594	K	9130 00 160 1818	MH	H	1.30			TRKLF 4000LB144LH	
X51585	3930 01 085 3767	K	9130 00 160 1818	MH	H	1.30			TRUCK LIFT FORK 4000 LBS	
X51654	3930 00 017 9079	K	9130 00 160 1818	MH	H	1.50			TRK LF 4000LB180LH	
X51654	3930 00 064 6564	K	9130 00 160 1818	MH	H	1.00			TRK LF4000LBM40MRS	
X51654	3930 00 214 1025	K	9130 00 160 1818	MH	H	1.50			SC S-4024-RS-10000	
X51654	3930 00 214 1026	K	9130 00 160 1818	MH	H	1.50			YAL-TOWKG-51T-40RS	
X51654	3930 00 257 4869	K	9130 00 160 1818	MH	H	1.50			TRK LF S-4024-8000	
X51654	3930 00 273 8224	K	9130 00 160 1818	MH	H	1.50			TRK LF 4000LBLT-48	

Figure 6. Equipment Combat Fuel Consumption Rates – Bulk POL Table A (continued)

LI	EI NSN	SNSN CMD	FUEL NSN	EQUIP TYP	CONSUMP CD	CONSUMPTION RATES IDL/AV	XCNTRY	2NDRDS	NOMENCLATURE	MULTIFUEL
X51654	3930 00 459 5948	K	9130 00 160 1818	MH	H	1.50			TRUCK LF F40-24-PS	
X51654	3930 00 542 2176	K	9130 00 160 1818	MH	H	1.50			TRK LF4000LBSL4024	
X51654	3930 00 556 4955	K	9130 00 160 1818	MH	H	1.50			TRK LF ACC440FS180	
X51654	3930 00 678 9916	K	9130 00 160 1818	MH	H	1.50			TRK LF 461-RS SRT	
X51654	3930 00 752 9464	K	9130 00 160 1818	MH	H	1.50			TRK LF 4000 LB 461	
X51654	3930 00 781 3855	K	9130 00 160 1818	MH	H	1.50			TRK LF462SG4024144	
X51654	3930 00 935 7865	K	9130 00 160 1818	MH	H	1.50			TRK LF 4000LBS40PC	
X51654	3930 00 937 5638	K	9130 00 160 1818	MH	H	1.50			CLARK 4024 1481NLH	
X51654	3930 00 954 1303	K	9130 00 160 1818	MH	H	1.50			TRKLFC40B1615159RS	
X51654	3930 01 039 8292	K	9130 00 160 1818	MH	H	1.25			TRK LF ACC 40PS180	
X51791	3930 00 025 1015	K	9130 00 160 1818	MH	H	1.50			TRK LF6000LBLT60RS	
X51791	3930 00 064 5869	K	9130 00 160 1818	MH	H	1.50			TRK LF MY-60-MCNRS	
X51791	3930 00 064 5870	K	9130 00 160 1818	MH	H	1.50			TRK LF MDLM460MCRS	
X51791	3930 00 235 4674	K	9130 00 160 1818	MH	H	1.50			TRKLF FJF06CMDL210	
X51791	3930 00 266 8957	K	9130 00 160 1818	MH	H	1.50			TRKLF6000LBMDL4024	
X51791	3930 00 266 8958	K	9130 00 160 1818	MH	H	1.50			TRK LF MDL6024RS50	
X51791	3930 00 266 8963	K	9130 00 160 1818	MH	H	1.50			TRK LF 6000LB 60RS	
X51791	3930 00 271 1892	K	9130 00 160 1818	MH	H	1.50			TRKLF 6000LBSP6024	
X51791	3930 00 272 9289	K	9130 00 160 1818	MH	H	1.50			TRK LF 6000LB LT60	
X51791	3930 00 272 9290	K	9130 00 160 1818	MH	H	1.50			TRKLF6000LBLT60-RS	
X51791	3930 00 273 8207	K	9130 00 160 1818	MH	H	1.50			CLARK MDL 6024RS52	
X51791	3930 00 724 3569	K	9130 00 160 1818	MH	H	1.50			TRK LF 6000LBMONO2	
X51791	3930 00 738 5938	K	9130 00 160 1818	MH	H	1.50			TRK LF6000LBFJF060	
X51791	3930 00 897 4633	K	9130 00 160 1818	MH	H	1.50			TRKLFGASKGPA51AT60	
X51791	3930 00 935 7979	K	9130 00 160 1818	MH	H	1.50			TRK LF ACFP-6-24PS	
X51791	3930 00 958 3684	K	9130 00 160 1818	MH	H	1.50			TRKLF GASFP60-24PS	
X51791	3930 01 052 5050	K	9130 00 160 1818	MH	H	1.50			TRK LF ACC 60PS180	
X51928	3930 00 679 4458	K	9130 00 160 1818	MH	H	1.50			TRKLF GASMDLRJF060	
X52065	3930 00 223 0624	K	9130 00 160 1818	MH	H	1.30			TRUCK, LIFT FORK	
X52065	3930 00 935 7856	K	9130 00 160 1818	MH	H	1.30			TRUCK, LIFT FORK	
X52065	3930 00 937 5637	K	9130 00 160 1818	MH	H	1.30			TRUCK, LIFT FORK	
X52202	3930 00 292 1100	K	9130 00 160 1818	MH	H	1.30			TRUCK, LIFT FORK	
X52202	3930 00 554 2318	K	9130 00 160 1818	MH	H	1.30			TRUCK, LIFT FORK	
X52202	3930 00 935 7855	K	9130 00 160 1818	MH	H	1.30			TRUCK, LIFT FORK	
X52339	3930 00 292 1098	K	9130 00 160 1818	MH	H	1.30			TRUCK, LIFT FORK	
X52339	3930 00 554 4592	K	9130 00 160 1818	MH	H	1.30			TRUCK, LIFT FORK	
X52339	3930 00 935 7857	K	9130 00 160 1818	MH	H	1.30			TRUCK, LIFT FORK	
X52407	3930 00 489 0263	K	9130 00 160 1818	MH	H	1.30			TRUCK, LIFT FORK	
X52476	3930 00 554 2700	K	9130 00 160 1818	MH	H	1.50			TRK LF GAS MR100RS	
X52476	3930 00 678 9056	K	9130 00 160 1818	MH	H	1.50			TRK LF MR 100SIZE2	
X52476	3930 00 799 9956	K	9130 00 160 1818	MH	H	1.50			TRK LF GAS HR-100	
X52476	3930 00 973 0659	K	9130 00 160 1818	MH	H	1.50			TRK LF GAS 390012	
X52613	3930 00 679 4457	K	9130 00 160 1818	MH	H	3.00			TRUCK, LIFT FORK	
X52613	3930 01 054 3832	K	9130 00 160 1818	MH	H	3.00			TRUCK, LIFT FORK	
X52750	3930 00 038 4410	K	9130 00 160 1818	MH	H	.70			TRK LF15000LBRT100	
X52750	3930 00 038 4411	K	9130 00 160 1818	MH	H	2.00			TRK LFGASRT-100-RS	
X52750	3930 00 038 4412	K	9130 00 160 1818	MH	H	2.00			TRK LFYL-158-53-RS	
X52750	3930 00 151 4434	K	9130 00 160 1818	MH	H	2.00			TRK LFGASHYSH130F	
X52750	3930 00 271 1893	K	9130 00 160 1818	MH	H	2.00			TRK LFGAS RT-150RS	
X52750	3930 00 271 1894	K	9130 00 160 1818	MH	H	2.00			TRK LFGAS RT-150	
X52750	3930 00 273 8203	K	9130 00 160 1818	MH	H	2.00			TRK LF15000LB-150	
X52750	3930 00 351 9946	K	9130 00 160 1818	MH	H	2.00			TRK LF GAS FL-100	
X52750	3930 00 514 3477	K	9130 00 160 1818	MH	H	2.00			TRKLF15000LBPH130	
X52750	3930 00 621 7413	K	9130 00 160 1818	MH	H	2.00			TRK LF15000LBCY150	
X52750	3930 00 897 4632	K	9130 00 160 1818	MH	H	2.00			TRK LF15000LBM150C	
X52784	3930 00 740 3190	K	9130 00 160 1818	MH	H	4.00			TRUCK, LIFT FORK	
X52810	3930 00 832 7043	K	9130 00 160 1818	MH	H	.70			TRK LF FL 4000LB	
X53366	2320 00 437 1137	K	9140 00 273 2377	WV	K	0.1305			TRUCK MAINT LINE	
X53371	2320 00 463 4580	K	9140 00 273 2377	WV	K	0.1305			TRUCK MAINT LINE	
X53376	2320 00 463 4582	K	9140 00 273 2377	WV	K	0.1305			TRUCK MAINT LINE	
X53400	2320 00 437 1140	K	9140 00 273 2377	WV	K	0.1305			TRUCK MAINT LINE	
X53402	2320 00 224 8859	K	9140 00 273 2377	WV	K	0.1305			TRUCK MAINT LINE	
X53406	2320 00 117 3418	K	9140 00 273 2377	WV	K	0.1305			TRUCK MAINT LINE	
X53572	2320 00 287 1991	K	9130 00 160 1818	WV	K	0.0621			TRUCK MAINT TELEPH	
X53572	2320 00 392 8190	K	9130 00 160 1818	WV	K	0.0621			TRUCK MAINT TELEPH	
X53572	2320 00 542 4150	K	9130 00 160 1818	WV	K	0.0621			TRUCK MAINT TELEPH	
X53572	2320 00 761 2855	K	9130 00 160 1818	WV	K	0.0621			TRUCK MAINT TELEPH	
X53572	2320 00 782 6886	K	9130 00 160 1818	WV	K	0.0621			TRUCK MAINT TELEPH	
X53572	2320 00 782 6889	K	9130 00 160 1818	WV	K	0.0621			TRUCK MAINT TELEPH	
X53572	2320 00 892 2154	K	9130 00 160 1818	WV	K	0.0621			TRUCK MAINT TELEPH	
X53572	2320 00 962 3703	K	9130 00 160 1818	WV	K	0.0621			TRUCK MAINT TELEPH	
X53572	2320 00 926 3704	K	9130 00 160 1818	WV	K	0.0621			TRUCK MAINT TELEPH	
X53572	2320 00 926 3707	K	9130 00 160 1818	WV	K	0.0621			TRUCK MAINT TELEPH	
X53572	2320 00 926 7000	K	9130 00 160 1818	WV	K	0.0621			TRUCK MAINT TELEPH	
X53572	2320 00 926 7001	K	9130 00 160 1818	WV	K	0.0621			TRUCK MAINT TELEPH	
X53572	2320 00 926 7032	K	9130 00 160 1818	WV	K	0.0621			TRUCK MAINT TELEPH	
X53709	2320 00 392 3703	K	9130 00 160 1818	WV	K	0.0621			M201 TRK MNT TEL	
X53709	2320 00 630 6801	K	9130 00 160 1818	WV	K	0.0621			M201B1 TRK MNT TEL	
X53775	2320 00 921 6833	K	9130 00 160 1818	WV	K	0.0746			M726 TRK MNT TEL	
X53790	2320 00 235 4815	K	9130 00 160 1818	WV	K	0.0621			TRUCK MAINT	
X53846	2320 00 498 8377	K	9130 00 160 1818	WV	K	0.1305			TRK MNT TEL V17AMT	
X53848	2320 00 410 7313	K	9130 00 160 1818	WV	K	0.0621			TRUCK MAINT UTILIT	
X53851	2320 00 411 3970	K	9130 00 160 1818	WV	K	0.0621			TRUCK MAINT UTILIT	
X53856	2320 00 277 1396	K	9130 00 160 1818	WV	K	0.0621			TRUCK MAINT UTILIT	
X53983	2320 00 498 8378	K	9130 00 160 1818	WV	K	0.1305			TRK MNT V18A/MTQ W	
X53983	2320 00 937 5980	K	9140 00 273 2377	WV	K	0.1305			M764 TRK MNT BORER	
X53983	2320 00 973 4577	K	9130 00 160 1818	WV	K	0.1305			TRK MNT V18B/MTQ W	
X54428	2320 00 279 0683	K	9130 00 160 1818	WV	K	0.0621			TRUCK MATL HANDLIN	
X54433	2320 00 275 7932	K	9130 00 160 1818	WV	K	0.0621			TRUCK MATL HANDLIN	
X54445	2320 00 460 2564	K	9130 00 160 1818	WV	K	0.0621			TRUCK MATL HANDLIN	

Figure 6. Equipment Combat Fuel Consumption Rates— Bulk POL Table A (continued)

LI	EI NSN	SNSN CMD	FUEL NSN	EQUIP TYP	CONSUMP CD	CONSUMPTION RATES			NOMENCLATURE	MULTIFUEL
						IDL/AV	XCNTRY	2NDRDS		
X54448	2320 00 458 9765	K	9130 00 160 1818	WV	K	0.0621			TRUCK MATL HANDLIN	
X54805	2320 01 090 7837	K	9130 00 160 1818	WV	K	0.0621			TRK PNL 3/4T 4500	M
X54805	2320 01 090 7838	K	9130 00 160 1818	WV	K	0.0435			TRK PNL 3/4T 5200	
X54805	2320 01 090 7840	K	9130 00 160 1818	WV	K	0.0435			TRK PHL 3/4T	
X55216	2320 00 904 3277	K	9140 00 273 2377	WV	K	0.0932			M756A2 TRK MNT PPL	M
X55627	2320 00 049 4804	K	9130 00 160 1818	WV	K	0.0559			M274 TRK PLTFM UTL	
X55627	2320 00 064 6373	K	9130 00 160 1818	WV	K	0.0435			274A1 TRK PLT UTL	
X55627	2320 00 074 1167	K	9130 00 160 1818	WV	K	0.0435			M274A2 TRK PLT UTL	
X55627	2320 00 782 5792	K	9130 00 160 1818	WV	K	0.0435			M274A3 TRK PLT UTL	
X55627	2320 00 782 5793	K	9130 00 160 1818	WV	K	0.0435			M274A4 TRK PLT UTL	
X55627	2320 00 930 1976	K	9130 00 160 1818	WV	K	0.0435			M274A5 TRK PLT UTL	
X55820	2320 00 489 8323	K	9130 00 160 1818	WV	K	0.0621			TRUCK REFUSE COLL	
X55832	2320 00 174 1610	K	9130 00 160 1818	WV	K	0.0621			TRUCK REFUSE COLL	
X55837	2320 00 411 5798	K	9130 00 160 1818	WV	K	0.0621			TRUCK REFUSE COLL	
X55839	2320 00 489 8324	K	9140 00 273 2377	WV	K	0.1305			TRUCK REFUSE COLL	
X55842	2320 00 963 6229	K	9140 00 273 2377	WV	K	0.1305			TRUCK REFUSE COLL	
X55847	2320 00 963 6270	K	9140 00 273 2377	WV	K	0.1305			TRUCK REFUSE COLL	
X56449	2320 01 090 7905	K	9140 00 273 2377	WV	K	0.1119			TKSTK 3-1/2T14MGVM	
X56449	2320 01 090 7906	K	9140 00 273 2377	WV	K	0.1243			TKSTK 4-1/2T16MGVM	
X56586	2320 00 050 9015	K	9140 00 273 2377	WV	K	0.1554			M821 TRK STK BR TR	
X56586	2320 00 200 1682	K	9130 00 160 1818	WV	K	0.1554			TRK STK BRDGE TRSP	
X56586	2320 00 880 4652	K	9140 00 273 2377	WV	K	0.1119			M328A1 TRK STKBRTR	
X56997	3930 00 179 1147	K	9130 00 160 1818	WV	K	0.0684			TRUCK STRADDLE	
X57271	2320 00 077 1631	K	9140 00 273 2377	WV	K	0.0932			M49A2C TRK TNK FS	M
X57271	2320 00 141 8235	K	9130 00 160 1818	WV	K	0.1305			M49C TRK TNK FS	
X57271	2320 00 440 3349	K	9130 00 160 1818	WV	K	0.0932			M49A1C TRK TNK FS	
X57408	2320 00 077 1632	K	9140 00 273 2377	WV	K	0.0932			M49A2C TRK TNK FS	M
X57408	2320 00 141 8237	K	9130 00 160 1818	WV	K	0.1305			M49C TRK TNK FS	
X57408	2320 00 440 3346	K	9130 00 160 1818	WV	K	0.0932			M49A1C TRK TNK FS	
X58078	2320 00 445 7250	K	9130 00 160 1818	WV	K	0.0621			M559 TRK TNK FS	
X58093	2320 00 873 5420	K	9130 00 160 1818	WV	K	0.0621			M559 TRK TNK FS WW	
X58367	2320 00 077 1633	K	9140 00 273 2377	WV	K	0.1243			M50A2 TRK TNK WTR	M
X58367	2320 00 440 8307	K	9140 00 273 2377	WV	K	0.1243			M50A1 TRK TNK WTR	
X58367	2320 00 835 8344	K	9140 00 273 2377	WV	K	0.1243			M50 TRK TNK WTR	
X58367	2320 00 937 4036	K	9140 00 273 2377	WV	K	0.1243			M50A3 TRK TNK WTR	
X58504	2320 00 077 1634	K	9140 00 273 2377	WV	K	0.1243			M50A2TRK TK WTR WW	M
X58504	2320 00 174 1601	K	9140 00 273 2377	WV	K	0.1243			M50 TRK TNK WTR WW	
X58504	2320 00 440 8305	K	9140 00 273 2377	WV	K	0.1243			M50A1TRK TK WTR WW	
X58504	2320 00 937 5264	K	9140 00 273 2377	WV	K	0.1243			M50A3TRK TK WTR WW	
X59052	2320 00 077 1640	K	9140 00 273 2377	WV	K	0.1305			M275A2 TRK TRAC	M
X59052	2320 00 446 2479	K	9140 00 273 2377	WV	K	0.1305			M275A1 TRK TRAC	M
X59052	2320 00 835 8345	K	9130 00 160 1818	WV	K	0.1305			M48 TRK TRAC	
X59052	2320 00 835 8609	K	9130 00 160 1818	WV	K	0.1305			M275 TRK TRAC	
X59189	2320 00 077 1641	K	9140 00 273 2377	WV	K	0.1305			M275A2 TRK TRAC WW	M
X59189	2320 00 835 8346	K	9130 00 160 1818	WV	K	0.1305			M48 TRK TRAC W/W	
X59189	2320 00 835 8611	K	9130 00 160 1818	WV	K	0.1305			M275 TRK TRAC W/W	
X59326	2320 00 050 8984	K	9140 00 273 2377	WV	K	0.1491			M818 TRK TRAC	
X59326	2320 00 055 9260	K	9140 00 273 2377	WV	K	0.1429			M52A2 TRK TRAC	M
X59326	2320 00 086 7479	K	9140 00 273 2377	WV	K	0.1184			M52A1 TRK TRAC	
X59326	2320 00 835 8326	K	9130 00 160 1818	WV	K	0.2237			M52 TRK TRAC	
X59326	2320 01 047 8753	K	9140 00 273 2377	WV	K	0.1554			M931 TRK TRACT 5T	
X59463	2320 00 050 8978	K	9140 00 273 2377	WV	K	0.1491			M818 TRK TRAC W/W	
X59463	2320 00 855 9261	K	9140 00 273 2377	WV	K	0.1429			M52A2 TRK TRAC W/W	M
X59463	2320 00 086 7480	K	9140 00 273 2377	WV	K	0.1184			M52A1 TRK TRAC W/W	
X59463	2320 00 835 8329	K	9140 00 273 2377	WV	K	0.1367			M52 TRK TRAC W/W	
X59463	2320 01 047 8752	K	9140 00 273 2377	WV	K	0.1491			M932 TRK TRACT 5T	
X59505	2320 00 937 1846	K	9140 00 273 2377	WV	K	0.1119			M757 TRK TRAC W/W	
X59600	2320 00 395 1875	K	9130 00 160 1818	WV	K	0.3418			M123 TRK TRAC W/W	
X59737	2320 00 542 2509	K	9130 00 160 1818	WV	K	0.3418			M123D TRK TRAC W/W	
X59874	2320 00 226 6081	K	9140 00 273 2377	WV	K	0.3107			M123A1C TRK TRAC	
X59874	2320 00 294 9552	K	9130 00 160 1818	WV	K	0.3418			M123C TRK TRAC	
X59874	2320 00 879 6177	K	9140 00 273 2377	WV	K	0.3107			TRK TRACXM12352	
X60185	2320 01 090 7781	K	9140 00 273 2377	WV	K	0.0808			TK TCTR 26K GTW	M
X60185	2320 01 090 7782	K	9140 00 273 2377	WV	K	0.0808			TK TCTR 32K GTW	M
X60422	2320 01 090 7784	K	9140 00 273 2377	WV	K	0.1491			TRK TCTR 34500 GVW	
X60422	2320 01 090 7785	K	9140 00 273 2377	WV	K	0.1491			TRK TCTR 39500 GVW	
X60440	2320 01 090 7786	K	9140 00 273 2377	WV	K	0.1491			TRK TCTR 44500 GVW	
X60440	2320 01 090 7787	K	9140 00 273 2377	WV	K	0.1491			TRK TCTR 51000 GVW	
X60440	2320 01 090 7788	K	9140 00 273 2377	WV	K	0.1491			TRK TCTR 64000 GVW	
X60696	2320 00 050 9004	K	9140 00 273 2377	WV	K	0.1243			M819 TRK TRAC W/W	
X60696	2320 00 073 8251	K	9140 00 273 2377	WV	K	0.1429			M246A2 TRK TRAC WW	
X60696	2320 00 695 9375	K	9140 00 273 2377	WV	K	0.1243			M246A1 TRK TRAC WW	
X60696	2320 00 835 8639	K	9130 00 160 1818	WV	K	0.2237			M246 TRK TRAC W/W	
X60696	2320 00 047 8768	K	9130 00 273 2377	WV	K	0.1491			TRK TRAC M933 51	
X60833	2320 00 177 9258	K	9130 00 160 1818	WV	K	0.0435			TRK UTIL M151A2	
X60833	2320 00 542 4783	K	9130 00 160 1818	WV	K	0.0435			TRK UTIL M151	
X60833	2320 00 763 1092	K	9130 00 160 1818	WV	K	0.0435			TRK UTIL M151A1	
X60833	2320 00 835 8318	K	9130 00 160 1818	WV	K	0.0373			M38 TRK UTIL	
X60833	2320 00 835 8319	K	9130 00 160 1818	WV	K	0.0373			TK UTIL 1/4TM38A1	
X60967	2320 00 089 7264	K	9130 00 160 1818	WV	K	1.3795			M746 TRK TRAC HET	
X61244	2320 00 141 8841	K	9130 00 160 1818	WV	K	0.0311			M38A1C TRK UTIL	
X61244	2320 00 177 9257	K	9130 00 160 1818	WV	K	0.0373			M825 TRK UTIL	
X61244	2320 00 763 1091	K	9130 00 160 1818	WV	K	0.0435			TRK UTIL M151A1C	
X61381	2320 00 445 0867	K	9130 00 160 1818	WV	K	0.0373			M38AID TRK UTIL	
X61518	2320 01 090 7826	K	9130 00 160 1818	WV	K	0.0373			TRK UTIL 4X2	
X61518	2320 01 090 7827	K	9130 00 160 1818	WV	K	0.0373			TRK UTIL WAGON	
X61655	2320 01 090 7828	K	9130 00 160 1818	WV	K	0.0373			TRK UTIL 1/2T 4X4	
X61792	2320 01 090 7771	K	9140 00 273 2377	WV	K	0.1554			TRK VAN CGO 16000G	
X61792	2320 01 090 7772	K	9140 00 273 2377	WV	K	0.1554			TRK VAN CGO 19000G	
X61929	2320 00 077 1642	K	9140 00 273 2377	WV	K	0.0932			M292A2 TRK VAN EXP	

Figure 6. Equipment Combat Fuel Consumption Rates— Bulk POL Table A (continued)

						CONSUMPTION RATES				
LI	EI NSN	SNSN CMD	FUEL NSN	EQUIP TYP	CONSUMP CD	IDL/AV	XCNTRY	2NDRDS	NOMENCLATURE	MULTIFUEL
X61929	2320 00 325 6574	K	9130 00 160 1818	WV	K	0.1305			M292TRK VAN EXP	
X61929	2320 00 440 8318	K	9140 00 273 2377	WV	K	0.0870			M292A1 TRK VAN EXP	
X61929	2320 00 077 1642	K	9140 00 273 2377	WV	K					
X62081	2320 00 832 5619	K	9140 00 273 2377	WV	K	0.1119			TRUCK VAN M791	
X62203	2320 00 699 3746	K	9140 00 273 2377	WV	K	0.0932			TRUCK VAN M292A5	
X62237	2320 00 050 9006	K	9140 00 273 2377	WV	K	0.1119			M820 TRK VAN EXP	
X62237	2320 00 880 4642	K	9140 00 273 2377	WV	K	0.1119			M291A1 TRK VAN EXP	M
X62237	2320 00 047 8750	K	9140 00 273 2377	WV	K	0.1491			M934 TRK VAN 5T	
X62271	2320 00 050 9010	K	9140 00 273 2377	WV	K	0.1119			M820A2 TRK VAN EXP	
X62271	2320 00 880 4647	K	9140 00 273 2377	WV	K	0.1119			M291A1D TRK VAN EXP	
X62271	2320 01 047 8751	K	9140 00 273 2377	WV	K	0.1740			TRK VAN EX 5T M935	
X62291	2320 01 091 3203	K	9140 00 273 2377	WV	K	0.2237			TRK VAN MOB TV	
X62291	2320 01 091 9060	K	9140 00 273 2377	WV	K	0.2237			TRK VAN TV RECORD	
X62340	2320 00 077 1636	K	9140 00 273 2377	WV	K	0.0932			M109A3 TRK VAN SHP	M
X62340	2320 00 440 8313	K	9140 00 273 2377	WV	K	0.0932			M109A3 TRK VAN SHP	M
X62340	2320 00 690 8365	K	9130 00 160 1818	WV	K	0.1305			M109A1 TRK VAN SHP	
X62340	2320 00 835 8515	K	9130 00 160 1818	WV	K	0.1305			M109 TRK VAN SHOP	
X62340	2320 00 835 8600	K	9130 00 160 1818	WV	K	0.1119			M220 TRK VAN SHOP	
X62477	2320 00 077 1637	K	9140 00 273 2377	WV	K	0.0932			M109A3TRKVANSHP WW	
X62477	2320 00 289 6473	K	9130 00 160 1818	WV	K	0.1305			M109TRK VAN SHP WW	
X62477	2320 00 440 8308	K	9140 00 273 2377	WV	K	0.0932			M109A2TRKVANSHP WW	M
X62477	2320 00 706 2224	K	9130 00 160 1818	WV	K	0.1367			M109A1TRKVANSHP WW	
X62477	2320 01 090 7777	K	9140 00 273 2377	WV	K	0.1305			TRK VAN SHOP 4X2	
X62614	2320 01 091 1662	K	9140 00 273 2377	WV	K	0.1305			TRK VAN OFFICE	
X63094	2320 00 911 5068	K	9130 00 160 1818	WV	K	0.0621			M711 TRK WRK 3/4 T	
X63299	2320 00 051 0489	K	9140 00 273 2377	WV	K	0.1616			M816 TRK WRK 5 TON	
X63299	2320 00 055 9258	K	9140 00 273 2377	WV	K	0.1429			M543A2 TRK WRK 5 T	M
X63299	2320 00 445 0866	K	9130 00 160 1818	WV	K	0.2237			M543 TRK WRK 5 TON	
X63299	2320 00 835 8325	K	9130 00 160 1818	WV	K	0.2237			M62 TRK WRKR 5 TON	
X63299	2320 01 047 4618	K	9140 00 273 2377	WV	K	0.1429			M543A1 TRK WRK 5T	
X63299	2320 01 047 8754	K	9140 00 273 2377	WV	K	0.1491			M936 TRK WRECK 5T	
X63436	2320 00 873 5426	K	9140 00 273 2377	WV	K	0.6214			TRK WRKR 10T M553	
X63573	2320 01 090 7797	K	9140 00 273 2377	WV	K	0.2237			TRK WRECK 34500GVW	
X63847	2320 01 090 7794	K	9140 00 273 2377	WV	K	0.2237			TRK WRECK 1600GVW	
X63984	2320 01 090 7798	K	9140 00 273 2377	WV	K	0.2237			TRK WRECK 3600GVW	
X63984	2320 01 090 7799	K	9140 00 273 2377	WV	K	0.2237			TRK WRECK 44500GVW	
X70772	1925 00 651 5685	B	9140 00 273 2377	AB	H	25.60			TUG DSN 3013	
X70909	1925 00 216 1848	B	9140 00 273 2377	AB	H	59.80			TUG DSN 327DS	
X70909	1925 00 375 3002	B	9140 00 273 2377	AB	H	36.40			TUG DSN 33004	
X71046	1925 00 216 1845	B	9140 00 273 2377	AB	H	24.00			TUG OCN DSN377A	
X71046	1925 00 375 3003	B	9140 00 273 2377	AB	H	73.00			TUG OCN DSN 3006	
Y00039	1915 00 217 2295	B	9140 00 273 2377	OV	H	65.40			VESSEL FRGHT 381	
Y00039	1915 00 217 2299	B	9140 00 273 2377	OV	H	65.40			VSL FRT SPY DS 210	
Y00039	1915 00 317 2300	B	9140 00 273 2377	OV	H	65.40			VESSEL FRGHT 427	
Y00039	1915 00 375 2981	B	9140 00 273 2377	OV	H	92.50			VESSEL FRGHT 7013	
Y00176	1915 00 375 2984	B	9140 00 273 2377	AB	H	44.19			DESIGN 294A	
Y00176	1915 00 375 2985	B	9140 00 273 2377	AB	H	49.70			DESIGN 294AB	
Y00176	1915 00 375 2987	B	9140 00 273 2377	AB	H	49.70			VSL LQDCGODSNG7014	
Y35143	4610 00 165 4964	B	9130 00 160 1818	SG	H	.75			WTRPURIF 420GPHE13	
Y35143	4610 00 937 0223	B	9130 00 160 1818	SG	H	.75			WTR PURIF 420 GPH	
Y35486	4610 00 202 6925	B	9130 00 160 1818	SV	H	2.50			WTR PURIF TM 1500	
Y36034	4610 00 202 8701	B	9130 00 160 1818	SV	H	3.50			WTR PURIF TM 3M GM	
Y44282	3431 00 542 0598	M	9140 00 273 2377	SG	H	1.60			WELD GEN ARCH52275	
Y44282	3431 00 894 1573	M	9140 00 273 2377	SG	H	1.60			WELD GEN ARCCOW300	
Y45652	3431 00 248 9327	M	9130 00 160 1818	SG	H	1.60			WELD GEN ARCGR202	
Y46200	3431 00 021 8696	M	9130 00 160 1818	SG	H	1.60			WLD MCH ARC WNG300	
Y46200	3431 00 072 0327	M	9130 00 160 1818	SG	H	1.60			WLD MCH ARC LEB300	
Y46200	3431 00 163 4345	M	9130 00 160 1818	SG	H	1.60			WLDMCH ARC GR300-S	
Y46200	3431 00 204 3831	M	9130 00 160 1818	SG	H	1.60			WLD MCH ARC 326-SK	
Y46200	3431 00 239 8186	M	9130 00 160 1818	SG	H	1.60			WLD MCH ARC 3153-S	
Y46200	3431 00 351 9209	M	9130 00 160 1818	SG	H	1.60			WLDMCH ARC CH-3153	
Y46200	3431 00 360 2787	M	9130 00 160 1818	SG	H	1.60			WLD MCH ASRC SK-300	
Y46200	3431 00 529 1409	M	9130 00 160 1818	SG	H	1.60			WLDMACHARCGH-31835	
Y46200	3431 00 633 4652	M	9130 00 160 1818	SG	H	1.60			WLD MCH ARC GB-318	
Y46200	3431 00 810 9696	M	9130 00 160 1818	SG	H	1.60			WELD GEN LE300	
Y46200	3431 00 845 9487	M	9130 00 160 1818	SG	H	2.00			WLD MCH CHB-3183-S	
Y46200	3431 00 991 2961	M	9130 00 160 1818	SG	H	2.00			WLD MACH LE H-300	
Y46234	3431 00 253 0558	M	9130 00 160 1818	SG	H	2.60			WELD MACH LTO 300	
Y46234	3431 01 032 6289	M	9130 00 160 1818	SG	H	2.60			WLD MCH ARC7550000	
Y51851	3950 00 298 3443	K	9140 00 273 2377	SV	H	2.30			WINCHDR P/0 5-3/4T	
Y86199	2230 00 356 7427	B	9130 00 160 1818	OV	H	2.33			NORDBERG MDL DH	
Z04615	1510 00 124 0914	H	9130 00 256 8613	AV	H	100.87			RU21J AIRPLA NE REC	
Z13217		K	9130 00 160 1818	WV	M	.18			CAR ARMORED, PER CA	
Z13288		K	9140 00 273 2377	TO	M	0.3356			CARRIER CARGO	
Z13321		K	9140 00 273 2377	TO	M	.33			CARRIER CARGO	
Z13323		S M	9140 00 273 2377	TV	H	1.00	11.80	16.10	CARRIER CARGO XM 1015	
Z13323	2350 01 136 8745	K	9140 00 273 2377	TV	H	1.00	11.80	16.10	CARR VEH XM1015A1	
Z13354	2320 01 163 1437	K	9140 00 273 2377	TO	K	0.2796			CARR AMMO 71XM1050	
Z13398	2350 01 203 0188	K	9140 00 273 2377	TO	K	0.1616			CARR SMO GN XM1059	
Z15142	4940 01 025 9856	M	9140 00 273 2377	SG	H	5.00			STEAM CLEANER	
Z20149		K	9140 00 273 2377	CE	H	7.00			CRANE 7-1/2 TYPE 1	
Z20160	3810 Z2 016 0001	K	9140 00 273 2377	CE	H	3.00			CRANE WHL MTD 7-1/2	
Z29542	10KW GE N02 9542	B	9140 00 273 2377	GN	H	1.00			10 KW DIESEL GEN	
Z29554	10KW GE N02 9554	B	9140 00 273 2377	GN	H	1.00			10 KW DIESEL GEN	
Z29554	6115 00 033 13S9	B	9140 00 273 2377	GN	H	1.09			GEN ST, PU 753/M	
Z30172	6115 23 017 2001	B	9130 00 160 1818	GN	H	2.00			GEN SET GTE 10KW	
Z30353	6115 01 078 3044	B	9140 00 273 2377	GN	H	18.00			GEN ST MEH 404B	
Z32325	1450 01 134 9359	L	9140 00 273 2377	WV	K	0.3107			CARR TR GM ROLAND	
Z32420	2350 01 169 2833	M	9140 00 273 2377	TV	H	1.00	5.20	13.00	GUN ADA SP M163A2	
Z32890	4520 01 081 0773	B	9130 00 160 1818	HG	H	3.25			HEAT DUCT PORTABLE	

Figure 6. Equipment Combat Fuel Consumption Rates— Bulk POL Table A (continued)

						CONSUMPTION RATES				
LI	EI NSN	SNSN CMD	FUEL NSN	EQUIP TYP	CONSUMP CD	IDL/AV	XCNTRY	2NDRDS	NOMENCLATURE	MULTIFUEL
Z38195	2320 01 123 1602	K	9140 00 273 2377	WV	K	0.1367			LT ARMD VEH M1047	
Z44650	2340 Z4 465 0001	K	9130 00 160 1818	WV	K	0.0249			MOTORCYCLE XM1030	
Z46347	1520 01 125 5476	H	9130 00 256 8613	AV	H	39.90			CPTR RECON OH-58D	
Z47542	2805 01 118 1275	B	9130 00 160 1818	OV	H	5.00			OUTBOARD MTR 35HP	
Z48447		B	9140 00 273 2377	SV	H	37.00			PETRO HOSELINE SYS	
Z48875		B	9140 00 273 2377	SG	H	36.00			PIPELINE OUTFIT	
Z77257	2350 01 087 1095	K	9140 00 273 2377	TV	H	10.80	56.60	44.64	M1E1 TANK 120MM	
Z90436		K	9140 00 273 2377	WV	K	0.0870			TRACTOR FULL TRCKD	
Z90445		K	9140 00 273 2377	WV	K	1.0875			EXCAVATOR SMALL EQ	
Z93224	2320 Z9 322 4001	K	9140 00 273 2377	WV	K	0.2237			TRUCK CARGO	
Z93546	2320 01 108 0820	K	9140 00 273 2377	WV	K	0.0621			TRK SMEL XM1028A1	
Z93791	3930 01 172 7892	K	9140 00 273 2377	MH	H	1.25			TRK FL 6000 LBS CP	
Z93851	3930 01 172 7891	K	9140 00 273 2377	MH	H	1.25			TRK FL 4000 LBS CP	
Z93961		K	9140 00 273 2377	WV	K	0.0621			TRK MNT TEL XM1057	
Z94111	2320 01 146 7192	K	9140 00 273 2377	WV	K	0.0497			TRK UTILITY XM 1055	
Z94112	1925 Z9 411 2001	B	9140 00 273 2377	AB	H	85.00			TUG HARBOR WATERWAY	
Z94113	2320 01 148 1638	K	9140 00 273 2377	WV	K	0.0497			TRKSQUADCARRXM1054	
Z94114	1925 Z9 411 4001	B	9140 00 273 2377	AB	H	290.00			TUG ISLAND COASTAL	
Z94115	2320 01 148 1639	K	9140 00 273 2377	WV	K	0.0497			TRKUTILSTINGXN1056	
Z94116	2320 01 146 7187	K	9140 00 273 2377	WV	K	0.0435			TRK UTILITY M1042	
Z94362	2320 01 150 1035	K	9140 00 273 2377	WV	K	0.0497			TRKSQUADCARRXM1053	
Z94363	2320 01 436 4001	K	9130 00 160 1818	WV	K	0.0311			TRK UTIL XM1041	
Z94364		K	9130 00 160 1818	WV	K	0.0311			TRK UTIL FAST ATK	
Z94423	2320 Z9 442 3001	K	9140 00 273 2377	WV	K	0.0746			TRK UTIL GLLD1-1/4	
Z98025	3431 01 079 8439	M	9140 00 273 2377	SG	H	3.00			WLD MCH ARC	

Figure 7. Daily Usage Rates for Other than Tracked Vehicles (H = hours; M = miles; K = kilometers) — Bulk POL Table B

Equipment Type						
Code	Nomenclature	Alaska	Panama Canal Zone	CONUS	Europe	Korea
AB	Amphibious	15H	20H	10H	12H	10H
AV	Aviation	4H	4H	4H	4H	4H
CE	Construction	15H	20H	10H	12H	10H
GN	Generators	20H	20H	20H	12H	20H
HG	Heating	20H	10H	10H	12H	15H
MH	Material Handling	10H	20H	20H	12H	20H
OV	Other Vehicles	10H	10H	10H	12H	10H
SG	Stationary Equipment — Misc	10H	10H	10H	12H	10H
SV	Stationary Equipment — Vehicle Mounted	10H	10H	10H	12H	10H
TO	Tracked Vehicles — Other	40M/64K	25M/40K	50M/80K	62.5M/100K	30M/48K
WV	Wheeled Vehicles	40M/64K	25M/40K	50M/80K	62.5M/100K	30M/48K

Figure 8. Daily Usage Rates for Tracked Vehicles (Hours) — Bulk POL Table C

		KOREA			EUROPE			ALASKA			PANAMA CANAL ZONE			CONUS		
LIN	NOMENCLATURE	IDLE/AV	XCNTRY	2NRDS	IDLE/AV	XCNTRY	2NRDS	IDLE/AV	XCNTRY	2RNDS	IDLE/AV	XCNTRY	2RNDS	IDLE/AV	XCNTRY	2NRDS
A93125	M551 ARAAV 152MM	6.0	6.5	5.0	6.0	6.5	5.0							4.8	7.7	4.6
C76335	CAV FGT VEH XM3	3.0	5.5	5.5	3.0	5.5	5.5	3.0	5.5	5.5	3.0	5.5	5.5	3.0	5.5	5.5
D10726	M125A1 CARR 81MM	4.1	5.0	5.0	4.0	5.0	5.0	2.9	0.5	3.6				5.0	3.8	1.6
D10741	M106A1 CARR MORTAR	4.1	5.0	5.0	4.0	5.0	5.0	2.9	0.5	3.6				5.3	3.1	4.3
D11538	M577A1 CAR CMD POST	6.0	2.9	5.0	5.0	4.0	4.5	2.4	0.2	1.9	9.6	1.2	6.0	5.8	3.7	1.2
D11668	CARR GM E CHAP M730	4.0	6.0	5.5	4.0	6.0	5.5	4.0	6.0	5.5	4.0	6.0	5.5	4.0	6.0	5.5
D11681	CARR GM EQP LES WE	3.0	5.5	5.5	3.0	3.0	5.5	3.0	5.5	5.5	3.0	5.5	5.5	3.0	5.5	5.5
D12087	M113 CARRIER PERS	3.1	5.5	5.5	3.0	5.5	5.5	3.6	1.9	12.0	6.0	1.2	4.8	7.0	6.8	1.9
E56896	M901 CBT VEH ITV	3.0	5.5	5.5	3.0	5.5	5.5	3.0	5.5	5.5	3.0	5.5	5.5	3.0	5.5	5.5
J81750	INF FGT VEH XM2	3.0	5.5	5.5	3.0	5.5	5.5	3.0	5.5	5.5	3.0	5.5	5.5	3.0	5.5	5.5
J96694	GUN AIRDEF M163	4.1	6.0	5.5	4.0	6.0	5.5							2.4	7.2	4.8
K56981	HOW HV SP 8IN M110	6.5	3.6	6.0	4.0	6.0	5.5							4.1	1.9	4.1
K57667	M109 HOW SP 155MM	4.1	6.0	5.5	4.0	6.0	5.5							6.2	1.9	2.9
L44894	LAUN-LOAD MLRS	5.0	4.0	4.5	5.0	5.0	4.5	5.0	4.0	4.5	5.0	4.0	4.5	5.0	4.0	4.5
T13169	TANK, M60A3 TTS	4.6	6.5	4.6	5.0	6.5	5.0							4.2	8.5	2.9
T13374	M1 TANK 105MM	5.2	3.3	3.4	5.0	6.5	5.0	5.2	3.3	3.4				5.2	3.3	3.4
V13101	M60A1 TANK 105MM	4.6	6.5	4.6	4.5	6.5	4.5							4.2	8.5	2.9
Z32424	GUN AIR DEF XM247	5.0	6.5	5.0	5.0	6.5	5.0	5.0	6.5	5.0	5.0	6.5	5.0	5.0	6.5	5.0
Z77257	M1E1 TANK 120MM	5.2	3.3	3.4	5.0	6.5	5.0	5.2	3.3	3.4				5.2	3.3	3.4

Figure 9. Standard Usage Area Profiles—Bulk POL Table D

Profile	AB	CE	GN	HG	MH	SG	SV	TI	CC	SR	WV	OV	AV
Standard — 001	12	12	12	12	12	12	12	3.8	5.6	5.1	100	12	04
POL Intense — 002	12	12	12	12	12	12	12	3.9	5.8	5.3	100	12	04
WAFF Rates — 0	12	12	12	12	12	12	12	12	3.8	5.6	5.1	100	04
Light Division Europe — 004	12	12	12	12	12	12	12	3.8	5.6	5.1	100	12	06
Light Division Middle East — 005	0.1	12	12	12	12	12	12	3.8	5.6	5.1	100	12	06
Light Division Europe — 004	12	12	12	12	12	12	12	3.8	5.6	5.1	100	12	06
Light Division Middle East — 005	0.1	12	12	12	12	12	12	3.8	5.6	5.1	100	12	06
Ar tic — 006	15	15	20	20	10	10	10	10.7	1.1	1.0	64.4	08	04
Pacific — 007	10	10	20	15	20	10	10	15.7	1.5	1.4	48	10	04
CONUS — 071	10	10	20	10	20	10	10	4.5	5.2	3.9	80	10	04
Europe — 072	12	12	12	12	12	12	12	4.2	5.7	5.5	101	12	04
Korea — 073	10	10	20	15	20	10	10	4.4	5.2	5.0	48.3	10	04
Alaska — 074	15	15	20	20	10	10	10	3.7	3.7	5.0	64.4	10	04
Canal Zone — 075	20	20	20	10	20	10	10	4.6	4.5	5.3	40.2	10	4
Echelon Above Corp, Middle East — 850	10	20	20	10	20	12	12	3.8	5.6	5.1	64.4	12	2.1
Echelon Above Corp, Middle East — 851	10	10	20	15	20	10	10	4.4	5.2	5.1	48.3	10	2.1
Echelon Above Corp, Europe — 852	12	12	12	12	12	12	12	3.8	5.6	5.1	100	12	2.1

Figure 10. Bulk POL Planning Factors by Type Unit— Bulk POL Table E

SUMMARY OF BULK FUEL USAGE BY EQUIPMENT CATEGORY
INF DIV E/W RIB BRG (SRC 07000H010)

SRC	UNIT NAME	FUEL TYPE	AB	CE	GN	HG	MH	SG	SV	TI	CC	SR	WV	OV	AV
03087H700	NBC COMPANY	MOGAS	0.0	0.0	1.1	0.0	0.0	35.2	0.0	0.0	0.0	0.0	0.0	0.0	
		DIESEL	0.0	0.0	0.0	0.0	0.0	0.0	0.0	0.0	0.0	0.0	4.7	0.0	
03107H000	NBC COMPANY	MOGAS	0.0	0.0	0.8	77.5	0.0	73.0	0.0	0.0	0.0	0.0	0.0	0.0	
		DIESEL	0.0	0.0	0.6	0.0	0.0	5.0	0.0	5.0	43.0	44.5	7.3	0.0	
05155H710	ENGR BN, INF DIV	MOGAS	0.0	4.0	21.0	39.8	0.0	67.1	0.0	0.0	0.0	0.0	0.1	0.0	
		DIESEL	86.4	255.2	2.8	0.0	8.5	29.0	0.0	43.0	457.1	333.0	25.6	0.0	
05156H700	HHC, ENGR BN, INF DIV	MOGAS	0.0	2.5	10.1	9.4	0.0	16.4	0.0	0.0	0.0	0.0	0.1	0.0	
		DIESEL	0.0	39.5	0.6	0.0	8.5	7.0	0.0	2.0	36.8	25.5	7.3	0.0	
05157H700	ENGR CO, ENGR BN, INF DIV	MOGAS	0.0	0.5	3.4	7.6	0.0	13.0	0.0	0.0	0.0	0.0	0.0	0.0	
		DIESEL	0.0	67.5	0.6	0.0	0.0	5.0	0.0	10.5	100.6	74.3	3.3	0.0	
05158H710	BRG CO, EN BN, RIBBON	MOGAS	0.0	0.0	0.8	7.6	0.0	11.6	0.0	0.0	0.0	0.0	0.0	0.0	
		DIESEL	86.4	13.1	0.6	0.0	0.0	7.0	0.0	9.4	118.5	84.4	8.4	0.0	
06100H000	INF DIV ARTY	MOGAS	0.0	0.0	128.3	102.4	0.0	124.1	0.0	0.0	0.0	0.0	0.2	0.0	
		DIESEL	0.0	0.0	34.9	0.0	0.0	5.0	0.0	17.8	159.8	173.8	83.5	1.7	
06125H000	FA BN, 155MM TOWED (DS)	MOGAS	0.0	0.0	24.5	22.0	0.0	26.9	0.0	0.0	0.0	0.0	0.0	0.0	
		DIESEL	0.0	0.0	3.0	0.0	0.0	0.0	0.0	0.0	0.0	0.0	17.7	0.0	
06126H000	HHB 155MM T, FA BN	MOGAS	0.0	0.0	13.1	5.4	0.0	8.0	0.0	0.0	0.0	0.0	0.0	0.0	
		DIESEL	0.0	0.0	3.0	0.0	0.0	0.0	0.0	0.0	0.0	0.0	3.2	0.0	
06127H000	FA BTRY, 155MM T, FA BN	MOGAS	0.0	0.0	2.7	3.6	0.0	4.0	0.0	0.0	0.0	0.0	0.0	0.0	
		DIESEL	0.0	0.0	0.0	0.0	0.0	0.0	0.0	0.0	0.0	0.0	3.1	0.0	
06129H000	SVC BTRY, 155MM T, FA BN	MOGAS	0.0	0.0	3.3	5.8	0.0	6.9	0.0	0.0	0.0	0.0	0.0	0.0	
		DIESEL	0.0	0.0	0.0	0.0	0.0	0.0	0.0	0.0	0.0	0.0	4.9	0.0	
06155H000	FA BN, 105MM T, INF DIV	MOGAS	0.0	0.0	15.3	16.6	0.0	26.4	0.0	0.0	0.0	0.0	0.0	0.0	
		DIESEL	0.0	0.0	3.6	0.0	0.0	5.0	0.0	0.0	0.0	0.0	11.4	0.0	
06156H000	HHB, FA BN, 105MM TOWED	MOGAS	0.0	0.0	11.2	5.4	0.0	8.0	0.0	0.0	0.0	0.0	0.0	0.0	
		DIESEL	0.0	0.0	3.0	0.0	0.0	0.0	0.0	0.0	0.0	0.0	3.0	0.0	
06157H000	FA BTRY, 105MM T, FA BN	MOGAS	0.0	0.0	1.1	1.8	0.0	4.0	0.0	0.0	0.0	0.0	0.0	0.0	
		DIESEL	0.0	0.0	0.0	0.0	0.0	0.0	0.0	0.0	0.0	0.0	1.7	0.0	
06159H000	SVC BTRY, FA BN, 105MM T	MOGAS	0.0	0.0	0.8	5.8	0.0	6.4	0.0	0.0	0.0	0.0	0.0	0.0	
		DIESEL	0.0	0.0	0.6	0.0	0.0	5.0	0.0	0.0	0.0	0.0	3.2	0.0	
06165H000	FA BN, 155MM/8 IN, INF DIV	MOGAS	0.0	0.0	17.4	25.6	0.0	30.4	0.0	0.0	0.0	0.0	0.0	0.0	
		DIESEL	0.0	0.0	3.6	0.0	0.0	5.0	0.0	17.8	159.8	173.8	18.6	1.7	
06166H000	HHB, 155 T/8 IN SP, FA BN	MOGAS	0.0	0.0	12.4	5.4	0.0	8.0	0.0	0.0	0.0	0.0	0.0	0.0	
		DIESEL	0.0	0.0	3.0	0.0	0.0	0.0	0.0	2.0	17.2	17.8	2.8	1.7	
06167H000	FA BTRY, 155M T, FA BN	MOGAS	0.0	0.0	0.8	3.6	0.0	4.0	0.0	0.0	0.0	0.0	0.0	0.0	
		DIESEL	0.0	0.0	0.0	0.0	0.0	0.0	0.0	0.0	0.0	0.0	2.6	0.0	
06169H000	SVC BTRY, 155MM T/8 IN SP	MOGAS	0.0	0.0	1.7	5.8	0.0	6.4	0.0	0.0	0.0	0.0	0.0	0.0	
		DIESEL	0.0	0.0	0.6	0.0	0.0	5.0	0.0	2.0	36.8	25.5	5.6	0.0	
06302H020	HHB, DIV ARTY, INF DIV	MOGAS	0.0	0.0	26.0	5.4	0.0	8.4	0.0	0.0	0.0	0.0	0.0	0.0	
		DIESEL	0.0	0.0	10.4	0.0	0.0	0.0	0.0	0.0	0.0	0.0	6.3	0.0	
06307H600	TGT ACQ BTRY, AIM DIV	MOGAS	0.0	0.0	11.6	5.4	0.0	4.5	0.0	0.0	0.0	0.0	0.0	0.0	
		DIESEL	0.0	0.0	12.0	0.0	0.0	0.0	0.0	0.0	0.0	0.0	5.1	0.0	
06358H000	FA BTRY, FA BN 8 IN SP	MOGAS	0.0	0.0	0.8	3.6	0.0	4.0	0.0	0.0	0.0	0.0	0.0	0.0	
		DIESEL	0.0	0.0	0.0	0.0	0.0	0.0	0.0	13.8	105.8	130.5	2.3	0.0	
07000H010	INF DIV E/W RIB BRG	MOGAS	0.0	4.0	767.0	644.8	0.0	590.9	0.0	0.0	0.0	0.0	2.1	0.0	
		DIESEL	86.4	401.2	235.4	0.0	180.8	167.3	0.0	181.6	1554.5	1535.1	301.2	2.0	
		JP4													18918.6
07004H000	HHC, INF DIV	MOGAS	0.0	0.0	9.4	11.6	0.0	12.0	0.0	0.0	0.0	0.0	0.0	0.0	
		DIESEL	0.0	0.0	3.0	0.0	0.0	0.0	0.0	0.0	0.0	0.0	2.3	0.0	
07042H000	HHC, INF DIV BDE	MOGAS	0.0	0.0	12.7	5.8	0.0	3.5	0.0	0.0	0.0	0.0	0.0	0.0	
		DIESEL	0.0	0.0	0.0	0.0	0.0	0.0	0.0	0.0	0.0	0.0	2.1	0.0	
08035H000	MED BN, AIM DIV	MOGAS	0.0	0.0	45.1	36.2	0.0	53.0	0.0	0.0	0.0	0.0	0.0	0.0	
		DIESEL	0.0	0.0	0.6	0.0	0.0	5.0	0.0	0.0	0.0	0.0	12.6	0.0	
08036H000	H&S CO, MED BN, AIM DIV	MOGAS	0.0	0.0	13.8	13.4	0.0	14.0	0.0	0.0	0.0	0.0	0.0	0.0	
		DIESEL	0.0	0.0	0.6	0.0	0.0	5.0	0.0	0.0	0.0	0.0	4.6	0.0	
08037H000	'MED CO, MED BN, AIM DIV	MOGAS	0.0	0.0	10.4	7.6	0.0	13.0	0.0	0.0	0.0	0.0	0.0	0.0	
		DIESEL	0.0	0.0	0.0	0.0	0.0	0.0	0.0	0.0	0.0	0.0	2.7	0.0	
09557H520	MSL SPT CO, MAINT BN, INF DIV	MOGAS	0.0	0.0	17.8	11.6	0.0	4.0	0.0	0.0	0.0	0.0	0.0	0.0	
		DIESEL	0.0	0.0	30.3	0.0	0.0	5.0	0.0	0.0	0.0	0.0	7.2	0.0	
10007H000	SUP-SVC CO S&T BN INF DIV	MOGAS	0.0	0.0	6.4	5.0	0.0	8.1	0.0	0.0	0.0	0.0	0.0	0.0	
		DIESEL	0.0	70.0	0.0	0.0	77.6	9.3	0.0	0.0	0.0	0.0	2.4	0.0	
11035H000	SIGNAL BN, AIM DIV	MOGAS	0.0	0.0	150.6	34.0	0.0	14.9	0.0	0.0	0.0	0.0	0.2	0.0	
		DIESEL	0.0	0.0	11.3	0.0	0.0	20.0	0.0	0.0	0.0	0.0	17.4	0.0	
11036H000	HHC, SIG BN, AIM DIV	MOGAS	0.0	0.0	17.4	4.0	0.0	2.9	0.0	0.0	0.0	0.0	0.0	0.0	
		DIESEL	0.0	0.0	0.6	0.0	0.0	5.0	0.0	0.0	0.0	0.0	4.2	0.0	
11037H000	CMD OP CO, SIG BN, AIM DIV	MOGAS	0.0	0.0	48.1	11.2	0.0	4.0	0.0	0.0	0.0	0.0	0.1	0.0	
		DIESEL	0.0	0.0	6.6	0.0	0.0	5.0	0.0	0.0	0.0	0.0	5.4	0.0	
11038H000	FWD COMM CO, SIG BN, AIM DIV	MOGAS	0.0	0.0	49.6	9.4	0.0	4.0	0.0	0.0	0.0	0.0	0.1	0.0	
		DIESEL	0.0	0.0	0.6	0.0	0.0	5.0	0.0	0.0	0.0	0.0	3.5	0.0	
11039H000	SIG SPT OP CO, SIG BN	MOGAS	0.0	0.0	35.6	9.4	0.0	4.0	0.0	0.0	0.0	0.0	0.0	0.0	
		DIESEL	0.0	0.0	3.6	0.0	0.0	5.0	0.0	0.0	0.0	0.0	4.2	0.0	
12017H610	AG CO, SPT CMD, AMBL/AIM	MOGAS	0.0	0.0	1.1	7.2	0.0	7.0	0.0	0.0	0.0	0.0	0.1	0.0	
		DIESEL	0.0	0.0	13.5	0.0	0.0	0.0	0.0	0.0	0.0	0.0	1.2	0.0	
14037H610	FIN CO, SPT CMD, AIM/AMBL	MOGAS	0.0	0.0	2.4	0.0	0.0	0.0	0.0	0.0	0.0	0.0	0.0	0.0	
		DIESEL	0.0	0.0	0.6	0.0	0.0	0.0	0.0	0.0	0.0	0.0	0.5	0.0	
17205H230	AIR CAV SQDN, INF DIV/SEP	MOGAS	0.0	0.0	41.9	57.2	0.0	29.5	0.0	0.0	0.0	0.0	0.7	0.0	
		DIESEL	0.0	24.0	1.7	0.0	11.7	15.0	0.0	32.4	408.9	304.1	22.3	0.0	
		JP4													7216.0
17206H200	HHT AIR CAV SQDN INF/SEP	MOGAS	0.0	0.0	12.6	33.2	0.0	22.8	0.0	0.0	0.0	0.0	0.1	0.0	
		DIESEL	0.0	0.0	0.0	0.0	0.0	0.0	0.0	0.0	0.0	0.0	6.9	0.0	
		JP4													436.0
17208H200	AIR CAV TRP, AIR CAV SQDN	MOGAS	0.0	0.0	9.8	8.0	0.0	1.9	0.0	0.0	0.0	0.0	0.2	0.0	
		DIESEL	0.0	8.0	0.6	0.0	3.9	5.0	0.0	0.0	0.0	0.0	4.9	0.0	
		JP4													2260.0

Figure 10. Bulk POL Planning Factors by Type Unit— Bulk POL Table E (continued)

SUMMARY OF BULK FUEL USAGE BY EQUIPMENT CATEGORY
INF DIV E/W RIB BRG (SRC 07000H010)

SRC	UNIT NAME	FUEL TYPE	AB	CE	GN	HG	MH	SG	SV	TI	CC	SR	WV	OV	AV
17307H700	AR CAV TP, AR CV SQ	MOGAS	0.0	0.0	0.0	0.0	0.0	1.0	0.0	0.0	0.0	0.0	0.0	0.0	
		DIESEL	0.0	0.0	0.0	0.0	0.0	0.0	0.0	32.4	408.9	304.1	0.4	0.0	
17387H720	ATTACK HELICOPTER COMPANY	MOGAS	0.0	0.0	10.6	5.4	0.0	5.9	0.0	0.0	0.0	0.0	0.0	0.0	
		DIESEL	0.0	8.0	0.6	0.0	0.0	5.0	0.0	0.0	0.0	0.0	5.1	0.0	
		JP4													3391.8
19017H710	MP CO, AIM DIV	MOGAS	0.0	0.0	3.5	4.0	0.0	1.0	0.0	0.0	0.0	0.0	0.0	0.0	
		DIESEL	0.0	0.0	1.1	0.0	0.0	5.0	0.0	0.0	0.0	0.0	2.0	0.0	
29001H000	SUPPORT COMMAND, INF DIV	MOGAS	0.0	0.0	137.0	183.1	0.0	164.2	0.0	0.0	0.0	0.0	0.2	0.0	
		DIESEL	0.0	98.0	148.3	0.0	122.7	56.3	0.0	8.6	74.3	68.4	75.8	0.0	
29002H700	HHC, SPT COMD, AIM DIV	MOGAS	0.0	0.0	0.8	3.6	0.0	4.0	0.0	0.0	0.0	0.0	0.1	0.0	
		DIESEL	0.0	0.0	3.0	0.0	0.0	0.0	0.0	0.0	0.0	0.0	0.8	0.0	
29003H500	DIV MMC, AIM DIV	MOGAS	0.0	0.0	0.0	0.0	0.0	2.0	0.0	0.0	0.0	0.0	0.0	0.0	
		DIESEL	0.0	0.0	15.0	0.0	0.0	0.0	0.0	0.0	0.0	0.0	1.6	0.0	
29005H000	S&T BN, INF DIV	MOGAS	0.0	0.0	11.0	23.8	0.0	18.4	0.0	0.0	0.0	0.0	0.0	0.0	
		DIESEL	0.0	70.0	0.6	0.0	77.6	18.3	0.0	0.0	0.0	0.0	20.9	0.0	
29006H000	HHD, S&T BN, AIM DIV	MOGAS	0.0	0.0	0.8	10.8	0.0	7.0	0.0	0.0	0.0	0.0	0.0	0.0	
		DIESEL	0.0	0.0	0.0	0.0	0.0	0.0	0.0	0.0	0.0	0.0	0.8	0.0	
29015H000	MAINT BN, INF DIV	MOGAS	0.0	0.0	76.5	112.3	0.0	79.8	0.0	0.0	0.0	0.0	0.0	0.0	
		DIESEL	0.0	28.0	115.1	0.0	45.1	33.0	0.0	8.6	74.3	68.4	37.9	0.0	
29016H000	HQ & LT MAINT CO, MAINT BN	MOGAS	0.0	0.0	11.4	12.5	0.0	5.0	0.0	0.0	0.0	0.0	0.0	0.0	
		DIESEL	0.0	0.0	18.0	0.0	19.6	0.0	0.0	0.0	0.0	0.0	7.2	0.0	
29017H000	FWD SPT CO, MAINT BN	MOGAS	0.0	0.0	11.3	19.6	0.0	17.7	0.0	0.0	0.0	0.0	0.0	0.0	
		DIESEL	0.0	7.0	15.2	0.0	8.5	7.0	0.0	2.2	12.5	14.3	5.8	0.0	
29018H000	HEAVY MAINT CO, MAINT BN	MOGAS	0.0	0.0	13.3	29.4	0.0	17.5	0.0	0.0	0.0	0.0	0.0	0.0	
		DIESEL	0.0	7.0	21.2	0.0	0.0	7.0	0.0	2.0	36.8	25.5	6.0	0.0	
34165H810	CEWI BN, INF DIV	MOGAS	0.0	0.0	114.6	20.6	0.0	19.7	0.0	0.0	0.0	0.0	0.0	0.0	
		DIESEL	0.0	0.0	1.5	0.0	0.0	17.0	0.0	0.0	0.0	0.0	13.9	0.3	
		JP4													438.0
34166H810	HQ/HQ & OP CO, CEWI BN	MOGAS	0.0	0.0	21.0	5.0	0.0	0.0	0.0	0.0	0.0	0.0	0.0	0.0	
		DIESEL	0.0	0.0	1.5	0.0	0.0	12.0	0.0	0.0	0.0	0.0	3.5	0.0	
		JP4													438.0
34167H810	C&J CO. CEWI BN (INF DIV)	MOGAS	0.0	0.0	44.1	0.0	0.0	0.0	0.0	0.0	0.0	0.0	0.0	0.0	
		DIESEL	0.0	0.0	0.0	0.0	0.0	0.0	0.0	0.0	0.0	0.0	2.6	0.3	
34168H810	GND SURVL CO, CEWI BN	MOGAS	0.0	0.0	2.3	0.0	0.0	0.0	0.0	0.0	0.0	0.0	0.0	0.0	
		DIESEL	0.0	0.0	0.0	0.0	0.0	0.0	0.0	0.0	0.0	0.0	2.0	0.0	
34169H810	SVC SPT CO, CEWI BN, INF DI	MOGAS	0.0	0.0	47.2	15.6	0.0	19.7	0.0	0.0	0.0	0.0	0.0	0.0	
		DIESEL	0.0	0.0	0.0	0.0	0.0	5.0	0.0	0.0	0.0	0.0	5.7	0.0	
44325H000	ADA BN, AIM DIVISION	MOGAS	0.0	0.0	64.6	25.6	0.0	30.5	0.0	0.0	0.0	0.0	0.1	0.0	
		DIESEL	0.0	0.0	7.1	0.0	0.0	5.0	0.0	74.8	411.4	611.2	19.6	0.0	
44326H000	HHB, ADA BN, C/V, SP	MOGAS	0.0	0.0	25.7	7.6	0.0	8.9	0.0	0.0	0.0	0.0	0.0	0.0	
		DIESEL	0.0	0.0	7.1	0.0	0.0	5.0	0.0	2.0	17.2	17.8	4.1	0.0	
44327H000	ADA BTRY, VUL (SP) STINGER	MOGAS	0.0	0.0	8.6	3.6	0.0	5.4	0.0	0.0	0.0	0.0	0.0	0.0	
		DIESEL	0.0	0.0	0.0	0.0	0.0	0.0	0.0	18.2	109.3	205.9	4.1	0.0	
44328H000	ADA BTRY, CHAP (SP) STINGER	MOGAS	0.0	0.0	10.8	5.4	0.0	5.4	0.0	0.0	0.0	0.0	0.0	0.0	
		DIESEL	0.0	0.0	0.0	0.0	0.0	0.0	0.0	18.2	87.8	90.8	3.6	0.0	
55088H000	TRANS MTR TRANS CO, INF DIV	MOGAS	0.0	0.0	3.8	8.0	0.0	3.3	0.0	0.0	0.0	0.0	0.0	0.0	
		DIESEL	0.0	0.0	0.6	0.0	0.0	9.0	0.0	0.0	0.0	0.0	17.7	0.0	
55427H010	TRANS ACFT MNT CO INF/ABN DIV	MOGAS	0.0	0.0	6.4	16.2	0.0	4.4	0.0	0.0	0.0	0.0	0.0	0.0	
		DIESEL	0.0	8.0	20.6	0.0	18.3	5.0	0.0	0.0	0.0	0.0	5.3	0.0	
		JP4													236.0
57055H320	CBT AVIATION BN, INF DIV	MOGAS	0.0	0.0	57.1	71.5	0.0	44.3	0.0	0.0	0.0	0.0	0.4	0.0	
		DIESEL	0.0	24.0	22.9	0.0	37.9	10.0	0.0	0.0	0.0	0.0	24.5	0.0	
		JP4													11264.6
57056H320	HHC, CBT AVN BN, INF DIV	MOGAS	0.0	0.0	3.3	0.0	0.0	6.0	0.0	0.0	0.0	0.0	0.3	0.0	
		DIESEL	0.0	0.0	0.6	0.0	0.0	0.0	0.0	0.0	0.0	0.0	1.0	0.0	
57057H320	CBT SPT AVN CO	MOGAS	0.0	0.0	11.7	21.1	0.0	9.0	0.0	0.0	0.0	0.0	0.0	0.0	
		DIESEL	0.0	0.0	0.0	0.0	1.3	0.0	0.0	0.0	0.0	0.0	4.3	0.0	
		JP4													2438.0
57058H320	AVN GEN SPT CO, CBT AVN BN	MOGAS	0.0	0.0	13.3	7.6	0.0	9.9	0.0	0.0	0.0	0.0	0.0	0.0	
		DIESEL	0.0	8.0	1.1	0.0	17.0	0.0	0.0	0.0	0.0	0.0	4.3	0.0	
		JP4													2760.8

SUMMARY OF BULK FUEL USAGE BY EQUIPMENT CATEGORY
SEP INF BDE WM4T6 1005 ADP (SRC 07100H020)

SRC	UNIT NAME	FUEL TYPE	AB	CE	GN	HG	MH	SG	SV	TI	CC	SR	WV	OV	AV
05107H020	ENGR CO, SEP IN BDE, M4T6	MOGAS	0.0	0.5	5.0	11.2	0.0	24.0	0.0	0.0	0.0	0.0	0.0	0.0	
		DIESEL	57.6	37.1	0.6	0.0	8.5	7.0	0.0	22.5	270.0	193.8	12.5	0.0	
06157H000	FA BTRY, 105MM T, FA BN	MOGAS	0.0	0.0	1.1	1.8	0.0	4.0	0.0	0.0	0.0	0.0	0.0	0.0	
		DIESEL	0.0	0.0	0.0	0.0	0.0	0.0	0.0	0.0	0.0	0.0	1.7	0.0	
06159H000	SVC BTRY, FA BN, 105MM T	MOGAS	0.0	0.0	0.8	5.8	0.0	6.4	0.0	0.0	0.0	0.0	0.0	0.0	
		DIESEL	0.0	0.0	0.6	0.0	0.0	5.0	0.0	0.0	0.0	0.0	3.2	0.0	
06185H000	FA BN, 105MM T SEP INF BD	MOGAS	0.0	0.0	21.5	18.4	0.0	26.4	0.0	0.0	0.0	0.0	0.0	0.0	
		DIESEL	0.0	0.0	3.6	0.0	0.0	5.0	0.0	0.0	0.0	0.0	12.7	0.3	
06186H000	HHB, FA BN, 105MM T	MOGAS	0.0	0.0	17.5	7.2	0.0	8.0	0.0	0.0	0.0	0.0	0.0	0.0	
		DIESEL	0.0	0.0	3.0	0.0	0.0	0.0	0.0	0.0	0.0	0.0	4.2	0.3	
07100H020	SEP INF BDE WM4T6, 1005 AD	MOGAS	0.0	0.5	145.7	107.3	0.0	133.3	0.0	0.0	0.0	0.0	0.3	0.0	
		DIESEL	57.6	80.1	82.5	0.0	40.9	29.0	0.0	56.9	715.7	523.5	58.7	0.5	
		JP4													1075.2
07102H000	HHC SEP INF BDE	MOGAS	0.0	0.0	37.0	11.2	0.0	9.6	0.0	0.0	0.0	0.0	0.1	0.0	
		DIESEL	0.0	8.0	5.2	0.0	0.0	0.0	0.0	0.0	0.0	0.0	5.8	0.0	
		JP4													637.2
08147H000	MED CO, SEP AIM BDE, ACR	MOGAS	0.0	0.0	10.4	11.6	0.0	13.0	0.0	0.0	0.0	0.0	0.0	0.0	
		DIESEL	0.0	0.0	0.0	0.0	0.0	5.0	0.0	0.0	0.0	0.0	3.1	0.0	

Figure 10. Bulk POL Planning Factors by Type Unit— Bulk POL Table E (continued)

SUMMARY OF BULK FUEL USAGE BY EQUIPMENT CATEGORY
SEP INF BDE WM4T6 1005 ADP (SRC 07100H020) — Cont'd

SRC	UNIT NAME	FUEL TYPE	AB	CE	GN	HG	MH	SG	SV	TI	CC	SR	WV	OV	AV
12147H600	ADMIN CO, SEP BDE	MOGAS	0.0	0.0	2.2	3.6	0.0	3.0	0.0	0.0	0.0	0.0	0.0	0.0	
		DIESEL	0.0	0.0	13.5	0.0	0.0	0.0	0.0	0.0	0.0	0.0	1.2	0.0	
17307H700	AR CAV TP, AR CV SQ, AM D	MOGAS	0.0	0.0	0.0	0.0	0.0	1.0	0.0	0.0	0.0	0.0	0.0	0.0	
		DIESEL	0.0	0.0	0.0	0.0	0.0	0.0	0.0	32.4	408.9	304.1	0.4	0.0	
29076H000	HHD, SPT BN, SEP AIM BDE	MOGAS	0.0	0.0	3.9	0.0	0.0	1.0	0.0	0.0	0.0	0.0	0.1	0.0	
		DIESEL	0.0	0.0	0.6	0.0	0.0	0.0	0.0	0.0	0.0	0.0	1.1	0.0	
29077H000	S&T CO, SPT BN, SEP AIM BDE	MOGAS	0.0	0.0	3.4	7.6	0.0	13.6	0.0	0.0	0.0	0.0	0.0	0.0	
		DIESEL	0.0	28.0	12.0	0.0	22.6	0.0	0.0	0.0	0.0	0.0	9.5	0.0	
29099H000	MNT CO, SPT BN SEP INF BDE	MOGAS	0.0	0.0	11.9	27.6	0.0	30.6	0.0	0.0	0.0	0.0	0.0	0.0	
		DIESEL	0.0	7.0	28.1	0.0	9.8	7.0	0.0	2.0	36.8	25.5	5.9	0.0	
29135H000	SPT BN SEP INF BDE	MOGAS	0.0	0.0	28.7	57.5	0.0	65.2	0.0	0.0	0.0	0.0	0.1	0.0	
		DIESEL	0.0	35.0	73.1	0.0	32.4	12.0	0.0	2.0	36.8	25.5	22.2	0.0	
29176H910	HHC, SPT BN, SEP AIM/ABN/ID(L)	MOGAS	0.0	0.0	0.8	7.1	0.0	5.0	0.0	0.0	0.0	0.0	0.1	0.0	
		DIESEL	0.0	0.0	19.5	0.0	0.0	0.0	0.0	0.0	0.0	0.0	2.4	0.0	
34114H110	MI CO (CEWI) SEP INF BDE	MOGAS	0.0	0.0	53.4	9.0	0.0	7.1	0.0	0.0	0.0	0.0	0.0	0.0	
		DIESEL	0.0	0.0	0.0	0.0	0.0	5.0	0.0	0.0	0.0	0.0	4.9	0.2	
		JP4													438.0

SUMMARY OF BULK FUEL USAGE BY EQUIPMENT CATEGORY
ARMD DIV E/W M4T6/CL60 BRG (SRC 17000H020)

SRC	UNIT NAME	FUEL TYPE	AB	CE	GN	HG	MH	SG	SV	TI	CC	SR	WV	OV	AV
05145H720	ENGR BN, ARMD/MECH DIV	MOGAS	40.0	4.5	24.0	49.2	0.0	81.7	0.0	0.0	0.0	0.0	0.1	0.0	
		DIESEL	72.0	141.1	3.4	0.0	8.5	38.0	0.0	106.5	1070.4	890.8	28.3	0.0	
05146H700	HHC, ENGR BN	MOGAS	0.0	2.5	8.1	9.4	0.0	15.5	0.0	0.0	0.0	0.0	0.1	0.0	
		DIESEL	0.0	37.9	0.6	0.0	8.5	11.0	0.0	7.0	99.3	77.8	8.8	0.0	
05147H700	ENGR CO, ENGR BN	MOGAS	0.0	0.5	3.4	7.6	0.0	13.0	0.0	0.0	0.0	0.0	0.0	0.0	
		DIESEL	0.0	22.5	0.6	0.0	0.0	5.0	0.0	22.5	213.2	182.1	1.7	0.0	
05148H720	BRG CO, EN BN, M4T6/CL60	MOGAS	40.0	0.0	2.5	9.4	0.0	14.1	0.0	0.0	0.0	0.0	0.0	0.0	
		DIESEL	72.0	13.1	0.6	0.0	0.0	7.0	0.0	9.4	118.5	84.4	12.7	0.0	
06300H000	ARMD DIV ARTILLERY	MOGAS	0.0	0.0	87.3	98.8	0.0	118.8	0.0	0.0	0.0	0.0	0.3	0.0	
		DIESEL	0.0	0.0	36.1	0.0	0.0	25.0	0.0	212.8	1375.2	1694.5	62.1	30.5	
06302H000	HHB, DIV ARTY, ARMD/INF (MECH)	MOGAS	0.0	0.0	26.3	5.4	0.0	8.4	0.0	0.0	0.0	0.0	0.1	0.0	
		DIESEL	0.0	0.0	9.8	0.0	0.0	5.0	0.0	1.0	8.6	8.9	5.9	0.0	
06307H600	TGT ACQ BTRY, AIM DIV	MOGAS	0.0	0.0	11.6	5.4	0.0	4.5	0.0	0.0	0.0	0.0	0.0	0.0	
		DIESEL	0.0	0.0	12.0	0.0	0.0	0.0	0.0	0.0	0.0	0.0	5.1	0.0	
06365H000	FA BN, 155MM SP, ARMD/MEC	MOGAS	0.0	0.0	11.0	22.0	0.0	26.4	0.0	0.0	0.0	0.0	0.0	0.0	
		DIESEL	0.0	0.0	3.6	0.0	0.0	5.0	0.0	53.0	314.8	398.5	13.0	9.3	
06366H000	HHB, FA BN, 155MM SP	MOGAS	0.0	0.0	6.8	5.4	0.0	8.0	0.0	0.0	0.0	0.0	0.0	0.0	
		DIESEL	0.0	0.0	3.0	0.0	0.0	0.0	0.0	6.0	51.6	53.4	2.8	4.3	
06367H000	FA BTRY, FA BN, 155MM, SP	MOGAS	0.0	0.0	0.8	3.6	0.0	4.0	0.0	0.0	0.0	0.0	0.0	0.0	
		DIESEL	0.0	0.0	0.0	0.0	0.0	0.0	0.0	14.2	79.4	105.5	1.7	1.7	
06369H000	SVC BTRY, FA BN, 155MM SP	MOGAS	0.0	0.0	1.7	5.8	0.0	6.4	0.0	0.0	0.0	0.0	0.0	0.0	
		DIESEL	0.0	0.0	0.6	0.0	0.0	5.0	0.0	4.4	25.0	28.6	4.9	0.0	
06395H000	FA BN, 8IN SP, ARMD DIV	MOGAS	0.0	0.0	16.5	22.0	0.0	26.4	0.0	0.0	0.0	0.0	0.0	0.0	
		DIESEL	0.0	0.0	3.6	0.0	0.0	5.0	0.0	52.8	422.2	490.1	11.8	2.6	
06396H000	HHB, FA BN, 8 INCH SP	MOGAS	0.0	0.0	10.7	5.4	0.0	8.0	0.0	0.0	0.0	0.0	0.0	0.0	
		DIESEL	0.0	0.0	3.0	0.0	0.0	0.0	0.0	5.0	43.0	44.5	2.8	2.6	
06397H000	FA BTRY, FA BN 8 IN SP	MOGAS	0.0	0.0	1.4	3.6	0.0	4.0	0.0	0.0	0.0	0.0	0.0	0.0	
		DIESEL	0.0	0.0	0.0	0.0	0.0	0.0	0.0	13.8	105.8	130.5	1.4	0.0	
06399H000	SVC BTRY, FA BN, 8 IN SP	MOGAS	0.0	0.0	1.7	5.8	0.0	6.4	0.0	0.0	0.0	0.0	0.0	0.0	
		DIESEL	0.0	0.0	0.6	0.0	0.0	5.0	0.0	6.4	61.8	54.1	4.6	0.0	
08035H000	MED BN, AIM DIV	MOGAS	0.0	0.0	45.1	36.2	0.0	53.0	0.0	0.0	0.0	0.0	0.0	0.0	
		DIESEL	0.0	0.0	0.6	0.0	0.0	5.0	0.0	0.0	0.0	0.0	12.6	0.0	
08036H000	H&S CO, MED BN, AIM DIV	MOGAS	0.0	0.0	13.8	13.4	0.0	14.0	0.0	0.0	0.0	0.0	0.0	0.0	
		DIESEL	0.0	0.0	0.6	0.0	0.0	5.0	0.0	0.0	0.0	0.0	4.6	0.0	
08037H000	MED CO, MED BN, AIM DIV	MOGAS	0.0	0.0	10.4	7.6	0.0	13.0	0.0	0.0	0.0	0.0	0.0	0.0	
		DIESEL	0.0	0.0	0.0	0.0	0.0	0.0	0.0	0.0	0.0	0.0	2.7	0.0	
09557H510	MSL SPT CO, MAINT BN, ARM	MOGAS	0.0	0.0	15.6	13.4	0.0	4.0	0.0	0.0	0.0	0.0	0.0	0.0	
		DIESEL	0.0	0.0	28.8	0.0	0.0	5.0	0.0	0.0	0.0	0.0	7.1	0.0	
10007H000	SUP-SVC CO S&T BN INF DIV	MOGAS	0.0	0.0	6.4	5.0	0.0	8.1	0.0	0.0	0.0	0.0	0.0	0.0	
		DIESEL	0.0	70.0	0.0	0.0	77.6	9.3	0.0	0.0	0.0	0.0	2.4	0.0	
10007H020	S&S CO, S&T BN ARM/MECH DIV	MOGAS	0.0	0.0	3.8	4.0	0.0	18.8	0.0	0.0	0.0	0.0	0.0	0.0	
		DIESEL	0.0	70.0	30.0	0.0	77.6	9.3	0.0	0.0	0.0	0.0	3.9	0.0	
11035H000	SIGNAL BN, AIM DIV	MOGAS	0.0	0.0	150.6	34.0	0.0	14.9	0.0	0.0	0.0	0.0	0.2	0.0	
		DIESEL	0.0	0.0	11.3	0.0	0.0	20.0	0.0	0.0	0.0	0.0	17.4	0.0	
11036H000	HHC, SIG BN, AIM DIV	MOGAS	0.0	0.0	17.4	4.0	0.0	2.9	0.0	0.0	0.0	0.0	0.0	0.0	
		DIESEL	0.0	0.0	0.6	0.0	0.0	5.0	0.0	0.0	0.0	0.0	4.2	0.0	
11037H000	CMD OP CO, SIG BN, AIM DIV	MOGAS	0.0	0.0	48.1	11.2	0.0	4.0	0.0	0.0	0.0	0.0	0.1	0.0	
		DIESEL	0.0	0.0	6.6	0.0	0.0	5.0	0.0	0.0	0.0	0.0	5.4	0.0	
11038H000	FWD COMM CO, SIG BN, AIM DIV	MOGAS	0.0	0.0	49.6	9.4	0.0	4.0	0.0	0.0	0.0	0.0	0.1	0.0	
		DIESEL	0.0	0.0	0.6	0.0	0.0	5.0	0.0	0.0	0.0	0.0	3.5	0.0	
11039H000	SIG SPT OP CO, SIG BN	MOGAS	0.0	0.0	35.6	9.4	0.0	4.0	0.0	0.0	0.0	0.0	0.0	0.0	
		DIESEL	0.0	0.0	3.6	0.0	0.0	5.0	0.0	0.0	0.0	0.0	4.2	0.0	
12017H610	AG CO, SPT CMD, AMBL/AIM DIV	MOGAS	0.0	0.0	1.1	7.2	0.0	7.0	0.0	0.0	0.0	0.0	0.1	0.0	
		DIESEL	0.0	0.0	13.5	0.0	0.0	0.0	0.0	0.0	0.0	0.0	1.2	0.0	
14037H610	FIN CO, SPT CMD, AIM/AMBL DIV	MOGAS	0.0	0.0	2.4	0.0	0.0	0.0	0.0	0.0	0.0	0.0	0.0	0.0	
		DIESEL	0.0	0.0	0.6	0.0	0.0	0.0	0.0	0.0	0.0	0.0	0.5	0.0	
17000H020	AR DIV EQP/W M4T6/CL60 BR	MOGAS	40.0	4.5	678.4	576.9	3.0	646.2	0.0	0.0	0.0	0.0	2.1	0.0	
		DIESEL	72.0	279.1	280.4	0.0	160.6	198.8	0.0	552.1	4698.3	4675.3	291.3	30.8	
		JP4													14916.4
17004H000	HHC ARMD DIV	MOGAS	0.0	0.0	9.8	9.4	0.0	12.0	0.0	0.0	0.0	0.0	0.0	0.0	
		DIESEL	0.0	0.0	3.0	0.0	0.0	0.0	0.0	1.0	8.6	8.9	2.5	0.0	

Figure 10. Bulk POL Planning Factors by Type Unit— Bulk POL Table E (continued)

SUMMARY OF BULK FUEL USAGE BY EQUIPMENT CATEGORY
ARMD DIV E/W M4T6/CL60 BRG (SRC 17000H020)

SRC	UNIT NAME	FUEL TYPE	AB	CE	GN	HG	MH	SG	SV	TI	CC	SR	WV	OV	AV
17042H000	HHC ARMD DIV BDE	MOGAS	0.0	0.0	8.9	7.6	0.0	4.0	0.0	0.0	0.0	0.0	0.0	0.0	
		DIESEL	0.0	0.0	0.0	0.0	0.0	0.0	0.0	8.2	64.1	67.7	1.9	0.0	
17085H700	CBT AVN BN, ARMD/MECH DIV	MOGAS	0.0	0.0	60.1	58.0	0.0	41.7	0.0	0.0	0.0	0.0	0.1	0.0	
		DIESEL	0.0	32.0	22.3	0.0	19.6	20.0	0.0	0.0	0.0	0.0	26.4	0.0	
		JP4													12218.4
17086H700	HHC CBT AVN BN, AR/MECH DIV	MOGAS	0.0	0.0	6.2	9.8	0.0	12.4	0.0	0.0	0.0	0.0	0.0	0.0	
		DIESEL	0.0	0.0	0.6	0.0	0.0	0.0	0.0	0.0	0.0	0.0	3.4	0.0	
17087H000	AVN CO, ARMD/INF (MECH)	MOGAS	0.0	0.0	14.5	0.0	0.0	3.9	0.0	0.0	0.0	0.0	0.0	0.0	
		DIESEL	0.0	8.0	0.6	0.0	0.0	5.0	0.0	0.0	0.0	0.0	3.0	0.0	
		JP4													2760.8
17105H020	ARMD CAV SQDN AR/MECH DIV	MOGAS	0.0	0.0	20.9	37.6	0.0	28.4	0.0	0.0	0.0	0.0	0.4	0.0	
		DIESEL	0.0	8.0	0.6	0.0	1.3	12.0	0.0	110.2	1377.7	1043.5	15.1	0.0	
		JP4													2260.0
17106H000	HHT ARMD CAV SQDN	MOGAS	0.0	0.0	6.1	29.6	0.0	22.4	0.0	0.0	0.0	0.0	0.1	0.0	
		DIESEL	0.0	0.0	0.0	0.0	0.0	7.0	0.0	13.0	150.9	131.2	9.3	0.0	
17108H000	AIR CAV TRP ARMD CAV SQDN	MOGAS	0.0	0.0	14.9	8.0	0.0	3.0	0.0	0.0	0.0	0.0	0.2	0.0	
		DIESEL	0.0	8.0	0.6	0.0	1.3	5.0	0.0	0.0	0.0	0.0	4.4	0.0	
		JP4													2260.0
17307H700	AR CAV TP, AR CV SQDN	MOGAS	0.0	0.0	0.0	0.0	0.0	1.0	0.0	0.0	0.0	0.0	0.0	0.0	
		DIESEL	0.0	0.0	0.0	0.0	0.0	0.0	0.0	32.4	408.9	304.1	0.4	0.0	
17387H720	ATTACK HELICOPTER COMPANY	MOGAS	0.0	0.0	10.6	5.4	0.0	5.9	0.0	0.0	0.0	0.0	0.0	0.0	
		DIESEL	0.0	8.0	0.6	0.0	0.0	5.0	0.0	0.0	0.0	0.0	5.1	0.0	
		JP4													3391.8
19017H710	MP CO, AIM DIV	MOGAS	0.0	0.0	3.5	4.0	0.0	1.0	0.0	0.0	0.0	0.0	0.0	0.0	
		DIESEL	0.0	0.0	1.1	0.0	0.0	5.0	0.0	0.0	0.0	0.0	2.0	0.0	
29002H700	HHC, SPT COMD, AIM DIV	MOGAS	0.0	0.0	0.8	3.6	0.0	4.0	0.0	0.0	0.0	0.0	0.1	0.0	
		DIESEL	0.0	0.0	3.0	0.0	0.0	0.0	0.0	0.0	0.0	0.0	0.8	0.0	
29003H500	DIV MMC, AIM DIV	MOGAS	0.0	0.0	0.0	0.0	0.0	2.0	0.0	0.0	0.0	0.0	0.0	0.0	
		DIESEL	0.0	0.0	15.0	0.0	0.0	0.0	0.0	0.0	0.0	0.0	1.6	0.0	
29006H000	HHD, S&T BN, AIM DIV	MOGAS	0.0	0.0	0.8	10.8	0.0	7.0	0.0	0.0	0.0	0.0	0.0	0.0	
		DIESEL	0.0	0.0	0.0	0.0	0.0	0.0	0.0	0.0	0.0	0.0	0.8	0.0	
29021H000	SUPPORT COMMAND, ARMD DIV	MOGAS	0.0	0.0	141.8	216.8	3.0	250.2	0.0	0.0	0.0	0.0	0.2	0.0	
		DIESEL	0.0	98.0	190.9	0.0	131.2	61.8	0.0	8.0	147.0	102.2	94.4	0.0	
29035H000	MAINT BN, ARMD DIV	MOGAS	0.0	0.0	115.3	128.4	0.0	188.0	0.0	0.0	0.0	0.0	0.0	0.0	
		DIESEL	0.0	28.0	110.7	0.0	53.6	40.5	0.0	8.0	147.0	102.2	50.6	0.0	
29036H000	HQ & LT MAINT CO, MAINT B	MOGAS	0.0	0.0	9.7	7.6	0.0	4.0	0.0	0.0	0.0	0.0	0.0	0.0	
		DIESEL	0.0	0.0	23.3	0.0	19.6	0.0	0.0	0.0	0.0	0.0	7.8	0.0	
29037H000	FORWARD SPT CO, MAINT BN	MOGAS	0.0	0.0	25.6	21.4	0.0	45.5	0.0	0.0	0.0	0.0	0.0	0.0	
		DIESEL	0.0	7.0	12.8	0.0	8.5	7.0	0.0	2.0	36.8	25.5	9.0	0.0	
29038H000	HEAVY MAINT CO, MAINT BN	MOGAS	0.0	0.0	13.3	43.2	0.0	43.3	0.0	0.0	0.0	0.0	0.0	0.0	
		DIESEL	0.0	7.0	20.2	0.0	8.5	14.5	0.0	2.0	36.8	25.5	8.6	0.0	
29115H000	S&T BN, ARMD DIV	MOGAS	0.0	0.0	8.5	22.8	0.0	29.5	0.0	0.0	0.0	0.0	0.0	0.0	
		DIESEL	0.0	70.0	30.6	0.0	77.6	18.3	0.0	0.0	0.0	0.0	26.4	0.0	
29255H920	MAINT BN, ARMORED DIVISION	MOGAS	0.0	0.0	83.9	147.0	3.0	154.7	0.0	0.0	0.0	0.0	0.0	0.0	
		DIESEL	0.0	28.0	127.7	0.0	53.6	38.5	0.0	8.0	147.0	102.2	51.0	0.0	
29256H920	HH & LT MAINT CO, MAINT BN	MOGAS	0.0	0.0	8.2	12.5	3.0	5.0	0.0	0.0	0.0	0.0	0.0	0.0	
		DIESEL	0.0	0.0	21.6	0.0	19.6	0.0	0.0	0.0	0.0	0.0	8.2	0.0	
29257H920	FORWARD SPT CO, MAINT BN	MOGAS	0.0	0.0	16.0	24.5	0.0	34.7	0.0	0.0	0.0	0.0	0.0	0.0	
		DIESEL	0.0	7.0	18.2	0.0	8.5	7.0	0.0	2.0	36.8	25.5	8.9	0.0	
29258H920	HEAVY MAINT CO, MAINT BN	MOGAS	0.0	0.0	12.2	47.6	0.0	41.6	0.0	0.0	0.0	0.0	0.0	0.0	
		DIESEL	0.0	7.0	22.7	0.0	8.5	12.5	0.0	2.0	36.8	25.5	9.0	0.0	
44325H000	ADA BN, AIM DIVISION	MOGAS	0.0	0.0	64.6	25.6	0.0	30.5	0.0	0.0	0.0	0.0	0.1	0.0	
		DIESEL	0.0	0.0	7.1	0.0	0.0	5.0	0.0	74.8	411.4	611.2	19.6	0.0	
44326H000	HHB, ADA BN, C/V, SP	MOGAS	0.0	0.0	25.7	7.6	0.0	8.9	0.0	0.0	0.0	0.0	0.0	0.0	
		DIESEL	0.0	0.0	7.1	0.0	0.0	5.0	0.0	2.0	17.2	17.8	4.1	0.0	
44327H000	ADA BTRY, VUL(SP)STINGER	MOGAS	0.0	0.0	8.6	3.6	0.0	5.4	0.0	0.0	0.0	0.0	0.0	0.0	
		DIESEL	0.0	0.0	0.0	0.0	0.0	0.0	0.0	18.2	109.3	205.9	4.1	0.0	
44328H000	ADA BTRY, CHAP(SP)STINGER	MOGAS	0.0	0.0	10.8	5.4	0.0	5.4	0.0	0.0	0.0	0.0	0.0	0.0	
		DIESEL	0.0	0.0	0.0	0.0	0.0	0.0	0.0	18.2	87.8	90.8	3.6	0.0	
55087H000	TRANS MTR TRANS CO, ARMD	MOGAS	0.0	0.0	3.8	8.0	0.0	3.7	0.0	0.0	0.0	0.0	0.0	0.0	
		DIESEL	0.0	0.0	0.6	0.0	0.0	9.0	0.0	0.0	0.0	0.0	21.7	0.0	
55427H020	TRANS ACFT MNT CO AR/MECH DIV	MOGAS	0.0	0.0	6.4	16.2	0.0	4.4	0.0	0.0	0.0	0.0	0.0	0.0	
		DIESEL	0.0	8.0	20.1	0.0	18.3	5.0	0.0	0.0	0.0	0.0	5.3	0.0	
		JP4													236.0
57057H320	CBT SPT AVN CO	MOGAS	0.0	0.0	11.7	21.1	0.0	9.0	0.0	0.0	0.0	0.0	0.0	0.0	
		DIESEL	0.0	0.0	0.0	0.0	1.3	0.0	0.0	0.0	0.0	0.0	4.3	0.0	
		JP4													2438.0

SUMMARY OF BULK FUEL USAGE BY EQUIPMENT CATEGORY
ARMD CAV REGT E/W M60 (SRC 17051H040)

SRC	UNIT NAME	FUEL TYPE	AB	CE	GN	HG	MH	SG	SV	TI	CC	SR	WV	OV	AV
05108H600	ENGINEER COMPANY, ACR	MOGAS	0.0	0.5	4.2	9.4	0.0	24.0	0.0	0.0	0.0	0.0	0.0	0.0	
		DIESEL	0.0	27.5	0.6	0.0	8.5	7.0	0.0	35.5	381.8	309.5	5.6	0.0	
06037H000	FA BTRY, 155MM SP, ACS	MOGAS	0.0	0.0	3.0	3.6	0.0	4.0	0.0	0.0	0.0	0.0	0.0	0.0	
		DIESEL	0.0	0.0	0.0	0.0	0.0	0.0	0.0	14.2	79.4	105.5	2.4	2.8	
08147H000	MED CO, SEP AIM BDE, ACR	MOGAS	0.0	0.0	10.4	11.6	0.0	13.0	0.0	0.0	0.0	0.0	0.0	0.0	
		DIESEL	0.0	0.0	0.0	0.0	0.0	5.0	0.0	0.0	0.0	0.0	3.1	0.0	
12147H600	ADMIN CO, SEP BDE	MOGAS	0.0	0.0	2.2	3.6	0.0	3.0	0.0	0.0	0.0	0.0	0.0	0.0	
		DIESEL	0.0	0.0	13.5	0.0	0.0	0.0	0.0	0.0	0.0	0.0	1.2	0.0	
17027H010	TK CO AR CAV SQ EQP/W MBT	MOGAS	0.0	0.0	0.0	7.6	0.0	4.0	0.0	0.0	0.0	0.0	0.0	0.0	
		DIESEL	0.0	0.0	0.0	0.0	0.0	0.0	0.0	37.0	496.4	353.9	0.7	0.0	
17051H040	ARMD CAV REG EQ/W M60	MOGAS	0.0	0.5	112.9	264.8	0.0	191.7	5.0	0.0	0.0	0.0	1.3	0.0	
		DIESEL	0.0	79.5	52.7	0.0	50.7	55.0	0.0	550.3	6646.6	5175.4	99.6	8.4	
		JP4													7269.2

Figure 10. Bulk POL Planning Factors by Type Unit— Bulk POL Table E (continued)

SUMMARY OF BULK FUEL USAGE BY EQUIPMENT CATEGORY
ARMD CAV REGT E/W M60 (SRC 17051H040) — Cont'd

SRC	UNIT NAME	FUEL TYPE	AB	CE	GN	HG	MH	SG	SV	TI	CC	SR	WV	OV	AV
17052H000	HHT ARMD CAV REGT	MOGAS	0.0	0.0	12.4	17.8	0.0	11.4	0.0	0.0	0.0	0.0	0.1	0.0	
		DIESEL	0.0	8.0	0.6	0.0	9.8	5.0	0.0	10.2	81.3	85.5	6.8	0.0	
		JP4													1617.4
17055H040	ARMD CAV SQDN ACR (CARCAV)	MOGAS	0.0	0.0	7.4	40.8	0.0	30.4	0.0	0.0	0.0	0.0	0.3	0.0	
		DIESEL	0.0	0.0	0.0	0.0	0.0	7.0	0.0	163.2	1979.0	1533.5	15.4	2.8	
17056H010	HHT ARMD CAV SQ ACR	MOGAS	0.0	0.0	4.4	13.4	0.0	10.4	0.0	0.0	0.0	0.0	0.1	0.0	
		DIESEL	0.0	0.0	0.0	0.0	0.0	7.0	0.0	19.0	230.5	187.5	10.3	0.0	
17058H000	AIR CAV TRP ARMD CAV REGT	MOGAS	0.0	0.0	11.2	12.5	0.0	6.0	0.0	0.0	0.0	0.0	0.2	0.0	
		DIESEL	0.0	8.0	0.6	0.0	1.3	5.0	0.0	0.0	0.0	0.0	5.0	0.0	
		JP4													2260.0
17157H700	AR CAV TRP, AR CAV SQ, ACR	MOGAS	0.0	0.0	0.0	5.4	0.0	4.0	0.0	0.0	0.0	0.0	0.0	0.0	
		DIESEL	0.0	0.0	0.0	0.0	0.0	0.0	0.0	31.0	390.9	295.5	0.6	0.0	
17387H720	ATTACK HELICOPTER COMPANY	MOGAS	0.0	0.0	10.6	5.4	0.0	5.9	0.0	0.0	0.0	0.0	0.0	0.0	
		DIESEL	0.0	8.0	0.6	0.0	0.0	5.0	0.0	0.0	0.0	0.0	5.1	0.0	
		JP4													3391.8
29165H920	SUPPORT SQDN, ACR	MOGAS	0.0	0.0	52.2	97.2	0.0	53.0	5.0	0.0	0.0	0.0	0.1	0.0	
		DIESEL	0.0	28.0	50.4	0.0	31.1	12.0	0.0	15.0	246.4	179.9	30.7	0.0	
29166H920	HHT,SPT SQDN,ACR	MOGAS	0.0	0.0	3.6	7.6	0.0	3.5	0.0	0.0	0.0	0.0	0.1	0.0	
		DIESEL	0.0	0.0	19.5	0.0	0.0	0.0	0.0	0.0	0.0	0.0	2.4	0.0	
29167H900	S & T TRP SPT SQDN, ACR	MOGAS	0.0	0.0	8.7	9.4	0.0	4.4	5.0	0.0	0.0	0.0	0.0	0.0	
		DIESEL	0.0	21.0	0.0	0.0	21.3	0.0	0.0	0.0	0.0	0.0	11.4	0.0	
29168H900	MAINT TRP SPT SQDN ACR	MOGAS	0.0	0.0	27.2	65.0	0.0	29.1	0.0	0.0	0.0	0.0	0.0	0.0	
		DIESEL	0.0	7.0	17.4	0.0	9.8	7.0	0.0	15.0	246.4	179.9	12.5	0.0	

SUMMARY OF BULK FUEL USAGE BY EQUIPMENT CATEGORY
ARMD CAV REGT E/W M113/M60 (SRC 17051J210)

SRC	UNIT NAME	FUEL TYPE	AB	CE	GN	HG	MH	SG	SV	TI	CC	SR	WV	OV	AV
05108H600	ENGINEER COMPANY, ACR	MOGAS	0.0	0.5	4.2	9.4	0.0	24.0	0.0	0.0	0.0	0.0	0.0	0.0	
		DIESEL	0.0	27.5	0.6	0.0	8.5	7.0	0.0	35.5	381.8	309.5	5.6	0.0	
06037H000	FA BTRY, 155MM SP, ACS	MOGAS	0.0	0.0	3.0	3.6	0.0	4.0	0.0	0.0	0.0	0.0	0.0	0.0	
		DIESEL	0.0	0.0	0.0	0.0	0.0	0.0	0.0	14.2	79.4	105.5	2.4	2.8	
08117J300	MEDICAL COMPANY, ACR	MOGAS	0.0	0.0	10.4	9.4	0.0	13.0	0.0	0.0	0.0	0.0	0.0	0.0	
		DIESEL	0.0	0.0	1.7	0.0	0.0	5.0	0.0	8.0	68.8	71.2	3.5	0.0	
12207J300	AG CO/TRP, SEP BDE/REGT	MOGAS	0.0	0.0	0.0	5.4	0.0	3.0	0.0	0.0	0.0	0.0	0.0	0.0	
		DIESEL	0.0	0.0	23.4	0.0	0.0	0.0	0.0	0.0	0.0	0.0	1.1	0.0	
12207J302	AUG ARMORED CAV REGT 5200	MOGAS	0.0	0.0	0.0	0.0	0.0	0.0	0.0	0.0	0.0	0.0	0.0	0.0	
		DIESEL	0.0	0.0	0.0	0.0	0.0	0.0	0.0	0.0	0.0	0.0	0.0	0.0	
17027J310	TANK COMPANY, ACS (M60)	MOGAS	0.0	0.0	0.0	9.4	0.0	1.0	0.0	0.0	0.0	0.0	0.0	0.0	
		DIESEL	0.0	0.0	0.0	0.0	0.0	0.0	0.0	31.0	416.8	297.5	0.4	0.0	
17051J310	ARMD CAV REGT E/W M113/M6	MOGAS	0.0	0.5	92.5	260.9	0.0	247.6	0.0	0.0	0.0	0.0	0.7	0.0	
		DIESEL	0.0	71.5	90.5	0.0	46.8	80.0	0.0	624.1	7107.7	5838.8	98.9	8.4	
		JP4													5420.2
17052J310	HHT, ACR	MOGAS	0.0	0.0	9.7	5.4	0.0	9.4	0.0	0.0	0.0	0.0	0.1	0.0	
		DIESEL	0.0	0.0	0.6	0.0	0.0	0.0	0.0	10.0	105.6	96.7	4.5	0.0	
17055J310	ARMD CAV SQDN ACR M113/M6	MOGAS	0.0	0.0	8.0	41.6	0.0	35.3	0.0	0.0	0.0	0.0	0.1	0.0	
		DIESEL	0.0	0.0	0.6	0.0	0.0	17.0	0.0	185.2	2101.7	1727.1	15.9	2.8	
17056J310	HHT, ARMD CAV SWDN (XXX-86)	MOGAS	0.0	0.0	5.0	16.6	0.0	27.3	0.0	0.0	0.0	0.0	0.1	0.0	
		DIESEL	0.0	0.0	0.6	0.0	0.0	17.0	0.0	32.0	380.5	313.0	11.3	0.0	
17057J310	ARMD CAV TRP, ACS 113/M60	MOGAS	0.0	0.0	0.0	4.0	0.0	1.0	0.0	0.0	0.0	0.0	0.0	0.0	
		DIESEL	0.0	0.0	0.0	0.0	0.0	0.0	0.0	36.0	408.3	337.0	0.5	0.0	
17059H700	AVN SPT TRP ACR	MOGAS	0.0	0.0	10.6	11.1	0.0	7.4	0.0	0.0	0.0	0.0	0.0	0.0	
		DIESEL	0.0	8.0	0.6	0.0	0.0	5.0	0.0	0.0	0.0	0.0	4.0	0.0	
		JP4													2028.4
17387H720	ATTACK HELICOPTER COMPANY	MOGAS	0.0	0.0	10.6	5.4	0.0	5.9	0.0	0.0	0.0	0.0	0.0	0.0	
		DIESEL	0.0	8.0	0.6	0.0	0.0	5.0	0.0	0.0	0.0	0.0	5.1	0.0	
		JP4													3391.8
42077J310	S&T TRP SPT SQDN,ACR	MOGAS	0.0	0.0	3.9	9.4	0.0	6.9	0.0	0.0	0.0	0.0	0.0	0.0	
		DIESEL	0.0	21.0	12.0	0.0	21.3	0.0	0.0	0.0	0.0	0.0	10.4	0.0	
43087J310	MAINT TRP, SPT-M60 & M113	MOGAS	0.0	0.0	13.3	73.0	0.0	66.9	0.0	0.0	0.0	0.0	0.1	0.0	
		DIESEL	0.0	7.0	30.0	0.0	17.0	7.0	0.0	15.0	246.4	179.9	14.1	0.0	
63065J310	SPT SQDN ACR (M60/M113)	MOGAS	0.0	0.0	33.5	104.8	0.0	94.8	0.0	0.0	0.0	0.0	0.1	0.0	
		DIESEL	0.0	28.0	86.5	0.0	38.3	12.0	0.0	23.0	315.2	251.1	31.9	0.0	
63066J300	HHT,SPT SQDN,ACR	MOGAS	0.0	0.0	5.9	7.6	0.0	5.0	0.0	0.0	0.0	0.0	0.1	0.0	
		DIESEL	0.0	0.0	19.5	0.0	0.0	0.0	0.0	0.0	0.0	0.0	2.6	0.0	

SUMMARY OF BULK FUEL USAGE BY EQUIPMENT CATEGORY
ARMD CAV REGT E/W M1/M3 (SRC 17051J320)

SRC	UNIT NAME	FUEL TYPE	AB	CE	GN	HG	MH	SG	SV	TI	CC	SR	WV	OV	AV
05108J300	ENGINEER COMPANY, ACR	MOGAS	0.0	0.5	4.2	9.4	0.0	24.0	0.0	0.0	0.0	0.0	0.0	0.0	
		DIESEL	0.0	27.5	0.6	0.0	8.5	7.0	0.0	35.5	381.8	309.5	5.2	0.0	
06037H000	FA BTRY, 155MM SP, ACS	MOGAS	0.0	0.0	3.0	3.6	0.0	4.0	0.0	0.0	0.0	0.0	0.0	0.0	
		DIESEL	0.0	0.0	0.0	0.0	0.0	0.0	0.0	14.2	79.4	105.5	2.4	2.8	
08177J300	MEDICAL COMPANY, ACR	MOGAS	0.0	0.0	10.4	9.4	0.0	13.0	0.0	0.0	0.0	0.0	0.0	0.0	
		DIESEL	0.0	0.0	1.7	0.0	0.0	5.0	0.0	8.0	68.8	71.2	3.5	0.0	
12207J300	AG CO/TRP, SEP BDE/REGT	MOGAS	0.0	0.0	0.0	5.4	0.0	3.0	0.0	0.0	0.0	0.0	0.0	0.0	
		DIESEL	0.0	0.0	23.4	0.0	0.0	0.0	0.0	0.0	0.0	0.0	1.1	0.0	
12207J302	AUG ARMORED CAV REGT 5200	MOGAS	0.0	0.0	0.0	0.0	0.0	0.0	0.0	0.0	0.0	0.0	0.0	0.0	
		DIESEL	0.0	0.0	0.0	0.0	0.0	0.0	0.0	0.0	0.0	0.0	0.0	0.0	
17027J320	TANK COMPANY, ACS (M1)	MOGAS	0.0	0.0	0.0	4.0	0.0	1.0	0.0	0.0	0.0	0.0	0.0	0.0	
		DIESEL	0.0	0.0	0.0	0.0	0.0	0.0	0.0	154.2	837.8	659.4	0.4	0.0	

Figure 10. Bulk POL Planning Factors by Type Unit—Bulk POL Table E (continued)

SUMMARY OF BULK FUEL USAGE BY EQUIPMENT CATEGORY
ARMD CAV REGT E/W M1/M3 (SRC 17051J320) — Cont'd

SRC	UNIT NAME	FUEL TYPE	AB	CE	GN	HG	MH	SG	SV	TI	CC	SR	WV	OV	AV
17051J320	ARMD CAV REGT E/W M1/M3	MOGAS	0.0	0.5	93.3	254.3	0.0	242.9	0.0	0.0	0.0	0.0	0.5	0.0	
		DIESEL	0.0	71.5	101.6	0.0	46.8	80.0	0.0	1743.1	11744.5	8898.1	102.4	8.4	
		JP4													5420.2
17052J310	HHT, ACR	MOGAS	0.0	0.0	9.7	5.4	0.0	9.4	0.0	0.0	0.0	0.0	0.1	0.0	
		DIESEL	0.0	0.0	0.6	0.0	0.0	0.0	0.0	10.0	105.6	96.7	4.5	0.0	
17055J320	ARMD CAV SQDN ACR M1/M3	MOGAS	0.0	0.0	6.9	43.4	0.0	35.3	0.0	0.0	0.0	0.0	0.1	0.0	
		DIESEL	0.0	0.0	0.6	0.0	0.0	17.0	0.0	558.2	3647.3	2746.9	15.8	2.8	
17056J320	HHT, ARMD CAV SQDN	MOGAS	0.0	0.0	3.9	23.8	0.0	27.3	0.0	0.0	0.0	0.0	0.1	0.0	
		DIESEL	0.0	0.0	0.6	0.0	0.0	17.0	0.0	29.8	354.9	283.7	11.6	0.0	
17057J320	ARMD CAV TRP, ACS M1/M3	MOGAS	0.0	0.0	0.0	4.0	0.0	1.0	0.0	0.0	0.0	0.0	0.0	0.0	
		DIESEL	0.0	0.0	0.0	0.0	0.0	0.0	0.0	120.0	791.8	566.1	0.4	0.0	
17059H700	AVN SPT TRP ACR	MOGAS	0.0	0.0	10.6	11.1	0.0	7.4	0.0	0.0	0.0	0.0	0.0	0.0	
		DIESEL	0.0	8.0	0.6	0.0	0.0	5.0	0.0	0.0	0.0	0.0	4.0	0.0	
		JP4													2028.4
17387H720	ATTACK HELICOPTER COMPANY	MOGAS	0.0	0.0	10.6	5.4	0.0	5.9	0.0	0.0	0.0	0.0	0.0	0.0	
		DIESEL	0.0	8.0	0.6	0.0	0.0	5.0	0.0	0.0	0.0	0.0	5.1	0.0	
		JP4													3391.8
42077J320	S&T TRP SPT SQDN,ACR	MOGAS	0.0	0.0	3.9	9.4	0.0	6.9	0.0	0.0	0.0	0.0	0.0	0.0	
		DIESEL	0.0	21.0	12.0	0.0	21.3	0.0	0.0	0.0	0.0	0.0	12.9	0.0	
43087J320	MAINT TRP SPT M1, M3, FSE	MOGAS	0.0	0.0	17.3	61.0	0.0	62.3	0.0	0.0	0.0	0.0	0.0	0.0	
		DIESEL	0.0	7.0	41.0	0.0	17.0	7.0	0.0	15.0	246.4	179.9	15.6	0.0	
63065J320	SPT SQDN ACR (M1/M3)	MOGAS	0.0	0.0	37.5	92.8	0.0	90.2	0.0	0.0	0.0	0.0	0.1	0.0	
		DIESEL	0.0	28.0	97.6	0.0	38.3	12.0	0.0	23.0	315.2	251.1	35.9	0.0	
63066J300	HHT,SPT SQDN,ACR	MOGAS	0.0	0.0	5.9	7 6	0.0	5.0	0.0	0.0	0.0	0.0	0.1	0.0	
		DIESEL	0.0	0.0	19.5	0.0	0.0	0.0	0.0	0.0	0.0	0.0	2.6	0.0	

SUMMARY OF BULK FUEL USAGE BY EQUIPMENT CATEGORY
ARMD CAV REGT (SRC 17051J330)

SRC	UNIT NAME	FUEL TYPE	AB	CE	GN	HG	MH	SG	SV	TI	CC	SR	WV	OV	AV
01257J430	CBT SPT AVN CO (ACR) UH-6	MOGAS	0.0	0.0	0.0	0.0	0.0	0.0	0.0	0.0	0.0	0.0	0.0	0.0	
		DIESEL	0.0	0.0	0.0	0.0	0.0	0.0	0.0	0.0	0.0	0.0	0.4	0.0	
		JP4													2130.0
03207J300	NBC CO - ACR (XXX-86)	MOGAS	0.0	0.0	0.8	4.0	0.0	16.7	.0.0	0.0	0.0	0.0	0.0	0.0	
		DIESEL	0.0	0.0	0.6	0.0	0.0	5.0	0.0	9.0	77.4	80.1	2.8	0.0	
05108J300	ENGINEER COMPANY, ACR	MOGAS	0.0	0.5	4.2	9.4	0.0	24.0	0.0	0.0	0.0	0.0	0.0	0.0	
		DIESEL	0.0	27.5	0.6	0.0	8.5	7.0	0.0	35.5	381.8	309.5	5.8	0.0	
06565J300	FA BN 155 SP ACR	MOGAS	0.0	0.0	19.9	23.8	0.0	26.4	0.0	0.0	0.0	0.0	0.0	0.0	
		DIESEL	0.0	0.0	3.6	0.0	0.0	5.0	0.0	72.4	432.5	545.0	15.3	11.0	
06566J300	HHB,FA BN 155SP (ACR)	MOGAS	0.0	0.0	12.8	5.4	0.0	8.0	0.0	0.0	0.0	0.0	0.0	0.0	
		DIESEL	0.0	0.0	3.0	0.0	0.0	0.0	0.0	7.0	60.2	62.3	2.8	4.3	
06567J300	FA BTRY,155SP (ACR)	MOGAS	0.0	0.0	1.1	3.6	0.0	4.0	0.0	0.0	0.0	0.0	0.0	0.0	
		DIESEL	0.0	0.0	0.0	0.0	0.0	0.0	0.0	19.6	111.6	146.6	2.3	2.2	
06569J300	SVC BTRY, 155SP (ACR)	MOGAS	0.0	0.0	3.8	7.6	0.0	6.4	0.0	0.0	0.0	0.0	0.0	0.0	
		DIESEL	0.0	0.0	0.6	0.0	0.0	5.0	0.0	6.6	37.5	42.9	5.5	0.0	
08177J300	MEDICAL COMPANY (ACR)	MOGAS	0.0	0.0	10.4	9.4	0.0	13.0	0.0	0.0	0.0	0.0	0.0	0.0	
		DIESEL	0.0	0.0	1.7	0.0	0.0	5.0	0.0	8.0	68.8	71.2	3.5	0.0	
12207J300	AG CO/TRP, SEP BDE/REGT	MOGAS	0.0	0.0	0.0	5.4	0.0	3.0	0.0	0.0	0.0	0.0	0.0	0.0	
		DIESEL	0.0	0.0	23.4	0.0	0.0	0.0	0.0	0.0	0.0	0.0	1.1	0.0	
12207J302	AUG ARMORED CAV REGT 5200	MOGAS	0.0	0.0	0.0	0.0	0.0	0.0	0.0	0.0	0.0	0.0	0.0	0.0	
		DIESEL	0.0	0.0	0.0	0.0	0.0	0.0	0.0	0.0	0.0	0.0	0.0	0.0	
17027J320	TANK COMPANY, ACS (MI)	MOGAS	0.0	0.0	0.0	4.0	0.0	1.0	0.0	0.0	0.0	0.0	0.0	0.0	
		DIESEL	0.0	0.0	0.0	0.0	0.0	0.0	0.0	154.2	837.8	659.4	0.4	0.0	
17051J330	ARMD CAV REGT	MOGAS	0.0	0.5	171.0	302.6	0.0	276.1	0.0	0.0	0.0	0.0	0.5	0.0	
		DIESEL	0.0	63.5	99.6	0.0	46.8	90.0	0.0	1806.1	12182.6	9453.0	130.0	11.2	
		JP4													7116.1
17052J320	HHT, ACR	MOGAS	0.0	0.0	8.9	3.6	0.0	9.4	0.0	0.0	0.0	0.0	0.1	0.0	
		DIESEL	0.0	0.0	0.0	0.0	0.0	0.0	0.0	9.8	115.8	87.2	3.3	0.0	
17055J330	ARMD CAV SQDN ACR	MOGAS	0.0	0.0	5.6	39.8	0.0	25.9	0.0	0.0	0.0	0.0	0.0	0.0	
		DIESEL	0.0	0.0	0.6	0.0	0.0	17.0	0.0	542.0	3550.7	2623.6	12.4	0.0	
17056J330	HHT, ARMD CAV SQDN	MOGAS	0.0	0.0	5.6	23.8	0.0	21.9	0.0	0.0	0.0	0.0	0.0	0.0	
		DIESEL	0.0	0.0	0.6	0.0	0.0	17.0	0.0	27.8	337.7	265.9	10.8	0.0	
17057J320	ARMD CAV TRP, ACS M1/M3	MOGAS	0.0	0.0	0.0	4.0	0.0	1.0	0.0	0.0	0.0	0.0	0.0	0.0	
		DIESEL	0.0	0.0	0.0	0.0	0.0	0.0	0.0	120.0	791.8	566.1	0.4	0.0	
17187J210	ATK HEL CO	MOGAS	0.0	0.0	0.0	0.0	0.0	0.0	0.0	0.0	0.0	0.0	0.0	0.0	
		DIESEL	0.0	0.0	0.0	0.0	0.0	0.0	0.0	0.0	0.0	0.0	0.2	0.0	
		JP4													1020.6
17208J210	AIR CAV TRP, CAV SQDN	MOGAS	0.0	0.0	0.0	0.0	0.0	0.0	0.0	0.0	0.0	0.0	0.0	0.0	
		DIESEL	0.0	0.0	0.0	0.0	0.0	0.0	0.0	0.0	0.0	0.0	0.2	0.0	
		JP4													731.4
17265J310	CBT AVN SQDN, ACR	MOGAS	0.0	0.0	41.3	32.2	0.0	20.0	0.0	0.0	0.0	0.0	0.1	0.0	
		DIESEL	0.0	8.0	0.0	0.0	0.0	0.0	0.0	0.0	0.0	0.0	19.5	0.0	
		JP4													7116.1
17266J310	HQ & HQ TRP (XXX-86)	MOGAS	0.0	0.0	41.3	32.2	0.0	20.0	0.0	0.0	0.0	0.0	0.1	0.0	
		DIESEL	0.0	8.0	0.0	0.0	0.0	0.0	0.0	0.0	0.0	0.0	17.9	0.0	
		JP4													750.7
34114J300	MI CO (CEWI) ACR	MOGAS	0.0	0.0	29.0	8.0	0.0	7.1	0.0	0.0	0.0	0.0	0.2	0.0	
		DIESEL	0.0	0.0	0.6	0.0	0.0	5.0	0.0	11.2	89.9	94.4	4.1	0.2	
42077J320	S&T TRP SPT SQDN, ACR	MOGAS	0.0	0.0	3.9	9.4	0.0	6.9	0.0	0.0	0.0	0.0	0.0	0.0	
		DIESEL	0.0	21.0	12.0	0.0	21.3	0.0	0.0	0.0	0.0	0.0	12.9	0.0	
43087J330	MAINT TRP CORPS 86, M1/M3	MOGAS	0.0	0.0	19.9	61.0	0.0	62.3	0.0	0.0	0.0	0.0	0.0	0.0	
		DIESEL	0.0	7.0	36.1	0.0	17.0	7.0	0.0	15.0	246.4	179.9	16.9	0.0	
44468J310	ADA BTRY VUL/STINGER, ACR	MOGAS	0.0	0.0	10.0	9.4	0.0	4.4	0.0	0.0	0.0	0.0	0.0	0.0	
		DIESEL	0.0	0.0	0.0	0.0	0.0	5.0	0.0	19.2	117.9	214.8	4.9	0.0	
63065J330	SPT SQDN ACR (M1/M3)	MOGAS	0.0	0.0	40.1	92.8	0.0	90.2	0.0	0.0	0.0	0.0	0.1	0.0	
		DIESEL	0.0	28.0	92.6	0.0	38.3	12.0	0.0	23.0	315.2	251.1	37.1	0.0	
63066J300	HHT, SPT SQDN, ACR	MOGAS	0.0	0.0	5.9	7.6	0.0	5.0	0.0	0.0	0.0	0.0	0.1	0.0	
		DIESEL	0.0	0.0	19.5	0.0	0.0	0.0	0.0	0.0	0.0	0.0	2.6	0.0	

Figure 10. *Bulk POL Planning Factors by Type Unit—Bulk POL Table E* (continued)

SUMMARY OF BULK FUEL USAGE BY EQUIPMENT CATEGORY
SEP ARMD BDE WM4T6 1005 ADP (SRC 17100H020)

SRC	UNIT NAME	FUEL TYPE	AB	CE	GN	HG	MH	SG	SV	TI	CC	SR	WV	OV	AV
05127H020	ENGR CO, SEP ARMD BDE,M4T	MOGAS	0.0	0.5	4.2	11.2	0.0	24.0	0.0	0.0	0.0	0.0	0.0	0.0	
		DIESEL	43.2	37.1	0.6	0.0	8.5	7.0	0.0	35.5	381.8	309.5	10.8	0.0	
06367H000	FA BTRY, FA BN, 155MM, SP	MOGAS	0.0	0.0	0.8	3.6	0.0	4.0	0.0	0.0	0.0	0.0	0.0	0.0	
		DIESEL	0.0	0.0	0.0	0.0	0.0	0.0	0.0	14.2	79.4	105.5	1.7	1.7	
06369H000	SVC BTRY, FA BN, 155MM SP	MOGAS	0.0	0.0	1.7	5.8	0.0	6.4	0.0	0.0	0.0	0.0	0.0	0.0	
		DIESEL	0.0	0.0	0.6	0.0	0.0	5.0	0.0	4.4	25.0	28.6	4.9	0.0	
06375H000	FA BN, 155 SP, SEP AR BDE	MOGAS	0.0	0.0	23.8	22.0	0.0	26.4	0.0	0.0	0.0	0.0	0.0	0.0	
		DIESEL	0.0	0.0	3.6	0.0	0.0	5.0	0.0	53.0	314.8	398.5	13.7	7.9	
06376H000	HHB, FA BN, 155MM SP	MOGAS	0.0	0.0	19.6	5.4	0.0	8.0	0.0	0.0	0.0	0.0	0.0	0.0	
		DIESEL	0.0	0.0	3.0	0.0	0.0	0.0	0.0	6.0	51.6	53.4	3.6	2.8	
08147H000	MED CO, SEP AIM BDE, ACR	MOGAS	0.0	0.0	10.4	11.6	0.0	13.0	0.0	0.0	0.0	0.0	0.0	0.0	
		DIESEL	0.0	0.0	0.0	0.0	0.0	5.0	0.0	0.0	0.0	0.0	3.1	0.0	
12147H600	ADMIN CO, SEP BDE	MOGAS	0.0	0.0	2.2	3.6	0.0	3.0	0.0	0.0	0.0	0.0	0.0	0.0	
		DIESEL	0.0	0.0	13.5	0.0	0.0	0.0	0.0	0.0	0.0	0.0	1.2	0.0	
17100H020	SEP ARMD BDE WM4T6,1005AD	MOGAS	0.0	0.5	134.6	126.5	0.0	138.8	0.2	0.0	0.0	0.0	0.0	0.0	
		DIESEL	43.2	72.1	79.3	0.0	40.9	29.0	0.0	140.1	1283.8	1185.5	60.0	8.1	
		JP4													889.4
17102H000	HHC SEPARATE ARMORED BDE	MOGAS	0.0	0.0	37.5	11.2	0.0	9.4	0.0	0.0	0.0	0.0	0.1	0.0	
		DIESEL	0.0	0.0	3.6	0.0	0.0	0.0	0.0	6.0	51.6	53.4	6.0	0.0	
		JP4													451.4
17307H700	AR CAV TP, AR CV SQ, AM DIV	MOGAS	0.0	0.0	0.0	0.0	0.0	1.0	0.0	0.0	0.0	0.0	0.0	0.0	
		DIESEL	0.0	0.0	0.0	0.0	0.0	0.0	0.0	32.4	408.9	304.1	0.4	0.0	
29075H000	SPT BN, SEP ARMD BDE	MOGAS	0.0	0.0	34.9	69.1	0.0	70.8	0.2	0.0	0.0	0.0	0.1	0.0	
		DIESEL	0.0	35.0	71.6	0.0	32.4	12.0	0.0	2.0	36.8	25.5	24.7	0.0	
29076H000	HHD, SPT BN, SEP AIM BDE	MOGAS	0.0	0.0	3.9	0.0	0.0	1.0	0.0	0.0	0.0	0.0	0.1	0.0	
		DIESEL	0.0	0.0	0.6	0.0	0.0	0.0	0.0	0.0	0.0	0.0	1.1	0.0	
29077H000	S&T CO, SPT BN, SEP AIM BDE	MOGAS	0.0	0.0	3.4	7.6	0.0	13.6	0.0	0.0	0.0	0.0	0.0	0.0	
		DIESEL	0.0	28.0	12.0	0.0	22.6	0.0	0.0	0.0	0.0	0.0	9.5	0.0	
29079H010	MNT CO,SPT BN,SEP ARMD BDE	MOGAS	0.0	0.0	18.1	39.2	0.0	36.3	0.2	0.0	0.0	0.0	0.0	0.0	
		DIESEL	0.0	7.0	26.6	0.0	9.8	7.0	0.0	2.0	36.8	25.5	8.3	0.0	
29176H910	HHC,SPT BN,SEP AIM/ABN/ID(L)	MOGAS	0.0	0.0	0.8	7.1	0.0	5.0	0.0	0.0	0.0	0.0	0.0	0.0	
		DIESEL	0.0	0.0	19.5	0.0	0.0	0.0	0.0	0.0	0.0	0.0	2.4	0.0	
34114H120	MI CO (CEWI)ACR/SEP HV BDE	MOGAS	0.0	0.0	34.1	13.0	0.0	7.1	0.0	0.0	0.0	0.0	0.0	0.0	
		DIESEL	0.0	0.0	0.0	0.0	0.0	5.0	0.0	11.2	89.9	94.4	4.1	0.2	
		JP4													438.0

SUMMARY OF BULK FUEL USAGE BY EQUIPMENT CATEGORY
AIR CAV CBT BDE (SRC 17200H500)

SRC	UNIT NAME	FUEL TYPE	AB	CE	GN	HG	MH	SG	SV	TI	CC	SR	WV	OV	AV
11059H500	SIGNAL CO, ACCB	MOGAS	0.0	0.0	26.1	0.0	0.0	2.0	0.0	0.0	0.0	0.0	0.0	0.0	
		DIESEL	0.0	0.0	0.6	0.0	0.0	5.0	0.0	0.0	0.0	0.0	2.0	0.0	
17200H500	AIR CAV CBT BDE	MOGAS	0.0	25.0	253.6	182.3	0.0	168.6	12.0	0.0	0.0	0.0	2.0	2.6	
		DIESEL	0.0	119.6	92.8	0.0	132.7	62.0	0.0	0.0	0.0	0.0	90.0	0.0	
		JP4													41448.8
17202H500	HHT AIR CAB CBT BDE	MOGAS	0.0	0.0	6.4	3.6	0.0	6.4	0.0	0.0	0.0	0.0	0.0	0.0	
		DIESEL	0.0	0.0	1.1	0.0	0.0	0.0	0.0	0.0	0.0	0.0	4.0	0.0	
		JP4													689.6
17205H220	AIR CAV SQDN ACCB	MOGAS	0.0	0.0	58.5	51.8	0.0	24.6	0.0	0.0	0.0	0.0	1.0	0.0	
		DIESEL	0.0	24.0	1.7	0.0	7.8	15.0	0.0	0.0	0.0	0.0	20.0	0.0	
		JP4													7216.0
17206H220	HHT AIR CAV SQDN ACCB	MOGAS	0.0	0.0	13.9	27.8	0.0	18.9	0.0	0.0	0.0	0.0	0.0	0.0	
		DIESEL	0.0	0.0	0.0	0.0	0.0	0.0	0.0	0.0	0.0	0.0	5.0	0.0	
		JP4													436.0
17208H220	AIR CAV TRP ACS ACCB	MOGAS	0.0	0.0	14.9	8.0	0.0	1.9	0.0	0.0	0.0	0.0	0.0	0.0	
		DIESEL	0.0	8.0	0.6	0.0	2.6	5.0	0.0	0.0	0.0	0.0	5.0	0.0	
		JP4													2260.0
17385H500	ATTACK HELICOPTER BN	MOGAS	0.0	0.0	58.6	25.6	0.0	29.3	0.0	0.0	0.0	0.0	0.0	0.0	
		DIESEL	0.0	24.0	1.7	0.0	0.0	15.0	0.0	0.0	0.0	0.0	16.0	0.0	
		JP4													10599.4
17386H500	HHC ATK HEL BN	MOGAS	0.0	0.0	11.5	25.6	0.0	19.0	0.0	0.0	0.0	0.0	0.0	0.0	
		DIESEL	0.0	0.0	0.0	0.0	0.0	0.0	0.0	0.0	0.0	0.0	4.0	0.0	
		JP4													424.0
17387H710	ATK HEL CO, ATK HEL BN	MOGAS	0.0	0.0	15.7	0.0	0.0	3.4	0.0	0.0	0.0	0.0	0.0	0.0	
		DIESEL	0.0	8.0	0.6	0.0	0.0	5.0	0.0	0.0	0.0	0.0	4.0	0.0	
		JP4													3391.8
29155H500	SUPPORT BATTALION, ACCB	MOGAS	0.0	25.0	45.4	75.8	0.0	76.8	12.0	0.0	0.0	0.0	1.0	2.6	
		DIESEL	0.0	47.6	85.9	0.0	124.9	12.0	0.0	0.0	0.0	0.0	33.0	0.0	
		JP4													12344.4
29156H500	HQ-HQ CO,SPT BN ACCB	MOGAS	0.0	0.0	1.6	9.4	0.0	9.0	0.0	0.0	0.0	0.0	0.0	0.0	
		DIESEL	0.0	0.0	18.0	0.0	0.0	0.0	0.0	0.0	0.0	0.0	3.0	0.0	
29157H500	SUP-TRANS CO, SPT BN, ACC	MOGAS	0.0	7.0	5.0	15.2	0.0	27.9	0.0	0.0	0.0	0.0	0.0	0.0	
		DIESEL	0.0	14.6	13.5	0.0	98.1	0.0	0.0	0.0	0.0	0.0	17.0	0.0	
29158H500	MAINT CO, SPT BN, ACCB	MOGAS	0.0	0.0	6.0	23.6	0.0	18.7	0.0	0.0	0.0	0.0	0.0	0.0	
		DIESEL	0.0	7.0	25.1	0.0	9.8	7.0	0.0	0.0	0.0	0.0	5.0	0.0	
55167H700	TRANS HEL CO (MED)	MOGAS	0.0	6.0	14.3	12.2	0.0	12.3	6.0	0.0	0.0	0.0	1.0	0.0	
		DIESEL	0.0	6.0	1.7	0.0	8.5	0.0	0.0	0.0	0.0	0.0	3.0	0.0	
		JP4													12036.4
55417H500	TRANS ACFT MAINT CO	MOGAS	0.0	12.0	18.5	15.3	0.0	8.9	6.0	0.0	0.0	0.0	0.0	2.6	
		DIESEL	0.0	20.0	27.6	0.0	8.5	5.0	0.0	0.0	0.0	0.0	6.0	0.0	
		JP4													308.0

Figure 10. Bulk POL Planning Factors by Type Unit— Bulk POL Table E (continued)

SUMMARY OF BULK FUEL USAGE BY EQUIPMENT CATEGORY
AIRBORNE SF GROUP (SRC 31101H000)

SRC	UNIT NAME	FUEL TYPE	AB	CE	GN	HG	MH	SG	SV	TI	CC	SR	WV	OV	AV
11257H400	SIG CO, ABN SF GROUP	MOGAS	0.0	0.0	2.4	0.0	0.0	0.0	0.0	0.0	0.0	0.0	0.0	0.0	
		DIESEL	0.0	0.0	6.1	0.0	0.0	24.0	0.0	0.0	0.0	0.0	3.0	0.0	
31101H000	AIRBORNE SF GROUP	MOGAS	0.0	12.0	21.6	9.0	0.0	13.3	0.0	0.0	0.0	0.0	0.0	0.0	
		DIESEL	0.0	0.0	8.8	0.0	8.5	35.0	0.0	0.0	0.0	0.0	8.0	0.0	
		JP4													775.0
31102H000	HHC, ABN SF GROUP	MOGAS	0.0	0.0	1.4	0.0	0.0	0.0	0.0	0.0	0.0	0.0	0.0	0.0	
		DIESEL	0.0	0.0	0.0	0.0	0.0	0.0	0.0	0.0	0.0	0.0	0.0	0.0	
31105H000	SF BN, ABN SF GROUP	MOGAS	0.0	0.0	0.0	0.0	0.0	0.0	0.0	0.0	0.0	0.0	0.0	0.0	
		DIESEL	0.0	0.0	0.0	0.0	0.0	0.0	0.0	0.0	0.0	0.0	0.0	0.0	
31106H000	HQ, SF BN (C DET)	MOGAS	0.0	0.0	0.0	0.0	0.0	0.0	0.0	0.0	0.0	0.0	0.0	0.0	
		DIESEL	0.0	0.0	0.0	0.0	0.0	0.0	0.0	0.0	0.0	0.0	0.0	0.0	
31107H000	SF CO, ABN SF GROUP	MOGAS	0.0	0.0	0.0	0.0	0.0	0.0	0.0	0.0	0.0	0.0	0.0	0.0	
		DIESEL	0.0	0.0	0.0	0.0	0.0	0.0	0.0	0.0	0.0	0.0	0.0	0.0	
31127H400	SVC CO, ABN SF GROUP	MOGAS	0.0	12.0	7.2	9.0	0.0	13.3	0.0	0.0	0.0	0.0	0.0	0.0	
		DIESEL	0.0	0.0	2.7	0.0	8.5	11.0	0.0	0.0	0.0	0.0	4.0	0.0	
		JP4													775.0
34137H800	MI CO, CEWI, SF GROUP	MOGAS	0.0	0.0	10.6	0.0	0.0	0.0	0.0	0.0	0.0	0.0	0.0	0.0	
		DIESEL	0.0	0.0	0.0	0.0	0.0	0.0	0.0	0.0	0.0	0.0	1.0	0.0	

SUMMARY OF BULK FUEL USAGE BY EQUIPMENT CATEGORY
INF DIV (MECH) E/W M4T6 (SRC 37000H020)

SRC	UNIT NAME	FUEL TYPE	AB	CE	GN	HG	MH	SG	SV	TI	CC	SR	WV	OV	AV
05145H720	ENGR BN, ARMD/MECH DIV	MOGAS	40.0	4.5	24.0	49.2	0.0	81.7	0.0	0.0	0.0	0.0	0.0	0.0	
		DIESEL	72.0	141.1	3.4	0.0	8.5	38.0	0.0	106.5	1070.4	890.8	28.3	0.0	
05146H700	HHC, ENGR BN	MOGAS	0.0	2.5	8.1	9.4	0.0	15.5	0.0	0.0	0.0	0.0	0.1	0.0	
		DIESEL	0.0	37.9	0.6	0.0	8.5	11.0	0.0	7.0	99.3	77.8	8.8	0.0	
05147H700	ENGR CO, ENGR BN	MOGAS	0.0	0.5	3.4	7.6	0.0	13.0	0.0	0.0	0.0	0.0	0.0	0.0	
		DIESEL	0.0	22.5	0.6	0.0	0.0	5.0	0.0	22.5	213.2	182.1	1.7	0.0	
05148H720	BRG CO, EN BN, M4T6/CL60	MOGAS	40.0	0.0	2.5	9.4	0.0	14.1	0.0	0.0	0.0	0.0	0.0	0.0	
		DIESEL	72.0	13.1	0.6	0.0	0.0	7.0	0.0	9.4	118.5	84.4	12.7	0.0	
06300H020	INF(M) DIV ARTILLERY	MOGAS	0.0	0.0	85.7	98.8	0.0	118.8	0.0	0.0	0.0	0.0	0.3	0.0	
		DIESEL	0.0	0.0	36.1	0.0	0.0	25.0	0.0	211.8	1366.6	1685.6	61.8	29.7	
06302H000	HHB, DIVARTY, ARMD/INF(MECH)	MOGAS	0.0	0.0	26.3	5.4	0.0	8.4	0.0	0.0	0.0	0.0	0.1	0.0	
		DIESEL	0.0	0.0	9.8	0.0	0.0	5.0	0.0	1.0	8.6	8.9	5.9	0.0	
06307H600	TGT ACQ BTRY, AIM DIV	MOGAS	0.0	0.0	11.6	5.4	0.0	4.5	0.0	0.0	0.0	0.0	0.0	0.0	
		DIESEL	0.0	0.0	12.0	0.0	0.0	0.0	0.0	0.0	0.0	0.0	5.1	0.0	
06365H000	FA BN, 155MM SP, RMD/MEC	MOGAS	0.0	0.0	11.0	22.0	0.0	26.4	0.0	0.0	0.0	0.0	0.0	0.0	
		DIESEL	0.0	0.0	3.6	0.0	0.0	5.0	0.0	53.0	314.8	398.5	13.0	9.3	
06366H000	HHB, FA BN, 155MM SP	MOGAS	0.0	0.0	6.8	5.4	0.0	8.0	0.0	0.0	0.0	0.0	0.0	0.0	
		DIESEL	0.0	0.0	3.0	0.0	0.0	0.0	0.0	6.0	51.6	53.4	2.8	4.3	
06367H000	FA BTRY, FA BN, 155MM, SP	MOGAS	0.0	0.0	0.8	3.6	0.0	4.0	0.0	0.0	0.0	0.0	0.0	0.0	
		DIESEL	0.0	0.0	0.0	0.0	0.0	0.0	0.0	14.2	79.4	105.5	1.7	1.7	
06369H000	SVC BTRY, FA BN, 155MM SP	MOGAS	0.0	0.0	1.7	5.8	0.0	6.4	0.0	0.0	0.0	0.0	0.0	0.0	
		DIESEL	0.0	0.0	0.6	0.0	0.0	5.0	0.0	4.4	25.0	28.6	4.9	0.0	
06395H020	FA BN, 8IN SP, INF(M) DIV	MOGAS	0.0	0.0	14.9	22.0	0.0	26.4	0.0	0.0	0.0	0.0	0.0	0.0	
		DIESEL	0.0	0.0	3.6	0.0	0.0	5.0	0.0	51.8	413.6	481.2	11.5	1.7	
06396H020	FA BN, 8 INCH SP	MOGAS	0.0	0.0	9.1	5.4	0.0	8.0	0.0	0.0	0.0	0.0	0.0	0.0	
		DIESEL	0.0	0.0	3.0	0.0	0.0	0.0	0.0	4.0	34.4	35.6	2.6	1.7	
06397H000	FA BTRY, FA BN 8 IN SP	MOGAS	0.0	0.0	1.4	3.6	0.0	4.0	0.0	0.0	0.0	0.0	0.0	0.0	
		DIESEL	0.0	0.0	0.0	0.0	0.0	0.0	0.0	13.8	105.8	130.5	1.4	0.0	
06399H000	SVC BTRY, FA BN, 8 IN SP	MOGAS	0.0	0.0	1.7	5.8	0.0	6.4	0.0	0.0	0.0	0.0	0.0	0.0	
		DIESEL	0.0	0.0	0.6	0.0	0.0	5.0	0.0	6.4	61.8	54.1	4.6	0.0	
08035H000	MED BN, AIM DIV	MOGAS	0.0	0.0	45.1	36.2	0.0	53.0	0.0	0.0	0.0	0.0	0.0	0.0	
		DIESEL	0.0	0.0	0.6	0.0	0.0	5.0	0.0	0.0	0.0	0.0	12.6	0.0	
08036H000	H&S CO, MED BN, AIM DIV	MOGAS	0.0	0.0	13.8	13.4	0.0	14.0	0.0	0.0	0.0	0.0	0.0	0.0	
		DIESEL	0.0	0.0	0.6	0.0	0.0	5.0	0.0	0.0	0.0	0.0	4.6	0.0	
08037H000	MED CO, MED BN, AIM DIV	MOGAS	0.0	0.0	10.4	7.6	0.0	13.0	0.0	0.0	0.0	0.0	0.0	0.0	
		DIESEL	0.0	0.0	0.0	0.0	0.0	0.0	0.0	0.0	0.0	0.0	2.7	0.0	
09557H530	MSL SPT CO, MAINT BN, MECH	MOGAS	0.0	0.0	15.1	13.4	0.0	4.0	0.0	0.0	0.0	0.0	0.0	0.0	
		DIESEL	0.0	0.0	28.8	0.0	0.0	5.0	0.0	0.0	0.0	0.0	7.6	0.0	
10007H000	SUP-SVC CO S&T BN INF DIV	MOGAS	0.0	0.0	6.4	5.0	0.0	8.1	0.0	0.0	0.0	0.0	0.0	0.0	
		DIESEL	0.0	70.0	0.0	0.0	77.6	9.3	0.0	0.0	0.0	0.0	2.4	0.0	
10007H020	S&S CO,S&T BN ARM/MECH DIV	MOGAS	0.0	0.0	3.8	4.0	0.0	18.8	0.0	0.0	0.0	0.0	0.0	0.0	
		DIESEL	0.0	70.0	30.0	0.0	77.6	9.3	0.0	0.0	0.0	0.0	3.9	0.0	
11035H000	SIGNAL BN, AIM DIV	MOGAS	0.0	0.0	150.6	34.0	0.0	14.9	0.0	0.0	0.0	0.0	0.2	0.0	
		DIESEL	0.0	0.0	11.3	0.0	0.0	20.0	0.0	0.0	0.0	0.0	17.4	0.0	
11036H000	HHC, SIG BN, AIM DIV	MOGAS	0.0	0.0	17.4	4.0	0.0	2.9	0.0	0.0	0.0	0.0	0.0	0.0	
		DIESEL	0.0	0.0	0.6	0.0	0.0	5.0	0.0	0.0	0.0	0.0	4.2	0.0	
11037H000	CMD OP CO, SIG BN, AIM DIV	MOGAS	0.0	0.0	48.1	11.2	0.0	4.0	0.0	0.0	0.0	0.0	0.1	0.0	
		DIESEL	0.0	0.0	6.6	0.0	0.0	5.0	0.0	0.0	0.0	0.0	5.4	0.0	
11038H000	FWD COMM CO, SIG BN, AIM DIV	MOGAS	0.0	0.0	49.6	9.4	0.0	4.0	0.0	0.0	0.0	0.0	0.1	0.0	
		DIESEL	0.0	0.0	0.6	0.0	0.0	5.0	0.0	0.0	0.0	0.0	3.5	0.0	
11039H000	SIG SPT OP CO, SIG BN, AIM DIV	MOGAS	0.0	0.0	35.6	9.4	0.0	4.0	0.0	0.0	0.0	0.0	0.0	0.0	
		DIESEL	0.0	0.0	3.6	0.0	0.0	5.0	0.0	0.0	0.0	0.0	4.2	0.0	
12017H610	AG CO, SPT CMD, AMBL/AIM DIV	MOGAS	0.0	0.0	1.1	7.2	0.0	7.0	0.0	0.0	0.0	0.0	0.1	0.0	
		DIESEL	0.0	0.0	13.5	0.0	0.0	0.0	0.0	0.0	0.0	0.0	1.2	0.0	
14037H610	FIN CO, SPT CMD,AIM/AMBL DIV	MOGAS	0.0	0.0	2.4	0.0	0.0	0.0	0.0	0.0	0.0	0.0	0.0	0.0	
		DIESEL	0.0	0.0	0.6	0.0	0.0	0.0	0.0	0.0	0.0	0.0	0.5	0.0	
17085H700	CBT AVN BN, ARMD/MECH DIV	MOGAS	0.0	0.0	60.1	58.0	0.0	41.7	0.0	0.0	0.0	0.0	0.1	0.0	
		DIESEL	0.0	32.0	22.3	0.0	19.6	20.0	0.0	0.0	0.0	0.0	26.4	0.0	
		JP4													12218.4
17086H700	HHC CBT AVN BN, AR/MECH DIV	MOGAS	0.0	0.0	6.2	9.8	0.0	12.4	0.0	0.0	0.0	0.0	0.0	0.0	
		DIESEL	0.0	0.0	0.6	0.0	0.0	0.0	0.0	0.0	0.0	0.0	3.4	0.0	

Figure 10. Bulk POL Planning Factors by Type Unit— Bulk POL Table E (continued)

SUMMARY OF BULK FUEL USAGE BY EQUIPMENT CATEGORY
INF DIV (MECH) E/W M4T6 (SRC 37000H020)

SRC	UNIT NAME	FUEL TYPE	AB	CE	GN	HG	MH	SG	SV	TI	CC	SR	WV	OV	AV
17087H000	AVN CO,ARMD/INF (MECH)	MOGAS	0.0	0.0	14.5	0.0	0.0	3.9	0.0	0.0	0.0	0.0	0.0	0.0	
		DIESEL	0.0	8.0	0.6	0.0	0.0	5.0	0.0	0.0	0.0	0.0	3.0	0.0	
		JP4													2760.8
17105H020	ARMD CAV SQDN AR/MECH DIV	MOGAS	0.0	0.0	20.9	37.6	0.0	28.4	0.0	0.0	0.0	0.0	0.0	0.0	
		DIESEL	0.0	8.0	0.6	0.0	1.3	12.0	0.0	110.2	1377.7	1043.5	15.1	0.0	
		JP4													2260.0
17106H000	HHT ARMD CAV SQ	MOGAS	0.0	0.0	6.1	29.6	0.0	22.4	0.0	0.0	0.0	0.0	0.0	0.0	
		DIESEL	0.0	0.0	0.0	0.0	0.0	7.0	0.0	13.0	150.9	131.2	9.3	0.0	
17108H000	AIR CAV TRP ARMD CAV SQDN	MOGAS	0.0	0.0	14.9	8.0	0.0	3.0	0.0	0.0	0.0	0.0	0.2	0.0	
		DIESEL	0.0	8.0	0.6	0.0	1.3	5.0	0.0	0.0	0.0	0.0	4.4	0.0	
		JP4													2260.0
17307H700	AR CAV TP, AR CV SQ, AM DIV	MOGAS	0.0	0.0	0.0	0.0	0.0	1.0	0.0	0.0	0.0	0.0	0.0	0.0	
		DIESEL	0.0	0.0	0.0	0.0	0.0	0.0	0.0	32.4	408.9	304.1	0.4	0.0	
17387H720	ATTACK HELICOPTER COMPANY	MOGAS	0.0	0.0	10.6	5.4	0.0	5.9	0.0	0.0	0.0	0.0	0.0	0.0	
		DIESEL	0.0	8.0	0.6	0.0	0.0	5.0	0.0	0.0	0.0	0.0	5.1	0.0	
		JP4													3391.8
19017H710	MP CO, AIM DIV	MOGAS	0.0	0.0	3.5	4.0	0.0	1.0	0.0	0.0	0.0	0.0	0.0	0.0	
		DIESEL	0.0	0.0	1.1	0.0	0.0	5.0	0.0	0.0	0.0	0.0	2.0	0.0	
29002H700	HHC, SPT COMD, AIM DIV	MOGAS	0.0	0.0	0.8	3.6	0.0	4.0	0.0	0.0	0.0	0.0	0.1	0.0	
		DIESEL	0.0	0.0	3.0	0.0	0.0	0.0	0.0	0.0	0.0	0.0	0.8	0.0	
29003H500	DIV MMC, AIM DIV	MOGAS	0.0	0.0	0.0	0.0	0.0	2.0	0.0	0.0	0.0	0.0	0.0	0.0	
		DIESEL	0.0	0.0	15.0	0.0	0.0	0.0	0.0	0.0	0.0	0.0	1.6	0.0	
29006H000	HHD, S&T BN, AIM DIV	MOGAS	0.0	0.0	0.8	10.8	0.0	7.0	0.0	0.0	0.0	0.0	0.0	0.0	
		DIESEL	0.0	0.0	0.0	0.0	0.0	0.0	0.0	0.0	0.0	0.0	0.8	0.0	
29011H000	SUPPORT CMD, INF DIV (MECH)	MOGAS	0.0	0.0	140.8	216.8	4.0	227.6	0.0	0.0	0.0	0.0	0.2	0.0	
		DIESEL	0.0	98.0	190.9	0.0	131.2	61.8	0.0	8.0	147.0	102.2	92.5	0.0	
29025H000	MAINT BN, INF DIV (MECH)	MOGAS	0.0	0.0	97.3	128.4	0.0	127.2	0.0	0.0	0.0	0.0	0.0	0.0	
		DIESEL	0.0	28.0	123.8	0.0	53.6	83.5	0.0	8.0	147.0	102.2	46.1	0.0	
29026H000	HQ & LT MAINT CO, MAINT BN	MOGAS	0.0	0.0	5.5	7.6	0.0	4.0	0.0	0.0	0.0	0.0	0.0	0.0	
		DIESEL	0.0	0.0	37.8	0.0	19.6	0.0	0.0	0.0	0.0	0.0	8.3	0.0	
29027H000	FORWARD SPT CO, MAINT BN	MOGAS	0.0	0.0	22.6	25.4	0.0	23.6	0.0	0.0	0.0	0.0	0.0	0.0	
		DIESEL	0.0	7.0	12.8	0.0	8.5	22.0	0.0	2.0	36.8	25.5	7.4	0.0	
29028H000	HEAVY MAINT CO, MAINT BN	MOGAS	0.0	0.0	8.9	31.2	0.0	48.2	0.0	0.0	0.0	0.0	0.0	0.0	
		DIESEL	0.0	7.0	18.9	0.0	8.5	12.5	0.0	2.0	36.8	25.5	7.8	0.0	
29065H000	S&T BN, IFN DIV (MECH)	MOGAS	0.0	0.0	8.5	22.8	0.0	29.5	0.0	0.0	0.0	0.0	0.0	0.0	
		DIESEL	0.0	70.0	30.6	0.0	77.6	18.3	0.0	0.0	0.0	0.0	25.3	0.0	
29255H900	MAINT BN INF DIV (MECH)	MOGAS	0.0	0.0	82.8	147.0	4.0	132.1	0.0	0.0	0.0	0.0	0.0	0.0	
		DIESEL	0.0	28.0	127.7	0.0	53.6	38.5	0.0	8.0	147.0	102.2	50.3	0.0	
29256H900	HH & LT MAINT CO MAINT BN	MOGAS	0.0	0.0	8.2	12.5	4.0	5.0	0.0	0.0	0.0	0.0	0.0	0.0	
		DIESEL	0.0	0.0	21.6	0.0	19.6	0.0	0.0	0.0	0.0	0.0	7.9	0.0	
29257H900	FORWARD SPT CO, MAINT BN	MOGAS	0.0	0.0	16.0	24.5	0.0	29.0	0.0	0.0	0.0	0.0	0.0	0.0	
		DIESEL	0.0	7.0	18.2	0.0	8.5	7.0	0.0	2.0	36.8	25.5	8.6	0.0	
29258H900	HEAVY MAINT CO, MAINT BN	MOGAS	0.0	0.0	11.7	47.6	0.0	35.9	0.0	0.0	0.0	0.0	0.0	0.0	
		DIESEL	0.0	7.0	22.7	0.0	8.5	12.5	0.0	2.0	36.8	25.5	8.6	0.0	
37000H020	INF DIV (MECH), E/W M4T6	MOGAS	40.0	4.5	675.3	579.1	4.0	623.6	0.0	0.0	0.0	0.0	2.1	0.0	
		DIESEL	72.0	279.1	280.4	0.0	160.6	198.8	0.0	551.1	4689.7	4666.4	289.3	30.0	
		JP4													14916.4
37004H000	HHC, INF DIV (MECH)	MOGAS	0.0	0.0	9.4	13.0	0.0	12.0	0.0	0.0	0.0	0.0	0.0	0.0	
		DIESEL	0.0	0.0	3.0	0.0	0.0	0.0	0.0	1.0	8.6	8.9	2.5	0.0	
37042H000	HHC, INF DIV (MECH) BDE	MOGAS	0.0	0.0	8.9	7.1	0.0	4.0	0.0	0.0	0.0	0.0	0.0	0.0	
		DIESEL	0.0	0.0	0.0	0.0	0.0	0.0	0.0	8.2	64.1	67.7	1.9	0.0	
44325H000	ADA BN, AIM DIVISION	MOGAS	0.0	0.0	64.6	25.6	0.0	30.5	0.0	0.0	0.0	0.0	0.1	0.0	
		DIESEL	0.0	0.0	7.1	0.0	0.0	5.0	0.0	74.8	411.4	611.2	19.6	0.0	
44326H000	HHB, ADA BN, C/V, SP	MOGAS	0.0	0.0	25.7	7.6	0.0	8.9	0.0	0.0	0.0	0.0	0.0	0.0	
		DIESEL	0.0	0.0	7.1	0.0	0.0	5.0	0.0	2.0	17.2	17.8	4.1	0.0	
44327H000	ADA BTRY, VUL(SP)STINGER	MOGAS	0.0	0.0	8.6	3.6	0.0	5.4	0.0	0.0	0.0	0.0	0.0	0.0	
		DIESEL	0.0	0.0	0.0	0.0	0.0	0.0	0.0	18.2	109.3	205.9	4.1	0.0	
44328H000	ADA BTRY, C HAPS(SP)STINGER	MOGAS	0.0	0.0	10.8	5.4	0.0	5.4	0.0	0.0	0.0	0.0	0.0	0.0	
		DIESEL	0.0	0.0	0.0	0.0	0.0	0.0	0.0	18.2	87.8	90.8	3.6	0.0	
55084H000	TRANS MTR TRANS CO, MECH	MOGAS	0.0	0.0	3.8	8.0	0.0	3.7	0.0	0.0	0.0	0.0	0.0	0.0	
		DIESEL	0.0	0.0	0.6	0.0	0.0	9.0	0.0	0.0	0.0	0.0	20.5	0.0	
55427H020	TRANS ACFT MNT CO AR/MECH	MOGAS	0.0	0.0	6.4	16.2	0.0	4.4	0.0	0.0	0.0	0.0	0.0	0.0	
		DIESEL	0.0	8.0	20.1	0.0	18.3	5.0	0.0	0.0	0.0	0.0	5.3	0.0	
		JP4													236.0
57057H320	CBT SPT AVN CO	MOGAS	0.0	0.0	11.7	21.1	0.0	9.0	0.0	0.0	0.0	0.0	0.0	0.0	
		DIESEL	0.0	0.0	0.0	0.0	1.3	0.0	0.0	0.0	0.0	0.0	4.3	0.0	
		JP4													2438.0

Figure 10. Bulk POL Planning Factors by Type Unit— Bulk POL Table E (continued)

SUMMARY OF BULK FUEL USAGE BY EQUIPMENT CATEGORY SEP INF BDE M WM4T6 1005 (SRC 37100H020)

SRC	UNIT NAME	FUEL TYPE	AB	CE	GN	HG	MH	SG	SV	TI	CC	SR	WV	OV	AV
05127H020	ENGR CO, SEP ARMD BDE,M4T	MOGAS	0.0	0.5	4.2	11.2	0.0	24.0	0.0	0.0	0.0	0.0	0.0	0.0	
		DIESEL	43.2	37.1	0.6	0.0	8.5	7.0	0.0	35.5	381.8	309.5	10.8	0.0	
06367H000	FA BTRY, FA BN, 155MM, SP	MOGAS	0.0	0.0	0.8	3.6	0.0	4.0	0.0	0.0	0.0	0.0	0.0	0.0	
		DIESEL	0.0	0.0	0.0	0.0	0.0	0.0	0.0	14.2	79.4	105.5	1.7	1.7	
06369H000	SVC BTRY, FA BN, 155MM SP	MOGAS	0.0	0.0	1.7	5.8	0.0	6.4	0.0	0.0	0.0	0.0	0.0	0.0	
		DIESEL	0.0	0.0	0.6	0.0	0.0	5.0	0.0	4.4	25.0	28.6	4.9	0.0	
06375H020	FA BN, 155 SP, SEP I (M)	MOGAS	0.0	0.0	23.8	23.8	0.0	26.4	0.0	0.0	0.0	0.0	0.0	0.0	
		DIESEL	0.0	0.0	3.6	0.0	0.0	5.0	0.0	53.0	314.8	398.5	14.0	7.9	
06376H020	HHB, FA BN, 155MM SP	MOGAS	0.0	0.0	19.6	7.2	0.0	8.0	0.0	0.0	0.0	0.0	0.0	0.0	
		DIESEL	0.0	0.0	3.0	0.0	0.0	0.0	0.0	6.0	51.6	53.4	3.8	2.8	
08147H000	MED CO, SEP AIM BDE, ACR	MOGAS	0.0	0.0	10.4	11.6	0.0	13.0	0.0	0.0	0.0	0.0	0.0	0.0	
		DIESEL	0.0	0.0	0.0	0.0	0.0	5.0	0.0	0.0	0.0	0.0	3.1	0.0	
12147H600	ADMIN CO, SEP BDE	MOGAS	0.0	0.0	2.2	3.6	0.0	3.0	0.0	0.0	0.0	0.0	0.0	0.0	
		DIESEL	0.0	0.0	13.5	0.0	0.0	0.0	0.0	0.0	0.0	0.0	1.2	0.0	
17307H700	AR CAV TP, AR CV SQ, AM D	MOGAS	0.0	0.0	0.0	0.0	0.0	1.0	0.0	0.0	0.0	0.0	0.0	0.0	
		DIESEL	0.0	0.0	0.0	0.0	0.0	0.0	0.0	32.4	408.9	304.1	0.4	0.0	
29075H020	SPT BN, SEP INF BDE (MECH)	MOGAS	0.0	0.0	34.9	73.1	0.0	70.8	0.2	0.0	0.0	0.0	0.1	0.0	
		DIESEL	0.0	35.0	71.6	0.0	32.4	12.0	0.0	2.0	36.8	25.5	25.2	0.0	
29076H000	HHD, SPT BN, SEP AIM BDE	MOGAS	0.0	0.0	3.9	0.0	0.0	1.0	0.0	0.0	0.0	0.0	0.1	0.0	
		DIESEL	0.0	0.0	0.6	0.0	0.0	0.0	0.0	0.0	0.0	0.0	1.1	0.0	
29077H000	S&T CO, SPT BN, SEP AIM B	MOGAS	0.0	0.0	3.4	7.6	0.0	13.6	0.0	0.0	0.0	0.0	0.0	0.0	
		DIESEL	0.0	28.0	12.0	0.0	22.6	0.0	0.0	0.0	0.0	0.0	9.5	0.0	
29079H020	MNT CO,SPT BN,SEP INF(M)	MOGAS	0.0	0.0	18.1	43.2	0.0	36.3	0.2	0.0	0.0	0.0	0.0	0.0	
		DIESEL	0.0	7.0	26.6	0.0	9,8	7.0	0.0	2.0	36.8	25.5	8.9	0.0	
29176H910	HHC,SPT BN,SEP AIM/ABN/LI	MOGAS	0.0	0.0	0.8	7.1	0.0	5.0	0.0	0.0	0.0	0.0	0.1	0.0	
		DIESEL	0.0	0.0	19.5	0.0	0.0	0.0	0.0	0.0	0.0	0.0	2.4	0.0	
34114H120	MI CO (CEWI)ACR/SEP HV BD	MOGAS	0.0	0.0	34.1	13.0	0.0	7.1	0.0	0.0	0.0	0.0	0.0	0.0	
		DIESEL	0.0	0.0	0.0	0.0	0.0	5.0	0.0	11.2	89.9	94.4	4.1	0.2	
		JP4													438.0
37100H020	SEP INF BDE M WM4T6,1005	MOGAS	0.0	0.5	133.8	132.3	0.0	138.8	0.2	0.0	0.0	0.0	0.3	0.0	
		DIESEL	43.2	72.1	78.8	0.0	40.9	29.0	0.0	140.1	1283.8	1185.5	60.9	8.1	
		JP4													889.4
37102H000	HHC, SEP INF BDE (MECH)	MOGAS	0.0	0.0	36.7	11.2	0.0	9.4	0.0	0.0	0.0	0.0	0.1	0.0	
		DIESEL	0.0	0.0	3.0	0.0	0.0	0.0	0.0	6.0	51.6	53.4	6.3	0.0	
		JP4													451.4

SUMMARY OF BULK FUEL USAGE BY EQUIPMENT CATEGORY AIRBORNE DIVISION E/W TOW (SRC 57000L000)

SRC	UNIT NAME	FUEL TYPE	AB	CE	GN	HG	MH	SG	SV	TI	CC	SR	WV	OV	AV
01070L000	AVIATION BRIGADE	MOGAS	0.0	0.0	65.2	55.2	0.0	34.6	0.0	0.0	0.0	0.0	2.3	0.0	
		DIESEL	0.0	32.0	2.3	0.0	7,8	0.0	0.0	0.0	0.0	0.0	16.7	0.0	
		JP4													11767.7
01072L000	HHC, AVIATION BRIGADE	MOGAS	0.0	0.0	9.0	3.6	0.0	17.6	0.0	0.0	0.0	0.0	0.1	0.0	
		DIESEL	0.0	0.0	0.0	0.0	2.6	0.0	0.0	0.0	0.0	0.0	6.6	0.0	
		JP4													478.8
01075L000	AIR RECON SQUADRON (AH-1)	MOGAS	0.0	0.0	20.4	12.6	0.0	6.0	0.0	0.0	0.0	0.0	2.1	0.0	
		DIESEL	0.0	8.0	2.3	0.0	1.3	0.0	0.0	0.0	0.0	0.0	4.7	0.0	
		JP4													3609.2
01076L000	HHT, AIR RECON SQUADRON	MOGAS	0.0	0.0	17.7	12.6	0.0	6.0	0.0	0.0	0.0	0.0	0.2	0.0	
		DIESEL	0.0	8.0	0.0	0.0	1.3	0.0	0.0	0.0	0.0	0.0	3.7	0.0	
		JP4													1415.0
01078L000	AIR RECON TRP, RECON SQDN	MOGAS	0.0	0.0	0.5	0.0	0.0	0.0	0.0	0.0	0.0	0.0	0.0	0.0	
		DIESEL	0.0	0.0	0.0	0.0	0.0	0.0	0.0	0.0	0.0	0.0	0.3	0.0	
		JP4													731.4
01277L000	ASSAULT HEL CO (UH-60)	MOGAS	0.0	0.0	9.4	13.0	0.0	4.0	0.0	0.0	0.0	0.0	0.0	0.0	
		DIESEL	0.0	8.0	0.0	0.0	1.3	0.0	0.0	0.0	0.0	0.0	1.1	0.0	
		JP4													2130.0
01375L000	ATTACK HEL BN (AH-1)	MOGAS	0.0	0.0	16.9	13.0	0.0	3.0	0.0	0.0	0.0	0.0	0.0	0.0	
		DIESEL	0.0	8.0	0.0	0.0	1.3	0.0	0.0	0.0	0.0	0.0	3.1	0.0	
		JP4													3419.7
01376L000	HQ AND SVC CO (AH-1)	MOGAS	0.0	0.0	15.3	13.0	0.0	3.0	0.0	0.0	0.0	0.0	0.0	0.0	
		DIESEL	0.0	8.0	0.0	0.0	1.3	0.0	0.0	0.0	0.0	0.0	2.3	0.0	
		JP4													357.9
01377L000	ATK HEL CO (AH-1)	MOGAS	0.0	0.0	0.5	0.0	0.0	0.0	0.0	0.0	0.0	0.0	0.0	0.0	
		DIESEL	0.0	0.0	0.0	0.0	0.0	0.0	0.0	0.0	0.0	0.0	0.3	0.0	
		JP4													1020.6
01973L000	AMC, ABN DIV (AOE)	MOGAS	0.0	0.0	4.2	20.0	0.0	2.0	0.0	0.0	0.0	0.0	0.0	0.0	
		DIESEL	0.0	8.0	25.5	0.0	20.9	0.0	0.0	0.0	0.0	0.0	4.4	0.0	
		JP4													308.0
03023L000	CHEM CO (SMK/DECON)	MOGAS	0.0	0.0	109.1	4.0	0.0	33.5	0.0	0.0	0.0	0.0	0.9	0.0	
		DIESEL	0.0	0.0	0.0	0.0	0.0	0.0	0.0	0.0	0.0	0.0	6.8	0.0	
05025L000	ENGR BN, ABN DIV	MOGAS	0.0	0.0	5.0	4.0	0.7	45.4	0.0	0.0	0.0	0.0	8.3	0.0	
		DIESEL	0.0	73.0	0.0	0.0	0.0	0.0	0.0	0.0	0.0	0.0	5.5	0.0	
05026L000	HHC, ENGR BN, ABN DIV	MOGAS	0.0	0.0	5.0	4.0	0.7	18.4	0.0	0.0	0.0	0.0	2.2	0.0	
		DIESEL	0.0	73.0	0.0	0.0	0.0	0.0	0.0	0.0	0.0	0.0	2.8	0.0	
05027L000	ENGR CO, ENGR BN, ABN DIV	MOGAS	0.0	0.0	0.0	0.0	0.0	9.0	0.0	0.0	0.0	0.0	2.0	0.0	
		DIESEL	0.0	0.0	0.0	0.0	0.0	0.0	0.0	0.0	0.0	0.0	0.9	0.0	
06200L000	AIRBORNE DIV ARTILLERY-AOE	MOGAS	0.0	0.0	77.2	17.4	0.0	26.8	0.0	0.0	0.0	0.0	5.3	0.0	
		DIESEL	0.0	0.0	0.0	0.0	0.0	0.0	0.0	0.0	0.0	0.0	22.0	0.0	
06202L000	HHB, DIVARTY AIRBORNE	MOGAS	0.0	0.0	14.7	0.0	0.0	1.4	0.0	0.0	0.0	0.0	0.7	0.0	
		DIESEL	0.0	0.0	0.0	0.0	0.0	0.0	0.0	0.0	0.0	0.0	2.3	0.0	

Figure 10. Bulk POL Planning Factors by Type Unit—Bulk POL Table E (continued)

SUMMARY OF BULK FUEL USAGE BY EQUIPMENT CATEGORY
AIRBORNE DIVISION E/W TOW (SRC 57000L000)

SRC	UNIT NAME	FUEL TYPE	AB	CE	GN	HG	MH	SG	SV	TI	CC	SR	WV	OV	AV
06205L000	FA BN, 105MM T (ABN) AOE	MOGAS	0.0	0.0	20.8	5.8	0.0	8.4	0.0	0.0	0.0	0.0	1.5	0.0	
		DIESEL	0.0	0.0	0.0	0.0	0.0	0.0	0.0	0.0	0.0	0.0	6.6	0.0	
06206L000	HHS FA BATTALION	MOGAS	0.0	0.0	12.7	5.8	0.0	8.4	0.0	0.0	0.0	0.0	1.4	0.0	
		DIESEL	0.0	0.0	0.0	0.0	0.0	0.0	0.0	0.0	0.0	0.0	2.6	0.0	
06207L000	FA BATTERY 105MM T	MOGAS	0.0	0.0	2.7	0.0	0.0	0.0	0.0	0.0	0.0	0.0	0.0	0.0	
		DIESEL	0.0	0.0	0.0	0.0	0.0	0.0	0.0	0.0	0.0	0.0	1.3	0.0	
07035L000	INF BN (ABN)	MOGAS	0.0	0.0	5.0	7.6	0.0	5.0	0.0	0.0	0.0	0.0	5.2	0.0	
		DIESEL	0.0	0.0	0.0	0.0	0.0	0.0	0.0	0.0	0.0	0.0	2.0	0.0	
07036L000	HHC INF BN (ABN)	MOGAS	0.0	0.0	4.4	7.6	0.0	5.0	0.0	0.0	0.0	0.0	1.4	0.0	
		DIESEL	0.0	0.0	0.0	0.0	0.0	0.0	0.0	0.0	0.0	0.0	2.0	0.0	
07037L000	RIFLE CO (ABN)	MOGAS	0.0	0.0	0.0	0.0	0.0	0.0	0.0	0.0	0.0	0.0	0.0	0.0	
		DIESEL	0.0	0.0	0.0	0.0	0.0	0.0	0.0	0.0	0.0	0.0	0.0	0.0	
07038L000	ANTIARMOR COMPANY	MOGAS	0.0	0.0	0.5	0.0	0.0	0.0	0.0	0.0	0.0	0.0	3.7	0.0	
		DIESEL	0.0	0.0	0.0	0.0	0.0	0.0	0.0	0.0	0.0	0.0	0.0	0.0	
07109L000	LRS DET REC SQN ID(LIGHT)	MOGAS	0.0	0.0	0.0	0.0	0.0	0.0	0.0	0.0	0.0	0.0	0.0	0.0	
		DIESEL	0.0	0.0	2.3	0.0	0.0	0.0	0.0	0.0	0.0	0.0	0.2	0.0	
08065L000	MEDICAL BATTALION AIRBORNE	MOGAS	0.0	0.0	8.4	16.2	0.0	7.0	0.0	0.0	0.0	0.0	0.0	0.0	
		DIESEL	0.0	0.0	10.6	0.0	1.3	0.0	0.0	0.0	0.0	0.0	10.8	0.0	
08066L000	HQS & CO A, MED BN (ABN)	MOGAS	0.0	0.0	5.9	5.4	0.0	2.5	0.0	0.0	0.0	0.0	0.0	0.0	
		DIESEL	0.0	0.0	3.9	0.0	1.3	0.0	0.0	0.0	0.0	0.0	3.9	0.0	
08067L000	FWD SPT MEDICAL CO (ABN)	MOGAS	0.0	0.0	0.8	3.6	0.0	1.5	0.0	0.0	0.0	0.0	0.0	0.0	
		DIESEL	0.0	0.0	2.2	0.0	0.0	0.0	0.0	0.0	0.0	0.0	2.3	0.0	
11215L000	SIGNAL BATTALION (ABN)	MOGAS	0.0	0.0	122.6	0.0	0.0	6.4	0.0	0.0	0.0	0.0	2.5	0.0	
		DIESEL	0.0	0.0	6.0	0.0	0.0	0.0	0.0	0.0	0.0	0.0	6.1	0.0	
11216L000	HHC SIG BN (ABN)	MOGAS	0.0	0.0	10.6	0.0	0.0	2.4	0.0	0.0	0.0	0.0	0.3	0.0	
		DIESEL	0.0	0.0	0.0	0.0	0.0	0.0	0.0	0.0	0.0	0.0	1.5	0.0	
11217L000	CMD COMM CO (ABN)	MOGAS	0.0	0.0	42.5	0.0	0.0	2.0	0.0	0.0	0.0	0.0	0.8	0.0	
		DIESEL	0.0	0.0	6.0	0.0	0.0	0.0	0.0	0.0	0.0	0.0	2.5	0.0	
11218L000	FWD COMM CO (ABN)	MOGAS	0.0	0.0	69.4	0.0	0.0	2.0	0.0	0.0	0.0	0.0	1.4	0.0	
		DIESEL	0.0	0.0	0.0	0.0	0.0	0.0	0.0	0.0	0.0	0.0	2.0	0.0	
12113L000	DIVISION BAND	MOGAS	0.0	0.0	0.0	0.0	0.0	0.0	0.0	0.0	0.0	0.0	0.0	0.0	
		DIESEL	0.0	0.0	0.0	0.0	0.0	0.0	0.0	0.0	0.0	0.0	0.0	0.0	
17207L000	RECON TRP (GROUND)	MOGAS	0.0	0.0	1.1	0.0	0.0	0.0	0.0	0.0	0.0	0.0	1.9	0.0	
		DIESEL	0.0	0.0	0.0	0.0	0.0	0.0	0.0	0.0	0.0	0.0	0.0	0.0	
19313L000	MP COMPANY AIR ASSAULT DIV	MOGAS	0.0	0.0	6.3	0.0	0.0	1.0	0.0	0.0	0.0	0.0	1.3	0.0	
		DIESEL	0.0	0.0	0.0	0.0	0.0	0.0	0.0	0.0	0.0	0.0	0.4	0.0	
34265L000	MI BN (CEWI) ABN DIVISION	MOGAS	0.0	0.0	33.8	0.0	0.0	9.1	0.0	0.0	0.0	0.0	1.8	0.0	
		DIESEL	0.0	0.0	0.6	0.0	0.0	5.0	0.0	0.0	0.0	0.0	4.7	0.3	
34266L000	HQ,HQ OP CO MI BN ABN DIV	MOGAS	0.0	0.0	4.6	0.0	0.0	0.0	0.0	0.0	0.0	0.0	0.3	0.0	
		DIESEL	0.0	0.0	0.0	0.0	0.0	0.0	0.0	0.0	0.0	0.0	0.9	0.0	
34267L000	C&J CO MI BN ABN DIV	MOGAS	0.0	0.0	8.4	0.0	0.0	0.0	0.0	0.0	0.0	0.0	0.2	0.0	
		DIESEL	0.0	0.0	0.0	0.0	0.0	0.0	0.0	0.0	0.0	0.0	1.6	0.3	
34268L000	INTEL&SURVL CO MI BN ABN	MOGAS	0.0	0.0	1.3	0.0	0.0	0.0	0.0	0.0	0.0	0.0	0.6	0.0	
		DIESEL	0.0	0.0	0.0	0.0	0.0	0.0	0.0	0.0	0.0	0.0	0.3	0.0	
34269L000	SVC SPT CO MI BN ABN DIV	MOGAS	0.0	0.0	19.5	0.0	0.0	9.1	0.0	0.0	0.0	0.0	0.6	0.0	
		DIESEL	0.0	0.0	0.6	0.0	0.0	5.0	0.0	0.0	0.0	0.0	1.8	0.0	
42055L000	S&T BN ABN DIV	MOGAS	0.0	0.0	23.2	58.4	0.0	94.9	0.0	0.0	0.0	0.0	0.9	0.0	
		DIESEL	0.0	7.0	25.5	0.0	182.3	4.0	0.0	0.0	0.0	0.0	16.0	0.0	
42056L000	HQ & SUP CO S&T BN ABN DIV	MOGAS	0.0	0.0	7.3	7.6	0.0	27.1	0.0	0.0	0.0	0.0	0.4	0.0	
		DIESEL	0.0	7.0	25.5	0.0	48.5	4.0	0.0	0.0	0.0	0.0	4.5	0.0	
42057L000	FWD SUP CO S&T BN ABN DIV	MOGAS	0.0	0.0	3.1	7.6	0.0	19.3	0.0	0.0	0.0	0.0	0.1	0.0	
		DIESEL	0.0	0.0	0.0	0.0	44.6	0.0	0.0	0.0	0.0	0.0	0.9	0.0	
42556LA00	AUG-CEB SECTION	MOGAS	0.0	0.0	5.9	28.0	0.0	0.0	0.0	0.0	0.0	0.0	0.0	0.0	
		DIESEL	0.0	0.0	0.0	0.0	0.0	0.0	0.0	0.0	0.0	0.0	1.3	0.0	
42556LB00	AUG-GRREG SECTION	MOGAS	0.0	0.0	0.0	0.0	0.0	0.0	0.0	0.0	0.0	0.0	0.0	0.0	
		DIESEL	0.0	0.0	0.0	0.0	0.0	0.0	0.0	0.0	0.0	0.0	0.3	0.0	
42556LC00	AUG – ARID ENV WATER SEC	MOGAS	0.0	0.0	0.0	0.0	0.0	6.5	0.0	0.0	0.0	0.0	0.0	0.0	
		DIESEL	0.0	0.0	0.0	0.0	0.0	0.0	0.0	0.0	0.0	0.0	0.0	0.0	
43055L000	MAINT BN ABN	MOGAS	0.0	0.0	83.6	0.0	0.0	23.9	0.0	0.0	0.0	0.0	0.9	0.0	
		DIESEL	0.0	0.0	45.5	0.0	35.3	90.0	0.0	0.0	0.0	0.0	15.1	0.0	
43056L000	HQ & LT ORD (MT) CO (ABN)	MOGAS	0.0	0.0	34.0	0.0	0.0	1.0	0.0	0.0	0.0	0.0	0.0	0.0	
		DIESEL	0.0	0.0	24.5	0.0	9.8	15.0	0.0	0.0	0.0	0.0	4.6	0.0	
43057L000	FWD SPT CO ORD BN (ABN)	MOGAS	0.0	0.0	14.5	0.0	0.0	1.0	0.0	0.0	0.0	0.0	0.3	0.0	
		DIESEL	0.0	0.0	2.6	0.0	8.5	15.0	0.0	0.0	0.0	0.0	2.5	0.0	
43058L000	HVY ORD (MT) CO (ABN)	MOGAS	0.0	0.0	6.0	0.0	0.0	19.9	0.0	0.0	0.0	0.0	0.1	0.0	
		DIESEL	0.0	0.0	13.1	0.0	0.0	30.0	0.0	0.0	0.0	0.0	2.9	0.0	
44135L000	ADA BN, SHORAD (ABN DIV)	MOGAS	0.0	0.0	27.7	0.0	0.0	4.0	0.0	0.0	0.0	0.0	4.4	0.0	
		DIESEL	0.0	0.0	0.0	0.0	0.0	0.0	0.0	0.0	0.0	0.0	6.5	0.0	
44136L000	HHB ADA BN (ABN DIV)	MOGAS	0.0	0.0	11.3	0.0	0.0	1.0	0.0	0.0	0.0	0.0	0.4	0.0	
		DIESEL	0.0	0.0	0.0	0.0	0.0	0.0	0.0	0.0	0.0	0.0	1.4	0.0	
44137L000	ADA BTRY VUL/MPDS (ABN DIV)	MOGAS	0.0	0.0	5.5	0.0	0.0	1.0	0.0	0.0	0.0	0.0	1.3	0.0	
		DIESEL	0.0	0.0	0.0	0.0	0.0	0.0	0.0	0.0	0.0	0.0	1.7	0.0	
55158L000	TMT CO S&T BN (ABN DIV)	MOGAS	0.0	0.0	0.8	0.0	0.0	3.3	0.0	0.0	0.0	0.0	0.1	0.0	
		DIESEL	0.0	0.0	0.0	0.0	0.0	0.0	0.0	0.0	0.0	0.0	7.3	0.0	
57000L000	AIRBORNE DIVISION AOE	MOGAS	0.0	0.0	665.2	267.4	0.7	348.8	0.0	0.0	0.0	0.0	78.1	0.0	
		DIESEL	0.0	120.0	138.1	0.0	247.6	99.0	0.0	0.0	0.0	0.0	142.0	0.3	
		JP4													12075.7
57004L000	HHC AIRBORNE DIVISION	MOGAS	0.0	0.0	19.2	10.8	0.0	5.0	0.0	0.0	0.0	0.0	0.7	0.0	
		DIESEL	0.0	0.0	0.0	0.0	0.0	0.0	0.0	0.0	0.0	0.0	2.8	0.0	
57042L000	HHC AIRBORNE BRIGADE	MOGAS	0.0	0.0	9.8	1.8	0.0	2.0	0.0	0.0	0.0	0.0	0.5	0.0	
		DIESEL	0.0	0.0	0.0	0.0	0.0	0.0	0.0	0.0	0.0	0.0	1.0	0.0	
63051L000	SPT COMD, ABN DIV	MOGAS	0.0	0.0	124.9	102.2	0.0	131.9	0.0	0.0	0.0	0.0	2.4	0.0	
		DIESEL	0.0	15.0	129.3	0.0	239.8	94.0	0.0	0.0	0.0	0.0	49.2	0.0	
		JP4													308.0
63052L000	HHC/MMC, SPT CMD, ABN DIV	MOGAS	0.0	0.0	5.5	7.6	0.0	4.0	0.0	0.0	0.0	0.0	0.5	0.0	
		DIESEL	0.0	0.0	22.1	0.0	0.0	0.0	0.0	0.0	0.0	0.0	2.7	0.0	
63552LA00	AUGMENTATION MAIT	MOGAS	0.0	0.0	0.0	0.0	0.0	0.0	0.0	0.0	0.0	0.0	0.0	0.0	
		DIESEL	0.0	0.0	0.0	0.0	0.0	0.0	0.0	0.0	0.0	0.0	0.0	0.0	

Figure 10. Bulk POL Planning Factors by Type Unit— Bulk POL Table E (continued)

**SUMMARY OF BULK FUEL USAGE BY EQUIPMENT CATEGORY
SEP ABN BDE W 1005 ADPE (SRC 57100H000)**

SRC	UNIT NAME	FUEL TYPE	AB	CE	GN	HG	MH	SG	SV	TI	CC	SR	WV	OV	AV
05137J200	ENGR CO, SEP ABN BDE	MOGAS	0.0	3.0	3.4	7.6	0.0	16.0	0.0	0.0	0.0	0.0	1.6	0.0	
		DIESEL	0.0	22.4	0.0	0.0	0.0	0.0	0.0	2.8	24.7	18.5	2.7	0.0	
06205H320	FA BN, 105 T, SEP ABN BDE	MOGAS	0.0	0.0	22.7	12.6	0.0	11.0	0.0	0.0	0.0	0.0	0.0	0.0	
		DIESEL	0.0	0.0	3.0	0.0	0.0	5.0	0.0	0.0	0.0	0.0	6.2	0.0	
06206H320	HHS BTRY 105MM T SEP ABN BDE	MOGAS	0.0	0.0	22.7	12.6	0.0	11.0	0.0	0.0	0.0	0.0	0.0	0.0	
		DIESEL	0.0	0.0	3.0	0.0	0.0	5.0	0.0	0.0	0.0	0.0	4.4	0.0	
06207H300	FA BTRY, FA BN, 105MM TOW	MOGAS	0.0	0.0	0.0	0.0	0.0	0.0	0.0	0.0	0.0	0.0	0.0	0.0	
		DIESEL	0.0	0.0	0.0	0.0	0.0	0.0	0.0	0.0	0.0	0.0	0.6	0.0	
08167H000	MEDICAL CO, SEP ABN BDE	MOGAS	0.0	0.0	10.4	11.6	0.0	13.0	0.0	0.0	0.0	0.0	0.0	0.0	
		DIESEL	0.0	0.0	0.0	0.0	0.0	0.0	0.0	0.0	0.0	0.0	2.0	0.0	
12147H600	ADMIN CO, SEP BDE	MOGAS	0.0	0.0	2.2	3.6	0.0	3.0	0.0	0.0	0.0	0.0	0.0	0.0	
		DIESEL	0.0	0.0	13.5	0.0	0.0	0.0	0.0	0.0	0.0	0.0	1.2	0.0	
17117H000	CAV TP LT INF/ABN BDE	MOGAS	0.0	0.0	1.9	7.6	0.0	4.0	0.0	0.0	0.0	0.0	0.0	0.0	
		DIESEL	0.0	0.0	0.0	0.0	0.0	0.0	0.0	0.0	0.0	0.0	3.0	0.0	
29105H000	SPT BN, SEP ABN BDE	MOGAS	0.0	6.0	41.0	61.1	0.0	72.5	0.0	0.0	0.0	0.0	0.1	0.0	
		DIESEL	0.0	7.0	58.2	0.0	47.9	7.0	0.0	0.0	0.0	0.0	12.5	0.0	
29106H000	HHD, SPT BN, SEP ABN BDE	MOGAS	0.0	0.0	2.8	0.0	0.0	1.0	0.0	0.0	0.0	0.0	0.1	0.0	
		DIESEL	0.0	0.0	0.0	0.0	0.0	0.0	0.0	0.0	0.0	0.0	0.7	0.0	
29107H000	S&S CO, SPT BN, SEP ABN BDE	MOGAS	0.0	6.0	5.0	11.1	0.0	22.9	0.0	0.0	0.0	0.0	0.0	0.0	
		DIESEL	0.0	7.0	13.5	0.0	38.1	0.0	0.0	0.0	0.0	0.0	3.2	0.0	
29109H000	MNT CO, SPT BN, SEP ABN BDE	MOGAS	0.0	0.0	22.5	27.6	0.0	28.6	0.0	0.0	0.0	0.0	0.0	0.0	
		DIESEL	0.0	0.0	11.7	0.0	9.8	7.0	0.0	0.0	0.0	0.0	3.6	0.0	
29176H910	HHC, SPT BN, SEP AIM/ABN/LI	MOGAS	0.0	0.0	0.8	7.1	0.0	5.0	0.0	0.0	0.0	0.0	0.1	0.0	
		DIESEL	0.0	0.0	19.5	0.0	0.0	0.0	0.0	0.0	0.0	0.0	2.4	0.0	
57100H000	SEP ABN BDE W 1005 ADPE	MOGAS	0.0	9.0	86.3	94.3	0.0	112.6	0.0	0.0	0.0	0.0	1.9	0.0	
		DIESEL	0.0	37.4	61.2	0.0	47.9	12.0	0.0	2.8	24.7	18.5	28.7	0.0	
		JP4													318.0
57102H000	HHC, SEP AIRBORNE BRIGADE	MOGAS	0.0	0.0	17.4	5.4	0.0	9.1	0.0	0.0	0.0	0.0	0.1	0.0	
		DIESEL	0.0	8.0	0.0	0.0	0.0	0.0	0.0	0.0	0.0	0.0	4.2	0.0	
		JP4													318.0

**SUMMARY OF BULK FUEL USAGE BY EQUIPMENT CATEGORY
AIR ASSAULT DIVISION (SRC 67000L000)**

SRC	UNIT NAME	FUEL TYPE	AB	CE	GN	HG	MH	SG	SV	TI	CC	SR	WV	OV	AV
01200L000	COMBAT AVIATION BRIGADE	MOGAS	0.0	0.0	155.7	204.8	0.0	131.4	12.0	0.0	0.0	0.0	10.3	10.4	
		DIESEL	0.0	96.0	0.0	0.0	23.4	0.0	0.0	0.0	0.0	0.0	88.9	0.0	
		JP4													46013.1
01202L000	HHC, COMBAT AVIATION BDE	MOGAS	0.0	0.0	7.3	0.0	0.0	1.0	0.0	0.0	0.0	0.0	0.0	0.0	
		DIESEL	0.0	0.0	0.0	0.0	0.0	0.0	0.0	0.0	0.0	0.0	2.1	0.0	
01205L000	COMBAT AVIATION BN (UH-60)	MOGAS	0.0	0.0	16.5	25.2	0.0	13.3	0.0	0.0	0.0	0.0	1.6	0.0	
		DIESEL	0.0	16.0	0.0	0.0	2.6	0.0	0.0	0.0	0.0	0.0	9.8	0.0	
		JP4													6426.0
01206L000	HHC, COMBAT AVN BN (UH-60)	MOGAS	0.0	0.0	14.9	25.2	0.0	13.3	0.0	0.0	0.0	0.0	0.8	0.0	
		DIESEL	0.0	16.0	0.0	0.0	2.6	0.0	0.0	0.0	0.0	0.0	9.8	0.0	
		JP4													36.0
01207L000	COMBAT AVIATION CO (UH-60)	MOGAS	0.0	0.0	0.5	0.0	0.0	0.0	0.0	0.0	0.0	0.0	0.2	0.0	
		DIESEL	0.0	0.0	0.0	0.0	0.0	0.0	0.0	0.0	0.0	0.0	0.0	0.0	
		JP4													2130.0
01215L000	COMMAND AVIATION BATTALION	MOGAS	0.0	0.0	20.5	25.2	0.0	15.8	0.0	0.0	0.0	0.0	0.7	0.0	
		DIESEL	0.0	16.0	0.0	0.0	2.6	0.0	0.0	0.0	0.0	0.0	9.1	0.0	
		JP4													3685.5
01216L000	HHC, COMMAND AVIATION BN	MOGAS	0.0	0.0	18.9	25.2	0.0	15.8	0.0	0.0	0.0	0.0	0.0	0.0	
		DIESEL	0.0	16.0	0.0	0.0	2.6	0.0	0.0	0.0	0.0	0.0	9.1	0.0	
01217L000	COMMAND AVIATION CO (UH-1)	MOGAS	0.0	0.0	0.5	0.0	0.0	0.0	0.0	0.0	0.0	0.0	0.2	0.0	
		DIESEL	0.0	0.0	0.0	0.0	0.0	0.0	0.0	0.0	0.0	0.0	0.0	0.0	
		JP4													1590.0
01218L000	COMMAND AVIATION CO (OH-58)	MOGAS	0.0	0.0	0.5	0.0	0.0	0.0	0.0	0.0	0.0	0.0	0.2	0.0	
		DIESEL	0.0	0.0	0.0	0.0	0.0	0.0	0.0	0.0	0.0	0.0	0.0	0.0	
		JP4													505.5
01245L100	COMBAT AVIATION BN (CH-47)	MOGAS	0.0	0.0	29.0	48.4	0.0	39.9	12.0	0.0	0.0	0.0	1.7	10.4	
		DIESEL	0.0	16.0	0.0	0.0	5.2	0.0	0.0	0.0	0.0	0.0	15.8	0.0	
		JP4													16119.2
01246L000	HHC, COMBAT AVN BN (CH-47)	MOGAS	0.0	0.0	7.3	3.6	0.0	2.0	0.0	0.0	0.0	0.0	0.6	0.0	
		DIESEL	0.0	0.0	0.0	0.0	0.0	0.0	0.0	0.0	0.0	0.0	1.3	0.0	
01247L000	COMBAT AVIATION CO (CH-47)	MOGAS	0.0	0.0	10.8	22.4	0.0	18.9	6.0	0.0	0.0	0.0	0.5	5.2	
		DIESEL	0.0	8.0	0.0	0.0	2.6	0.0	0.0	0.0	0.0	0.0	7.2	0.0	
		JP4													8059.6
01265L100	AIR RECON SQUADRON (AH-1)	MOGAS	0.0	0.0	21.0	25.2	0.0	14.3	0.0	0.0	0.0	0.0	1.4	0.0	
		DIESEL	0.0	16.0	2.3	0.0	2.6	0.0	0.0	0.0	0.0	0.0	13.3	0.0	
		JP4													4208.8
01266L100	HHT, AIR RECON SQUADRON	MOGAS	0.0	0.0	18.9	25.2	0.0	14.3	0.0	0.0	0.0	0.0	0.9	0.0	
		DIESEL	0.0	16.0	0.0	0.0	2.6	0.0	0.0	0.0	0.0	0.0	12.3	0.0	
		JP4													1432.0
01267L100	AIR RECON TRP, RECON SQDN	MOGAS	0.0	0.0	0.5	0.0	0.0	0.0	0.0	0.0	0.0	0.0	0.1	0.0	
		DIESEL	0.0	0.0	0.0	0.0	0.0	0.0	0.0	0.0	0.0	0.0	0.2	0.0	
		JP4													694.2

Figure 10. Bulk POL Planning Factors by Type Unit— Bulk POL Table E (continued)

SUMMARY OF BULK FUEL USAGE BY EQUIPMENT CATEGORY
AIR ASSAULT DIVISION (SRC 67000L000)

SRC	UNIT NAME	FUEL TYPE	AB	CE	GN	HG	MH	SG	SV	TI	CC	SR	WV	OV	AV
01385L100	ATTACK HEL BN (AH-1)	MOGAS	0.0	0.0	16.5	20.2	0.0	12.0	0.0	0.0	0.0	0.0	1.2	0.0	
		DIESEL	0.0	8.0	0.0	0.0	2.6	0.0	0.0	0.0	0.0	0.0	10.5	0.0	
		JP4													3339.1
01386L100	HQ AND SVC CO (AH-1)	MOGAS	0.0	0.0	16.5	20.2	0.0	12.0	0.0	0.0	0.0	0.0	0.8	0.0	
		DIESEL	0.0	8.0	0.0	0.0	2.6	0.0	0.0	0.0	0.0	0.0	10.0	0.0	
		JP4													351.7
01387L100	ATK HEL CO (AH-1)	MOGAS	0.0	0.0	0.0	0.0	0.0	0.0	0.0	0.0	0.0	0.0	0.1	0.0	
		DIESEL	0.0	0.0	0.0	0.0	0.0	0.0	0.0	0.0	0.0	0.0	0.2	0.0	
		JP4													995.8
01925L000	AVIATION MAINT BN AAD	MOGAS	0.0	0.0	28.3	23.6	6.0	10.3	0.0	0.0	0.0	0.0	0.0	5.2	
		DIESEL	0.0	16.0	63.0	0.0	53.6	0.0	0.0	0.0	0.0	0.0	7.2	0.0	
		JP4													568.0
01926L000	HHSC, AVN MAINT BN, AAD	MOGAS	0.0	0.0	2.2	3.6	2.0	4.5	0.0	0.0	0.0	0.0	0.0	0.0	
		DIESEL	0.0	0.0	0.0	0.0	17.0	0.0	0.0	0.0	0.0	0.0	1.7	0.0	
01927L000	AVN MAINT CO, AMBAASLT DIV	MOGAS	0.0	0.0	13.0	10.0	2.0	2.9	0.0	0.0	0.0	0.0	0.0	2.6	
		DIESEL	0.0	8.0	31.5	0.0	18.3	0.0	0.0	0.0	0.0	0.0	2.7	0.0	
		JP4													284.0
03057L000	CHEM CO (SMK/DECON)	MOGAS	0.0	0.0	109.1	4.0	0.0	33.5	0.0	0.0	0.0	0.0	0.9	0.0	
		DIESEL	0.0	0.0	0.0	0.0	0.0	0.0	0.0	0.0	0.0	0.0	6.8	0.0	
05215L000	ENGINEER BN AIR ASLT	MOGAS	0.0	0.0	3.4	4.0	0.0	45.4	0.0	0.0	0.0	0.0	8.2	0.0	
		DIESEL	0.0	96.9	0.0	0.0	0.0	0.0	0.0	0.0	0.0	0.0	7.1	0.0	
05216L000	HHC, ENGR BN AIR ASLT	MOGAS	0.0	0.0	3.4	4.0	0.0	18.4	0.0	0.0	0.0	0.0	2.1	0.0	
		DIESEL	0.0	96.9	0.0	0.0	0.0	0.0	0.0	0.0	0.0	0.0	3.1	0.0	
05217L000	ENGR CO ENGR BN AASLT	MOGAS	0.0	0.0	0.0	0.0	0.0	9.0	0.0	0.0	0.0	0.0	2.0	0.0	
		DIESEL	0.0	0.0	0.0	0.0	0.0	0.0	0.0	0.0	0.0	0.0	1.3	0.0	
06700L000	DIV ARTILLERY,AIR ASLT-AD	MOGAS	0.0	0.0	62.1	17.4	0.0	26.8	0.0	0.0	0.0	0.0	5.2	0.0	
		DIESEL	0.0	0.0	0.0	0.0	0.0	0.0	0.0	0.0	0.0	0.0	27.9	0.0	
06702L000	HHB,DIV ARTY,AIR ASSAULT	MOGAS	0.0	0.0	14.2	0.0	0.0	1.4	0.0	0.0	0.0	0.0	0.6	0.0	
		DIESEL	0.0	0.0	0.0	0.0	0.0	0.0	0.0	0.0	0.0	0.0	2.2	0.0	
06705L000	FA BN, 105MM T,AIR ASLT-A	MOGAS	0.0	0.0	16.0	5.8	0.0	8.4	0.0	0.0	0.0	0.0	1.5	0.0	
		DIESEL	0.0	0.0	0.0	0.0	0.0	0.0	0.0	0.0	0.0	0.0	8.5	0.0	
06706L000	HHS FA BATTALION	MOGAS	0.0	0.0	11.1	5.8	0.0	8.4	0.0	0.0	0.0	0.0	1.4	0.0	
		DIESEL	0.0	0.0	0.0	0.0	0.0	0.0	0.0	0.0	0.0	0.0	2.6	0.0	
06707L000	FA BATTERY 105MM T	MOGAS	0.0	0.0	1.6	0.0	0.0	0.0	0.0	0.0	0.0	0.0	0.0	0.0	
		DIESEL	0.0	0.0	0.0	0.0	0.0	0.0	0.0	0.0	0.0	0.0	2.0	0.0	
07055L000	INF BN (AASLT)	MOGAS	0.0	0.0	4.7	7.6	0.0	5.4	0.0	0.0	0.0	0.0	4.5	0.0	
		DIESEL	0.0	0.0	0.0	0.0	0.0	0.0	0.0	0.0	0.0	0.0	3.1	0.0	
07056L000	HHC INF BN (AASLT)	MOGAS	0.0	0.0	4.1	7.6	0.0	5.4	0.0	0.0	0.0	0.0	1.3	0.0	
		DIESEL	0.0	0.0	0.0	0.0	0.0	0.0	0.0	0.0	0.0	0.0	2.3	0.0	
07057L000	RIFLE CO (AASLT)	MOGAS	0.0	0.0	0.0	0.0	0.0	0.0	0.0	0.0	0.0	0.0	0.0	0.0	
		DIESEL	0.0	0.0	0.0	0.0	0.0	0.0	0.0	0.0	0.0	0.0	0.0	0.0	
07058L000	ANTIARMOR COMPANY	MOGAS	0.0	0.0	0.5	0.0	0.0	0.0	0.0	0.0	0.0	0.0	3.2	0.0	
		DIESEL	0.0	0.0	0.0	0.0	0.0	0.0	0.0	0.0	0.0	0.0	0.8	0.0	
07209L000	LRS DET, CAV SQDN	MOGAS	0.0	0.0	0.0	0.0	0.0	0.0	0.0	0.0	0.0	0.0	0.0	0.0	
		DIESEL	0.0	0.0	2.3	0.0	0.0	0.0	0.0	0.0	0.0	0.0	0.2	0.0	
08025L000	MEDICAL BATTALION AIR ASLT	MOGAS	0.0	0.0	30.8	31.0	0.0	8.0	0.0	0.0	0.0	0.0	0.9	0.0	
		DIESEL	0.0	8.0	1.7	0.0	1.3	0.0	0.0	0.0	0.0	0.0	8.1	0.0	
		JP4													1704.0
08026L000	HQ & COMPANY A, MED BN	MOGAS	0.0	0.0	9.0	7.2	0.0	3.0	0.0	0.0	0.0	0.0	0.2	0.0	
		DIESEL	0.0	0.0	0.6	0.0	1.3	0.0	0.0	0.0	0.0	0.0	2.6	0.0	
08027L000	FWD SPT MEDICAL COMPANY	MOGAS	0.0	0.0	5.6	3.6	0.0	1.0	0.0	0.0	0.0	0.0	0.2	0.0	
		DIESEL	0.0	0.0	0.0	0.0	0.0	0.0	0.0	0.0	0.0	0.0	1.5	0.0	
08028L000	MED AIR AMBULANCE CO	MOGAS	0.0	0.0	4.9	13.0	0.0	2.0	0.0	0.0	0.0	0.0	0.0	0.0	
		DIESEL	0.0	8.0	1.1	0.0	0.0	0.0	0.0	0.0	0.0	0.0	0.9	0.0	
		JP4													1704.0
11205L000	SIGNAL BN (AIR ASSAULT)	MOGAS	0.0	0.0	98.2	0.0	0.0	4.9	0.0	0.0	0.0	0.0	0.1	0.0	
		DIESEL	0.0	0.0	0.0	0.0	0.0	0.0	0.0	0.0	0.0	0.0	9.8	0.0	
11206L000	HHC SIG BN (AIR ASSAULT)	MOGAS	0.0	0.0	11.4	0.0	0.0	2.9	0.0	0.0	0.0	0.0	0.0	0.0	
		DIESEL	0.0	0.0	0.0	0.0	0.0	0.0	0.0	0.0	0.0	0.0	1.9	0.0	
11207L000	CMD COMM CO (AIR ASSAULT)	MOGAS	0.0	0.0	45.2	0.0	0.0	1.0	0.0	0.0	0.0	0.0	0.0	0.0	
		DIESEL	0.0	0.0	0.0	0.0	0.0	0.0	0.0	0.0	0.0	0.0	4.1	0.0	
11208L000	SIG SPT CO (AIR ASSAULT)	MOGAS	0.0	0.0	41.6	0.0	0.0	1.0	0.0	0.0	0.0	0.0	0.1	0.0	
		DIESEL	0.0	0.0	0.0	0.0	0.0	0.0	0.0	0.0	0.0	0.0	3.6	0.0	
12113L000	DIVISION BAND	MOGAS	0.0	0.0	0.0	0.0	0.0	0.0	0.0	0.0	0.0	0.0	0.0	0.0	
		DIESEL	0.0	0.0	0.0	0.0	0.0	0.0	0.0	0.0	0.0	0.0	0.0	0.0	
19343L000	MP COMPANY AIR ASSAULT DIV	MOGAS	0.0	0.0	6.3	0.0	0.0	1.0	0.0	0.0	0.0	0.0	1.3	0.0	
		DIESEL	0.0	0.0	0.0	0.0	0.0	0.0	0.0	0.0	0.0	0.0	0.4	0.0	
34275L000	MI BN CEWI AIR ASSAULT DIV	MOGAS	0.0	0.0	50.8	5.0	0.0	10.5	0.0	0.0	0.0	0.0	0.1	0.0	
		DIESEL	0.0	0.0	0.6	0.0	0.0	11.0	0.0	0.0	0.0	0.0	7.9	0.3	
		JP4													279.0
34276L000	HQ, HQ & OP CO MI BN AASLT	MOGAS	0.0	0.0	9.6	5.0	0.0	0.0	0.0	0.0	0.0	0.0	0.0	0.0	
		DIESEL	0.0	0.0	0.0	0.0	0.0	6.0	0.0	0.0	0.0	0.0	1.9	0.0	
		JP4													279.0
34277L000	C&J CO MI BN AASLT DIV	MOGAS	0.0	0.0	10.6	0.0	0.0	0.0	0.0	0.0	0.0	0.0	0.0	0.0	
		DIESEL	0.0	0.0	0.0	0.0	0.0	0.0	0.0	0.0	0.0	0.0	1.7	0.3	
34278L000	INTEL&SURVL CO MI BN AASLT	MOGAS	0.0	0.0	1.3	0.0	0.0	0.0	0.0	0.0	0.0	0.0	0.1	0.0	
		DIESEL	0.0	0.0	0.0	0.0	0.0	0.0	0.0	0.0	0.0	0.0	0.8	0.0	
34279L000	SVC SPT CO MI BN ASLT DI	MOGAS	0.0	0.0	29.2	0.0	0.0	10.5	0.0	0.0	0.0	0.0	0.0	0.0	
		DIESEL	0.0	0.0	0.6	0.0	0.0	5.0	0.0	0.0	0.0	0.0	3.6	0.0	
42065L000	S&T BN AIR ASSAULT	MOGAS	0.0	0.0	17.3	58.4	0.0	74.1	0.0	0.0	0.0	0.0	0.4	0.0	
		DIESEL	0.0	7.0	25.5	0.0	233.3	4.0	0.0	0.0	0.0	0.0	20.0	0.0	
42066L000	HQ & SUP CO S&T BN AA DIV	MOGAS	0.0	0.0	3.9	7.6	0.0	17.4	0.0	0.0	0.0	0.0	0.0	0.0	
		DIESEL	0.0	7.0	25.5	0.0	74.0	4.0	0.0	0.0	0.0	0.0	6.2	0.0	
42067L000	FWD SUP CO S&T BN AA DIV	MOGAS	0.0	0.0	2.2	7.6	0.0	18.9	0.0	0.0	0.0	0.0	0.0	0.0	
		DIESEL	0.0	0.0	0.0	0.0	53.1	0.0	0.0	0.0	0.0	0.0	1.0	0.0	
42566LA00	AUG-CEB SECTION	MOGAS	0.0	0.0	5.9	28.0	0.0	0.0	0.0	0.0	0.0	0.0	0.0	0.0	
		DIESEL	0.0	0.0	0.0	0.0	0.0	0.0	0.0	0.0	0.0	0.0	1.6	0.0	

Figure 10. Bulk POL Planning Factors by Type Unit— Bulk POL Table E (continued)

SUMMARY OF BULK FUEL USAGE BY EQUIPMENT CATEGORY
AIR ASSAULT DIVISION (SRC 67000L000)

SRC	UNIT NAME	FUEL TYPE	AB	CE	GN	HG	MH	SG	SV	TI	CC	SR	WV	OV	AV
42566LB00	AUG-GRREG SECTION	MOGAS	0.0	0.0	0.0	0.0	0.0	0.0	0.0	0.0	0.0	0.0	0.2	0.0	
		DIESEL	0.0	0.0	0.0	0.0	0.0	0.0	0.0	0.0	0.0	0.0	0.4	0.0	
43065L000	MAINT BN AASSLT	MOGAS	0.0	0.0	37.7	52.0	0.0	91.0	0.9	0.0	0.0	0.0	0.3	0.0	
		DIESEL	0.0	0.0	90.8	0.0	45.1	77.0	0.0	0.0	0.0	0.0	20.1	0.0	
43066L000	HQ LT MT CO MT BN ASSLT	MOGAS	0.0	0.0	11.1	4.0	0.0	1.0	0.0	0.0	0.0	0.0	0.1	0.0	
		DIESEL	0.0	0.0	46.1	0.0	19.6	0.0	0.0	0.0	0.0	0.0	7.2	0.0	
43067L000	FWD SPT CO MT BN ASSLT	MOGAS	0.0	0.0	6.8	8.0	0.0	17.9	0.0	0.0	0.0	0.0	0.0	0.0	
		DIESEL	0.0	0.0	10.1	0.0	8.5	15.0	0.0	0.0	0.0	0.0	3.2	0.0	
43068L000	HEAVY MAINT CO, MAINT BN	MOGAS	0.0	0.0	6.2	24.0	0.0	36.1	0.9	0.0	0.0	0.0	0.0	0.0	
		DIESEL	0.0	0.0	14.3	0.0	0.0	32.0	0.0	0.0	0.0	0.0	3.2	0.0	
44145L000	ADA BN (AIR ASSAULT DIV)	MOGAS	0.0	0.0	35.5	0.0	0.0	4.4	0.0	0.0	0.0	0.0	4.3	0.0	
		DIESEL	0.0	0.0	0.0	0.0	0.0	0.0	0.0	0.0	0.0	0.0	10.3	0.0	
44146L000	HHB ADA BN (AASLT)	MOGAS	0.0	0.0	19.1	0.0	0.0	1.4	0.0	0.0	0.0	0.0	1.2	0.0	
		DIESEL	0.0	0.0	0.0	0.0	0.0	0.0	0.0	0.0	0.0	0.0	2.4	0.0	
44147L000	ADA BTRY VUL/MPDS (AASLT)	MOGAS	0.0	0.0	5.5	0.0	0.0	1.0	0.0	0.0	0.0	0.0	1.0	0.0	
		DIESEL	0.0	0.0	0.0	0.0	0.0	0.0	0.0	0.0	0.0	0.0	2.6	0.0	
55168L000	TMT CO S&T BN AASLT DIV	MOGAS	0.0	0.0	0.8	0.0	0.0	0.0	0.0	0.0	0.0	0.0	0.1	0.0	
		DIESEL	0.0	0.0	0.0	0.0	0.0	0.0	0.0	0.0	0.0	0.0	8.8	0.0	
63041L000	SPT COMD, AASLT DIV	MOGAS	0.0	0.0	121.3	170.8	6.0	187.4	0.9	0.0	0.0	0.0	1.7	5.2	
		DIESEL	0.0	31.0	202.0	0.0	333.3	81.0	0.0	0.0	0.0	0.0	59.6	0.0	
		JP4													2272.0
63042L000	HHC/MMC,SPTCMD,AASLT DIV	MOGAS	0.0	0.0	7.2	5.8	0.0	4.0	0.0	0.0	0.0	0.0	0.2	0.0	
		DIESEL	0.0	0.0	21.0	0.0	0.0	0.0	0.0	0.0	0.0	0.0	4.0	0.0	
63542LA00	AUG - DIV MAINT	MOGAS	0.0	0.0	0.0	0.0	0.0	0.0	0.0	0.0	0.0	0.0	0.0	0.0	
		DIESEL	0.0	0.0	0.0	0.0	0.0	0.0	0.0	0.0	0.0	0.0	0.0	0.0	
67000L000	AIR ASSAULT DIVISION	MOGAS	0.0	0.0	751.7	508.6	6.0	529.3	12.9	0.0	0.0	0.0	76.9	15.6	
		DIESEL	0.0	239.9	204.9	0.0	359.3	92.0	0.0	0.0	0.0	0.0	266.2	0.3	
		JP4													52772.9
67004L000	HHC AIR ASSAULT DIVISION	MOGAS	0.0	0.0	24.5	3.6	0.0	11.5	0.0	0.0	0.0	0.0	0.8	0.0	
		DIESEL	0.0	0.0	0.0	0.0	0.0	0.0	0.0	0.0	0.0	0.0	2.7	0.0	
67042L000	HHC AIR ASSAULT BRIGADE	MOGAS	0.0	0.0	7.3	1.8	0.0	3.0	0.0	0.0	0.0	0.0	0.4	0.0	
		DIESEL	0.0	0.0	0.0	0.0	0.0	0.0	0.0	0.0	0.0	0.0	1.0	0.0	

SUMMARY OF BULK FUEL USAGE BY EQUIPMENT CATEGORY
LIGHT INFANTRY DIVISION (SRC 77000L000)

SRC	UNIT NAME	FUEL TYPE	AB	CE	GN	HG	MH	SG	SV	TI	CC	SR	WV	OV	AV
01100L000	COMBAT AVN BDE (ID(L))	MOGAS	0.0	0.0	52.1	96.0	4.0	34.1	0.0	0.0	0.0	0.0	7.9	0.0	
		DIESEL	0.0	0.0	3.4	0.0	5.2	4.0	0.0	0.0	0.0	0.0	13.1	0.0	
		JP4													10169.7
01102L000	HQ & HQ COMPANY, CAB (ID(L))	MOGAS	0.0	0.0	5.9	7.6	2.0	16.1	0.0	0.0	0.0	0.0	1.3	0.0	
		DIESEL	0.0	0.0	1.1	0.0	1.3	0.0	0.0	0.0	0.0	0.0	7.4	0.0	
		JP4													202.2
01103L200	COMBAT AVN CO (UH-1)	MOGAS	0.0	0.0	10.5	22.0	0.0	3.0	0.0	0.0	0.0	0.0	0.8	0.0	
		DIESEL	0.0	0.0	0.0	0.0	1.3	0.0	0.0	0.0	0.0	0.0	0.8	0.0	
		JP4													2438.0
01167L000	AIR CAV TRP, CAV SQDN	MOGAS	0.0	0.0	0.0	0.0	0.0	0.0	0.0	0.0	0.0	0.0	0.1	0.0	
		DIESEL	0.0	0.0	0.0	0.0	0.0	0.0	0.0	0.0	0.0	0.0	0.0	0.0	
		JP4													694.2
01185L100	ATTACK HEL BN (ID(L))	MOGAS	0.0	0.0	14.2	22.0	2.0	3.0	0.0	0.0	0.0	0.0	1.3	0.0	
		DIESEL	0.0	0.0	0.0	0.0	0.0	0.0	0.0	0.0	0.0	0.0	1.1	0.0	
		JP4													3339.1
011886L100	HQ AND SVC CO	MOGAS	0.0	0.0	14.2	22.0	2.0	3.0	0.0	0.0	0.0	0.0	1.0	0.0	
		DIESEL	0.0	0.0	0.0	0.0	0.0	0.0	0.0	0.0	0.0	0.0	1.1	0.0	
		JP4													351.7
01187L100	ATK HEL CO	MOGAS	0.0	0.0	0.0	0.0	0.0	0.0	0.0	0.0	0.0	0.0	0.1	0.0	
		DIESEL	0.0	0.0	0.0	0.0	0.0	0.0	0.0	0.0	0.0	0.0	0.0	0.0	
		JP4													995.8
01977L000	TRANS ACFT MNT CO LT INF	MOGAS	0.0	0.0	10.7	19.0	0.0	2.4	6.0	0.0	0.0	0.0	1.0	0.0	
		DIESEL	0.0	0.0	19.5	0.0	1.3	0.0	0.0	0.0	0.0	0.0	3.6	0.0	
		JP4													212.0
05155L000	ENGINEER BN ID(L)	MOGAS	0.0	0.0	3.1	0.0	0.0	24.9	0.0	0.0	0.0	0.0	6.5	0.0	
		DIESEL	0.0	99.2	0.0	0.0	0.0	0.0	0.0	0.0	0.0	0.0	3.9	0.0	
05156L000	HHC,ENGR BN ID(L)	MOGAS	0.0	0.0	3.1	0.0	0.0	18.9	0.0	0.0	0.0	0.0	6.0	0.0	
		DIESEL	0.0	99.2	0.0	0.0	0.0	0.0	0.0	0.0	0.0	0.0	3.0	0.0	
05157L000	ENGR CO ENGR BN ID(L)	MOGAS	0.0	0.0	0.0	0.0	0.0	2.0	0.0	0.0	0.0	0.0	0.2	0.0	
		DIESEL	0.0	0.0	0.0	0.0	0.0	0.0	0.0	0.0	0.0	0.0	0.3	0.0	
06100L000	DIVISION ARTILLERY, ID(L)	MOGAS	0.0	0.0	71.8	22.8	0.0	26.3	0.0	0.0	0.0	0.0	2.9	0.0	
		DIESEL	0.0	0.0	0.0	0.0	0.0	0.0	0.0	0.0	0.0	0.0	19.8	0.0	
06102L000	HHB,DIV ARTY, ID(L)	MOGAS	0.0	0.0	13.6	0.0	0.0	1.0	0.0	0.0	0.0	0.0	0.8	0.0	
		DIESEL	0.0	0.0	0.0	0.0	0.0	0.0	0.0	0.0	0.0	0.0	1.0	0.0	
06125L000	FA BN,105MM T, ID(L)	MOGAS	0.0	0.0	19.4	7.6	0.0	8.4	0.0	0.0	0.0	0.0	0.7	0.0	
		DIESEL	0.0	0.0	0.0	0.0	0.0	0.0	0.0	0.0	0.0	0.0	6.3	0.0	
06126L000	HHS DS BATTALION	MOGAS	0.0	0.0	9.5	7.6	0.0	8.4	0.0	0.0	0.0	0.0	0.5	0.0	
		DIESEL	0.0	0.0	0.0	0.0	0.0	0.0	0.0	0.0	0.0	0.0	2.5	0.0	
06127L000	FA BATTERY 105MM T	MOGAS	0.0	0.0	3.3	0.0	0.0	0.0	0.0	0.0	0.0	0.0	0.0	0.0	
		DIESEL	0.0	0.0	0.0	0.0	0.0	0.0	0.0	0.0	0.0	0.0	1.2	0.0	
07015L000	INFANTRY BATTALION ID(L)	MOGAS	0.0	0.0	1.9	0.0	0.0	0.0	0.0	0.0	0.0	0.0	0.9	0.0	
		DIESEL	0.0	0.0	0.0	0.0	0.0	0.0	0.0	0.0	0.0	0.0	1.3	0.0	

Figure 10. Bulk POL Planning Factors by Type Unit—Bulk POL Table E (continued)

SUMMARY OF BULK FUEL USAGE BY EQUIPMENT CATEGORY
LIGHT INFANTRY DIVISION (SRC 77000L000)

SRC	UNIT NAME	FUEL TYPE	AB	CE	GN	HG	MH	SG	SV	TI	CC	SR	WV	OV	AV
07016L000	HHC INFANTRY BN (LIGHT)	MOGAS	0.0	0.0	1.9	0.0	0.0	0.0	0.0	0.0	0.0	0.0	0.9	0.0	
		DIESEL	0.0	0.0	0.0	0.0	0.0	0.0	0.0	0.0	0.0	0.0	1.3	0.0	
07017L000	RIFLE CO INF BN (LIGHT)	MOGAS	0.0	0.0	0.0	0.0	0.0	0.0	0.0	0.0	0.0	0.0	0.0	0.0	
		DIESEL	0.0	0.0	0.0	0.0	0.0	0.0	0.0	0.0	0.0	0.0	0.0	0.0	
07109L000	LRS DET REC SQD ID(L)	MOGAS	0.0	0.0	0.0	0.0	0.0	0.0	0.0	0.0	0.0	0.0	0.0	0.0	
		DIESEL	0.0	0.0	2.3	0.0	0.0	0.0	0.0	0.0	0.0	0.0	0.2	0.0	
08045L000	MED BN LT INF DIV	MOGAS	0.0	0.0	25.9	0.0	0.0	1.0	0.0	0.0	0.0	0.0	4.7	0.0	
		DIESEL	0.0	0.0	0.6	0.0	0.0	0.0	0.0	0.0	0.0	0.0	4.3	0.0	
08046L000	HQS & SPT CO	MOGAS	0.0	0.0	9.0	0.0	0.0	1.0	0.0	0.0	0.0	0.0	1.6	0.0	
		DIESEL	0.0	0.0	0.6	0.0	0.0	0.0	0.0	0.0	0.0	0.0	1.7	0.0	
08047L000	FORWARD SPT MEDICAL CO	MOGAS	0.0	0.0	5.6	0.0	0.0	0.0	0.0	0.0	0.0	0.0	1.0	0.0	
		DIESEL	0.0	0.0	0.0	0.0	0.0	0.0	0.0	0.0	0.0	0.0	0.9	0.0	
11045L000	SIG BN ID(L)	MOGAS	0.0	0.0	86.9	0.0	0.0	3.9	0.0	0.0	0.0	0.0	6.9	0.0	
		DIESEL	0.0	0.0	0.0	0.0	0.0	0.0	0.0	0.0	0.0	0.0	3.6	0.0	
11046L000	HHC, SIG BN ID(L)	MOGAS	0.0	0.0	7.5	0.0	0.0	1.9	0.0	0.0	0.0	0.0	0.7	0.0	
		DIESEL	0.0	0.0	0.0	0.0	0.0	0.0	0.0	0.0	0.0	0.0	1.4	0.0	
11047L000	CMD COMM CO	MOGAS	0.0	0.0	38.0	0.0	0.0	1.0	0.0	0.0	0.0	0.0	2.9	0.0	
		DIESEL	0.0	0.0	0.0	0.0	0.0	0.0	0.0	0.0	0.0	0.0	0.6	0.0	
11048L000	SIG SPT CO	MOGAS	0.0	0.0	41.4	0.0	0.0	1.0	0.0	0.0	0.0	0.0	3.3	0.0	
		DIESEL	0.0	0.0	0.0	0.0	0.0	0.0	0.0	0.0	0.0	0.0	1.6	0.0	
12113L000	DIVISION BAND	MOGAS	0.0	0.0	0.0	0.0	0.0	0.0	0.0	0.0	0.0	0.0	0.0	0.0	
		DIESEL	0.0	0.0	0.0	0.0	0.0	0.0	0.0	0.0	0.0	0.0	0.0	0.0	
17185L000	RECON SQDN, ID(L)	MOGAS	0.0	0.0	11.1	22.4	0.0	9.0	0.0	0.0	0.0	0.0	3.6	0.0	
		DIESEL	0.0	0.0	2.3	0.0	1.3	4.0	0.0	0.0	0.0	0.0	3.0	0.0	
		JP4													1752.4
17186L000	HHT RECON SQDN ID(L)	MOGAS	0.0	0.0	11.1	22.4	0.0	9.0	0.0	0.0	0.0	0.0	1.4	0.0	
		DIESEL	0.0	0.0	0.0	0.0	1.3	4.0	0.0	0.0	0.0	0.0	2.8	0.0	
		JP4													364.0
17187L000	CAV TRP ID(L)	MOGAS	0.0	0.0	0.0	0.0	0.0	0.0	0.0	0.0	0.0	0.0	1.9	0.0	
		DIESEL	0.0	0.0	0.0	0.0	0.0	0.0	0.0	0.0	0.0	0.0	0.0	0.0	
19323L000	MP COMPANY ID(L)	MOGAS	0.0	0.0	4.1	0.0	0.0	1.0	0.0	0.0	0.0	0.0	1.1	0.0	
		DIESEL	0.0	0.0	0.0	0.0	0.0	0.0	0.0	0.0	0.0	0.0	0.5	0.0	
34295L000	MI BN (CEWI) ID(L)	MOGAS	0.0	0.0	23.8	0.0	0.0	5.3	0.0	0.0	0.0	0.0	2.3	0.0	
		DIESEL	0.0	0.0	0.0	0.0	0.0	0.0	0.0	0.0	0.0	0.0	0.7	0.0	
34296L000	HQ,HQ&SVC CO MI BN LIGHT	MOGAS	0.0	0.0	13.7	0.0	0.0	5.3	0.0	0.0	0.0	0.0	1.0	0.0	
		DIESEL	0.0	0.0	0.0	0.0	0.0	0.0	0.0	0.0	0.0	0.0	0.5	0.0	
34297L000	COLL CO MI BN LT DIV	MOGAS	0.0	0.0	10.0	0.0	0.0	0.0	0.0	0.0	0.0	0.0	0.8	0.0	
		DIESEL	0.0	0.0	0.0	0.0	0.0	0.0	0.0	0.0	0.0	0.0	0.2	0.0	
34298L000	INTEL&SURVL CO MI BN LT	MOGAS	0.0	0.0	0.0	0.0	0.0	0.0	0.0	0.0	0.0	0.0	0.5	0.0	
		DIESEL	0.0	0.0	0.0	0.0	0.0	0.0	0.0	0.0	0.0	0.0	0.0	0.0	
42025L000	S&T BN ID(L)	MOGAS	0.0	0.0	7.6	3.84	0.0	49.2	0.0	0.0	0.0	0.0	1.6	0.0	
		DIESEL	0.0	0.0	18.6	0.0	191.5	15.0	0.0	0.0	0.0	0.0	19.5	0.0	
42026L000	HQ & SUP CO S&T BN ID(L)	MOGAS	0.0	0.0	1.7	11.6	0.0	16.0	0.0	0.0	0.0	0.0	0.6	0.0	
		DIESEL	0.0	0.0	18.0	0.0	5.2	15.0	0.0	0.0	0.0	0.0	2.7	0.0	
42027L000	GWD SUP CO S&T BN ID(L)	MOGAS	0.0	0.0	0.8	3.6	0.0	11.0	0.0	0.0	0.0	0.0	0.2	0.0	
		DIESEL	0.0	0.0	0.0	0.0	62.1	0.0	0.0	0.0	0.0	0.0	1.3	0.0	
42526LA00	AUG-CEB SECTION	MOGAS	0.0	0.0	3.4	16.0	0.0	0.0	0.0	0.0	0.0	0.0	0.0	0.0	
		DIESEL	0.0	0.0	0.0	0.0	0.0	0.0	0.0	0.0	0.0	0.0	0.9	0.0	
42526LB00	AUG-GRREG SECTION	MOGAS	0.0	0.0	0.0	0.0	0.0	0.0	0.0	0.0	0.0	0.0	0.2	0.0	
		DIESEL	0.0	0.0	0.0	0.0	0.0	0.0	0.0	0.0	0.0	0.0	0.2	0.0	
43045L000	MAINT BN ID(L)	MOGAS	0.0	0.0	36.0	48.0	0.0	65.9	0.0	0.0	0.0	0.0	2.0	0.0	
		DIESEL	0.0	0.0	10.6	0.0	3.9	60.0	0.0	0.0	0.0	0.0	12.7	0.0	
43046L000	HQ + LT MT CO ID(L)	MOGAS	0.0	0.0	16.2	16.0	0.0	1.4	0.0	0.0	0.0	0.0	1.3	0.0	
		DIESEL	0.0	0.0	8.3	0.0	3.9	15.0	0.0	0.0	0.0	0.0	5.7	0.0	
43048L000	MAIN SPT CO ID(L)	MOGAS	0.0	0.0	19.8	32.0	0.0	64.5	0.0	0.0	0.0	0.0	0.7	0.0	
		DIESEL	0.0	0.0	2.3	0.0	0.0	45.0	0.0	0.0	0.0	0.0	6.9	0.0	
44115L000	ADA BN, ID(L)	MOGAS	0.0	0.0	34.5	4.0	0.0	3.4	0.0	0.0	0.0	0.0	3.7	0.0	
		DIESEL	0.0	0.0	0.0	0.0	0.0	0.0	0.0	0.0	0.0	0.0	4.5	0.0	
44116L000	HHB ADA BN ID(L)	MOGAS	0.0	0.0	8.8	4.0	0.0	1.4	0.0	0.0	0.0	0.0	0.5	0.0	
		DIESEL	0.0	0.0	0.0	0.0	0.0	0.0	0.0	0.0	0.0	0.0	0.9	0.0	
44117L000	ADA GUN/STGR BTRY ID(L)	MOGAS	0.0	0.0	12.8	0.0	0.0	1.0	0.0	0.0	0.0	0.0	1.6	0.0	
		DIESEL	0.0	0.0	0.0	0.0	0.0	0.0	0.0	0.0	0.0	0.0	1.8	0.0	
55178L000	TMT CO S&T BN ID(L)	MOGAS	0.0	0.0	0.0	0.0	0.0	0.0	0.0	0.0	0.0	0.0	0.1	0.0	
		DIESEL	0.0	0.0	0.6	0.0	0.0	0.0	0.0	0.0	0.0	0.0	11.6	0.0	
63021L000	SPT CMD, ID(L)	MOGAS	0.0	0.0	84.4	107.2	0.0	120.1	6.0	0.0	0.0	0.0	12.2	0.0	
		DIESEL	0.0	0.0	70.2	0.0	196.7	75.0	0.0	0.0	0.0	0.0	40.7	0.0	
		JP4													212.0
63022L000	HHC/MMC,SPT CMD, ID(L)	MOGAS	0.0	0.0	4.2	1.8	0.0	1.5	0.0	0.0	0.0	0.0	2.8	0.0	
		DIESEL	0.0	0.0	21.0	0.0	0.0	0.0	0.0	0.0	0.0	0.0	0.6	0.0	
63522LA00	AUG-DIVISION MAIT	MOGAS	0.0	0.0	0.0	0.0	0.0	0.0	0.0	0.0	0.0	0.0	0.0	0.0	
		DIESEL	0.0	0.0	0.0	0.0	0.0	0.0	0.0	0.0	0.0	0.0	0.0	0.0	
77000L000	LIGHT INFANTRY DIVISION	MOGAS	0.0	0.0	412.7	255.2	4.0	266.1	6.0	0.0	0.0	0.0	55.1	0.0	
		DIESEL	0.0	99.2	73.6	0.0	201.9	79.0	0.0	0.0	0.0	0.0	106.1	0.0	
		JP4													10381.7
77004L000	HHC LIGHT INFANTRY DIVISION	MOGAS	0.0	0.0	12.1	3.6	0.0	8.0	0.0	0.0	0.0	0.0	1.8	0.0	
		DIESEL	0.0	0.0	0.0	0.0	0.0	0.0	0.0	0.0	0.0	0.0	1.7	0.0	
77042L000	HHC INF DIV BDE ID(L)	MOGAS	0.0	0.0	7.5	7.2	0.0	13.0	0.0	0.0	0.0	0.0	0.4	0.0	
		DIESEL	0.0	0.0	0.0	0.0	0.0	0.0	0.0	0.0	0.0	0.0	1.8	0.0	

Figure 10. Bulk POL Planning Factors by Type Unit—Bulk POL Table E (continued)

SUMMARY OF BULK FUEL USAGE BY EQUIPMENT CATEGORY
SEP LT INF BDE W1005 ADPE (SRC 77100H000)

SRC	UNIT NAME	FUEL TYPE	AB	CE	GN	HG	MH	SG	SV	TI	CC	SR	WV	OV	AV
05207H000	ENGR CO, SEP LT INF BDE	MOGAS	0.0	0.5	4.2	9.4	0.0	21.0	0.0	0.0	0.0	0.0	0.9	0.0	
		DIESEL	0.0	32.5	0.6	0.0	1.3	7.0	0.0	8.5	74.1	55.6	6.5	0.0	
06115H000	FA BN, 105MM T, LT INF BDE	MOGAS	0.0	0.0	24.1	16.6	0.0	22.0	0.0	0.0	0.0	0.0	0.0	0.0	
		DIESEL	0.0	0.0	3.6	0.0	0.0	5.0	0.0	0.0	0.0	0.0	11.8	0.0	
06116H000	HH&S BTRY, FA BN, 105MM	MOGAS	0.0	0.0	21.5	11.2	0.0	10.0	0.0	0.0	0.0	0.0	0.0	0.0	
		DIESEL	0.0	0.0	3.6	0.0	0.0	5.0	0.0	0.0	0.0	0.0	6.5	0.0	
06117H000	FA BTRY, 105MM TOWED	MOGAS	0.0	0.0	0.8	1.8	0.0	4.0	0.0	0.0	0.0	0.0	0.0	0.0	
		DIESEL	0.0	0.0	0.0	0.0	0.0	0.0	0.0	0.0	0.0	0.0	1.7	0.0	
08197H000	MEDICAL CO, SEP LT INF BDE	MOGAS	0.0	0.0	10.4	11.6	0.0	13.0	0.0	0.0	0.0	0.0	0.0	0.0	
		DIESEL	0.0	0.0	0.0	0.0	0.0	0.0	0.0	0.0	0.0	0.0	1.9	0.0	
12147H600	ADMIN CO, SEP BDE	MOGAS	0.0	0.0	2.2	3.6	0.0	3.0	0.0	0.0	0.0	0.0	0.0	0.0	
		DIESEL	0.0	0.0	13.5	0.0	0.0	0.0	0.0	0.0	0.0	0.0	1.2	0.0	
17117H000	CAV TP LT INF/ABN BDE	MOGAS	0.0	0.0	1.9	7.6	0.0	4.0	0.0	0.0	0.0	0.0	0.0	0.0	
		DIESEL	0.0	0.0	0.0	0.0	0.0	0.0	0.0	0.0	0.0	0.0	3.0	0.0	
29176H910	HHC,SPT BN,SEP AIM/ABN/ID(L)	MOGAS	0.0	0.0	0.8	7.1	0.0	5.0	0.0	0.0	0.0	0.0	0.1	0.0	
		DIESEL	0.0	0.0	19.5	0.0	0.0	0.0	0.0	0.0	0.0	0.0	2.4	0.0	
29245H000	SUPPORT BN, SEP LT INF BDE	MOGAS	0.0	0.0	30.6	51.8	0.0	53.0	5.0	0.0	0.0	0.0	0.1	0.0	
		DIESEL	0.0	0.0	50.4	0.0	26.8	7.0	0.0	2.2	12.5	14.3	10.6	0.0	
29246H000	HQ AND HQ DET, SUPPORT BN	MOGAS	0.0	0.0	4.2	0.0	0.0	1.0	0.0	0.0	0.0	0.0	0.1	0.0	
		DIESEL	0.0	0.0	0.0	0.0	0.0	0.0	0.0	0.0	0.0	0.0	0.6	0.0	
29247H000	MNT&SUP CO, SPT BN	MOGAS	0.0	0.0	17.1	29.4	0.0	32.0	5.0	0.0	0.0	0.0	0.0	0.0	
		DIESEL	0.0	0.0	17.4	0.0	26.8	7.0	0.0	2.2	12.5	14.3	4.9	0.0	
77100H000	SEP LT INF BDE W1005 ADPE	MOGAS	0.0	0.5	103.4	96.5	0.0	109.2	5.0	0.0	0.0	0.0	1.2	0.0	
		DIESEL	0.0	40.5	57.5	0.0	28.1	19.0	0.0	10.7	86.6	69.9	37.4	0.0	
		JP4													637.2
77102H000	HHC, SEP LT INF BRIGADE	MOGAS	0.0	0.0	42.7	11.2	0.0	9.1	0.0	0.0	0.0	0.0	0.1	0.0	
		DIESEL	0.0	8.0	3.0	0.0	0.0	0.0	0.0	0.0	0.0	0.0	5.5	0.0	
		JP4													637.2

SUMMARY OF BULK FUEL USAGE BY EQUIPMENT CATEGORY
HVY DIV AR 6TK M60 4M M113 (SRC 87000J210)

SRC	UNIT NAME	FUEL TYPE	AB	CE	GN	HG	MH	SG	SV	TI	CC	SR	WV	OV	AV
01285J210	CBT SPT AVN BN (HVY DIV)	MOGAS	0.0	0.0	46.1	37.6	1.5	21.3	0.0	0.0	0.0	0.0	0.0	0.0	
		DIESEL	0.0	22.0	45.8	0.0	8.5	19.0	0.0	0.0	0.0	0.0	14.0	0.0	
		JP4													1872.8
01286J210	HHC, CBT SPT AVN BN (HVY)	MOGAS	0.0	0.0	7.5	12.6	0.0	10.4	0.0	0.0	0.0	0.0	0.0	0.0	
		DIESEL	0.0	0.0	0.0	0.0	0.0	5.0	0.0	0.0	0.0	0.0	3.0	0.0	
01287J200	GEN SPT AVN CO	MOGAS	0.0	0.0	21.9	12.0	0.0	6.4	0.0	0.0	0.0	0.0	0.0	0.0	
		DIESEL	0.0	6.0	0.6	0.0	0.0	9.0	0.0	0.0	0.0	0.0	5.3	0.0	
		JP4													1540.8
03387J200	CHEMICAL CO, HVY DIV	MOGAS	0.0	0.0	36.8	4.0	0.0	64.0	0.0	0.0	0.0	0.0	0.0	0.0	
		DIESEL	0.0	0.0	0.6	0.0	0.0	5.0	0.0	6.0	51.6	53.4	9.5	0.0	
05145J210	ENGR BN, HVY DIV - RIBBON	MOGAS	0.0	2.0	22.6	45.6	0.0	102.7	0.0	0.0	0.0	0.0	0.1	0.0	
		DIESEL	86.4	68.0	2.8	0.0	8.5	34.0	0.0	147.1	1583.2	1311.5	37.3	0.0	
05146J200	HQ-HQ COMPANY	MOGAS	0.0	0.0	4.1	7.6	0.0	11.5	0.0	0.0	0.0	0.0	0.1	0.0	
		DIESEL	0.0	0.0	0.6	0.0	8.5	7.0	0.0	1.0	8.6	8.9	7.8	0.0	
05147J200	ENGR CO, ENGR BN, HVY DIV	MOGAS	0.0	0.5	4.2	7.6	0.0	19.5	0.0	0.0	0.0	0.0	0.0	0.0	
		DIESEL	0.0	17.0	0.6	0.0	0.0	5.0	0.0	36.5	393.6	325.6	5.2	0.0	
05148J210	BRIDGE COMPANY - RIBBON	MOGAS	0.0	0.0	1.7	7.6	0.0	13.0	0.0	0.0	0.0	0.0	0.0	0.0	
		DIESEL	86.4	0.0	0.0	0.0	0.0	7.0	0.0	0.0	0.0	0.0	8.5	0.0	
06300J210	ARMD DIVARTY W/TACFIRE	MOGAS	0.0	0.0	112.5	109.6	0.0	121.5	0.0	0.0	0.0	0.0	0.3	0.0	
		DIESEL	0.0	0.0	41.2	0.0	0.0	100.0	0.0	288.5	1934.4	2272.6	82.0	30.7	
06302J200	HHB DIV ARTY HVY DIV	MOGAS	0.0	0.0	26.3	5.4	0.0	8.4	0.0	0.0	0.0	0.0	0.2	0.0	
		DIESEL	0.0	0.0	9.8	0.0	0.0	5.0	0.0	1.0	8.6	8.9	5.5	0.0	
06307J200	TGT ACQ BTRY HVY DIV	MOGAS	0.0	0.0	4.4	5.4	0.0	4.5	0.0	0.0	0.0	0.0	0.0	0.0	
		DIESEL	0.0	0.0	12.0	0.0	0.0	10.0	0.0	0.0	0.0	0.0	5.0	0.0	
06365J210	FA BN 155 SP HVY DIV	MOGAS	0.0	0.0	20.0	25.6	0.0	27.3	0.0	0.0	0.0	0.0	0.0	0.0	
		DIESEL	0.0	0.0	5.3	0.0	0.0	25.0	0.0	72.4	432.5	545.0	17.2	10.1	
06365J220	FA BN 155 SP HVY DIV	MOGAS	0.0	0.0	20.0	25.6	0.0	27.3	0.0	0.0	0.0	0.0	0.0	0.0	
		DIESEL	0.0	0.0	5.3	0.0	0.0	25.0	0.0	72.4	432.5	545.0	17.2	10.1	
06366J210	HHB FA BN 155SP HVY DIV	MOGAS	0.0	0.0	12.8	7.2	0.0	7.0	0.0	0.0	0.0	0.0	0.0	0.0	
		DIESEL	0.0	0.0	3.6	0.0	0.0	5.0	0.0	7.0	60.2	62.3	3.0	3.4	
06366J220	HHB FA BN 155SP HVY DIV	MOGAS	0.0	0.0	12.8	7.2	0.0	7.0	0.0	0.0	0.0	0.0	0.0	0.0	
		DIESEL	0.0	0.0	3.6	0	0.0	5.0	0.0	7.0	60.2	62.3	2.1	3.4	
06367J200	FA BTRY 155SP HVY DIV	MOGAS	0.0	0.0	1.1	3.6	0.0	3.0	0.0	0.0	0.0	0.0	0.0	0.0	
		DIESEL	0.0	0.0	0.6	0.0	0.0	5.0	0.0	19.6	111.6	146.6	2.0	2.2	
06369J200	SVC BTRY 155SP HVY DIV	MOGAS	0.0	0.0	3.9	7.6	0.0	11.3	0.0	0.0	0.0	0.0	0.0	0.0	
		DIESEL	0.0	0.0	0.0	0.0	0.0	5.0	0.0	6.6	37.5	42.9	8.2	0.0	
06395J200	FA BN,8IN/MLRS HVY DIV	MOGAS	0.0	0.0	21.4	22.0	0.0	26.5	0.0	0.0	0.0	0.0	0.0	0.0	
		DIESEL	0.0	0.0	3.6	0.0	0.0	10.0	0.0	69.3	619.7	619.8	19.7	0.0	
06396J200	HHB 8IN/MLRS BN HVY DIV	MOGAS	0.0	0.0	6.4	3.6	0.0	7.0	0.0	0.0	0.0	0.0	0.0	0.0	
		DIESEL	0.0	0.0	3.0	0.0	0.0	0.0	0.0	3.0	25.8	26.7	2.4	0.0	
06396J202	AUG- FIST, TANK BN	MOGAS	0.0	0.0	0.5	0.0	0.0	0.0	0.0	0.0	0.0	0.0	0.0	0.0	
		DIESEL	0.0	0.0	0.0	0.0	0.0	0.0	0.0	1.0	8.6	8.9	0.0	0.3	
06397J200	FA BTRY 8IN SP HVY DIV	MOGAS	0.0	0.0	3.2	3.6	0.0	3.0	0.0	0.0	0.0	0.0	0.0	0.0	
		DIESEL	0.0	0.0	0.0	0.0	0.0	0.0	0.0	21.2	163.0	200.2	2.1	0.0	
06398J200	FA BTRY MLRS	MOGAS	0.0	0.0	3.8	3.6	0.0	4.5	0.0	0.0	0.0	0.0	0.0	0.0	
		DIESEL	0.0	0.0	0.0	0.0	0.0	0.0	0.0	15.5	169.4	113.0	7.1	0.0	
06399J200	SVC BTRY 8IN/MLRS HVY DIV	MOGAS	0.0	0.0	4.7	7.6	0.0	9.0	0.0	0.0	0.0	0.0	0.0	0.0	
		DIESEL	0.0	0.0	0.6	0.0	0.0	10.0	0.0	8.4	98.5	79.7	5.7	0.0	
07245J220	INF BN-MECH E/W M113	MOGAS	0.0	0.0	4.4	23.4	0.0	29.0	0.0	0.0	0.0	0.0	0.1	0.0	
		DIESEL	0.0	0.0	5.1	0.0	0.0	45.0	0.0	124.8	1072.3	1105.1	7.1	0.0	
07246J220	HHC INF BN MECH M113	MOGAS	0.0	0.0	3.9	23.4	0.0	29.0	0.0	0.0	0.0	0.0	0.1	0.0	
		DIESEL	0.0	0.0	2.3	0.0	0.0	20.0	0.0	44.8	384.3	393.1	5.1	0.0	
07247J220	RIFLE CO INF BN MECH M113	MOGAS	0.0	0.0	0.0	0.0	0.0	0.0	0.0	0.0	0.0	0.0	0.0	0.0	
		DIESEL	0.0	0.0	0.6	0.0	0.0	5.0	0.0	16.0	137.6	142.4	0.4	0.0	

Figure 10. *Bulk POL Planning Factors by Type Unit—Bulk POL Table E* (continued)

SUMMARY OF BULK FUEL USAGE BY EQUIPMENT CATEGORY
HVY DIV AR 6TK M60 4M M113 (SRC 87000J210)—Cont'd

SRC	UNIT NAME	FUEL TYPE	AB	CE	GN	HG	MH	SG	SV	TI	CC	SR	WV	OV	AV
07248J200	ANTIARMOR CO INF BN(M) IT	MOGAS	0.0	0.0	0.5	0.0	0.0	0.0	0.0	0.0	0.0	0.0	0.0	0.0	
		DIESEL	0.0	0.0	0.6	0.0	0.0	5.0	0.0	16.0	137.6	142.4	0.4	0.0	
08205J200	MEDICAL BN HVY DIV	MOGAS	0.0	0.0	46.7	28.6	0.0	52.0	0.0	0.0	0.0	0.0	0.0	0.0	
		DIESEL	0.0	0.0	11.1	0.0	0.0	20.0	0.0	15.0	129.0	133.5	14.3	0.0	
08206J200	HHD MED BN HVY DIV	MOGAS	0.0	0.0	1.7	0.0	0.0	0.0	0.0	0.0	0.0	0.0	0.0	0.0	
		DIESEL	0.0	0.0	2.2	0.0	0.0	0.0	0.0	0.0	0.0	0.0	1.6	0.0	
08207J200	MED CO MED BN HVY DIV	MOGAS	0.0	0.0	10.4	5.8	0.0	13.0	0.0	0.0	0.0	0.0	0.0	0.0	
		DIESEL	0.0	0.0	2.2	0.0	0.0	5.0	0.0	5.0	43.0	44.5	2.8	0.0	
08208J200	MED SPT CO MED BN HVY DIV	MOGAS	0.0	0.0	13.7	11.2	0.0	13.0	0.0	0.0	0.0	0.0	0.0	0.0	
		DIESEL	0.0	0.0	2.2	0.0	0.0	5.0	0.0	0.0	0.0	0.0	4.1	0.0	
09558J200	MSL SPT CO HVY DIV	MOGAS	0.0	0.0	27.6	4.0	0.0	1.0	0.0	0.0	0.0	0.0	0.0	0.0	
		DIESEL	0.0	30.0	56.7	0.0	1.3	4.0	0.0	2.0	36.8	25.5	7.6	0.0	
11035J200	SIGNAL BN (HEAVY DIV)	MOGAS	0.0	0.0	79.3	37.6	0.0	15.3	0.0	0.0	0.0	0.0	0.2	0.0	
		DIESEL	0.0	0.0	2.3	0.0	0.0	20.0	0.0	0.0	0.0	0.0	12.1	0.0	
11036J200	HHC SIG BN (HEAVY DIV)	MOGAS	0.0	0.0	13.8	4.0	0.0	3.3	0.0	0.0	0.0	0.0	0.2	0.0	
		DIESEL	0.0	0.0	0.6	0.0	0.0	5.0	0.0	0.0	0.0	0.0	3.9	0.0	
11037J200	CMD OPNS CO (HEAVY DIV)	MOGAS	0.0	0.0	27.2	13.0	0.0	4.0	0.0	0.0	0.0	0.0	0.0	0.0	
		DIESEL	0.0	0.0	0.6	0.0	0.0	5.0	0.0	0.0	0.0	0.0	3.1	0.0	
11038J200	FWD COMM CO HEAVY DIVISION	MOGAS	0.0	0.0	24.3	9.4	0.0	4.0	0.0	0.0	0.0	0.0	0.0	0.0	
		DIESEL	0.0	0.0	0.6	0.0	0.0	5.0	0.0	0.0	0.0	0.0	2.2	0.0	
11039J200	SIG SPT OPNS CO HEAVY DIV	MOGAS	0.0	0.0	14.0	11.2	0.0	4.0	0.0	0.0	0.0	0.0	0.0	0.0	
		DIESEL	0.0	0.0	0.6	0.0	0.0	5.0	0.0	0.0	0.0	0.0	2.8	0.0	
12217J200	AG CO- ARMOR/INF(MECH) DIV	MOGAS	0.0	0.0	2.5	11.2	0.0	4.0	0.0	0.0	0.0	0.0	0.1	0.0	
		DIESEL	0.0	0.0	16.5	0.0	0.0	5.0	0.0	0.0	0.0	0.0	1.9	0.0	
17185J210	ATK HEL BN CBAA AHIS HV DIV	MOGAS	0.0	0.0	15.1	19.2	0.0	13.2	0.0	0.0	0.0	0.0	0.0	0.0	
		DIESEL	0.0	8.0	1.1	0.0	3.9	10.0	0.0	0.0	0.0	0.0	10.1	0.0	
		JP4													3539.7
17186J210	HQ AND SVC CO	MOGAS	0.0	0.0	15.1	19.2	0.0	13.2	0.0	0.0	0.0	0.0	0.0	0.0	
		DIESEL	0.0	8.0	1.1	0.0	3.9	10.0	0.0	0.0	0.0	0.0	9.4	0.0	
		JP4													477.9
17187J210	ATK HEL CO	MOGAS	0.0	0.0	0.0	0.0	0.0	0.0	0.0	0.0	0.0	0.0	0.0	0.0	
		DIESEL	0.0	0.0	0.0	0.0	0.0	0.0	0.0	0.0	0.0	0.0	0.2	0.0	
		JP4													1020.6
17201J210	CAV BDE AIR ATK (CBAA)AHI	MOGAS	0.0	0.0	103.8	109.2	1.5	75.6	0.0	0.0	0.0	0.0	0.0	0.0	
		DIESEL	0.0	46.0	49.8	0.0	18.9	59.0	0.0	89.0	1067.6	668.7	50.7	0.6	
		JP4													10557.0
17202J200	HQ & HQ TROOP, CBAA	MOGAS	0.0	0.0	7.6	4.0	0.0	4.4	0.0	0.0	0.0	0.0	0.0	0.0	
		DIESEL	0.0	0.0	0.6	0.0	0.0	0.0	0.0	0.0	0.0	0.0	3.0	0.0	
17205J210	CAV SQDN, CBAA AHIS HV DIV	MOGAS	0.0	0.0	20.0	29.2	0.0	23.4	0.0	0.0	0.0	0.0	0.0	0.0	
		DIESEL	0.0	8.0	1.1	0.0	2.6	20.0	0.0	89.0	1067.6	668.7	13.7	0.6	
		JP4													1604.8
17206J210	HQ AND HQ TRP, CAV SQDN	MOGAS	0.0	0.0	20.0	29.2	0.0	21.4	0.0	0.0	0.0	0.0	0.0	0.0	
		DIESEL	0.0	8.0	1.1	0.0	2.6	20.0	0.0	21.8	238.5	201.8	12.5	0.6	
		JP4													142.0
17207J210	CAV TRP, CAV SQDN	MOGAS	0.0	0.0	0.0	0.0	0.0	1.0	0.0	0.0	0.0	0.0	0.0	0.0	
		DIESEL	0.0	0.0	0.0	0.0	0.0	0.0	0.0	33.6	414.6	233.4	0.3	0.0	
17208J210	AIR CAV TRP, CAV SQDN	MOGAS	0.0	0.0	0.0	0.0	0.0	0.0	0.0	0.0	0.0	0.0	0.0	0.0	
		DIESEL	0.0	0.0	0.0	0.0	0.0	0.0	0.0	0.0	0.0	0.0	0.2	0.0	
		JP4													731.4
17235J210	TANK BATTALION, EQ/W, M60	MOGAS	0.0	0.0	5.5	36.2	0.0	29.8	0.0	0.0	0.0	0.0	0.0	0.0	
		DIESEL	0.0	0.0	0.6	0.0	0.0	7.0	0.0	51.4	619.0	490.5	12.9	0.0	
17236J110	HHC, TK BN, M60	MOGAS	0.0	0.0	5.5	36.2	0.0	29.8	0.0	0.0	0.0	0.0	0.0	0.0	
		DIESEL	0.0	0.0	0.6	0.0	0.0	7.0	0.0	51.4	619.0	490.5	11.8	0.0	
17237J110	TK CO. TK BN, M60	MOGAS	0.0	0.0	0.0	0.0	0.0	0.0	0.0	0.0	0.0	0.0	0.0	0.0	
		DIESEL	0.0	0.0	0.0	0.0	0.0	0.0	0.0	0.0	0.0	0.0	0.3	0.0	
19217J200	MP CO-HVY DIV	MOGAS	0.0	0.0	3.2	4.0	0.0	0	0.0	0.0	0.0	0.0	0.0	0.0	
		DIESEL	0.0	0.0	1.1	0.0	0.0	5.0	0.0	0.0	0.0	0.0	2.3	0.0	
34285J200	MI BN (CEWI) HVY DIV	MOGAS	0.0	0.0	63.4	18.8	0.0	17.5	0.0	0.0	0.0	0.0	0.0	0.0	
		DIESEL	0.0	0.0	16.5	0.0	0.0	17.0	0.0	11.4	85.2	90.9	13.4	0.4	
34286J200	HQ HQ-OP CO MI BN CEWI DIV	MOGAS	0.0	0.0	13.1	0.0	0.0	0.0	0.0	0.0	0.0	0.0	0.0	0.0	
		DIESEL	0.0	0.0	1.5	0.0	0.0	12.0	0.0	1.0	8.6	8.9	3.1	0.0	
34287J200	EW CO MI BN CEWI, DIV	MOGAS	0.0	0.0	15.2	0.0	0.0	0.0	0.0	0.0	0.0	0.0	0.0	0.0	
		DIESEL	0.0	0.0	15.0	0.0	0.0	0.0	0.0	0.0	0.0	0.0	1.3	0.4	
34288J200	INTL-SVL CO MI BN CEWI DIV	MOGAS	0.0	0.0	0.0	0.0	0.0	0.0	0.0	0.0	0.0	0.0	0.0	0.0	
		DIESEL	0.0	0.0	0.0	0.0	0.0	0.0	0.0	6.0	51.6	53.4	2.8	0.0	
34289J200	SVC SPT CO MI BN CEWI DIV	MOGAS	0.0	0.0	35.0	18.8	0.0	17.5	0.0	0.0	0.0	0.0	0.0	0.0	
		DIESEL	0.0	0.0	0.0	0.0	0.0	5.0	0.0	4.4	25.0	28.6	6.0	0.0	
42004J200	SUP CO FWD SPT BN HVY DIV	MOGAS	0.0	0.0	2.5	7.2	0.0	7.9	0.0	0.0	0.0	0.0	0.0	0.0	
		DIESEL	0.0	21.0	0.0	0.0	21.3	0.0	0.0	0.0	0.0	0.0	4.9	0.0	
42005J200	S&T BN HEAVY DIVISION	MOGAS	0.0	0.0	16.2	32.6	0.0	39.3	14.0	0.0	0.0	0.0	0.0	0.0	
		DIESEL	0.0	28.0	3.4	0.0	43.5	17.0	0.0	0.0	0.0	0.0	32.8	0.0	
42006J200	HHC S&T BN HEAVY DIVISION	MOGAS	0.0	0.0	0.8	21.0	0.0	8.0	0.0	0.0	0.0	0.0	0.0	0.0	
		DIESEL	0.0	0.0	1.1	0.0	0.0	5.0	0.0	0.0	0.0	0.0	2.1	0.0	
42007J200	S&S CO S&T BN HVY DIV	MOGAS	0.0	0.0	13.7	0.0	0.0	25.5	14.0	0.0	0.0	0.0	0.0	0.0	
		DIESEL	0.0	28.0	0.0	0.0	43.5	0.0	0.0	0.0	0.0	0.0	10.1	0.0	
43004J200	MAINT CO,FWD SPT BN,HVY DIV	MOGAS	0.0	0.0	33.2	16.0	0.0	15.5	0.0	0.0	0.0	0.0	0.0	0.0	
		DIESEL	0.0	7.0	11.8	0.0	9.8	11.0	0.0	3.0	45.4	34.4	9.3	0.0	
43004J201	TK SYSTEM SPT TM	MOGAS	0.0	0.0	0.5	0.0	0.0	5.6	0.0	0.0	0.0	0.0	0.0	0.0	
		DIESEL	0.0	0.0	0.0	0.0	0.0	0.0	0.0	1.0	8.6	8.9	0.7	0.0	
43004J202	INF SYS(M) SPT TM	MOGAS	0.0	0.0	3.5	0.0	0.0	5.6	0.0	0.0	0.0	0.0	0.0	0.0	
		DIESEL	0.0	0.0	0.0	0.0	0.0	0.0	0.0	1.0	8.6	8.9	0.8	0.0	
43005J200	MAINT BN,SPT COMD,HVY DIV	MOGAS	0.0	0.0	83.3	66.4	0.0	79.1	0.0	0.0	0.0	0.0	0.0	0.0	
		DIESEL	0.0	37.0	153.7	0.0	26.8	17.0	0.0	6.0	90.7	68.9	27.3	0.0	
43006J200	HQ&SUPPORT CO HVY DIV	MOGAS	0.0	0.0	7.3	7.6	0.0	4.0	0.0	0.0	0.0	0.0	0.0	0.0	
		DIESEL	0.0	0.0	5.2	0.0	17.0	0.0	0.0	0.0	0.0	0.0	6.2	0.0	

Figure 10. Bulk POL Planning Factors by Type Unit—Bulk POL Table E (continued)

SUMMARY OF BULK FUEL USAGE BY EQUIPMENT CATEGORY
HVY DIV AR 6TK M60 4M M113 (SRC 87000J210)

SRC	UNIT NAME	FUEL TYPE	AB	CE	GN	HG	MH	SG	SV	TI	CC	SR	WV	OV	AV
43007J200	LIGHT MAINT CO HVY DIV	MOGAS	0.0	0.0	32.9	25.4	0.0	20.9	0.0	0.0	0.0	0.0	0.0	0.0	
		DIESEL	0.0	0.0	88.2	0.0	0.0	0.0	0.0	0.0	0.0	0.0	6.3	0.0	
43008J200	HEAVY MAINT CO HVY DIV	MOGAS	0.0	0.0	15.5	29.4	0.0	53.2	0.0	0.0	0.0	0.0	0.0	0.0	
		DIESEL	0.0	7.0	3.6	0.0	8.5	13.0	0.0	4.0	54.0	43.3	7.1	0.0	
55087J200	TMT CO S&T BN HEAVY DIV	MOGAS	0.0	0.0	0.0	0.0	0.0	0.9	0.0	0.0	0.0	0.0	0.0	0.0	
		DIESEL	0.0	0.0	0.6	0.0	0.0	5.0	0.0	0.0	0.0	0.0	13.9	0.0	
55089J200	TMT CO (HY) S&T BN HY DIV	MOGAS	0.0	0.0	1.7	11,6	0.0	4.9	0.0	0.0	0.0	0.0	0.0	0.0	
		DIESEL	0.0	0.0	1.7	0.0	0.0	7.0	0.0	0.0	0.0	0.0	6.7	0.0	
55427J200	TAM CO,CBT SPT,AVN BN,CBA	MOGAS	0.0	0.0	16.7	13.0	1.5	4.4	0.0	0.0	0.0	0.0	0.0	0.0	
		DIESEL	0.0	16.0	45.2	0.0	8.5	5.0	0.0	0.0	0.0	0.0	5.1	0.0	
		JP4													332.0
63001J210	SPT COMD, 6×4, HVY DIV,AR	MOGAS	0.0	0.0	282.4	216.0	0.0	308.3	14.0	0.0	0.0	0.0	0.4	0.0	
		DIESEL	0.0	149.0	272.6	0.0	163.6	92.0	0.0	40.0	441.8	394.7	132.6	0.0	
63002J200	HHC, SPT COMD, HV DIV	MOGAS	0.0	0.0	0.8	7.6	0.0	4.0	0.0	0.0	0.0	0.0	0.1	0.0	
		DIESEL	0.0	0.0	6.0	0.0	0.0	0.0	0.0	0.0	0.0	0.0	1.2	0.0	
63003J200	DMMC,SPT COMD,HV DIV	MOGAS	0.0	0.0	0.0	0.0	0.0	0.0	0.0	0.0	0.0	0.0	0.0	0.0	
		DIESEL	0.0	0.0	37.5	0.0	0.0	0.0	0.0	0.0	0.0	0.0	2.5	0.0	
63005J210	FWD SPT BN 2×1 HVY DIV	MOGAS	0.0	0.0	43.1	23.2	0.0	41.4	0.0	0.0	0.0	0.0	0.1	0.0	
		DIESEL	0.0	28.0	14.8	0.0	31.1	11.0	0.0	6.0	71.2	61.1	17.2	0.0	
63005J220	FWD SPT BN 2×2 HVY DIV	MOGAS	0.0	0.0	46.6	23.2	0.0	47.0	0.0	0.0	0.0	0.0	0.1	0.0	
		DIESEL	0.0	28.0	14.8	0.0	31.1	11.0	0.0	7.0	79.8	70.0	17.9	0.0	
63002J200	HHD,FWD SPT BN,HEAVY DIV	MOGAS	0.0	0.0	2.8	0.0	0.0	1.0	0.0	0.0	0.0	0.0	0.1	0.0	
		DIESEL	0.0	0.0	3.0	0.0	0.0	0.0	0.0	0.0	0.0	0.0	0.8	0.0	
87000J210	HVY DIV,AR 6TK M60,4M M11	MOGAS	0.0	2.0	791.6	898.6	1.5	1024.2	14.0	0.0	0.0	0.0	1.3	0.0	
		DIESEL	86.4	263.0	410.9	0.0	191.0	569.0	0.0	1421.2	13419.5	12420.2	453.6	31.7	
		JP4													10557.0
87004J210	HHC ARMORED DIVISION	MOGAS	0.0	0.0	16.0	14.8	0.0	12.0	0.0	0.0	0.0	0.0	0.0	0.0	
		DIESEL	0.0	0.0	0.0	0.0	0.0	0.0	0.0	4.0	34.4	35.6	2.1	0.0	
87042J210	HHC ARMD DIV BDE	MOGAS	0.0	0.0	5.9	9.4	0.0	4.0	0.0	0.0	0.0	0.0	0.0	0.0	
		DIESEL	0.0	0.0	0.0	0.0	0.0	5.0	0.0	9.2	72.7	76.6	1.6	0.0	
87042J220	HHC INF DIV (MECH) BDE	MOGAS	0.0	0.0	8.9	9.4	0.0	4.0	0.0	0.0	0.0	0.0	0.0	0.0	
		DIESEL	0.0	0.0	0.0	0.0	0.0	5.0	0.0	9.2	72.7	76.6	1.6	0.0	

SUMMARY OF BULK FUEL USAGE BY EQUIPMENT CATEGORY
HVY DIV M 5TK M60 5M M113 (SRC 87000J220)

SRC	UNIT NAME	FUEL TYPE	AB	CE	GN	HG	MH	SG	SV	TI	CC	SR	WV	OV	AV
01285J210	CBT SPT AVN BN (HVY DIV)	MOGAS	0.0	0.0	46.1	37.6	1.5	21.3	0.0	0.0	0.0	0.0	0.0	0.0	
		DIESEL	0.0	22.0	45.8	0.0	8.5	19.0	0.0	0.0	0.0	0.0	13.6	0.0	
		JP4													1872.8
01286J210	HHC, CBT SPT AVN BN (HVY)	MOGAS	0.0	0.0	7.5	12.6	0.0	10.4	0.0	0.0	0.0	0.0	0.0	0.0	
		DIESEL	0.0	0.0	0.0	0.0	0.0	5.0	0.0	0.0	0.0	0.0	3.2	0.0	
01287J200	GEN SPT AVN CO	MOGAS	0.0	0.0	21.9	12.0	0.0	6.4	0.0	0.0	0.0	0.0	0.0	0.0	
		DIESEL	0.0	6.0	0.6	0.0	0.0	9.0	0.0	0.0	0.0	0.0	5.3	0.0	
		JP4													1540.8
03387J200	CHEMICAL CO, HVY DIV	MOGAS	0.0	0.0	36.8	4.0	0.0	64.0	0.0	0.0	0.0	0.0	0.0	0.0	
		DIESEL	0.0	0.0	0.6	0.0	0.0	5.0	0.0	6.0	51.6	53.4	9.5	0.0	
05145J210	ENGR BN, HVY DIV - RIBBON	MOGAS	0.0	2.0	22.6	45.6	0.0	102.7	0.0	0.0	0.0	0.0	0.1	0.0	
		DIESEL	86.4	68.0	2.8	0.0	8.5	34.0	0.0	147.1	1583.2	1311.5	36.9	0.0	
05146J200	HQ-HQ COMPANY	MOGAS	0.0	0.0	4.1	7.6	0.0	11.5	0.0	0.0	0.0	0.0	0.1	0.0	
		DIESEL	0.0	0.0	0.6	0.0	8.5	7.0	0.0	1.0	8.6	8.9	7.4	0.0	
05147J200	ENGR CO, ENGR BN, HVY DIV	MOGAS	0.0	0.5	4.2	7.6	0.0	19.5	0.0	0.0	0.0	0.0	0.0	0.0	
		DIESEL	0.0	17.0	0.6	0.0	0.0	5.0	0.0	36.5	393.6	325.6	5.3	0.0	
05148J210	BRIDGE COMPANY - RIBBON	MOGAS	0.0	0.0	1.7	7.6	0.0	13.0	0.0	0.0	0.0	0.0	0.0	0.0	
		DIESEL	86.4	0.0	0.0	0.0	0.0	7.0	0.0	0.0	0.0	0.0	8.2	0.0	
06300J220	MECH DIVARTY W/TACFIRE	MOGAS	0.0	0.0	112.5	109.6	0.0	121.5	0.0	0.0	0.0	0.0	0.0	0.0	
		DIESEL	0.0	0.0	41.2	0.0	0.0	100.0	0.0	288.5	1934.4	2272.6	82.2	30.7	
06302J200	HHB DIV ARTY HVY DIV	MOGAS	0.0	0.0	26.3	5.4	0.0	8.4	0.0	0.0	0.0	0.0	0.1	0.0	
		DIESEL	0.0	0.0	9.8	0.0	0.0	5.0	0.0	1.0	8.6	8.9	5.4	0.0	
06307J200	TGT ACQ BTRY HVY DIV	MOGAS	0.0	0.0	4.4	5.4	0.0	4.5	0.0	0.0	0.0	0.0	0.0	0.0	
		DIESEL	0.0	0.0	12.0	0.0	0.0	10.0	0.0	0.0	0.0	0.0	5.0	0.0	
06365J210	FA BN 155 SP HVY DIV	MOGAS	0.0	0.0	20.0	25.6	0.0	27.3	0.0	0.0	0.0	0.0	0.0	0.0	
		DIESEL	0.0	0.0	5.3	0.0	0.0	25.0	0.0	7.24	432.5	545.0	17.3	10.1	
06365J220	FA BN 155 SP HVY DIV	MOGAS	0.0	0.0	20.0	25.6	0.0	27.3	0.0	0.0	0.0	0.0	0.0	0.0	
		DIESEL	0.0	0.0	5.3	0.0	0.0	25.0	0.0	72.4	432.5	545.0	17.3	10.1	
06366J210	HHB FA BN 155SP HVY DIV	MOGAS	0.0	0.0	12.8	7.2	0.0	7.0	0.0	0.0	0.0	0.0	0.0	0.0	
		DIESEL	0.0	0.0	3.6	0.0	0.0	5.0	0.0	7.0	60.2	62.3	2.5	3.4	
06366J220	HHB FA BN 155SP HVY DIV	MOGAS	0.0	0.0	12.8	7.2	0.0	7.0	0.0	0.0	0.0	0.0	0.0	0.0	
		DIESEL	0.0	0.0	3.6	0.0	0.0	5.0	0.0	7.0	60.2	62.3	2.4	3.4	
06367J200	FA BTRY 155SP HVY DIV	MOGAS	0.0	0.0	1.1	3.6	0.0	3.0	0.0	0.0	0.0	0.0	0.0	0.0	
		DIESEL	0.0	0.0	0.6	0.0	0.0	5.0	0.0	19.6	111.6	146.6	2.2	2.2	
06369J200	SVC BTRY 155SP HVY DIV	MOGAS	0.0	0.0	3.9	7.6	0.0	11.3	0.0	0.0	0.0	0.0	0.0	0.0	
		DIESEL	0.0	0.0	0.0	0.0	0.0	5.0	0.0	6.6	37.5	42.9	8.2	0.0	
06395J200	FA BN, 8IN/MLRS HVY DIV	MOGAS	0.0	0.0	21.4	22.0	0.0	26.5	0.0	0.0	0.0	0.0	0.0	0.0	
		DIESEL	0.0	0.0	3.6	0.0	0.0	10.0	0.0	69.3	619.7	619.8	19.7	0.0	
06396J200	HHB 8IN/MLRS BN HVY DIV	MOGAS	0.0	0.0	6.4	3.6	0.0	7.0	0.0	0.0	0.0	0.0	0.0	0.0	
		DIESEL	0.0	0.0	3.0	0.0	0.0	0.0	0.0	3.0	25.8	26.7	2.4	0.0	
06396J201	AUG-FIST, MECH BN	MOGAS	0.0	0.0	0.5	0.0	0.0	0.0	0.0	0.0	0.0	0.0	0.0	0.0	
		DIESEL	0.0	0.0	0.0	0.0	0.0	0.0	0.0	1.0	8.6	8.9	0.0	0.3	

Figure 10. Bulk POL Planning Factors by Type Unit— Bulk POL Table E (continued)

SUMMARY OF BULK FUEL USAGE BY EQUIPMENT CATEGORY
HVY DIV M 5TK M60 5M M113 (SRC 87000J220)—Cont'd

SRC	UNIT NAME	FUEL TYPE	AB	CE	GN	HG	MH	SG	SV	TI	CC	SR	WV	OV	AV
06397J200	FA BTRY 8IN SP HVY DIV	MOGAS	0.0	0.0	3.2	3.6	0.0	3.0	0.0	0.0	0.0	0.0	0.0	0.0	
		DIESEL	0.0	0.0	0.0	0.0	0.0	0.0	0.0	21.2	163.0	200.2	2.1	0.0	
06398J200	FA BTRY MLRS	MOGAS	0.0	0.0	3.8	3.6	0.0	4.5	0.0	0.0	0.0	0.0	0.0	0.0	
		DIESEL	0.0	0.0	0.0	0.0	0.0	0.0	0.0	15.5	169.4	113.0	7.1	0.0	
06399J200	SVC BTRY 8IN/MLRS HVY DIV	MOGAS	0.0	0.0	4.7	7.6	0.0	9.0	0.0	0.0	0.0	0.0	0.0	0.0	
		DIESEL	0.0	0.0	0.6	0.0	0.0	10.0	0.0	8.4	98.5	79.7	5.7	0.0	
07245J220	INF BN-MECH E/W M113	MOGAS	0.0	0.0	4.4	23.4	0.0	29.0	0.0	0.0	0.0	0.0	0.0	0.0	
		DIESEL	0.0	0.0	5.1	0.0	0.0	45.0	0.0	124.8	1072.3	1105.1	7.1	0.0	
07246J220	HHC INF BN MECH M113	MOGAS	0.0	0.0	3.9	23.4	0.0	29.0	0.0	0.0	0.0	0.0	0.0	0.0	
		DIESEL	0.0	0.0	2.3	0.0	0.0	20.0	0.0	44.8	384.3	393.1	5.1	0.0	
07247J220	RIFLE CO INF BN MECH M113	MOGAS	0.0	0.0	0.0	0.0	0.0	0.0	0.0	0.0	0.0	0.0	0.0	0.0	
		DIESEL	0.0	0.0	0.6	0.0	0.0	5.0	0.0	16.0	137.6	142.4	0.4	0.0	
07248J200	ANTIARMOR CO INF BN(M) IT	MOGAS	0.0	0.0	0.5	0.0	0.0	0.0	0.0	0.0	0.0	0.0	0.0	0.0	
		DIESEL	0.0	0.0	0.6	0.0	0.0	5.0	0.0	16.0	137.6	142.4	0.4	0.0	
08205J200	MEDICAL BN HVY DIV	MOGAS	0.0	0.0	46.7	28.6	0.0	52.0	0.0	0.0	0.0	0.0	0.0	0.0	
		DIESEL	0.0	0.0	11.1	0.0	0.0	20.0	0.0	15.0	129.0	133.5	14.3	0.0	
08206J200	HHD MED BN HVY DIV	MOGAS	0.0	0.0	1.7	0.0	0.0	0.0	0.0	0.0	0.0	0.0	0.0	0.0	
		DIESEL	0.0	0.0	2.2	0.0	0.0	0.0	0.0	0.0	0.0	0.0	1.6	0.0	
08207J200	MED CO MED BN HVY DIV	MOGAS	0.0	0.0	10.4	5.8	0.0	13.0	0.0	0.0	0.0	0.0	0.0	0.0	
		DIESEL	0.0	0.0	2.2	0.0	0.0	5.0	0.0	5.0	43.0	44.5	2.8	0.0	
08208J200	MED SPT CO MED BN HVY DIV	MOGAS	0.0	0.0	13.7	11.2	0.0	13.0	0.0	0.0	0.0	0.0	0.0	0.0	
		DIESEL	0.0	0.0	2.2	0.0	0.0	5.0	0.0	0.0	0.0	0.0	4.1	0.0	
09558J200	MSL SPT CO HVY DIV	MOGAS	0.0	0.0	27.6	4.0	0.0	1.0	0.0	0.0	0.0	0.0	0.0	0.0	
		DIESEL	0.0	30.0	56.7	0.0	1.3	4.0	0.0	2.0	36.8	25.5	7.6	0.0	
11035J200	SIGNAL BN (HEAVY DIV)	MOGAS	0.0	0.0	79.3	37.6	0.0	15.3	0.0	0.0	0.0	0.0	0.2	0.0	
		DIESEL	0.0	0.0	2.3	0.0	0.0	20.0	0.0	0.0	0.0	0.0	12.1	0.0	
11036J200	HHC SIG BN (HEAVY DIV)	MOGAS	0.0	0.0	13.8	4.0	0.0	3.3	0.0	0.0	0.0	0.0	0.2	0.0	
		DIESEL	0.0	0.0	0.6	0.0	0.0	5.0	0.0	0.0	0.0	0.0	3.9	0.0	
11037J200	CMD OPNS CO (HEAVY DIV)	MOGAS	0.0	0.0	27.2	13.0	0.0	4.0	0.0	0.0	0.0	0.0	0.0	0.0	
		DIESEL	0.0	0.0	0.6	0.0	0.0	5.0	0.0	0.0	0.0	0.0	3.1	0.0	
11038J200	FWD COMM CO HEAVY DIVISION	MOGAS	0.0	0.0	24.3	9.4	0.0	4.0	0.0	0.0	0.0	0.0	0.0	0.0	
		DIESEL	0.0	0.0	0.6	0.0	0.0	5.0	0.0	0.0	0.0	0.0	2.2	0.0	
11039J200	SIG SPT OPNS CO HEAVY DIV	MOGAS	0.0	0.0	14.0	11.2	0.0	4.0	0.0	0.0	0.0	0.0	0.0	0.0	
		DIESEL	0.0	0.0	0.6	0.0	0.0	5.0	0.0	0.0	0.0	0.0	2.8	0.0	
12217J200	AG CO ARMOR/INF(MECH) DIV	MOGAS	0.0	0.0	2.5	11.2	0.0	4.0	0.0	0.0	0.0	0.0	0.1	0.0	
		DIESEL	0.0	0.0	16.5	0.0	0.0	5.0	0.0	0.0	0.0	0.0	1.9	0.0	
17185J210	ATK HEL BN CBAA AHIS HV DIV	MOGAS	0.0	0.0	15.1	19.2	0.0	13.2	0.0	0.0	0.0	0.0	0.0	0.0	
		DIESEL	0.0	8.0	1.1	0.0	3.9	10.0	0.0	0.0	0.0	0.0	10.1	0.0	
		JP4													3539.7
17186J210	HQ AND SVC CO	MOGAS	0.0	0.0	15.1	19.2	0.0	13.2	0.0	0.0	0.0	0.0	0.0	0.0	
		DIESEL	0.0	8.0	1.1	0.0	3.9	10.0	0.0	0.0	0.0	0.0	9.4	0.0	
		JP4													477.9
17187J210	ATK HEL CO	MOGAS	0.0	0.0	0.0	0.0	0.0	0.0	0.0	0.0	0.0	0.0	0.0	0.0	
		DIESEL	0.0	0.0	0.0	0.0	0.0	0.0	0.0	0.0	0.0	0.0	0.2	0.0	
		JP4													1020.6
17201J210	CAV BDE AIR ATK (CBAA) (AH-IS)	MOGAS	0.0	0.0	103.8	109.2	1.5	75.6	0.0	0.0	0.0	0.0	0.0	0.0	
		DIESEL	0.0	46.0	49.8	0.0	18.9	59.0	0.0	89.0	1067.6	668.7	50.7	0.6	
		JP4													10557.0
17202J200	HQ & HQ TROOP, CBAA	MOGAS	0.0	0.0	7.6	4.0	0.0	4.4	0.0	0.0	0.0	0.0	0.0	0.0	
		DIESEL	0.0	0.0	0.6	0.0	0.0	0.0	0.0	0.0	0.0	0.0	3.0	0.0	
17205J210	CAV SQDN, CBAA AH-IS HVY DIV	MOGAS	0.0	0.0	20.0	29.2	0.0	23.4	0.0	0.0	0.0	0.0	0.0	0.0	
		DIESEL	0.0	8.0	1.1	0.0	2.6	20.0	0.0	89.0	1067.6	668.7	13.7	0.6	
		JP4													1604.8
17206J210	HQ AND HQ TRP, CAV SQDN	MOGAS	0.0	0.0	20.0	29.2	0.0	21.4	0.0	0.0	0.0	0.0	0.0	0.0	
		DIESEL	0.0	8.0	1.1	0.0	2.6	20.0	0.0	21.8	238.5	201.8	12.5	0.6	
		JP4													142.0
17207J210	CAV TRP, CAV SQDN	MOGAS	0.0	0.0	0.0	0.0	0.0	1.0	0.0	0.0	0.0	0.0	0.0	0.0	
		DIESEL	0.0	0.0	0.0	0.0	0.0	0.0	0.0	33.6	414.6	233.4	0.3	0.0	
17208J210	AIR CAV TRP, CAV SQDN	MOGAS	0.0	0.0	0.0	0.0	0.0	0.0	0.0	0.0	0.0	0.0	0.0	0.0	
		DIESEL	0.0	0.0	0.0	0.0	0.0	0.0	0.0	0.0	0.0	0.0	0.2	0.0	
		JP4													731.4
17235J110	TANK BATTALION, EQ/W, M60	MOGAS	0.0	0.0	5.5	36.2	0.0	29.8	0.0	0.0	0.0	0.0	0.0	0.0	
		DIESEL	0.0	0.0	0.6	0.0	0.0	7.0	0.0	51.4	619.0	490.5	12.9	0.0	
17236J110	HHC, TK BN, M60	MOGAS	0.0	0.0	5.5	36.2	0.0	29.8	0.0	0.0	0.0	0.0	0.0	0.0	
		DIESEL	0.0	0.0	0.6	0.0	0.0	7.0	0.0	51.4	619.0	490.5	11.8	0.0	
17237J110	TK CO, TK BN, M60	MOGAS	0.0	0.0	0.0	0.0	0.0	0.0	0.0	0.0	0.0	0.0	0.0	0.0	
		DIESEL	0.0	0.0	0.0	0.0	0.0	0.0	0.0	0.0	0.0	0.0	0.3	0.0	
19217J200	MP CO-HVY DIV	MOGAS	0.0	0.0	3.2	4.0	0.0	0.0	0.0	0.0	0.0	0.0	0.0	0.0	
		DIESEL	0.0	0.0	1.1	0.0	0.0	5.0	0.0	0.0	0.0	0.0	2.3	0.0	
34285J200	MI BN (CEWI) HVY DIV	MOGAS	0.0	0.0	63.4	18.8	0.0	17.5	0.0	0.0	0.0	0.0	0.0	0.0	
		DIESEL	0.0	0.0	16.5	0.0	0.0	17.0	0.0	11.4	85.2	90.9	13.4	0.4	
34286J200	HQ HQ-OP CO MI BN CEWI DIV	MOGAS	0.0	0.0	13.1	0.0	0.0	0.0	0.0	0.0	0.0	0.0	0.0	0.0	
		DIESEL	0.0	0.0	1.5	0.0	0.0	12.0	0.0	1.0	8.6	8.9	3.1	0.0	
34287J200	EW CO MI BN CEWI, DIV	MOGAS	0.0	0.0	15.2	0.0	0.0	0.0	0.0	0.0	0.0	0.0	0.0	0.0	
		DIESEL	0.0	0.0	15.0	0.0	0.0	0.0	0.0	0.0	0.0	0.0	1.3	0.4	
34288J200	INTL-SVL CO MI BN CEWI DIV	MOGAS	0.0	0.0	0.0	0.0	0.0	0.0	0.0	0.0	0.0	0.0	0.0	0.0	
		DIESEL	0.0	0.0	0.0	0.0	0.0	0.0	0.0	6.0	51.6	53.4	2.8	0.0	
34289J200	SVC SPT CO MI BN CEWI DIV	MOGAS	0.0	0.0	35.0	18.8	0.0	17.5	0.0	0.0	0.0	0.0	0.0	0.0	
		DIESEL	0.0	0.0	0.0	0.0	0.0	5.0	0.0	4.4	25.0	28.6	6.0	0.0	
42004J200	SUP CO FWD SPT BN HVY DIV	MOGAS	0.0	0.0	2.5	7.2	0.0	7.9	0.0	0.0	0.0	0.0	0.0	0.0	
		DIESEL	0.0	21.0	0.0	0.0	21.3	0.0	0.0	0.0	0.0	0.0	4.9	0.0	
42005J200	S&T BN HEAVY DIVISION	MOGAS	0.0	0.0	16.2	32.6	0.0	39.3	14.0	0.0	0.0	0.0	0.0	0.0	
		DIESEL	0.0	28.0	3.4	0.0	43.5	17.0	0.0	0.0	0.0	0.0	32.8	0.0	
42006J200	HHC S&T BN HEAVY DIVISION	MOGAS	0.0	0.0	0.8	21.0	0.0	8.0	0.0	0.0	0.0	0.0	0.0	0.0	
		DIESEL	0.0	0.0	1.1	0.0	0.0	5.0	0.0	0.0	0.0	0.0	2.1	0.0	

Figure 10. Bulk POL Planning Factors by Type Unit—Bulk POL Table E (continued)

SUMMARY OF BULK FUEL USAGE BY EQUIPMENT CATEGORY
HVY DIV M 5TK M60 5M M113 (SRC 87000J220)—(Cont'd)

SRC	UNIT NAME	FUEL TYPE	AB	CE	GN	HG	MH	SG	SV	TI	CC	SR	WV	OV	AV
42007J200	S&S CO S&T BN HVY DIV	MOGAS	0.0	0.0	13.7	0.0	0.0	25.5	14.0	0.0	0.0	0.0	0.0	0.0	
		DIESEL	0.0	28.0	0.0	0.0	43.5	0.0	0.0	0.0	0.0	0.0	10.1	0.0	
43004J200	MAINT CO, FWD SPT BN, HVY DIV	MOGAS	0.0	0.0	33.2	16.0	0.0	15.5	0.0	0.0	0.0	0.0	0.0	0.0	
		DIESEL	0.0	7.0	11.8	0.0	9.8	11.0	0.0	3.0	45.4	34.4	9.3	0.0	
43004J201	TK SYSTEM SPT TM	MOGAS	0.0	0.0	0.5	0.0	0.0	5.6	0.0	0.0	0.0	0.0	0.0	0.0	
		DIESEL	0.0	0.0	0.0	0.0	0.0	0.0	0.0	1.0	8.6	8.9	0.7	0.0	
43004J202	INF SYS(M) SPT TM	MOGAS	0.0	0.0	3.5	0.0	0.0	5.6	0.0	0.0	0.0	0.0	0.0	0.0	
		DIESEL	0.0	0.0	0.0	0.0	0.0	0.0	0.0	1.0	8.6	8.9	0.8	0.0	
43005J200	MAINT BN, SPT COMD, HVY DIV	MOGAS	0.0	0.0	83.3	66.4	0.0	79.1	0.0	0.0	0.0	0.0	0.0	0.0	
		DIESEL	0.0	37.0	153.7	0.0	26.8	17.0	0.0	6.0	90.7	68.9	27.3	0.0	
43006J200	HQ&SUPPORT CO HVY DIV	MOGAS	0.0	0.0	7.3	7.6	0.0	4.0	0.0	0.0	0.0	0.0	0.0	0.0	
		DIESEL	0.0	0.0	5.2	0.0	17.0	0.0	0.0	0.0	0.0	0.0	6.2	0.0	
43007J200	LIGHT MAINT CO HVY DIV	MOGAS	0.0	0.0	32.9	25.4	0.0	20.9	0.0	0.0	0.0	0.0	0.0	0.0	
		DIESEL	0.0	0.0	88.2	0.0	0.0	0.0	0.0	0.0	0.0	0.0	6.3	0.0	
43008J200	HEAVY MAINT CO HVY DIV	MOGAS	0.0	0.0	15.5	29.4	0.0	53.2	0.0	0.0	0.0	0.0	0.0	0.0	
		DIESEL	0.0	7.0	3.6	0.0	8.5	13.0	0.0	4.0	54.0	43.3	7.1	0.0	
55087J200	TMT CO S&T BN HEAVY DIV	MOGAS	0.0	0.0	0.0	0.0	0.0	0.9	0.0	0.0	0.0	0.0	0.0	0.0	
		DIESEL	0.0	0.0	0.6	0.0	0.0	5.0	0.0	0.0	0.0	0.0	13.9	0.0	
55089J200	TMT CO (HV) S&T BN HY DIV	MOGAS	0.0	0.0	1.7	11.6	0.0	4.9	0.0	0.0	0.0	0.0	0.0	0.0	
		DIESEL	0.0	0.0	1.7	0.0	0.0	7.0	0.0	0.0	0.0	0.0	6.7	0.0	
55427J200	TAM CO, CBT, SPT, AVN BN, CBA	MOGAS	0.0	0.0	16.7	13.0	1.5	4.4	0.0	0.0	0.0	0.0	0.0	0.0	
		DIESEL	0.0	16.0	45.2	0.0	8.5	5.0	0.0	0.0	0.0	0.0	5.1	0.0	
		JP4													332.0
63001J220	SPT COMD, 6x4, HVY DIV, INF	MOGAS	0.0	0.0	285.4	216.0	0.0	308.3	14.0	0.0	0.0	0.0	0.4	0.0	
		DIESEL	0.0	149.0	272.6	0.0	163.6	92.0	0.0	40.0	441.8	394.7	132.7	0.0	
63002J200	HHC, SPT COMD, HV DIV	MOGAS	0.0	0.0	0.8	7.6	0.0	4.0	0.0	0.0	0.0	0.0	0.1	0.0	
		DIESEL	0.0	0.0	6.0	0.0	0.0	0.0	0.0	0.0	0.0	0.0	1.2	0.0	
63003J200	DMMC, SPT COMD, HV DIV	MOGAS	0.0	0.0	0.0	0.0	0.0	0.0	0.0	0.0	0.0	0.0	0.0	0.0	
		DIESEL	0.0	0.0	37.5	0.0	0.0	0.0	0.0	0.0	0.0	0.0	2.5	0.0	
63005J210	FWD SPT BN 2×1 HVY DIV	MOGAS	0.0	0.0	43.1	23.2	0.0	41.4	0.0	0.0	0.0	0.0	0.1	0.0	
		DIESEL	0.0	28.0	14.8	0.0	31.1	11.0	0.0	6.0	71.2	61.1	17.2	0.0	
63005J220	FWD SPT BN, 2x2 HVY DIV	MOGAS	0.0	0.0	46.6	23.2	0.0	47.0	0.0	0.0	0.0	0.0	0.1	0.0	
		DIESEL	0.0	28.0	14.8	0.0	31.1	11.0	0.0	7.0	79.8	70.0	17.9	0.0	
63005J230	FWD SPT BN 1×2 HVY DIV	MOGAS	0.0	0.0	46.1	23.2	0.0	41.4	0.0	0.0	0.0	0.0	0.1	0.0	
		DIESEL	0.0	28.0	14.8	0.0	31.1	11.0	0.0	6.0	71.2	61.1	17.3	0.0	
63006J200	HHD, FWD SPT BN, HEAVY DIV	MOGAS	0.0	0.0	2.8	0.0	0.0	1.0	0.0	0.0	0.0	0.0	0.1	0.0	
		DIESEL	0.0	0.0	3.0	0.0	0.0	0.0	0.0	0.0	0.0	0.0	0.8	0.0	
87000J220	HVY DIV, M 5TK M60, 5M M11	MOGAS	0.0	2.0	798.4	885.8	1.5	1023.3	14.0	0.0	0.0	0.0	1.4	0.0	
		DIESEL	86.4	263.0	415.5	0.0	191.0	607.0	0.0	1494.6	13872.8	13034.8	447.9	31.7	
		JP4													10557.0
87004J220	HHC INFANTRY DIVISION (MECH)	MOGAS	0.0	0.0	17.9	14.8	0.0	12.0	0.0	0.0	0.0	0.0	0.0	0.0	
		DIESEL	0.0	0.0	0.0	0.0	0.0	0.0	0.0	4.0	34.4	35.6	2.1	0.0	
87042J210	HHC ARMD DIV BDE	MOGAS	0.0	0.0	5.9	9.4	0.0	4.0	0.0	0.0	0.0	0.0	0.0	0.0	
		DIESEL	0.0	0.0	0.0	0.0	0.0	5.0	0.0	9.2	72.7	76.6	1.6	0.0	
87042J220	HHC INF DIV (MECH) BDE	MOGAS	0.0	0.0	8.9	9.4	0.0	4.0	0.0	0.0	0.0	0.0	0.0	0.0	
		DIESEL	0.0	0.0	0.0	0.0	0.0	5.0	0.0	9.2	72.7	76.6	1.6	0.0	

SUMMARY OF BULK FUEL USAGE BY EQUIPMENT CATEGORY
HVY DIV AR 6TK M1 4M FVS (SRC 87000J230)

SRC	UNIT NAME	FUEL TYPE	AB	CE	GN	HG	MH	SG	SV	TI	CC	SR	WV	OV	AV
01285J210	CBT SPT AVN BN (HVY DIV)	MOGAS	0.0	0.0	46.1	37.6	1.5	21.3	0.0	0.0	0.0	0.0	0.0	0.0	
		DIESEL	0.0	22.0	45.8	0.0	8.5	19.0	0.0	0.0	0.0	0.0	13.6	0.0	
		JP4													1872.8
01286J210	HHC, CBT SPT AVN BN (HVY)	MOGAS	0.0	0.0	7.5	12.6	0.0	10.4	0.0	0.0	0.0	0.0	0.0	0.0	
		DIESEL	0.0	0.0	0.0	0.0	0.0	5.0	0.0	0.0	0.0	0.0	3.2	0.0	
01287J200	GEN SPT AVN CO	MOGAS	0.0	0.0	21.9	12.0	0.0	6.4	0.0	0.0	0.0	0.0	0.0	0.0	
		DIESEL	0.0	6.0	0.6	0.0	0.0	9.0	0.0	0.0	0.0	0.0	5.3	0.0	
		JP4													1540.8
03387J200	CHEMICAL CO, HVY DIV	MOGAS	0.0	0.0	36.8	4.0	0.0	64.0	0.0	0.0	0.0	0.0	0.0	0.0	
		DIESEL	0.0	0.0	0.6	0.0	0.0	5.0	0.0	6.0	51.6	53.4	9.5	0.0	
05145J210	ENGR BN, HVY DIV - RIBBON	MOGAS	0.0	2.0	22.6	45.6	0.0	102.7	0.0	0.0	0.0	0.0	0.1	0.0	
		DIESEL	86.4	68.0	2.8	0.0	8.5	34.0	0.0	147.1	1583.2	1311.5	36.9	0.0	
05146J200	HQ-HQ COMPANY	MOGAS	0.0	0.0	4.1	7.6	0.0	11.5	0.0	0.0	0.0	0.0	0.1	0.0	
		DIESEL	0.0	0.0	0.6	0.0	8.5	7.0	0.0	1.0	8.6	8.9	7.4	0.0	
05147J200	ENGR CO, ENGR BN, HVY DIV	MOGAS	0.0	0.5	4.2	7.6	0.0	19.5	0.0	0.0	0.0	0.0	0.0	0.0	
		DIESEL	0.0	17.0	0.6	0.0	0.0	5.0	0.0	36.5	393.6	325.6	5.3	0.0	
05148J210	BRIDGE COMPANY RIBBON	MOGAS	0.0	0.0	1.7	7.6	0.0	13.0	0.0	0.0	0.0	0.0	0.0	0.0	
		DIESEL	86.4	0.0	0.0	0.0	0.0	7.0	0.0	0.0	0.0	0.0	8.2	0.0	
06300J210	ARMD DIVARTY W/TACFIRE	MOGAS	0.0	0.0	112.5	109.6	0.0	121.5	0.0	0.0	0.0	0.0	0.3	0.0	
		DIESEL	0.0	0.0	41.2	0.0	0.0	100.0	0.0	288.5	1934.4	2272.6	82.2	30.7	
06302J200	HHB DIV ARTY HVY DIV	MOGAS	0.0	0.0	26.3	5.4	0.0	8.4	0.0	0.0	0.0	0.0	0.1	0.0	
		DIESEL	0.0	0.0	9.8	0.0	0.0	5.0	0.0	1.0	8.6	8.9	5.4	0.0	
06307J200	TGT ACQ BTRY HVY DIV	MOGAS	0.0	0.0	4.4	5.4	0.0	4.5	0.0	0.0	0.0	0.0	0.0	0.0	
		DIESEL	0.0	0.0	12.0	0.0	0.0	10.0	0.0	0.0	0.0	0.0	5.0	0.0	
06365J210	FA BN 155 SP HVY DIV	MOGAS	0.0	0.0	20.0	25.6	0.0	27.3	0.0	0.0	0.0	0.0	0.0	0.0	
		DIESEL	0.0	0.0	5.3	0.0	0.0	25.0	0.0	72.4	432.5	545.0	17.3	10.1	
06365J220	FA BN 155 SP HVY DIV	MOGAS	0.0	0.0	20.0	25.6	0.0	27.3	0.0	0.0	0.0	0.0	0.0	0.0	
		DIESEL	0.0	0.0	5.3	0.0	0.0	25.0	0.0	72.4	432.5	545.0	17.3	10.1	
06366J210	HHB FA BN 155SP HVY DIV	MOGAS	0.0	0.0	12.8	7.2	0.0	7.0	0.0	0.0	0.0	0.0	0.0	0.0	
		DIESEL	0.0	0.0	3.6	0.0	0.0	5.0	0.0	7.0	60.2	62.3	2.5	3.4	
06366J220	HHB FA BN 155SP HVY DIV	MOGAS	0.0	0.0	12.8	7.2	0.0	7.0	0.0	0.0	0.0	0.0	0.0	0.0	
		DIESEL	0.0	0.0	3.6	0.0	0.0	5.0	0.0	7.0	60.2	62.3	2.4	3.4	
06367J220	FA BTRY 155SP HVY DIV	MOGAS	0.0	0.0	1.1	3.6	0.0	3.0	0.0	0.0	0.0	0.0	0.0	0.0	
		DIESEL	0.0	0.0	0.6	0.0	0.0	5.0	0.0	19.6	111.6	146.6	2.2	2.2	

Figure 10. Bulk POL Planning Factors by Type Unit—Bulk POL Table E (continued)

SUMMARY OF BULK FUEL USAGE BY EQUIPMENT CATEGORY
HVY DIV AR 6TK M1 4M FVS (SRC 87000J230) —Cont'd

SRC	UNIT NAME	FUEL TYPE	AB	CE	GN	HG	MH	SG	SV	TI	CC	SR	WV	OV	AV
06369J200	SVC BTRY 155SP HVY DIV	MOGAS	0.0	0.0	3.9	7.6	0.0	11.3	0.0	0.0	0.0	0.0	0.0	0.0	
		DIESEL	0.0	0.0	0.0	0.0	0.0	5.0	0.0	6.6	37.5	42.9	8.2	0.0	
06395J200	FA BN, 8IN/MLRS HVY DIV	MOGAS	0.0	0.0	21.4	22.0	0.0	26.5	0.0	0.0	0.0	0.0	0.0	0.0	
		DIESEL	0.0	0.0	3.6	0.0	0.0	10.0	0.0	69.3	619.7	619.8	19.7	0.0	
06396J200	HHB 8IN/MLRS BN HVY DIV	MOGAS	0.0	0.0	6.4	3.6	0.0	7.0	0.0	0.0	0.0	0.0	0.0	0.0	
		DIESEL	0.0	0.0	3.0	0.0	0.0	0.0	0.0	3.0	25.8	26.7	2.4	0.0	
06396J202	AUGFIST, TANK BN	MOGAS	0.0	0.0	0.5	0.0	0.0	0.0	0.0	0.0	0.0	0.0	0.0	0.0	
		DIESEL	0.0	0.0	0.0	0.0	0.0	0.0	0.0	1.0	8.6	8.9	0.0	0.3	
06397J200	FA BTRY 8IN SP HVY DIV	MOGAS	0.0	0.0	3.2	3.6	0.0	3.0	0.0	0.0	0.0	0.0	0.0	0.0	
		DIESEL	0.0	0.0	0.0	0.0	0.0	0.0	0.0	21.2	163.0	200.2	2.1	0.0	
06398J200	FA BTRY MLRS	MOGAS	0.0	0.0	3.8	3.6	0.0	4.5	0.0	0.0	0.0	0.0	0.0	0.0	
		DIESEL	0.0	0.0	0.0	0.0	0.0	0.0	0.0	15.5	169.4	113.0	7.1	0.0	
06399J200	SVC BTRY 8IN/MLRS HVY DIV	MOGAS	0.0	0.0	4.7	7.6	0.0	9.0	0.0	0.0	0.0	0.0	0.0	0.0	
		DIESEL	0.0	0.0	0.6	0.0	0.0	10.0	0.0	8.4	98.5	79.7	5.7	0.0	
07245J210	INF BN-MECH E/W BFVS	MOGAS	0.0	0.0	2.8	25.2	0.0	29.0	0.0	0.0	0.0	0.0	0.1	0.0	
		DIESEL	0.0	0.0	5.1	0.0	0.0	45.0	0.0	147.0	1744.3	1130.9	7.8	0.0	
07246J210	HHC INF BN MECH BFVS	MOGAS	0.0	0.0	2.2	25.2	0.0	29.0	0.0	0.0	0.0	0.0	0.1	0.0	
		DIESEL	0.0	0.0	2.3	0.0	0.0	20.0	0.0	54.2	636.3	505.7	5.8	0.0	
07247J210	RIFLE CO INF BN MECH BFVS	MOGAS	0.0	0.0	0.0	0.0	0.0	0.0	0.0	0.0	0.0	0.0	0.0	0.0	
		DIESEL	0.0	0.0	0.6	0.0	0.0	5.0	0.0	19.2	242.6	120.7	0.4	0.0	
07248J200	ANTIARMOR CO INF BN(M) IT	MOGAS	0.0	0.0	0.5	0.0	0.0	0.0	0.0	0.0	0.0	0.0	0.0	0.0	
		DIESEL	0.0	0.0	0.6	0.0	0.0	5.0	0.0	16.0	137.6	142.4	0.4	0.0	
08205J200	MEDICAL BN HVY DIV	MOGAS	0.0	0.0	46.7	28.6	0.0	52.0	0.0	0.0	0.0	0.0	0.0	0.0	
		DIESEL	0.0	0.0	11.1	0.0	0.0	20.0	0.0	15.0	129.0	133.5	14.3	0.0	
08206J200	HHD MED BN HVY DIV	MOGAS	0.0	0.0	1.7	0.0	0.0	0.0	0.0	0.0	0.0	0.0	0.0	0.0	
		DIESEL	0.0	0.0	2.2	0.0	0.0	0.0	0.0	0.0	0.0	0.0	1.6	0.0	
08207J200	MED CO MED BN HVY DIV	MOGAS	0.0	0.0	10.4	5.8	0.0	13.0	0.0	0.0	0.0	0.0	0.0	0.0	
		DIESEL	0.0	0.0	2.2	0.0	0.0	5.0	0.0	5.0	43.0	44.5	2.8	0.0	
08208J200	MED SPT CO MED BN HVY DIV	MOGAS	0.0	0.0	13.7	11.2	0.0	13.0	0.0	0.0	0.0	0.0	0.0	0.0	
		DIESEL	0.0	0.0	2.2	0.0	0.0	5.0	0.0	0.0	0.0	0.0	4.1	0.0	
09558J200	MSL SPT CO HVY DIV	MOGAS	0.0	0.0	27.6	4.0	0.0	1.0	0.0	0.0	0.0	0.0	0.0	0.0	
		DIESEL	0.0	30.0	56.7	0.0	1.3	4.0	0.0	2.0	36.8	25.5	7.6	0.0	
11035J200	SIGNAL BN (HEAVY DIV)	MOGAS	0.0	0.0	79.3	37.6	0.0	15.3	0.0	0.0	0.0	0.0	0.2	0.0	
		DIESEL	0.0	0.0	2.3	0.0	0.0	20.0	0.0	0.0	0.0	0.0	12.1	0.0	
11036J200	HHC SIG BN (HEAVY DIV)	MOGAS	0.0	0.0	13.8	4.0	0.0	3.3	0.0	0.0	0.0	0.0	0.2	0.0	
		DIESEL	0.0	0.0	0.6	0.0	0.0	5.0	0.0	0.0	0.0	0.0	3.9	0.0	
11037J200	CMD OPNS CO (HEAVY DIV)	MOGAS	0.0	0.0	27.2	13.0	0.0	4.0	0.0	0.0	0.0	0.0	0.0	0.0	
		DIESEL	0.0	0.0	0.6	0.0	0.0	5.0	0.0	0.0	0.0	0.0	3.1	0.0	
11038J200	FWD COMM CO HEAVY DIVISION	MOGAS	0.0	0.0	24.3	9.4	0.0	4.0	0.0	0.0	0.0	0.0	0.0	0.0	
		DIESEL	0.0	0.0	0.6	0.0	0.0	5.0	0.0	0.0	0.0	0.0	2.2	0.0	
11039J200	SIG SPT OPNS CO HEAVY DIV	MOGAS	0.0	0.0	144.0	11.2	0.0	4.0	0.0	0.0	0.0	0.0	0.0	0.0	
		DIESEL	0.0	0.0	0.6	0.0	0.0	5.0	0.0	0.0	0.0	0.0	2.8	0.0	
12217J200	AG CO- ARMOR/INF(MECH) DIV	MOGAS	0.0	0.0	2.5	11.2	0.0	4.0	0.0	0.0	0.0	0.0	0.1	0.0	
		DIESEL	0.0	0.0	16.5	0.0	0.0	5.0	0.0	0.0	0.0	0.0	1.9	0.0	
17185J220	ATK HEL BN CBAA (AH-64) HVDP	MOGAS	0.0	0.0	22.3	29.2	0.0	14.2	0.0	0.0	0.0	0.0	0.0	0.0	
		DIESEL	0.0	8.0	1.1	0.0	5.2	10.0	0.0	0.0	0.0	0.0	11.2	0.0	
		JP4													3884.7
17186J220	HQ AND SVC CO (AH-64)	MOGAS	0.0	0.0	22.3	29.2	0.0	14.2	0.0	0.0	0.0	0.0	0.0	0.0	
		DIESEL	0.0	8.0	1.1	0.0	5.2	10.0	0.0	0.0	0.0	0.0	10.6	0.0	
		JP4													525.9
17187J220	ATTACK HEL CO (AH-64)	MOGAS	0.0	0.0	0.0	0.0	0.0	0.0	0.0	0.0	0.0	0.0	0.0	0.0	
		DIESEL	0.0	0.0	0.0	0.0	0.0	0.0	0.0	0.0	0.0	0.0	0.2	0.0	
		JP4													1119.6
17201J220	CAV BDE AIR ATK (CBAA) (AH-64)	MOGAS	0.0	0.0	118.3	127.8	1.5	81.0	0.0	0.0	0.0	0.0	0.3	0.0	
		DIESEL	0.0	46.0	49.8	0.0	21.5	61.0	0.0	91.0	1084.8	686.5	54.1	0.0	
		JP4													11567.0
17202J200	HA & HQ TROOP, CBAA	MOGAS	0.0	0.0	7.6	4.0	0.0	4.4	0.0	0.0	0.0	0.0	0.0	0.0	
		DIESEL	0.0	0.0	0.6	0.0	0.0	0.0	0.0	0.0	0.0	0.0	3.0	0.0	
17205J220	CAV SQDN HVY DIV (AH-64)	MOGAS	0.0	0.0	20.0	27.8	0.0	26.8	0.0	0.0	0.0	0.0	0.0	0.0	
		DIESEL	0.0	8.0	1.1	0.0	2.6	22.0	0.0	91.0	1084.8	686.5	14.8	0.0	
		JP4													1924.8
17206J220	HQ & HQ TRP CAV SQN (AH-64)	MOGAS	0.0	0.0	20.0	27.8	0.0	24.8	0.0	0.0	0.0	0.0	0.3	0.0	
		DIESEL	0.0	8.0	1.1	0.0	2.6	22.0	0.0	23.8	255.7	219.6	13.6	0.0	
		JP4													166.0
17207J210	CAV TRP, CAV SQDN	MOGAS	0.0	0.0	0.0	0.0	0.0	1.0	0.0	0.0	0.0	0.0	0.0	0.0	
		DIESEL	0.0	0.0	0.0	0.0	0.0	0.0	0.0	33.6	414.6	233.4	0.3	0.0	
17208J220	AIR CAV TRP, CAV SQN (AH-64)	MOGAS	0.0	0.0	0.0	0.0	0.0	0.0	0.0	0.0	0.0	0.0	0.0	0.0	
		DIESEL	0.0	0.0	0.0	0.0	0.0	0.0	0.0	0.0	0.0	0.0	0.2	0.0	
		JP4													879.4
17235J120	TANK BATTALION EQ W/M1	MOGAS	0.0	0.0	1.4	36.2	0.0	12.0	0.0	0.0	0.0	0.0	0.2	0.0	
		DIESEL	0.0	0.0	0.0	0.0	0.0	0.0	0.0	638.2	3570.8	2804.9	8.9	0.0	
17236J120	HHC, TK BN (M1)	MOGAS	0.0	0.0	1.4	36.2	0.0	12.0	0.0	0.0	0.0	0.0	0.0	0.0	
		DIESEL	0.0	0.0	0.0	0.0	0.0	0.0	0.0	33.4	401.2	305.1	7.8	0.0	
17237J120	TANK CO, (M1)	MOGAS	0.0	0.0	0.0	0.0	0.0	0.0	0.0	0.0	0.0	0.0	0.0	0.0	
		DIESEL	0.0	0.0	0.0	0.0	0.0	0.0	0.0	151.2	792.4	625.0	0.3	0.0	
19217J200	MP CO-HVY DIV	MOGAS	0.0	0.0	3.2	4.0	0.0	0.0	0.0	0.0	0.0	0.0	0.0	0.0	
		DIESEL	0.0	0.0	1.1	0.0	0.0	5.0	0.0	0.0	0.0	0.0	2.3	0.0	
34285J200	MI BN (CEWI) HVY DIV	MOGAS	0.0	0.0	63.4	18.8	0.0	17.5	0.0	0.0	0.0	0.0	0.0	0.0	
		DIESEL	0.0	0.0	16.5	0.0	0.0	17.0	0.0	11.4	85.2	90.9	13.4	0.4	
34286J200	HQ HQ-OP CO MI BN CEWI DIV	MOGAS	0.0	0.0	13.1	0.0	0.0	0.0	0.0	0.0	0.0	0.0	0.0	0.0	
		DIESEL	0.0	0.0	1.5	0.0	0.0	12.0	0.0	1.0	8.6	8.9	3.1	0.0	
34287J200	EW CO MI BN CEWI DIV	MOGAS	0.0	0.0	15.2	0.0	0.0	0.0	0.0	0.0	0.0	0.0	0.0	0.0	
		DIESEL	0.0	0.0	15.0	0.0	0.0	0.0	0.0	0.0	0.0	0.0	1.3	0.4	
34288J200	INTL-SVL CO MI BN CEWI DIV	MOGAS	0.0	0.0	0.0	0.0	0.0	0.0	0.0	0.0	0.0	0.0	0.0	0.0	
		DIESEL	0.0	0.0	0.0	0.0	0.0	0.0	0.0	6.0	51.6	53.4	2.8	0.0	
34289J200	SVC SPT CO MI BN CEWI DIV	MOGAS	0.0	0.0	35.0	18.8	0.0	17.5	0.0	0.0	0.0	0.0	0.0	0.0	
		DIESEL	0.0	0.0	0.0	0.0	0.0	5.0	0.0	4.4	25.0	28.6	6.0	0.0	

Figure 10. Bulk POL Planning Factors by Type Unit—Bulk POL Table E (continued)

SUMMARY OF BULK FUEL USAGE BY EQUIPMENT CATEGORY
HVY DIV AR 6TK M1 4M FVS (SRC 87000J230)—(Cont'd)

SRC	UNIT NAME	FUEL TYPE	AB	CE	GN	HG	MH	SG	SV	TI	CC	SR	WV	OV	AV
42004J200	SUP CO FWD SPT BN HVY DIV	MOGAS	0.0	0.0	2.5	7.2	0.0	7.9	0.0	0.0	0.0	0.0	0.0	0.0	
		DIESEL	0.0	21.0	0.0	0.0	21.3	0.0	0.0	0.0	0.0	0.0	4.9	0.0	
42005J200	S&T BN HEAVY DIVISION	MOGAS	0.0	0.0	16.2	32.6	0.0	39.3	14.0	0.0	0.0	0.0	0.0	0.0	
		DIESEL	0.0	28.0	3.4	0.0	43.5	17.0	0.0	0.0	0.0	0.0	32.8	0.0	
42006J200	HHC S&T BN HEAVY DIVISION	MOGAS	0.0	0.0	0.8	21.0	0.0	8.0	0.0	0.0	0.0	0.0	0.0	0.0	
		DIESEL	0.0	0.0	1.1	0.0	0.0	5.0	0.0	0.0	0.0	0.0	2.1	0.0	
42007J200	S&S CO S&T BN HVY DIV	MOGAS	0.0	0.0	13.7	0.0	0.0	25.5	14.0	0.0	0.0	0.0	0.0	0.0	
		DIESEL	0.0	28.0	0.0	0.0	43.5	0.0	0.0	0.0	0.0	0.0	10.1	0.0	
43004J200	MAINT CO, FWD SPT BN, HVY DIV	MOGAS	0.0	0.0	33.2	16.0	0.0	15.5	0.0	0.0	0.0	0.0	0.0	0.0	
		DIESEL	0.0	7.0	11.8	0.0	9.8	11.0	0.0	3.0	45.4	34.4	9.3	0.0	
43004J201	TK SYSTEM SPT TM	MOGAS	0.0	0.0	0.5	0.0	0.0	5.6	0.0	0.0	0.0	0.0	0.0	0.0	
		DIESEL	0.0	0.0	0.0	0.0	0.0	0.0	0.0	1.0	8.6	8.9	0.7	0.0	
43004J202	INF SYS(M) SPT TM	MOGAS	0.0	0.0	3.5	0.0	0.0	5.6	0.0	0.0	0.0	0.0	0.0	0.0	
		DIESEL	0.0	0.0	0.0	0.0	0.0	0.0	0.0	1.0	8.6	8.9	0.8	0.0	
43005J200	MAINT BN, SPT COMD, HVY DIV	MOGAS	0.0	0.0	83.3	66.4	0.0	79.1	0.0	0.0	0.0	0.0	0.0	0.0	
		DIESEL	0.0	37.0	153.7	0.0	26.8	17.0	0.0	6.0	90.7	68.9	27.3	0.0	
43006J200	HQ&SUPPORT CO HVY DIV	MOGAS	0.0	0.0	7.3	7.6	0.0	4.0	0.0	0.0	0.0	0.0	0.0	0.0	
		DIESEL	0.0	0.0	5.2	0.0	17.0	0.0	0.0	0.0	0.0	0.0	6.2	0.0	
43007J200	LIGHT MAINT CO HVY DIV	MOGAS	0.0	0.0	32.9	25.4	0.0	20.9	0.0	0.0	0.0	0.0	0.0	0.0	
		DIESEL	0.0	0.0	88.2	0.0	0.0	0.0	0.0	0.0	0.0	0.0	6.3	0.0	
43008J200	HEAVY MAINT CO HVY DIV	MOGAS	0.0	0.0	15.5	29.4	0.0	53.2	0.0	0.0	0.0	0.0	0.0	0.0	
		DIESEL	0.0	7.0	3.6	0.0	8.5	13.0	0.0	4.0	54.0	43.3	7.1	0.0	
55087J200	TMT CO S&T BN HEAVY DIV	MOGAS	0.0	0.0	0.0	0.0	0.0	0.9	0.0	0.0	0.0	0.0	0.0	0.0	
		DIESEL	0.0	0.0	0.6	0.0	0.0	5.0	0.0	0.0	0.0	0.0	13.9	0.0	
55089J200	TMT CO (HY) S&T BN HY DIV	MOGAS	0.0	0.0	1.7	11.6	0.0	4.9	0.0	0.0	0.0	0.0	0.0	0.0	
		DIESEL	0.0	0.0	1.7	0.0	0.0	7.0	0.0	0.0	0.0	0.0	6.7	0.0	
55427J200	TAM CO, CBT SPT, AVN BN, CBA	MOGAS	0.0	0.0	16.7	13.0	1.5	4.4	0.0	0.0	0.0	0.0	0.0	0.0	
		DIESEL	0.0	16.0	45.2	0.0	8.5	5.0	0.0	0.0	0.0	0.0	5.1	0.0	
		JP4													332.0
63001J210	SPT COMD, 6 × 4, HVY DIV, AR	MOGAS	0.0	0.0	282.4	216.0	0.0	308.3	14.0	0.0	0.0	0.0	0.0	0.0	
		DIESEL	0.0	149.0	272.6	0.0	163.6	92.0	0.0	40.0	441.8	394.7	132.6	0.0	
63002J200	HHC, SPT COMD, HVY DIV	MOGAS	0.0	0.0	0.8	7.6	0.0	4.0	0.0	0.0	0.0	0.0	0.1	0.0	
		DIESEL	0.0	0.0	6.0	0.0	0.0	0.0	0.0	0.0	0.0	0.0	1.2	0.0	
63003J200	DMMC, SPT COMD, HVY DIV	MOGAS	0.0	0.0	0.0	0.0	0.0	0.0	0.0	0.0	0.0	0.0	0.0	0.0	
		DIESEL	0.0	0.0	37.5	0.0	0.0	0.0	0.0	0.0	0.0	0.0	2.5	0.0	
63005J210	FWD SPT BN 2 × 2 HVY DIV	MOGAS	0.0	0.0	43.1	23.2	0.0	41.4	0.0	0.0	0.0	0.0	0.1	0.0	
		DIESEL	0.0	28.0	14.8	0.0	31.1	11.0	0.0	6.0	71.2	61.1	17.2	0.0	
63005J220	FWD SPT BN 2 × 2 HVY DIV	MOGAS	0.0	0.0	46.6	23.2	0.0	47.0	0.0	0.0	0.0	0.0	0.1	0.0	
		DIESEL	0.0	28.0	14.8	0.0	31.1	11.0	0.0	7.0	79.8	70.0	17.9	0.0	
63006J200	HHD,FWD SPT BN,HEAVY DIV	MOGAS	0.0	0.0	2.8	0.0	0.0	1.0	0.0	0.0	0.0	0.0	0.1	0.0	
		DIESEL	0.0	0.0	3.0	0.0	0.0	0.0	0.0	0.0	0.0	0.0	0.8	0.0	
87000J230	HVY DIV,AR 6TK M1,4M FVS	MOGAS	0.0	2.0	774.5	924.4	1.5	922.4	14.0	0.0	0.0	0.0	3.2	0.0	
		DIESEL	86.4	263.0	407.5	0.0	193.6	529.0	0.0	5032.8	33835.8	26427.8	435.6	31.1	
		JP4													11567.0
87004J210	HHC ARMORED DIVISION	MOGAS	0.0	0.0	16.0	14.8	0.0	12.0	0.0	0.0	0.0	0.0	0.0	0.0	
		DIESEL	0.0	0.0	0.0	0.0	0.0	0.0	0.0	4.0	34.4	35.6	2.1	0.0	
87042J210	HHC ARMD DIV BDE	MOGAS	0.0	0.0	5.9	9.4	0.0	4.0	0.0	0.0	0.0	0.0	0.0	0.0	
		DIESEL	0.0	0.0	0.0	0.0	0.0	5.0	0.0	9.2	72.7	76.6	1.6	0.0	
87042J220	HHC INF DIV (MECH) BDE	MOGAS	0.0	0.0	8.9	9.4	0.0	4.0	0.0	0.0	0.0	0.0	0.0	0.0	
		DIESEL	0.0	0.0	0.0	0.0	0.0	5.0	0.0	9.2	72.7	76.6	1.6	0.0	

SUMMARY OF BULK FUEL USAGE BY EQUIPMENT CATEGORY
HVY DIV M 5TK M1 5M BFVS (SRC 87000J240)

SRC	UNIT NAME	FUEL TYPE	AB	CE	GN	HG	MH	SG	SV	TI	CC	SR	WV	OV	AV
01285J210	CBT SPT AVN BN (HVY DIV)	MOGAS	0.0	0.0	46.1	37.6	1.5	21.3	0.0	0.0	0.0	0.0	0.0	0.0	
		DIESEL	0.0	22.0	45.8	0.0	8.5	19.0	0.0	0.0	0.0	0.0	13.6	0.0	
		JP4													1872.8
01286J210	HHC, CBT SPT AVN BN (HVY)	MOGAS	0.0	0.0	7.5	12.6	0.0	10.4	0.0	0.0	0.0	0.0	0.0	0.0	
		DIESEL	0.0	0.0	0.0	0.0	0.0	5.0	0.0	0.0	0.0	0.0	3.2	0.0	
01287J200	GEN SPT AVN CO	MOGAS	0.0	0.0	21.9	12.0	0.0	6.4	0.0	0.0	0.0	0.0	0.0	0.0	
		DIESEL	0.0	6.0	0.6	0.0	0.0	9.0	0.0	0.0	0.0	0.0	5.3	0.0	
		JP4													1540.8
03387J200	CHEMICAL CO, HVY DIV	MOGAS	0.0	0.0	36.8	4.0	0.0	64.0	0.0	0.0	0.0	0.0	0.0	0.0	
		DIESEL	0.0	0.0	0.6	0.0	0.0	5.0	0.0	6.0	51.6	53.4	9.5	0.0	
05145J210	ENGR BN, HVY DIV - RIBBON	MOGAS	0.0	2.0	22.6	45.6	0.0	102.7	0.0	0.0	0.0	0.0	0.1	0.0	
		DIESEL	86.4	68.0	2.8	0.0	8.5	34.0	0.0	147.1	1583.2	1311.5	36.9	0.0	
05146J200	HQ-HQ COMPANY	MOGAS	0.0	0.0	4.1	7.6	0.0	11.5	0.0	0.0	0.0	0.0	0.1	0.0	
		DIESEL	0.0	0.0	0.6	0.0	8.5	7.0	0.0	1.0	8.6	8.9	7.4	0.0	
05147J200	ENGR CO, ENGR BN, HVY DIV	MOGAS	0.0	0.5	4.2	7.6	0.0	19.5	0.0	0.0	0.0	0.0	0.0	0.0	
		DIESEL	0.0	17.0	0.6	0.0	0.0	5.0	0.0	36.5	393.6	325.6	5.3	0.0	
05148J210	BRIDGE COMPANY - RIBBON	MOGAS	0.0	0.0	1.7	7.6	0.0	13.0	0.0	0.0	0.0	0.0	0.0	0.0	
		DIESEL	86.4	0.0	0.0	0.0	0.0	7.0	0.0	0.0	0.0	0.0	8.2	0.0	
06300J220	MECH DIVARTY W/TACFIRE	MOGAS	0.0	0.0	112.5	109.6	0.0	121.5	0.0	0.0	0.0	0.0	0.3	0.0	
		DIESEL	0.0	0.0	41.2	0.0	0.0	100.0	0.0	288.5	1934.4	2272.6	82.2	30.7	
06302J200	HHB DIV ARTY HVY DIV	MOGAS	0.0	0.0	26.3	5.4	0.0	8.4	0.0	0.0	0.0	0.0	0.1	0.0	
		DIESEL	0.0	0.0	9.8	0.0	0.0	5.0	0.0	1.0	8.6	8.9	5.4	0.0	
06307J200	TGT ACQ BTRY HVY DIV	MOGAS	0.0	0.0	4.5	5.4	0.0	4.5	0.0	0.0	0.0	0.0	0.0	0.0	
		DIESEL	0.0	0.0	12.0	0.0	0.0	10.0	0.0	0.0	0.0	0.0	5.0	0.0	
06365J210	FA BN 155 SP HVY DIV	MOGAS	0.0	0.0	20.0	25.6	0.0	27.3	0.0	0.0	0.0	0.0	0.0	0.0	
		DIESEL	0.0	0.0	5.3	0.0	0.0	25.0	0.0	72.4	432.5	545.0	17.3	10.1	
06365J220	FA BN 155 SP HVY DIV	MOGAS	0.0	0.0	20.0	25.6	0.0	27.3	0.0	0.0	0.0	0.0	0.0	0.0	
		DIESEL	0.0	0.0	5.3	0.0	0.0	25.0	0.0	72.4	432.5	545.0	17.3	10.1	
06366J210	HHB FA BN 155SP HVY DIV	MOGAS	0.0	0.0	12.8	7.2	0.0	7.0	0.0	0.0	0.0	0.0	0.0	0.0	
		DIESEL	0.0	0.0	3.6	0.0	0.0	5.0	0.0	7.0	60.2	62.3	2.5	3.4	

Figure 10. Bulk POL Planning Factors by Type Unit— Bulk POL Table E (continued)

SUMMARY OF BULK FUEL USAGE BY EQUIPMENT CATEGORY
HVY DIV M 5TK M1 5M BFVS (SRC 87000J240)—(Cont'd)

SRC	UNIT NAME	FUEL TYPE	AB	CE	GN	HG	MH	SG	SV	TI	CC	SR	WV	OV	AV
06366J220	HHB FA BN 155SP HVY DIV	MOGAS	0.0	0.0	12.8	7.2	0.0	7.0	0.0	0.0	0.0	0.0	0.0	0.0	
		DIESEL	0.0	0.0	3.6	0.0	0.0	5.0	0.0	7.0	60.2	62.3	2.4	3.4	
06367J200	FA BTRY 155SP HVY DIV	MOGAS	0.0	0.0	1.1	3.6	0.0	3.0	0.0	0.0	0.0	0.0	0.0	0.0	
		DIESEL	0.0	0.0	0.6	0.0	0.0	5.0	0.0	19.6	111.6	146.6	2.2	2.2	
06369J200	SVC BTRY 155SP HVY DIV	MOGAS	0.0	0.0	3.9	7.6	0.0	11.3	0.0	0.0	0.0	0.0	0.0	0.0	
		DIESEL	0.0	0.0	0.0	0.0	0.0	5.0	0.0	6.6	37.5	42.9	8.2	0.0	
06395J200	FA BN, 8IN/MLRS HVY DIV	MOGAS	0.0	0.0	21.4	22.0	0.0	26.5	0.0	0.0	0.0	0.0	0.0	0.0	
		DIESEL	0.0	0.0	3.6	0.0	0.0	10.0	0.0	69.3	619.7	619.8	19.7	0.0	
06396J200	HHB 8IN/MLRS BN HVY DIV	MOGAS	0.0	0.0	6.4	3.6	0.0	7.0	0.0	0.0	0.0	0.0	0.0	0.0	
		DIESEL	0.0	0.0	3.0	0.0	0.0	0.0	0.0	3.0	25.8	26.7	2.4	0.0	
06396J201	AUG-FIST, MECH BN	MOGAS	0.0	0.0	0.5	0.0	0.0	0.0	0.0	0.0	0.0	0.0	0.0	0.0	
		DIESEL	0.0	0.0	0.0	0.0	0.0	0.0	0.0	1.0	8.6	8.9	0.0	0.3	
06397J200	FA BTRY 8IN SP HVY DIV	MOGAS	0.0	0.0	3.2	3.6	0.0	3.0	0.0	0.0	0.0	0.0	0.0	0.0	
		DIESEL	0.0	0.0	0.0	0.0	0.0	0.0	0.0	21.2	163.0	200.2	2.1	0.0	
06398J200	FA BTRY MLRS	MOGAS	0.0	0.0	3.8	3.6	0.0	4.5	0.0	0.0	0.0	0.0	0.0	0.0	
		DIESEL	0.0	0.0	0.0	0.0	0.0	0.0	0.0	15.5	169.4	113.0	7.1	0.0	
06399J200	SVC BTRY 8IN/MLRS HVY DIV	MOGAS	0.0	0.0	4.7	7.6	0.0	9.0	0.0	0.0	0.0	0.0	0.0	0.0	
		DIESEL	0.0	0.0	0.6	0.0	0.0	10.0	0.0	8.4	98.5	79.7	5.7	0.0	
07245J210	INF BN-MECH E/W BFVS	MOGAS	0.0	0.0	2.8	25.2	0.0	29.9	0.0	0.0	0.0	0.0	0.1	0.0	
		DIESEL	0.0	0.0	5.1	0.0	0.0	45.0	0.0	147.0	1744.3	1130.9	7.8	0.0	
07246J210	HHC INF BN MECH BFVS	MOGAS	0.0	0.0	2.2	25.2	0.0	29.0	0.0	0.0	0.0	0.0	0.1	0.0	
		DIESEL	0.0	0.0	2.3	0.0	0.0	20.0	0.0	54.2	636.3	505.7	5.8	0.0	
07247J210	RIFLE CO INF BN MECH BFVS	MOGAS	0.0	0.0	0.0	0.0	0.0	0.0	0.0	0.0	0.0	0.0	0.0	0.0	
		DIESEL	0.0	0.0	0.6	0.0	0.0	5.0	0.0	19.2	242.6	120.7	0.4	0.0	
07248J200	ANTIARMOR CO INF BN(M) IT	MOGAS	0.0	0.0	0.5	0.0	0.0	0.0	0.0	0.0	0.0	0.0	0.0	0.0	
		DIESEL	0.0	0.0	0.6	0.0	0.0	5.0	0.0	16.0	137.6	142.4	0.4	0.0	
08205J200	MEDICAL BN HVY DIV	MOGAS	0.0	0.0	46.7	28.6	0.0	52.0	0.0	0.0	0.0	0.0	0.0	0.0	
		DIESEL	0.0	0.0	11.1	0.0	0.0	20.0	0.0	15.0	129.0	133.5	14.3	0.0	
08206J200	HHD MED BN HVY DIV	MOGAS	0.0	0.0	1.7	0.0	0.0	0.0	0.0	0.0	0.0	0.0	0.0	0.0	
		DIESEL	0.0	0.0	2.2	0.0	0.0	0.0	0.0	0.0	0.0	0.0	1.6	0.0	
08207J200	MED CO MED BN HVY DIV	MOGAS	0.0	0.0	10.4	5.8	0.0	13.0	0.0	0.0	0.0	0.0	0.0	0.0	
		DIESEL	0.0	0.0	2.2	0.0	0.0	5.0	0.0	5.0	43.0	44.5	2.8	0.0	
08208J200	MED SPT CO MED BN HVY DIV	MOGAS	0.0	0.0	13.7	11.2	0.0	13.0	0.0	0.0	0.0	0.0	0.0	0.0	
		DIESEL	0.0	0.0	2.2	0.0	0.0	5.0	0.0	0.0	0.0	0.0	4.1	0.0	
09558J200	MSL SPT CO HVY DIV	MOGAS	0.0	0.0	27.6	4.0	0.0	1.0	0.0	0.0	0.0	0.0	0.0	0.0	
		DIESEL	0.0	30.0	56.7	0.0	1.3	4.0	0.0	2.0	36.8	25.5	7.6	0.0	
11035J200	SIGNAL BN (HEAVY DIV)	MOGAS	0.0	0.0	79.3	37.6	0.0	15.3	0.0	0.0	0.0	0.0	0.2	0.0	
		DIESEL	0.0	0.0	2.3	0.0	0.0	20.0	0.0	0.0	0.0	0.0	12.1	0.0	
11036J200	HHC SIG BN (HEAVY DIV)	MOGAS	0.0	0.0	13.8	4.0	0.0	3.3	0.0	0.0	0.0	0.0	0.2	0.0	
		DIESEL	0.0	0.0	0.6	0.0	0.0	5.0	0.0	0.0	0.0	0.0	3.9	0.0	
11037J200	CMD OPNS CO (HEAVY DIV)	MOGAS	0.0	0.0	27.2	13.0	0.0	4.0	0.0	0.0	0.0	0.0	0.0	0.0	
		DIESEL	0.0	0.0	0.6	0.0	0.0	5.0	0.0	0.0	0.0	0.0	3.1	0.0	
11038J200	FWD COMM CO HEAVY DIVISION	MOGAS	0.0	0.0	24.3	9.4	0.0	4.0	0.0	0.0	0.0	0.0	0.0	0.0	
		DIESEL	0.0	0.0	0.6	0.0	0.0	5.0	0.0	0.0	0.0	0.0	2.2	0.0	
11039J200	SGT SPT OPNS CO HEAVY DIV	MOGAS	0.0	0.0	14.0	11.2	0.0	4.0	0.0	0.0	0.0	0.0	0.0	0.0	
		DIESEL	0.0	0.0	0.6	0.0	0.0	5.0	0.0	0.0	0.0	0.0	2.8	0.0	
12217J200	AG CO - ARMOR/INF (MECH) DIV	MOGAS	0.0	0.0	2.5	11.2	0.0	4.0	0.0	0.0	0.0	0.0	0.1	0.0	
		DIESEL	0.0	0.0	16.5	0.0	0.0	5.0	0.0	0.0	0.0	0.0	1.9	0.0	
17185J220	ATK HEL BN CBAA (AH-64) HVD	MOGAS	0.0	0.0	22.3	29.2	0.0	14.2	0.0	0.0	0.0	0.0	0.0	0.0	
		DIESEL	0.0	8.0	1.1	0.0	5.2	10.0	0.0	0.0	0.0	0.0	11.2	0.0	
		JP4													3884.7
17186J220	HQ ANC SVC CO (AH-64)	MOGAS	0.0	0.0	22.3	29.2	0.0	14.2	0.0	0.0	0.0	0.0	0.0	0.0	
		DIESEL	0.0	8.0	1.1	0.0	5.2	10.0	0.0	0.0	0.0	0.0	10.6	0.0	
		JP4													525.9
17187J220	ATTACK HEL CO (AH-64)	MOGAS	0.0	0.0	0.0	0.0	0.0	0.0	0.0	0.0	0.0	0.0	0.0	0.0	
		DIESEL	0.0	0.0	0.0	0.0	0.0	0.0	0.0	0.0	0.0	0.0	0.2	0.0	
		JP4													1119.6
17201J220	CAV BDE AIR ATK (CBAA) (AH-64)	MOGAS	0.0	0.0	118.3	127.8	1.5	81.0	0.0	0.0	0.0	0.0	0.3	0.0	
		DIESEL	0.0	46.0	49.8	0.0	21.5	61.0	0.0	91.0	1084.8	686.5	54.1	0.0	
		JP4													11567.0
17202J200	HQ & HQ TROOP, CBAA	MOGAS	0.0	0.0	7.6	4.0	0.0	4.4	0.0	0.0	0.0	0.0	0.0	0.0	
		DIESEL	0.0	0.0	0.6	0.0	0.0	0.0	0.0	0.0	0.0	0.0	3.0	0.0	
17205J220	CAV SQDN HVY DIV (AH-64)	MOGAS	0.0	0.0	20.0	27.8	0.0	26.8	0.0	0.0	0.0	0.0	0.3	0.0	
		DIESEL	0.0	8.0	1.1	0.0	2.6	22.0	0.0	91.0	1084.8	686.5	14.8	0.0	
		JP4													1924.8
17206J220	HQ & HQ TRP, CAV SQDN (AH-64)	MOGAS	0.0	0.0	20.0	27.8	0.0	24.8	0.0	0.0	0.0	0.0	0.3	0.0	
		DIESEL	0.0	8.0	1.1	0.0	2.6	22.0	0.0	23.8	255.7	219.6	13.6	0.0	
		JP4													166.0
17207J210	CAV TRP, CAV SQDN	MOGAS	0.0	0.0	0.0	0.0	0.0	1.0	0.0	0.0	0.0	0.0	0.0	0.0	
		DIESEL	0.0	0.0	0.0	0.0	0.0	0.0	0.0	33.6	414.6	233.4	0.3	0.0	
17208J220	AIR CAV TRP, CAV SQDN (AH-64)	MOGAS	0.0	0.0	0.0	0.0	0.0	0.0	0.0	0.0	0.0	0.0	0.0	0.0	
		DIESEL	0.0	0.0	0.0	0.0	0.0	0.0	0.0	0.0	0.0	0.0	0.2	0.0	
		JP4													879.4
17235J120	TANK BATTALION EQ W/M1	MOGAS	0.0	0.0	1.4	36.2	0.0	12.0	0.0	0.0	0.0	0.0	0.2	0.0	
		DIESEL	0.0	0.0	0.0	0.0	0.0	0.0	0.0	638.2	3570.8	2804.9	8.9	0.0	
17236J120	HHC, TK BN (M1)	MOGAS	0.0	0.0	1.4	36.2	0.0	12.0	0.0	0.0	0.0	0.0	0.0	0.0	
		DIESEL	0.0	0.0	0.0	0.0	0.0	0.0	0.0	33.4	401.2	305.1	7.8	0.0	
17237J120	TANK CO (M1)	MOGAS	0.0	0.0	0.0	0.0	0.0	0.0	0.0	0.0	0.0	0.0	0.0	0.0	
		DIESEL	0.0	0.0	0.0	0.0	0.0	0.0	0.0	151.2	792.4	625.0	0.3	0.0	
19217J200	MP CO-HVY DIV	MOGAS	0.0	0.0	3.2	4.0	0.0	0.0	0.0	0.0	0.0	0.0	0.0	0.0	
		DIESEL	0.0	0.0	1.1	0.0	0.0	5.0	0.0	0.0	0.0	0.0	2.3	0.0	
34285J200	MI BN (CEWI) HVY DIV	MOGAS	0.0	0.0	63.4	18.8	0.0	17.5	0.0	0.0	0.0	0.0	0.0	0.0	
		DIESEL	0.0	0.0	16.5	0.0	0.0	17.0	0.0	11.4	85.2	90.9	13.4	0.4	
34286J200	HQ HQ-OP CO MI BN CEWI DIV	MOGAS	0.0	0.0	13.1	0.0	0.0	0.0	0.0	0.0	0.0	0.0	0.0	0.0	
		DIESEL	0.0	0.0	1.5	0.0	0.0	12.0	0.0	1.0	8.6	8.9	3.1	0.0	
34287J200	EW CO MI BN CEWI, DIV	MOGAS	0.0	0.0	15.2	0.0	0.0	0.0	0.0	0.0	0.0	0.0	0.0	0.0	
		DIESEL	0.0	0.0	15.0	0.0	0.0	0.0	0.0	0.0	0.0	0.0	1.3	0.4	

Figure 10. Bulk POL Planning Factors by Type Unit— Bulk POL Table E (continued)

SUMMARY OF BULK FUEL USAGE BY EQUIPMENT CATEGORY
HVY DIV M 5TK M1 5M BFVS (SRC 87000J240)—(Cont'd)

SRC	UNIT NAME	FUEL TYPE	AB	CE	GN	HG	MH	SG	SV	TI	CC	SR	WV	OV	AV
34288J200	INTL-SVL CO MI BN CEWI DIV	MOGAS	0.0	0.0	0.0	0.0	0.0	0.0	0.0	0.0	0.0	0.0	0.0	0.0	
		DIESEL	0.0	0.0	0.0	0.0	0.0	0.0	0.0	6.0	51.6	53.4	2.8	0.0	
34289J200	SVC SPT CO MI BN CEWI DIV	MOGAS	0.0	0.0	35.0	18.8	0.0	17.5	0.0	0.0	0.0	0.0	0.0	0.0	
		DIESEL	0.0	0.0	0.0	0.0	0.0	5.0	0.0	4.4	25.0	28.6	6.0	0.0	
42004J200	SUP CO FWD SPT BN HVY DIV	MOGAS	0.0	0.0	2.5	7.2	0.0	7.9	0.0	0.0	0.0	0.0	0.0	0.0	
		DIESEL	0.0	21.0	0.0	0.0	21.3	0.0	0.0	0.0	0.0	0.0	4.9	0.0	
42005J200	S&T BN HEAVY DIVISION	MOGAS	0.0	0.0	16.2	32.6	0.0	39.3	14.0	0.0	0.0	0.0	0.0	0.0	
		DIESEL	0.0	28.0	3.4	0.0	43.5	17.0	0.0	0.0	0.0	0.0	32.8	0.0	
42006J200	HHC S&T BN HEAVY DIVISION	MOGAS	0.0	0.0	0.8	21.0	0.0	8.0	0.0	0.0	0.0	0.0	0.0	0.0	
		DIESEL	0.0	0.0	1.1	0.0	0.0	5.0	0.0	0.0	0.0	0.0	2.1	0.0	
42007J200	S&S CO S&T BN HVY DIV	MOGAS	0.0	0.0	13.7	0.0	0.0	25.5	14.0	0.0	0.0	0.0	0.0	0.0	
		DIESEL	0.0	28.0	0.0	0.0	43.5	0.0	0.0	0.0	0.0	0.0	10.1	0.0	
43004J200	MAINT CO,FWD SPT BN, HVY DIV	MOGAS	0.0	0.0	33.2	16.0	0.0	15.5	0.0	0.0	0.0	0.0	0.0	0.0	
		DIESEL	0.0	7.0	11.8	0.0	9.8	11.0	0.0	3.0	45.4	34.4	9.3	0.0	
43004J201	TK SYSTEM SPT TM	MOGAS	0.0	0.0	0.5	0.0	0.0	5.6	0.0	0.0	0.0	0.0	0.0	0.0	
		DIESEL	0.0	0.0	0.0	0.0	0.0	0.0	0.0	1.0	8.6	8.9	0.7	0.0	
43004J202	INF SYS(M) SPT TM	MOGAS	0.0	0.0	3.5	0.0	0.0	5.6	0.0	0.0	0.0	0.0	0.0	0.0	
		DIESEL	0.0	0.0	0.0	0.0	0.0	0.0	0.0	1.0	8.6	8.9	0.8	0.0	
43005J200	MAINT BN,SPT COMD,HVY DIV	MOGAS	0.0	0.0	83.3	66.4	0.0	79.1	0.0	0.0	0.0	0.0	0.0	0.0	
		DIESEL	0.0	37.0	153.7	0.0	26.8	17.0	0.0	6.0	90.7	68.9	27.3	0.0	
43006J200	HQ&SUPPORT CO HVY DIV	MOGAS	0.0	0.0	7.3	7.6	0.0	4.0	0.0	0.0	0.0	0.0	0.0	0.0	
		DIESEL	0.0	0.0	5.2	0.0	17.0	0.0	0.0	0.0	0.0	0.0	6.2	0.0	
43007J200	LIGHT MAINT CO HVY DIV	MOGAS	0.0	0.0	32.9	25.4	0.0	20.9	0.0	0.0	0.0	0.0	0.0	0.0	
		DIESEL	0.0	0.0	88.2	0.0	0.0	0.0	0.0	0.0	0.0	0.0	6.3	0.0	
43008J200	HEAVY MAINT CO HVY DIV	MOGAS	0.0	0.0	15.5	29.4	0.0	53.2	0.0	0.0	0.0	0.0	0.0	0.0	
		DIESEL	0.0	7.0	3.6	0.0	8.5	13.0	0.0	4.0	54.0	43.3	7.1	0.0	
55087J200	TMT CO S&T BN HEAVY DIV	MOGAS	0.0	0.0	0.0	0.0	0.0	0.9	0.0	0.0	0.0	0.0	0.0	0.0	
		DIESEL	0.0	0.0	0.6	0.0	0.0	5.0	0.0	0.0	0.0	0.0	13.9	0.0	
55089J200	TMT CO (HY) S&T BN HY DIV	MOGAS	0.0	0.0	1.7	11.6	0.0	4.9	0.0	0.0	0.0	0.0	0.0	0.0	
		DIESEL	0.0	0.0	1.7	0.0	0.0	7.0	0.0	0.0	0.0	0.0	6.7	0.0	
55427J200	TAM CO,CBT SPT,AVN BN,CBA	MOGAS	0.0	0.0	16.7	13.0	1.5	4.4	0.0	0.0	0.0	0.0	0.0	0.0	
		DIESEL	0.0	16.0	45.2	0.0	8.5	5.0	0.0	0.0	0.0	0.0	5.1	0.0	
		JP4													332.0
63001J220	SPT COMD,6 × 4,HVY DIV,INF	MOGAS	0.0	0.0	285.4	216.0	0.0	308.3	14.0	0.0	0.0	0.0	0.4	0.0	
		DIESEL	0.0	149.0	272.6	0.0	163.6	92.0	0.0	40.0	441.8	394.7	132.7	0.0	
63002J200	HHC, SPT COMD, HV DIV	MOGAS	0.0	0.0	0.8	7.6	0.0	4.0	0.0	0.0	0.0	0.0	0.1	0.0	
		DIESEL	0.0	0.0	6.0	0.0	0.0	0.0	0.0	0.0	0.0	0.0	1.2	0.0	
63003J200	DMMC,SPT COMD,HV DIV	MOGAS	0.0	0.0	0.0	0.0	0.0	0.0	0.0	0.0	0.0	0.0	0.0	0.0	
		DIESEL	0.0	0.0	37.5	0.0	0.0	0.0	0.0	0.0	0.0	0.0	2.5	0.0	
63005J210	FWD SPT BN 2 × 1 HVY DIV	MOGAS	0.0	0.0	43.1	23.2	0.0	41.4	0.0	0.0	0.0	0.0	0.1	0.0	
		DIESEL	0.0	28.0	14.8	0.0	31.1	11.0	0.0	6.0	71.2	61.1	17.2	0.0	
63005J220	FWD SPT BN 2 × 2 HVY DIV	MOGAS	0.0	0.0	46.6	23.2	0.0	47.0	0.0	0.0	0.0	0.0	0.1	0.0	
		DIESEL	0.0	28.0	14.8	0.0	31.1	11.0	0.0	7.0	79.8	70.0	17.9	0.0	
63005J230	FWD SPT BN 1 × 2 HVY DIV	MOGAS	0.0	0.0	46.1	23.2	0.0	41.4	0.0	0.0	0.0	0.0	0.1	0.0	
		DIESEL	0.0	28.0	14.8	0.0	31.1	11.0	0.0	6.0	71.2	61.1	17.3	0.0	
63006J200	HHD,FWD SPT BN,HEAVY DIV	MOGAS	0.0	0.0	2.8	0.0	0.0	1.0	0.0	0.0	0.0	0.0	0.1	0.0	
		DIESEL	0.0	0.0	3.0	0.0	0.0	0.0	0.0	0.0	0.0	0.0	0.8	0.0	
87000J240	HVY DIV M 5TK M1,5M (BFVS)	MOGAS	0.0	2.0	783.7	913.4	1.5	939.4	14.0	0.0	0.0	0.0	3.0	0.0	
		DIESEL	86.4	263.0	412.6	0.0	193.6	574.0	0.0	4541.6	32009.3	24753.8	434.6	31.1	
		JP4													11567.0
87004J220	HHC INFANTRY DIVISION (MECH)	MOGAS	0.0	0.0	17.9	14.8	0.0	12.0	0.0	0.0	0.0	0.0	0.0	0.0	
		DIESEL	0.0	0.0	0.0	0.0	0.0	0.0	0.0	4.0	34.4	35.6	2.1	0.0	
87042J210	HHC ARMD DIV BDE	MOGAS	0.0	0.0	5.9	9.4	0.0	4.0	0.0	0.0	0.0	0.0	0.0	0.0	
		DIESEL	0.0	0.0	0.0	0.0	0.0	5.0	0.0	9.2	72.7	76.6	1.6	0.0	
87042J220	HHC INF DIV (MECH) BDE	MOGAS	0.0	0.0	8.9	9.4	0.0	4.0	0.0	0.0	0.0	0.0	0.0	0.0	
		DIESEL	0.0	0.0	0.0	0.0	0.0	5.0	0.0	9.2	72.7	76.6	1.6	0.0	

SUMMARY OF BULK FUEL USAGE BY EQUIPMENT CATEGORY
HVY DIV FULL 6TK M1 4MB FVS (SRC 87000J250)

SRC	UNIT NAME	FUEL TYPE	AB	CE	GN	HG	MH	SG	SV	TI	CC	SR	WV	OV	AV
01285J210	CBT SPT AVN BN (HVY DIV)	MOGAS	0.0	0.0	46.1	37.6	1.5	21.3	0.0	0.0	0.0	0.0	0.0	0.0	
		DIESEL	0.0	22.0	45.8	0.0	8.5	19.0	0.0	0.0	0.0	0.0	13.6	0.0	
		JP4													1872.8
01286J210	HHC, CBT SPT AVN BN (HVY)	MOGAS	0.0	0.0	7.5	12.6	0.0	10.0	0.0	0.0	0.0	0.0	0.0	0.0	
		DIESEL	0.0	0.0	0.0	0.0	0.0	5.0	0.0	0.0	0.0	0.0	3.2	0.0	
01286J211	HHC, CSAB, CBAA AAPRS	MOGAS	0.0	0.0	0.0	9.0	0.0	2.5	0.0	0.0	0.0	0.0	0.0	0.0	
		DIESEL	0.0	0.0	0.0	0.0	17.0	0.0	0.0	0.0	0.0	0.0	7.1	0.0	
01287J200	GEN SPT AVN CO	MOGAS	0.0	0.0	21.9	12.0	0.0	6.4	0.0	0.0	0.0	0.0	0.0	0.0	
		DIESEL	0.0	6.0	0.6	0.0	0.0	9.0	0.0	0.0	0.0	0.0	5.3	0.0	
		JP4													1540.8
01287J201	GSAC, CSAB, CBAA AAPRS	MOGAS	0.0	0.0	0.0	0.0	0.0	0.0	0.0	0.0	0.0	0.0	0.0	0.0	
		DIESEL	0.0	0.0	0.0	0.0	0.0	0.0	0.0	0.0	0.0	0.0	0.0	0.0	
03387J200	CHEMICAL CO, HVY DIV	MOGAS	0.0	0.0	36.8	4.0	0.0	64.0	0.0	0.0	0.0	0.0	0.0	0.0	
		DIESEL	0.0	0.0	0.6	0.0	0.0	5.0	0.0	6.0	51.6	53.4	9.5	0.0	
03387J201	DECON PLT	MOGAS	0.0	0.0	0.0	0.0	0.0	15.7	0.0	0.0	0.0	0.0	0.0	0.0	
		DIESEL	0.0	0.0	0.0	0.0	0.0	0.0	0.0	0.0	0.0	0.0	2.1	0.0	
05145J210	ENGR BN, HVY DIV - RIBBON	MOGAS	0.0	2.0	22.6	45.6	0.0	102.7	0.0	0.0	0.0	0.0	0.1	0.0	
		DIESEL	86.4	68.0	2.8	0.0	8.5	34.0	0.0	147.1	1583.2	1311.5	36.9	0.0	
05146J200	HQ-HQ COMPANY	MOGAS	0.0	0.0	4.1	7.6	0.0	11.5	0.0	0.0	0.0	0.0	0.1	0.0	
		DIESEL	0.0	0.0	0.6	0.0	8.5	7.0	0.0	1.0	8.6	8.9	7.4	0.0	
05147J200	ENGR CO, ENGR BN, HVY DIV	MOGAS	0.0	0.5	4.2	7.6	0.0	19.5	0.0	0.0	0.0	0.0	0.0	0.0	
		DIESEL	0.0	17.0	0.6	0.0	0.0	5.0	0.0	36.5	393.6	325.6	5.3	0.0	

Figure 10. Bulk POL Planning Factors by Type Unit— Bulk POL Table E (continued)

SUMMARY OF BULK FUEL USAGE BY EQUIPMENT CATEGORY
HVY DIV FULL 6TK M1 4MB FVS (SRC 87000J250)

SRC	UNIT NAME	FUEL TYPE	AB	CE	GN	HG	MH	SG	SV	TI	CC	SR	WV	OV	AV
05147J201	ARMD VEH LAUNCHED BR AUG	MOGAS	0.0	0.0	0.0	0.0	0.0	0.0	0.0	0.0	0.0	0.0	0.0	0.0	
		DIESEL	0.0	0.0	0.0	0.0	0.0	0.0	0.0	4.0	53.1	37.6	0.0	0.0	
05148J210	BRIDGE COMPANY - RIBBON	MOGAS	0.0	0.0	1.7	7.6	0.0	13.0	0.0	0.0	0.0	0.0	0.0	0.0	
		DIESEL	86.4	0.0	0.0	0.0	0.0	7.0	0.0	0.0	0.0	0.0	8.2	0.0	
06300J210	ARMD DIVARTY W/TACFIRE	MOGAS	0.0	0.0	112.5	109.6	0.0	121.5	0.0	0.0	0.0	0.0	0.3	0.0	
		DIESEL	0.0	0.0	41.2	0.0	0.0	100.0	0.0	288.5	1934.4	2272.6	82.2	30.7	
06302J200	HHB DIV ARTY HVY DIV	MOGAS	0.0	0.0	26.3	5.4	0.0	8.4	0.0	0.0	0.0	0.0	0.1	0.0	
		DIESEL	0.0	0.0	9.8	0.0	0.0	5.0	0.0	1.0	8.6	8.9	5.4	0.0	
06307J200	TGT ACQ BTRY HVY DIV	MOGAS	0.0	0.0	4.4	5.4	0.0	4.5	0.0	0.0	0.0	0.0	0.0	0.0	
		DIESEL	0.0	0.0	12.0	0.0	0.0	10.0	0.0	0.0	0.0	0.0	5.0	0.0	
06365J210	FA BN 155 SP HVY DIV	MOGAS	0.0	0.0	20.0	25.6	0.0	27.3	0.0	0.0	0.0	0.0	0.0	0.0	
		DIESEL	0.0	0.0	5.3	0.0	0.0	25.0	0.0	72.4	432.5	545.0	17.3	10.1	
06365J220	FA BN 155 SP HVY DIV	MOGAS	0.0	0.0	20.0	25.6	0.0	27.3	0.0	0.0	0.0	0.0	0.0	0.0	
		DIESEL	0.0	0.0	5.3	0.0	0.0	25.0	0.0	72.4	432.5	545.0	17.3	10.1	
06366J210	HHB FA BN 155SP HVY DIV	MOGAS	0.0	0.0	12.8	7.2	0.0	7.0	0.0	0.0	0.0	0.0	0.0	0.0	
		DIESEL	0.0	0.0	3.6	0.0	0.0	5.0	0.0	7.0	60.2	62.3	2.5	3.4	
06366J220	HHB FA BN 155SP HVY DIV	MOGAS	0.0	0.0	12.8	7.2	0.0	7.0	0.0	0.0	0.0	0.0	0.0	0.0	
		DIESEL	0.0	0.0	3.6	0.0	0.0	5.0	0.0	7.0	60.2	62.3	2.4	3.4	
06367J200	FA BTRY 155SP HVY DIV	MOGAS	0.0	0.0	1.1	3.6	0.0	3.0	0.0	0.0	0.0	0.0	0.0	0.0	
		DIESEL	0.0	0.0	0.6	0.0	0.0	5.0	0.0	19.6	111.6	146.6	2.2	2.2	
06369J200	SVC BTRY 155SP HVY DIV	MOGAS	0.0	0.0	3.9	7.6	0.0	11.3	0.0	0.0	0.0	0.0	0.0	0.0	
		DIESEL	0.0	0.0	0.0	0.0	0.0	5.0	0.0	6.6	37.5	42.9	8.2	0.0	
06395J200	FA BN, 8IN/MLRS HVY DIV	MOGAS	0.0	0.0	21.4	22.0	0.0	26.5	0.0	0.0	0.0	0.0	0.0	0.0	
		DIESEL	0.0	0.0	3.6	0.0	0.0	10.0	0.0	69.3	619.7	619.8	19.7	0.0	
06396J200	HHB 8IN/MLRS HVY DIV	MOGAS	0.0	0.0	6.4	3.6	0.0	7.0	0.0	0.0	0.0	0.0	0.0	0.0	
		DIESEL	0.0	0.0	3.0	0.0	0.0	0.0	0.0	3.0	25.8	26.7	2.4	0.0	
06396J202	AUG- FIST, TANK BN	MOGAS	0.0	0.0	0.5	0.0	0.0	0.0	0.0	0.0	0.0	0.0	0.0	0.0	
		DIESEL	0.0	0.0	0.0	0.0	0.0	0.0	0.0	1.0	8.6	8.9	0.0	0.3	
06397J200	FA BTRY 8IN SP HVY DIV	MOGAS	0.0	0.0	3.2	3.6	0.0	3.0	0.0	0.0	0.0	0.0	0.0	0.0	
		DIESEL	0.0	0.0	0.0	0.0	0.0	0.0	0.0	21.2	163.0	200.2	2.1	0.0	
06398J200	FA BTRY MLRS	MOGAS	0.0	0.0	3.8	3.6	0.0	4.5	0.0	0.0	0.0	0.0	0.0	0.0	
		DIESEL	0.0	0.0	0.0	0.0	0.0	0.0	0.0	15.5	169.4	113.0	7.1	0.0	
06399J200	SVC BTRY 8IN/MLRS HVY DIV	MOGAS	0.0	0.0	4.7	7.6	0.0	9.0	0.0	0.0	0.0	0.0	0.0	0.0	
		DIESEL	0.0	0.0	0.6	0.0	0.0	10.0	0.0	8.4	98.5	79.7	5.7	0.0	
07245J210	INF BN-MECH E/W BFVS	MOGAS	0.0	0.0	2.8	25.2	0.0	29.0	0.0	0.0	0.0	0.0	0.1	0.0	
		DIESEL	0.0	0.0	5.1	0.0	0.0	45.0	0.0	147.0	1744.3	1130.0	7.8	0.0	
07246J210	HHC INF BN MECH BFVS	MOGAS	0.0	0.0	2.2	25.2	0.0	29.0	0.0	0.0	0.0	0.0	0.1	0.0	
		DIESEL	0.0	0.0	2.3	0.0	0.0	20.0	0.0	54.2	636.3	505.7	5.8	0.0	
07247J210	RIFLE CO INF BN MECH BFVS	MOGAS	0.0	0.0	0.0	0.0	0.0	0.0	0.0	0.0	0.0	0.0	0.0	0.0	
		DIESEL	0.0	0.0	0.6	0.0	0.0	5.0	0.0	19.2	242.6	120.7	0.4	0.0	
07248J200	ANTIARMOR CO INF BN(M) IT	MOGAS	0.0	0.0	0.5	0.0	0.0	0.0	0.0	0.0	0.0	0.0	0.0	0.0	
		DIESEL	0.0	0.0	0.6	0.0	0.0	5.0	0.0	16.0	137.6	142.4	0.4	0.0	
08205J200	MEDICAL BN HVY DIV	MOGAS	0.0	0.0	46.7	28.6	0.0	52.0	0.0	0.0	0.0	0.0	0.0	0.0	
		DIESEL	0.0	0.0	11.1	0.0	0.0	20.0	0.0	15.0	129.0	133.5	14.3	0.0	
08206J200	HHD MED BN HVY DIV	MOGAS	0.0	0.0	1.7	0.0	0.0	0.0	0.0	0.0	0.0	0.0	0.0	0.0	
		DIESEL	0.0	0.0	2.2	0.0	0.0	0.0	0.0	0.0	0.0	0.0	1.6	0.0	
08207J200	MED CO MED BN HVY DIV	MOGAS	0.0	0.0	10.4	5.8	0.0	13.0	0.0	0.0	0.0	0.0	0.0	0.0	
		DIESEL	0.0	0.0	2.2	0.0	0.0	5.0	0.0	5.0	43.0	44.5	2.8	0.0	
08207J201	AUG-PAT DECON	MOGAS	0.0	0.0	0.0	0.0	0.0	1.0	0.0	0.0	0.0	0.0	0.0	0.0	
		DIESEL	0.0	0.0	0.0	0.0	0.0	0.0	0.0	0.0	0.0	0.0	0.0	0.0	
08208J200	MED SPT CO MED BN HVY DIV	MOGAS	0.0	0.0	13.7	11.2	0.0	13.0	0.0	0.0	0.0	0.0	0.0	0.0	
		DIESEL	0.0	0.0	2.2	0.0	0.0	5.0	0.0	0.0	0.0	0.0	4.1	0.0	
08208J201	AUG-PAT DECON	MOGAS	0.0	0.0	0.0	0.0	0.0	1.0	0.0	0.0	0.0	0.0	0.0	0.0	
		DIESEL	0.0	0.0	0.0	0.0	0.0	0.0	0.0	0.0	0.0	0.0	0.0	0.0	
09558J200	MSL SPT CO HVY DIV	MOGAS	0.0	0.0	27.6	4.0	0.0	1.0	0.0	0.0	0.0	0.0	0.0	0.0	
		DIESEL	0.0	30.0	56.7	0.0	1.3	4.0	0.0	2.0	36.8	25.5	7.6	0.0	
11035J200	SIGNAL BN (HEAVY DIV)	MOGAS	0.0	0.0	79.3	37.6	0.0	15.3	0.0	0.0	0.0	0.0	0.2	0.0	
		DIESEL	0.0	0.0	2.3	0.0	0.0	20.0	0.0	0.0	0.0	0.0	12.1	0.0	
11036J200	HHC SIG BN (HEAVY DIV)	MOGAS	0.0	0.0	13.8	4.0	0.0	3.3	0.0	0.0	0.0	0.0	0.2	0.0	
		DIESEL	0.0	0.0	0.6	0.0	0.0	5.0	0.0	0.0	0.0	0.0	3.9	0.0	
11037J200	CMD OPNS CO (HEAVY DIV)	MOGAS	0.0	0.0	27.2	13.0	0.0	4.0	0.0	0.0	0.0	0.0	0.0	0.0	
		DIESEL	0.0	0.0	0.6	0.0	0.0	5.0	0.0	0.0	0.0	0.0	3.1	0.0	
11038J200	FWD COMM CO HEAVY DIVISION	MOGAS	0.0	0.0	24.3	9.4	0.0	4.0	0.0	0.0	0.0	0.0	0.0	0.0	
		DIESEL	0.0	0.0	0.6	0.0	0.0	5.0	0.0	0.0	0.0	0.0	2.2	0.0	
11039J200	SIG SPT OPNS CO HEAVY DIV	MOGAS	0.0	0.0	14.0	11.2	0.0	4.0	0.0	0.0	0.0	0.0	0.0	0.0	
		DIESEL	0.0	0.0	0.6	0.0	0.0	5.0	0.0	0.0	0.0	0.0	2.8	0.0	
12217J200	AG CO, ARMOR/INF (MECH) DIV	MOGAS	0.0	0.0	2.5	11.2	0.0	4.0	0.0	0.0	0.0	0.0	0.1	0.0	
		DIESEL	0.0	0.0	16.5	0.0	0.0	5.0	0.0	0.0	0.0	0.0	1.9	0.0	
12217J201	AUG-REPL DET MESS + SUPPL	MOGAS	0.0	0.0	0.0	7.2	0.0	3.0	0.0	0.0	0.0	0.0	0.0	0.0	
		DIESEL	0.0	0.0	0.0	0.0	0.0	0.0	0.0	0.0	0.0	0.0	0.2	0.0	
12217J202	AUG-PERS SVCS DIV + POSTAL	MOGAS	0.0	0.0	0.0	0.0	0.0	0.0	0.0	0.0	0.0	0.0	0.0	0.0	
		DIESEL	0.0	0.0	0.0	0.0	0.0	0.0	0.0	0.0	0.0	0.0	0.0	0.0	
12217J203	AUG-BAND	MOGAS	0.0	0.0	0.0	0.0	0.0	0.0	0.0	0.0	0.0	0.0	0.0	0.0	
		DIESEL	0.0	0.0	0.0	0.0	0.0	0.0	0.0	0.0	0.0	0.0	0.0	0.0	
17185J220	ATK HEL BN CBAA AH-64 HVD	MOGAS	0.0	0.0	22.3	29.2	0.0	14.2	0.0	0.0	0.0	0.0	0.0	0.0	
		DIESEL	0.0	8.0	1.1	0.0	5.2	10.0	0.0	0.0	0.0	0.0	11.2	0.0	
		JP4													3884.7
17186J211	ATK HEL BN, CBAA AAPRS	MOGAS	0.0	0.0	0.0	1.8	0.0	1.0	0.0	0.0	0.0	0.0	0.0	0.0	
		DIESEL	0.0	0.0	0.0	0.0	0.0	0.0	0.0	0.0	0.0	0.0	0.0	0.0	
17186J220	HQ AND SVC CO (AH-64)	MOGAS	0.0	0.0	22.3	29.2	0.0	14.2	0.0	0.0	0.0	0.0	0.0	0.0	
		DIESEL	0.0	8.0	1.1	0.0	5.2	10.0	0.0	0.0	0.0	0.0	10.6	0.0	
		JP4													525.9
17187J220	ATTACK HEL CO (AH-64)	MOGAS	0.0	0.0	0.0	0.0	0.0	0.0	0.0	0.0	0.0	0.0	0.0	0.0	
		DIESEL	0.0	0.0	0.0	0.0	0.0	0.0	0.0	0.0	0.0	0.0	0.2	0.0	
		JP4													1119.6

Figure 10. Bulk POL Planning Factors by Type Unit— Bulk POL Table E (continued)

SUMMARY OF BULK FUEL USAGE BY EQUIPMENT CATEGORY
HVY DIV FULL 6TK MI 4MB FVS (SRC87000J250)—(Cont'd)

SRC	UNIT NAME	FUEL TYPE	AB	CE	GN	HG	MH	SG	SV	TI	CC	SR	WV	OV	AV
17202J200	HQ & HQ TROOP, CBAA	MOGAS	0.0	0.0	7.6	4.0	0.0	4.4	0.0	0.0	0.0	0.0	0.0	0.0	
		DIESEL	0.0	0.0	0.6	0.0	0.0	0.0	0.0	0.0	0.0	0.0	3.0	0.0	
17202J201	HQ & HQ TROOP, CBAA AAPRS	MOGAS	0.0	0.0	0.0	0.0	0.0	0.0	0.0	0.0	0.0	0.0	0.0	0.0	
		DIESEL	0.0	0.0	0.0	0.0	0.0	0.0	0.0	0.0	0.0	0.0	0.0	0.0	
17205J210	CAV SQDN, CBAA AHIS HVY DIV	MOGAS	0.0	0.0	20.0	29.2	0.0	23.4	0.0	0.0	0.0	0.0	0.0	0.0	
		DIESEL	0.0	8.0	1.1	0.0	2.6	20.0	0.0	89.0	1067.6	668.7	13.7	0.6	
		JP4													1604.8
17206J210	HQ AND HQ TRP, CAV SQDN	MOGAS	0.0	0.0	20.0	29.2	0.0	21.4	0.0	0.0	0.0	0.0	0.0	0.0	
		DIESEL	0.0	8.0	1.1	0.0	2.6	20.0	0.0	21.8	238.5	201.8	12.5	0.6	
		JP4													142.0
17206J211	CAV SQDN, CBAA AAPRS	MOGAS	0.0	0.0	0.0	1.8	0.0	1.5	0.0	0.0	0.0	0.0	0.0	0.0	
		DIESEL	0.0	0.0	0.0	0.0	0.0	0.0	0.0	0.0	0.0	0.0	0.0	0.0	
17207J210	CAV TRP, CAV SQDN	MOGAS	0.0	0.0	0.0	0.0	0.0	1.0	0.0	0.0	0.0	0.0	0.0	0.0	
		DIESEL	0.0	0.0	0.0	0.0	0.0	0.0	0.0	33.6	414.6	233.4	0.3	0.0	
17208J210	AIR CAV TRP, CAV SQDN	MOGAS	0.0	0.0	0.0	0.0	0.0	0.0	0.0	0.0	0.0	0.0	0.0	0.0	
		DIESEL	0.0	0.0	0.0	0.0	0.0	0.0	0.0	0.0	0.0	0.0	0.2	0.0	
		JP4													731.4
17235J120	TANK BATTALION EQ W/M1	MOGAS	0.0	0.0	1.4	36.2	0.0	12.0	0.0	0.0	0.0	0.0	0.2	0.0	
		DIESEL	0.0	0.0	0.0	0.0	0.0	0.0	0.0	638.2	3570.8	2804.9	8.9	0.0	
17236J120	HHC, TK BN (M1)	MOGAS	0.0	0.0	1.4	36.2	0.0	12.0	0.0	0.0	0.0	0.0	0.0	0.0	
		DIESEL	0.0	0.0	0.0	0.0	0.0	0.0	0.0	33.4	401.2	305.1	7.8	0.0	
17237J120	TANK CO (M1)	MOGAS	0.0	0.0	0.0	0.0	0.0	0.0	0.0	0.0	0.0	0.0	0.0	0.0	
		DIESEL	0.0	0.0	0.0	0.0	0.0	0.0	0.0	151.2	792.4	625.0	0.3	0.0	
19217J200	MP CO-HVY DIV	MOGAS	0.0	0.0	3.2	4.0	0.0	0.0	0.0	0.0	0.0	0.0	0.0	0.0	
		DIESEL	0.0	0.0	1.1	0.0	0.0	5.0	0.0	0.0	0.0	0.0	2.3	0.0	
34285J200	MI BN (CEWI) HVY DIV	MOGAS	0.0	0.0	63.4	18.8	0.0	17.5	0.0	0.0	0.0	0.0	0.0	0.0	
		DIESEL	0.0	0.0	16.5	0.0	0.0	17.0	0.0	11.4	85.2	90.9	13.4	0.4	
34286J200	HQ HQ-OP CO MI BN CEWI DIV	MOGAS	0.0	0.0	13.1	0.0	0.0	0.0	0.0	0.0	0.0	0.0	0.0	0.0	
		DIESEL	0.0	0.0	1.5	0.0	0.0	12.0	0.0	1.0	8.6	8.9	3.1	0.0	
34287J200	EW CO MI BN CEWI, DIV	MOGAS	0.0	0.0	15.2	0.0	0.0	0.0	0.0	0.0	0.0	0.0	0.0	0.0	
		DIESEL	0.0	0.0	15.0	0.0	0.0	0.0	0.0	0.0	0.0	0.0	1.3	0.4	
34287J201	AUG-3 ELINT TMS	MOGAS	0.0	0.0	7.2	0.0	0.0	0.0	0.0	0.0	0.0	0.0	0.0	0.0	
		DIESEL	0.0	0.0	0.0	0.0	0.0	0.0	0.0	0.0	0.0	0.0	0.3	0.0	
34287J202	AUG-3 VHF ECM TMS	MOGAS	0.0	0.0	7.2	0.0	0.0	0.0	0.0	0.0	0.0	0.0	0.0	0.0	
		DIESEL	0.0	0.0	0.0	0.0	0.0	0.0	0.0	0.0	0.0	0.0	0.1	0.0	
34289J200	SVC SPT CO MI BN CEWI DIV	MOGAS	0.0	0.0	35.0	18.8	0.0	17.5	0.0	0.0	0.0	0.0	0.0	0.0	
		DIESEL	0.0	0.0	0.0	0.0	0.0	5.0	0.0	4.4	25.0	28.6	6.0	0.0	
34289J201	AUG-MAINTENANCE	MOGAS	0.0	0.0	0.0	0.0	0.0	0.0	0.0	0.0	0.0	0.0	0.0	0.0	
		DIESEL	0.0	0.0	0.0	0.0	0.0	0.0	0.0	0.0	0.0	0.0	0.0	0.0	
42004J200	SUP CO FWD SPT BN HVY DIV	MOGAS	0.0	0.0	2.5	7.2	0.0	7.9	0.0	0.0	0.0	0.0	0.0	0.0	
		DIESEL	0.0	21.0	0.0	0.0	21.3	0.0	0.0	0.0	0.0	0.0	4.9	0.0	
42005J200	S&T BN HEAVY DIVISION	MOGAS	0.0	0.0	16.2	32.6	0.0	39.3	14.0	0.0	0.0	0.0	0.0	0.0	
		DIESEL	0.0	28.0	3.4	0.0	43.5	17.0	0.0	0.0	0.0	0.0	32.8	0.0	
42006J200	HHC S&T BN HEAVY DIVISION	MOGAS	0.0	0.0	0.8	21.0	0.0	8.0	0.0	0.0	0.0	0.0	0.0	0.0	
		DIESEL	0.0	0.0	1.1	0.0	0.0	5.0	0.0	0.0	0.0	0.0	2.1	0.0	
42007J200	S&S CO S&T BN HVY DIV	MOGAS	0.0	0.0	13.7	0.0	0.0	25.5	14.0	0.0	0.0	0.0	0.0	0.0	
		DIESEL	0.0	28.0	0.0	0.0	43.5	0.0	0.0	0.0	0.0	0.0	10.1	0.0	
42007J201	AUG - GRREG PLT	MOGAS	0.0	0.0	0.0	0.0	0.0	0.0	0.0	0.0	0.0	0.0	0.0	0.0	
		DIESEL	0.0	0.0	0.0	0.0	0.0	0.0	0.0	0.0	0.0	0.0	0.6	0.0	
42007J202	AUG - CEB PLT	MOGAS	0.0	0.0	7.6	36.0	0.0	0.0	0.0	0.0	0.0	0.0	0.0	0.0	
		DIESEL	0.0	0.0	0.0	0.0	0.0	0.0	0.0	0.0	0.0	0.0	1.6	0.0	
43004J200	MAINT CO, FWD SPT BN, HVY DIV	MOGAS	0.0	0.0	33.2	16.0	0.0	15.5	0.0	0.0	0.0	0.0	0.0	0.0	
		DIESEL	0.0	7.0	11.8	0.0	9.8	11.0	0.0	3.0	45.4	34.4	9.3	0.0	
43004J201	TK SYSTEM SPT TM	MOGAS	0.0	0.0	0.5	0.0	0.0	5.6	0.0	0.0	0.0	0.0	0.0	0.0	
		DIESEL	0.0	0.0	0.0	0.0	0.0	0.0	0.0	1.0	8.6	8.9	0.7	0.0	
43004J202	INF SYS(M) SPT TM	MOGAS	0.0	0.0	3.5	0.0	0.0	5.6	0.0	0.0	0.0	0.0	0.0	0.0	
		DIESEL	0.0	0.0	0.0	0.0	0.0	0.0	0.0	1.0	8.6	8.9	0.8	0.0	
43005J200	MAINT BN, SPT COMD, HVY DIV	MOGAS	0.0	0.0	83.3	66.4	0.0	79.1	0.0	0.0	0.0	0.0	0.0	0.0	
		DIESEL	0.0	37.0	153.7	0.0	26.8	17.0	0.0	6.0	90.7	68.9	27.3	0.0	
43006J200	HQ&SUPPORT CO HVY DIV	MOGAS	0.0	0.0	7.3	7.6	0.0	4.0	0.0	0.0	0.0	0.0	0.0	0.0	
		DIESEL	0.0	0.0	5.2	0.0	17.0	0.0	0.0	0.0	0.0	0.0	6.2	0.0	
43007J200	LIGHT MAINT CO HVY DIV	MOGAS	0.0	0.0	32.9	25.4	0.0	20.9	0.0	0.0	0.0	0.0	0.0	0.0	
		DIESEL	0.0	0.0	88.2	0.0	0.0	0.0	0.0	0.0	0.0	0.0	6.3	0.0	
43008J200	HEAVY MAINT CO HVY DIV	MOGAS	0.0	0.0	15.5	29.4	0.0	53.2	0.0	0.0	0.0	0.0	0.0	0.0	
		DIESEL	0.0	7.0	3.6	0.0	8.5	13.0	0.0	4.0	54.0	43.3	7.1	0.0	
55087J200	TMET CO S&T BN HEAVY DIV	MOGAS	0.0	0.0	0.0	0.0	0.0	0.9	0.0	0.0	0.0	0.0	0.0	0.0	
		DIESEL	0.0	0.0	0.6	0.0	0.0	5.0	0.0	0.0	0.0	0.0	13.9	0.0	
55089J200	TMT CO (HY) S&T BN HY DIV	MOGAS	0.0	0.0	1.7	11.6	0.0	4.9	0.0	0.0	0.0	0.0	0.0	0.0	
		DIESEL	0.0	0.0	1.7	0.0	0.0	7.0	0.0	0.0	0.0	0.0	6.7	0.0	
55427J200	TAM CO, CBT SPT, AVN BN, CBA	MOGAS	0.0	0.0	16.7	13.0	1.5	4.4	0.0	0.0	0.0	0.0	0.0	0.0	
		DIESEL	0.0	16.0	45.2	0.0	8.5	5.0	0.0	0.0	0.0	0.0	5.1	0.0	
		JP4													332.0
55427J201	TAMC, CSAB, CBAA AAPRS	MOGAS	0.0	0.0	0.0	0.0	0.0	0.0	0.0	0.0	0.0	0.0	0.0	0.0	
		DIESEL	0.0	0.0	0.0	0.0	0.0	0.0	0.0	0.0	0.0	0.0	0.0	0.0	
55427J202	TAM CO AUG (UH-1)	MOGAS	0.0	0.0	0.0	0.0	0.0	0.0	0.0	0.0	0.0	0.0	0.0	0.0	
		DIESEL	0.0	0.0	0.0	0.0	0.0	0.0	0.0	0.0	0.0	0.0	0.0	0.0	
63001J210	SPT COMD, 6X4, HVY DIV, AR	MOGAS	0.0	0.0	282.4	216.0	0.0	308.3	14.0	0.0	0.0	0.0	0.4	0.0	
		DIESEL	0.0	149.0	272.6	0.0	163.6	92.0	0.0	40.0	441.8	394.7	132.6	0.0	
63002J200	HHC, SPT COMD, HV DIV	MOGAS	0.0	0.0	0.8	7.6	0.0	4.0	0.0	0.0	0.0	0.0	0.1	0.0	
		DIESEL	0.0	0.0	6.0	0.0	0.0	0.0	0.0	0.0	0.0	0.0	1.2	0.0	
63002J201	AUG-DIVISION MAIT	MOGAS	0.0	0.0	0.0	0.0	0.0	0.0	0.0	0.0	0.0	0.0	0.0	0.0	
		DIESEL	0.0	0.0	0.0	0.0	0.0	0.0	0.0	0.0	0.0	0.0	0.0	0.0	
63003J200	DMMC, SPT COMD, HV DIV	MOGAS	0.0	0.0	0.0	0.0	0.0	0.0	0.0	0.0	0.0	0.0	0.0	0.0	
		DIESEL	0.0	0.0	37.5	0.0	0.0	0.0	0.0	0.0	0.0	0.0	2.5	0.0	
63005J210	FWD SPT BN 2 × 1 HVY DIV	MOGAS	0.0	0.0	43.1	23.2	0.0	41.4	0.0	0.0	0.0	0.0	0.1	0.0	
		DIESEL	0.0	28.0	14.8	0.0	31.1	11.0	0.0	6.0	71.2	61.1	17.2	0.0	

Figure 10. Bulk POL Planning Factors by Type Unit– Bulk POL Table E (continued)

SUMMARY OF BULK FUEL USAGE BY EQUIPMENT CATEGORY
HVY DIV FULL 6TK MI 4MB FVS (SRC 87000J250)–(Cont'd)

SRC	UNIT NAME	FUEL TYPE	AB	CE	GN	HG	MH	SG	SV	TI	CC	SR	WV	OV	AV
63005J220	FWD SPT BN 2 × 2 HVY DIV	MOGAS	0.0	0.0	46.6	23.2	0.0	47.0	0.0	0.0	0.0	0.0	0.1	0.0	
		DIESEL	0.0	28.0	14.8	0.0	31.1	11.0	0.0	7.0	79.8	70.0	17.9	0.0	
63006J200	HHD, FWD SPT BN, HEAVY DIV	MOGAS	0.0	0.0	2.8	0.0	0.0	1.0	0.0	0.0	0.0	0.0	0.1	0.0	
		DIESEL	0.0	0.0	3.0	0.0	0.0	0.0	0.0	0.0	0.0	0.0	0.8	0.0	
87000J250	HVY DIV FULL 6TK M1 4MBFV	MOGAS	0.0	2.0	830.5	1023.6	1.5	1017.8	14.0	0.0	0.0	0.0	2.8	0.0	
		DIESEL	86.4	275.0	407.5	0.0	213.2	527.0	0.0	5073.6	34332.9	26752.5	464.9	31.7	
		JP4													15827.0
87004J210	HHC ARMORED DIVISION	MOGAS	0.0	0.0	16.0	14.8	0.0	12.0	0.0	0.0	0.0	0.0	0.0	0.0	
		DIESEL	0.0	0.0	0.0	0.0	0.0	0.0	0.0	4.0	34.4	35.6	2.1	0.0	
87004J211	AUG-STAFF JUDGE ADVOCATE	MOGAS	0.0	0.0	0.0	0.0	0.0	0.0	0.0	0.0	0.0	0.0	0.0	0.0	
		DIESEL	0.0	0.0	0.0	0.0	0.0	0.0	0.0	0.0	0.0	0.0	0.0	0.0	
87004J212	AUG-AUTOMATION MGT OFFICE	MOGAS	0.0	0.0	0.0	0.0	0.0	0.0	0.0	0.0	0.0	0.0	0.0	0.0	
		DIESEL	0.0	0.0	0.0	0.0	0.0	0.0	0.0	0.0	0.0	0.0	0.1	0.0	
87042J210	HHC ARMD DIV BDE	MOGAS	0.0	0.0	5.9	9.4	0.0	4.0	0.0	0.0	0.0	0.0	0.0	0.0	
		DIESEL	0.0	0.0	0.0	0.0	0.0	5.0	0.0	9.2	72.7	76.6	1.6	0.0	
87042J211	AUG-RIFLE PLATOON	MOGAS	0.0	0.0	0.0	0.0	0.0	0.0	0.0	0.0	0.0	0.0	0.0	0.0	
		DIESEL	0.0	0.0	0.0	0.0	0.0	0.0	0.0	5.6	72.0	34.4	0.0	0.0	
87042J220	HHC INF DIV (MECH) BDE	MOGAS	0.0	0.0	8.9	9.4	0.0	4.0	0.0	0.0	0.0	0.0	0.0	0.0	
		DIESEL	0.0	0.0	0.0	0.0	0.0	5.0	0.0	9.2	72.7	76.6	1.6	0.0	
87042J221	AUG-RIFLE PLATOON	MOGAS	0.0	0.0	0.0	0.0	0.0	0.0	0.0	0.0	0.0	0.0	0.0	0.0	
		DIESEL	0.0	0.0	0.0	0.0	0.0	0.0	0.0	5.6	72.0	34.4	0.0	0.0	

SUMMARY OF BULK FUEL USAGE BY EQUIPMENT CATEGORY
AR DIV 6-M60 4-M113 2-AHB (SRC 87000J410)

SRC	UNIT NAME	FUEL TYPE	AB	CE	GN	HG	MH	SG	SV	TI	CC	SR	WV	OV	AV
01257J410	CBT SPT AVN CO (CBAA) (UH-1)	MOGAS	0.0	0.0	9.4	21.0	0.0	7.3	0.0	0.0	0.0	0.0	0.0	0.0	
		DIESEL	0.0	6.0	0.0	0.0	1.3	0.0	0.0	0.0	0.0	0.0	6.0	0.0	
		JP4													2438.0
01287J400	GEN SPT AVN CO	MOGAS	0.0	0.0	21.9	12.0	0.0	6.4	0.0	0.0	0.0	0.0	0.0	0.0	
		DIESEL	0.0	6.0	0.6	0.0	0.0	9.0	0.0	0.0	0.0	0.0	5.0	0.0	
		JP4													1540.8
01385J410	ATTACK HEL BN (AH-1)	MOGAS	0.0	0.0	13.3	14.8	0.0	9.0	0.0	0.0	0.0	0.0	0.0	0.0	
		DIESEL	0.0	8.0	0.0	0.0	2.6	0.0	0.0	0.0	0.0	0.0	10.0	0.0	
		JP4													3551.7
01386J410	HQ AND SVC CO (AH-1)	MOGAS	0.0	0.0	13.3	14.8	0.0	9.0	0.0	0.0	0.0	0.0	0.0	0.0	
		DIESEL	0.0	8.0	0.0	0.0	2.6	0.0	0.0	0.0	0.0	0.0	9.0	0.0	
		JP4													489.9
01387J410	ATK HEL CO (AH-1)	MOGAS	0.0	0.0	0.0	0.0	0.0	0.0	0.0	0.0	0.0	0.0	0.0	0.0	
		DIESEL	0.0	0.0	0.0	0.0	0.0	0.0	0.0	0.0	0.0	0.0	0.0	0.0	
		JP4													1020.6
03387J400	CHEMICAL CO, HVY DIV	MOGAS	0.0	0.0	36.8	4.0	0.0	64.0	0.0	0.0	0.0	0.0	0.0	0.0	
		DIESEL	0.0	0.0	0.6	0.0	0.0	5.0	0.0	6.0	51.6	53.4	1.0	0.0	
05145J410	ENGR BN, HVY DIV - RIBBON	MOGAS	0.0	2.0	24.2	33.0	0.0	104.2	0.0	0.0	0.0	0.0	0.0	0.0	
		DIESEL	86.4	68.0	3.4	0.0	8.5	34.0	0.0	150.5	1612.7	1338.5	37.0	0.0	
05146J400	HQ-HQ COMPANY	MOGAS	0.0	0.0	5.0	5.8	0.0	15.5	0.0	0.0	0.0	0.0	0.0	0.0	
		DIESEL	0.0	0.0	0.6	0.0	8.5	7.0	0.0	3.0	25.8	26.7	8.0	0.0	
05147J400	ENGR CO, ENGR BN, HVY DIV	MOGAS	0.0	0.5	4.2	5.8	0.0	19.5	0.0	0.0	0.0	0.0	0.0	0.0	
		DIESEL	0.0	17.0	0.6	0.0	0.0	5.0	0.0	36.5	393.6	325.6	5.0	0.0	
05148J410	BRIDGE COMPANY - RIBBON	MOGAS	0.0	0.0	2.5	4.0	0.0	10.4	0.0	0.0	0.0	0.0	0.0	0.0	
		DIESEL	86.4	0.0	0.6	0.0	0.0	7.0	0.0	1.4	12.3	9.3	9.0	0.0	
06300J410	AR DIVARTY	MOGAS	0.0	0.0	89.4	42.6	0.0	78.5	0.0	0.0	0.0	0.0	0.0	0.0	
		DIESEL	0.0	0.0	38.2	0.0	0.0	75.0	0.0	234.7	1484.1	1765.8	68.0	32.4	
06302J400	HHB DIV ARTY HVY DIV	MOGAS	0.0	0.0	23.5	1.8	0.0	8.4	0.0	0.0	0.0	0.0	0.0	0.0	
		DIESEL	0.0	0.0	9.8	0.0	0.0	5.0	0.0	1.0	8.6	8.9	6.0	0.0	
06307J400	TGT ACQ BTRY HVY DIV	MOGAS	0.0	0.0	4.4	0.0	0.0	1.5	0.0	0.0	0.0	0.0	0.0	0.0	
		DIESEL	0.0	0.0	12.6	0.0	0.0	10.0	0.0	0.0	0.0	0.0	4.0	0.0	
06365J410	FA BN 155 SP HVY DIV	MOGAS	0.0	0.0	18.1	13.0	0.0	21.3	0.0	0.0	0.0	0.0	0.0	0.0	
		DIESEL	0.0	0.0	5.3	0.0	0.0	20.0	0.0	72.4	432.5	545.0	17.0	10.4	
06365J430	FA BN 155 SP HVY DIV	MOGAS	0.0	0.0	20.2	13.0	0.0	21.3	0.0	0.0	0.0	0.0	0.0	0.0	
		DIESEL	0.0	0.0	5.3	0.0	0.0	20.0	0.0	73.4	441.1	553.9	17.0	11.6	
06366J410	HHB FA BN 155SP HVY DIV	MOGAS	0.0	0.0	10.4	5.4	0.0	13.0	0.0	0.0	0.0	0.0	0.0	0.0	
		DIESEL	0.0	0.0	3.6	0.0	0.0	0.0	0.0	7.0	60.2	62.3	3.0	3.7	
06366J430	HHB FA BN 155SP HVY DIV	MOGAS	0.0	0.0	12.5	5.4	0.0	13.0	0.0	0.0	0.0	0.0	0.0	0.0	
		DIESEL	0.0	0.0	3.6	0.0	0.0	0.0	0.0	8.0	68.8	71.2	3.1	4.8	
06367J410	FA BTRY 155SP HVY DIV	MOGAS	0.0	0.0	1.1	0.0	0.0	0.0	0.0	0.0	0.0	0.0	0.0	0.0	
		DIESEL	0.0	0.0	0.6	0.0	0.0	5.0	0.0	19.6	111.6	146.6	2.0	2.2	
06369J410	SVC BTRY 155SP HVY DIV	MOGAS	0.0	0.0	4.5	7.6	0.0	8.3	0.0	0.0	0.0	0.0	0.0	0.0	
		DIESEL	0.0	0.0	0.0	0.0	0.0	5.0	0.0	6.6	37.5	42.9	8.0	0.0	
06398J400	FA BTRY MLRS	MOGAS	0.0	0.0	5.2	1.8	0.0	4.5	0.0	0.0	0.0	0.0	0.0	0.0	
		DIESEL	0.0	0.0	0.0	0.0	0.0	0.0	0.0	15.5	169.4	113.0	7.2	0.0	
07209J400	LRS DET, CAV SQDN, HVY DIV	MOGAS	0.0	0.0	5.6	0.0	0.0	0.0	0.0	0.0	0.0	0.0	0.0	0.0	
		DIESEL	0.0	0.0	0.0	0.0	0.0	0.0	0.0	0.0	0.0	0.0	0.2	0.0	
07245J420	INF BN-MECH E/W M113	MOGAS	0.0	0.0	8.8	7.6	0.0	24.1	0.0	0.0	0.0	0.0	0.1	0.0	
		DIESEL	0.0	0.0	1.1	0.0	0.0	12.0	0.0	124.8	1072.3	1105.1	12.0	0.0	
07246J420	HHC INF BN MECH M113	MOGAS	0.0	0.0	6.1	7.6	0.0	24.1	0.0	0.0	0.0	0.0	0.1	0.0	
		DIESEL	0.0	0.0	1.1	0.0	0.0	12.0	0.0	44.8	384.3	393.1	9.9	0.0	
07247J420	RIFLE CO INF BN MECH M113	MOGAS	0.0	0.0	0.5	0.0	0.0	0.0	0.0	0.0	0.0	0.0	0.0	0.0	
		DIESEL	0.0	0.0	0.0	0.0	0.0	0.0	0.0	16.0	137.6	142.4	0.4	0.0	
07248J400	ANTIARMOR CO INF BN(M) IT	MOGAS	0.0	0.0	0.5	0.0	0.0	0.0	0.0	0.0	0.0	0.0	0.0	0.0	
		DIESEL	0.0	0.0	0.0	0.0	0.0	0.0	0.0	16.0	137.6	142.4	0.4	0.0	
08077J400	MEDICAL CO (MSB) HVY DIV	MOGAS	0.0	0.0	13.7	7.2	0.0	13.0	0.0	0.0	0.0	0.0	0.0	0.0	
		DIESEL	0.0	0.0	2.8	0.0	0.0	5.0	0.0	0.0	0.0	0.0	5.5	0.0	

Figure 10. Bulk POL Planning Factors by Type Unit—Bulk POL Table E (continued)

SUMMARY OF BULK FUEL USAGE BY EQUIPMENT CATEGORY
AR DIV 6-M60 4-M113 2-AHB (SRC 87000J410)—(Cont'd)

SRC	UNIT NAME	FUEL TYPE	AB	CE	GN	HG	MH	SG	SV	TI	CC	SR	WV	OV	AV
08078J400	MEDICAL CO (FSB) HVY DIV	MOGAS	0.0	0.0	10.4	5.8	0.0	13.0	0.0	0.0	0.0	0.0	0.0	0.0	
		DIESEL	0.0	0.0	2.2	0.0	0.0	5.0	0.0	5.0	43.0	44.5	3.1	0.0	
09558J400	MSL SPT CO HVY DIV	MOGAS	0.0	0.0	22.7	4.0	0.0	1.0	0.0	0.0	0.0	0.0	0.0	0.0	
		DIESEL	0.0	0.0	40.2	0.0	1.3	5.0	0.0	0.0	0.0	0.0	6.9	0.0	
09558J402	SGT YORK AUG, MSL SPT CO	MOGAS	0.0	0.0	3.0	0.0	0.0	0.0	0.0	0.0	0.0	0.0	0.0	0.0	
		DIESEL	0.0	30.0	26.1	0.0	0.0	0.0	0.0	2.0	36.8	25.5	2.4	0.0	
11035J500	SIG BN HVY DIV	MOGAS	0.0	0.0	141.8	17.8	0.0	15.4	0.0	0.0	0.0	0.0	0.3	0.0	
		DIESEL	0.0	0.0	17.3	0.0	0.0	20.0	0.0	0.0	0.0	0.0	18.4	0.0	
11036J500	HHC SIG BN HEAVY DIV	MOGAS	0.0	0.0	25.1	4.0	0.0	9.4	0.0	0.0	0.0	0.0	0.3	0.0	
		DIESEL	0.0	0.0	0.6	0.0	0.0	5.0	0.0	0.0	0.0	0.0	5.8	0.0	
11037J500	CMD OPS CO	MOGAS	0.0	0.0	35.6	4.0	0.0	1.0	0.0	0.0	0.0	0.0	0.0	0.0	
		DIESEL	0.0	0.0	6.6	0.0	0.0	5.0	0.0	0.0	0.0	0.0	4.4	0.0	
11038J500	FWD COMM CO	MOGAS	0.0	0.0	38.3	4.0	0.0	1.0	0.0	0.0	0.0	0.0	0.0	0.0	
		DIESEL	0.0	0.0	0.6	0.0	0.0	5.0	0.0	0.0	0.0	0.0	3.3	0.0	
11039J500	AREA SIGNAL CO	MOGAS	0.0	0.0	42.8	5.8	0.0	4.0	0.0	0.0	0.0	0.0	0.0	0.0	
		DIESEL	0.0	0.0	9.6	0.0	0.0	5.0	0.0	0.0	0.0	0.0	4.8	0.0	
12114J400	DIVISION BAND	MOGAS	0.0	0.0	0.0	0.0	0.0	0.0	0.0	0.0	0.0	0.0	0.0	0.0	
		DIESEL	0.0	0.0	0.0	0.0	0.0	0.0	0.0	0.0	0.0	0.0	0.0	0.0	
17201J410	CAV BDE AIR ATK (AH-1) (AOE)	MOGAS	0.0	0.0	89.9	86.8	0.0	62.5	0.0	0.0	0.0	0.0	0.0	0.0	
		DIESEL	0.0	36.0	1.7	0.0	9.1	21.0	0.0	81.0	998.8	597.5	46.6	0.6	
		JP4													12687.0
17202J400	HQ & HQ TROOP, CBAA	MOGAS	0.0	0.0	13.2	7.6	0.0	7.4	0.0	0.0	0.0	0.0	0.0	0.0	
		DIESEL	0.0	0.0	0.6	0.0	0.0	0.0	0.0	0.0	0.0	0.0	3.0	0.0	
17205J410	CAV SQDN, CBAA AHIS HVY DIV	MOGAS	0.0	0.0	18.7	16.6	0.0	23.4	0.0	0.0	0.0	0.0	0.0	0.0	
		DIESEL	0.0	8.0	0.6	0.0	2.6	12.0	0.0	81.0	998.8	597.5	13.7	0.6	
		JP4													1604.8
17206J410	HQ AND HQ TRP, CAV SQDN	MOGAS	0.0	0.0	13.1	16.6	0.0	21.4	0.0	0.0	0.0	0.0	0.0	0.0	
		DIESEL	0.0	8.0	0.6	0.0	2.6	12.0	0.0	13.8	169.7	130.6	12.4	0.6	
		JP4													142.0
17207J410	CAV TRP, CAV SQDN	MOGAS	0.0	0.0	0.0	0.0	0.0	1.0	0.0	0.0	0.0	0.0	0.0	0.0	
		DIESEL	0.0	0.0	0.0	0.0	0.0	0.0	0.0	33.6	414.6	233.4	0.3	0.0	
17208J410	AIR CAV TRP, CAV SQDN	MOGAS	0.0	0.0	0.0	0.0	0.0	0.0	0.0	0.0	0.0	0.0	0.0	0.0	
		DIESEL	0.0	0.0	0.0	0.0	0.0	0.0	0.0	0.0	0.0	0.0	0.2	0.0	
		JP4													731.4
17235J410	TANK BATTALION, EQ/W, M60	MOGAS	0.0	0.0	3.9	23.6	0.0	16.0	0.0	0.0	0.0	0.0	0.0	0.0	
		DIESEL	0.0	0.0	0.6	0.0	0.0	7.0	0.0	165.4	2121.9	1560.5	11.4	0.0	
17236J410	HHC, TK BN, M60	MOGAS	0.0	0.0	3.9	23.6	0.0	16.0	0.0	0.0	0.0	0.0	0.0	0.0	
		DIESEL	0.0	0.0	0.6	0.0	0.0	7.0	0.0	53.4	636.2	508.3	10.3	0.0	
17237J410	TK CO, TK BN, M60	MOGAS	0.0	0.0	0.0	0.0	0.0	0.0	0.0	0.0	0.0	0.0	0.0	0.0	
		DIESEL	0.0	0.0	0.0	0.0	0.0	0.0	0.0	28.0	371.4	263.1	0.3	0.0	
19217J400	MP CO-HVY DIV	MOGAS	0.0	0.0	4.6	4.0	0.0	1.0	0.0	0.0	0.0	0.0	0.0	0.0	
		DIESEL	0.0	0.0	1.1	0.0	0.0	5.0	0.0	0.0	0.0	0.0	2.5	0.0	
34285J400	MI BN (CEWI) HVY DIV	MOGAS	0.0	0.0	42.9	13.4	0.0	12.0	0.0	0.0	0.0	0.0	0.0	0.0	
		DIESEL	0.0	0.0	15.6	0.0	0.0	17.0	0.0	16.2	132.9	138.9	7.8	0.3	
34286J400	HQ HQ-OP CO MI BN CEWI DIV	MOGAS	0.0	0.0	0.8	0.0	0.0	0.0	0.0	0.0	0.0	0.0	0.0	0.0	
		DIESEL	0.0	0.0	0.0	0.0	0.0	12.0	0.0	2.0	17.2	17.8	1.8	0.0	
34287J400	C&J CO MI BN CEWI, DIV	MOGAS	0.0	0.0	7.2	0.0	0.0	0.0	0.0	0.0	0.0	0.0	0.0	0.0	
		DIESEL	0.0	0.0	15.0	0.0	0.0	0.0	0.0	12.0	103.2	106.8	1.6	0.3	
34289J400	SVC SPT CO MI BN CEWI DIV	MOGAS	0.0	0.0	34.8	13.4	0.0	12.0	0.0	0.0	0.0	0.0	0.0	0.0	
		DIESEL	0.0	0.0	0.6	0.0	0.0	5.0	0.0	2.2	12.5	14.3	4.4	0.0	
42004J400	SUP CO FWD SPT BN HVY DIV	MOGAS	0.0	0.0	1.7	3.6	0.0	7.9	0.0	0.0	0.0	0.0	0.0	0.0	
		DIESEL	0.0	14.0	0.6	0.0	27.6	5.0	0.0	0.0	0.0	0.0	5.2	0.0	
42007J400	S&S CO MAINT SPT BN HVY DIV	MOGAS	0.0	0.0	6.6	11.6	0.0	35.8	0.0	0.0	0.0	0.0	0.0	0.0	
		DIESEL	0.0	21.0	30.6	0.0	35.9	5.0	0.0	0.0	0.0	0.0	10.9	0.0	
43004J400	MAINT CO,FWD SPT BN,HVY DIV	MOGAS	0.0	0.0	25.4	16.0	0.0	20.4	0.0	0.0	0.0	0.0	0.0	0.0	
		DIESEL	0.0	7.0	11.1	0.0	9.8	7.0	0.0	3.0	45.4	34.4	10.4	0.0	
43004J401	TK SYSTEM SPT TM	MOGAS	0.0	0.0	1.1	0.0	0.0	5.6	0.0	0.0	0.0	0.0	0.0	0.0	
		DIESEL	0.0	0.0	0.6	0.0	0.0	0.0	0.0	1.0	8.6	8.9	0.8	0.0	
4004J402	INF SYS(M) SPT TM	MOGAS	0.0	0.0	2.4	0.0	0.0	5.6	0.0	0.0	0.0	0.0	0.0	0.0	
		DIESEL	0.0	0.0	0.0	0.0	0.0	0.0	0.0	1.0	8.6	8.9	0.8	0.0	
43007J400	LIGHT MAINT CO HVY DIV	MOGAS	0.0	0.0	42.3	11.6	1.4	24.9	0.0	0.0	0.0	0.0	0.0	0.0	
		DIESEL	0.0	0.0	64.0	0.0	17.0	0.0	0.0	0.0	0.0	0.0	15.0	0.0	
43008J400	HEAVY MAINT CO HVY DIV	MOGAS	0.0	0.0	14.5	28.0	0.0	41.3	0.0	0.0	0.0	0.0	0.0	0.0	
		DIESEL	0.0	14.0	13.5	0.0	8.5	7.0	0.0	4.0	54.0	43.3	7.7	0.0	
44165J400	ADA BN HVY DIV	MOGAS	0.0	0.0	59.4	14.8	0.0	17.8	0.0	0.0	0.0	0.0	0.1	0.0	
		DIESEL	0.0	36.0	2.3	0.0	0.0	28.0	0.0	45.0	503.3	553.3	18.0	0.0	
44166J400	HHB, ADA BN, HEAVY DIV	MOGAS	0.0	0.0	20.2	14.8	0.0	11.9	0.0	0.0	0.0	0.0	0.0	0.0	
		DIESEL	0.0	0.0	0.6	0.0	0.0	13.0	0.0	3.0	25.8	26.7	4.7	0.0	
44167J400	ADA BTRY, GUN(SP)/STINGER	MOGAS	0.0	0.0	13.1	0.0	0.0	1.9	0.0	0.0	0.0	0.0	0.0	0.0	
		DIESEL	0.0	12.0	0.6	0.0	0.0	5.0	0.0	14.0	159.2	175.5	4.4	0.0	
55087J400	TMET CO MAIN SPT VH HVY DIV	MOGAS	0.0	0.0	1.7	8.0	0.0	2.4	0.0	0.0	0.0	0.0	0.0	0.0	
		DIESEL	0.0	0.0	1.1	0.0	0.0	5.0	0.0	0.0	0.0	0.0	19.9	0.0	
55427J410	TAMC, SPT CMD, HVY DIV	MOGAS	0.0	0.0	16.7	13.0	1.5	4.4	0.0	0.0	0.0	0.0	0.0	0.0	
		DIESEL	0.0	16.0	45.2	0.0	8.5	5.0	0.0	0.0	0.0	0.0	5.1	0.0	
		JP4													332.0
63001J410	SPT CMD, 6X4X2, HVY DIV	MOGAS	0.0	0.0	250.7	167.2	2.9	314.3	0.0	0.0	0.0	0.0	0.1	0.0	
		DIESEL	0.0	144.0	303.0	0.0	183.4	101.0	0.0	40.0	441.8	394.7	146.1	0.0	
		JP4													332.0
63002J400	HHC/MMC, SPT CMD, HVY DIV	MOGAS	0.0	0.0	0.8	7.6	0.0	7.0	0.0	0.0	0.0	0.0	0.0	0.0	
		DIESEL	0.0	0.0	25.5	0.0	0.0	0.0	0.0	0.0	0.0	0.0	3.8	0.0	
63005J410	FWD SPT BN (2X1) HVY DIV	MOGAS	0.0	0.0	42.1	25.4	0.0	59.2	0.0	0.0	0.0	0.0	0.1	0.0	
		DIESEL	0.0	21.0	16.5	0.0	37.4	23.0	0.0	11.0	114.2	105.6	22.1	0.0	
63005J420	FWD SPT BN (2X2) HVY DIV	MOGAS	0.0	0.0	44.5	25.4	0.0	64.9	0.0	0.0	0.0	0.0	0.0	0.0	
		DIESEL	0.0	21.0	16.5	0.0	37.4	23.0	0.0	12.0	122.8	114.5	22.9	0.0	
63006J400	HHD,FWD SPT BN,HEAVY DIV	MOGAS	0.0	0.0	0.0	0.0	0.0	1.0	0.0	0.0	0.0	0.0	0.1	0.0	
		DIESEL	0.0	0.0	1.5	0.0	0.0	6.0	0.0	0.0	0.0	0.0	1.0	0.0	

Figure 10. Bulk POL Planning Factors by Type Unit— Bulk POL Table E (continued)

SUMMARY OF BULK FUEL USAGE BY EQUIPMENT CATEGORY
AR DIV 6-M60 4-M113 2-AHB (SRC 87000J410)—(Cont'd)

SRC	UNIT NAME	FUEL TYPE	AB	CE	GN	HG	MH	SG	SV	TI	CC	SR	WV	OV	AV
63135J400	MAIN SUPPORT BN, HVY DIV	MOGAS	0.0	0.0	104.4	70.4	1.4	119.4	0.0	0.0	0.0	0.0	0.0	0.0	
		DIESEL	0.0	65.0	182.8	0.0	62.7	27.0	0.0	6.0	90.7	68.9	69.6	0.0	
63136J400	HHD,MAIN SPT BN, HVY DIV	MOGAS	0.0	0.0	0.0	0.0	0.0	1.0	0.0	0.0	0.0	0.0	0.0	0.0	
		DIESEL	0.0	0.0	4.5	0.0	0.0	0.0	0.0	0.0	0.0	0.0	1.0	0.0	
87000J410	AR DIV, 6-M60, 4-M113, 2-AH	MOGAS	0.0	2.0	859.0	580.6	2.9	886.4	0.0	0.0	0.0	0.0	1.5	0.0	
		DIESEL	86.4	284.0	392.7	0.0	201.0	411.0	0.0	2097.6	22506.8	18899.7	482.0	33.3	
		JP4													13019.0
87004J410	HHC ARMORED DIVISION	MOGAS	0.0	0.0	39.6	7.6	0.0	12.0	0.0	0.0	0.0	0.0	0.0	0.0	
		DIESEL	0.0	0.0	1.5	0.0	0.0	0.0	0.0	5.0	43.0	44.5	5.2	0.0	
87042J410	HHC ARMD DIV BDE	MOGAS	0.0	0.0	6.2	5.8	0.0	4.0	0.0	0.0	0.0	0.0	0.0	0.0	
		DIESEL	0.0	0.0	0.0	0.0	0.0	5.0	0.0	9.2	72.7	76.6	1.6	0.0	
87042J420	HHC INF DIV (MECH) BDE	MOGAS	0.0	0.0	8.9	5.8	0.0	4.0	0.0	0.0	0.0	0.0	0.0	0.0	
		DIESEL	0.0	0.0	0.0	0.0	0.0	5.0	0.0	9.2	72.7	76.6	1.6	0.0	

SUMMARY OF BULK FUEL USAGE BY EQUIPMENT CATEGORY
MX DIV 5-M60 5-M113 2-AHB (SRC 87000J420)

SRC	UNIT NAME	FUEL TYPE	AB	CE	GN	HG	MH	SG	SV	TI	CC	SR	WV	OV	AV
01257J410	CBT SPT AVN CO (CBAA) (UH-1)	MOGAS	0.0	0.0	9.4	21.0	0.0	7.3	0.0	0.0	0.0	0.0	0.0	0.0	
		DIESEL	0.0	6.0	0.0	0.0	1.3	0.0	0.0	0.0	0.0	0.0	5.5	0.0	
		JP4													2438.0
01287J400	GEN SPT AVN CO	MOGAS	0.0	0.0	21.9	12.0	0.0	6.4	0.0	0.0	0.0	0.0	0.0	0.0	
		DIESEL	0.0	6.0	0.6	0.0	0.0	9.0	0.0	0.0	0.0	0.0	5.3	0.0	
		JP4													1540.8
01385J410	ATTACK HEL BN (AH-1)	MOGAS	0.0	0.0	13.3	14.8	0.0	9.0	0.0	0.0	0.0	0.0	0.0	0.0	
		DIESEL	0.0	8.0	0.0	0.0	2.6	0.0	0.0	0.0	0.0	0.0	9.5	0.0	
		JP4													3551.7
01386J410	HQ AND SVC CO (AH-1)	MOGAS	0.0	0.0	13.3	14.8	0.0	9.0	0.0	0.0	0.0	0.0	0.0	0.0	
		DIESEL	0.0	8.0	0.0	0.0	2.6	0.0	0.0	0.0	0.0	0.0	8.6	0.0	
		JP4													489.9
01387J410	ATK HEL CO (AH-1)	MOGAS	0.0	0.0	0.0	0.0	0.0	0.0	0.0	0.0	0.0	0.0	0.0	0.0	
		DIESEL	0.0	0.0	0.0	0.0	0.0	0.0	0.0	0.0	0.0	0.0	0.3	0.0	
		JP4													1020.6
03387J400	CHEMICAL CO, HVY DIV	MOGAS	0.0	0.0	36.8	4.0	0.0	64.0	0.0	0.0	0.0	0.0	0.0	0.0	
		DIESEL	0.0	0.0	0.6	0.0	0.0	5.0	0.0	6.0	51.6	53.4	9.5	0.0	
05145J410	ENGR BN, HVY DIV - RIBBON	MOGAS	0.0	2.0	24.2	33.0	0.0	104.2	0.0	0.0	0.0	0.0	0.1	0.0	
		DIESEL	86.4	68.0	3.4	0.0	8.5	34.0	0.0	150.5	1612.7	1338.5	37.3	0.0	
05146J400	HQ-HQ COMPANY	MOGAS	0.0	0.0	5.0	5.8	0.0	15.5	0.0	0.0	0.0	0.0	0.1	0.0	
		DIESEL	0.0	0.0	0.6	0.0	8.5	7.0	0.0	3.0	25.8	26.7	7.8	0.0	
05147J400	ENGR CO, ENGR BN, HVY DIV	MOGAS	0.0	0.5	4.2	5.8	0.0	19.5	0.0	0.0	0.0	0.0	0.0	0.0	
		DIESEL	0.0	17.0	0.6	0.0	0.0	5.0	0.0	36.5	393.6	325.6	5.2	0.0	
05148J410	BRIDGE COMPANY - RIBBON	MOGAS	0.0	0.0	2.5	4.0	0.0	10.4	0.0	0.0	0.0	0.0	0.0	0.0	
		DIESEL	86.4	0.0	0.6	0.0	0.0	7.0	0.0	1.4	12.3	9.3	8.5	0.0	
06300J420	MECH DIVARTY	MOGAS	0.0	0.0	89.4	42.6	0.0	78.5	0.0	0.0	0.0	0.0	0.3	0.0	
		DIESEL	0.0	0.0	38.2	0.0	0.0	75.0	0.0	234.7	1484.1	1765.8	67.9	32.4	
06302J400	HHB DIV ARTY HVY DIV	MOGAS	0.0	0.0	23.5	1.8	0.0	8.4	0.0	0.0	0.0	0.0	0.2	0.0	
		DIESEL	0.0	0.0	9.8	0.0	0.0	5.0	0.0	1.0	8.6	8.9	5.5	0.0	
06307J400	TGT ACQ BTRY HVY DIV	MOGAS	0.0	0.0	4.4	0.0	0.0	1.5	0.0	0.0	0.0	0.0	0.0	0.0	
		DIESEL	0.0	0.0	12.6	0.0	0.0	10.0	0.0	0.0	0.0	0.0	3.5	0.0	
06365J410	FA BN 155 SP HVY DIV	MOGAS	0.0	0.0	18.1	13.0	0.0	21.3	0.0	0.0	0.0	0.0	0.0	0.0	
		DIESEL	0.0	0.0	5.3	0.0	0.0	20.0	0.0	72.4	432.5	545.0	17.2	10.4	
06365J420	FA BN 155 SP HVY DIV	MOGAS	0.0	0.0	18.1	13.0	0.0	21.3	0.0	0.0	0.0	0.0	0.0	0.0	
		DIESEL	0.0	0.0	5.3	0.0	0.0	20.0	0.0	72.4	432.5	545.0	17.1	10.4	
06365J430	FA BN 155 SP HVY DIV	MOGAS	0.0	0.0	20.2	13.0	0.0	21.3	0.0	0.0	0.0	0.0	0.0	0.0	
		DIESEL	0.0	0.0	5.3	0.0	0.0	20.0	0.0	73.4	441.1	553.9	17.2	11.6	
06366J410	HHB FA BN 155SP HVY DIV	MOGAS	0.0	0.0	10.4	5.4	0.0	13.0	0.0	0.0	0.0	0.0	0.0	0.0	
		DIESEL	0.0	0.0	3.6	0.0	0.0	0.0	0.0	7.0	60.2	62.3	3.0	3.7	
06366J420	HHB FA BN 155SP HVY DIV	MOGAS	0.0	0.0	10.4	5.4	0.0	13.0	0.0	0.0	0.0	0.0	0.0	0.0	
		DIESEL	0.0	0.0	3.6	0.0	0.0	0.0	0.0	7.0	60.2	62.3	3.0	3.7	
06366J430	HHB FA BN 155SP HVY DIV	MOGAS	0.0	0.0	12.5	5.4	0.0	13.0	0.0	0.0	0.0	0.0	0.0	0.0	
		DIESEL	0.0	0.0	3.6	0.0	0.0	0.0	0.0	8.0	68.8	71.2	3.1	4.8	
06367J410	FA BTRY 155SP HVY DIV	MOGAS	0.0	0.0	1.1	0.0	0.0	0.0	0.0	0.0	0.0	0.0	0.0	0.0	
		DIESEL	0.0	0.0	0.6	0.0	0.0	5.0	0.0	19.6	111.6	146.6	2.0	2.2	
06369J410	SVC BTRY 155SP HVY DIV	MOGAS	0.0	0.0	4.5	7.6	0.0	8.3	0.0	0.0	0.0	0.0	0.0	0.0	
		DIESEL	0.0	0.0	0.0	0.0	0.0	5.0	0.0	6.6	37.5	42.9	8.0	0.0	
06398J400	FA BTRY MLRS	MOGAS	0.0	0.0	5.2	1.8	0.0	4.5	0.0	0.0	0.0	0.0	0.0	0.0	
		DIESEL	0.0	0.0	0.0	0.0	0.0	0.0	0.0	15.5	169.4	113.0	7.2	0.0	
07209J400	LRS DET, CAV SQDN, HVY DIV	MOGAS	0.0	0.0	5.6	0.0	0.0	0.0	0.0	0.0	0.0	0.0	0.0	0.0	
		DIESEL	0.0	0.0	0.0	0.0	0.0	0.0	0.0	0.0	0.0	0.0	0.2	0.0	
07245J420	INF BN-MECH E/W M113	MOGAS	0.0	0.0	8.8	7.6	0.0	24.1	0.0	0.0	0.0	0.0	0.1	0.0	
		DIESEL	0.0	0.0	1.1	0.0	0.0	12.0	0.0	124.8	1072.3	1105.1	12.0	0.0	
07246J420	HHC INF BN MECH M113	MOGAS	0.0	0.0	6.1	7.6	0.0	24.1	0.0	0.0	0.0	0.0	0.1	0.0	
		DIESEL	0.0	0.0	1.1	0.0	0.0	12.0	0.0	44.8	384.3	393.1	9.9	0.0	
07247J420	RIFLE CO INF BN MECH M113	MOGAS	0.0	0.0	0.5	0.0	0.0	0.0	0.0	0.0	0.0	0.0	0.0	0.0	
		DIESEL	0.0	0.0	0.0	0.0	0.0	0.0	0.0	16.0	137.6	142.4	0.4	0.0	
07248J400	ANTIARMOR CO INF BN(M) IT	MOGAS	0.0	0.0	0.5	0.0	0.0	0.0	0.0	0.0	0.0	0.0	0.0	0.0	
		DIESEL	0.0	0.0	0.0	0.0	0.0	0.0	0.0	16.0	137.6	142.4	0.4	0.0	
08077J400	MEDICAL CO (MSB) HVY DIV	MOGAS	0.0	0.0	13.7	7.2	0.0	13.0	0.0	0.0	0.0	0.0	0.0	0.0	
		DIESEL	0.0	0.0	2.8	0.0	0.0	5.0	0.0	0.0	0.0	0.0	5.5	0.0	
08078J400	MEDICAL CO (FSB) HVY DIV	MOGAS	0.0	0.0	10.4	5.8	0.0	13.0	0.0	0.0	0.0	0.0	0.0	0.0	
		DIESEL	0.0	0.0	2.2	0.0	0.0	5.0	0.0	5.0	43.0	44.5	3.1	0.0	
09558J400	MSL SPT CO HVY DIV	MOGAS	0.0	0.0	22.7	4.0	0.0	1.0	0.0	0.0	0.0	0.0	0.0	0.0	
		DIESEL	0.0	0.0	40.2	0.0	1.3	5.0	0.0	0.0	0.0	0.0	6.9	0.0	
09558J402	SGT YORK AUG, MSL SPT CO	MOGAS	0.0	0.0	3.0	0.0	0.0	0.0	0.0	0.0	0.0	0.0	0.0	0.0	
		DIESEL	0.0	30.0	26.1	0.0	0.0	0.0	0.0	2.0	36.8	25.5	2.4	0.0	

Figure 10. Bulk POL Planning Factors by Type Unit—Bulk POL Table E (continued)

SUMMARY OF BULK FUEL USAGE BY EQUIPMENT CATEGORY
MX DIV 5-M60 5-M113 2-AHB (SRC 87000J420)—(Cont'd)

SRC	UNIT NAME	FUEL TYPE	AB	CE	GN	HG	MH	SG	SV	TI	CC	SR	WV	OV	AV
11035J500	SIG BN HVY DIV	MOGAS	0.0	0.0	141.8	17.8	0.0	15.4	0.0	0.0	0.0	0.0	0.3	0.0	
		DIESEL	0.0	0.0	17.3	0.0	0.0	20.0	0.0	0.0	0.0	0.0	18.4	0.0	
11036J500	HHC SIG BN HEAVY DIV	MOGAS	0.0	0.0	25.1	4.0	0.0	9.4	0.0	0.0	0.0	0.0	0.3	0.0	
		DIESEL	0.0	0.0	0.6	0.0	0.0	5.0	0.0	0.0	0.0	0.0	5.8	0.0	
11037J500	CMD OPS CO	MOGAS	0.0	0.0	35.6	4.0	0.0	1.0	0.0	0.0	0.0	0.0	0.0	0.0	
		DIESEL	0.0	0.0	6.6	0.0	0.0	5.0	0.0	0.0	0.0	0.0	4.4	0.0	
11038J500	FWD COMM CO	MOGAS	0.0	0.0	38.3	4.0	0.0	1.0	0.0	0.0	0.0	0.0	0.0	0.0	
		DIESEL	0.0	0.0	0.6	0.0	0.0	5.0	0.0	0.0	0.0	0.0	3.3	0.0	
11039J500	AREA SIGNAL CO	MOGAS	0.0	0.0	42.8	5.8	0.0	4.0	0.0	0.0	0.0	0.0	0.0	0.0	
		DIESEL	0.0	0.0	9.6	0.0	0.0	5.0	0.0	0.0	0.0	0.0	4.8	0.0	
12114J400	DIVISION BAND	MOGAS	0.0	0.0	0.0	0.0	0.0	0.0	0.0	0.0	0.0	0.0	0.0	0.0	
		DIESEL	0.0	0.0	0.0	0.0	0.0	0.0	0.0	0.0	0.0	0.0	0.0	0.0	
17201J410	DAV BDE AIR ATK (AH-1) (AOE)	MOGAS	0.0	0.0	89.9	86.8	0.0	62.5	0.0	0.0	0.0	0.0	0.0	0.0	
		DIESEL	0.0	36.0	1.7	0.0	9.1	21.0	0.0	81.0	998.8	597.5	46.6	0.6	
		JP4													12687.0
17202J400	HQ & HQ TROOP, CBAA	MOGAS	0.0	0.0	13.2	7.6	0.0	7.4	0.0	0.0	0.0	0.0	0.0	0.0	
		DIESEL	0.0	0.0	0.6	0.0	0.0	0.0	0.0	0.0	0.0	0.0	3.0	0.0	
17205J410	CAV SQDN, CBAA AHIS HVY DIV	MOGAS	0.0	0.0	18.7	16.6	0.0	23.4	0.0	0.0	0.0	0.0	0.0	0.0	
		DIESEL	0.0	8.0	0.6	0.0	2.6	12.0	0.0	81.0	998.8	597.5	13.7	0.6	
		JP4													1604.8
17206J410	HQ AND HQ TRP, CAV SQDN	MOGAS	0.0	0.0	13.1	16.6	0.0	21.4	0.0	0.0	0.0	0.0	0.0	0.0	
		DIESEL	0.0	8.0	0.6	0.0	2.6	12.0	0.0	13.8	169.7	130.6	12.4	0.6	
		JP4													142.0
17207J410	CAV TRP, CAV SQDN	MOGAS	0.0	0.0	0.0	0.0	0.0	1.0	0.0	0.0	0.0	0.0	0.0	0.0	
		DIESEL	0.0	0.0	0.0	0.0	0.0	0.0	0.0	33.6	414.6	233.4	0.3	0.0	
17208J410	AIR CAV TRP, CAV SQDN	MOGAS	0.0	0.0	0.0	0.0	0.0	0.0	0.0	0.0	0.0	0.0	0.0	0.0	
		DIESEL	0.0	0.0	0.0	0.0	0.0	0.0	0.0	0.0	0.0	0.0	0.2	0.0	
		JP4													731.4
17235J410	TANK BATTALION, EQ/W, M60	MOGAS	0.0	0.0	3.9	23.6	0.0	16.0	0.0	0.0	0.0	0.0	0.0	0.0	
		DIESEL	0.0	0.0	0.6	0.0	0.0	7.0	0.0	165.4	2121.9	1560.5	11.4	0.0	
17236J410	HHC, TK BN, M60	MOGAS	0.0	0.0	3.9	23.6	0.0	16.0	0.0	0.0	0.0	0.0	0.0	0.0	
		DIESEL	0.0	0.0	0.6	0.0	0.0	7.0	0.0	53.4	636.2	508.3	10.3	0.0	
17237J410	TK CO, TK BN, M60	MOGAS	0.0	0.0	0.0	0.0	0.0	0.0	0.0	0.0	0.0	0.0	0.0	0.0	
		DIESEL	0.0	0.0	0.0	0.0	0.0	0.0	0.0	28.0	371.4	263.1	0.3	0.0	
19217J400	MP CO-HVY DIV	MOGAS	0.0	0.0	4.6	4.0	0.0	1.0	0.0	0.0	0.0	0.0	0.0	0.0	
		DIESEL	0.0	0.0	1.1	0.0	0.0	5.0	0.0	0.0	0.0	0.0	2.5	0.0	
34285J400	MI BN (CEWI) HVY DIV	MOGAS	0.0	0.0	42.9	13.4	0.0	12.0	0.0	0.0	0.0	0.0	0.0	0.0	
		DIESEL	0.0	0.0	15.6	0.0	0.0	17.0	0.0	16.2	132.9	138.9	7.8	0.3	
34286J400	HQ & HQ-HP-OP CO MI BN CEWI DIV	MOGAS	0.0	0.0	0.8	0.0	0.0	0.0	0.0	0.0	0.0	0.0	0.0	0.0	
		DIESEL	0.0	0.0	0.0	0.0	0.0	12.0	0.0	2.0	17.2	17.8	1.8	0.0	
34287J400	C&J CO MI BN CEWI DIV	MOGAS	0.0	0.0	7.2	0.0	0.0	0.0	0.0	0.0	0.0	0.0	0.0	0.0	
		DIESEL	0.0	0.0	15.0	0.0	0.0	0.0	0.0	12.0	103.2	106.8	1.6	0.3	
34289J400	SVC SPT CO MI BN CEWI DIV	MOGAS	0.0	0.0	34.8	13.4	0.0	12.0	0.0	0.0	0.0	0.0	0.0	0.0	
		DIESEL	0.0	0.0	0.6	0.0	0.0	5.0	0.0	2.2	12.5	14.3	4.4	0.0	
42004J400	SUP CO FWD SPT BN HVY DIV	MOGAS	0.0	0.0	1.7	3.6	0.0	7.9	0.0	0.0	0.0	0.0	0.0	0.0	
		DIESEL	0.0	14.0	0.6	0.0	27.6	5.0	0.0	0.0	0.0	0.0	5.2	0.0	
42007J400	S&S CO MAINT SPT BN HVY DIV	MOGAS	0.0	0.0	6.6	11.6	0.0	35.8	0.0	0.0	0.0	0.0	0.0	0.0	
		DIESEL	0.0	21.0	30.6	0.0	35.9	5.0	0.0	0.0	0.0	0.0	10.9	0.0	
43004J400	MAINT CO, FWD SPT BN, HVY DIV	MOGAS	0.0	0.0	25.4	16.0	0.0	20.4	0.0	0.0	0.0	0.0	0.0	0.0	
		DIESEL	0.0	7.0	11.1	0.0	9.8	7.0	0.0	3.0	45.4	34.4	10.4	0.0	
43004J401	TK SYSTEM SPT TM	MOGAS	0.0	0.0	1.1	0.0	0.0	5.6	0.0	0.0	0.0	0.0	0.0	0.0	
		DIESEL	0.0	0.0	0.6	0.0	0.0	0.0	0.0	1.0	8.6	8.9	0.8	0.0	
43004J402	INF SYS(M) SPT TM	MOGAS	0.0	0.0	2.4	0.0	0.0	5.6	0.0	0.0	0.0	0.0	0.0	0.0	
		DIESEL	0.0	0.0	0.0	0.0	0.0	0.0	0.0	1.0	8.6	8.9	0.8	0.0	
43007J400	LIGHT MAINT CO HVY DIV	MOGAS	0.0	0.0	42.3	11.6	1.4	24.9	0.0	0.0	0.0	0.0	0.0	0.0	
		DIESEL	0.0	0.0	64.0	0.0	17.0	0.0	0.0	0.0	0.0	0.0	15.0	0.0	
43008J400	HEAVY MAINT CO HVY DIV	MOGAS	0.0	0.0	14.5	28.0	0.0	41.3	0.0	0.0	0.0	0.0	0.0	0.0	
		DIESEL	0.0	14.0	13.5	0.0	8.5	7.0	0.0	4.0	54.0	43.3	7.7	0.0	
44165J400	ADA BN HVY DIV	MOGAS	0.0	0.0	59.4	14.8	0.0	17.8	0.0	0.0	0.0	0.0	0.1	0.0	
		DIESEL	0.0	36.0	2.3	0.0	0.0	28.0	0.0	45.0	503.3	553.3	18.0	0.0	
44166J400	HHB, ADA BN, HEAVY DIV	MOGAS	0.0	0.0	20.2	14.8	0.0	11.9	0.0	0.0	0.0	0.0	0.0	0.0	
		DIESEL	0.0	0.0	0.6	0.0	0.0	13.0	0.0	3.0	25.8	26.7	4.7	0.0	
44167J400	ADA BTRY, GUN(SP)/STINGER	MOGAS	0.0	0.0	13.1	0.0	0.0	1.9	0.0	0.0	0.0	0.0	0.0	0.0	
		DIESEL	0.0	12.0	0.6	0.0	0.0	5.0	0.0	14.0	159.2	175.5	4.4	0.0	
55087J400	TMET CO MAIN SPT BN HVY DIV	MOGAS	0.0	0.0	1.7	8.0	0.0	2.4	0.0	0.0	0.0	0.0	0.0	0.0	
		DIESEL	0.0	0.0	1.1	0.0	0.0	5.0	0.0	0.0	0.0	0.0	19.9	0.0	
55427J410	TAMC, SPT CMD, HVY DIV	MOGAS	0.0	0.0	16.7	13.0	1.5	4.4	0.0	0.0	0.0	0.0	0.0	0.0	
		DIESEL	0.0	16.0	45.2	0.0	8.5	5.0	0.0	0.0	0.0	0.0	5.1	0.0	
		JP4													332.0
63001J420	SPT CMD, 5x5x2, HVY DIV	MOGAS	0.0	0.0	252.0	167.2	2.9	314.3	0.0	0.0	0.0	0.0	0.3	0.0	
		DIESEL	0.0	144.0	302.5	0.0	183.4	101.0	0.0	40.0	441.8	394.7	146.1	0.0	
		JP4													332.0
63002J400	HHC/MMC, SPT CMD, HVY DIV	MOGAS	0.0	0.0	0.8	7.6	0.0	7.0	0.0	0.0	0.0	0.0	0.0	0.0	
		DIESEL	0.0	0.0	25.5	0.0	0.0	0.0	0.0	0.0	0.0	0.0	3.8	0.0	
63005J410	FWD SPT BN (2X1) HVY DIV	MOGAS	0.0	0.0	42.1	25.4	0.0	59.2	0.0	0.0	0.0	0.0	0.0	0.0	
		DIESEL	0.0	21.0	16.5	0.0	37.4	23.0	0.0	11.0	114.2	105.6	22.1	0.0	
63005J420	FWD SPT BN (2X2) HVY DIV	MOGAS	0.0	0.0	44.5	25.4	0.0	64.9	0.0	0.0	0.0	0.0	0.0	0.0	
		DIESEL	0.0	21.0	16.5	0.0	37.4	23.0	0.0	12.0	122.8	114.5	22.9	0.0	
63005J430	FWD SPT BN (1X2) HVY DIV	MOGAS	0.0	0.0	43.4	25.4	0.0	59.2	0.0	0.0	0.0	0.0	0.0	0.0	
		DIESEL	0.0	21.0	15.9	0.0	37.4	23.0	0.0	11.0	114.2	105.6	22.1	0.0	
63006J400	HHD, FWD SPT BN, HEAVY DIV	MOGAS	0.0	0.0	0.0	0.0	0.0	1.0	0.0	0.0	0.0	0.0	0.1	0.0	
		DIESEL	0.0	0.0	1.5	0.0	0.0	6.0	0.0	0.0	0.0	0.0	1.0	0.0	
63135J400	MAIN SUPPORT BN, HVY DIV	MOGAS	0.0	0.0	104.4	70.4	1.4	119.4	0.0	0.0	0.0	0.0	0.0	0.0	
		DIESEL	0.0	65.0	182.8	0.0	62.7	27.0	0.0	6.0	90.7	68.9	69.6	0.0	
63136J400	HHD, MAINT SPT BN, HVY DIV	MOGAS	0.0	0.0	0.0	0.0	0.0	1.0	0.0	0.0	0.0	0.0	0.0	0.0	
		DIESEL	0.0	0.0	4.5	0.0	0.0	0.0	0.0	0.0	0.0	0.0	1.0	0.0	

Figure 10. Bulk POL Planning Factors by Type Unit– Bulk POL Table E (continued)

SUMMARY OF BULK FUEL USAGE BY EQUIPMENT CATEGORY
MX DIV 5-M60 5-M113 2-AHB (SRC 87000J420) – (Cont)

SRC	UNIT NAME	FUEL TYPE	AB	CE	GN	HG	MH	SG	SV	TI	CC	SR	WV	OV	AV
87000J420	MX DIV, 5-M60, 5-M113, 2-AHB	MOGAS	0.0	2.0	868.4	564.6	2.9	894.6	0.0	0.0	0.0	0.0	1.6	0.0	
		DIESEL	86.4	284.0	392.7	0.0	201.0	416.0	0.0	2057.0	21457.2	18444.3	482.4	33.3	
		JP4													13019.0
87004J420	HHC INFANTRY DIVISION (MECH)	MOGAS	0.0	0.0	40.2	7.6	0.0	12.0	0.0	0.0	0.0	0.0	0.0	0.0	
		DIESEL	0.0	0.0	1.5	0.0	0.0	0.0	0.0	5.0	43.0	44.5	5.1	0.0	
87042J410	HHC ARMD DIV BDE	MOGAS	0.0	0.0	6.2	5.8	0.0	4.0	0.0	0.0	0.0	0.0	0.0	0.0	
		DIESEL	0.0	0.0	0.0	0.0	0.0	5.0	0.0	9.2	72.7	76.6	1.6	0.0	
87042J420	HHC INF DIV (MECH) BDE	MOGAS	0.0	0.0	8.9	5.8	0.0	4.0	0.0	0.0	0.0	0.0	0.0	0.0	
		DIESEL	0.0	0.0	0.0	0.0	0.0	5.0	0.0	9.2	72.7	76.6	1.6	0.0	

SUMMARY OF BULK FUEL USAGE BY EQUIPMENT CATEGORY
AR DIV 6-M1 4-BFVS 2-AHB (SRC 87000J430)

SRC	UNIT NAME	FUEL TYPE	AB	CE	GN	HG	MH	SG	SV	TI	CC	SR	WV	OV	AV
01257J420	CBT SPT AVN CO (CBAA) (UH-60)	MOGAS	0.0	0.0	9.4	21.0	0.0	7.3	0.0	0.0	0.0	0.0	0.0	0.0	
		DIESEL	0.0	6.0	0.0	0.0	1.3	0.0	0.0	0.0	0.0	0.0	5.3	0.0	
		JP4													2142.0
01287J400	GEN SPT AVN CO	MOGAS	0.0	0.0	21.9	12.0	0.0	6.4	0.0	0.0	0.0	0.0	0.0	0.0	
		DIESEL	0.0	6.0	0.6	0.0	0.0	9.0	0.0	0.0	0.0	0.0	5.3	0.0	
		JP4													1540.9
01385J420	ATTACK HEL BN (AH-64)	MOGAS	0.0	0.0	13.3	14.8	0.0	9.0	0.0	0.0	0.0	0.0	0.0	0.0	
		DIESEL	0.0	8.0	0.0	0.0	2.6	0.0	0.0	0.0	0.0	0.0	9.5	0.0	
		JP4													3848.7
01386J420	HQ AND SVC CO (AH-64)	MOGAS	0.0	0.0	13.3	14.8	0.0	9.0	0.0	0.0	0.0	0.0	0.0	0.0	
		DIESEL	0.0	8.0	0.0	0.0	2.6	0.0	0.0	0.0	0.0	0.0	8.6	0.0	
		JP4													489.9
01387J420	ATK HEL CO (AH-64)	MOGAS	0.0	0.0	0.0	0.0	0.0	0.0	0.0	0.0	0.0	0.0	0.0	0.0	
		DIESEL	0.0	0.0	0.0	0.0	0.0	0.0	0.0	0.0	0.0	0.0	0.3	0.0	
		JP4													1119.6
03387J400	CHEMICAL CO, HVY DIV	MOGAS	0.0	0.0	36.8	4.0	0.0	64.0	0.0	0.0	0.0	0.0	0.0	0.0	
		DIESEL	0.0	0.0	0.6	0.0	0.0	5.0	0.0	6.0	51.6	53.4	9.5	0.0	
05145J410	ENGR BN, HVY DIV - RIBBON	MOGAS	0.0	0.0	24.2	33.0	0.0	104.2	0.0	0.0	0.0	0.0	0.1	0.0	
		DIESEL	86.4	68.0	3.4	0.0	8.5	34.0	0.0	150.5	1612.7	1338.5	37.3	0.0	
05146J400	HQ-HQ COMPANY	MOGAS	0.0	0.0	5.0	5.8	0.0	15.5	0.0	0.0	0.0	0.0	0.1	0.0	
		DIESEL	0.0	0.0	0.6	0.0	8.5	7.0	0.0	3.0	25.8	26.7	7.8	0.0	
05147J400	ENGR CO, ENGR BN, HVY DIV	MOGAS	0.0	0.5	4.2	5.8	0.0	19.5	0.0	0.0	0.0	0.0	0.0	0.0	
		DIESEL	0.0	17.0	0.6	0.0	0.0	5.0	0.0	36.5	393.6	325.6	5.2	0.0	
05148J410	BRIDGE COMPANY - RIBBON	MOGAS	0.0	0.0	2.5	4.0	0.0	10.4	0.0	0.0	0.0	0.0	0.0	0.0	
		DIESEL	86.4	0.0	0.6	0.0	0.0	7.0	0.0	1.4	12.3	9.3	8.5	0.0	
06300J410	AR DIVARTY	MOGAS	0.0	0.0	89.4	42.6	0.0	78.5	0.0	0.0	0.0	0.0	0.3	0.0	
		DIESEL	0.0	0.0	38.2	0.0	0.0	75.0	0.0	234.7	1484.1	1765.8	67.9	32.4	
06302J400	HHB DIV ARTY HVY DIV	MOGAS	0.0	0.0	23.5	1.8	0.0	8.4	0.0	0.0	0.0	0.0	0.2	0.0	
		DIESEL	0.0	0.0	9.8	0.0	0.0	5.0	0.0	1.0	8.6	8.9	5.5	0.0	
06307J400	TGT ACQ BTRY HVY DIV	MOGAS	0.0	0.0	4.4	0.0	0.0	1.5	0.0	0.0	0.0	0.0	0.0	0.0	
		DIESEL	0.0	0.0	12.6	0.0	0.0	10.0	0.0	0.0	0.0	0.0	3.5	0.0	
06365J410	FA BN 155 SP HVY DIV	MOGAS	0.0	0.0	18.1	13.0	0.0	21.3	0.0	0.0	0.0	0.0	0.0	0.0	
		DIESEL	0.0	0.0	5.3	0.0	0.0	20.0	0.0	72.4	432.5	545.0	17.2	10.4	
06365J430	FA BN 155 SP HVY DIV	MOGAS	0.0	0.0	20.2	13.0	0.0	21.3	0.0	0.0	0.0	0.0	0.0	0.0	
		DIESEL	0.0	0.0	5.3	0.0	0.0	20.0	0.0	73.4	441.1	553.9	17.2	11.6	
06366J410	HHB FA BN 155SP HVY DIV	MOGAS	0.0	0.0	10.4	5.4	0.0	13.0	0.0	0.0	0.0	0.0	0.0	0.0	
		DIESEL	0.0	0.0	3.6	0.0	0.0	0.0	0.0	7.0	60.2	62.3	3.0	3.7	
06366J430	HHB FA BN 155SP HVY DIV	MOGAS	0.0	0.0	12.5	5.4	0.0	13.0	0.0	0.0	0.0	0.0	0.0	0.0	
		DIESEL	0.0	0.0	3.6	0.0	0.0	0.0	0.0	8.0	68.8	71.2	3.1	4.8	
06367J410	FA BTRY 155SP HVY DIV	MOGAS	0.0	0.0	1.1	0.0	0.0	0.0	0.0	0.0	0.0	0.0	0.0	0.0	
		DIESEL	0.0	0.0	0.6	0.0	0.0	5.0	0.0	19.6	116.6	146.6	2.0	2.2	
06369J410	SBC BTRY 155SP HVY DIV	MOGAS	0.0	0.0	4.5	7.6	0.0	8.3	0.0	0.0	0.0	0.0	0.0	0.0	
		DIESEL	0.0	0.0	0.0	0.0	0.0	5.0	0.0	6.6	37.5	42.9	8.0	0.0	
06398J400	FA BTRY MLRS	MOGAS	0.0	0.0	5.2	1.8	0.0	4.5	0.0	0.0	0.0	0.0	0.0	0.0	
		DIESEL	0.0	0.0	0.0	0.0	0.0	0.0	0.0	15.5	169.4	113.0	7.2	0.0	
07209J400	LRS DET, CAB SQDN, HVY DIV	MOGAS	0.0	0.0	5.6	0.0	0.0	0.0	0.0	0.0	0.0	0.0	0.0	0.0	
		DIESEL	0.0	0.0	0.0	0.0	0.0	0.0	0.0	0.0	0.0	0.0	0.2	0.0	
07245J410	INF BN-MECH E/W BFVS	MOGAS	0.0	0.0	8.5	7.6	0.0	24.1	0.0	0.0	0.0	0.0	0.1	0.0	
		DIESEL	0.0	0.0	1.1	0.0	0.0	12.0	0.0	147.0	1744.3	1130.9	14.2	0.0	
07246J410	HHC INF BN MECH BFVS	MOGAS	0.0	0.0	5.8	7.6	0.0	24.1	0.0	0.0	0.0	0.0	0.1	0.0	
		DIESEL	0.0	0.0	1.1	0.0	0.0	12.0	0.0	54.2	636.3	505.7	12.2	0.0	
07247J410	RIFLE CO INF BN MECH BFVS	MOGAS	0.0	0.0	0.5	0.0	0.0	0.0	0.0	0.0	0.0	0.0	0.0	0.0	
		DIESEL	0.0	0.0	0.0	0.0	0.0	0.0	0.0	19.2	242.6	120.7	0.4	0.0	
07248J400	ANTIARMOR CO INF BN(M) IT	MOGAS	0.0	0.0	0.5	0.0	0.0	0.0	0.0	0.0	0.0	0.0	0.0	0.0	
		DIESEL	0.0	0.0	0.0	0.0	0.0	0.0	0.0	16.0	137.6	142.4	0.4	0.0	
08077J400	MEDICAL CO (MSB) HVY DIV	MOGAS	0.0	0.0	13.7	7.2	0.0	13.0	0.0	0.0	0.0	0.0	0.0	0.0	
		DIESEL	0.0	0.0	2.8	0.0	0.0	5.0	0.0	0.0	0.0	0.0	5.5	0.0	
08078J400	MEDICAL CO (FSB) HVY DIV	MOGAS	0.0	0.0	10.4	5.8	0.0	13.0	0.0	0.0	0.0	0.0	0.0	0.0	
		DIESEL	0.0	0.0	2.2	0.0	0.0	5.0	0.0	5.0	43.0	44.5	3.1	0.0	
09558J400	MSL SPT CO HVY DIV	MOGAS	0.0	0.0	22.7	4.0	0.0	1.0	0.0	0.0	0.0	0.0	0.0	0.0	
		DIESEL	0.0	0.0	40.2	0.0	1.3	5.0	0.0	0.0	0.0	0.0	6.9	0.0	
09558J402	SGT YORK AUG, MSL SPT CO	MOGAS	0.0	0.0	3.0	0.0	0.0	0.0	0.0	0.0	0.0	0.0	0.0	0.0	
		DIESEL	0.0	30.0	26.1	0.0	0.0	0.0	0.0	2.0	36.8	25.5	2.4	0.0	
11035J500	SIG BN HVY DIV	MOGAS	0.0	0.0	141.8	17.8	0.0	15.4	0.0	0.0	0.0	0.0	0.3	0.0	
		DIESEL	0.0	0.0	17.3	0.0	0.0	20.0	0.0	0.0	0.0	0.0	18.4	0.0	
11036J500	HHC SIG BN HEAVY DIV	MOGAS	0.0	0.0	25.1	4.0	0.0	9.4	0.0	0.0	0.0	0.0	0.3	0.0	
		DIESEL	0.0	0.0	0.6	0.0	0.0	5.0	0.0	0.0	0.0	0.0	5.8	0.0	
11037J500	CMD OPS CO	MOGAS	0.0	0.0	35.6	4.0	0.0	1.0	0.0	0.0	0.0	0.0	0.0	0.0	
		DIESEL	0.0	0.0	6.6	0.0	0.0	5.0	0.0	0.0	0.0	0.0	4.4	0.0	
11038J500	FWD COMM CO	MOGAS	0.0	0.0	38.3	4.0	0.0	1.0	0.0	0.0	0.0	0.0	0.0	0.0	
		DIESEL	0.0	0.0	0.6	0.0	0.0	5.0	0.0	0.0	0.0	0.0	3.3	0.0	

Figure 10. Bulk POL Planning Factors by Type Unit— Bulk POL Table E (continued)

SUMMARY OF BULK FUEL USAGE BY EQUIPMENT CATEGORY
AR DIV 6-M1 4-BFVS 2-AHB (SRC 87000J430)—(Cont'd)

SRC	UNIT NAME	FUEL TYPE	AB	CE	GN	HG	MH	SG	SV	TI	CC	SR	WV	OV	AV
11039J500	AREA SIGNAL CO	MOGAS	0.0	0.0	42.8	5.8	0.0	4.0	0.0	0.0	0.0	0.0	0.0	0.0	
		DIESEL	0.0	0.0	9.6	0.0	0.0	5.0	0.0	0.0	0.0	0.0	4.8	0.0	
12114J400	DIVISION BAND	MOGAS	0.0	0.0	0.0	0.0	0.0	0.0	0.0	0.0	0.0	0.0	0.0	0.0	
		DIESEL	0.0	0.0	0.0	0.0	0.0	0.0	0.0	0.0	0.0	0.0	0.0	0.0	
17201J420	CAV BDE AIR ATK (AH-64) (AOE)	MOGAS	0.0	0.0	89.9	86.8	0.0	62.5	0.0	0.0	0.0	0.0	0.0	0.0	
		DIESEL	0.0	36.0	1.7	0.0	9.1	21.0	0.0	81.0	998.8	597.5	46.4	0.6	
		JP4													12985.0
17202J400	HQ & HQ TROOP, CBAA	MOGAS	0.0	0.0	13.2	7.6	0.0	7.4	0.0	0.0	0.0	0.0	0.0	0.0	
		DIESEL	0.0	0.0	0.6	0.0	0.0	0.0	0.0	0.0	0.0	0.0	3.0	0.0	
17205J410	CAV SQDN, CBAA AH IS HVY DIV	MOGAS	0.0	0.0	18.7	16.6	0.0	23.4	0.0	0.0	0.0	0.0	0.0	0.0	
		DIESEL	0.0	8.0	0.6	0.0	2.6	12.0	0.0	81.0	998.8	597.5	13.7	0.6	
		JP4													1604.8
17206J410	HQ AND HQ TRP, CAV SQDN	MOGAS	0.0	0.0	13.1	16.6	0.0	21.4	0.0	0.0	0.0	0.0	0.0	0.0	
		DIESEL	0.0	8.0	0.6	0.0	2.6	12.0	0.0	13.8	169.7	130.6	12.4	0.6	
		JP4													142.0
17207J410	CAV TRP, CAV SQDN	MOGAS	0.0	0.0	0.0	0.0	0.0	1.0	0.0	0.0	0.0	0.0	0.0	0.0	
		DIESEL	0.0	0.0	0.0	0.0	0.0	0.0	0.0	33.6	414.6	233.4	0.3	0.0	
17208J410	AIR CAV TRP, CAV SQDN	MOGAS	0.0	0.0	0.0	0.0	0.0	0.0	0.0	0.0	0.0	0.0	0.0	0.0	
		DIESEL	0.0	0.0	0.0	0.0	0.0	0.0	0.0	0.0	0.0	0.0	0.2	0.0	
		JP4													731.4
17235J420	TANK BATTALION EQ W/M1	MOGAS	0.0	0.0	3.9	23.6	0.0	16.0	0.0	0.0	0.0	0.0	0.0	0.0	
		DIESEL	0.0	0.0	0.6	0.0	0.0	7.0	0.0	675.8	3865.9	3059.8	14.4	0.0	
17236J420	HHC, TK BN, (M1)	MOGAS	0.0	0.0	3.9	23.6	0.0	16.0	0.0	0.0	0.0	0.0	0.0	0.0	
		DIESEL	0.0	0.0	0.6	0.0	0.0	7.0	0.0	71.0	696.3	560.0	13.3	0.0	
17237J420	TANK CO, (M1)	MOGAS	0.0	0.0	0.0	0.0	0.0	0.0	0.0	0.0	0.0	0.0	0.0	0.0	
		DIESEL	0.0	0.0	0.0	0.0	0.0	0.0	0.0	151.2	792.4	625.0	0.3	0.0	
19217J400	MP CO-HVY DIV	MOGAS	0.0	0.0	4.6	4.0	0.0	1.0	0.0	0.0	0.0	0.0	0.0	0.0	
		DIESEL	0.0	0.0	1.1	0.0	0.0	5.0	0.0	0.0	0.0	0.0	2.5	0.0	
34285J400	MI BN (CEWI) HVY DIV	MOGAS	0.0	0.0	42.9	13.4	0.0	12.0	0.0	0.0	0.0	0.0	0.0	0.0	
		DIESEL	0.0	0.0	15.6	0.0	0.0	17.0	0.0	16.2	132.9	138.9	7.8	0.3	
34286J400	HQ & HQ-OP CO MI BN CEWI DIV	MOGAS	0.0	0.0	0.8	0.0	0.0	0.0	0.0	0.0	0.0	0.0	0.0	0.0	
		DIESEL	0.0	0.0	0.0	0.0	0.0	12.0	0.0	2.0	17.2	17.8	1.8	0.0	
34287J400	C&J CO MI BN CEWI, DIV	MOGAS	0.0	0.0	7.2	0.0	0.0	0.0	0.0	0.0	0.0	0.0	0.0	0.0	
		DIESEL	0.0	0.0	15.0	0.0	0.0	0.0	0.0	12.0	103.2	106.8	1.6	0.3	
34289J400	SVC SPT CO MI BN CEWI DIV	MOGAS	0.0	0.0	38.4	13.4	0.0	12.0	0.0	0.0	0.0	0.0	0.0	0.0	
		DIESEL	0.0	0.0	0.6	0.0	0.0	5.0	0.0	2.2	12.5	14.3	4.4	0.0	
42004J400	SUP CO FWD SPT BN HVY DIV	MOGAS	0.0	0.0	1.7	3.6	0.0	7.9	0.0	0.0	0.0	0.0	0.0	0.0	
		DIESEL	0.0	14.0	0.6	0.0	27.6	5.0	0.0	0.0	0.0	0.0	5.2	0.0	
42007J400	S&S CO MAIN SPT BN HVY DIV	MOGAS	0.0	0.0	6.6	11.6	0.0	35.8	0.0	0.0	0.0	0.0	0.0	0.0	
		DIESEL	0.0	21.0	30.6	0.0	35.9	5.0	0.0	0.0	0.0	0.0	10.9	0.0	
43004J400	MAINT CO, FWD SPT BN, HVY DIV	MOGAS	0.0	0.0	25.4	16.0	0.0	20.4	0.0	0.0	0.0	0.0	0.0	0.0	
		DIESEL	0.0	7.0	11.1	0.0	9.8	7.0	0.0	3.0	45.4	34.4	10.0	0.0	
43004J401	TK SYSTEM SPT TM	MOGAS	0.0	0.0	1.1	0.0	0.0	5.6	0.0	0.0	0.0	0.0	0.0	0.0	
		DIESEL	0.0	0.0	0.6	0.0	0.0	0.0	0.0	1.0	8.6	8.9	1.0	0.0	
43004J402	INF SYS(M) SPT TM	MOGAS	0.0	0.0	2.4	0.0	0.0	5.6	0.0	0.0	0.0	0.0	0.0	0.0	
		DIESEL	0.0	0.0	0.0	0.0	0.0	0.0	0.0	1.0	8.6	8.9	1.0	0.0	
43007J400	LIGHT MAINT CO HVY DIV	MOGAS	0.0	0.0	42.3	11.6	1.4	24.9	0.0	0.0	0.0	0.0	0.0	0.0	
		DIESEL	0.0	0.0	64.0	0.0	17.0	0.0	0.0	0.0	0.0	0.0	15.0	0.0	
43008J400	HEAVY MAINT CO HVY DIV	MOGAS	0.0	0.0	14.5	28.0	0.0	41.3	0.0	0.0	0.0	0.0	0.0	0.0	
		DIESEL	0.0	14.0	13.5	0.0	8.5	7.0	0.0	4.0	54.0	43.3	8.0	0.0	
44165J400	ADA BN HVY DIV	MOGAS	0.0	0.0	59.4	14.8	0.0	17.8	0.0	0.0	0.0	0.0	0.0	0.0	
		DIESEL	0.0	36.0	2.3	0.0	0.0	28.0	0.0	45.0	503.3	553.3	18.0	0.0	
44166J400	HHB, ADA BN, HEAVY DIV	MOGAS	0.0	0.0	20.2	14.8	0.0	11.9	0.0	0.0	0.0	0.0	0.0	0.0	
		DIESEL	0.0	0.0	0.6	0.0	0.0	13.0	0.0	3.0	25.8	26.7	5.0	0.0	
44167J400	ADA BTRY, GUN (SP)/STINGER	MOGAS	0.0	0.0	13.1	0.0	0.0	1.9	0.0	0.0	0.0	0.0	0.0	0.0	
		DIESEL	0.0	12.0	0.6	0.0	0.0	5.0	0.0	14.0	159.2	175.5	4.0	0.0	
55087J400	TMT CO MAIN SPT BN HVY DIV	MOGAS	0.0	0.0	1.7	8.0	0.0	2.4	0.0	0.0	0.0	0.0	0.0	0.0	
		DIESEL	0.0	0.0	1.1	0.0	0.0	5.0	0.0	0.0	0.0	0.0	20.0	0.0	
55427J410	TAMC, SPT CMD, HVY DIV	MOGAS	0.0	0.0	16.7	13.0	1.5	4.4	0.0	0.0	0.0	0.0	0.0	0.0	
		DIESEL	0.0	16.0	45.2	0.0	8.5	5.0	0.0	0.0	0.0	0.0	5.0	0.0	
		JP4													332.0
63001J410	SPT CMD, 6 x 4 x 2, HVY DIV	MOGAS	0.0	0.0	250.7	167.2	2.9	314.3	0.0	0.0	0.0	0.0	0.0	0.0	
		DIESEL	0.0	144.0	303.0	0.0	183.4	101.0	0.0	40.0	441.8	394.7	146.0	0.0	
		JP4													332.0
63002J400	HHC/MMC, SPT CMD, HVY DIV	MOGAS	0.0	0.0	0.8	7.6	0.0	7.0	0.0	0.0	0.0	0.0	0.0	0.0	
		DIESEL	0.0	0.0	25.5	0.0	0.0	0.0	0.0	0.0	0.0	0.0	4.0	0.0	
63005J410	FWD SPT BN (2 x 1) HVY DIV	MOGAS	0.0	0.0	42.1	25.4	0.0	59.2	0.0	0.0	0.0	0.0	0.0	0.0	
		DIESEL	0.0	21.0	16.5	0.0	37.4	23.0	0.0	11.0	114.2	105.6	22.0	0.0	
63005J420	FWD SPT BN (2 x 2) HVY DIV	MOGAS	0.0	0.0	44.5	25.4	0.0	64.9	0.0	0.0	0.0	0.0	0.0	0.0	
		DIESEL	0.0	21.0	16.5	0.0	37.4	23.0	0.0	12.0	122.8	114.5	23.0	0.0	
63006J400	HHD,FWD SPT BN,HEAVY DIV	MOGAS	0.0	0.0	0.0	0.0	0.0	1.0	0.0	0.0	0.0	0.0	0.0	0.0	
		DIESEL	0.0	0.0	1.5	0.0	0.0	6.0	0.0	0.0	0.0	0.0	1.0	0.0	
63135J400	MAIN SUPPORT BN, HVY DIV	MOGAS	0.0	0.0	104.4	70.4	1.4	119.4	0.0	0.0	0.0	0.0	0.0	0.0	
		DIESEL	0.0	65.0	182.8	0.0	62.7	27.0	0.0	6.0	90.7	68.9	70.0	0.0	
63136J400	HHD,MAIN SPT BN, HVY DIV	MOGAS	0.0	0.0	0.0	0.0	0.0	1.0	0.0	0.0	0.0	0.0	0.0	0.0	
		DIESEL	0.0	0.0	4.5	0.0	0.0	0.0	0.0	0.0	0.0	0.0	1.0	0.0	
87000J430	AR DIV, 6-M1, 4-BFVS,2-AH	MOGAS	0.0	2.0	857.8	580.6	2.9	886.4	0.0	0.0	0.0	0.0	2.0	0.0	
		DIESEL	86.4	284.0	392.7	0.0	201.0	411.0	0.0	5248.8	35659.1	27998.7	508.0	33.3	
		JP4													13317.0
87004J410	HHC ARMORED DIVISION	MOGAS	0.0	0.0	39.6	7.6	0.0	12.0	0.0	0.0	0.0	0.0	0.0	0.0	
		DIESEL	0.0	0.0	1.5	0.0	0.0	0.0	0.0	5.0	43.0	44.5	5.0	0.0	
87042J410	HHC ARMD DIV BDE	MOGAS	0.0	0.0	6.2	5.8	0.0	4.0	0.0	0.0	0.0	0.0	0.0	0.0	
		DIESEL	0.0	0.0	0.0	0.0	0.0	5.0	0.0	9.2	72.7	76.6	2.0	0.0	
87042J420	HHC INF DIV (MECH) BDE	MOGAS	0.0	0.0	8.9	5.8	0.0	4.0	0.0	0.0	0.0	0.0	0.0	0.0	
		DIESEL	0.0	0.0	0.0	0.0	0.0	5.0	0.0	9.2	72.7	76.6	2.0	0.0	

Figure 10. Bulk POL Planning Factors by Type Unit— Bulk POL Table E (continued)

SUMMARY OF BULK FUEL USAGE BY EQUIPMENT CATEGORY
MX DIV 5-M1 5-BFVS 2-AHB (SRC 87000J440)

SRC	UNIT NAME	FUEL TYPE	AB	CE	GN	HG	MH	SG	SV	TI	CC	SR	WV	OV	AV
01257J420	CBT SPT AVN CO (CBAA) (UH-6)	MOGAS	0.0	0.0	9.4	21.0	0.0	7.3	0.0	0.0	0.0	0.0	0.0	0.0	
		DIESEL	0.0	6.0	0.0	0.0	1.3	0.0	0.0	0.0	0.0	0.0	5.3	0.0	
		JP4													2142.0
01287J400	GEN SPT AVN CO	MOGAS	0.0	0.0	21.9	12.0	0.0	6.4	0.0	0.0	0.0	0.0	0.0	0.0	
		DIESEL	0.0	6.0	0.6	0.0	0.0	9.0	0.0	0.0	0.0	0.0	5.3	0.0	
		JP4													1540.8
01385J420	ATTACK HEL BN (AH-64)	MOGAS	0.0	0.0	13.3	14.8	0.0	9.0	0.0	0.0	0.0	0.0	0.0	0.0	
		DIESEL	0.0	8.0	0.0	0.0	2.6	0.0	0.0	0.0	0.0	0.0	9.5	0.0	
		JP4													3848.7
01386J420	HQ AND SVC CO (AH-64)	MOGAS	0.0	0.0	13.3	14.8	0.0	9.0	0.0	0.0	0.0	0.0	0.0	0.0	
		DIESEL	0.0	8.0	0.0	0.0	2.6	0.0	0.0	0.0	0.0	0.0	8.6	0.0	
		JP4													489.9
01387J420	ATK HEL CO (AH-64)	MOGAS	0.0	0.0	0.0	0.0	0.0	0.0	0.0	0.0	0.0	0.0	0.0	0.0	
		DIESEL	0.0	0.0	0.0	0.0	0.0	0.0	0.0	0.0	0.0	0.0	0.3	0.0	
		JP4													1119.6
03387J400	CHEMICAL CO, HVY DIV	MOGAS	0.0	0.0	36.8	4.0	0.0	64.0	0.0	0.0	0.0	0.0	0.0	0.0	
		DIESEL	0.0	0.0	0.6	0.0	0.0	5.0	0.0	6.0	51.6	53.4	9.5	0.0	
05145J410	ENGR BN, HVY DIV - RIBBON	MOGAS	0.0	0.0	24.2	33.0	0.0	104.2	0.0	0.0	0.0	0.0	0.1	0.0	
		DIESEL	86.4	68.0	3.4	0.0	8.5	34.0	0.0	150.5	1612.7	1338.5	37.3	0.0	
05146J400	HQ-HQ COMPANY	MOGAS	0.0	0.0	5.0	5.8	0.0	15.5	0.0	0.0	0.0	0.0	0.1	0.0	
		DIESEL	0.0	0.0	0.6	0.0	8.5	7.0	0.0	3.0	25.8	26.7	7.8	0.0	
05147J400	ENGR CO, ENGR BN, HVY DIV	MOGAS	0.0	0.5	4.2	5.8	0.0	19.5	0.0	0.0	0.0	0.0	0.0	0.0	
		DIESEL	0.0	17.0	0.6	0.0	0.0	5.0	0.0	36.5	393.6	325.6	5.2	0.0	
05148J410	BRIDGE COMPANY - RIBBON	MOGAS	0.0	0.0	2.5	4.0	0.0	10.4	0.0	0.0	0.0	0.0	0.0	0.0	
		DIESEL	86.4	0.0	0.6	0.0	0.0	7.0	0.0	1.4	12.3	9.3	8.5	0.0	
06300J420	MECH DIVARTY	MOGAS	0.0	0.0	89.4	42.6	0.0	78.5	0.0	0.0	0.0	0.0	0.3	0.0	
		DIESEL	0.0	0.0	38.2	0.0	0.0	75.0	0.0	234.7	1484.1	1765.8	67.9	32.4	
06302J400	HHB DIV ARTY HVY DIV	MOGAS	0.0	0.0	23.5	1.8	0.0	8.4	0.0	0.0	0.0	0.0	0.2	0.0	
		DIESEL	0.0	0.0	9.8	0.0	0.0	5.0	0.0	1.0	8.6	8.9	5.5	0.0	
06307J400	TGT ACQ BTRY HVY DIV	MOGAS	0.0	0.0	4.4	0.0	0.0	1.5	0.0	0.0	0.0	0.0	0.0	0.0	
		DIESEL	0.0	0.0	12.6	0.0	0.0	10.0	0.0	0.0	0.0	0.0	3.5	0.0	
06365J410	FA BN 155 SP HVY DIV	MOGAS	0.0	0.0	18.1	13.0	0.0	21.3	0.0	0.0	0.0	0.0	0.0	0.0	
		DIESEL	0.0	0.0	5.3	0.0	0.0	20.0	0.0	72.4	432.5	545.0	17.2	10.4	
06365J420	FA BN 155 SP HVY DIV	MOGAS	0.0	0.0	18.1	13.0	0.0	21.3	0.0	0.0	0.0	0.0	0.0	0.0	
		DIESEL	0.0	0.0	5.3	0.0	0.0	20.0	0.0	72.4	432.5	545.0	17.1	10.4	
06365J430	FA BN 155 SP HVY DIV	MOGAS	0.0	0.0	20.2	13.0	0.0	21.3	0.0	0.0	0.0	0.0	0.0	0.0	
		DIESEL	0.0	0.0	5.3	0.0	0.0	20.0	0.0	73.4	441.1	553.9	17.2	11.6	
06366J410	HHB FA BN 155SP HVY DIV	MOGAS	0.0	0.0	10.4	5.4	0.0	13.0	0.0	0.0	0.0	0.0	0.0	0.0	
		DIESEL	0.0	0.0	3.6	0.0	0.0	0.0	0.0	7.0	60.2	62.3	3.0	3.7	
06366J420	HHB FA BN 155SP HVY DIV	MOGAS	0.0	0.0	10.4	5.4	0.0	13.0	0.0	0.0	0.0	0.0	0.0	0.0	
		DIESEL	0.0	0.0	3.6	0.0	0.0	0.0	0.0	7.0	60.2	62.3	3.0	3.7	
06366J430	HHB FA BN 155SP HVY DIV	MOGAS	0.0	0.0	12.5	5.4	0.0	13.0	0.0	0.0	0.0	0.0	0.0	0.0	
		DIESEL	0.0	0.0	3.6	0.0	0.0	0.0	0.0	8.0	68.8	71.2	3.1	4.8	
06367J410	FA BTRY 155SP HVY DIV	MOGAS	0.0	0.0	1.1	0.0	0.0	0.0	0.0	0.0	0.0	0.0	0.0	0.0	
		DIESEL	0.0	0.0	0.6	0.0	0.0	5.0	0.0	19.6	111.6	146.6	2.0	2.2	
06369J410	SVC BTRY 155SP HVY DIV	MOGAS	0.0	0.0	4.5	7.6	0.0	8.3	0.0	0.0	0.0	0.0	0.0	0.0	
		DIESEL	0.0	0.0	0.0	0.0	0.0	5.0	0.0	6.6	37.5	42.9	8.0	0.0	
06398J400	FA BTRY MLRS	MOGAS	0.0	0.0	5.2	1.8	0.0	4.5	0.0	0.0	0.0	0.0	0.0	0.0	
		DIESEL	0.0	0.0	0.0	0.0	0.0	0.0	0.0	15.5	169.4	113.0	7.2	0.0	
07209J400	LRS DET, CAV SQDN, HVY DIV	MOGAS	0.0	0.0	5.6	0.0	0.0	0.0	0.0	0.0	0.0	0.0	0.0	0.0	
		DIESEL	0.0	0.0	0.0	0.0	0.0	0.0	0.0	0.0	0.0	0.0	0.2	0.0	
07245J410	INF BN-MECH E/W BFVS	MOGAS	0.0	0.0	8.5	7.6	0.0	24.1	0.0	0.0	0.0	0.0	0.1	0.0	
		DIESEL	0.0	0.0	1.1	0.0	0.0	12.0	0.0	147.0	1744.3	1130.9	14.2	0.0	
07246J410	HHC INF BN MECH BFVS	MOGAS	0.0	0.0	5.8	7.6	0.0	24.1	0.0	0.0	0.0	0.0	0.1	0.0	
		DIESEL	0.0	0.0	1.1	0.0	0.0	12.0	0.0	54.2	636.3	505.7	12.1	0.0	
07247J410	RIFLE CO INF BN MECH BFVS	MOGAS	0.0	0.0	0.5	0.0	0.0	0.0	0.0	0.0	0.0	0.0	0.0	0.0	
		DIESEL	0.0	0.0	0.0	0.0	0.0	0.0	0.0	19.2	242.6	120.7	0.4	0.0	
07248J400	ANTIARMOR CO INF BN(M) IT	MOGAS	0.0	0.0	0.5	0.0	0.0	0.0	0.0	0.0	0.0	0.0	0.0	0.0	
		DIESEL	0.0	0.0	0.0	0.0	0.0	0.0	0.0	16.0	137.6	142.4	0.4	0.0	
08077J400	MEDICAL CO (MSB) HVY DIV	MOGAS	0.0	0.0	13.7	7.2	0.0	13.0	0.0	0.0	0.0	0.0	0.0	0.0	
		DIESEL	0.0	0.0	2.8	0.0	0.0	5.0	0.0	0.0	0.0	0.0	5.5	0.0	
08078J400	MEDICAL CO (FSB) HVY DIV	MOGAS	0.0	0.0	10.4	5.8	0.0	13.0	0.0	0.0	0.0	0.0	0.0	0.0	
		DIESEL	0.0	0.0	2.2	0.0	0.0	5.0	0.0	5.0	43.0	44.5	3.1	0.0	
09558J400	MSL SPT CO HVY DIV	MOGAS	0.0	0.0	22.7	4.0	0.0	1.0	0.0	0.0	0.0	0.0	0.0	0.0	
		DIESEL	0.0	0.0	40.2	0.0	1.3	5.0	0.0	0.0	0.0	0.0	6.9	0.0	
09558J402	SGT YORK AUG, MSL SPT CO	MOGAS	0.0	0.0	3.0	0.0	0.0	0.0	0.0	0.0	0.0	0.0	0.0	0.0	
		DIESEL	0.0	30.0	26.1	0.0	0.0	0.0	0.0	2.0	36.8	25.5	2.4	0.0	
11035J500	SIG BN HVY DIV	MOGAS	0.0	0.0	141.8	17.8	0.0	15.4	0.0	0.0	0.0	0.0	0.3	0.0	
		DIESEL	0.0	0.0	17.3	0.0	0.0	20.0	0.0	0.0	0.0	0.0	18.4	0.0	
11036J500	HHC SIG BN HEAVY DIV	MOGAS	0.0	0.0	25.1	4.0	0.0	9.4	0.0	0.0	0.0	0.0	0.3	0.0	
		DIESEL	0.0	0.0	0.6	0.0	0.0	5.0	0.0	0.0	0.0	0.0	5.8	0.0	
11037J500	CMB OPS CO	MOGAS	0.0	0.0	35.6	4.0	0.0	1.0	0.0	0.0	0.0	0.0	0.0	0.0	
		DIESEL	0.0	0.0	6.6	0.0	0.0	5.0	0.0	0.0	0.0	0.0	4.4	0.0	
11038J500	FWD COMM CO	MOGAS	0.0	0.0	38.3	4.0	0.0	1.0	0.0	0.0	0.0	0.0	0.0	0.0	
		DIESEL	0.0	0.0	0.6	0.0	0.0	5.0	0.0	0.0	0.0	0.0	3.3	0.0	
11039J500	AREA SIGNAL CO	MOGAS	0.0	0.0	42.8	5.8	0.0	4.0	0.0	0.0	0.0	0.0	0.0	0.0	
		DIESEL	0.0	0.0	9.6	0.0	0.0	5.0	0.0	0.0	0.0	0.0	4.8	0.0	
12114J400	DIVISION BAND	MOGAS	0.0	0.0	0.0	0.0	0.0	0.0	0.0	0.0	0.0	0.0	0.0	0.0	
		DIESEL	0.0	0.0	0.0	0.0	0.0	0.0	0.0	0.0	0.0	0.0	0.0	0.0	
17201J420	CAV BDE AIR ATK (AH-64) (AOE)	MOGAS	0.0	0.0	89.9	86.8	0.0	62.5	0.0	0.0	0.0	0.0	0.0	0.0	
		DIESEL	0.0	36.0	1.7	0.0	9.1	21.0	0.0	81.0	998.8	597.5	46.4	0.6	
		JP4													12985.0
17202J400	HQ & HQ TROOP, CBAA	MOGAS	0.0	0.0	13.2	7.6	0.0	7.4	0.0	0.0	0.0	0.0	0.0	0.0	
		DIESEL	0.0	0.0	0.6	0.0	0.0	0.0	0.0	0.0	0.0	0.0	3.0	0.0	

Figure 10. Bulk POL Planning Factors by Type Unit— Bulk POL Table E (continued)

SUMMARY OF BULK FUEL USAGE BY EQUIPMENT CATEGORY
MX DIV 5-M1 5-BFVS 2-AHB (SRC 87000J440)—(Cont'd)

SRC	UNIT NAME	FUEL TYPE	AB	CE	GN	HG	MH	SG	SV	TI	CC	SR	WV	OV	AV
17205J410	CAV SQDN, CBAA AH-IS HVY DIV	MOGAS	0.0	0.0	18.7	16.6	0.0	23.4	0.0	0.0	0.0	0.0	0.0	0.0	
		DIESEL	0.0	8.0	0.6	0.0	2.6	12.0	0.0	81.0	998.8	597.5	13.7	0.6	
		JP4													1604.8
17206J410	HQ AND HQ TRP, CAV SQDN	MOGAS	0.0	0.0	13.1	16.6	0.0	21.4	0.0	0.0	0.0	0.0	0.0	0.0	
		DIESEL	0.0	8.0	0.6	0.0	2.6	12.0	0.0	13.8	169.7	130.6	12.4	0.6	
		JP4													142.0
17207J410	CAV TRP, CAV SQDN	MOGAS	0.0	0.0	0.0	0.0	0.0	1.0	0.0	0.0	0.0	0.0	0.0	0.0	
		DIESEL	0.0	0.0	0.0	0.0	0.0	0.0	0.0	33.6	414.6	233.4	0.3	0.0	
17208J410	AIR CAV TRP, CAV SQDN	MOGAS	0.0	0.0	0.0	0.0	0.0	0.0	0.0	0.0	0.0	0.0	0.0	0.0	
		DIESEL	0.0	0.0	0.0	0.0	0.0	0.0	0.0	0.0	0.0	0.0	0.2	0.0	
		JP4													731.4
17235J420	TANK BATTALION EQ W/M1	MOGAS	0.0	0.0	3.9	23.6	0.0	16.0	0.0	0.0	0.0	0.0	0.0	0.0	
		DIESEL	0.0	0.0	0.6	0.0	0.0	7.0	0.0	675.8	3865.9	3059.8	14.4	0.0	
17236J420	HHC, TK BN, (M1)	MOGAS	0.0	0.0	3.9	23.6	0.0	16.0	0.0	0.0	0.0	0.0	0.0	0.0	
		DIESEL	0.0	0.0	0.6	0.0	0.0	7.0	0.0	71.0	696.3	560.0	13.3	0.0	
17237J420	TANK CO, (M1)	MOGAS	0.0	0.0	0.0	0.0	0.0	0.0	0.0	0.0	0.0	0.0	0.0	0.0	
		DIESEL	0.0	0.0	0.0	0.0	0.0	0.0	0.0	151.2	792.4	625.0	0.3	0.0	
19217J400	MP CO-HVY DIV	MOGAS	0.0	0.0	4.6	4.0	0.0	1.0	0.0	0.0	0.0	0.0	0.0	0.0	
		DIESEL	0.0	0.0	1.1	0.0	0.0	5.0	0.0	0.0	0.0	0.0	2.5	0.0	
34285J400	MI BN (CEWI) HVY DIV	MOGAS	0.0	0.0	42.9	13.4	0.0	12.0	0.0	0.0	0.0	0.0	0.0	0.0	
		DIESEL	0.0	0.0	15.6	0.0	0.0	17.0	0.0	16.2	132.9	138.9	7.8	0.3	
34286J400	HQ & HQ-OP CO MI BN CEWI DIV	MOGAS	0.0	0.0	0.8	0.0	0.0	0.0	0.0	0.0	0.0	0.0	0.0	0.0	
		DIESEL	0.0	0.0	0.0	0.0	0.0	12.0	0.0	2.0	17.2	17.8	1.8	0.0	
34287J400	C&J CO MI BN CEWI DIV	MOGAS	0.0	0.0	7.2	0.0	0.0	0.0	0.0	0.0	0.0	0.0	0.0	0.0	
		DIESEL	0.0	0.0	15.0	0.0	0.0	0.0	0.0	12.0	103.2	106.8	1.6	0.3	
34289J400	SVC SPT CO MI BN CEWI DIV	MOGAS	0.0	0.0	34.8	13.4	0.0	12.0	0.0	0.0	0.0	0.0	0.0	0.0	
		DIESEL	0.0	0.0	0.6	0.0	0.0	5.0	0.0	2.2	12.5	14.3	4.4	0.0	
42004J400	SUP CO FWD SPT BN HVY DIV	MOGAS	0.0	0.0	1.7	3.6	0.0	7.9	0.0	0.0	0.0	0.0	0.0	0.0	
		DIESEL	0.0	14.0	0.6	0.0	27.6	5.0	0.0	0.0	0.0	0.0	5.2	0.0	
42007J400	S&S CO MAIN SPT BN HVY DIV	MOGAS	0.0	0.0	6.6	11.6	0.0	35.8	0.0	0.0	0.0	0.0	0.0	0.0	
		DIESEL	0.0	21.0	30.6	0.0	35.9	5.0	0.0	0.0	0.0	0.0	10.9	0.0	
43004J400	MAINT CO, FWD SPT BN, HVY DIV	MOGAS	0.0	0.0	25.4	16.0	0.0	20.4	0.0	0.0	0.0	0.0	0.0	0.0	
		DIESEL	0.0	7.0	11.1	0.0	9.8	7.0	0.0	3.0	45.4	34.4	10.4	0.0	
43004J401	TK SYSTEM SPT TM	MOGAS	0.0	0.0	1.1	0.0	0.0	5.6	0.0	0.0	0.0	0.0	0.0	0.0	
		DIESEL	0.0	0.0	0.6	0.0	0.0	0.0	0.0	1.0	8.6	8.9	0.8	0.0	
43004J402	INF SYS(M) SPT TM	MOGAS	0.0	0.0	2.4	0.0	0.0	5.6	0.0	0.0	0.0	0.0	0.0	0.0	
		DIESEL	0.0	0.0	0.0	0.0	0.0	0.0	0.0	1.0	8.6	8.9	0.8	0.0	
43007J400	LIGHT MAINT CO HVY DIV	MOGAS	0.0	0.0	42.3	11.6	1.4	24.9	0.0	0.0	0.0	0.0	0.0	0.0	
		DIESEL	0.0	0.0	64.0	0.0	17.0	0.0	0.0	0.0	0.0	0.0	15.0	0.0	
43008J400	HEAVY MAINT CO HVY DIV	MOGAS	0.0	0.0	14.5	28.0	0.0	41.3	0.0	0.0	0.0	0.0	0.0	0.0	
		DIESEL	0.0	14.0	13.5	0.0	8.5	7.0	0.0	4.0	54.0	43.3	7.7	0.0	
44165J400	ADA BN HVY DIV	MOGAS	0.0	0.0	59.4	14.8	0.0	17.8	0.0	0.0	0.0	0.0	0.1	0.0	
		DIESEL	0.0	36.0	2.3	0.0	0.0	28.0	0.0	45.0	503.3	553.3	18.0	0.0	
44166J400	HHB, ADA BN, HEAVY DIV	MOGAS	0.0	0.0	20.2	14.8	0.0	11.9	0.0	0.0	0.0	0.0	0.0	0.0	
		DIESEL	0.0	0.0	0.6	0.0	0.0	13.0	0.0	3.0	25.8	26.7	4.7	0.0	
44167J400	ADA BTRY, GUN (SP)/STINGER	MOGAS	0.0	0.0	13.1	0.0	0.0	1.9	0.0	0.0	0.0	0.0	0.0	0.0	
		DIESEL	0.0	12.0	0.6	0.0	0.0	5.0	0.0	14.0	159.2	175.5	4.4	0.0	
55087J400	TMT CO MAIN SPT BN HVY DIV	MOGAS	0.0	0.0	1.7	8.0	0.0	2.4	0.0	0.0	0.0	0.0	0.0	0.0	
		DIESEL	0.0	0.0	1.1	0.0	0.0	5.0	0.0	0.0	0.0	0.0	19.9	0.0	
55427J410	TAMC, SPT CMD, HVY DIV	MOGAS	0.0	0.0	16.7	13.0	1.5	4.4	0.0	0.0	0.0	0.0	0.0	0.0	
		DIESEL	0.0	16.0	45.2	0.0	8.5	5.0	0.0	0.0	0.0	0.0	5.1	0.0	
		JP4													332.0
63001J420	SPT CMD, 5 × 5 × 2, HVY DIV	MOGAS	0.0	0.0	252.0	167.2	2.9	314.3	0.0	0.0	0.0	0.0	0.3	0.0	
		DIESEL	0.0	144.0	302.5	0.0	183.4	101.0	0.0	40.0	441.8	394.7	146.1	0.0	
		JP4													332.0
63002J400	HHC/MMC, SPT CMD, HVY DIV	MOGAS	0.0	0.0	0.8	7.6	0.0	7.0	0.0	0.0	0.0	0.0	0.0	0.0	
		DIESEL	0.0	0.0	25.5	0.0	0.0	0.0	0.0	0.0	0.0	0.0	3.8	0.0	
63005J410	FWD SPT BN (2 × 1) HVY DIV	MOGAS	0.0	0.0	42.1	25.4	0.0	59.2	0.0	0.0	0.0	0.0	0.1	0.0	
		DIESEL	0.0	21.0	16.5	0.0	37.4	23.0	0.0	11.0	114.2	105.6	22.1	0.0	
63005J420	FWD SPT BN (2 × 2) HVY DIV	MOGAS	0.0	0.0	44.5	25.4	0.0	64.9	0.0	0.0	0.0	0.0	0.1	0.0	
		DIESEL	0.0	21.0	16.5	0.0	37.4	23.0	0.0	12.0	122.8	114.5	22.9	0.0	
63005J430	FWD SPT BN (1 × 2) HVY DIV	MOGAS	0.0	0.0	43.4	25.4	0.0	59.2	0.0	0.0	0.0	0.0	0.1	0.0	
		DIESEL	0.0	21.0	15.9	0.0	37.4	23.0	0.0	11.0	114.2	105.6	22.1	0.0	
63006J400	HHD,FWD SPT BN,HEAVY DIV	MOGAS	0.0	0.0	0.0	0.0	0.0	1.0	0.0	0.0	0.0	0.0	0.1	0.0	
		DIESEL	0.0	0.0	1.5	0.0	0.0	6.0	0.0	0.0	0.0	0.0	1.0	0.0	
63135J400	MAIN SUPPORT BN, HVY DIV	MOGAS	0.0	0.0	104.4	70.4	1.4	119.4	0.0	0.0	0.0	0.0	0.0	0.0	
		DIESEL	0.0	65.0	182.8	0.0	62.7	27.0	0.0	6.0	90.7	68.9	69.6	0.0	
63136J400	HHD,MAIN SPT BN, HVY DIV	MOGAS	0.0	0.0	0.0	0.0	0.0	1.0	0.0	0.0	0.0	0.0	0.0	0.0	
		DIESEL	0.0	0.0	4.5	0.0	0.0	0.0	0.0	0.0	0.0	0.0	1.0	0.0	
87000J440	MX DIV, 5-M1, 5-BFVS, 2-AH	MOGAS	0.0	2.0	866.9	564.6	2.9	894.6	0.0	0.0	0.0	0.0	1.6	0.0	
		DIESEL	86.4	284.0	392.7	0.0	201.0	416.0	0.0	4720.0	33537.5	26069.8	508.0	33.3	
		JP4													13317.0
87004J420	HHC INFANTRY DIVISION (MECH)	MOGAS	0.0	0.0	40.2	7.6	0.0	12.0	0.0	0.0	0.0	0.0	0.0	0.0	
		DIESEL	0.0	0.0	1.5	0.0	0.0	0.0	0.0	5.0	43.0	44.5	5.1	0.0	
87042J410	HHC ARMD DIV BDE	MOGAS	0.0	0.0	6.2	5.8	0.0	4.0	0.0	0.0	0.0	0.0	0.0	0.0	
		DIESEL	0.0	0.0	0.0	0.0	0.0	5.0	0.0	9.2	72.7	76.6	1.6	0.0	
87042J420	HHC INF DIV (MECH) BDE	MOGAS	0.0	0.0	8.9	5.8	0.0	4.0	0.0	0.0	0.0	0.0	0.0	0.0	
		DIESEL	0.0	0.0	0.0	0.0	0.0	5.0	0.0	9.2	72.7	76.6	1.6	0.0	

Figure 10. Bulk POL Planning Factors by Type Unit—Bulk POL Table E (continued)

SUMMARY OF BULK FUEL USAGE BY EQUIPMENT CATEGORY
HSB MECH 1 BN TMK-60 2BN MECH M-113 (SRC 87100J420)

SRC	UNIT NAME	FUEL TYPE	AB	CE	GN	HG	MH	SG	SV	TI	CC	SR	WV	OV	AV
05127J400	ENGR CO HVY SEP BDE	MOGAS	0.0	0.0	3.9	9.4	0.0	21.4	0.0	0.0	0.0	0.0	0.0	0.0	
		DIESEL	0.0	22.0	0.0	0.0	0.0	0.0	0.0	43.5	485.0	398.1	6.2	0.0	
06375J420	FA BN, 155-MM SP, HSB (AOE)	MOGAS	0.0	0.0	24.3	35.8	0.0	26.4	0.0	0.0	0.0	0.0	0.0	0.0	
		DIESEL	0.0	0.0	3.6	0.0	0.0	0.0	0.0	72.4	432.5	545.0	16.5	11.3	
06376J420	HHB, FA BN, 155 SP SEP BD	MOGAS	0.0	0.0	19.6	7.2	0.0	8.0	0.0	0.0	0.0	0.0	0.0	0.0	
		DIESEL	0.0	0.0	3.0	0.0	0.0	0.0	0.0	7.0	60.2	62.3	4.2	4.6	
06377J400	FA BATTERY, 155-MM SP	MOGAS	0.0	0.0	0.8	7.6	0.0	4.0	0.0	0.0	0.0	0.0	0.0	0.0	
		DIESEL	0.0	0.0	0.0	0.0	0.0	0.0	0.0	19.6	111.6	146.6	2.3	2.2	
06379J400	SVC BTRY, FA BN, 155-MM SP	MOGAS	0.0	0.0	2.2	5.8	0.0	6.4	0.0	0.0	0.0	0.0	0.0	0.0	
		DIESEL	0.0	0.0	0.6	0.0	0.0	0.0	0.0	6.6	37.5	42.9	5.3	0.0	
07245J420	INF BN-MECH E/W M113	MOGAS	0.0	0.0	8.8	7.6	0.0	26.1	0.0	0.0	0.0	0.0	0.0	0.0	
		DIESEL	0.0	0.0	1.1	0.0	0.0	12.0	0.0	124.8	1072.3	1105.1	12.0	0.0	
07246J420	HHC INF BN MECH M113	MOGAS	0.0	0.0	6.1	7.6	0.0	26.1	0.0	0.0	0.0	0.0	0.1	0.0	
		DIESEL	0.0	0.0	1.1	0.0	0.0	12.0	0.0	44.8	384.3	393.1	9.9	0.0	
07247J420	RIFLE CO INF BN MECH M113	MOGAS	0.0	0.0	0.5	0.0	0.0	0.0	0.0	0.0	0.0	0.0	0.0	0.0	
		DIESEL	0.0	0.0	0.0	0.0	0.0	0.0	0.0	16.0	137.6	142.4	0.4	0.0	
07248J400	ANTIARMOR CO INF BN(M) IT	MOGAS	0.0	0.0	0.5	0.0	0.0	0.0	0.0	0.0	0.0	0.0	0.0	0.0	
		DIESEL	0.0	0.0	0.0	0.0	0.0	0.0	0.0	16.0	137.6	142.4	0.4	0.0	
08247J500	MEDICAL CO SEP BDE (HEAVY)	MOGAS	0.0	0.0	11.3	9.4	0.0	13.0	0.0	0.0	0.0	0.0	0.0	0.0	
		DIESEL	0.0	0.0	2.2	0.0	0.0	5.0	0.0	6.0	51.6	53.4	2.9	0.0	
17007J410	SEPARATE CAV TRP (M113)	MOGAS	0.0	0.0	0.5	3.6	0.0	4.4	0.0	0.0	0.0	0.0	0.0	0.0	
		DIESEL	0.0	0.0	0.0	0.0	0.0	0.0	0.0	27.2	220.3	236.8	1.6	0.0	
17235J410	TANK BATTALION, EQ/W, M60	MOGAS	0.0	0.0	3.9	23.6	0.0	16.0	0.0	0.0	0.0	0.0	0.0	0.0	
		DIESEL	0.0	0.0	0.6	0.0	0.0	7.0	0.0	165.4	2121.9	1560.5	11.4	0.0	
17236J410	HHC, TK BN, M60	MOGAS	0.0	0.0	3.9	23.6	0.0	16.0	0.0	0.0	0.0	0.0	0.0	0.0	
		DIESEL	0.0	0.0	0.6	0.0	0.0	7.0	0.0	53.4	636.2	508.3	10.3	0.0	
17237J410	TK CO, TK BN, M60	MOGAS	0.0	0.0	0.0	0.0	0.0	0.0	0.0	0.0	0.0	0.0	0.0	0.0	
		DIESEL	0.0	0.0	0.0	0.0	0.0	0.0	0.0	28.0	371.4	263.1	0.3	0.0	
34144J400	MI CO (CEWI) HVY SEP BDE	MOGAS	0.0	0.0	17.2	0.0	0.0	2.4	0.0	0.0	0.0	0.0	0.0	0.0	
		DIESEL	0.0	0.0	0.6	0.0	0.0	5.0	0.0	8.0	68.8	71.2	3.1	0.0	
42084J400	S&T CO, SPT BN, SEP HVY B	MOGAS	0.0	0.0	3.1	7.6	0.0	14.0	0.0	0.0	0.0	0.0	0.0	0.0	
		DIESEL	0.0	28.0	12.6	0.0	22.6	5.0	0.0	0.0	0.0	0.0	12.3	0.0	
43079J400	ORG (MT) CO SPT BN HSB	MOGAS	0.0	0.0	12.6	23.2	0.0	15.7	0.0	0.0	0.0	0.0	0.0	0.0	
		DIESEL	0.0	7.0	25.1	0.0	11.1	12.0	0.0	2.0	36.8	25.5	9.3	0.0	
43079J401	TK SYSTEM SPT TM	MOGAS	0.0	0.0	1.1	0.0	0.0	5.6	0.0	0.0	0.0	0.0	0.0	0.0	
		DIESEL	0.0	0.0	0.0	0.0	0.0	0.0	0.0	1.0	8.6	8.9	0.8	0.0	
43079J402	INF SYS(M) SPT TM	MOGAS	0.0	0.0	2.4	0.0	0.0	5.6	0.0	0.0	0.0	0.0	0.0	0.0	
		DIESEL	0.0	0.0	0.0	0.0	0.0	0.0	0.0	1.0	8.6	8.9	0.8	0.0	
43079J403	1-ARTY SYS SPT TM	MOGAS	0.0	0.0	4.3	0.0	0.0	5.6	0.0	0.0	0.0	0.0	0.0	0.0	
		DIESEL	0.0	0.0	0.0	0.0	0.0	0.0	0.0	1.0	8.6	8.9	0.8	0.0	
43079J404	1-MSL SPT SEC	MOGAS	0.0	0.0	1.6	0.0	0.0	0.0	0.0	0.0	0.0	0.0	0.0	0.0	
		DIESEL	0.0	0.0	1.5	0.0	0.0	0.0	0.0	0.0	0.0	0.0	0.3	0.0	
43079J405	1-ELEC/COMSEC REP SEC	MOGAS	0.0	0.0	4.8	0.0	0.0	0.0	0.0	0.0	0.0	0.0	0.0	0.0	
		DIESEL	0.0	0.0	0.0	0.0	0.0	0.0	0.0	0.0	0.0	0.0	0.5	0.0	
63085J420	SPT BN, HVY BDE, (SEP) (1x2)	MOGAS	0.0	0.0	53.9	47.8	0.0	70.4	0.0	0.0	0.0	0.0	0.0	0.0	
		DIESEL	0.0	35.0	84.9	0.0	33.7	22.0	0.0	12.0	122.8	114.5	31.8	0.0	
63086J400	HHS, SPT BN HVY BDE (SEP)	MOGAS	0.0	0.0	8.7	7.6	0.0	5.0	0.0	0.0	0.0	0.0	0.0	0.0	
		DIESEL	0.0	0.0	42.0	0.0	0.0	0.0	0.0	0.0	0.0	0.0	3.0	0.0	
87100J420	HSB, ME, 1BN TKM60, 2BN MECH M11	MOGAS	0.0	0.0	153.6	148.4	0.0	200.9	0.0	0.0	0.0	0.0	0.0	0.0	
		DIESEL	0.0	57.0	91.9	0.0	33.7	58.0	0.0	589.3	5685.0	5230.7	10.1	11.3	
87102J420	HHC HVY SEP BDE (MECH)	MOGAS	0.0	0.0	32.3	13.0	0.0	7.4	0.0	0.0	0.0	0.0	0.0	0.0	
		DIESEL	0.0	0.0	0.0	0.0	0.0	0.0	0.0	11.2	89.9	94.4	6.2	0.0	

SUMMARY OF BULK FUEL USAGE BY EQUIPMENT CATEGORY
HSB, ARM 2 BN TMK1, BN MECH BFV (SRC 87100J430)—(Cont'd)

SRC	UNIT NAME	FUEL TYPE	AB	CE	GN	HG	MH	SG	SV	TI	CC	SR	WV	OV
05127J400	ENGR CO HVY SEP BDE	MOGAS	0.0	0.0	3.9	9.4	0.0	21.4	0.0	0.0	0.0	0.0	0.0	0.0
		DIESEL	0.0	22.0	0.0	0.0	0.0	0.0	0.0	43.5	485.0	398.1	6.2	0.0
06375J410	FA BN, 155-MM SP, HSB (AOE)	MOGAS	0.0	0.0	24.3	35.8	0.0	26.4	0.0	0.0	0.0	0.0	0.0	0.0
		DIESEL	0.0	0.0	3.6	0.0	0.0	0.0	0.0	72.4	432.5	545.0	16.5	11.3
06376J410	HHB, FA BN, 155 SP SEP BD	MOGAS	0.0	0.0	19.6	7.2	0.0	8.0	0.0	0.0	0.0	0.0	0.0	0.0
		DIESEL	0.0	0.0	3.0	0.0	0.0	0.0	0.0	7.0	60.2	62.3	4.1	4.6
06377J400	FA BATTERY, 155MM SP	MOGAS	0.0	0.0	0.8	7.6	0.0	4.0	0.0	0.0	0.0	0.0	0.0	0.0
		DIESEL	0.0	0.0	0.0	0.0	0.0	0.0	0.0	19.6	111.6	146.6	2.3	2.2
06379J400	SVC BTRY, FA BN, 155-MM SP	MOGAS	0.0	0.0	2.2	5.8	0.0	6.4	0.0	0.0	0.0	0.0	0.0	0.0
		DIESEL	0.0	0.0	0.6	0.0	0.0	0.0	0.0	6.6	37.5	42.9	5.3	0.0
07245J410	INF BN-MECH E/W BFVS	MOGAS	0.0	0.0	8.5	7.6	0.0	26.1	0.0	0.0	0.0	0.0	0.1	0.0
		DIESEL	0.0	0.0	1.1	0.0	0.0	12.0	0.0	147.0	1744.3	1130.9	14.2	0.0
07246J410	HHC INF BN MECH BFVS	MOGAS	0.0	0.0	5.8	7.6	0.0	26.1	0.0	0.0	0.0	0.0	0.1	0.0
		DIESEL	0.0	0.0	1.1	0.0	0.0	12.0	0.0	54.2	636.3	505.7	12.1	0.0
07247J410	RIFLE CO INF BN MECH BFVS	MOGAS	0.0	0.0	0.5	0.0	0.0	0.0	0.0	0.0	0.0	0.0	0.0	0.0
		DIESEL	0.0	0.0	0.0	0.0	0.0	0.0	0.0	19.2	242.6	120.7	0.4	0.0
07248J400	ANTIARMOR CO INF BN(M) IT	MOGAS	0.0	0.0	0.5	0.0	0.0	0.0	0.0	0.0	0.0	0.0	0.0	0.0
		DIESEL	0.0	0.0	0.0	0.0	0.0	0.0	0.0	16.0	137.6	142.4	0.4	0.0
08247J500	MEDICAL CO SEP BDE (HVY DIV)	MOGAS	0.0	0.0	11.3	9.4	0.0	13.0	0.0	0.0	0.0	0.0	0.0	0.0
		DIESEL	0.0	0.0	2.2	0.0	0.0	5.0	0.0	6.0	51.6	53.4	2.9	0.0
17007J420	SEPARATE CAV TRP (M3)	MOGAS	0.0	0.0	0.5	3.6	0.0	4.0	0.0	0.0	0.0	0.0	0.0	0.0
		DIESEL	0.0	0.0	0.0	0.0	0.0	0.0	0.0	34.6	423.2	242.3	2.0	0.0
17235J420	TANK BATTALION EQ W/M1	MOGAS	0.0	0.0	3.9	23.6	0.0	16.0	0.0	0.0	0.0	0.0	0.0	0.0
		DIESEL	0.0	0.0	0.6	0.0	0.0	7.0	0.0	675.8	3865.9	3059.8	14.4	0.0
17236J420	HHC, TK BN, (M1)	MOGAS	0.0	0.0	3.9	23.6	0.0	16.0	0.0	0.0	0.0	0.0	0.0	0.0
		DIESEL	0.0	0.0	0.6	0.0	0.0	7.0	0.0	71.0	696.3	560.0	13.3	0.0
17237J420	TANK CO, (M1)	MOGAS	0.0	0.0	0.0	0.0	0.0	0.0	0.0	0.0	0.0	0.0	0.0	0.0
		DIESEL	0.0	0.0	0.0	0.0	0.0	0.0	0.0	151.2	792.4	625.0	0.3	0.0
34144J400	MI CO (CEWI) HVY SEP BDE	MOGAS	0.0	0.0	17.2	0.0	0.0	2.4	0.0	0.0	0.0	0.0	0.0	0.0
		DIESEL	0.0	0.0	0.6	0.0	0.0	5.0	0.0	8.0	68.8	71.2	3.1	0.0

Figure 10. Bulk POL Planning Factors by Type Unit—Bulk POL Table E (continued)

SUMMARY OF BULK FUEL USAGE BY EQUIPMENT CATEGORY
1BN TMK-60 2BN MECH M-11 (SRC 87100J420)—(Cont'd)

SRC	UNIT NAME	FUEL TYPE	AB	CE	GN	HG	MH	SG	SV	TI	CC	SR	WV	OV	AV
42084J400	S&T CO, SPT BN, SEP HVY B	MOGAS	0.0	0.0	0.0	3.1	7.6	0.0	14.0	0.0	0.0	0.0	0.0	0.0	
		DIESEL	0.0	0.0	28.0	12.6	0.0	22.6	5.0	0.0	0.0	0.0	12.3	0.0	
43079J400	ORD (MT) CO SPT BN HSB	MOGAS	0.0	0.0	0.0	12.6	23.2	0.0	15.7	0.0	0.0	0.0	0.0	0.0	
		DIESEL	2.0	0.0	7.0	25.1	0.0	11.1	12.0	0.0	36.8	25.5	9.3	0.0	
43079J401	TK SYSTEM SPT TM	MOGAS	0.0	0.0	1.1	0.0	0.0	5.6	0.0	0.0	0.0	0.0	0.0	0.0	
		DIESEL	0.0	0.0	0.0	0.0	0.0	0.0	0.0	1.0	8.6	8.9	0.8	0.0	
43079J402	INF SYS(M) SPT TM	MOGAS	0.0	0.0	2.4	0.0	0.0	5.6	0.0	0.0	0.0	0.0	0.0	0.0	
		DIESEL	0.0	0.0	0.0	0.0	0.0	0.0	0.0	1.0	8.6	8.9	0.8	0.0	
43079J403	1-ARTY SYS SPT TM	MOGAS	0.0	0.0	4.3	0.0	0.0	5.6	0.0	0.0	0.0	0.0	0.0	0.0	
		DIESEL	0.0	0.0	0.0	0.0	0.0	0.0	0.0	1.0	8.6	8.9	0.8	0.0	
43079J404	1-MSL SPT SEC	MOGAS	0.0	0.0	1.6	0.0	0.0	0.0	0.0	0.0	0.0	0.0	0.0	0.0	
		DIESEL	0.0	0.0	1.5	0.0	0.0	0.0	0.0	0.0	0.0	0.0	0.3	0.0	
43079J405	1-ELEC/COMSEC REP SEC	MOGAS	0.0	0.0	4.8	0.0	0.0	0.0	0.0	0.0	0.0	0.0	0.0	0.0	
		DIESEL	0.0	0.0	0.0	0.0	0.0	0.0	0.0	0.0	0.0	0.0	0.5	0.0	
63085J410	SPT BN, HVY BDE, (SEP) (2 × 1)	MOGAS	0.0	0.0	50.9	47.8	0.0	70.4	0.0	0.0	0.0	0.0	0.0	0.0	
		DIESEL	0.0	35.0	83.4	0.0	33.7	22.0	0.0	12.0	122.8	114.5	31.8	0.0	
63086J400	HHC, SPT BN, HVY BDE (SEP)	MOGAS	0.0	0.0	8.7	7.6	0.0	5.0	0.0	0.0	0.0	0.0	0.0	0.0	
		DIESEL	0.0	0.0	42.0	0.0	0.0	0.0	0.0	0.0	0.0	0.0	2.7	0.0	
87100J430	HSB, AR 2BN TKM1, 1BN MECH FV	MOGAS	0.0	0.0	150.3	164.4	0.0	191.7	0.0	0.0	0.0	0.0	0.2	0.0	
		DIESEL	0.0	57.0	89.9	0.0	33.7	53.0	0.0	1680.3	11098.3	8716.1	111.1	11.3	
87102J410	HHC HVY SEP BDE (ARMOR)	MOGAS	0.0	0.0	37.1	13.0	0.0	8.8	0.0	0.0	0.0	0.0	0.0	0.0	
		DIESEL	0.0	0.0	0.0	0.0	0.0	0.0	0.0	11.2	89.9	94.4	6.2	0.0	

Figure 11. Weights, Volumes, and Conversion Factors for Petroleum Products

	1	2	3	4	5	6	7	8	9	10	11	12	13	14	15	16	17
				Cu Ft		Conversion factors									Cap of veh for carrying filled containers[3]		
1	Product	Packaging	Wt (lb)	Actual	Planning factor	Gal to lb	Lb to gal	Gal per STON	Gal per LTON	Gal per MTON[1]	Bbl per LTON[1]	Packages per STON	Packages per LTON	Packages per MTON	1½-ton trk	2½-ton trk	5-ton trk
2	AVGAS	Bulk				5.90	0.169	339.0	379.7		9.04						
3		55-gal drums[3]	373.0	9.03	11	6.91	0.145	289.4	324.2	187.8		5.36	6.00	3.48	8	14	28
4		55-gal drums[4]	389.0	8.80	11	7.20	0.139	277.8	311.1	192.8		5.14	5.76	3.57	8	13	26
5		55-gal drums[5]	364.0	9.20	11	6.90	0.145	289.9	324.6	181.2		5.49	6.15	3.42	9	14	28
6		5-gal cans[6]	40.5	0.81	1	8.00	0.125	250.0	280.0	200.0		49.40	55.30	40.00	74	124	248
7	Jet fuel (JP-4)	Bulk				6.42	0.156	312.0	349.4		8.058						
8		55-gal drums[3]	399.0	9.03	11	7.39	0.135	270.0	302.4	187.8		5.01	5.61	3.48	8	13	25
9		55-gal drums[4]	415.0	8.80	11	7.68	0.130	260.0	291.2	192.7		4.82	5.40	3.57	8	12	24
10		55-gal drums[5]	392.0	9.20	11	7.40	0.135	270.0	302.4	181.2		5.10	5.71	3.42	8	14	28
11	MOGAS	Bulk				6.11	0.164	327.3	366.6		8.73						
12		55-gal drums[3]	384.0	9.03	11	7.11	0.141	281.2	315.1	187.8		5.21	5.83	3.48	8	13	26
13		55-gal drums[4]	400.0	8.80	11	7.41	0.135	269.9	302.3	192.8		5.00	5.60	3.57	8	13	26
14		55-gal drums[5]	376.0	9.20	11	7.09	0.141	282.1	315.9	181.2		5.32	5.96	3.42	8	14	28
15		5-gal cans[6]	41.6	0.81	1	8.32	0.120	240.4	269.2	200.0		48.10	53.80	40.00	73	121	242
16	Diesel Fuel	Bulk				6.99	0.143	286.1	320.5		7.63						
17		55-gal drums[3]	432.0	9.03	11	8.00	0.125	250.0	280.0	187.8		4.63	5.19	3.48	7	12	24
18		55-gal drums[4]	448.0	8.80	11	8.30	0.120	241.0	269.9	192.7		4.66	5.00	3.57	7	12	24
19		55-gal drums[5]	430.0	9.20	11	8.11	0.123	246.6	276.2	181.2		4.65	5.21	3.42	7	12	24
20		5-gal cans[6]	46.0	0.81	1	9.20	0.109	317.4	243.5	200.0		43.50	48.70	40.00	66	109	218
21	Kerosene	Bulk				6.80	0.147	294.1	329.4		7.84						
22		55-gal drums[3]	421.0	9.03	11	7.80	0.128	256.4	287.1	187.8		4.75	5.32	3.48	8	12	24
23		55-gal drums[4]	437.0	8.80	11	8.09	0.124	247.2	276.9	192.8		4.58	5.13	3.57	7	12	24
24		55-gal drums[5]	351.0	9.20	11	6.62	0.151	302.1	338.3	181.2		5.70	6.38	3.42	9	15	30
25		5-gal cans[6]	45.0	0.81	1	9.00	0.111	222.2	248.9	200.0		44.40	49.80	40.00	67	112	224
26	Lub oils	Bulk				7.60	0.132	263.2	294.7		7.02						
27		55-gal drums[3]	472.0	9.03	11	8.58	0.117	233.1	261.0	191.3		4.24	4.75	3.48	7	11	22
28		55-gal drums[4]	488.0	8.80	11	8.87	0.113	225.5	252.5	196.4		4.10	4.59	3.57	7	11	22
29		55-gal drums[5]	462.0	9.20	11	8.56	0.117	233.6	261.7	184.6		4.33	4.85	3.42	7	11	22
30		5-gal cans[6]	49.0	0.81	1	9.80	0.102	204.1	228.6	181.2		40.80	45.70	40.00	62	103	206
31		1-qt cans (12 per case)	35.0	0.88	1							58.00	64.90	40.00	86	143	286
32		1-qt cans (24 per case)	60.0	1.60	2							33.40	37.30	20.00	50	84	168
33		5-qt cans (6 per case)	77.0	1.90	2							26.00	29.10	20.00	39	65	130
34	Greases	25-lb pails	29.0	0.95	1							69.00	77.20	40.00	104	173	346
35		5-lb cans (6 per case)	44.0	1.10	2							45.40	50.90	20.00	69	114	227
	Fog oils:																
36	SGF1	Bulk				7.11	0.140	281.0	314.0		7.49						
37		55-gal drums[3]	438.0	9.03	11	8.11	0.123	246.6	276.2	191.3		4.50	5.02	3.48	7	11	22
38		55-gal drums[4]	588.0	8.80	11	8.40	0.110	238.0	266.6	196.4		4.32	4.84	3.57	7	11	22
39		55-gal drums[5]	421.0	9.20	11	8.10	0.123	246.9	276.5	184.6		4.57	5.12	3.42	7	11	22

Figure 11. Weights, Volumes, and Conversion Factors for Petroleum Products (continued)

1		2	3	4	5	6	7	8	9	10	11	12	13	14	15	16	17
				Cu Ft		Conversion factors									Cap of veh for carrying filled containers[3]		
1	Product	Packaging	Wt (lb)	Actual	Planning factor	Gal to lb	Lb to gal	Gal per STON	Gal per LTON	Gal per MTON[1]	Bbl per LTON[1]	Packages per STON	Packages per LTON	Packages per MTON	1½-ton trk	2½-ton trk	5-ton trk
40	SGF2	Bulk				6.99	0.143	286.0	320.0		7.63						
41		55-gal drums[3]	431.0	9.03	11	7.99	0.120	250.3	280.3	191.3		4.54	5.09	3.48	7	11	22
42		55-gal drums[4]	616.0	8.80	11	8.28	0.120	241.5	270.5	196.4		4.39	4.90	3.57	7	11	22
43		55-gal drums[5]	478.0	9.20	11	7.90	0.121	253.1	283.5	184.6		4.68	5.25	3.42	7	11	23

FOOTNOTES:

[1]For ocean-shipping, storage, and pipeline computations, bulk petroleum products usually are measured in bbl of 42 gal each or in LTON.

[2]Based on authorized loads in STON. When overloads are authorized, these quantities may be increased to the cubic capacity of the veh or to 100-percent overweight, whichever limit is reached first.

[3]18-gauge standard — weighs 54 lb empty — filled to 54 gal with light products, 55 gal with heavy products. Federal Specification PPP-D-729, Amendment 1.

[4]16-gauge standard — weighs 70 lb empty — filled to 54 gal with light products, 55 gal with heavy products. Federal Specification PPP-D-729, Amendment 1.

[5]18-gauge limited standard — weighs 52 lb empty — filled to 53 lb with light products, 54 gal with heavy products, Federal Specification PPP-D-729.

[6]For planning purposes, wt of MOGAS may be taken as 42 lb and wt of lub oil for engines as 50 lb per 5-gal can, including wt of can. Cans, 5-gal, weigh approximately 11 lb empty.

CONSIDERATION:

- Factors in this table are based on US gal: 1 imperial gallon = 1.2010 US gallons
1 liter = 0.2642 US gallons

Figure 12. Ammunition Expenditures per Type Unit per Weapon per Day in STONs

Weapon	No. of wpns	Packed wt/rd	Defense of Position: First day Rds/wpn	Total rds	STON	Succeeding days Rds/wpn	Total rds	STON	Attack of Position (deliberately organized): First day Rds/wpn	Total rds	STON	Succeeding days Rds/wpn	Total rds	STON	Protracted period Rds/wpn	Total rds	STON
Armored Division (AIM)			Part A. Armored Division (AIM)														
Armament pod, acft, 7.62-mm mg, M18	6	.093	6,000	36,000	1.7	3,600	21,600	1.0	4,980	29,880	1.4	2,689	16,134	.8	1,500	9,000	.4
Armament subsystem, helicopter, 20mm auto-gun, M35	4	.80	3,000	12,000	4.8	1,800	7,200	2.9	2,490	9,960	4.0	1,345	5,380	2.2	750	3,000	1.2
Armament subsystem, helicopter, 7.62mm mg, lt, M23	13	.093	840	10,920	.5	509	6,617	.3	700	9,100	.4	382	4,966	.2	213	2,769	.1
Armament subsystem, helicopter																	
7.62mm mg	9	.093	2,250	20,250	1.0	1,350	12,150	.6	1,868	16,812	.8	1,009	9,081	.4	563	5,067	.2
40mm lchr	9	.750	321	2,889	1.1	193	1,737	.7	266	2,394	.9	144	1,296	.5	80	720	.3
Hi rate, M28, A1																	
Armored reconnaissance airborne assault vehicle, M551																	
Ctg, 152mm	27	60.00	9	243	7.3	5	135	4.1	7	189	5.7	4	108	3.2	2	54	1.6
S1B (Shillelagh)	27	112.00	7	189	10.6	9	243	13.6	6	162	9.1	7	189	10.6	3	81	4.5
Gun, ADA SP, 20mm, M163	24	1.00	6,000	144,000	72.0	3,600	86,400	43.2	4,980	119,520	60.0	2,689	64,536	32.3	1,500	36,000	18.0
Howitzer, 155mm, SP, M109	54	135.7	203	10,962	743.8	207	11,178	758.4	146	7,884	534.9	153	8,262	560.6	166	8,964	608.2
Howitzer, 8 in, SP, M110	12	262.50	177	2,124	278.8	164	1,968	258.3	130	1,560	204.8	127	1,524	200.0	118	1,416	185.9
Lchr, GM, M222 (Dragon)	137	67.00	3	411	13.8	4	548	18.4	2	274	9.2	3	411	13.8	1	137	4.6
Lchr, grenade, 40mm, M203	1,061	.750	32	33,952	12.7	19	20,159	7.6	27	28,647	10.8	15	15,915	6.0	8	8,488	3.2
Lchr, rkt acft, 2.75 in, M158A41	18	27.00	42	756	10.2	25	450	6.1	35	630	8.5	19	342	4.6	11	198	2.7
Lchr, rkt acft, 2.75 in, 19 tube (repairable), M200A1	10	27.00	114	1,140	15.4	68	680	9.2	95	950	12.8	51	510	6.9	29	290	3.9
Lchr, rkt, multiple, 155 mm, M91	9	93.33	See note 2														
Lchr, rkt, 66 mm, M72 (LAW)	2,400	7.80	NA	700	2.7	NA	455	1.7	NA	595	2.3	NA	301	1.2	NA	175	0.7
Lchr, rkt, 66 mm, 4-tube, M202, A1	85	8.75	16	1,360	5.9	10	850	3.7	14	1,190	5.2	7	595	2.6	4	340	1.5
Lchr, tubular, GM (TOW)	90	87.00	9	810	35.2	10	900	39.2	7	630	27.4	8	720	31.3	4	360	15.7
Machine gun, .50 cal, M2	1,195	.395	263	314,285	62.1	159	190,005	37.5	219	261,705	51.7	120	143,400	28.3	67	80,065	15.8
Machine gun, 7.62mm, M60	611	.093	649	396,539	18.4	393	240,123	11.2	541	330.551	15.4	295	180.245	8.4	164	100,204	4.7
Machine gun, 7.62mm, six barrels, M134	9	.093	6,000	54,000	2.5	3,600	32,400	1.5	4,980	44,820	2.1	2,689	24,201	1.1	1,500	13,500	.6
Mortar, 81mm, M29, A1	45	17.32	145	6,525	56.5	88	3,960	34.3	121	5,445	47.2	66	2,970	25.7	37	1,665	14.4
Mortar, 4.2 in, M24, A1	53	40.00	163	8,639	172.8	99	5,274	104.9	136	7,208	144.2	74	3,922	78.4	41	2,173	43.5
Rifle, 5.56mm, M16, A1	13,160	.042	148	1,947,680	40.9	90	1,184,400	24.9	124	1,631,840	34.3	67	881,720	18.5	38	500,080	10.5
Rifle, recoilless, 90mm, M67	8	27.50	19	144	1.9	11	88	1.2	15	120	1.7	8	64	.9	5	40	.6
Submachinegun, 45 cal, M3, A1	889	.056	44	29,116	1.1	27	24,003	.7	37	32,893	.9	20	17,780	.5	11	9,779	.3
Tank, combat, full tracked, 105mm gun, M60, A1	324	68.49	78	25,272	865.4	47	15,228	5,215.0	65	21,060	721.2	35	11,340	388.3	20	6,480	221.9
Armored division total (STON)					2,432.6			1,902.8			1,911.5			1424.3			1,163.4
Infantry Division (AIM)			Part B. Infantry Division (AIM)														
Armament subsystem, helicopter, 20mm auto gun, M35	12	.80	3,000	36,000	14.4	1,800	21,600	8.6	2,490	29,880	12.0	1,345	16,140	6.5	750	9,000	3.6
Armament subsystem, helicopter, 7.62mm mg, lt, M23	35	.093	840	29,400	1.4	509	17,815	.8	700	24,500	1.1	382	13,370	.6	213	7,455	.3
Armament subsystem helicopter																	
7.62mm mg	27	.093	2,250	60,750	2.8	1,350	35,450	1.7	1,868	50,436	2.3	1,009	27,243	1.3	563	15,201	.7
40mm lchr	27	.750	321	8,667	3.3	193	5,211	2.0	266	7,182	2.7	144	3,888	1.5	80	2,160	.8
Hi rate, M28, A1																	
Armored reconnaissance airborne assault vehicle, M551																	
Ctg, 152mm	9	60.00	9	81	2.4	5	45	1.4	7	63	1.9	4	36	1.1	2	18	.5
S1B (Shillelagh)	9	112.00	7	63	3.5	9	81	4.5	6	54	3.0	7	63	3.5	3	27	1.5
Gun, ADA, SP, 20mm, M163	24	1.00	6,000	144,000	72.0	3,600	86,400	43.2	4,980	119,520	60.0	2,689	64,536	32.3	1,500	36,000	18.0
Howitzer, 105mm, towed, M102	54	68.50	423	22,842	782.3	467	25,218	863.7	376	20,304	695.4	381	20,574	704.6	210	11,340	388.4
Howitzer, 155 mm, towed M114	18	135.70	203	3,365	247.9	207	3,726	252.8	146	2,628	178.3	153	2,754	186.9	166	2,988	202.7

Figure 12. Ammunition Expenditures per Type Unit per Weapon per Day in STONs (continued)

Weapon	No. of wpns	Packed wt/rd	Defense of Position: First day Rds/wpn	Total rds	STON	Succeeding days Rds/wpn	Total rds	STON	Attack of Position (deliberately organized): First day Rds/wpn	Total rds	STON	Succeeding days Rds/wpn	Total rds	STON	Protracted period Rds/wpn	Total rds	STON
Part B. Infantry Division (continued)																	
Howitzer, 8 in, SP, M110	4	262.50	177	708	92.9	164	656	86.1	130	520	68.3	127	508	66.7	118	472	61.9
Lchr, GM, M222 (Dragon)	249	67.00	3	747	25.0	4	996	33.4	2	498	16.7	3	747	25.0	1	249	8.3
Lchr, grenade, 40mm, M203	1,193	.750	32	38,176	14.3	19	22,667	8.5	27	32,211	12.1	15	17,895	6.7	8	9,544	3.6
Lchr, rkt acft, 2.75 in, M158A1	54	27.00	42	2,268	30.6	25	1,350	18.2	35	1,890	25.5	19	1,026	13.9	11	594	8.0
Lchr, rkt acft, 2.75 in, 19 tube, M159	12	27.00	114	1,368	18.5	68	816	11.0	95	1,140	15.4	51	612	8.2	29	348	4.7
Lchr, rkt acft, 2.75 in, 19 tube (repairable), M200A1	30	27.00	114	3,420	46.2	68	2,040	27.5	95	2,850	38.5	51	1,530	20.7	29	870	11.7
Lchr, rkt multiple, 115mm, M91	9	93.33	See note 2														
Lchr, rkt, 66mm, M72 (LAW)	2,400	7.80	NA	700	2.7	NA	455	1.7	NA	595	2.3	NA	301	1.2	NA	175	0.7
Lchr, rkt, 66mm, 4 tube, M202, A1	92	8.75	16	1,472	6.4	10	920	4.0	14	1,288	5.6	7	644	2.8	4	368	1.6
Lchr, tubular, GM (TOW)	162	87.00	9	1,458	63.4	10	1,620	70.5	7	1,134	49.3	8	1,296	56.4	4	648	28.2
Machinegun, .50 cal, M2	373	.395	263	98,099	19.4	159	59,307	11.7	219	81,687	16.1	120	44,760	8.8	67	24,991	4.9
Machinegun, 7.62mm, M60	705	.093	649	457,545	21.3	393	277,065	12.9	541	381,405	17.7	295	207,975	9.7	164	115,620	5.4
Machinegun, 7.62mm, six barrels, M134	27	.093	6,000	162,000	7.5	3,600	97,200	4.5	4,980	13,446	6.3	2,698	72,603	3.4	1,500	40,500	1.9
Mortar, 81mm, M29, A1	81	17.32	145	11,745	101.7	88	7,128	61.7	121	9,801	84.9	66	5,346	46.3	37	2,997	26.0
Mortar, 4.2 in, M24, A1	43	40.00	163	7,009	140.2	99	4,257	85.1	136	5,848	117.0	74	3,182	63.6	41	1,763	35.3
Rifle, 5.56mm, M16A1	14,242	.042	148	2,107,816	44.3	90	1,281,700	26.9	124	1,766,009	37.1	67	954,214	20.0	38	541,196	11.4
Rifle, recoilless, 90-mm, M67	8	27.50	18	144	1.9	11	88	1.2	15	120	1.7	8	64	.9	5	40	.6
Submachinegun, .45 cal, M3, A1	159	.056	44	7,348	.2	27	4.509	1.0	37	6,179	.2	20	4,843	.1	11	1,837	.1
Tank, combat, full-tracked, 105-mm gun, M60, A1	54	68.49	78	4,212	144.2	47	2,538	86.9	65	3,510	120.2	35	1,890	64.7	20	1,080	37.0
Infantry division total (STON)					1,896.3			1,722.0			1,579.6			1,350.9			864.2
Mechanized Division (AIM) — Part C. Mechanized Division (AIM)																	
Armament Pod, acft, 7.62mm mg, M18, A1	6	.093	6,000	36,000	1.7	3,600	21,600	1.0	4,980	29,880	1.4	2,689	16.134	.8	1,500	9,000	.4
Armament subsystem, helicopter, 20mm auto gun, M35	4	.80	3,000	12,000	4.8	1,800	7,200	2.9	2,490	9,960	4.0	1,345	5,380	2.2	750	3,000	1.2
Armament subsystem, helicopter, 7.62mm, M23	13	.093	840	10,920	.5	509	6,617	.3	700	9,100	.4	382	4.966	.2	213	2,769	.1
Armament subsystem, helicopter																	
7.62mm mg	9	.093	2,250	20,250	.9	1,350	12,150	.6	1,868	16,812	.8	1,009	9,081	.4	563	5,067	.2
20mm lchr	9	.750	321	2,889	1.1	193	1,737	.7	266	2,394	.9	144	1,296	.5	80	720	.3
Armored reconnaissance airborne assault vehicle, M551																	
Ctg, 152-mm	27	60.00	9	243	7.3	5	135	4.1	7	189	5.7	4	108	3.2	2	54	1.6
S1B (Shillelagh)	27	112.00	7	189	10.6	9	243	13.6	6	162	9.1	7	189	10.6	3	81	4.5
Gun, ADA, SP, 20-mm, M163	24	1.00	6,000	144,000	72.0	3,600	86,400	43.2	4,980	119,520	59.8	2,689	64,536	32.3	1,500	36,000	18.0
Howitzer, 155-mm, SP, M109	54	135.70	203	10,962	743.8	207	11,178	758.4	146	7,884	534.9	153	8,262	560.6	166	8,964	608.2
Howitzer, 8-in, SP, M110	12	262.50	177	2,124	278.8	164	1,968	258.3	130	1,660	204.8	127	1,524	200.0	118	1,416	185.9
Lchr, GM, M222 (Dragon)	164	67.00	3	492	16.5	4	656	22.0	2	328	11.0	3	492	16.5	1	164	5.5
Lchr, grenade, 40-mm, M203	1,113	.750	32	35,616	13.4	19	21,147	8.0	27	30,051	11.3	15	16,695	6.3	8	8,904	3.3
Lchr, rkt acft, 2.75-in, M158A1	18	27.00	42	756	10.2	25	450	6.1	35	630	8.5	19	342	4.6	11	198	2.7
Lchr, rkt, acft, 2.75 in, 19-tube (repairable), M200A1	10	27.00	114	1,140	15.4	68	680	9.2	95	950	12.8	51	510	6.9	29	290	3.9
Lchr, rkt, multiple, 115mm, M91	9	93.33	See note 2														
Lchr, rkt, 66mm, M72 (LAW)	2,400	7.80	NA	700	2.7	NA	455	1.7	NA	595	2.3	NA	301	1.2	NA	75	0.7
Lchr, rkt, 66mm, 4-tube, M202, A1	84	8.75	16	1,344	5.9	10	840	3.7	14	1,176	5.1	7	588	2.6	4	336	1.5
Lchr, tubular, GM (TOW)	108	87.00	9	972	42.3	10	1,080	47.0	7	756	32.9	8	864	37.6	4	432	18.8
Machinegun, .50 cal, M2	1,238	.395	263	325,594	64.3	159	196,842	38.9	219	271,122	53.5	120	148,560	29.3	67	82,946	16.4
Machinegun, 7.62mm, M60	660	.093	649	428,340	19.9	393	259,380	12.1	541	357,060	16.6	295	194,700	9.1	164	108,240	5.0
Machinegun, 7.62mm, 6-barrel, M134	9	.093	6,000	54,000	2.5	3,600	32,400	1.5	4,980	44,820	2.1	2,689	24,201	1.1	1,500	13,500	.6

Figure 12. Ammunition Expenditures per Type Unit per Weapon per Day in STONs (continued)

Mortar, 81-mm, M29, A1	54	17.32	145	7,830	67.8	88	4,752	41.2	121	6,534	56.6	66	3,564	30.9	37	1,998	17.3
Mortar, 4.2-in, M24, A1	49	40.0	163	7,987	159.7	99	4,851	97.0	136	6,664	133.3	74	3,636	62.5	41	2,009	40.2
Rifle, 5.56-mm, M16, A1	13,387	.042	148	1,980,240	41.6	90	1,204,200	25.3	124	1,659,120	34.8	67	896,460	18.8	38	508,440	10.7
Rifle, recoilless, 90-mm, M67	8	27.50	18	144	1.9	11	88	1.2	15	120	1.7	8	64	.9	5	40	.6
Submachine gun, .45 cal, M3, A1	673	.056	44	29.612	.8	27	18,171	.5	37	24,901	.7	20	13,460	.4	11	7,403	.2
Tank, combat, full-tracked, 105-mm gun, M60, A1	216	68.49	78	16,848	576.9	47	10,152	347.7	65	14,040	480.8	35	7,560	258.9	20	4,320	147.9
Mechanized division total (STON)					2,156.8			1,742.3			1,680.4			1,295.4			1,094.1
Airborne Division				Part D. Airborne Division													
Armament pod, acft, 7.62-mm, mg, M18, A1	22	.093	6,000	132,000	6.1	3,600	79,200	3.7	4,980	109,560	5.1	2,689	59,158	2.8	1,500	33,000	1.5
Armament subsystem, helicopter, 20-mm auto-gun, M35	14	.80	3,000	42,000	16.8	1,800	25,200	10.1	2,490	34,860	13.9	1,345	18,830	7.5	750	10,500	4.2
Armament subsystem, helicopter, 7.62mm mg, lt, M23	65	.093	840	54,600	2.5	509	33,085	1.5	700	45,500	2.1	382	24,830	1.2	2.3	13,845	.6
Armament subsystem helicopter																	
7.62-mm mg	33	.093	2,250	74,250	3.5	1,350	44,550	2.1	1,868	61,644	2.9	1,009	33,297	1.6	563	18,579	.9
40-mm lchr	33	.750	321	10.593	4.0	193	6,369	2.4	266	8,778	3.3	144	4,752	1.8	80	2,640	1.0
Hi rate, M28, A1																	
Armored reconnaissance airborne assault vehicle, M551																	
Ctg, 152-mm	54	60.00	9	486	14.6	5	270	8.1	7	387	11.3	4	216	6.5	2	108	3.2
S1B (Shillelagh)	54	112.00	7	378	21.2	9	486	27.2	6	324	18.1	7	378	21.2	3	162	9.1
Gun, ADA, towed, 20-mm, M167	48	1.00	4,000	192,000	96.0	2,400	115,200	57.6	3,320	159,360	79.7	1,793	86,064	43.0	1,000	48,000	24.0
Howitzer, 105-mm, towed, M102	54	68.5	423	22,842	782.3	467	25,218	863.7	376	20,304	695.4	381	20,574	704.6	210	11,340	388.4
Lchr, GM, M222 (Dragon)	285	67.00	3	855	28.6	4	1,140	38.2	2	570	19.1	3	855	28.6	1	285	9.5
Lchr, grenade, 40-mm, M203	1,164	.750	32	37,248	14.0	19	22,116	8.3	27	31.428	11.8	15	17,460	6.5	8	9,312	3.5
Lchr, rkt acft, 2.75 in, M158, A1	66	27.00	42	2,772	37.4	25	1,650	22.3	35	2,310	31.2	19	1,254	16.9	11	726	9.8
Lchr, rkt acft, 2.75 in, 19 tube (repairable), M200A1	12	27.00	114	1,368	18.5	68	816	11.0	95	1,140	15.4	51	612	8.3	29	348	4.7
Lchr, rkt, 66-mm, M72 (LAW)	2,400	7.80	NA	700	2.7	NA	455	1.7	NA	595	2.3	NA	301	1.2	NA	175	0.7
Lchr, rkt, 66mm, 4-tube, M202, A1	65	8.75	16	1,040	4.6	10	650	2.8	14	910	4.0	7	455	2.0	4	260	1.1
Lchr, tubular, GM (TOW)	114	87.00	9	1,026	44.6	10	1,140	49.6	7	798	34.7	8	912	39.7	4	456	19.8
Machine gun, .50 cal, M2	94	.395	293	24,722	4.9	159	14,946	3.0	219	20,586	4.1	120	11,280	2.2	67	6,298	1.2
Machine gun, 7.62mm, M60	691	.093	649	448,459	20.9	393	271,563	12.6	541	373,831	17.4	295	203,845	9.5	164	113,324	5.3
Machine gun, 7.62-mm, six barrels, M134	33	.093	6,000	198,000	9.2	3,600	118,800	5.5	4,980	164,340	7.6	2,689	88,737	4.1	1,500	49,500	2.3
Mortar, 81-mm, M29, A1	84	17.32	145	12,180	105.5	88	7,392	64.0	212	10,164	88.0	66	5,544	48.0	37	3,108	27.0
Mortar, 4.2-in, M24, A1	36	40.00	163	5,868	117.4	99	3,564	71.3	136	4,896	97.9	74	2,664	53.2	41	1,476	29.5
Rifle, 5.56-mm, M16A1	13,159	.042	148	1,947,532	40.9	90	1,184,310	24.9	124	1,631,716	34.3	67	881,653	18.5	38	500,042	10.5
Submachinegun, .45 cal, M3, A1	108	.056	44	4,752	.1	27	2,916	.1	37	3,996	.1	20	2,160	.1	11	1,188	.1
Airborne division total (STON)					1,373.4			1,277.9			1,180.7			1,018.7			552.2
Air Assault Division				Part E. Air Assault Division													
Armament pod, acft, 7.62-mm mg, M18, A1	78	.093	6,000	468,000	21.8	3,600	280,800	13.1	4,980	388,440	18.1	2,689	209,742	9.8	1,500	117,000	5.4
Armament subsystem, helicopter, 20-mm auto-gun, M35	20	.80	3,000	60,000	24.0	1,800	36,000	14.4	2,490	49,800	19.9	1,345	26,900	10.8	750	15,000	6.0
Armament subsystem, helicopter, 7.62-mm mg, lt, M23	188	.093	840	157,920	7.3	509	95,692	4.5	700	131,600	6.1	382	71,816	3.3	213	40,044	1.9
Armament subsystem, helicopter																	
7.62-mm	87	.093	2,250	195,750	9.1	1,350	117,450	5.5	1,868	162,516	7.6	1,009	87,783	4.1	563	48,981	2.3
40-mm lchr	87	.750	321	27,927	10.5	193	16,791	6.3	266	23,142	8.7	144	12,528	4.7	80	6,960	2.6
Hi-rate, M28, A1																	
Gun, ADA, towed, 20-mm, M167	48	1.00	4,000	192,000	96.0	2,400	115,200	57.6	3,320	159,360	79.7	1,793	86,064	43.0	1,000	48,000	24.0
Howitzer, 105-mm, towed, M102	54	68.50	423	22,842	782.3	467	25,218	863.7	376	20,304	695.4	381	20,574	704.6	210	11,340	388.4
Howitzer, 105-mm, towed, M114	18	135.70	203	3,654	247.9	207	3,726	252.8	146	2,628	178.3	153	2,754	186.9	166	2,988	202.7
Lchr, GM, M222 (Dragon)	342	67.00	3	1,026	34.4	4	1,368	45.8	2	684	22.9	3	1,026	34.4	1	342	11.5
Lchr, grenade, 40-mm, M203	1,200	.750	32	38,400	14.4	19	22,800	8.6	27	32,400	12.2	15	18,000	6.8	8	9,600	3.6
Lchr, rkt, acft, 2.75-in, M158A1	174	27.00	42	7,308	98.7	25	4,350	58.7	35	6,090	82.2	19	3,306	44.6	11	1,914	25.8
Lchr, rkt, acft, 2.75-in, 19-tube (repairable), M200A1	120	27.00	114	13,680	184.7	68	8,160	110.2	95	11,400	153.9	51	6,120	82.6	29	3,480	47.0
Lchr, rkt, 66-mm, M72 (LAW)	2,400	7.80	NA	700	2.7	NA	455	1.7	NA	595	2.3	NA	301	1.2	NA	175	0.7
Lchr, rkt, 66-mm, 4-tube, M202, A1	87	8.75	16	1,392	6.1	10	870	3.8	14	1,218	5.3	7	609	2.7	4	348	1.5

Figure 12. Ammunition Expenditures per Type Unit per Weapon per Day in STONs (continued)

Weapon	No. of wpns	Packed wt/rd	Defense of Position						Attack of Position (deliberately organized)								
			First day			Succeeding days			First day			Succeeding days			Protracted period		
			Rds/ wpn	Total rds	STON	Rds/ wpn	Total rds	STON	Rds/ wpn	Total rds	STON	Rds/ wpn	Total rds	STON	Rds/ wpn	Total rds	STON
			Part E. Air Assault Division — Cont'd														
Lchr, tubular, GM (TOW)	168	87.00	9	1,512	65.8	10	1,680	73.1	7	1,176	51.2	8	1,344	58.5	4	672	29.2
Machinegun, .50 cal, M2	13	.395	263	3,419	.7	159	2,067	.4	219	2,847	.6	120	1,560	.3	67	871	.2
Machine gun, 7.62-mm, M60	1,012	.093	649	656,788	30.5	393	397,716	18.5	541	547,492	25.5	295	298,540	13.9	164	165,968	7.7
Machine gun, 7.62-mm, six barrels, M134	123	.093	6,000	738,000	34.3	3,600	442,800	20.6	4,980	612,540	28.5	2,689	330.747	15.4	1,500	184,500	8.6
Mortar, 81-mm, M29, A1	120	17.32	145	17,400	150.7	88	10,560	91.4	121	14,520	125.7	66	7,920	68.6	37	4,440	38.5
Rifle, 5.56-mm, M16, A1	15,231	.042	148	2,254,188	47.3	90	1,370,790	28.8	124	1,888,644	39.7	67	1,020,477	21.4	38	578,778	12.2
Rifle, recoilless, 90-mm, M67	7	27.50	18	126	1.7	11	77	1.1	15	105	1.4	8	56	.8	5	35	.5
Air assault division total (STON)					1,825.1			1.653.1			1,572.2			1,297.8			808.9
Separate Armored Brigade			Part F. Separate Armored Brigade														
Armored reconnaissance airborne assault vehicle, M551																	
152-mm, Ctg	9	60.00	9	81	2.4	5	45	1.4	7	63	1.9	4	36	1.1	2	18	0.5
S1B (Shillelagh)	9	112.00	7	63	3.5	9	81	4.5	6	54	3.0	7	63	3.5	3	27	1.5
Howitzer, 155-mm, towed SP, M114 & M109	18	135.7	203	3,654	247.9	207	3,726	252.8	146	2,628	178.3	153	2,754	186.9	166	2,988	202.7
Launcher, grenade, 40-mm, M203	216	750	32	6,912	2.6	19	4,104	1.5	27	5,832	2.2	15	3,240	1.2	8	1,728	0.6
Launcher, GM, M222 (Dragon)	30	67.00	3	90	3.0	4	120	4.0	2	60	2.0	3	90	3.0	1	30	1.0
Launcher, rkt, multiple, 115-mm, M91	3	93.33	See note 2														
Launcher, rkt, 66-mm 4-tube, M202, A1	18	8.75	16	288	1.3	10	180	0.8	14	252	1.1	7	126	0.6	4	72	0.3
Launcher, rkt, 66-mm, M72 (LAW)	610	7.80	NA	183	0.7	NA	115	.04	NA	153	0.6	NA	79	0.3	NA	43	0.2
Launcher, tubular, GM (TOW)	18	87.00	19	162	7.0	10	180	7.8	7	126	5.5	8	144	6.3	4	72	3.1
Machine gun, .50 cal, M2	251	.395	263	66,013	13.0	159	39,909	7.9	219	54,969	10.9	120	30.120	5.9	67	16,817	3.3
Machine gun, 7.62-mm, M60	131	.093	649	85,019	4.0	393	51,483	2.4	541	70,871	3.3	295	38,645	1.8	164	21,484	1.0
Mortar, 81-mm, M29A1	9	17.32	145	1,305	11.3	88	792	6.9	121	1,089	9.4	66	594	5.1	37	333	2.9
Mortar, 4.2-in, M24A1	11	40.00	163	1,793	35.9	99	1,089	21.8	136	1,496	29.9	74	814	16.3	41	451	9.0
Rifle, 5.56-mm, M16A1	2,738	.042	148	405,224	8.5	90	246,420	5.2	124	339,512	7.1	67	183,446	3.9	38	104,044	2.2
Rifle, recoilless, 90-mm, M67	1	27.50	19	19	0.26	11	11	0.15	15	15	0.20	8	8	0.11	5	5	0.07
Submachine gun, .45 cal, M3A1	159	.056	44	6,996	0.19	27	4,293	0.12	37	5,883	0.16	20	3,180	0.09	11	1,749	0.05
Tank, combat, full-tracked, 105-mm gun, M60A1	54	68.49	78	4,212	144.2	47	2,538	86.9	65	3,510	120.2	35	1,890	64.7	20	1,080	36.9
Total STON					485.8			404.6			375.8			300.8			265.4
Separate Mechanized Brigade			Part G. Separate Mechanized Brigade														
Armament subsystem, hel, 7.62-mm MG, lt, M23	2	.093	840	1,680	.08	509	1,018	.05	700	1,400	.07	382	764	.04	213	426	.02
Armored reconnaissance airborne assault vehicle, M551																	
152-mm Ctg	9	60.00	9	81	2.4	5	45	1.4	7	63	1.9	4	36	1.1	2	18	0.5
S1B (Shillelagh)	9	112.00	7	63	3.5	9	81	4.5	6	54	3.0	7	63	3.5	3	27	1.5
Howitzer, 155-mm, Towed & SP, M114 & M109	18	135.7	203	3,654	247.9	207	3,726	252.8	146	2,628	178.3	153	2,754	186.9	166	2,988	202.7
Launcher, grenade, 40-mm, M203	220	.750	32	7,040	2.6	19	4,180	1.6	27	5,940	2.2	15	3,300	1.2	8	1,760	0.7
Launcher, GM, M222 (Dragon)	30	67.00	3	90	3.0	4	120	4.0	2	60	2.0	3	90	3.0	1	30	1.0
Launcher, rkt, multiple, 115-mm, M91	3	93.33	See note 2														
Launcher, rkt, 66 mm, 4-tube, M202, A1	17	8.75	16	272	1.2	10	170	0.7	14	238	1.0	7	119	0.5	4	68	0.3
Launcher, rkt, 66-mm, M72 (LAW)	610	7.80	NA	183	0.7	NA	115	0.4	NA	153	0.6	NA	79	0.3	NA	43	0.2
Launcher, tubular, GM (TOW)	18	87.00	19	162	7.0	10	180	7.8	7	126	5.5	8	144	6.3	4	72	3.1
Machine gun, .50 cal, M2	252	.395	263	66,276	13.1	159	40,068	7.9	219	55,188	10.9	120	30,240	6.0	67	16,884	3.3
Machine gun, 7.62-mm, M60	131	.093	649	85,019	4.0	393	51,483	2.4	541	70,871	3.3	295	38,645	1.8	164	21,484	1.0
Mortar, 81-mm, M29A1	9	17.32	145	1,305	11.3	88	792	6.9	121	1,089	9.4	66	594	5.1	37	333	2.9
Mortar, 4.2-in, M24A1	11	40.00	163	1,793	35.9	99	1,089	21.8	136	2,496	29.9	74	814	16.3	41	451	9.0

Figure 12. Ammunition Expenditures per Type Unit per Weapon per Day in STONs (continued)

Rifle, 5.56-mm, M16A1	2,733	.042	148	404,484	8.5	90	245,970	5.2	124	338,892	7.1	67	183,111	3.8	38	103,854	2.2
Submachine gun, .45 cal, M3A1	159	.056	44	6,996	0.19	27	4,293	0.12	37	5,883	0.16	20	3,180	0.09	11	1,749	0.05
Tank, combat, full-tracked, 105-mm gun, M60A1	54	68.49	78	4,212	144.2	47	2,538	86.9	65	3,510	120.2	35	1,890	64.7	20	1,080	36.9
Total STON					485.6			404.5			375.5			300.6			265.4
Separate Infantry Brigade			Part H. Separate Infantry Brigade														
Armored reconnaissance airborne assault vehicle, M551																	
152-mm Ctg	9	60.00	9	81	2.4	5	45	1.4	7	63	1.9	4	36	1.1	2	18	0.5
S1B (Shillelagh)	9	112.00	7	63	3.5	9	81	4.5	6	54	3.0	7	63	3.5	3	27	1.5
Howitzer, 105-mm, Towed, M102	18	68.50	423	7,614	260.8	467	8,406	287.9	376	6,768	231.8	381	6,858	234.9	210	3,780	129.5
Launcher, grenade, 40-mm, M203	191	.750	32	6,112	2.3	19	3,629	1.4	27	5,157	1.9	15	2,865	1.1	8	1,528	0.6
Launcher, GM, M222 (Dragon)	30	67.00	3	90	3.0	4	120	4.0	2	60	2.0	3	90	3.0	1	30	1.0
Launcher, rkt, multiple, 115-mm, M91	3	93.33	See note 2														
Launcher, rkt, 66-mm 4 tube, M202, A1	17	8.75	16	272	1.2	10	170	0.7	14	238	1.0	7	119	0.5	4	68	0.3
Launcher, rkt, 66-mm, M72 (LAW)	610	7.80	NA	183	0.7	NA	115	0.4	NA	153	0.6	NA	79	0.3	NA	43	0.2
Launcher, tubular, GM, TOW	18	87.00	9	162	7.0	10	180	7.8	7	126	5.5	8	144	6.3	4	72	3.1
Machine gun, .50 cal, M2	93	.395	263	24,459	4.8	159	14,787	2.9	219	20,367	4.0	120	11,160	2.2	67	6,231	1.2
Machine gun, 7.62-mm, M60	108	.093	649	70,092	3.3	393	42,444	2.0	541	58,428	2.7	295	31,860	1.5	164	17,712	0.8
Mortar, 81-mm, M29A1	9	10.32	145	1,305	11.3	88	792	6.9	121	1,089	9.4	66	594	5.1	37	333	2.9
Mortar, 4.2-in, M24A1	11	40.00	163	1,793	35.9	99	1,089	21.8	136	1,496	29.9	74	814	16.3	41	451	9.0
Rifle, 5.56-mm, M16A1	2,542	.042	148	376,216	7.9	90	228,780	4.8	124	315,208	6.6	67	170,314	3.6	38	96,596	2.0
Rifle, recoilless, 90-mm, M67	1	27.50	19	19	0.26	11	11	0.15	15	15	0.2	8	8	0.11	5	5	0.07
Submachine gun, .45 cal, M3A1	142	.056	44	6,248	0.17	27	3,834	0.10	37	5,254	0.15	20	2,840	0.08	11	1,562	0.04
Tank, combat, full-tracked, 105-mm gun, M60A1	54	68.49	78	4,212	144.2	47	2,538	86.9	65	3,510	120.2	35	1,890	64.7	20	1,080	36.9
Total STON					488.8			433.7			420.9			344.3			189.6
Separate Light Infantry Brigade			Part I. Separate Light Infantry Brigade														
Armament subsystem, hel, 7.62-mm mg, lt, M23	3	.093	840	2,520	.11	509	1,527	.07	700	2,100	.10	382	1,146	.05	213	639	.03
Armored reconnaissance airborne assault vehicle, M551																	
152-mm Ctg	6	60.00	9	54	1.6	5	30	0.9	7	42	1.3	4	24	0.7	2	12	0.4
S1B (Shillelagh)	6	122.00	7	42	2.4	9	54	3.0	6	36	2.0	7	42	2.4	3	18	1.0
Howitzer, 105-mm, towed, M102	18	68.50	423	7,614	260.8	467	8,406	287.9	376	6,768	231.8	381	6,858	234.9	210	3,780	129.5
Launcher, grenade, 40-mm, M203	148	.750	32	4,736	1.8	19	2,812	1.1	27	3,996	1.5	15	2,220	0.8	8	1,184	0.4
Launcher, GM, M222 (Dragon)	30	67.00	3	90	3.0	4	120	4.0	2	60	2.0	3	90	3.0	1	30	1.0
Launcher, rkt, multiple, 115-mm, M91	3	93.33	See note 2														
Launcher, rkt, 66-mm, 4-tube, M202, A1	12	8.75	16	192	0.8	10	120	0.5	14	168	0.7	7	84	0.4	4	48	0.2
Launcher, rkt, 66-mm, M72 (LAW)	476	7.80	NA	143	0.6	NA	90	0.4	NA	119	0.5	NA	62	0.2	NA	33	0.1
Launcher, tubular, GM, (TOW)	18	87.00	9	162	7.0	10	180	7.8	7	126	5.5	8	144	6.3	4	72	3.1
Machine gun, .50 cal, M2	8	.395	263	2,104	0.4	159	1,272	0.3	219	1,752	0.3	120	960	0.2	67	536	0.1
Machine gun, 7.62-mm, M60	94	.093	649	61,006	2.8	393	36,942	1.7	541	50,854	2.4	295	27,730	1.3	164	15,416	0.7
Mortar, 81-mm, M29A1	16	17.32	145	2,320	20.1	88	1,408	12.2	121	1,936	16.8	66	1,056	9.1	37	592	5.1
Rifle, 5.56-mm, M16A1	2,025	.042	148	299,700	6.3	90	182,250	3.8	124	251,100	5.3	67	135,675	2.8	38	76,950	1.6
Submachine gun, .45 cal, M3A1	16	.056	44	704	0.02	27	432	0.01	37	592	0.02	20	320	0.008	11	176	0.005
Total STON					307.8			323.3			270.2			262.2			143.2
Separate Airborne Brigade			Part J. Separate Airborne Brigade (Equipped with 106RR and TOW)														
Armament subsystem, hel, 7.62-mm mg, lt, M23	3	.093	840	2,520	.11	509	1,527	.07	700	2,100	.10	382	1,146	.05	213	639	.03
Armored reconnaissance airborne assault vehicle, M551																	
152-mm Ctg	6	60.00	9	54	1.6	5	30	0.9	7	42	1.3	4	24	0.7	2	12	0.4
S1B (Shillelagh)	6	112.00	7	42	2.4	9	54	3.0	6	36	2.0	7	42	2.4	3	18	1.0
Howitzer, 105-mm, towed, M102	18	68.50	423	7,614	260.8	467	8,406	287.9	376	6,768	231.8	381	6,858	234.9	210	3,780	129.5
Launcher, grenade, 40-mm, M203	186	.750	32	5,952	2.2	19	3,534	1.3	27	5,022	1.9	15	2,790	1.0	8	1,488	0.6
Launcher, GM, M222 (Dragon)	30	67.00	3	90	3.0	4	120	4.0	2	60	2.0	3	90	3.0	1	30	1.0
Launcher, rkt, 66-mm, 4 tube, M202, A1	9	8.75	16	144	0.6	10	90	0.4	14	126	0.5	7	63	0.3	4	36	0.2

Figure 12. *Ammunition Expenditures per Type Unit per Weapon per Day in STONs* (continued)

Weapon	No. of wpns	Packed wt/rd	Defense of Position: First day Rds/wpn	Total rds	STON	Succeeding days Rds/wpn	Total rds	STON	Attack of Position (deliberately organized): First day Rds/wpn	Total rds	STON	Succeeding days Rds/wpn	Total rds	STON	Protracted period Rds/wpn	Total rds	STON
			Part J. Separate Airborne Brigade (Equipped with 106RR and TOW)—Cont'd														
Launcher, rkt, 66-mm, M72 (LAW)	476	7.80	NA	143	0.6	NA	90	0.4	NA	119	0.5	NA	62	0.2	NA	33	0.1
Machine gun, .50 cal, M2	7	.395	263	1,841	0.4	159	1,113	0.2	219	1,533	0.3	120	840	0.2	67	469	0.1
Machine gun, 7.62-mm, M60	101	.093	649	65,549	3.0	393	39,693	1.8	541	54,641	2.5	295	29,795	1.4	164	16,564	0.8
Mortar, 81-mm, M29A1	12	17.32	145	1,740	15.1	88	1,056	9.1	121	1,452	12.6	66	792	6.9	37	444	3.8
Mortar, 4.2-in, M24A1	4	40.00	163	652	13.0	99	396	7.9	136	544	10.9	74	296	5.9	41	164	3.3
Rifle, 5.56-mm, M16A1	2,033	.042	148	300,884	6.4	90	182,970	3.8	124	252,092	5.3	67	136,211	2.9	38	77,254	1.6
Rifle, recoilless, 106-mm	8	60.00	19	152	4.6	11	88	2.6	15	120	3.6	8	64	1.9	5	40	1.2
Submachine gun, .45 cal, M3A1	14	.056	44	616	0.017	27	378	0.010	37	518	0.014	20	280	0.007	11	154	0.004
Total STON (These totals are minus TOW tonnage)					313.7			323.4			275.3			261.8			143.6
Air Cavalry Combat Brigade			Part K. Air Cavalry Combat Brigade														
Armament subsystem, hel, 7.62-mm mg, lt, M23	61	.093	840	51,240	2.4	509	31,049	1.4	700	42,700	2.0	382	23,302	1.1	213	12,993	0.6
Armament subsystem, hel, 7.62-mm mg/40-mm lchr hi-rate, M28A1																	
7.62-mm mg	153	.093	2,250	344,250	16.0	1,350	206,550	9.6	1,868	285,804	13.3	1,009	154,377	7.2	563	86,139	4.0
40-mm lchr	153	.750	321	49,113	18.4	193	29.529	11.1	266	40,698	15.3	144	22,032	8.3	80	12,240	4.6
Launcher, grenade, 40-mm, M203	173	.750	32	5,536	2.1	19	3,287	1.2	27	4.671	1.8	15	2,595	1.0	8	1,384	0.5
Launcher, GM, M222 (Dragon)	6	67.00	3	18	0.6	4	24	0.8	2	12	0.4	3	18	0.6	1	6	0.2
Launcher, rkt acft, 2.75 in, M158A41	222	27.00	42	9,324	125.9	25	5,550	74.9	35	7,770	104.9	19	4,218	56.9	11	2,442	33.0
Launcher, rkt, acft, 2.75-in, 19-tube (repairable), M200A1	114	27.00	114	12,996	175.4	68	7,752	104.7	95	10,830	146.2	51	5,814	78.5	29	3,306	44.6
Launcher, rkt, 66-mm, 4 tube, M202, A1	3	8.75	16	48	0.2	10	30	0.13	14	42	0.18	7	21	0.09	4	12	0.05
Launcher, rkt, 66-mm, M72 (LAW)	276	7.80	NA	83	0.3	NA	50	0.2	NA	69	0.26	NA	36	0.14	NA	19	0.07
Machine gun, .50 cal, M2	23	.375	263	6,049	1.2	159	3,657	0.7	219	5,037	1.0	120	2,760	0.5	67	1,541	0.3
Machine gun, 7.62-mm, M60	301	.093	649	195,349	9.1	393	118,293	5.5	541	162,841	7.6	295	88,795	4.1	164	49,364	2.3
Machine gun, 7.62-mm, six barrels, M134	153	.093	6,000	918,000	42.7	3,600	550,800	25.6	4,980	761,940	35.4	2,689	411,417	19.1	1,500	229,500	10.7
Rifle, 5.56-mm, M16A1	3,109	.042	148	460,132	9.7	90	279,810	5.9	124	385,516	8.1	67	208,303	4.4	38	118,142	2.5
Total STON					404.0			241.7			336.4			181.9			103.4
Armored Cavalry Regiment (w/ARAAV)			Part L. Armored Cavalry Regiment (Equipped with ARAAV)														
Armament subsystem, hel, 7.62-mm mg, lt, M23	22	.093	840	18,480	0.9	509	11,198	0.5	700	15,400	0.7	382	8,404	0.4	213	4,686	0.2
Armament subsystem, hel, 7.62-mm mg/40-mm lchr hi-rate, M28A1																	
7.62-mm mg	9	.093	2,250	20,250	1.0	1,350	12,150	0.6	1,868	16,812	0.8	1,009	9,081	0.4	563	5,067	0.2
40-mm lchr	9	.750	321	2,889	1.1	193	1,737	0.7	266	2,394	0.9	144	1,296	0.5	80	720	0.3
Armored reconnaissance airborne assault vehicle, M551																	
152-mm Ctg	132	60.00	9	1,188	35.6	5	660	19.8	7	924	27.7	4	528	15.8	2	264	7.9
S1B (Shillelagh)	132	112.00	7	924	51.7	9	1,188	66.5	6	792	44.4	7	924	51.7	3	396	22.2
Howitzer, 155-mm, towed SP, M114 & M109	18	135.7	203	3,654	247.9	207	3,726	252.8	146	2,628	178.3	153	2,754	186.9	166	2,988	202.7
Launcher, grenade, 40-mm, M203	238	.750	32	7,616	2.9	19	4,522	1.7	27	6,426	2.4	15	3,570	1.3	8	1,904	0.7
Launcher, rkt, acft, 2.75-in, M158A41	18	27.00	42	756	10.2	25	450	6.1	35	630	8.5	19	342	4.6	11	198	2.7
Launcher, rkt, acft, 2.75-in, 19-tube (repairable), M200A1	10	27.00	114	1,140	15.4	68	680	9.2	95	950	12.8	51	510	6.9	29	290	3.9
Launcher, rkt, 66-mm, 4 tube, M202, A1	31	8.75	16	496	2.2	10	310	1.4	14	434	1.9	7	217	0.9	4	124	0.5
Launcher, rkt, 66-mm, M72 (LAW)	408	7.80	NA	122	0.5	NA	73	0.3	NA	102	0.4	NA	61	0.2	NA	29	0.1
Machine gun, .50 cal, M2	524	.095	263	137,812	27.2	159	83,316	16.5	219	114,756	22.7	120	62,880	12.4	67	35,108	6.9
Machine gun, 7.62-mm, M60	214	.093	649	138,886	6.5	393	84,102	3.9	541	115,774	5.4	295	63,130	2.9	164	35,096	1.6

Figure 12. Ammunition Expenditures per Type Unit per Weapon per Day in STONs (continued)

Machine gun, 7.62-mm, six barrels, M134	9	.093	6,000	54,000	2.5	3,600	32,400	1.5	4,980	44,820	2.1	2,689	24,201	1.1	1,500	13,500	0.6
Mortar, 4.2 in, M24A1	27	40.00	163	4,401	88.0	99	2,673	53.5	136	3,672	73.4	74	1,998	40.0	41	1,107	22.1
Rifle, 5.56-mm, M16A1	2,091	.042	148	309,468	6.5	90	188,190	4.0	124	259,284	5.4	67	140,097	2.9	38	79,458	1.7
Submachine gun, .45 cal, M3A1	338	.056	44	14,872	0.4	27	9,126	0.3	37	12,506	0.4	20	6,760	0.2	11	3,718	0.1
Total STON					500.7			439.6			388.3			329.3			274.5
Armored Cavalry Regiment (w/M60A1)					Part M. Armored Cavalry Regiment (Equipped with M60A1)												
Armament subsystem, hel, 7.62-mm mg, lt, M23	22	.093	840	18,480	0.9	509	11,198	0.5	700	15,400	0.7	382	8,404	0.4	213	4,686	0.2
Armament subsystem, hel, 7.62-mm mg/40-mm lchr, hi-rate, M28A1																	
7.62-mm mg	9	.093	2,250	20,250	1.0	1,350	12,150	0.6	1,868	16,812	0.8	1,009	9,081	0.4	563	5,067	0.2
40-mm lchr	9	.750	321	2,889	1.1	193	1,737	0.7	266	2,394	0.9	144	1,296	0.5	80	720	0.3
Howitzer, 155-mm, towed SP, M114 & M109	18	135.7	203	3,654	247.9	207	3,726	252.8	146	2,628	178.3	153	2,754	186.9	166	2,988	202.7
Launcher, grenade, 40-mm	238	.750	32	7,616	2.9	19	4,522	1.7	27	6,426	2.4	15	3,570	1.3	8	1,904	0.7
Launcher, rkt acft, 2.75-in, M158A41	18	28.00	42	756	10.2	25	450	6.1	35	630	8.5	19	342	4.6	11	198	2.7
Launcher, rkt acft, 2.75-in, 19-tube (repairable), M200A1	10	27.00	114	1,140	15.4	68	680	9.2	95	950	12.8	51	510	6.9	29	290	3.9
Launcher, rkt, 66-mm, 4-tube, M202, A1	31	8.75	16	496	2.2	10	310	1.4	14	434	1.9	7	217	0.9	4	124	0.5
Launcher, rkt, 66-mm, M72 (LAW)	408	7.80	NA	122	0.5	NA	73	0.3	NA	102	0.4	NA	61	0.2	NA	29	0.1
Machine gun, .50 cal, M2	392	.395	263	103,096	20.4	159	62,328	12.3	219	85,848	17.0	120	47,040	9.3	67	26,264	5.2
Machine gun, 7.62-mm, M60	214	.093	649	138,886	6.5	393	84,102	3.9	541	115,774	5.4	295	63,130	2.9	164	35,096	1.6
Machinegun, 7.62-mm, six barrels, M134	9	.093	6,000	54,000	2.5	3,600	32,400	1.5	4,980	44,820	2.1	2,689	24,201	1.1	1,500	13,500	0.6
Mortar, 4.2-in, M24A1	27	40.00	163	4,401	88.0	99	2,673	53.5	136	3,672	73.4	74	1,998	40.0	41	1,107	22.1
Rifle, 5.56-mm, M16A1	2,098	.042	148	310,800	6.5	90	189,000	4.0	124	260,400	5.5	67	140,700	2.9	38	79,800	1.7
Submachine gun, .45 cal, M3A1	338	.056	44	14,872	0.4	27	9,126	0.3	37	12,506	0.4	20	6,760	0.2	11	3,718	0.1
Tank, combat, full-tracked, 105-mm gun, M60A1	132	68.49	78	10,296	352.6	47	6,204	212.5	65	8,580	293.8	35	4,620	158.2	20	2,640	90.4
Total STON					759.2			561.6			604.4			416.9			330.1
Heavy Division Armor (87000J430)																	
CFV 25mm[1]	100	1.66	277	27,700	23.0	216	21,600	17.9	225	22,500	18.7	166	16,600	13.8	98	9,800	8.1
(TOW)		87.00	9	900	39.2	10	1,000	43.5	7	700	30.5	8	800	34.8	4	400	17.4
CEV[1]	8	92.40	21	168	7.8	16	128	5.9	17	136	6.3	12	96	4.4	7	56	2.6
ITV TOW[1]	48	87.00	13	624	27.1	15	720	31.3	10	480	20.9	12	576	25.1	6	288	12.5
AH-64 hel 30mm[1]	36	1.75	770	27,720	24.3	602	21,672	19.0	628	22,608	19.8	463	16,668	14.6	274	9,864	8.6
2.75 rocket	72	11.83	26	936	5.5	15	540	3.2	21	756	4.5	12	432	2.6	7	252	1.5
Hellfire	36	185.00	16	576	53.3	17	612	56.6	12	432	40.0	13	468	43.3	7	252	23.3
AH-IS TOW	8	87.00	12	864	37.6	13	468	20.4	9	324	14.1	10	360	15.7	5	360	15.7
2.75 rocket	16	11.83	42	1,512	8.9	25	900	5.3	35	1,260	7.5	19	684	4.0	11	396	2.3
20 mm	8	0.8	3,000	24,000	9.6	1,800	64,800	25.9	2,490	89,640	35.9	1,345	48,420	19.4	750	6,000	2.4
IFV 25mm[1]	216	1.66	214	46,224	38.4	167	36,072	29.9	174	37,584	31.2	129	27,864	23.1	76	16,416	13.6
(TOW)		87.00	6	1,296	56.4	7	1,512	65.8	5	1,080	47.0	6	1,296	56.4	3	648	28.2
ADA, SP, 20mm	24	0.80	4,800	115,200	46.1	2,880	69,120	27.6	3,984	95,616	38.2	2,151	51,624	20.6	1,200	28,800	11.5
155mm Howitzer	72	99.62	203	14,616	728.0	207	14,904	742.4	146	10,512	523.6	153	11,016	548.7	166	11,952	595.3
Prop chg		31.95	213	15,347	245.2	217	15,649	250.0	153	11,038	176.3	161	11,567	184.8	174	12,550	200.5
Fuze		3.75	213	15,347	28.8	217	15,649	29.3	153	11,038	20.7	161	11,567	21.7	174	12,550	23.5
40mm M203	1,047	0.75	32	33,504	12.6	19	19,893	7.5	27	28,269	10.6	15	15,705	5.9	8	8,376	3.1
Launcher, 66mm, M202	48	8.75	16	768	3.4	10	480	2.1	14	672	2.9	7	336	1.5	4	192	0.8
Launcher (TOW)	48	87.00	9	432	18.8	10	480	20.9	7	336	14.6	8	384	16.7	4	192	8.4
MG .50 Cal	1,140	0.40	263	299,820	59.2	159	181,620	35.8	219	249,660	49.3	120	136,800	27.0	67	76,380	15.1
MG 7.62mm ACFT	60	0.09	840	50,400	2.3	509	30,540	1.4	700	42,000	2.0	382	22,920	1.1	213	12,780	0.6
MG 7.62mm fixed	704	0.09	649	456,896	21.2	393	276,672	12.9	541	380,864	17.7	295	207,680	9.7	164	115,456	5.4
MG 7-62mm lt flex	660	0.09	649	428,340	19.9	393	259,380	12.1	541	357,060	16.6	295	194,700	9.1	164	108,240	5.0
SAW 5.56mm	618	0.09	243	150,174	6.8	147	90,846	4.1	202	124,836	5.6	110	67,980	3.1	61	37,698	1.7
4.2in Mortar	66	40.00	163	10,758	215.2	99	6,534	130.7	136	8,976	179.5	74	4,884	97.7	41	2,706	54.1
MG 7.62mm RH Feed	316	0.09	840	265,440	12.3	509	160,844	7.5	700	221,200	10.3	382	120,712	5.6	213	67,308	3.1

Figure 12. Ammunition Expenditures per Type Unit per Weapon per Day in STONs (continued)

Weapon	No. of wpns	Packed wt/rd	Defense of Position: First day Rds/wpn	Total rds	STON	Defense of Position: Succeeding days Rds/wpn	Total rds	STON	Attack of Position (deliberately organized): First day Rds/wpn	Total rds	STON	Attack: Succeeding days Rds/wpn	Total rds	STON	Protracted period Rds/wpn	Total rds	STON
Part M. Armored Cavalry Regiment (Equipped with M60A1) — Cont'd																	
M16 A1 rifle	13,266	0.04	148	1,963,368	41.2	90	1,193,940	25.1	124	1,644,984	34.5	67	888,822	18.7	38	504,108	10.6
90mm recoil, rfl	24	27.50	19	456	6.3	11	264	3.6	15	360	5.0	8	192	2.6	5	120	1.7
SMG 5.56mm[1]	1,296	0.09	153	198,288	8.9	92	119,232	5.4	127	164,592	7.4	69	89,424	4.0	38	49,248	2.2
Tank M1[1]	348	68.49	37	12,876	440.9	22	7,656	262.2	31	10,788	369.4	16	5,568	190.7	9	3,132	107.3
SMG 45cal	288	0.06	44	12,672	0.4	27	7,776	0.2	37	10,656	0.3	20	5,760	0.2	11	3,168	0.1
Dragon	144	67.00	3	432	14.5	4	576	19.3	2	288	9.6	3	432	14.5	1	144	4.8
MLRS[1]	9	872.57	99	891	388.7	98	882	384.8	75	675	294.5	76	684	298.4	67	603	263.1
					2,651.6			2,309.4			2,064.8			1,739.1			1,454.2
Heavy Division Mech (87000J440)																	
CFV 25mm[1]	100	1.66	277	27,700	23.0	216	21,600	17.9	225	22,500	18.7	166	16,600	13.8	98	9,800	8.1
TOW		87.00	9	900	39.2	10	1,000	43.5	7	700	30.5	8	800	34.8	4	400	17.4
CEV	8	92.40	21	168	7.8	16	128	5.9	17	136	6.3	12	96	4.4	7	56	2.6
ITV TOW[1]	60	87.00	13	780	33.9	15	900	39.2	10	600	26.1	12	720	31.3	6	360	15.7
AH-64 hel .30mm[1]	36	1.75	770	27,720	24.3	602	21,672	19.0	628	22,608	19.8	463	16,668	14.6	274	9,864	8.6
2.75 rocket	72	11.83	26	936	5.5	15	540	3.2	21	756	4.5	12	432	2.6	7	252	1.5
Hellfire	36	185.00	16	576	53.3	17	612	56.6	12	432	40.0	13	468	43.3	7	252	23.3
AH-1S TOW	8	87.00	12	864	37.6	13	468	20.4	9	324	14.1	10	360	15.7	5	360	15.7
2.75 rocket	16	11.83	42	1,512	8.9	25	900	5.3	35	1,260	7.5	19	684	4.0	11	396	2.3
20 mm	8	0.8	3,000	24,000	9.6	1,800	64,800	25.9	2,490	89,640	35.9	1,345	48,420	19.4	750	6,000	2.4
IFV 25 mm	270	1.66	214	57,780	48.0	167	45,090	37.4	174	46,980	39.0	129	34,830	28.9	76	20,520	17.0
TOW		87.00	6	1,620	70.5	7	1,890	82.2	5	1,350	58.7	6	1,620	70.5	3	810	35.2
ADA, SP, 20mm	24	0.80	4,800	115,200	46.1	2,880	69,120	27.6	3,984	95,616	38.2	2,151	51,624	20.6	1,200	28,800	11.5
155mm Howitzer	72	99.62	203	14,616	728.0	207	14,904	742.4	146	10,512	523.6	153	11,016	548.7	166	11,952	595.3
prop chg		31.95	3,150	25,200	402.6	1,890	15,120	241.5	2,615	20,916	334.1	1,412	11,298	180.5	788	6,300	100.6
fuze		3.75	3,150	25,200	47.3	1,890	15,120	28.4	2,615	20,916	39.2	1,412	11,298	21.2	788	6,300	11.8
40mm M203	1,146	0.75	32	36,672	13.8	19	21,774	8.2	27	30,942	11.6	15	17,190	6.4	8	9,168	3.4
Launcher, 66mm, M202	60	8.75	16	960	4.2	10	600	2.6	14	840	3.7	7	420	1.8	4	240	1.1
Launcher TOW	60	87.00	9	540	23.5	10	600	26.1	7	420	18.3	8	480	20.9	4	240	10.4
MG .50 Cal	1,087	0.40	263	285,881	56.5	159	172,833	34.1	219	238,053	47.0	120	130,440	25.8	67	72,829	14.4
MG 7.62mm acft	60	0.09	840	50,400	2.3	509	30,540	1.4	700	42,000	2.0	382	22,920	1.1	213	12,780	0.6
MG 7.62mm fixed	588	0.09	649	381,612	17.7	393	231,084	10.7	541	318,108	14.8	295	173,460	8.1	164	96,432	4.5
MG 7.62 lt flex	685	0.09	649	444,565	20.7	393	269,205	12.5	541	370,585	17.2	295	202,075	9.4	164	112,340	5.2
SAW 5.56mm[1]	690	0.09	243	167,670	7.5	147	101,430	4.6	202	139,380	6.3	110	75,900	3.4	61	42,090	1.9
4.2in mortar	66	40.00	163	10,758	215.2	99	6,534	130.7	136	8,976	179.5	74	4,884	97.7	41	2,706	54.1
MG 7.62 RH feed	370	0.09	840	310,800	14.5	509	188,330	8.8	700	259,000	12.0	382	141,340	6.6	213	78,810	3.7
M16 A1 rifle	13,705	0.04	148	2,028,340	42.6	90	1,233,450	25.9	124	1,699,420	35.7	67	918,235	19.3	38	520,790	10.9
90mm recoil, rfl	24	27.50	19	456	6.3	11	264	3.6	15	360	5.0	8	192	2.6	5	120	1.7
SMG 5.56mm[1]	1,620	0.09	153	247,860	11.2	92	149,040	6.7	127	205,740	9.3	69	111,780	5.0	38	61,560	2.8
Tank M1[1]	290	68.49	37	10,730	367.4	22	6,380	218.5	31	8,990	307.9	16	4,640	158.9	9	2,160	89.4
SMG .45cal	288	0.06	44	12,672	0.4	27	7,776	0.2	37	10,656	0.3	20	5,760	0.2	11	3,168	0.1
Dragon	180	67.00	3	540	18.1	4	720	24.1	2	360	12.1	3	540	18.1	1	180	6.0
MLRS[1]	9	872.57	99	891	388.7	98	882	384.8	75	675	294.5	76	684	298.4	67	603	263.1
Total					2,795.8			2,299.9			2,213.0			1,737.8			1,342.4

Figure 12. Ammunition Expenditures per Type Unit per Weapon per Day in STONs (continued)

Light Inf Div (77000L000)																	
ADA 20mm towed	18	0.80	4,800	86,400	34.6	2,880	51,840	20.7	3,984	71,712	28.7	2,151	38,718	15.5	1,200	21,600	8.6
AH-1S Hel TOW	29	87.00	12	348	15.1	13	377	16.4	9	261	11.4	10	290	12.6	5	145	6.3
Heli. 20mm	29	0.80	3,000	87,000	34.8	1,800	52,200	20.9	2,490	72,210	28.9	1,345	39,005	15.6	750	21,750	8.7
2.75 rocket	58	11.83	42	2,436	14.4	25	1,450	8.6	35	2,030	12.0	19	1,102	6.5	11	638	3.8
105mm How rds	54	60.00	423	22,842	685.3	467	25,218	756.5	376	20,304	609.1	381	20,574	617.2	210	11,340	340.2
Fuzes		3.92	444	23,984	47.0	490	26,479	51.9	395	21,319	41.8	400	21,603	648.0	221	11,907	23.3
40mm M203	831	0.75	32	26,592	10.0	19	15,789	5.9	27	22,437	8.4	15	12,465	4.7	8	6,648	2.5
Launcher 66mm, M202	81	8.75	16	1,296	5.7	10	810	3.5	14	1,134	5.0	7	567	2.5	4	324	1.4
Launcher TOW	44	87.00	9	396	17.2	10	440	19.1	7	308	13.4	8	352	15.3	4	176	7.7
MG .50 Cal	17	0.40	263	4,471	0.9	159	2,703	0.5	219	3,723	0.7	120	2,040	0.4	67	1,139	0.2
MG 7.62mm acft	104	0.09	840	87,360	4.1	509	52,936	2.5	700	72,800	3.4	382	39,728	1.8	213	22,152	1.0
MG 7.62mm 6-brl	2	0.09	6,000	12,000	0.5	3,600	7,200	0.3	4,980	9,960	0.4	2,698	5,396	0.2	1,500	3,000	0.1
MG 7.62 lt flex	465	0.09	649	301,785	14.0	393	182,745	8.5	541	251,565	11.7	295	137,175	6.4	164	76,260	3.5
MG 5.56mm M249	33	0.09	243	112,995	5.3	147	68,355	3.2	202	93,930	4.4	110	51,150	2.4	61	28,365	1.3
60mm mortar[2]	54	7.00	145	7,830	27.4	88	4,752	16.6	121	6,534	22.9	66	3,564	12.5	37	1,998	7.0
81mm mortar	36	17.32	145	5,220	45.2	88	3,168	27.4	121	4,356	37.7	66	2,376	20.6	37	1,332	11.5
M16 A1 rifle	9,587	0.04	148	1,418,876	29.8	90	862,830	18.1	124	1,188,788	25.0	67	642,329	13.5	38	364,306	7.7
Dragon	162	67.00	3	486	16.3	4	648	21.7	2	324	10.9	3	486	16.3	1	162	5,4
					1,007.5			1,002.5			875.66			1,412.0			440.39

FOOTNOTES:

[1]Ammunition expenditure rates for new items based on scaling factor from theater-level rates.

[2]Ammunition expenditure rates are the same as 81-mm mortar rates.

Figure 13. Ammunition Expenditures per Weapon per Day and STONs per Day by Level of Operation for All Types of Divisions

Weapon	Level of Operation	Defense of Position				Attack of Position				Protracted Period	
		First Day		Succeeding Days		First Day		Succeeding Days			
		Rounds	STON	Rounds	STON	Rounds	STON	Rounds	STON	Rounds	STON
1. MG 7.62 M18	Heavy	6000	0.300	3600	0.180	4980	0.249	2689	0.134	1500	0.075
	Moderate	4260	0.213	2556	0.128	3536	0.177	1909	0.095	1065	0.053
	Light	2580	0.129	1548	0.077	2141	0.107	1156	0.058	645	0.032
2. HEL ATK AH-1S 20MM GUN	Heavy	3000	1.200	1800	0.720	2490	0.996	1345	0.538	750	0.300
	Moderate	2130	0.852	1278	0.511	1768	0.707	955	0.382	533	0.213
	Light	1290	0.516	774	0.310	1071	0.428	578	0.231	323	0.129
3. HEL ATK AH-1S 7.62 MG	Heavy	840	0.042	509	0.025	700	0.035	382	0.019	213	0.011
	Moderate	596	0.030	361	0.018	497	0.025	271	0.014	151	0.008
	Light	361	0.018	219	0.011	301	0.015	164	0.008	92	0.005
4. HEL ATK AH-1S TOW	Heavy	12	0.593	13	0.642	9	0.445	10	0.494	5	0.247
	Moderate	9	0.445	9	0.445	6	0.296	7	0.346	4	0.198
	Light	5	0.247	6	0.296	4	0.198	4	0.198	2	0.099
5. ARAAV M551 SHILLELAGH	Heavy	7	0.392	9	0.504	6	0.336	7	0.392	3	0.168
	Moderate	5	0.280	6	0.336	4	0.224	5	0.280	2	0.112
	Light	3	0.168	4	0.224	3	0.168	3	0.168	1	0.056
6. ARAAV M551 152MM CTG	Heavy	9	0.270	5	0.150	7	0.210	4	0.120	2	0.060
	Moderate	6	0.180	4	0.120	5	0.150	3	0.090	1	0.030
	Light	4	0.120	2	0.060	3	0.090	2	0.060	1	0.030
7. ADA SP 20MM M163	Heavy	4800	2.400	2880	1.440	3984	1.992	2151	1.076	1200	0.600
	Moderate	3408	1.704	2045	1.023	2829	1.415	1527	0.764	852	0.426
	Light	2064	1.032	1238	0.619	1713	0.857	925	0.463	516	0.258
8. HOW SP 105MM M108	Heavy	423	14.488	467	15.995	376	12.878	381	13.049	210	7.193
	Moderate	300	10.275	332	11.371	267	9.145	271	9.282	149	5.103
	Light	182	6.234	201	6.884	162	5.549	164	5.617	90	3.083
9. HOW SP 155MM M109	Heavy	203	13.774	207	14.045	146	9.906	153	10.381	166	11.263
	Moderate	144	9.770	147	9.974	104	7.056	109	7.396	118	8.006
	Light	87	5.903	89	6.039	63	4.275	66	4.478	71	4.817
10. HOW SP 8" M110	Heavy	177	23.231	164	21.525	130	17.063	127	16.669	118	15.488
	Moderate	126	16.538	116	15.225	92	12.075	90	11.813	84	11.025
	Light	76	9.975	71	9.319	56	7.350	55	7.219	51	6.694
11. LCHR GREN 40MM M203	Heavy	32	0.017	19	0.010	27	0.015	15	0.008	8	0.004
	Moderate	23	0.013	13	0.007	19	0.010	11	0.006	6	0.003
	Light	14	0.008	8	0.004	12	0.007	6	0.003	3	0.002
12. LCHR GM DRAGON	Heavy	3	0.109	4	0.145	2	0.073	3	0.109	1	0.036
	Moderate	2	0.073	3	0.109	1	0.036	2	0.073	1	0.036
	Light	1	0.036	2	0.073	1	0.036	1	0.036	0	0.000
13. HEL ATK AH-1S 2.75" RKT	Heavy	42	0.693	25	0.413	35	0.578	19	0.014	11	0.182
	Moderate	30	0.495	18	0.297	25	0.413	13	0.215	8	0.132
	Light	18	0.297	11	0.182	15	0.248	8	0.132	5	0.083
14. LCHR RKT 66MM M202	Heavy	16	0.070	10	0.044	14	0.061	7	0.031	4	0.116
	Moderate	11	0.048	7	0.031	10	0.044	5	0.022	3	0.113
	Light	7	0.031	4	0.018	6	0.026	3	0.013	2	0.009
15. LCHR GM TOW	Heavy	9	0.445	10	0.494	7	0.046	8	0.395	4	0.198
	Moderate	6	0.296	7	0.346	5	0.247	6	0.296	3	0.148
	Light	4	0.198	4	0.198	3	0.148	3	0.148	2	0.099
16. MG .50 CAL, M2	Heavy	263	0.059	159	0.036	219	0.048	120	0.027	67	0.015
	Moderate	187	0.042	113	0.025	155	0.035	85	0.019	48	0.110
	Light	113	0.025	68	0.015	94	0.021	52	0.012	29	0.007
17. MG 7.62 6-BARREL	Heavy	6000	0.300	3600	0.180	4980	0.248	2689	0.134	1500	0.075
	Moderate	4260	0.213	2556	0.128	3536	0.177	1909	0.095	1065	0.053
	Light	2580	0.129	1548	0.077	2141	0.107	1156	0.058	645	0.032

Figure 13. Ammunition Expenditures per Weapon per Day and STONs per Day by Level of Operation for All Types of Divisions (continued)

Weapon	Level of Operation	Defense of Position				Attack of Position				Protracted Period	
		First Day		Succeeding Days		First Day		Succeeding Days			
		Rounds	STON	Rounds	STON	Rounds	STON	Rounds	STON	Rounds	STON
18. MORTAR 81MM	Heavy	145	1.256	88	0.762	121	1.048	66	0.572	37	0.320
	Moderate	103	0.892	62	0.537	86	0.745	47	0.407	26	0.225
	Light	62	0.537	38	0.329	52	0.450	28	0.242	16	0.139
19. MORTAR 4.2" M30	Heavy	163	3.260	99	1.980	136	2.720	74	1.480	41	0.820
	Moderate	116	2.320	70	0.400	97	1.940	53	0.060	29	0.580
	Light	70	1.400	43	0.860	58	1.160	32	0.640	18	0.760
20. RIFLE 5.56MM M16A1	Heavy	148	0.003	90	0.002	124	0.002	67	0.001	38	0.001
	Moderate	105	0.002	64	0.001	88	0.001	48	0.001	27	0.001
	Light	64	0.001	39	0.001	53	0.001	29	0.001	16	0.000
21. RIFLE RECOIL 90MM M67	Heavy	14	0.193	9	0.124	12	0.165	6	0.083	4	0.055
	Moderate	10	0.138	6	0.083	9	0.124	4	0.055	3	0.041
	Light	6	0.083	4	0.055	5	0.069	3	0.041	2	0.028
22. SUB MG CAL .45 M3	Heavy	44	0.001	27	0.001	37	0.001	20	0.001	11	0.000
	Moderate	31	0.001	19	0.001	26	0.001	14	0.000	8	0.000
	Light	19	0.001	12	0.000	16	0.000	9	0.000	5	0.000
23. TANK, M60A3 105MM	Heavy	78	2.808	47	0.692	65	2.340	35	0.260	20	0.720
	Moderate	55	1.980	33	1.188	46	1.656	25	0.900	14	0.504
	Light	34	1.224	20	0.720	28	1.008	15	0.540	9	0.324
24. CFV M3 25MM CTR	Heavy	277	0.259	216	0.202	225	0.210	166	0.155	98	0.082
	Moderate	197	0.184	153	0.143	160	0.150	118	0.110	70	0.065
	Light	119	0.111	93	0.087	97	0.091	71	0.066	42	0.039
25. CFV M3 TOW	Heavy	9	0.445	10	0.494	7	0.046	8	0.395	4	1.198
	Moderate	6	0.296	7	0.346	5	0.247	6	0.296	3	0.148
	Light	4	0.198	4	0.198	3	0.148	3	0.148	2	0.099
26. ITV M901 TOW	Heavy	13	0.642	15	0.741	10	0.494	12	0.593	6	0.296
	Moderate	9	0.445	11	0.543	7	0.346	9	0.445	4	0.198
	Light	6	0.296	6	0.296	4	0.198	5	0.247	3	0.148
27. IFV 25MM CTG	Heavy	214	0.200	167	0.156	174	0.163	129	0.121	76	0.071
	Moderate	152	0.142	119	0.111	124	0.116	92	0.086	54	0.050
	Light	92	0.086	72	0.067	75	0.070	55	0.051	33	0.031
28. IFV TOW	Heavy	6	0.296	7	0.346	5	0.247	6	0.296	3	0.148
	Moderate	4	0.198	5	0.247	4	0.198	4	0.198	2	0.099
	Light	3	0.148	3	0.148	2	0.099	3	0.148	1	0.049
29. HEL ATK AH-64 (30 MM)	Heavy	770	0.527	602	0.412	628	0.430	463	0.317	274	0.188
	Moderate	547	0.375	427	0.292	446	0.306	329	0.225	195	0.134
	Light	331	0.227	259	0.177	270	0.185	199	0.136	118	0.081
30. HEL ATK AH-64 (HELLFIRE)	Heavy	16	1.554	17	1.652	12	1.166	13	1.263	7	0.680
	Moderate	11	1.069	12	1.166	9	0.874	9	0.847	5	0.486
	Light	7	0.680	7	0.680	5	0.486	6	0.583	3	0.291

Figure 14. Daily Artillery Ammunition in Rounds per Weapon

Type of operation	Level of operation	First day Rounds	First day STON[3]	Succeeding days[1] Rounds	Succeeding days[1] STON	Protracted period[2] Rounds	Protracted period[2] STON
		Part A. 105-mm Howitzer					
Covering Force	1-Heavy	491	16.8	511	17.5	198	6.8
	2-Moderate	319	10.9	332	11.4	129	4.4
	3-Light	172	5.9	179	6.1	69	2.4
Defense of Position	1-Heavy	423	14.5	467	16.0	222	7.6
	2-Moderate	275	9.4	304	10.4	144	4.9
	3-Light	148	5.1	163	5.6	78	2.7
Attack of Position	1-Heavy	376	12.9	381	13.0	210	7.2
	2-Moderate	244	8.4	248	8.5	137	4.7
	3-Light	132	4.5	133	4.6	74	2.5
		Part B. 155-mm Howitzer (Divisional)					
Covering Force	1-Heavy	254	17.2	274	18.6	174	11.8
	2-Moderate	165	11.2	178	12.1	113	7.7
	3-Light	89	6.0	96	6.5	61	4.1
Defense of Position	1-Heavy	203	13.8	207	14.0	183	12.4
	2-Moderate	132	9.0	135	9.2	119	8.1
	3-Light	71	4.8	72	4.9	64	4.3
Attack of Position	1-Heavy	146	9.9	153	10.4	140	9.5
	2-Moderate	95	6.4	99	6.7	91	6.2
	3-Light	51	3.5	54	3.7	49	3.3
		Part C. 155-mm Howitzer (Nondivisional)					
Covering Force	1-Heavy	309	21.0	333	22.6	212	14.4
	2-Moderate	201	13.6	216	14.7	138	9.4
	3-Light	108	7.3	117	7.9	74	5.0
Defense of Position	1-Heavy	227	15.4	235	15.9	199	13.5
	2-Moderate	148	10.0	153	10.4	129	8.8
	3-Light	79	5.3	82	5.6	70	4.7
Attack of Position	1-Heavy	176	11.9	183	12.4	170	11.5
	2-Moderate	114	7.7	119	8.1	111	7.5
	3-Light	62	4.2	64	4.3	60	4.1
		Part D. 8-in Howitzer (Divisional)					
Covering Force	1-Heavy	360	47.3	361	47.4	207	27.2
	2-Moderate	234	30.7	235	30.8	135	17.7
	3-Light	126	16.5	126	16.5	73	9.6
Defense of Position	1-Heavy	177	23.2	164	21.5	90	11.8
	2-Moderate	115	15.1	107	14.0	59	7.7
	3-Light	62	8.1	57	7.5	32	4.2
Attack of Position	1-Heavy	130	17.1	127	16.7	56	7.4
	2-Moderate	85	11.1	83	10.9	36	4.7
	3-Light	46	6.0	45	5.9	20	2.6
		Part E. 8-in Howitzer (Nondivisional)					
Covering Force	1-Heavy	446	58.5	448	58.8	257	33.7
	2-Moderate	290	38.1	291	38.2	167	21.9
	3-Light	156	20.5	157	20.6	90	11.8
Defense of Position	1-Heavy	177	23.3	164	21.5	90	11.8
	2-Moderate	115	15.1	107	14.0	59	7.7
	3-Light	62	8.1	57	7.5	32	4.2
Attack of Position	1-Heavy	161	21.1	158	20.7	69	9.1
	2-Moderate	105	13.8	103	13.5	45	5.9
	3-Light	56	7.4	55	7.3	24	3.2
		Part F. 175-mm Gun (Nondivisional)					
Covering Force	1-Heavy	372	51.2	481	66.2	221	30.4
	2-Moderate	242	33.3	313	43.1	144	19.8
	3-Light	130	17.9	168	23.1	74	10.2
Defense of Position	1-Heavy	166	22.9	180	24.8	64	8.8
	2-Moderate	108	14.9	117	16.1	42	5.8
	3-Light	58	8.0	63	8.7	22	3.0
Attack of Position	1-Heavy	113	15.6	113	15.6	53	7.3
	2-Moderate	74	10.2	74	10.2	35	4.8
	3-Light	40	5.5	40	5.5	19	2.6

FOOTNOTES:

[1]Succeeding days are the second, third, and fourth days of the battle. For the fifth-day ammunition requirements, take the average of the succeeding-days' rate and the protracted rate.

[2]Protracted period refers to days 6 through 15. For estimating ammunition requirements for periods greater than 15 days, use rates provided in SB 38-26, as amended by DA message 262258Z Aug 76, subject: FY 77 USAREUR Ammunition-Theater Combat Rates.

[3]STON are computed on total weight per complete round: 105-mm—68.5 lb/rd
155-mm—135.7 lb/rd
175-mm—275.4 lb/rd
8-mm—262.5 lb/rd

Figure 15. Daily Anti-Tank Guided Missile Requirements in Rounds per Launcher and STONS

Type of operation	Level of operation	First day Missiles	First day STON[3]	Succeeding days[1] Missiles	Succeeding days[1] STON	Protracted period[2] Missiles	Protracted period[2] STON
	Part A. TOW (Mounted/Unmounted) Ground System						
Covering Force	1-Heavy	9	.39	10	.44	4	.17
	2-Moderate	5	.22	6	.26	2	.08
	3-Light	2	.08	3	.13	1	.04
Defense of Position	1-Heavy	9	.39	10	.44	4	.17
	2-Moderate	6	.26	7	.30	2	.08
	3-Light	4	.17	4	.17	1	.04
Attack of Position	1-Heavy	7	.30	8	.34	4	.17
	2-Moderate	4	.17	5	.22	2	.08
	3-Light	2	.08	3	.13	1	.04
Recon and Security	1-Heavy	5	.22	6	.26	4	.17
	2-Moderate	3	.13	4	.17	2	.08
	3-Light	2	.08	2	.08	1	.04
	Part B. TOW Aerial System						
Covering Force	1-Heavy	11	.48	12	.52	1	.22
	2-Moderate	6	.26	7	.30	3	.13
	3-Light	2	.08	3	.13	1	.04
Defense of Position	1-Heavy	12	.52	13	.57	5	.22
	2-Moderate	7	.30	8	.34	3	.13
	3-Light	3	.13	4	.17	1	.04
Attack of Position	1-Heavy	9	.39	10	.44	5	.22
	2-Moderate	5	.22	6	.26	3	.13
	3-Light	2	.08	3	.13	1	.04
Recon and Security	1-Heavy	7	.30	8	.34	5	.22
	2-Moderate	4	.17	5	.22	3	.13
	3-Light	2	.08	2	.08	1	.04
	Part C. Dragon						
Covering Force	1-Heavy	2	.06	2	.06	1	.03
	2-Moderate	2	.06	2	.06	1	.03
	3-Light	1	.03	1	.03	1	.03
Defense of Position	1-Heavy	3	.10	4	.13	1	.03
	2-Moderate	2	.06	2	.06	1	.03
	3-Light	1	.03	1	.03	1	.03
Attack of Position	1-Heavy	2	.06	3	.10	1	.03
	2-Moderate	1	.03	2	.06	1	.03
	3-Light	1	.03	1	.03	1	.03
Recon and Security	1-Heavy	2	.06	2	.06	1	.03
	2-Moderate	1	.03	1	.03	1	.03
	3-Light	1	.03	1	.03	1	.03
	Part D. Shillelagh						
Covering Force	1-Heavy	7	.39	8	.45	3	.17
	2-Moderate	3	.17	4	.22	2	.11
	3-Light	2	.11	2	.11	1	.06
Defense of Position	1-Heavy	7	.39	9	.50	3	.17
	2-Moderate	5	.28	6	.34	2	.11
	3-Light	3	.17	3	.17	1	.06
Attack of Position	1-Heavy	6	.34	7	.39	3	.17
	2-Moderate	3	.17	4	.22	2	.11
	3-Light	2	.11	3	.17	1	.06
Recon and Security	1-Heavy	4	.22	5	.28	3	.17
	2-Moderate	2	.11	3	.17	2	.11
	3-Light	1	.06	1	.06	1	.06

FOOTNOTES:

[1]Succeeding days are the second, third, and fourth days of the battle. For the fifth-day ammunition requirements, take the average of the succeeding-days' rate and the protracted rate.

[2]Protracted period refers to days 6 through 15. For estimating ammunition requirements for periods greater than 15 days, use rates provided in SB 38-26, as amended by DA message 262258Z Aug 76, subject: FY 77 USAREUR Ammunition-Theater Combat Rates.

[3]STON are computed with packaged weight per missile: Dragon — 67.0 lb/msl
Shillelagh — 112.0 lb/msl
TOW — 92.4 lb/msl

the demands for ammunition support. You as a logistician must remember that the problem will not be with small arms ammunition normally, but with larger caliber needs, such as artillery and main gun rounds. The movement of the massive weights represented by these commodities requires a great deal of planning and forethought.

Ammunition per Type Unit per Weapon

The accompanying table provides the expected expenditure data for most tactical situations and will enable you to predict the quantity of ammunition required for resupply. Note that the expenditures appear as quantities per day of operation, indicating that ammunition resupply must be a daily function to maintain operational stocks immediately available to the supported units.

Ammunition Expenditure by Level of Operation

The accompanying table *(Figure 13)* indicates the usage rates of ammunition as modified by the level of intensity involved in an action. This information can modify the predictable resupply needs extracted from the previous expenditure table.

Daily Artillery Ammunition Requirements and Anti-Tank Guided Missile Requirements

The artillery expenditure table *(Figure 14)* provides ammunition requirements in rounds per weapon per day and short tons (STON), by level of operation. An expenditure table also appears for anti-tank guided missile requirements *(See figure 15)*. These two tables give the data necessary for the logistician to plan resupply operations for these two categories of ammunition. Their tactical importance in modern warfare warrants separate discussion.

ESTABLISHING TRANSPORTATION PRIORITIES

The Army will never have enough transportation assets available to transport all required cargo simultaneously. Therefore, the logistician must separate the requirements into priorities according to the needs and the requirements of the supported combat units. The commanders of every formation are responsible for establishing the transportation priorities within their areas of operation, but logisticians must interpret the commanders' desires and assign specific priorities to every transportation commitment. As a logistician, you must consider several factors in assigning cargo priorities.

The first consideration should be the essentiality of the cargo to the combat units. Items that will have a direct effect on the outcome of the operation in progress would obviously be of high priority, but the logistician must also assign priorities in accordance with the projected needs of the supported units in the future. A particular load might guarantee a favorable outcome of today's battle, but if the battle is probably won with what is on the ground already, then maybe the load that will help get ready for tomorrow's battle is more important. The logistician on the ground must measure and assign the essentiality of a particular load in accordance with the needs of the supported combat unit.

Logisticians must also consider quantity, kind, and capabilities of lift available. Trucks are the most common type of transport on the battlefield, but rail assets, waterway assets, and aircraft may also be available. For example, aircraft are seldom capable of carrying the outsized or heavy cargo required on the battlefield, but they are the fastest way to deliver small emergency items or small quantities to the front lines.

The tactical situation and the type of operation being conducted also affect transportation priorities. The tactical situation influences the assignment of transportation priorities in two ways. First, the combat situation dictates what the most essential cargo to be transported is. Second, logisticians must consider the risk of losing transportation assets to enemy action. The danger of not having the truck or aircraft tomorrow when the priorities may be different can sometimes outweigh the needs of the combat units in today's battle. The logistician in support who has a broader overview of the situation is often in a better position to judge this dilemma than the combat commander at the front. At the very least, the combat service support officer must advise the overall combat commander of the risks involved in any transportation mission that endangers the commander's assets or ability to sustain support operations in the future.

In general, the following items have top priority in specific operations. If the supported unit is moving forward in the offense, the highest priority cargo for transport is normally fuel, with ammunition a very close second. In the defense, ammunition and fuel exchange order of importance with most combat units identifying ammunition and barrier/construction material as the most important items. When the unit is in a retrograde operation, the most important transport requirement is normally evacuation of materiel and personnel. Finally, for the combat unit in a retrofit or reconstitution situation, repair parts, major end items, and rations usually have a high priority.

Assigning priorities to transport requirements is not an easy task, especially when the best answer for most logistics problems is that it depends on the situation. Logisticians must ensure that those items that the combat unit must have arrive on time and in sufficient quantities. Further, they must ensure that delivery of nonessential cargo does not hinder the combat unit.

TRUCK PLANNING FACTORS

In the absence of specific data, use the following factors in motor transport planning for computing truck and truck company requirements.

• *Vehicle availability.* The average number of task vehicles available for daily operations out of the total task vehicles assigned to a truck unit:

—Operational short-range, 83 percent (maximum sustained effort; used only for an all-out effort and then only for periods of less than 30 days).

–Long-range planning, 75 percent.

• *Anticipated payload per vehicle.* Previously, vehicle payload was either off-road or highway. The planning factor or allowable load for highway operations exceeded those loads for off-road operations. Now, however, logisticians use only the off-road payload factor. The offroad capacity equals the rated capacity of vehicles, except 5,000-gal tankers, which are rated at 3,000-gal capacity for offroad operations.

• *Trips per day.* The daily round trips that a vehicle averages. Because trips vary with running times and loading and unloading times, the following figures are only general:

–Line-haul: one per operating shift.

–Local-haul: two per operating shift.

• *Length of haul.* The one-way distance to haul cargo from which to compute round-trip distance. The following figures are rule of thumb only:

–Line-haul, 144 km one way per operating shift.

–Local-haul, 32 km one way per trip.

• *Rate of movement.* The average number of kilometers traveled in one hour (KPH), including halts during the period of movement. To calculate rate of movement, also consider road conditions, such as surface, terrain, weather, and hostile activity. For long-range planning, use the following estimates:

–Poor roads, 16 KPH.

–Good roads, 32 KPH.

• *Turnaround time.* The time used in loading, unloading, and moving from origin to destination and return.

• *Delay time.* Time used in loading and unloading (includes time waiting, spotting [location at loading and unloading point], documenting, and handling cargo on and off vehicles) or relay time (hookup and drop trailers) in line-haul operations or both. When planning, also consider mess halts and rest halts. These figures are only general:

–Semitrailers and straight trucks, 2.5 hours loading and unloading time per round trip (direct haul).

–Container transporters, 1.5 hours loading and unloading time per round trip (direct haul).

–Truck tractors in semitrailer relay operations, 1 hour per relay (round trip per line-haul leg).

• *Operational day.* The number of hours per day in which vehicles with drivers normally are employed.

–One operating shift, 10 hours.

–Round the clock (two operating shifts), 20 hours.

• *Unit lift and daily lift.* Unit lift is the amount of cargo a truck unit can move at one time; daily lift is the number of trips a unit can move in a day. FM 55-15 discusses unit capabilities.

• *Ton-kilometers and passenger-kilometers.* The product of the tons or passengers times the actual distance traveled.

Figure 16. Local Haul Unit Capabilities for Cargo

(Vehicle availability × average tons per vehicle × trips per day = short-ton capability per day.)

	No. Vehicles Available (75% of Total Authorized)	Average STON Carried Per Trip	No. Trips	Total STON Cargo Moved Per Day
Light truck company (2-1/2 ton truck)	45	45	2-1/2	450
Light truck company (5-ton truck)	45	5	4	900
Medium truck company (cargo) (12-ton stake and platform)	45	12	4	2,160
Medium truck company (cargo) Flatbed break bulk/transporter (22-1/2-ton trailer)	45	15	4	2,700
Medium truck company (cargo) Flatbed break bulk/transporter (34-ton trailer)	45	25	4	4,500
Medium truck company (petroleum) (5,000-gallon tanker)	45	5,000	4	90,000 gal
Medium truck company (reefer) (7-1/2-ton reefer van)	45	6	4	1,080
Heavy truck company (60-ton semitrailer)	18	40	4	2,880
Light-medium truck company (2-1/2-ton truck)	45	2-1/2	4	450
(12-ton stake and platform)	8	12	4	384
Total light-medium truck company				834

Figure 17. Line Haul Unit Capabilities for Cargo

(Vehicle availability × average tons per vehicle × trips per day = short-ton capability per day.)

	No. Vehicles Available (75% of Total Authorized)	Average STON Carried Per Trip	No. Trips	Total STON Cargo Moved Per Day
Light truck company (2-1/2 ton truck)	45	2-1/2	2	225
Light truck company (5-ton truck)	45	5	2	450
Medium truck company (cargo) (12-ton stake and platform)	45	12	2	1,080
Medium truck company (cargo) (22-1/2-ton flatbed break bulk/transporter)	45	15	2	1,350
Medium truck company flatbed break bulk/transporter (34-ton trailer)	45	25	2	2,250
Medium truck company (petroleum) (5,000-gallon tanker)	45	5,000	2	450,000
Medium truck company (reefer) (7-1/2-ton reefer van)	45	6	2	540
Heavy truck company (60-ton semitrailer)	18	40	2	1,440
Light-medium truck company (2-1/2-ton truck)	45	2-1/2	2	225
(12-ton stake and platform)	8	2-1/2	2	192
Total light-medium truck company				417

Figure 18. Local Haul Unit Capabilities for Passengers

(Vehicle availability × passengers per vehicle × trips per day = passenger capability per day.)

	No. Vehicles Available (75% of Total Authorized)	Average Passengers Carried Per Trip	No. Trips	Passengers
Light truck company (2-1/2 ton truck)	45	20	4	3,600
Light truck company (5-ton truck)	45	20	4	3,600
Medium truck company (cargo) (12-ton stake and platform)[2]	45	50	4	9,000
Light-medium truck company (2-1/2-ton truck)	45	20	62	5,400
(12-ton stake and platform)[2]	8	50	62	7,800
Total light-medium truck company				13,200

FOOTNOTES:

[1]Recommended for emergency use only; no troop seats provided.

[2]Number of trips based on employment of unit in tactical situation. For general troop movements, planner should plan on four trips per day.

Figure 19. Line Haul Unit Capabilities for Passengers

(Vehicle availability x passengers per vehicle × trips per day = passenger capability per day.)

	No. Vehicles Available (75% of Total Authorized)	Average Passengers Carried Per Trip	No. Trips	Passengers
Light truck company (2-1/2-ton truck)	45	16	2	1,440
Light truck company (5-ton truck)	45	18	2	1,620
Medium truck company (cargo) (12-ton stake and platform)[1]	45	50	2	4,500
Light-medium truck company (2-1/2-ton truck)	45	202	2	1,800
(12-ton stake and platform)[2]	8	50	2	800
Total light-medium truck company				2,600

FOOTNOTES:

[1]Recommended for emergency use only; no troop seats provided.

[2]Number of personnel per vehicle based on employment of unit in tactical situation. For general troop movements, planner should recompute using 16 troops per vehicle.

TRUCK UNIT CARGO AND PASSENGER CAPABILITIES

For planning purposes, the unit capability tables *(Figures 16, 17, 18, and 19)* provide estimates of unit lift capabilities based on current Tables of Organization and Equipment. In the absence of specific operational data, they should enable logisticians to estimate truck requirements.

ESTIMATING TRUCK REQUIREMENTS

One-lift Hauls

To determine the number of truck companies required to move a given number of tons in one lift, use the following formula:

$$\text{Truck companies required} = \frac{\text{Tons to be lifted}}{\text{Tons per vehicle} \times \text{Vehicles available per company}}$$

Sustained Haul

Sustained haul is one continuous operation. In most operations, supplies flow continuously forward from supply points, depots, beaches, or terminals. In such cases, tonnages move forward only, and trucks return for another load. Compute the average turnaround time by dividing the round-trip distance by the rate of movement and adding delays:

$$\text{Turnaround time} = 2 \times \frac{\text{distance}}{\text{rate}} + \text{delays}$$

The formula used for sustained operations becomes:

$$\text{Truck companies required} = \frac{\text{Daily tonnage forward} \times \text{Turnaround time}}{\text{Tons per vehicle} \times \text{Vehicles available per company} \times \text{Operating time per day}}$$

AIR TRANSPORT PLANNING

Fixed-wing and rotary-wing aircraft can provide rapid movement of cargo, personnel, and equipment. Generally, fixed-wing aircraft are for long-distance movement, and rotary-wing are for shorter distances that require their ability to land with little or no ground run in unimproved areas. Planners must balance the selection of aircraft as a mode of transport against the availability of other transport. If the troops can perform the mission as quickly by trucks or any other mode of transport, planners should not use air transport.

AIR TRANSPORT PLANNING FACTORS

When planning for airlift of cargo, troops, or equipment, consider the following factors:

• *Availability.* Scheduled and unscheduled maintenance, repair parts supply, combat losses, and the geographical location of the operating and supporting service units affect availability of aircraft.

• *Landing sites.* In planning for helicopter support, provide adequate landing sites. Allow at least the following landing zone (LZ) dimensions:

OH-58, OH-6	80-ft diameter (25m)
UH-1	125-ft diameter (38m)
UH-60	160-ft diameter (49m)
CH-47, CH-54	264-ft diameter (80m)

• *Load/unload time.* Presume that the aircraft has been properly prepared for the type of cargo planned. The times reflected by the following data do not include palletizing cargo for internal loading or rigging time for external sling loads:

Personnel–	
Troops	3 minutes
Patients	10 minutes
Internal Cargo–	
Single vehicles	10 minutes
Vehicles and trailer	15 minutes
Palletized cargo	25 minutes
External Cargo–	
Hook-up time only	30 seconds

AIRCRAFT CHARACTERISTICS

The accompanying table *(Figure 20)* provides basic planning data for Army aircraft.

Figure 20. US Army Aircraft Characteristics

(Fixed Wing)

A. **AIRCRAFT**[1]	**UNIT**	**C-12A**	**C-12C**	**C-12D**	**OV-1B**	**OV-1C**	**OV-1D**	**RC-12D**	**RV-1D**	**T-42A**	**U-8F**
B. NORMAL CREW	PER AIRCRAFT	2	2	2	2 (Pilot & Radar Operator)	2 (Pilot & Ir (Operator)	2 (Pilot & Operator)	2	2 (Pilot & Operator)	2 for IFR	1 (2 for IFR)
C. OPERATIONAL CHARACTERISTICS[2,3,4]											
(1) MAX ALLOWABLE GROSS WEIGHT	LBS	12,500	12,500	12,500	15,795	14,823	18,109	14,200	18,109	5,100	7,700
(2) BASIC WEIGHT	LBS	7,869	8,084	8,084	10,983	10,011	12,054	8,143	12,054	3,480	5,490
(3) USEFUL LOAD	LBS	2,131	4,416	4,416	4,812	4,812	6,055	2,078	6,055	1,620	2,210
(4) PAYLOAD/NORMAL MISSION	LBS	2,000	2,000	2,000	NA	NA	NA	2,000	NA	1,115	590
(5) FUEL CAPACITY[9]	LBS/GAL (INTERNAL EXTERNAL)	2,470/386	2,470/386	2,470/386	1,930/297 1,950/300	1,930/297 1,950/300	1,790/276 1,950/300	2,470/386	1,790/276 1,950/300	852/142	1,380/230
(6) FUEL CONSUMPTION RATE[9]	LBS/GAL PER HOUR	350/538	456/70	456/70	826/126.9	826/126.9	900/130	456/70	900/130	154.8/ 25.8	204.5/35
(7) NORMAL CRUISE SPEED	KNOTS	240	260	260	225	225	220	260	220	177	160
(8) ENDURANCE AT CRUISE (PLUS 30 MIN RESERVE)	HOURS + MINUTES	6+30	5+15	5+15	1+55[14] 3+55[15]	1+55[14] 3+55[15]	1+40[14] 3+30[15]	5+15	1+40[14] 3+30[15]	5+00	5+30
(9) GRADE OF FUEL	OCTANE	JP-4/5	JP-4/5	JP-4/5	JP-4	JP-4	JP-4	JP-4/5	JP-4	115/145	115/145
D. PASSENGER CAPACITY											
(1) TROOP SEATS	EACH	8	8	8	1	1	1	8	1	3	5
(2) NORMAL CAPACITY	EACH	8	8	8	1	1	1	8	1	3	5
(3) TOTAL CAPACITY W/CREW	EACH	10	10	10	2	2	2	10	2	4	6
(4) LITTERS & AMBULATORY	EACH	NA	NA	NA	NA	NA	NA	NA	NA	NA	NA

Figure 20. US Army Aircraft Characteristics (continued)

E. EXTERNAL CARGO											
(1) MAXIMUM RECOMMENDED EXTERNAL LOAD[5]	LBS	NA	NA	NA	EACH WING 2000	EACH WING 2000	EACH WING 2000	NA	EACH WING 2000	NA	NA
F. DIMENSIONS											
(1) LENGTH — FUSELAGE[6]	FT-IN	43′-10″	43′-10″	43′-10″	41′-9″	41′-9″	41′-9″	43′-10″	41′-9″	27′-3″	33′-4″
(5) WIDTH — TREAD	FT-IN	17′-2″	17′-2″	17′-2″	9′-2″	9′-2″	9′-2″	17′-2″	9′-2″	9′-7″	12′-9″
(6) HEIGHT — EXTREME	FT-IN	15′-5″	15′-5″	14′-9″	13′-0″	13′-0″	13′-0″	15′-5″	13′-0″	9′-7″	14′-2″
(9) WING SPAN	FT-IN	54′-6″	54′-6″	55′-6.5″	48′-0″	42′-0″	48′-0″	54′-6″	48′-0″	37′-10″	45′-11″
G. CARGO DOOR											
(1) DIMENSIONS — WIDTH/HEIGHT	IN	27.7″ × 51.5″	27.7″ × 51.5″	52″ × 52″	NA	NA	NA	27.7″ × 51.5″	NA	13.5″ × 22.5″	50.5″ × 26.5″
(2) LOCATION — SIDE OF FUSELAGE	(LEFT/RIGHT FRONT/REAR)	LEFT REAR	LEFT REAR	LEFT REAR	NA	NA	NA	LEFT REAR	NA	NA	LEFT
H. CARGO COMPARTMENT											
(1) FLOOR — ABOVE GROUND	IN	47″	47″	42″	NA	NA	NA	47″	NA	NA	48″
(2) USABLE LENGTH	IN	128″	128″	128″	NA	NA	NA	128″	NA	NA	110.5″
(3) FLOOR WIDTH	IN	54″	54″	54″	NA	NA	NA	54″	NA	NA	5″
(4) HEIGHT (CLEAR OF OBSTRUCTIONS)	IN	57″	57″	57″	NA	NA	NA	57″	NA	NA	55″
(5) MAXIMUM CARGO SPACE	CU FT	306.5	306.5	306.5	NA	NA	NA	306.5	NA	NA	158

Figure 20. US Army Aircraft Characteristics (continued)

(Fixed Wing)

A. **AIRCRAFT**[1]	**UNIT**	**U-21A**	**U-21A**	**U-21F**	**U-21G**	**U-21H**	**RU-21A**	**RU-21B**	**RU-21C**	**RU-21D**	**RU-21H**
B. NORMAL CREW	PER AIRCRAFT	2	2	2	2	2	4 (2 Pilots & 2 Operators)	4 (2 Pilots & 2 Operators)	4 (2 Pilots & 2 Operators)	4 (2 Pilots & 2 Operators)	4 (2 Pilots & 2 Operators)
C. OPERATIONAL CHARACTERISTICS [2], [3], [4]											
(1) MAX ALLOWABLE GROSS WEIGHT	LBS	9,500	9,500	11,568	9,650	9,650	10,200	10,900	10,900	9,650	10,200
(2) BASIC WEIGHT	LBS	5,383	5,383	7,012	5,434	5,434	5,450	5,945	5,945	7,170	6,814
(3) USEFUL LOAD	LBS	4,117	4,117	2,756	4,216	4,216	4,750	4,945	4,945	2,480	3,386
(4) PAYLOAD/NORMAL MISSION	LBS	2,000	2,000	1,800	2,000	2,000	1,845	1,845	1,845	0	962
(5) FUEL CAPACITY[9]	LBS/GAL (INTERNAL EXTERNAL)	2,457/378	2,457/378	2,405/370	2,457/378	2,457/378	2,405/370	2,574/396	2,574/396	2,405/370	2,405/370
(6) FUEL CONSUMPTION RATE[9]	LBS/GAL PER HOUR	450/72	450/72	450/72	450/72	450/72	580/89.2	580/89.2	580/89.2	580/89.2	580/89.2
(7) NORMAL CRUISE SPEED	KNOTS	210	210	220	210	210	205	205	205	205	205
(8) ENDURANCE AT CRUISE (PLUS 30 MIN RESERVE)	HOURS + MINUTES	5+00	5+00	4+45	5+00	5+00	3+45	5+00	4+15	3+45	3+45
(9) GRADE OF FUEL	OCTANE	JP-4	JP-4	JP-4	JP-4	JP-4	JP-4/5	JP-4/5	JP-4/5	JP-4/5	JP-4/5
D. PASSENGER CAPACITY											
(1) TROOP SEATS	EACH	10	10	10	10	10	NA	NA	NA	NA	NA
(2) NORMAL CAPACITY	EACH	6	6	7	6	6	NA	NA	NA	NA	NA
(3) TOTAL CAPACITY W/CREW	EACH	12	12	12	12	12	4	5	4	4	4
(4) LITTERS & AMBULATORY	EACH	3/3	3/3	3/3	3/3	3/3	NA	NA	NA	NA	NA
E. EXTERNAL CARGO											
(1) MAXIMUM RECOMMENDED EXTERNAL LOAD[5]	LBS	NA	NA	NA	NA	NA	NA	NA	NA	NA	NA
F. DIMENSIONS											
(1) LENGTH — FUSELAGE[6]	FT-IN	35′-10″	35′-10″	39′-11″	35′-10″	35′-10″	35′-10″	35′-10″	35′-10″	35′-10″	35′-10″
(5) WIDTH — TREAD	FT-IN	12′-9″	12′-9″	13′-0″	12′-9″	12′-9″	12′-9″	12′-9″	12′-9″	12′-9″	12′-9″
(6) HEIGHT — EXTREME	FT-IN	14′-2″	14′-2″	15′-4″	14′-2″	14′-2″	14′-2″	14′-2″	14′-2″	14′-2″	14′-2″
(9) WING SPAN	FT-IN	45′-11″	45′-11″	45′-11″	45′-11″	50′-11″	50′-11″	45′-11″	45′-11″	45′-11″	50′-11″

Figure 20. US Army Aircraft Characteristics (continued)

G. CARGO DOOR											
(1) DIMENSIONS — WIDTH/HEIGHT	IN	50.5″ × 53″	50.5″ × 53″	17″ × 51.7″	50.5″ × 53″	50.5″ × 53″	50.5″ × 53″	50.5″ × 53″	33″ × 51.5″	50.5″ × 53″	50.5″ × 53″
(2) LOCATION — SIDE OF FUSELAGE	(LEFT/RIGHT FRONT/REAR)	LEFT	LEFT	LEFT	LEFT	LEFT	LEFT	LEFT	LEFT	LEFT	LEFT
H. CARGO COMPARTMENT											
(1) FLOOR — ABOVE GROUND	IN	48″	48″	45″	48″	48″	48″	48″	48″	48″	48″
(2) USABLE LENGTH	IN	110.5″	110.5″	132″	110.5″	110.5″	110.5″	110.5″	110.5″	110.5″	110.5″
(3) FLOOR WIDTH	IN	55″	55″	54″	55″	55″	55″	55″	55″	55″	55″
(4) HEIGHT (CLEAR OF OBSTRUCTIONS)	IN	55″	55″	57″	55″	55″	55″	55″	55″	55″	55″
(5) MAXIMUM CARGO SPACE	CU FT	230	230	306	230	158	158	158	158	158	158

(Rotary Wing)

A. AIRCRAFT[1]	UNIT	OH-6A	OH-58A	OH-58C	CH-47A	CH-47B	CH-47C	CH-47D	CH-54A
B. NORMAL CREW	PER AIRCRAFT	1 + Observer	1 + Observer	1 + Observer	4	4	4	4	4
C. OPERATIONAL CHARACTERISTICS [2], [3], [4]									
(1) MAX ALLOWABLE GROSS WEIGHT	LBS	2,400	3,000	3,200	33,000	40,000	46,000	50,000	42,000
(2) BASIC WEIGHT	LBS	1,163	1,586	1,898	18,153	19,591	20,481	22,499	20,800
(3) USEFUL LOAD	LBS	1,237	1,417	1,302	14,888	20,455	23,380	27,501	21,200
(4) PAYLOAD/NORMAL MISSION	LBS	650[8]	760[8]	837[8]	10,000	15,000	18,200	20,206	11,650[8]
(5) FUEL CAPACITY[9]	LBS/GAL (INTERNAL EXTERNAL)	400/61.5	475/73	465/71.5	4,036/621	4,036/621	7,351/1131	6,695/1030	8,794/1,353
(6) FUEL CONSUMPTION RATE[9]	LBS/GAL PER HOUR	143/22	189/29	175/27	2,120/342	2,780/427	3,038/467	2,600/400	3,624/556
(7) NORMAL CRUISE SPEED	KNOTS	121	120	120	120	150	155	155	95
(8) ENDURANCE AT CRUISE (PLUS 30 MIN RESERVE)	HOURS + MINUTES	3 + 15	3 + 30	3 + 00	1 + 30	1 + 00	2 + 00	2 + 30	2 + 00
(9) GRADE OF FUEL	OCTANE	JP-4	JP-4	JP-4	JP-4	JP-4	JP-4	JP-4	JP-4/5
D. PASSENGER CAPACITY									
(1) TROOP SEATS	EACH	3	4	4	33	33	33	33	1
(2) NORMAL CAPACITY	EACH	3	4	4	33	33	33	33	1
(3) TOTAL CAPACITY W/CREW	EACH	4	4	4	37	37	37	37	5
(4) LITTERS & AMBULATORY	EACH	NA	2/4	2	24	24	24	24	0
E. EXTERNAL CARGO									
(1) MAXIMUM RECOMMENDED EXTERNAL LOAD[5]	LBS	NA	NA	NA	16,000	20,000	20,000	20,000	20,000
(2) RESCUE HOIST CAPACITY	LBS	NA	NA	NA	600	600	600	600	NA
(3) CARGO WINCH CAPACITY	LBS	NA	NA	NA	3,000	3,000	3,000	3,000	15,000

Figure 20. US Army Aircraft Characteristics (continued)

(7) NORMAL CRUISE SPEED	KNOTS	110	92-140	90-120	145	0-190[19]	0-190[19]	0-161[19]
(8) ENDURANCE AT CRUISE (PLUS 30 MIN RESERVE)	HOURS + MINUTES	1+30	3+00 – 2+45	2+15	2+15	2+007	2+30	1+45
(9) GRADE OF FUEL	OCTANE	JP-4/5	JP-4/5	JP-4/5	JP-4/5/8	JP-4	JP-4	JP-4/5/8
D. PASSENGER CAPACITY								
(1) TROOP SEATS	EACH	1	7	11	14	0	0	0
(2) NORMAL CAPACITY	EACH	1	7	11	14	0	0	0
(3) TOTAL CAPACITY W/CREW	EACH	5	9	13	17	0	0	0
(4) LITTERS & AMBULATORY	EACH	0	3	6	4/6	0	0	0
E. EXTERNAL CARGO								
(1) MAXIMUM RECOMMENDED EXTERNAL LOAD[5]	LBS	25,000	3,787	4,000	8,000	NA	1,380[18]	6,200[18]
(2) RESCUE HOIST CAPACITY	LBS	NA	300[17]	300[17]	600	NA	NA	NA
(3) CARGO WINCH CAPACITY	LBS	25,000	NA	NA	NA	NA	NA	NA
F. DIMENSIONS								
(1) LENGTH — FUSELAGE[6]	FT-IN	70′-0″	42′-7″	40′-7″	50′-7.5″	44′-5.2″	44′-7″	49′-3″
(2) LENGTH — BLADES UNFOLDED	FT-IN	88′-5″	52′-10″	57′-1″	64′-10″	52′-11.7″	53′-1″	57′-1″
(3) LENGTH — BLADES FOLDED	FT-IN	NA	NA	NA	40′-4″	NA	NA	NA
(4) WIDTH — BLADES FOLDED	FT-IN	NA	NA	8′-7″	9′-8.1″	10′-4″	10′-9″	16′-3″
(5) WIDTH — TREAD	FT-IN	19′-9″	8′-4″	8′-7″	8′-10.2″	7′-0″	7′-0″	6′-6″
(6) HEIGHT — EXTREME	FT-IN	24′-5″	12′-8″	14′-6″	17′-6″	11′-7″	13′-9″	12′-6″
(7) DIAMETER — MAIN OR FORWARD ROTOR	FT-IN	72′-0″	44′-0″	48′	53′-8″	44′-0″	44′-0″	49′-0″
(8) DIAMETER — TAIL OR REAR ROTOR	FT-IN	16′-0″	8′-6″	8′-6″	11′-0″	8′-6″	8′-6″	9′-3″
(9) WING SPAN	FT-IN	NA	NA	NA	NA	10′4″	10′4″	16′3″
G. CARGO DOOR								
(1) DIMENSIONS — WIDTH/HEIGHT	IN	104.5″ (POD)	48″ × 48″	74″ × 48″	68″ × 54″	NA	NA	NA
(2) LOCATION — SIDE OF FUSELAGE	(LEFT/RIGHT FRONT/REAR)	REAR	LEFT & RIGHT	LEFT & RIGHT	LEFT & RIGHT	NA NA	NA NA	NA NA
H. CARGO COMPARTMENT								
(1) FLOOR — ABOVE GROUND	IN	27″ (POD)	14″	24″	19″	NA	NA	NA
(2) USABLE LENGTH	IN	329″	60″	92″	110″	NA	NA	NA
(3) FLOOR WIDTH	IN	104.52″	80.5″	96″	72″	NA	NA	NA
(4) HEIGHT (CLEAR OF OBSTRUCTIONS)	IN	78″	54″	49″	54″	NA	NA	NA
(5) MAXIMUM CARGO SPACE	CU FT	1,552	140	220	246.8	NA	NA	NA
I. WEAPONS[10]	NA	NA	XM-3 M-5 M-6 XM-16 XM-21 M-22 XM-156	M-23 M-56 M-5923	M-23	M-18 M-28 M-35 M-1,571[11] M-158A1[11] M-159[12] M-200[12]	M-65 M-97 M-158 M-200[12] M-260 M-261	XM-430 HELLFIRE M-200[12] M-260 M-261 M-230

Figure 20. US Army Aircraft Characteristics (continued)

(Rotary Wing)

AIRCRAFT[1]	UNIT	OH-6A	OH-58A	OH-58C	CH-47A	CH-47B	CH-47C	CH-47D	CH-54A
F. DIMENSIONS									
(1) LENGTH — FUSELAGE[6]	FT-IN	23′-0″	32′-3.5″	32′-8.8″	51′-0″	51′-0″	51′-0″	51′-0″	70′-0″
(2) LENGTH — BLADES UNFOLDED	FT-IN	30′-4″	40′-11.8″	40′-11.8″	98′-3″	99′-0″	99′-0″	99′-0″	88′-5″
(3) LENGTH — BLADES FOLDED	FT-IN	23′-0″	NA	NA	51′-0″	51′-0″	51′-0″	51′-0″	NA
(4) WIDTH — BLADES FOLDED	FT-IN	5′-6″	NA	NA	12′-5″	12′-5″	12′-5″	12′-5″	NA
(5) WIDTH — TREAD	FT-IN	6′-9″	6′-3.5″	6′-5.4″	11′-11″	11′-11″	11′-11″	11′-11″	19′-9″
(6) HEIGHT — EXTREME	FT-IN	8′-3″	9′-6.5″	12′-0″	18′-6″	18′-8″	18′-8″	18′-8″	24′-5″
(7) DIAMETER — MAIN OR FORWARD ROTOR	FT-IN	26′-4″	35′-4″	35′-4″	59′-1″	60′-0″	60′-0″	60′-0″	72′-0″
(8) DIAMETER — TAIL OR REAR ROTOR	FT-IN	4′-3″	5′-2″	5′-2″	59′-1″	60′-0″	60′-0″	60′-0″	16′-0″
(9) WING SPAN	FT-IN	NA	NA	NA	NA	NA	NA	NA	NA
G. CARGO DOOR									
(1) DIMENSIONS — WIDTH/HEIGHT	IN	41″ × 34.5″	40″ × 35″	40″ × 35″	90″ × 78″	90″ × 78″	90″ × 78″	90″ × 78″	104.5″ (POD)
(2) LOCATION — SIDE OF FUSELAGE	(LEFT & RIGHT FRONT REAR)	LEFT & RIGHT	LEFT & RIGHT	REAR RIGHT	REAR	REAR	REAR	REAR	REAR
H. CARGO COMPARTMENT									
(1) FLOOR — ABOVE GROUND	IN	14.5″	22.5″	22.5″	30″	31.2″	31.2″	31.2″	27″ (POD)
(2) USABLE LENGTH	IN	5′-9″	39″	39″	360″	360″	30′-2″	30′-2″	329″
(3) FLOOR WIDTH	IN	3′-2″	50″	50″	90″	90″	7′-6″	7′-6″	104.5″
(4) HEIGHT (CLEAR OF OBSTRUCTIONS)	IN	3′-2″	50″	50″	78″	78″	6′-6″	6′-6″	78″
(5) MAXIMUM CARGO SPACE	CU FT	40	20	20	1,474	1,474	1,474	1,474	1,552
I. WEAPONS[10]	NA	XM-27E-1	XM-27E-1	NA	M-24 XM-41	M-24 XM-41	M-24 XM-41	M-24 XM-41	NA

(Rotary Wing)

A. AIRCRAFT[1]	UNIT	CH-54B	UH-1C/M	UH-1H/V	UH-60	TH/AH-1G	AH-1S	AH-64[13,22]
B. NORMAL CREW	PER AIRCRAFT	4	2	2	3	2	2	2
C. OPERATIONAL CHARACTERISTICS[2, 3, 4]								
(1) MAX ALLOWABLE GROSS WEIGHT	LBS	47,000	9,500	9,500	20,250	9,500	10,000	17,400
(2) BASIC WEIGHT	LBS	21,200	4,827	5,132	10,500	5,560	6,598	10,505
(3) USEFUL LOAD	LBS	25,800	4,673	4,368	6,195	3,940	4,302	6,895
(4) PAYLOAD/NORMAL MISSION	LBS	16,258	2,685	2,900	3,360[16]	1,785[20]	1,293[20]	4,090[20]
(5) FUEL CAPACITY[9]	LBS/GAL (INTERNAL EXTERNAL)	8,794/1,353	15,573/242	1,358/209	2,360/362	1,755/270	1,703/262	2,405/370
(6) FUEL CONSUMPTION RATE[9]	LBS/GAL PER HOUR	4,230/65[1]	500/77 550/84[21]	550/84	960/148	546/83.6	640/98	810/124

Figure 20. US Army Aircraft Characteristics (continued)

FOOTNOTES:

[1]A — Attack, C — Cargo, O — Observation, U — Utility.
[2]All data computed at standard conditions at sea level.
[3]Detailed weight computations and characteristics taken from current 55-series TMs.
[4]Data subject to change due to developmental testing.
[5]Maximum load the aircraft is capable of lifting.
[6]Dimension from nose to end of tail.
[7]Varies with load carried. Figure given is for normal mission profile.
[8]Does not meet 200-NM range requirement of normal mission definition.
[9]Aviation gas figured on 6 lbs/gal. JP-4 computed on 6.5 lbs/gal.
[10]Indicates type of weapons aircraft can carry. Specific armament based on unit assignment.
[11]Seven-round 2.75-inch rocket pod.
[12] Nineteen-round 2.75-inch rocket pod.
[13]Subject to final development configuration.
[14]Without external fuel.
[15]With external fuel.
[16]Normal mission, internal load, probability exists to cube out before weight out. Max load on the floor is 300 lbs/sq ft.
[17]UH-1 is restricted to hoist capacity of 300 lbs because of center of gravity conditions.
[18] External wing stores.
[19]Due to armament configurations and flight profiles.
[20]Considers gross weight minus basic weight minus 400 lbs for crew and total fuel weight.
[21]Fuel consumption at 92 kts, 77 gal/hr; at 140 kts, 84 gal/hr.
[22]Weapons are not applicable to UH-1V, medical evacuation helicopters.

CONSIDERATIONS:

- This chart is for general reference use only. Refer to the appropriate operator's manual for detailed information.
  Definitions of terms used in this table include the following:
- Maximum allowable gross weight. The maximum allowed total weight of the aircraft prior to takeoff. The ''basic weight'' of the aircraft plus the crew, personnel equipment, special device, passengers and cargo, and usable fuel and oil. This is limited by structure, power available, or landing load.
- Basic weight. The empty weight of an aircraft configuration to include all appointments, integral equipment, instrumentation, and trapped fuel and oil, but excluding passengers, cargo, crew, fuel, and oil.
- Useful load. The load-carrying capability of an aircraft including payload, crew, oil, and usable fuel required for the mission. This is the difference between ''maximum allowable gross weight'' and ''basic weight'' as defined above. Thus, a reduction of the fuel load will decrease the endurance and increase the payload. Fuel oil is required for all missions.
- Payload. The useful load less the crew, full oil, and the required fuel for the mission.
- Normal mission. Payload available computed under the follow conditions:
  - Fuel for 200 NM plus 30-minute reserve.
  - Flight altitude 2000′ mean sea level, standard temperature.
  - Takeoff maximum gross weight (weight of crew included).
- Normal cruising speed. The true airspeed which an aircraft can normally be expected to maintain at some standard power setting below rated military power. This speed will vary with altitude (for example, the U-8F's normal is 165 at 65% power at 8,000 feet).
- Endurance at cruising speed. The time that an aircraft can remain airborne at normal cruising speed with fuel aboard without using the required fuel reserve. The data listed under ''Operational Characteristics'' are computed using full fuel minus a 30-minute reserve.

ESTIMATING AIRCRAFT REQUIREMENTS

Most close support airlift missions require helicopters. These operations will generally be less than 35 nautical miles and may require more than one sortie in support of the total required lift. To determine the number of helicopters or units required to accomplish a specific mission or the capabilities of aircraft to perform a specific mission, use the following formulas.

- To determine the number of trips per aircraft per day:

$$N = \frac{(H\text{-}R) \times S}{D}$$

Where: N = number of round trips per day per type of aircraft.
H = number of operational hours per day.
R = refueling/service stops (in hours).
S = Average sortie speed of aircraft in knots. For planning, use cruising speed unless otherwise specified.
D = round-trip distance in nautical miles. This distance must be the actual distance flown rather than a straight-line course from origin to destination. When estimating distance, consider terrain, weather, enemy situation, and aids to navigation.

- To determine the number of aircraft required:

$$O = \frac{T}{N \times P}$$

Where: O = the number of aircraft required.
T = tonnage to be moved.
N = number of trips per day per type aircraft.
P = payload of type aircraft used.

- To determine the capability of a given number of aircraft (or units):

$$T = N \times P \times A$$

Where: T = tonnage that available aircraft can move.
N = number of round trips per day per type of aircraft.
P = payload per type of aircraft.
A = number of aircraft available.

RECOVERY AND EVACUATION PROCEDURES AND RESPONSIBILITIES

Recovery is the first action in returning mired, damaged, or broken equipment to the battlefield. It is the removal of materiel from hazardous areas or areas of active operations to a repair place or to an evacuation location. Recovery operations stop at the direct support maintenance collection point. Recovery has several purposes:

- Retrieve weapons and materiel so they can be repaired and returned to service or cannibalized.
- Retrieve equipment that has become mired or stuck.
- Prevent the enemy from gaining use of friendly equipment.
- Remove enemy materiel from the battlefield for either friendly use or intelligence purposes.

The owning unit is responsible for recovery of its own equipment with assistance from direct support units if available. The owning unit can take any of the following measures:

- Self-recovery by the crew or operator to a secure area or collection point.
- Recovery by similar or larger tactical equipment.
- Recovery by recovery equipment, such as wreckers or tracked recovery vehicles.
- Requesting assistance from support units when recovery is beyond the capability of the owning unit, perhaps simply notifying the support unit of the location of the equipment if it is in a secure area.

Evacuation starts where recovery stops. Evacuation is a coordinated effort of maintenance, supply, and transportation elements. Unserviceable equipment is either repaired at the direct support collection point or evacuated to other locations where support units can repair, cannibalize, or salvage it. Logisticians should coordinate evacuation to preclude multiple handling of the item. They should use all backhaul capability, but the equipment being evacuated should go from the collection point directly to its final destination if possible. If evacuation capabilities are not sufficient to backhaul entire items, then support units should attempt to evacuate components and major assemblies. They should leave nothing that is reusable on the battlefield if the means to recover and evacuate are available.

In the process of recovery and evacuation, logisticians may use two other actions to return the greatest quantity of equipment to the battlefield: controlled substitution and cannibalization. Controlled substitution is the removal of serviceable parts, components, and major assemblies from unserviceable but repairable equipment for installation in a like unserviceable item. The intent is to return items to the battlefield as quickly as possible and to prevent the evacuation of serviceable parts and assemblies if a need exists for them in the forward areas. Support units need to use caution to replace the serviceable parts with the unserviceable parts for which they are being substituted. This procedure ensures evacuation of a complete item of equipment, a process that eases repair by higher levels of maintenance. Cannibalization is the removal of serviceable parts and components from items of equipment that cannot be repaired, for installation on like items of equipment to return them to operational status. Support units need not return the cannibalized item to a complete status because other units will salvage rather than repair it. If any level has declared an item irreparable, support units should immediately begin the removal and recovery of usable parts for either application to other equipment or evacuation to the rear for redistribution.

Commanders at all levels must establish priorities for recovery and evacuation of equipment. The aim of these priorities should be, first, to return the greatest quantity of equipment to the battle and, second, to save as much materiel as possible, including components and parts, for future use.

LOGISTICS OPERATIONS IN A NUCLEAR, BIOLOGICAL, OR CHEMICAL ENVIRONMENT

A nuclear, biological, or chemical (NBC) environment poses a distinct and menacing challenge to combat service support (CSS) operations. In an NBC environment, all aspects of CSS will become more difficult with an increase in workloads and a decrease in productivity and capability. In general, casualties will increase greatly, thus not only increasing the medical workload but also posing a transportation problem for evacuation. Supply points will sustain damage from nuclear blasts and will suffer from the same predictable increase of casualties that will deplete the combat forces. Maintenance support requirements will increase, and the necessity of working in protective masks and bulky protective suits will reduce the productivity of maintenance personnel. Full protective equipment will also encumber supply personnel. CSS units will respond more slowly and require more time to accomplish their functions. Contaminated equipment will hamper salvage, recovery, supply, medical, maintenance, and transportation operations. Decontamination procedures are time-consuming but essential to reduce the CSS vulnerability to contamination casualties. In some cases, support units will have to distribute contaminated supplies of ammunition and equipment and repair contaminated equipment before decontamination because of the battlefield situation, but CSS commanders must carefully consider the risks involved for their personnel.

The key to lessening the effects of an NBC environment on CSS operations is to train all personnel to operate under these conditions before they confront an NBC environment.

CSS commanders must plan for and train their soldiers to operate in an NBC environment. This preparation must include these procedures:

- Analysis of vulnerability and effects of NBC warfare on CSS operations.
- Identification of alternate methods of CSS support capable of coping with the effects of NBC warfare.
- Flexibility in planning to allow for continuation of support operations with reduced capability.
- Identification and coordination of required augmentation from decontamination units.
- Plans for transportation and medical augmentation to support large numbers of casualties.
- Support estimates and plans that reflect the reduced response of support units in the NBC environment.

• Development of operational procedures to minimize contamination of supplies and equipment.

RECOVERY, EVACUATION, AND MAINTENANCE OF CONTAMINATED EQUIPMENT

Owning units are responsible for the decontamination to the extent of their capabilities. Logisticians should develop standard operating procedures (SOPs) for recovery, handling, and decontamination of equipment before its submission to support maintenance personnel. This SOP should address the prevention of contamination of materiel, as well as its decontamination. Decontamination is time-consuming and can cause further damage to some items of unserviceable equipment. Providing overhead cover or tarpaulins for unused/unserviceable parked equipment and stocks of supplies will assist in preventing liquid contamination of materiel and will also help in reducing contamination by nuclear fallout.

If owning units do not have the capability for decontamination of their own unserviceable equipment, they should mark the equipment with the date/time of its contamination and the type of contamination. They should also ensure that such items are separate from other unserviceable equipment.

When owning units turn in contaminated equipment to support maintenance units, the support units must decide whether to decontaminate it or repair it as it is. This decision involves weighing the criticality of the equipment to the supported unit against the time required to complete decontamination. The support unit must consider that, if the decision is to repair as it is, the repair personnel will not be able to work as quickly, as efficiently, or as long while they are wearing protective gear as they could normally.

SUPPLY OPERATIONS IN AN NBC ENVIRONMENT

In an NBC environment, support units must protect supplies, no matter which class, as much as possible. Although support units should store all stocks under overhead cover when it is available, covers of any sort, such as tarpaulins or plastic sheets, will provide some degree of protection against contamination. Before issuing any supplies suspected of being contaminated or exposed to contamination, support units must have qualified personnel survey and evaluate them. Support units should very carefully protect water sources and Class I stocks as much as possible and get them special attention in surveying before issue in an NBC environment.

Any stocks of contaminated supplies must be decontaminated and resurveyed before issue. Some types of supplies, such as paper products or fresh food items, would be destroyed by decontamination and should be discarded.

MEDICAL OPERATIONS IN AN NBC ENVIRONMENT

The number of casualties requiring medical care in the NBC environment will increase enormously over the usual number of battlefield casualties. Medical units will require assistance in the decontamination of patients and facilities. Transporting casualties to the rear will require assistance. Most forward medical elements will require augmentation to provide treatment to the great number of casualties they will have to handle. Commanders should train all troops in self- or buddy-aid decontamination to assist medical personnel in giving aid more rapidly.

TRANSPORTATION SUPPORT OPERATIONS IN AN NBC ENVIRONMENT

Just as it does all other CSS functions, an NBC environment complicates transportation support. Alternate supply routes become very important, and strict traffic control measures are necessary to prevent the use of contaminated routes. The necessary detours and rerouting will increase turnaround times and require additional transportation assets to maintain the flow of materiel forward. The use of aviation support will increase on a contaminated battlefield because of the aircraft's ability to fly over contaminated areas and the great dispersion of the combat elements. Aircraft will also prove very helpful in responding to transportation requests from medical units for evacuation of casualties.

DECONTAMINATION PROCEDURES

Commanders must train their soldiers to conduct decontamination procedures for four reasons. First, contamination by chemical, biological, or radiological agents is lethal. It kills some soldiers immediately and goes on killing others for an extended period of time. Second, soldiers must wear protective clothing and equipment under mission oriented protective posture (MOPP) guidelines, and this additional clothing and equipment protection greatly degrades their performance and hampers all aspects of military operations. Third, MOPP gear has limitations and will not provide protection for extended periods of use. Finally, the only way to prevent the spread of contamination is by elimination. These points all lead to the necessity of decontamination.

Decontamination occurs on two levels. Partial decontamination consists of those minimum requirements necessary to keep a weapon system or a unit operating on the battlefield, such as the decontamination of weapon controls, driving controls, entrance surfaces, and other such areas to allow operation. Complete decontamination includes all the steps necessary to allow the operation of equipment for extended periods of time at reduced MOPP levels.

Decontamination is very time-consuming and requires the commitment and expenditure of a great deal of assets and manpower. Although they should eventually completely decontaminate all equipment, unit commanders may well find that they are capable of only partial decontamination while on the battlefield and that they have to wait for a period of reconstitution to finish the job.

Contamination exposes soldiers to four general types of hazards:

• *Transfer.* If a surface is contaminated with a solid or a liquid agent, then physical contact with that surface will result in a casualty. Such an injury is by transfer.

• *Vapor.* Any agent that can be breathed constitutes a vapor hazard, such as dust, atomized liquids, or gas. A dusty contaminated surface can also produce a vapor hazard if it is disturbed. For example, if a tracked vehicle drove over a contaminated area, the surface of the vehicle itself would be a transfer hazard, but the dust kicked up into the air would actually be a vapor hazard.

• *Desorption.* Liquid contaminants absorbed into the pores of equipment that slowly evaporate into the surrounding air establish a desorption hazard. This condition is related to temperature and can injure soldiers long after the NBC environment has been eliminated.

• *Radiation.* Often called fallout, this hazard comes from radioactive dust and dirt. Treat this contaminant as a solid contamination.

Four principles form the basic doctrine for decontamination operations. The first and most important principle is to decontaminate as soon as possible. A contaminated environment forces soldiers to stay in MOPP gear, which degrades combat power and combat service support operations. Begin restoring combat power as soon as possible by decontaminating.

The second principle is to decontaminate only what is necessary because decontamination requires a large commitment of resources that should not be wasted on equipment that will not influence the battlefield. Commanders must consider several things: unit mission, available time, degree of contamination, length of time the unit has been MOPP-4, and decontamination assets available.

Third, decontaminate as far forward as possible. This procedure will limit the spread of contamination to other areas. Bring decontamination apparatus and units forward instead of bringing contaminated units or equipment to the rear.

Fourth, decontaminate by priority. As in all other aspects of combat service support, decontamination requires setting priorities. Commanders must decide which items are most important to the unit's mission and have them decontaminated first.

Hasty Decontamination Procedures

Hasty decontamination procedures normally occur at the organizational level. Two techniques can limit the spread of liquid and particle contamination. For the soldiers, an exchange of MOPP gear will reduce the contamination level of the unit. The equipment of the unit must be at least partially decontaminated or very quickly washed down if possible. Take these steps as early as possible for maximum effectiveness.

Deliberate Decontamination Procedures

Deliberate decontamination includes detailed troop decontamination and detailed equipment decontamination. These procedures require considerable resources and normally occur at company level or higher in units in reconstitution status. Units cannot complete a deliberate decontamination while still engaged in combat. Even deliberate decontamination measures, however, cannot completely remove the effects of contamination. They allow the unit to operate for extended periods of time at reduced MOPP levels. Desorption hazards will still exist, and the unit NBC personnel must continually monitor to prevent casualties.

Casualty Decontamination Procedures

Combat service support units will see the first results of NBC warfare in the medical units. Decontamination of casualties starts at the organization level. To reduce the danger of contaminating the supporting medical units as much as possible, units should not transport contaminated casualties to the rear before decontamination, except in the most severe combat conditions.

Patient Decontamination Procedures

The first place that a patient should be decontaminated is where he falls on the battlefield. If this method is not possible, then the patient should be decontaminated at the battalion aid station (BAS). The principle is to decontaminate as forward as possible. At the BAS, nonmedical personnel from the unit must accomplish the decontamination. If contaminated casualties arrive at supporting medical units before decontamination, they must be decontaminated before treatment. Commanders must augment the medical units with manpower from any assets available in the area to decontaminate patients if the workload is beyond their capabilities.

Fatality Decontamination Procedures

The NBC environment will produce a large number of fatalities as well as casualties. These dead soldiers will constitute a distinct hazard to the remaining personnel on the battlefield. The remains must be decontaminated and interred as soon as possible. The threat of spreading contamination can be greatly reduced by burial of contaminated remains within the theater of operations. They should not be evacuated through normal graves registration channels. If they must be evacuated, they must be clearly marked as contaminated to alert the personnel involved in handling them.

Contaminated remains must be decontaminated as soon as possible. Induced radioactive contamination cannot be removed, and biological contamination cannot normally be detected in normal graves registration procedures. These two types of contaminated remains must be clearly tagged, identified, and interred very quickly.

When decontaminating remains, graves registration personnel must wear protective equipment. Chemically contaminated remains can be decontaminated using the M258 series personal decontamination kit. Remains contaminated by radiological debris must be thoroughly washed with soap and water, and biological contamination can be reduced by washing the remains with 10 percent calcium hypochlorite solution or full-strength household bleach followed by rinsing with clean water. Clothing and equipment must be destroyed and decontaminated quickly to prevent the spread of contamination.

When contaminated remains have been interred, the burial sites must be clearly marked as contaminated areas.

Maintenance Decontamination Procedures

The requirement to wear MOPP gear greatly hampers the conduct of maintenance operations in the NBC environment. Mechanics are further hindered because MOPP equipment loses its protective ability when exposed to grease, oil, and dirt. Thus, extra MOPP gear must be available for maintenance personnel. Placing wet weather clothing over MOPP gear gains some added protection, but the buildup of heat also slows maintenance efforts.

It is essential that maintenance personnel stay in MOPP gear when working on equipment that has been used on a contaminated battlefield even if it has undergone decontamination procedures. Because petroleum products trap chemical contaminants, equipment that is safe to operate can still be hazardous to repair or maintain. Casualties to support maintenance personnel become a high risk unless they use MOPP gear.

In general, contaminated equipment should not be evacuated to support maintenance operations. It should be fixed in place if possible or decontaminated before it reaches the support activity. Maintenance units must monitor and survey all incoming equipment because the risk of casualties is too high to depend on decontamination in the forward areas. Remember that decontaminated equipment is still hazardous to maintenance personnel. Monitor, segregate, and mark all contaminated equipment. If in doubt, assume that all equipment is contaminated. Also, segregate all tools used on contaminated equipment. Do not mix contaminated and clean tools. Maintenance units should have extra vehicle on-board decontamination apparatus on hand and immediately available in the shop areas. Further, all contaminated markings must be left on the repaired equipment, even if it has been decontaminated, to remind the owning unit that the item must be monitored in the future.

All decontamination personnel and all maintenance personnel should be constantly monitored and decontaminated at least once each day.

Decontamination of Supplies

Support units cannot use the same method to decontaminate all supply items. Some supplies require specialized treatment. Other items cannot be decontaminated at all. Most decontaminants are highly corrosive and must be used carefully, if at all, on many items. Most military equipment has not been evaluated for the best method of decontamination, but some general guidance is available.

Electronics equipment is normally sealed to make it watertight or dust proof. This seal is very helpful because it also means that contamination very seldom gets inside tactical electronic equipment. Decontaminate this equipment by wiping the outside with a decontaminant or hot soapy water. Then wipe it with a clean damp cloth and allow it to dry. The final step is to wipe the surface with oil.

Because of the corrosive nature of most decontaminants, optical equipment, especially plastic lenses, will be very vulnerable to damage during decontamination. The best method of decontamination for optical equipment is to wash it with hot soapy water or to use the wipes from the M258A1 personal decontamination kit. If you use the kit, use wipe #2 before wipe #1 to prevent leaving residue on lenses. The final step is to wipe all surfaces again with a clean damp cloth.

Ammunition should be wiped or washed gently with cool soapy water. No other decontaminant can be used. Most would remove the markings on the ammunition, rendering it unidentifiable. Other decontaminants are highly flammable and greatly increase the explosive hazard of the ammunition.

It is very difficult to decontaminate canvas items, including slings and web gear. It is usually easier to destroy and replace such items. If they must be decontaminated, they should be boiled for one hour and then rinsed in clean water.

Food items are also very difficult to decontaminate and obviously very vulnerable to hazardous conditions. The first step in handling food is to try to prevent contamination by proper storage. Store food under cover if at all possible. Even under cover, food should remain in its wrappers, boxes, or containers. Store those containers in a reefer, in a building, or at least under canvas.

Contaminated food falls into three groups:

Group I is packaged food with protective covering that has been exposed to chemical vapor contamination. This category includes items inside bottles, cans, aluminum foil, heavy waxed paper, or sealed plastic. These items can be decontaminated by weathering with continuous monitoring. When readings are negative, these food items are safe for consumption. Each item, however, should be carefully examined to ensure that there is no break in the container and that it has remained sealed.

Group II includes packaged items with protective covering that has been exposed to liquid chemical or biological contamination or radioactive fallout. These items should be decontaminated according to the material of the package. Food in this category packaged in paper or cardboard must be discarded. Guidance on the appropriate decontaminant to use is available in the accompanying charts.

Group III includes food items stored in unsealed and unprotected containers that have been exposed to any type of contamination. Discard and destroy these items.

In all three categories of contaminated food, any item suspected of being contaminated inside its package must be discarded and destroyed.

Contaminated water supplies must be tested by medical personnel and decontaminated by water supply specialists.

Standard Decontaminants

1. Decontaminating Solution No. 2 (DS2)
   Use: Biological and Chemical Contamination

Remarks

Effective against all known toxic chemical agents and biological materials (except bacterial spores) if sufficient contact time is allowed.

Allow to remain in contact with contaminated surface for approximately 30 minutes for VX or 8 to 10 minutes for mustard and G agents. Rinse off with water. Recheck for contamination.

Can be used at temperatures from −15°F.

Used with the ABC-Mill 1½-quart portable decon apparatus, M13 DAP, or can be applied with brooms and swabs.

Most effective when application is accompanied by scrubbing action.

Cautions

Extremely irritating to the eyes and skin. Protective mask and rubber gloves must be worn. If DS2 contacts skin, wash the area with water. Do not inhale vapors.

Will cause a green to black color change upon contact with ABC M8 detector paper and cause a false/positive with M9 paper.

Ignites spontaneously on contact with STB and HTH.

Avoid spilling DS2 on chemical protective overgarment.

Combustible. Do not confuse with fire extinguisher. DS2 is a combustible liquid with a flash point of 160°F. Spraying DS2 onto heated surfaces above 168°F will ignite the DS2.

Do not use on M17-series mask (damages Mylar diaphragm in voicemitter assembly).

Preparations

No mixing is required; issued in ready-to-use solutions.

Remarks	Cautions	Preparations
	Corrodes aluminum, cadium, tin, and zinc; softens leather. May soften, remove, or discolor paint. Rinse well after use, and oil metal surfaces.	
	Ineffective against bacterial spores.	

2. Super Tropical Bleach (STB)
   Use: Biological and Chemical Contamination

Remarks	Cautions	Preparations
Effective against lewisite, V and G agents, and biological agents.	Ignites spontaneously on contact with liquid blister agent or DS2.	Slurry Paste: mix one 50-lb drum of STB with 6 gals water. Slurry paste consists of approximately equal parts (by weight) of STB and water.
Allow to remain in contact with contaminated surface for at least 30 minutes, then wash off with clear water.	Gives off toxic vapors on contact with G agent.	Dry Mix: 2 shovels STB to 3 shovels earth or inert material (such as ashes).
	Not recommended for ship use. Top deck storage only.	
	Corrosive to most metals and injurious to most fabrics (rinse thoroughly and oil metal surfaces).	Slurry Mix: *a*. Chemical-slurry mix will consist of 40 parts STB to 60 parts water (by weight). To mix in M12A1, use 1300 lbs STB, 225 gals water, 12½ lbs antiset, 24 oz antifoam. *b*. Biological-slurry mix will consist of 7 parts STB to 93 parts water (by weight). To mix in M12A1, use 150 lbs STB, 225 gals water, 1½ lbs antiset, 24 oz antifoam.
	STB mixtures (dry and slurry) do not effectively decon mustard if it has solidified at low temperatures.	
	Porous surfaces may require several applications.	
	Should not be inhaled or come in contact with the skin.	Camouflage: Lampblack or dye mixes may be added for camouflage.

(continued)

Remarks	Cautions	Preparations
	Protective mask or other respiratory protection device should be worn when mixing slurry. Store in unheated warehouse isolated from combustibles and metals subject to corrosion.	No mixing.

3. Mask Sanitizing Solution
   Use: Chemical and Biological Contamination

Remarks	Cautions	Preparations
Used on previously cleaned mask with filter elements removed.	1 gal of solution needed for every ten masks.	Fill standard plastic canteen to shoulder with water. Add 0.5-gram tube calcium hypochorite from water purification kit (NSN 6810-00-266-6979). Cover canteen and shake vigorously for 30 seconds.
Place mask face up. Attach canteen to mask at the drinking tube. Drain one canteen full of sanitizing solution through the mask. Follow with two canteens of clean water as a rinse.		Mix bulk quantities as follows: add 2 grams (.08 oz) of calcium hypochlorite from 6-oz jar (NSN 6810-00-255-0471) to 1 gal water.
Immerse mask and outserts in sanitizing solution. Agitate for 5 minutes. Rinse twice in clear water, agitating 2 or 3 minutes each time.		
Dry all parts and reassemble mask.		

4. Soap and Detergents (Detergent, general purpose, liquid, NSN 7930-00-282-9699)
   Use: Nuclear, Biological, and Chemical Contamination

Remarks	Cautions	Preparations
Scrub contaminated surfaces twice with hot, soapy water solution or immerse item in the solution.	Soaps and detergents are effective in physically removing contamination. However, casualty-producing levels of contamination may remain, so the runoff water must be considered contaminated.	Mix 75 lbs of powdered soap in 350 gal of water. If powdered soap is not available, bar laundry soap may be used (75 lbs of soap, cut into 1-inch pieces and dissolved in 350 gals hot water). For smaller amounts of soap solution, use a ration of approximately 1 lb soap per gal of water. Mix 2 pints detergent to 450 gals water in M12A1 PDDE.

Natural Decontaminants

1. Water
   Use: Nuclear, Biological, and Chemical Contamination

Remarks	Cautions
Flush contamination from surfaces with large amounts of water.	Effective in physically removing contamination, but does not neutralize the contamination.

2. Steam
   Use: Nuclear, Biological, and Chemical Contamination

Remarks	Cautions
The use of steam accompanied by scrubbing is more effective than the use of steam alone.	Effective in physically removing contamination. However, contamination may not be neutralized.

3. Absorbents (earth, sawdust, ashes, rags, etc.)
   Use: Chemical Contamination

Remarks	Cautions
Used to physically remove gross contamination from surfaces.	The contamination is transferred from the surface to the absorbent. The absorbent becomes contaminated and must be disposed of accordingly.

4. Sealants (concrete, asphalt, earth, paint, etc.)
   Use: Nuclear, Biological, and Chemical Contamination

Remarks	Cautions
Used to physically seal in or shield contamination.	A break in the surface of the sealant will expose the contamination.
Various sealants are effective as follows:	Contaminated areas covered with sealants must be marked with appropriate NBC warning signs.
12 inches of earth provides good protection from fallout (3 inches will reduce the dose rate by about one half).	
4 inches of earth provides good protection from chemical contamination.	
1 inch of asphalt or concrete completely absorbs alpha and beta radiation.	
¼ inch of grout shields alpha and beta radiation.	
Burying items contaminated with biological agents is an effective means of sealing off contamination.	

8

Formats for Orders, Plans, and Estimates

One of the keys to good support is standardization of administrative information systems and effective formulation of orders and directives. This chapter presents several standard formats and examples to aid the logistician in conducting and controlling combat service support operations. The proper use of these formats will ensure that the information needed by the logistician is available in a usable form. Further, it will ensure that the information passed to the supported and supporting elements is understandable and useful.

OPERATIONS ORDER FORMAT

The first and most basic standard format is the operations order (OPORD). In its five paragraphs, it identifies and stipulates the conditions of an operation or series of operations in a logical and easily understandable sequence. With the addition of annexes to cover the details of the operation, it becomes the instruction booklet from the commanding element on what is expected to be accomplished, what all of the factors affecting the operation are, and how the commander wants the units to proceed. The operations order applies to all levels of command and all types of units.

There are two illustrations of the operations order provided. One example is an annotated operations order, which will aid in understanding the intricacies of an operations order. The other is a blank operations order format. It is provided as a "fill-in-the-blank" format, which you could photocopy and use for taking notes, or use as a worksheet for operations order composition.

When confronting the operations order and all of its various details, the planner's first question will be where to find the data to include in the operations order. Therefore, the sources of information for an operations order are also noted on the blank format.

Annotated Operations Order

NOTES

Abbreviations may be used to save time and space if there is no loss of clarity. Except for abbreviations in common international use; e.g., mm (for millimeters), abbreviations normally are not used in an order that is to be circulated for inter-Allied use.

3. *a.* G3 provides except for message reference number (YZ 51). See *f* below.

b. Copy number: Must be shown.

c. Issuing unit: May be in code.

d. Place of issue: Show name of town or place, coordinate location in parentheses, and country. May be in code.

e. Date-time group: Time order is signed and time order is effective unless otherwise indicated in the body of the order. Time must include time zone suffix.

f. Message reference number: Assigned by G3 from a block of numbers provided by the division C-E officer. Its use facilitates acknowledgement of the order. (See note 21)

8. Paragraph 1 will always contain three subparagraphs.

a. Subparagraph a. Provided by G2 and contains enemy information only. Instructions are not included. Reference may be made to an intelligence annex, operation overlay (if enemy information is shown), periodic intelligence report, or intelligence summary. Only enemy information vital to the entire command is included. Letter designation of the annex is provided by G3.

b. Subparagraph b. G3 includes information concerning higher, adjacent, supporting, and reinforcing units, as applicable. Information should be limited to that which subordinate commanders need to know to accomplish their assigned mission.

(Classification) (Note 1)

(No change from oral orders.) (Note 2)

(Note 3)
Copy No 2 of ___ copies
52d Mech Div
XRAYVILLE (QU6271), MISSOURI
131800S Jan ___
YZ 51

OPERATION ORDER 7 (Note 4)

Reference: Map, series V661, KANSAS-MISSOURI, sheet 7061 (METROPOLIS-JUNCTION CITY), edition 1, 1:50,000 (Note 5)

Time Zone Used Throughout the Order: SIERRA. (Note 6)

Task Organization: (Note 7)

1st Bde
- 1-77 Mech
- 1-78 Mech
- 1-2 Armor
- 1-4 Armor
- C/52d Avn (OPCON)
- A/1-23 Cav
- 1-40 FA (DS)
- A/1-441 ADA (DS)
- 500th Engr Cbt Bn (Corps) (-) (DS)
  - 5045th Engr Aslt Fltbrg Co (Ribbon)
  - A/52d Engr (OPCON)

2d Bde
- 1-79 Mech
- 1-80 Mech
- 1-5 Armor
- D/52d Avn (OPCON)
- 1-41 FA (DS)
- B/1-441 ADA (DS)
- B/52d Engr (DS)
  - B/500th Engr (OPCON)

3d Bde
- 1-81 Mech
- 1-82 Mech
- 1-3 Armor
- C/52d Engr (DS)
  - C/500th Engr (OPCON)

Div Arty
- 1-42 FA
- 1-43 FA
- 2d Bn (155, SP), 631st FA
  - (atch eff 132000 Jan)
- 52d Tgt Acq Brty

Div Trp
- 1-23 Cav (-)
- 1-441 ADA (C/V)
- 52d Cbt Avn (-)
- 52d CEWI
  - 1st Plt, Co C (EW), 219th CEWI Tac Xplt Bn (remains atch)
- 52d Engr (-)
- 52d MP Co
- 52d NBC Def Co
- 52d Sig
- 500th CA Tac Spt Co (remains atch)

DISCOM
- 52d AG Co
- 52d Fin Co
- 52d Maint
- 52d Med
- 52d S&T

1. SITUATION (Note 8)

a. Enemy Forces. Annex A (Intelligence).

NOTES

1. Determined by G3. Classified per Army Regulation 380-5. Classification is shown at top and bottom of each page of the order.

2. Each staff officer having a responsibility in the preparation of the operation order provides G3 with status of oral orders pertaining to his activity and, when appropriate, applicable remark. If no oral orders were issued, this comment will be left out. If there were oral orders, such expressions as "No change from oral orders" or "No change from oral orders except for paragraph 4" will be used as appropriate.

4. Operation order number is provided by G3. Numbers run serially throughout the calendar year.

5. Each staff officer providing information or entries for the operation order provides G3 with references as appropriate. List any maps, charts, or other documents required to understand the order. Reference to a map will include the map series number (and country or geographic area, if required), sheet number (and name if required), edition, and scale (if required).

6. The zone applicable to the operation. Times in other zones are converted to this time zone for this operation.

7. *a.* Task organization indicates how the command is organized to accomplish the mission. Task organization may be shown in one of three places.

(1) Immediately preceding paragraph 1. This technique is normal at the division.

(2) In an annex. This technique is used when a large number of units are involved.

(3) In paragraph 3 of the operation order. This technique is most adaptable to brigade and lower levels.

b. G3 develops the task organization based on the commander's decision and concept, if given, and in coordination with staff officers having responsibilities in combat and combat support operations. Selection of specific units, except for maneuver battalion,

Annotated Operations Order (continued)

b. Friendly Forces.

(1) 1st Corps atk 140900 Jan to secure METROPOLIS (QU3069). 53d Mech Div on our left atks as part of corps atk. The 201st ACR protects corps north flank.

(2) Elm 10th AF spt 52d Mech Div.

(3) 2d Bn (Imprv Hawk), 461st ADA reinf 1-441 ADA (C/V)

(4) 61st FA Bde reinf 52d Mech Div Arty.

c. Attachments and Detachments. Task organization.

2. MISSION (Note 9)

Div atk 140900 Jan, secures JUNCTION CITY (QU4873) and high ground from Hill 984 (QU4469) to Hill 892 (QU4578), and prepares to continue the atk to the west to penetrate the enemy main defensive belt.

3. EXECUTION (Note 10)

a. Concept of Operation. Annex B (Operation Overlay).

(1) Maneuver. Div atk with 1st Bde making the main atk in the north (right), 2d Bde in the south (left), and 3d Bde in reserve to penetrate enemy positions in zone and secure the div objectives and prepares to continue the atk to the west.

(2) Fires. A 15-minute conventional arty preparation will be fired beginning H-10 min. Priority of arty and close air spt to 1st Bde.

(3) Obstacles. * * *

b. 1st Bde: Be prepared to receive up to two bns reinf.

c. 2d Bde.

d. 1-23 Cav (-):

(1) Maintain contact with 53d Mech Div on the south.

(2) Prepare to release one troop to DISCOM for rear area security.

e. Fire Support: (Note 11)

(1) Chemical Support: Appendix 1 (Chemical Support) to Annex C (Fire Support.

(2) Close Air Support:

(a) General.

1. Seventy-six air sorties allocated to 52d Mech Div for planning purposes only.

2. Priority of employment to 1st Bde, 2d Bde and counterfire targets in that order.

(b) Allocation for planning purposes only.

1. 1st Bde: 36 sorties daily.
2. 2d Bde: 16 sorties daily.
3. Div control: 24 sorties daily.

(c) Appendix 2 (Close Air Support) to Annex C (Fire Support).

c. Subparagraph c. G3 determines from the operation order of the next higher headquarters units attached to or detached from the division. He lists these units together with the effective times. If these units are listed in the "Task Organization," they need not be included in subparagraph c. G3 recommends further attachments to subordinate elements of the division to the division commander.

9. The mission is a clear, concise statement of the task to be accomplished by the command and its purpose. It includes the essential tasks determined by the commander as a result of his mission analysis. This paragraph has no subparagraphs. The mission is stated in full, even if portions are shown on the overlay.

10. *a.* The first subparagraph in paragraph 3 of the operation order is the concept of operation. The concept of operation is a statement of the commander's visualization of the conduct of the operation. The concept clarifies the purpose of the operation and is stated in sufficient detail to insure appropriate action by subordinates in the absence of additional specific instructions. The concept of operation may be a single paragraph or may be divided into two or more sub-subparagraphs: maneuver, fires, obstacles and others the commander considers appropriate. If the operation is to be phased, a sub-subparagraph for each phase may be appropriate. If lengthy, the concept of operation may be prepared as an annex. As a minimum, the concept of operation states the scheme of maneuver and plan of fire support. It includes priority of artillery fire when appropriate and, if a preparation is to be fired, its time and duration, and employment of nuclear and chemical fires.

b. In subsequent lettered subparagraphs, specific tasks to be accomplished by each element of the command charged with the execution of a tactical mission are shown. Tasks adequately shown on the operation overlay need not be repeated in the body of the order (e.g., 2d Bde.) If there is a priority or sequence for accomplishment, it is stated. G3 determines tasks from the command is the prerogative of unit commanders who provide unit designations to staff officer concerned. Staff officer concerned provides to G3 for inclusion in the operation order.

c. The task organization may be depicted by phase of the operation, if appropriate.

d. Units are grouped by command and control headquarters appropriate to the operation to be conducted. Major subordinate maneuver units (e.g., 1st Bde) are listed first in alphabetical or numerical order (task forces, when formed, that are a major subordinate command precede brigade listings), followed by Divarty, Division troops and DISCOM.

e. Units listed under a major subordinate control of headquarters are in an attached status unless otherwise indicated in parentheses following the unit designation (examples: A/52d Engr (DS) or 1-41 FA (DS)) The parenthetical term indicates a command relationship other than attachment, not a mission assignment. Mission assignments must be made in paragraph 3. The order of listing units under the major subordinate headquarters is as follows.

(1) Maneuver units (task forces, infantry, mechanized, air assault, airborne, infantry, armor. Armor units are listed in this order: tank, attack helicopter, armored cavalry, and air cavalry.

(2) Artillery fire support elements.

(3) Other combat support elements in alphabetical order.

(4) Combat service support elements in alphabetical order.

f. Organic units of a major subordinate control headquarters (such as DISCOM and elements of division troops) that are performing routine combat support and combat service support activities for other major subordinate elements, i.e., brigades, may be omitted in the listing underneath the brigade.

g. Attachments reflected in "Task Organization" need not be repeated in paragraph 1c or in paragraph 3.

Annotated Operations Order (continued)

mander's decision and any explanation and amplification thereof. Subordinate elements are listed in the following order:

(1) Major subordinate maneuver commands. Named or numbered task forces are listed first followed by brigades.

(2) Infantry elements.

(3) Armored elements. (Tank, atk hel, cav, air cav.)

(4) Fire support elements. (In alphabetical order, if practicable.)

(5) Combat support elements (in alphabetical order).

(6) Division troops (tactical instructions only.

(7) Support command (tactical instructions only).

(3) Field Artillery Support

(a) General.

1. Priority of fires to 1st Bde.
2. Counterfire priorities: enemy mortars and FA affecting committed brigades, then the nuclear capable fire systems.

(b) Organization for Combat.

1-40 FA: DS 1st Bde
1-41 FA: DS 2d Bde
1-42 FA: GSR 1-40 FA; on order DS 3d Bde.
1-43 FA: GSR 1-40 FA
2-631 FA (155, SP): GSR 1-41 FA

(c) Appendix 3 (Field Artillery Support to Annex C (Fire Support).

(4) Naval Gunfire Support: Appendix 4 (Naval Gunfire Support) to Annex C (Fire Support).

(5) Nuclear Support: Appendix 5 (Nuclear Support) to Annex C (Fire Support).

(6) Annex C (Fire Support).

f. Air Defense: (Note 12)

(1) 1-441 ADA (CV): GS; protect in priority 1-43 FA, Div Main CP.

(2) Annex D (Air Defense).

g. 52d CEWI:

(1) Priority of coverage to 1st Bde zone then to 2d Bde.

(2) Annex A (Intelligence).

(3) Annex E (Electronic Warfare).

h. Engr Support: (Note 13)

(1) General.

(a) Priority of engr support to attacking bdes, reserve in order.
(b) Priority of engrs with attacking bdes: to mobility, countermobility, and survivability in that order.
(c) Priority of engrs with reserve: to survivability, mobility, and countermobility in that order.

(2) Organization for Combat.

(a) Div engrs: 52d Engr (-) GS.
(b) Attached engrs: 500th Engr Cbt Bn (-) DS 1st Bde.

(3) Annex F (Engineer).

11. *a* Recommended by division artillery commander except for priority of fire, which is determined by the division commander.

b As a minimum, the fire support subparagraph will include the organization for combat and assigned tactical missions of organic and attached field artillery and the reference to the fire support annex, if applicable.

c The fire support subparagraph may contain a sub-subparagraph for each fire support means applicable to the operation (i.e., chemical, close air support, field artillery, naval gunfire, and nuclear) Each means is listed in alphabetical order, if practicable. A fire support annex should be used if data required is too extensive.

12. Recommended by air defense artillery staff officer. Priorities of air defense are provided by the division commander. The air defense subparagraph is divided into two or more subparagraphs to allow for statement of air defense priorities, organization for combat and assigned tactical missions of organic and attached air defense artillery and reference to the air defense annex, if applicable.

13. Recommended by G3 in coordination with division engineer. Letter designation of annex is provided by G3. Provides information on priority of engineer effort, organization/for combat of organic and attached engineer units, missions, and reference to the engineer annex and obstacle annex if applicable.

14. Provided by G3 based on guidance received from the commander (these instructions do not conflict with tactical instructions previously issued to elements listed under div trp. These instructions pertain to

Annotated Operations Order (continued)

their administrative and logistic elements as well as those combat support and combat service support units not specifically listed in the subpara of para 3).

15. Provided by G4 in coordination with G1, G2, and G3, G5, support command commander, and appropriate special staff officers.

16. Reserve: G3 determines from the commander's decision and any explanation and amplification thereof. It is always included as the next to the last subparagraph in paragraph 3 unless there are no coordinating instructions, in which case it becomes the last subparagraph.

i. 52d NBC Def Co: Prepare to release one plt to each committed bde.

j. Div Trp (-): on order, follow 2d Bde. (Note 14)

k. DISCOM.

(1) Prepare to receive one cav trp for rear area security.

(2) Move to vicinity of BEANTOWN (QU5275) on order. (Note 15)

l. Res: 3d Bde: follow 1st Bde, prepared for employment in zone of 1st or 2d Bde in priority; establish liaison and communications with 201st ACR; be prepared to protect div north flank. (Note 16)

m. Coordinating Instructions: (Note 17)

(1) Task organization effective 132000 Jan.

(2) EEI: Will the enemy 312 TKD be used in a counterattack in our zone? If so, when and where?

(3) Troop safety: negligible risk to warned, exposed personnel.

(4) Operation exposure guide: moderate risk.

(5) MOPP: Personnel will wear protective clothing (open) and carry protective masks.

(6) Annex G (Deception)

(7) Annex H (Phychological Operations).

4. SERVICE SUPPORT (Note 18)

a. General. Div installations remain in present locations. Annex I (Service Support).

b. Materiel and Services.

(1) Supply.

(a) Cl III. SUPPT 506, cl III, 1st COSCOM, at QU7283.

(b) Cl V.

1. ASP 950, 1st COSCOM, at QU8391, open 141000 Jan.
2. SASP 915, 1st COSCOM, at QU8592, open 141000 Jan.
3. CSR 14-15 Jan.

	HE	ICM(AP)	ICM(DP)	WP	ILLUM
4.2-in	75				
155-mm	95	30	25	10	10
8-in	80	20	10		

(2) Transportation.

(3) Services.

c. Civil-Military Cooperation. Annex J (Civil Affairs). (Note 19)

17. Coordinating instructions are included as the last subparagraph in paragraph 3. This subparagraph contains instructions applicable to two or more elements of the command. Signal instructions are not included in this subparagraph. EEI, when included, are provided by the G2. The operation exposure guide (OEG) is included in this subparagraph to express the commander's guide to exposure of personnel to radiation during the operation. Mission-oriented protective posture (MOPP) normally will be included in the SOP; exceptions are included here. Annexes not listed elsewhere in the order will be referenced in coordinating instructions.

18. Provided by G4 in coordination with G1, G5, support command commander, and appropriate special staff officers. If these instructions are numerous or voluminous, they may be included in an annex and reference made to the annex in paragraph 4. Letter designations of annexes are provided by G3.

19. If civil affairs (CA) units are also assigned tactical mission, the reference to the CA annex will also be listed in para 3 with other combat support elements.

Annotated Operations Order (continued)

5. COMMAND AND SIGNAL (Note 20)

a. Command. Div Tactical CP initially QU520710.

b. Signal.

(1) CEOI Index 3.

(2) Annex K (Communications-Electronics)

Acknowledge. (Note 21)

von STEUBEN (Note 22)
MG

OFFICIAL:

GEORGE
G3

Annexes: A–Intelligence
B–Operation Overlay
(Note 23) C–Fire Support
D–Air Defense
E–Electronic Warfare
F–Engineer
G–Deception
H–Psychological Operations
I–Service Support
J–Civil Affairs
K–Communications-Electronics

Distribution: B

1st Corps
53d Mech Div
201st ACR
(Note 24) 61st FA Bde

(Classification)

20 This paragraph contains command and signal instructions. As a minimum, reference will be made to the communications-electronics annex (if used), current index to the CEOI, and the location of the division command post and axis of command post displacement (unless shown graphically). When both command and signal entries are made, command data is listed first, followed by signal.

21 Directs the recipient of the order to acknowledge receipt and understanding. Acknowledgement may be made in the clear using the message reference number contained in the heading.

22 *a*. The commander or a designated representative signs the original copy of the operation order. If this signature cannot be reproduced, the G3 authenticates subsequent copies. Annexes, appendixes, tabs, and inclosures issued with the order do not require signature or authentication. Those issued separately do require signature (or authentication) in the same manner as the order. Authentication is performed by the appropriate coordinating staff officer.

b. Examples of signature blocks for copy 1 of the order, and of annexes, appendixes, tabs, and inclosures if issued separately.

(1)

von STEUBEN
MG

(2) FOR THE COMMANDER:

NICKSON
Chief of Staff

23. Annexes are lettered alphabetically and are listed in the order in which they appear in the operation order. G3 designates the letter to be associated with a given annex. Annexes are associated with a given annex. Annexes are prepared by the appropriate officer having staff responsibility for the activity, arm, or service covered by the annex.

24 G3 establishes distribution in coordination with other coordinating and special staff officers. A distribution formula may be included in standing operating procedures.

LEGEND

Notes 1—6—Heading.
Notes 7—20—Body.
Notes 21—24—Ending.

NOTE: This example is not designed to convey tactical doctrine but to establish a format for conveying a commander's intent without stifling the initiative of subordinate commanders.

Operations Order Format

....
(Classification)

	Sources
Task Organization:	• Task organization of higher HQ • Your commander's concept
OPORD # _____	
1. SITUATION	
a. Enemy (situation, location, capabilities):	• Higher HQ's OPORD – Para 1a – Intelligence annex • G2/S2
b. Friendly (mission, designation, location): (1) Higher:	• Higher HQ's OPORD – Para 2
(2) Adjacent:	• Higher HQ's OPORD – Para 1b – Para 3a
(3) Supporting:	• Higher HQ's OPORD – Para 1b – Subunit paragraphs – Task organization
c. Attachment/Effective Time:	• Higher HQ's OPORD – Task organization – Para 1c – Para 3g (Coordinating Inst)

Operations Order Format (continued)

d. Detachment/Effective Time:

- Higher HQ's OPORD
  - Task organization
  - Para 1c
  - Para 3g (Coordinating Inst)

2. MISSION (who, what, when)

- Higher HQ's OPORD
  - Para 2
  - Para 3a
  - Subunit paragraphs
- Your commander

3. EXECUTION

a. Concept (maneuver and fires):

(1) Route:

- Higher HQ's OPORD
  - Para 3a
- Your commander
  - Commander's decision
  - Commander's concept

(2) Formation: Order of march:

(3) Final CL:

(4) Consolidation:

(5) Fire support:

b. 1st:

- Higher HQ's OPORD
  - Para 3a
- Your commander
  - Commander's decision
  - Commander's concept

Operations Order Format (continued)

c. 2nd:	• Higher HQ's OPORD – Para 3a • Your commander – Commander's decision – Commander's concept
d. 3rd:	• Higher HQ's OPORD – Para 3a • Your commander – Commander's decision – Commander's concept
e. Weapons:	• Higher HQ's OPORD – Para 3a • Your commander – Commander's decision – Commander's concept
f. Attachments:	• Higher HQ's OPORD – Para 3a • Your commander – Commander's decision – Commander's concept
g. Coordinating instructions: (1) LD:	• Higher HQ's OPORD – Para 3g (Coordinating Inst) • Your commander's concept • Your G2/S2
(2) Final CL:	

Operations Order Format (continued)

(3) Aircraft movement data:
(a) Route:

(b) Formation:

(c) Type load (ACL):

(d) No. of aircraft:

(4) Additional information:

4. ADMIN AND LOGISTICS
a. Rations:

b. Ammo:

c. Transportation:

d. Med evac:

- Higher HQ's OPORD –Para 4
- Your commander's order
- Your G1/S1
- Your G4/S4
- Supporting units

Operations Order Format (continued)

5. COMMAND AND SIGNAL
   a. Signal instructions and information:
   b. CP and location of commander:

- Higher HQ's OPORD
  – Para 5
- Your commander's concept
- Your commo-elect officer

....
(Classification)

Warning Order (example)

JOINT MESSAGEFORM

SECURITY CLASSIFICATION: (CLASSIFICATION)

PAGE	DTG/RELEASER TIME			PRECEDENCE		CLASS	SPECAT	LMF	CIC	ORIG/MSG IDENT
	DATE-TIME	MONTH	YR	ACT	INFO					
01 OF 01	131200Z	JUL	87	PP	PP	(CLASS)			ZYUW	3281200Z

BOOK	MESSAGE HANDLING INSTRUCTIONS
NO	

FROM: CDR 20TH INF DIV//USAID-HD//

TO: CDR 1ST BDE//USAID-FB//
CDR 2D BDE//USAID-SB//
CDR 3D BDE//USAID-TB//
CDR DIV ARTY//USAID-DA//
CDR DISCOM//USAID-DS//
CDR 1-21 CAV//USAID-AR//
CDR 20TH AVN BDE//USAID-AV//
CDR 20TH ENGR BN//USAID-EN//
CDR 20TH CML CO//USAID-CM//
CDR 20TH MP CO//USAID-MP//
CDR 20TH SIG BN//USAID-CE//
CDR 404TH TRANS BN (MT)//USATR-HD//

(CLASSIFICATION)

SUBJECT: WARNING ORDER ( )

( ) DIV MOVES NIGHT OF 13-14 JUL TO ASSY AREA VIC YR1016; PREP TO ADV EARLY 7 AUG TO SECURE CROSSINGS OVER WARTA RIVER TO COVER DEPLOYMENT OF 1ST CORPS. FIVE TRANS TRK CO ATTCH EFF 131900Z. RD MOV PLAN AND OPLAN TO BE ISS AT CDR CONF AT 131500Z.

DISTR:
G1, G2, G4, G5

DRAFTER TYPED NAME, TITLE, OFFICE SYMBOL, PHONE
ROBERT YOUNG MAJ ASST G3 USAID-HT HAWK 3

SPECIAL INSTRUCTIONS

RELEASER
TYPED NAME, TITLE, OFFICE SYMBOL AND PHONE
L. WALLACE LTC G3 USAID-HT HAWK 3

SIGNATURE

SECURITY CLASSIFICATION (CLASSIFICATION)

DATE TIME GROUP

Fragmentary Order (example)

JOINT MESSAGEFORM

SECURITY CLASSIFICATION: (CLASSIFICATION)

PAGE	DATE-TIME	MONTH	YR	ACT	INFO	CLASS	SPECAT	LMF	CIC	ORIG/MSG IDENT
01 OF 01	141049Z	JUL	87	PP	PP	(CLASS)			ZYUW	3292200Z

BOOK: NO

MESSAGE HANDLING INSTRUCTIONS

FROM: CDR 52D MECH DIV

TO: CDR 2D BDE

CDR 3D BDE

CDR DIVARTY

CDR 1-23 CAV (-)

CDR DISCOM

INFO: CDR 1ST CORPS

CDR 54TH MECH DIV

CDR 23D ARMD DIV

CDR 1ST BDE

(CLASSIFICATION)

SUBJ: CHANGE TO OPORD 11 ( )

A. REFERENCE OPORD 11 ( )

1. ( ) EN FORCE EST TO BE ONE TK REGT PREPARING TO COUNTERATTACK 2D BDE.

2. ( ) 3D BDE: ATK 141300 JULY TO REPULSE EN COUNTERATTACK AND SECURE HILL 322; BE PREPARED TO CONTINUE ATTACK TO THE SOUTH. BE PREPARED TO ACCEPT A MECH AND TANK BN FROM THE 2D BDE.

3. ( ) 2D BDE: DETACH A MECH AND A TANK BN TO THE 3D BDE WITH DS MAINT TM'S, EFFECTIVE 141200; BECOME THE DIV RESERVE AND FOLLOW 3D BDE; BE PREPARED FOR COMMITMENT IN ZONE OF 3D BDE AND 1ST BDE IN PRIORITY.

4. ( ) 1-23 CAV (-): CONTINUE TO SCREEN DIV EAST FLANK.

5. ( ) PRIORITY OF ARTY AND TAC AIR TO 3D BDE EFFECTIVE 141245 JULY.

6. ( ) ACKNOWLEDGE.

DISTR:

G1, G2, G4, G5, FSE, DCEO, ALO, DAME, COFS

DRAFTER TYPED NAME, TITLE, OFFICE SYMBOL, PHONE: D. SMITH MAJ ASST G3 SAFARI 123/14 JUL

SPECIAL INSTRUCTIONS

RELEASER — TYPED NAME, TITLE, OFFICE SYMBOL AND PHONE: E. YOUNG LTC G3 SAFARI 121

SIGNATURE

SECURITY CLASSIFICATION: (CLASSIFICATION)

DATE TIME GROUP

DD FORM 1 MAR 79 173/2 (OCR)   PREVIOUS EDITION IS OBSOLETE S/N 0102-LF-000-1736   ☆U.S. GOVERNMENT PRINTING OFFICE: 1985-485-135

Like most staff-composed documents, the operations order is more a compilation of many important points than a single comprehensive statement. Each paragraph addresses a different area of concern and therefore is in the bailiwick of a different staff officer. Officers will read most intently the items that most directly affect their own areas of responsibility. In like manner, the data used to write the operations order to subordinate units comes from many different sources.

WARNING ORDER

A warning order is exactly what its name implies. It is advance notice of an upcoming operation or action. It is short and concise and includes only enough information to allow subordinate units to begin basic preparations and planning. The warning order must include the warning and the essential details of impending operations, as well as the amount of planning time available.

Warning orders have no prescribed format. They are usually brief verbal or written messages. The words *warning order* precede the message text, and an acknowledgment is usually required. The message should also clearly identify which parts are for execution and which parts are for information. When movement is involved, the warning order should state a time before which there will be no move.

A coordinating or special staff officer may issue a warning order; however, completion of appropriate staff coordination must be assured. The accompanying example shows the concise and efficient nature of the warning order.

FRAGMENTARY ORDER

A fragmentary order (FRAGO) is a form of an operations order. It contains information of immediate concern to the subordinate units. It will be a brief and concise verbal or written message and will include specific instructions stated in simple terms for clarity. A FRAGO is normally issued to change or modify an operations order. There is no prescribed format for a FRAGO.

Fragmentary orders are normally issued by coordinating staff officers with command approval. In the interest of speed and clarity, the elements normally found in a complete order may be omitted when these elements have not changed, are not essential to the mission, might delay or complicate transmission, or are unavailable or incomplete at the time of issue.

As a general rule, a fragmentary order is addressed to each commander required to take action and to higher and adjacent headquarters for information, if applicable. It refers to a previous order, when appropriate, and indicates task organization changes if applicable. If required for clarity, it includes a brief outline of the situation that generated the requirement for a fragmentary order, including a statement of the mission, if changed. In short, it provides brief and specific instructions in the most concise manner possible and requires acknowledgment.

Although a fragmentary order has no prescribed format, it may follow the five-paragraph Operations Order format, and it must indicate proper classification. See the accompanying example of a fragmentary Order.

SERVICE SUPPORT ANNEX TO THE OPERATIONS ORDER

The service support annex to an operations order is an integral part of that order and is normally written by the logistics officer of the command. It is also the part of the operations order that is most carefully read by subordinate combat service support elements. This annex contains all of the specific instructions for combat service support functions during the prescribed operation. The service support annex should not contain information that should be in standard operating procedures (SOPs), nor should it omit items that the logistician might consider basic knowledge but that the unit SOP does not address. The service support annex is the vehicle for the logistician to tell the supported units how to obtain support and to give the supporting units necessary specific instructions on how to provide support during the current operation. See the accompanying annotated example of a service support annex.

REAR AREA SECURITY OPERATIONS ORDER

The rear area security operations order is written in almost the same format as any other operations order. The differences stem from the primary missions of the units to which it is issued. The rear area units generally will have a mission that is not directly involved with confronting the enemy. This situation requires additional information in the first and third paragraphs. The situation described must stress the enemy capabilities to project combat power into the rear areas, including all forms of airborne or air assault capabilities, indirect fire, and irregular forces. The execution paragraph must address coordination of civil authorities, cooperation between units that are not necessarily in the same command, and a specific listing of the combat capabilities of the units in the rear, both while maintaining support operations and with the cessation of primary mission requirements.

The accompanying rear area security operations order format is a simplified example of the basic requirements that this order must include.

TACTICAL CONTROL MEASURES

Control measures are necessary for proper organization and control of operations. They are used to provide coordination and reference points on the ground. Logisticians need to use control measures to develop operations orders, but more important, they must understand them to interpret the details of the orders issued by the supported tactical units.

The accompanying illustration and the definitions that are keyed to it will give a good understanding of control measures and their use on the battlefield.

Annotated Service Support Annex to an Operations Order

Determined by G4 in coordination with G1 and G5. Classified per AR 380—5. Classification is shown at the top and bottom of each page.

Copy 2 of ___ copies
23d Armd Div
PRADIA (884039), POLAND
082200R Aug 19___
GX 36

Identical with OPORD heading if issued with, but on different distribution than, the OPORD. If issued separately the date-time group is changed and a new message reference number is used.

Letter designation of annex provided by G3.

ANNEX F (SERVICE SUPPORT) to OPERATION ORDER 33

Each staff officer providing information or entries for the annex provides G4 with references as appropriate. List any maps, charts, or other documents required to understand the annex. Reference to a map will include the map series number (and country or geographical area, if required), sheet number (and sheet name, if required), edition, and scale.

Reference: Map, series M651, POLAND, sheet R12 (CZESTOCHOWA), edition 1, 1:100,000.

Time Zone Used Throughout the Order: ROMEO.

1. GENERAL

This annex provides for CSS to 23d Armd Div vic PRADIA. Div is supported by the 10th Spt Gp and the 82d Med Gp. Div instl open not later than 090800 Aug. 1-53 FA supported from 1st Bde Tn area. 501st Engr Cbt Bn (Corps) supported from 2d bde Spt area

Paragraph 1 outlines the general plan for the provision of combat service support and the purpose of the annex. It is prepared by the G4 in coordination with the G1, G5, other coordinating and special staff officers, and the support command commander, as appropriate.

2. MATERIEL AND SERVICES

Paragraph 2 contains information and instructions pertaining to supplies, transport, transportation services, maintenance, construction, other services, and allocation of labor for logistic purposes. It may contain supply, transportation, and services subparagraphs, as appropriate. It is prepared by the G4 in coordination with the support command commander and coordinating and special staff officers, as appropriate.

a. Supply. At division this subparagraph may be further divided according to class of supply. Unless shown graphically, this subparagraph will include as a minimum the location of the supporting class V supply points. When all or a portion of class III supplies are to be issued by supply point distribution, the location of the supporting class III GS supply installation will be shown.

b. Transportation. This subparagraph contains information and instructions pertaining to transportation facilities, the main supply route, classification of roads and bridges,

a. Supply.

(1) Cl I.

(a) Supply point distribution for all units supported from div spt area on 9 Aug only. Schedule-SOP.

Determined by G4 in coordination with support command commander.

(b) All units maintain two rations in reserve during period 9 Aug to 12 Aug inclusive.

Obtained from corps admin/log order by G4.

(2) Cl II. Priority of cl II to 1st Bde for 9 and 10 Aug.

Determined by G4 in coordination with G3.

(3) Cl III.

(a) SUPPT 522, cl III, 1st Corps (BB320820).

Obtained from supporting spt group by G4.

(b) Appendix 1 (Fuel Allocations).

Determined by G4 in coordination with G3.

(4) Cl V.

(a) ASP 955, 1st Corps (BB316972); and SASP 956, 1st Corps (BB312969).

Obtained from corps admin/log order by G4.

(b) CSR, 9-12 Aug.

1. 81-mm mortar (WP) . . . . 5.
2. 4.2-in mortar (HE). . . . . 55.
3. 155-mm how (HE) .75.
4. Other types-no restriction.

Obtained from corps OPORD by G4.

(c) Prescribed nuclear load.

1-53 FA . . . . Three MRC/8/6-38 (2 KT).

Obtained from corps OPORD and division artillery commander by G4.

Annotated Service Support Annex to an Operations Order (continued)

Annotation	Annex text
Provided by G4 in coordination with support command commander and division aviation officer, as appropriate.	(5) Appendix 2 (Aerial Resupply).
	b. Transportation.
Provided by G4 in coordination with division engineer.	(1) Bridges on main roads are two way, cl 60; on secondary roads, they are one way, cl 5 or better.
Provided by G4 in coordination with G3 and provost marshal.	(2) Route YOKE (BB1545 to BB3985) closed for movement of armor from 090100 Aug to 090500 Aug.
Provided by G4 in coordination with the transportation officer, division engineer, and provost marshal.	(3) Appendix 3 (Traffic Circulation and Control).
	c. Services.
Provided by G4 in coordination with the support command commander.	(1) Effective 090800 Aug exchange of socks and underwear will be resumed at all clothing exchange and bath points (CEB).
Provided by G4 in coordination with G3 and the support command commander.	(2) Decon Sec, 223d Fld Svc Co (GS) (Fwd), provides spt to unit decontaminating activities beginning 090800 Aug.
Provided by G4 in coordination with G3 and the support command commander.	d. Maintenance. Priority of maintenance. (1) 1-53 FA. (2) 1-10 Armor. (3) 1-22 Cav. (4) 1-14 Armor.

and traffic control and regulating measures. Reference the traffic circulation and control appendix here.

c. Services. This subparagraph contains information and instructions pertaining to services that are available and what action must be taken by the supported units to obtain the service.

d. Maintenance. This subparagraph contains information and instructions pertaining to maintenance facilities; priorities, as appropriate; and evacuation policies.

Annotation	Annex text
Provided by G1 in coordination with the division surgeon, the support command commander, and the supporting medical group.	3. MEDICAL EVACUATION AND HOSPITALIZATION a. Current cholera and typhus inoculations will be completed prior to 102400 Aug. b. 809th CSH (BB293847) supports 23d Armd Div, opens at 090800 Aug.

Paragraph 3 This paragraph contains information and instructions pertaining to evacuation policy, medical evacuation and hospitalization. Unless shown graphically, location of the supporting combat support hospital should be shown in this paragraph. Opening and closing times are also included

Annotation	Annex text
	4. PERSONNEL
Provided by G1 in accordance with instructions from higher headquarters.	a. During period 10 Aug to 12 Aug inclusive, submit personnel daily summary as of 1500 to reach this headquarters by 1900.
Provided by G1 in coordination with the provost marshal.	b. Guards delivering prisoners of war to prisoner of war coll pt remain under control of PM until released.
Provided by G1 in coordination with the support command commander.	c. Contaminated remains will be segregated and moved by separate transportation.
Provided by G1 in coordination with G5 and provost marshal.	d. All local food establishments off limits.

Paragraph 4. This paragraph contains information and instructions pertaining to personnel matters. It is prepared by the G1 in coordination with other coordinating and special staff officers and the support command commander, as appropriate. May include a subparagraph for each of the G1's functional areas of responsibility.

Annotation	Annex text
	5. CIVIL-MILITARY COOPERATION
Obtained from corps admin/log order by G5.	a. Curfew for civilians is 1800 to 0800.
Provided by G5; number of appendix designated by G4.	b. Appendix 4 (Civil Affairs).

Paragraph 5. This paragraph contains information and instructions pertaining to the allocation of civil affairs units, control of refugees, and the feeding and treatment of the civil population. It is prepared by the G5 in coordination with other coordinating and special staff officers and the support command commander, as appropriate.

Annotation	Annex text
	6. MISCELLANEOUS
Obtained from corps admin/log order by G4.	a. Div rear boundary is div light line.
Provided by G1 in coordination with the chief of staff.	b. Div chaplain located at div rear effective 091200 Aug.
Provided by G4 in coordination with G3 and the support command commander.	c. Proposed DSA in the vic of CA9405.

Paragraph 6. This paragraph contains information and instructions not covered elsewhere in the annex. It is prepared by the G4 in coordination with the G1, G5, other coordinating and special staff officers, and the support command commander, as appropriate.

Annotated Service Support Annex to an Operations Order (continued)

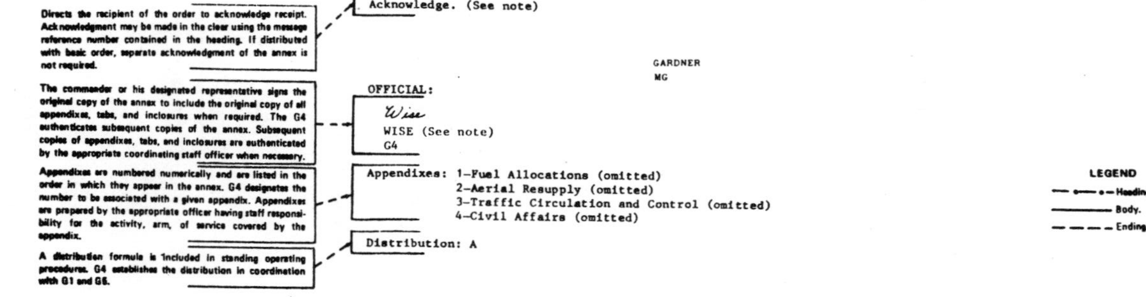

Directs the recipient of the order to acknowledge receipt. Acknowledgment may be made in the clear using the message reference number contained in the heading. If distributed with basic order, separate acknowledgment of the annex is not required.

Acknowledge. (See note)

GARDNER
MG

The commander or his designated representative signs the original copy of the annex to include the original copy of all appendixes, tabs, and inclosures when required. The G4 authenticates subsequent copies of the annex. Subsequent copies of appendixes, tabs, and inclosures are authenticated by the appropriate coordinating staff officer when necessary.

OFFICIAL:
Wise
WISE (See note)
G4

Appendixes are numbered numerically and are listed in the order in which they appear in the annex. G4 designates the number to be associated with a given appendix. Appendixes are prepared by the appropriate officer having staff responsibility for the activity, arm, of service covered by the appendix.

Appendixes: 1–Fuel Allocations (omitted)
2–Aerial Resupply (omitted)
3–Traffic Circulation and Control (omitted)
4–Civil Affairs (omitted)

A distribution formula is included in standing operating procedures. G4 establishes the distribution in coordination with G1 and G5.

Distribution: A

LEGEND
—•—•— Heading.
———— Body.
– – – – Ending.

Rear Area Security Operations Order Format

....
(Classification)

Copy no ___ of ___ copies
Issuing headquarters
Place of issue (may be in code)
Date-time group of signature
Message reference number ___

REAR AREA SECURITY OPERATIONS ORDER NUMBER _______

References: Maps, charts, and relevant documents

Time zone used throughout the order:

Task organization:

1. SITUATION

The following points will normally be covered:

a. Enemy forces. Enemy capabilities to—

(1) Use nuclear, biological, and chemical weapons

(2) Assault with airborne elements and other regular units

(3) Mount an attack with irregular forces

(4) Execute air or guided missile attacks

....
(Classification)

Rear Area Security Operations Order Format (continued)

....
(Classification)

(Short title identification)

(5) Employ psychological warfare

b. Friendly forces/Civilian authorities

c. Attachments and detachments

d. Commander's evaluation

2. MISSION

3. EXECUTION

The following points will normally be covered:

a. Concept of operations

b. Combat and security units

c. Technical and administrative units/agencies

....
(Classification)

Rear Area Security Operations Order Format (continued)

....
(Classification)

(Short title identification)

d. Coordination within the forces

e. Cooperation within the forces

4. SERVICE SUPPORT

5. COMMAND AND SIGNAL

Acknowledgment instructions

/s/......................
Commander

Authentication:

Annexes:

Distribution:

....
(Classification)

Control Measures on the Battlefield

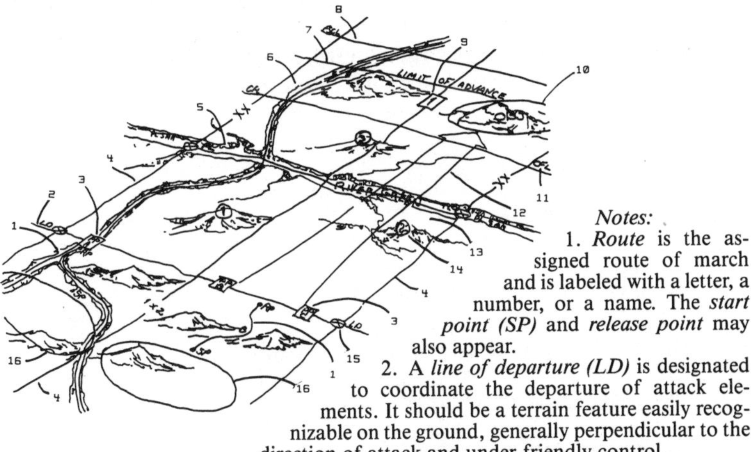

Notes:

1. *Route* is the assigned route of march and is labeled with a letter, a number, or a name. The *start point (SP)* and *release point* may also appear.

2. A *line of departure (LD)* is designated to coordinate the departure of attack elements. It should be a terrain feature easily recognizable on the ground, generally perpendicular to the direction of attack and under friendly control.

3. *Passage points (PPs)* are designated locations in the unit being passed through. They are the points through which, by commander's agreement, passing units should move.

4. *Boundaries* mark areas of tactical responsibility. Commanders must not, however, allow boundaries to prevent fires on an enemy force simply because the enemy is on the other side of the boundary.

5. *Phase line (PL)* is a line used for control and coordination of military operations. It usually is a recognizable terrain feature extending across the zone of action. Units always report crossing phase lines but do not halt unless specifically directed. Phase lines are often used to prescribe the timing of operations.

6. *Direction of attack* is a specific direction or route for the main attack or the main body of the force to follow. If used, it is normally at battalion or lower levels. Direction of attack is a more restrictive control measure than axis of advance, and units are not free to maneuver off the assigned route. It is usually associated with infantry units conducting night attacks, units involved in limited visibility operations, or units in counterattacks.

7. A *limit of advance* is an easily recognizable terrain feature beyond which attacking elements will not advance.

8. *Fire support coordination lines (FSCLs)* are those lines forward of which all targets may be attacked by any weapon system without danger to, or additional coordination with, the establishing headquarters.

9. *Contact points* are designated places where two or more units are required to make physical contact.

10. *Objectives* are normally assigned in an attack to battalions of a brigade. They may be the only control measures assigned and are used to direct the efforts of attacking units.

11. *Coordinated fire lines (CFLs)* delineate the area beyond which field artillery, mortars, and ships may fire at any time without additional coordination. Normally, they are established by brigade or division, but they may be established by battalion. For heliborne or airmobile operations with linkup forces, see restrictive fire line (RFL).

12. *Axis of advance* indicates a general axis of movement for an attacking unit.

13. *Zone of attack* is an area forward of contact assigned to a force having a mission to attack, normally delineated by boundaries extending forward into enemy territory. It delineates an area that requires close coordination and cooperation between adjacent units.

14. *Checkpoints* are reference points used to facilitate control. They may be selected throughout the zone of action or along an axis of advance or direction of attack.

15. *Coordination point* is a designated point at which, in all types of combat, adjacent units or formations must make contact for purposes of control and coordination.

16. *Assembly areas* are specified for organization, maintenance, supply, issuance of orders, and rest. The command assembles in an assembly area to prepare for operations.

Format for Commander's Estimate of the Situation

....
(Classification)

Headquarters
Place
Date, Time, Zone

COMMANDER'S ESTIMATE OF THE SITUATION

References: Maps, charts, and other relevant documents

1. MISSION

2. THE SITUATION AND COURSES OF ACTION

   a. Considerations affecting the possible courses of action

      (1) Characteristics of the area of operations

         (a) Weather

         (b) Terrain

         (c) Other pertinent factors

      (2) Enemy situation

      (3) Own situation

      (4) Relative combat power

....
(Classification)

Format for Commander's
Estimate of the Situation (continued)

....
(Classification)

b. Enemy capabilities

c. Own courses of action

3. ANALYSIS OF COURSES OF ACTION

4. COMPARISON OF COURSES OF ACTION

5. DECISION (RECOMMENDATIONS)

/s/......................
Commander

Annexes (as required)

....
(Classification)

Format for Supporting Commander's Estimate of the Situation

....
(Classification)

Headquarters
Place
Date, Time, Zone

SUPPORTING COMMANDER'S ESTIMATE OF THE SITUATION

References: Maps, charts, and other relevant documents

1. MISSION

2. THE SITUATION AND COURSES OF ACTION

   a. Considerations affecting the possible courses of action

      (1) Operations to be supported

      (2) Characteristics of the area of operations

         (a) Weather

         (b) Terrain

         (c) Other pertinent factors

      (3) Enemy situations

....
(Classification)

Format for Supporting Commander's Estimate of the Situation (continued)

....
(Classification)

(4) Own situation

(a) Tactical situation

(b) Personnel situation

(c) Logistic situation

(d) Civil-military operations situation

b. Anticipated difficulties or difficulty patterns

c. Own courses of action

3. ANALYSIS OF COURSES OF ACTION

4. COMPARISON OF COURSES OF ACTION

5. DECISION (RECOMMENDATIONS)

/s/......................
Commander

Annexes (as required)

....
(Classification)

Intelligence Estimate Format

....
(Classification)

Headquarters
Place
Date, Time, Zone

INTELLIGENCE ESTIMATE NO _____

References: Maps, charts, or other documents

1. MISSION

The restated mission determined by the commander

2. THE AREA OF OPERATIONS

Summarizes the analysis of the area of operation

a. Weather

(1) Existing situation. Include light data and either a weather forecast or climatic information, as appropriate. Use appendices for graphic representations of weather factors and other detailed information.

(2) Effect on enemy courses of action. Discuss the effects of weather on each enemy course of action such as attack, defend, in terms of mobility and optical and electronic line of sight. Also include the effects of weather factors on biological and chemical agents, nuclear weapons, and special methods, techniques, equipment, procedures, or forces, such as airborne or airmobile, surveillance devices, radio electronic combat, and deception. Each discussion should conclude with how the weather affects the course of action.

(3) Effects on own courses of action. Discuss in the same manner as for (2) above, except that the estimate excludes the use of biological agents.

b. Terrain

....
(Classification)

Intelligence Estimate Format (continued)

....
(Classification)
(Short title identification)

(1) Existing situation. Use graphic representations where possible. Use annexes for detailed material. Include as much information as necessary for an understanding of cover and concealment, observation and fire, obstacles, key terrain, and avenues of approach. Include effects on each of the factors, as appropriate, of nuclear fires, enemy biological and chemical agents, and any other pertinent considerations.

(2) Effect on enemy courses of action. Discuss in the same manner as for the effects of weather in a. (2) above. For defensive courses of action, state the best defense area and the best terrain avenues of approach leading to it. For the attack courses of action, state the best avenues of approach.

(3) Effect on own courses of action. Discuss in the same manner as for effects of weather in a. (3) above.

c. Other characteristics. Include the following characteristics in separate subparagraphs: sociology, politics, economics, psychology, and other factors. Other factors may include such items as science and technology, materiel, transportation, manpower, and hydrography. Analyze these factors under the same headings as weather and terrain.

3. ENEMY SITUATION

Information on the enemy that will permit later development of enemy capabilities and vulnerabilities and refinement of these capabilities into a specific course of action and its adoption.

a. Disposition. Refer to overlays, enemy situation maps, or previously published documents.

....
(Classification)

Intelligence Estimate Format (continued)

....
(Classification)
(Short title identification)

b. Composition. Summary of order of battle of opposing forces and other enemy forces that can influence the accomplishment of the mission. Refer to previously published documents. Mention units capable of electronic warfare and other special operations.

c. Strength. List enemy strength as committed forces, reinforcements, artillery, air, nuclear weapons, chemical and biological agents, and other forces, such as electronic warfare, air defense, antitank, unconventional warfare, and combat surveillance. The purpose of this listing is to assist in developing enemy capabilities and vulnerabilities for the use of the commander and staff in selecting courses of action. The unit mission, location of the enemy, enemy doctrine, and the level of command at which the estimate is prepared are factors to consider.

(1) Committed forces. List those enemy ground maneuver units currently in contact and those ground maneuver units with which imminent contact can be expected regardless of the specific friendly course of action implemented. Designation of enemy forces as committed forces depends on their disposition, location, controlling headquarters, and doctrine. The intelligence officer usually accounts for committed forces by the size unit to oppose the friendly size unit used in his headquarters as a basis for planning operations. For example, a brigade S2 normally considers committed forces in terms of companies; a division G2, in terms of battalions; and a corps G2, in terms of regiments. If there is doubt whether a unit is a committed force or a reinforcement, consider it a reinforcement. This method ensures maximum consideration of the enemy's capability to reinforce his forces.

(2) Reinforcements. Include designation and location. Reinforcements are those enemy maneuver units that may or may not be employed against us, depending on our choice of a specific course of action and enemy plans. Reinforcements are enemy units that are not committed in or out of the friendly sector, but that can react to the friendly course of action, subject to time and distance considerations, in time to influence the accomplishment of the mission. Imminent contact is not expected. Disposition,

....
(Classification)

Intelligence Estimate Format (continued)

....
(Classification)
(Short title identification)

location, level of control, or other factors considered at the time of the estimate help determine which enemy forces are reinforcements.

(3) Artillery. List enemy artillery units, including those organic to maneuver units identified above as being committed or reinforcing. All artillery units that can be identified as being within supporting range should be listed in support of the committed force.

(4) Air. List the number of enemy aircraft by type within the operational radius. Include the number of possible sorties per day by type of aircraft, if known.

(5) Nuclear weapons and chemical and biological agents. Estimate the number, type, yield, and delivery means of enemy nuclear weapons and chemical and biological munitions or agents available to the enemy.

(6) Other Forces. List forces not previously considered that have special capabilities, such as electronic warfare, air defense, antitank, unconventional warfare, or combat surveillance.

d. Recent and present significant activities. List selected items or information to provide bases for analysis to determine relative probability of adoption of specific courses of action and enemy vulnerabilities. List enemy failure to take expected actions, as well as positive information.

e. Peculiarities and weaknesses. Based on knowledge of enemy tactical doctrine, practices, the principles of war, the area of operations, and the enemy situation previously described, list peculiarities and weaknesses, and briefly discuss each, indicating the extent to which they may be vulnerabilities and how they influence possible friendly courses of action. The items listed are grouped under the headings indicated below. Only pertinent headings are used.

(1) Personnel. Include an estimate of the strength if less than 80 percent of authorized strength. Include status of morale, if known.

....
(Classification)

Intelligence Estimate Format (continued)

....
(Classification)
(Short title identification)

(2) Intelligence. Include an estimate of enemy intelligence success, effectiveness, and susceptibility to deception and detection.

(3) Operations. Include an estimate of combat effectiveness if less than excellent.

(4) Logistics. Include an estimate of the enemy's ability to support his forces logistically if weakness is apparent.

(5) Civil-military operations. Include an estimate of the attitudes of the enemy and the civilian populace and the status of food, supply, medical facilities, and communications.

4. Enemy capabilities

Based on all the previous information and analysis, develop and list enemy capabilities. The listing provides a basis for analyzing available information to arrive at those capabilities that the enemy can adopt as specific courses of action and their relative probability of adoption.

a. Enumeration. State what, when, where, and in what strength for each capability.

b. Analysis and discussion. To provide a basis for conclusions on the adoption of enemy capabilities and their relative probability of adoption, discuss each capability, or appropriate combination thereof, in a separate subparagraph. Include consideration of enemy deception measures. Tabulate all the pertinent previous information and conclusions as either supporting or rejecting the adoption of the capability. After listing all the evidence, judge each capability from the enemy point of view of whether the adoption of the capability is advantageous to the enemy. Such judgments are not necessary if the conclusion is obvious or if there is no evidence that the enemy will adopt the capability, except when the capability is one that will make the accomplishment of the friendly mission highly doubtful or impossible. This exception is to focus attention on dangerous threats.

....
(Classification)

Intelligence Estimate Format (continued)

....
(Classification)
(Short title identification)

5. Conclusions

Based on all the previous information and analysis, state conclusions concerning the total effect of the area of operation on friendly courses of action: the courses of action most probable for adoption by the enemy, including their relative probability of adoption and the effects of the enemy vulnerabilities that can be exploited. These conditions assist in the selection of a friendly course of action.

a. Effects of intelligence considerations on operations. Indicate whether the mission set forth in paragraph 1 above can be supported from an intelligence standpoint. Indicate which course(s) of action can best be supported from an intelligence standpoint.

b. Effects of the area of operations on own courses of action. For attack courses of action, indicate the best avenues of approach. For defense courses of action, indicate the best defense areas and the best avenues of approach leading to and into the defense areas. (Omit this subparagraph if the discussion of the effects of the area on own courses of action in paragraph 2 has been omitted because of the availability of a current analysis of the area of operations.)

c. Probable enemy courses of action. List courses of action in order of relative probability of adoption. A listed course of action may include several subordinate courses of action that can be executed concurrently. Usually, no more than two or three courses of action, in order of probability of adoption, can be justified by the available evidence.

d. Enemy vulnerabilities. List the effects of peculiarities and weaknesses that result in vulnerabilities that are exploitable at own, higher, or lower levels of command. The order of listing these vulnerabilities has no significance.

/s/......................
Commander

Annexes (as required)

....
(Classification)

Personnel Estimate Format

....
(Classification)

Headquarters
Place
Date, Time, Zone

PERSONNEL ESTIMATE NO _____

References: Maps, charts, or other documents

1. MISSION

The restated mission determined by the commander

2. THE SITUATION AND CONSIDERATIONS

a. Intelligence situation. Information obtained from the intelligence officer. When the details make it appropriate and the estimate is written, a brief summary and reference to appropriate intelligence documents or an annex of the estimate may be used.

(1) Characteristics of the area of operations

(2) Enemy strength and dispositions

(3) Enemy capabilities

(a) Affecting the mission

(b) Affecting personnel activities

b. Tactical situation. Information received from the commander's planning guidance and from the operations officer.

(1) Present dispositions of major tactical elements.

....
(Classification)

Personnel Estimate Format (continued)

....
(Classification)
(Short title identification)

(2) Possible courses of action to accomplish the mission. (These courses of action are carried forward through the remainder of the estimate.)

(3) Projected operations, if known, and other planning factors as required for coordination and integration of staff estimates.

c. Logistic situation. Information obtained from the logistics officer.

(1) Present dispositions of logistic units and installations that have an effect on the personnel situation.

(2) Projected developments within the logistics field likely to influence personnel operations.

d. Civil-military operations situation. Information obtained from the civil-military affairs officer.

(1) Present dispositions of civil-military operations units and installations that have an effect on personnel operations.

(2) Projected developments within the civil-military field likely to influence personnel operations.

e. Troop preparedness situation. In this subparagraph, show the status under appropriate headings. In the case of detailed information at higher levels of command, a summary may appear under the subheading with reference to an annex to the estimate.

(1) Unit strength. Indicate authorized, assigned, and attached strengths, and include the effect of deployability, losses (combat/noncombat), critical shortages, projections (gains/losses), and any local situations affecting strength, such as restrictions on the number of soldiers allowed in an area by treaty.

(2) Other personnel. Indicate personnel, other than unit soldiers, whose presence affects the unit mission. Include in this paragraph prisoners

....
(Classification)

Personnel Estimate Format (continued)

....
(Classification)
(Short title identification)

of war, third country nationals, augmentees (non–U.S. forces), civilian internees and detainees, Department of the Army civilians, and others, depending on local circumstances.

(3) Soldier personal readiness. Indicate those elements of quality of life and personnel administration and management that provide services, facilities, and policies affecting soldier personal readiness.

(a) Soldier services.

1. Administrative services (pay, orders, evaluation reports, decorations, awards, reenlistments, eliminations, separations, promotions, assignments, transfers, personal affairs, leaves, and passes).

2. Health services (field medical support, disease, mental health, and other services).

3. Support services (transportation, commissary, PX, clothing, laundry, legal, spiritual, law and order, and so forth).

4. Health care (medical, dental, entitlements, eligibility, and physical fitness).

5. Personal development (education, professional development, and job enhancement).

6. Housing (soldier and family, quality, availability, distance, and adequacy).

7. Community relations (partnership programs and orientations).

8. Morale support activities (Army community/child support, libraries, community centers, clubs, movies, and postal).

....
(Classification)

Personnel Estimate Format (continued)

....
(Classification)
(Short title identification)

9. Dependents assistance planning.

(b) Duty Conditions.

1. Work facilities (location and quality of facility).

2. Work requirements (effect of length of duty day, frequency and length of field duty, and rotation between remote and nonremote duty locations).

3. Equipment (adequacy).

4. Safety and accident prevention.

(c) Other.

(4) Human potential. Indicate factors affecting the stability and human potential of individual soliders, teams, and crews to accomplish the mission. Consider such factors as turbulence and turnover, experience, personal problems, individual stress, status of crews, and military occupational specialty (MOS) match within the unit.

(5) Organizational climate. Indicate factors affecting personnel readiness.

(a) Performance and discipline standards.

(b) Job satisfaction.

(c) Incentives.

(d) Drug and alcohol abuse standards.

(e) Counseling.

....
(Classification)

Personnel Estimate Format (continued)

....
(Classification)
(Short title identification)

(f) Human relations.

(g) Supervision.

(h) Planning.

(i) Ethics.

(j) Organizational stress.

(k) Other.

(6) Commitment. Indicate the relative strength of the soldiers' identification and involvement with the unit.

(a) Morale.

(b) Motivation.

(c) Confidence.

(d) Trust.

(7) Cohesion. Indicate factors that unite and commit soldiers to accomplish the mission.

(a) Esprit.

(b) Team work.

f. Assumptions. Any assumptions required as a basis for initiating planning or preparing the estimate. Modify assumptions as factual data when specific planning guidance becomes available.

....
(Classification)

Personnel Estimate Format (continued)

....
(Classification)
(Short title identification)

3. ANALYSIS

For each course of action, analyze cause (2e (1), (2), and (3)), effect (2e (4) and (5)), and outcome (2e (6) and (7)) relationships, indicating problems and deficiencies.

4. COMPARISON

a. Evaluate deficiencies from a personnel standpoint and list the advantages and disadvantages, if any, to the accomplishment of the mission.

b. Discuss the advantages and disadvantages of each course of action under consideration. In each course of action, include methods for overcoming deficencies or modifications required.

5. CONCLUSIONS

a. Indicate whether the mission set forth in paragraph 1 above can be supported from a personnel standpoint.

b. Indicate which course of action can best be supported from the personnel standpoint.

c. List the major personnel deficiencies that must be brought to the commander's attention. Include specific recommendations concerning the methods of eliminating or reducing the effect of these deficiencies.

/s/......................
Commander

Annexes (as required)

....
(Classification)

COMMANDER'S ESTIMATE

Each commander must provide his staff and subordinate commanders his estimate of the situation. This requirement is just as true for the combat service support commander as it is for the combat commander. The commander's estimate is based on personal knowledge and experience, as well as on the estimates provided to him by his staff. It contains his modifications to courses of action being considered and his judgment of known factors, assumptions, and unknown data. The commander's estimate must present workable solutions allowing execution with available resources.

There are two accompanying formats for the commander's estimate. The first is a general purpose format any commander could use regardless of the type of unit he commands. The second format is specifically designed for supporting commanders. The supporting commander's estimate differs from the basic format by emphasizing combat support and combat service support units. The primary difference is in paragraph 2, which stresses aspects more appropriate to support operations.

INTELLIGENCE ESTIMATE

The intelligence estimate is a complex and lengthy document that provides the commander vital information about the enemy. Normally prepared by the G2/S2, it gives the logistician essential data necessary for planning the support mission. The tactical situation depicted in the intelligence estimate allows the planner to predict the quantity, priority, and most effective location of his support efforts. The accompanying intelligence estimate example explains the complete format.

PERSONNEL ESTIMATE

The personnel estimate is a very useful tool for the commander in his continuous appraisal of the tactical situation. It is equally useful for the commander in garrison, providing vital information necessary for sound managerial decisions. A complex and lengthy document, it is usually prepared by the G1/S1. The logistician can also draw a great deal of valuable planning data from the personnel estimate. The format presented is self-explanatory.

ROAD MOVEMENT PLANNING

The atmosphere of moving the massive amount of equipment and materiel of a modern army can be visualized as pouring rice through a funnel. As long as all the grains stay straight and slide past one another, there is no problem. If, however, one grain is sideways or sticky, the funnel clogs up and nothing moves. Road movement of convoys and troop formations is exactly the same. If the movement is organized and every unit does exactly what it is instructed to do, there are no problems, but a single unit can prevent the movement of the entire force. The next section gives logisticians the fundamental procedures and tools for organizing the road movement of their combat service support units: first, the planning factors that logisticians must consider in planning for road movements; second, an explanation of the procedures logisticians must follow to coordinate and organize the movements of units in modern armies.

Road Movement Planning Factors

Consider the following factors in the planning of road movements. They apply to all units regardless of type or size.

• Distance factors:

– *Vehicle distance.* The space between two consecutive vehicles of an organized element of a column.

– *Column gap.* The space between two organized elements following each other on the same route.

– *Traffic density.* The average number of vehicles that occupy 1 mile or 1 kilometer, expressed in VPM or VPKM.

– *Length of a column.* The length of roadway occupied by a column, including gaps, measured from front to rear inclusive.

– *Road gap.* The distance between two march elements.

• Rate factors:

– *Speed.* The actual rate of speed at a given moment.

– *Pace.* The regulated speed of a column or element, set by the head vehicle, to maintain the prescribed average speed.

– *Rate of march.* The average number of miles or kilometers traveled in any given period of time, including short delays or periodic halts. Expressed in miles or kilometers in the hour (MIH or KMIH).

• Time factors:

– *Arrival time.* The time when the head of the column arrives at a designated point.

– *Clearance time.* The time when the last of a column passes a designated point.

– *Completion time.* The time when the last vehicle of a column passes the release point.

– *Extra time allowance (EXTAL).* Always add 1 minute per 25 vehicles to the pass time. If the column has more than 600 vehicles, the EXTAL will be 2 minutes per 25 vehicles.

– *Pass time.* Actual time required for a column, from the first to the last vehicles inclusive, to pass a given point.

– *Road clearance time.* The total time a column requires to travel over and clear a section of road.

– *Time distance (TDIS).* The time required to move from one point to another at a given rate of march.

—*Time gap.* Time measured between the rear and front of successive vehicles as they move past any given point.

- Formulas:

$$\text{Rate} = \frac{\text{Distance}}{\text{Time}}$$

$$\text{Distance} = \text{Rate} \times \text{Time}$$

$$\text{Time} = \frac{\text{Distance}}{\text{Rate}}$$

$$\text{Time Distance} = \frac{\text{Distance}}{\text{Rate of March (MIH or KMIH)}}$$

Example: Determine TDIS of a serial traveling 135 kilometers at a rate of march of 20 KMIH.

$$\text{TDIS} = \frac{135}{20} = 6.75 \text{ hrs} = 6 \text{ hrs and } 45 \text{ min}$$

$$\text{Pass time} = \frac{\#\text{ of Vehicles} \times 60}{\text{density} \times \text{speed}} + \frac{\#\text{ of Vehicles}}{25} + (\text{time gaps} \times \text{min})$$

Example: Determine pass time (PST) of a serial of 150 vehicles organized into march units of 25 vehicles, traveling at a speed of 24 KMIH, with a density of 15 VPKM and using a 2-minute time gap between march units.

$$\text{PST} = \frac{150 \times 60}{15 \times 24} + \frac{150}{25} + (5 \times 2) = 25 + 6 + 10 = 41 \text{ minutes}$$

Note: Add EXTAL of 1 minute per 25 vehicles

Road Movement Graph

A road movement graph is a time-space diagram that visually depicts a movement from start point (SP) to release point (RP). (See the accompanying example.) Use it during the movement planning stage to avoid conflicts and discrepancies and to prevent congestion along the route of march. Also use it to prepare or check the road movement table. It shows the relative time and location of the head and tail of each march element at any point along the route, arrival and clearance times of march elements at critical points, and restrictions.

Transfer information derived from march formulas or obtained from march tables directly to the graph. To complete the road movement graph, the planner must have already organized the march column into serials and the serials into march units, determined time-distance, arrival time, and completion time, and computed pass time for each serial or march unit as appropriate.

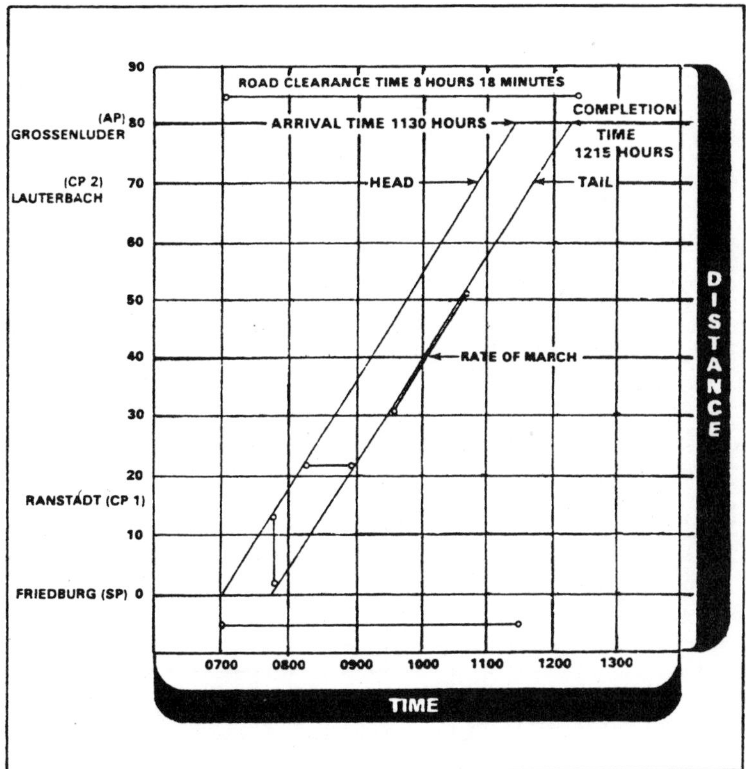

Road movement graph (example).

Road Movement Table

A road movement table is normally an annex to a movement order. It is a convenient way of transmitting time schedules and other essential details of a move. The accompanying example of a road movement table is a general-use blank form. It is virtually self-explanatory, but the following notes may help you use it.

- Use only the minimum number of headings. Include any information common to two or more movement numbers under general data paragraphs of the movement order.
- Because the table may be issued to personnel concerned with control of traffic, remember the security aspect. Including dates and locations may not be desirable.
- If the table is issued by itself and not as an annex to a detailed order, the table must be signed and authenticated in the normal way.

Road Movement Table Format

ANNEX....(Road Movement Table) to OPORD#......................

Colums:

a=March Unit #
b=Date
c=Unit
d=No. of Veh.
e=Load Class (Hvy)
f=From
g=To
h=Route

i=Route to SP
j=Reference
k=Due
l=Clear
m=Route to RP
n=Remarks

General Information:

1. Speed.................
2. Rate of March.........
3. Open/Closed Column
4. Traffic Density........
5. Time Gap..............
6. Halts.................
7. Route........
8. From.........
9. To.........
10. Critical Points:

SPa.......... d.........
RPb.......... e.........
c.......... f.........

11. Route to SP.........
12. Route From RP........

									Critical Points				
a	b	c	d	e	f	g	h	i	j	k	l	m	n

• *Critical point* is a selected point along a route used for reference in giving instructions. It includes start points, release points, and other points along a route where interference with movement may occur or where timings are critical.

• The movement number (column a) identifies a column (or element of a column) during the whole of the movement.

• If an annex has the same distribution as an operation order, it is not necessary to include the complete heading.

• To obtain due times for march units, transfer directly from the road movement graph or calculate using time distance table and strip map.

• To obtain clear times, add march unit pass time to due time.

• To complete the schedule for successive march units, add pass time plus gap time to due time.

Road Movement Annex to the Operations Order

If an operations order includes the movement of units, an annex to the order must be written to ensure coordinated movement of the elements involved. This organization and control is necessary to prevent confusion and assist subordinate units to arrive at required destinations in the proper sequence and on the proper schedule to accomplish the mission. See the accompanying example of the format for a road movement annex to an operations order.

Format for Road Movement Annex to an Operations Order

. . . .
(Classification)

(Change from verbal orders, if any)

Copy no ___ of ___ copies
Issuing headquarters
Place of issue (may be in code)
Date-time group of signature
Message reference number ___

ANNEX _____ (ROAD MOVEMENT) to OPERATION ORDER NO _____

References: Maps, charts, and other relevant documents

Time zone used throughout the order:

1. SITUATION

Any items of information that affect the movement and were not covered in paragraph 1 of the operation order or that need to be amplified.

2. MISSION

3. EXECUTION

a. Concept of movement.

b. Tasks to subordinate units.

c. Detailed timings.

d. Coordinating instructions.

(1) Order of march.

. . . .
(Classification)

Format for Road Movement Annex to an Operations Order (continued)

....
(Classification)
(Short title identification)

(2) Routes.

(3) Density.

(4) Speed.

(5) Method of movement.

(6) Defense on move.

(7) Start, release, or other critical points.

(8) Convoy control.

(9) Harbor areas (see note at end of annex).

(10) Instructions for halts.

(11) Lighting.

(12) Air support.

4. SERVICE SUPPORT

a. Traffic control.

b. Recovery.

c. Medical.

d. Petroleum, oil, and lubricants.

e. Water.

....
(Classification)

Format for Road Movement Annex to an Operations Order (continued)

....
(Classification)
(Short title identification)

5. COMMAND AND SIGNAL

   a. Commander(s).

   b. Communications.

   c. Position of key vehicles.

Acknowledgment instructions.

/s/......................
Commander

Authentication:

Appendixes:

Distribution:

Note: A *harbor area* is an area designated for normal halts, for traffic control, and to avoid congestion in emergencies.

....
(Classification)

9

Staff Action Formats

Combat service support officers find themselves serving most often as staff officers. Even commanders of combat service support units usually have a second implied role as a special staff officer to the commander of the supported units. This chapter presents a few essential items for effective communication from staff positions. These items are very important to the logistician in the field. The first is the military briefing, a formal verbal communication key to effective exchanges of information. The next is a series of checklists to enable the logistician to conduct more productive meetings. The chapter will then discuss the most often used written format in the U.S. Army, the Disposition Form. Finally, the chapter presents a detailed description and format for the Joint Message Form because of its great importance to the communications system of the entire Department of Defense. These formats will help the logistician communicate effectively regardless of the situation.

MILITARY BRIEFINGS

Logisticians are constantly involved in briefings. This involvement includes meetings with the visiting dignitary, the supported commander who must be briefed, the combat service support commander who must receive a daily briefing, or the subordinate unit commanders who have to be informed of their role in pending operations. These requirements for formal verbal presentation of data make it necessary for the logistician to understand the principles of preparing a useful and informative briefing.

Most verbal communication is informal and follows the pattern of normal conversational habits. The military briefing, however, is a formal presentation of selected information to commanders, staffs, or other designated audiences. The briefing may be meticulously prepared, or it may be given extemporaneously from the briefer's knowledge of the situation. In general, the briefing techniques are set by the purpose of the briefing, desired response, or role of the briefer. The Army uses four main types of briefings: information, decision, mission, and staff. Logisticians can use the following explanations and suggestions as aids in organizing briefings required to accomplish their mission. Although, officially, the Army has no designated formats, the following structures will ensure effective communication in an efficiently organized manner.

The Information Briefing

The purpose of the information briefing is to inform the listener. It deals with facts and does not include conclusions or recommendations. It should contain a brief introduction sufficient to name the subject and limit scope of the briefing. The format is not rigid, but the briefing should be orderly, objective, honest, clear, and concise, such as in the following outline for a briefing.

1. Introduction.

a. Greeting. Address the primary or ranking person being briefed with military courtesy, and introduce yourself by name and position.

b. Purpose. Announce and explain the purpose and scope of the briefing.

c. Procedure. Describe the schedule of events or structure of the briefing. Explain any demonstration, tour, or display so that the audience will understand any required movement or actions on their part, if necessary.

d. Classification. Announce the classification of the material being presented. This announcement may not be appropriate at all briefings, but do not omit it if you discuss any classified material. In the case of briefing unclassified data to civilian personnel, you could omit it.

2. Body.

a. Arrange the material in a logical manner. The ideas or data presented should flow smoothly, and the sequence should aid audience comprehension.

b. The transitions between main points should effectively move the information being briefed to its final point.

3. Closing.

a. After the formal briefing, ask whether the audience has any questions. This feedback is a good way to figure out whether you've gotten your point across to your audience. Answer all questions as quickly as possible, and explain any confusion that the questions reveal.

b. Make your final statement after you have answered all the questions.

The Decision Briefing

The decision briefing is similar to the information briefing, but it has a different purpose. This type of briefing is given to a commander to provide the data to make a decision and to obtain that decision at the end of the briefing. The decision briefing could be called a verbal staff study because the format for this briefing contains each of the elements of the staff study. As with the information briefing, the decision briefing has no official structure, but it does require more specific evidence plus analysis.

1. Introduction.

a. Greeting. Address the ranking person being briefed, and identify yourself and your position.

b. Announce the problem statement. State the purpose of the briefing and ensure that the commander understands that the briefing is attempting to draw a decision from him.

c. Procedure. Explain any demonstrations or special procedures to be used, if necessary.

d. Coordination. The commander should always be informed of any completed coordination that could affect his decision. A summary of all coordination should be presented at the start of the briefing, if necessary.

e. Classification. Announce the classification of the material to be covered if it includes any classified information.

2. Body.

a. Assumptions. Present all assumptions that affect the decision. They should be valid, logical, and essential to the decision.

b. Facts bearing on the problem. Present relevant and supportable facts. Even if supporting material is not presented, it should be available for discussion as required by the commander.

c. Discussion. Analyze each identified course of action. Ensure that transitions between courses of action are smooth and lead the commander through a logical consideration of all valid and essential factors influencing the decision.

d. Conclusions. State the degree of acceptance or merit of each course of action discussed. A logical reasoning process should be apparent in the ordering of the courses of action from the best to the least appropriate.

e. Recommendation. Clearly and concisely recommend a specific course(s) of action. (It is important to not request an opinion from the commander during this process.)

3. Close.

a. Ask for questions. (If you have presented necessary and sufficient evidence, analyzed that evidence in terms of your recommendation, refuted all valid objectives, coordinated your recommendation with your peers, rehearsed your briefing, you shouldn't get many questions here.)

b. Request the decision.

The Staff Briefing

The staff briefing is the most widely used briefing. It is used at all levels to keep commanders and staff officers abreast of situations. It may involve the exchange of information, the announcement of decisions, the issuance of directives, or the presentation of guidance. The purpose of the staff briefing is to coordinate the efforts and organize the operations of the entire unit.

There is no set format for the staff briefing. It is normally a recurring briefing at intervals designated by the commander. In some situations, it could occur daily, whereas other circumstances don't require that frequency. Each unit will design its own staff briefing format to suit its own needs.

The Mission Briefing

The mission briefing is used to publish or elaborate on an order, to give specific instructions, or to instill a general appreciation of a unit mission. The intended result is to establish a complete understanding of the mission involved. The mission briefing is very similar to the information briefing.

MEETING PLANNING CHECKLISTS

The coordination of operations both in the field and in garrison requires every officer to conduct and attend meetings. Unfortunately, one of the most wasteful things that people must endure is participation in a poorly organized or poorly executed meeting. The checklists presented in this section should assist logisticians in ensuring that their meetings are efficiently structured and conducted in a productive manner.

Premeeting Checklist

The premeeting checklist is a guide for personnel involved in problem-solving or decision-making meetings.

- For the person calling the meeting:
  - Why is the meeting necessary?
  - Can I gather the right people to attend the meeting at this time?
  - What outcomes or results do I expect to achieve?
- For the person conducting the meeting:
  - Do I have a thorough understanding of the purpose of this meeting?
  - Do I have the necessary background or knowledge to conduct this meeting?
  - Can I clearly communicate the purpose of this meeting to the attendees?
- For the person attending the meeting:
  - Why am I attending this meeting?
  - What can I contribute?
  - Do I understand the purpose of the meeting?

The Agenda Checklist

One of the keys to effective meetings is the proper construction of the agenda. An agenda is a list or schedule of topics that will be discussed at the meeting. It should be carefully developed to match the announced purpose of the meeting planned.

- For the person who calls the meeting:
  - Is the agenda properly prepared?
  - Did I send it to the right persons?
  - Did I send it in time?
  - Did I allow for additions or subtractions?
  - Did I list all the presentations?
- For the person conducting the meeting:
  - Am I satisfied with the agenda?
  - Is the agenda clear?
  - Are the time limitations appropriate?
  - Does the agenda fit the purpose of the meeting?
- For the person attending the meeting:
  - Do I understand this agenda?
  - Can I add or subtract from the agenda?
  - Where can I be most active at the meeting?
  - Does the agenda meet my personal purpose for attending the meeting?

The Meeting Checklist

The following checklists serve as a guide for all personnel involved in a meeting. The points should remind all attendees of their responsibility to contribute to the success of the meeting.

- For the person calling the meeting:
  - Is it clear that the members know what type of meeting this is, informal or decisionmaking?
  - Have I established appropriate priorities for agenda items?
  - Has the agenda been sent in time for the members to do appropriate planning?
  - Has adequate time been allotted to each presenter?
- For the person conducting the meeting:
  - Is there sufficient time for all members to express their opinions?
  - Am I inclined to favor some members' opinions more than others?
  - Is there enough time for questions?
  - Are members satisfied with the decisions?
- For persons attending the meeting:
  - Do I have some knowledge or expertise on the matter under discussion?
  - Do I feel free to express my opinions? If not, why not?
  - How can I best make use of this information?
  - Am I willing to be cooperative in making decisions?
  - Am I prepared to take notes on any presentations?
  - Am I willing to assume personal responsibility for the decisions?

DISPOSITION FORM

This section explains, through the use of an example, the correct format for the preparation of a DA Form 2496, *Disposition Form,* known

DISPOSITION FORM

For use of this form, see AR 340-15; the proponent agency is TAGO.

S: SUSPENSE DATE

REFERENCE OR OFFICE SYMBOL	SUBJECT
DAIM-FAR (MARKS NUMBER)	Preparation of a Disposition Form

TO	FROM	DATE	
DAPE-ZX DALO-ZX DAMI-ZX DAPC-ZX	DAIM	17 March 1986 SFC Horner/nm/699-4676	CMT 1

1. When preparing a Disposition Form (DF), align the typewriter on the first space to the right of the border marking. Type or print the reference symbol of the originator of the DF and the subject on the first line below the block titles. Begin each at the left edge of the respective box. This positioning will accommodate a two-line office symbol or two-line subject. Block the "TO" and "FROM" addressees approximately two spaces behind the printed designations. Stamp or type the date two spaces behind the word "DATE." Use the identification of the writer on all DFs or CMTs and type it on the next line below the date, ending approximately at the right margin.

2. If a suspense date is used, type it on the proponent agency line, ending at the right margin, as shown above.

3. Begin the text of the DF on the second line below the last line of the address or the writer identification, whichever is lower. Margins of the DF are established by the vertical lines on the form.

a. The horizontal mark, which may be at the left side of the form, identifies the maximum text that may be typed on the form and still leave room for the signature block.

b. If it can be determined that two pages will be required to complete CMT 1, the typing may continue to the bottom of the form.

c. If the DF is classified, stop the text at the horizontal mark to leave space for the required reclassification stamp, classifier identification, and general downgrading schedule information.

4. Place the authority line (if applicable), the signature block, the enclosure listing, and information copy notation as specified for a memorandum.

5. On a DF the "FROM" addressee will always agree with either the authority line or the signer's title.

DA FORM AUG 80 **2496** PREVIOUS EDITIONS WILL BE USED

Disposition Form (example).

Example of a Disposition Form Continuation Sheet

DAIM-FAR-P
SUBJECT: Continuation of a Disposition Form CMT 1

6. If a continuation page is required, use plain bond paper. The following rules apply:

a. The right and left margins are the same as for the printed Disposition Form.

b. Type the office symbol at the left margin on the eighth line from the top of the page. Place the identification of the comment, "CMT 1," "CMT 2," etc., at the far right margin on the same line as the office symbol.

c. Do not divide a paragraph of three lines or less between pages. At least two lines of a divided paragraph must be on each page.

d. Include at least two words on each page of any sentence divided between pages.

e. Do not type the authority line and the signature block on the continuation page without at least two lines of the last paragraph. If, however, a paragraph or subparagraph contains only one line, it may be placed alone on the continuation page with the authority line and signature block.

f. Number continuation pages the same as for the memorandum, approximately 1 to ½ inches from the bottom of the page and centered.

FOR THE ASSISTANT CHIEF OF STAFF FOR INFORMATION MANAGEMENT:

JAMES S. HARRIS
LTC, GS
Director, Reserve Affairs

2 Encls
1. Ltr, NGB, 5 Mar 86
2. Ltr, ARNG, 5 Mar 86

Example of a Disposition Form Comment 2

S: 20 Mar 86

DAIM-FAR-PM (DAIG-CC/1 Mar 86) (MARKS NUMBER)
SUBJECT: Preparing a Separate-Page Comment

TO	DAIG-CC	FROM	DAIM-FAR	DATE	6 Mar 86	CMT 2
	Pentagon		Hoffman I		SFC Harris/mn/325-6090	

1. Type the office symbol or reference symbol of the office or action officer preparing the comment at the left margin on the eighth line from the top of the page; include the office or reference symbol and date of the basic comment in parentheses. Add the MARKS number, in parentheses, following the office symbol and date of the basic comment.

2. The right and left margins are the same as for the printed Disposition Form.

3. If a suspense date is used, type it on the sixth line from the top of the page ending at the right margin.

4. Type the subject line on the next line below the office or reference symbol. Type the word “TO” at the left margin on the second line below the subject. Type the words “FROM,” “DATE,” and designation of the number of the comment; CMT 2, CMT 3, etc., on the same line, spaced in the same position as on the printed form itself, or as close as possible.

5. Begin the text on the second line below the last line of the addressee or writer identification, whichever is lower, beginning at the left margin.

6. Place the authority line (if applicable), the signature block, the enclosure listing, and information copy notation as specified for the memorandum.

FOR THE ASSISTANT CHIEF OF STAFF FOR INFORMATION MANAGEMENT:

LAWRENCE F. DELANEY
Colonel, GS
Director, Resources and Manpower

2 Encls
nc

Elements of the Joint Message Format

Item No.	*Tab Position***	*Number and Type of Characters*	*Description of Entry*
* 1	1	2—numeric	Page number.
2	5	2—numeric	Total page count.
3	9	6—numeric 1—alpha	First two digits represent the day of the month, next two digits represent the hour of the day using the 24-hour clock, and last two digits represent the minutes. It will contain the suffix "Z" indicating time in GMT.
4	18	3—alpha	Authorized abbreviation of the current month.
5	23	2—numeric	Last two digits of the current year.
* 6	27	2—alpha	Action precedence.
* 7	31	2—alpha	There must be an info precedence entry if action field is not used.
* 8	35	4—alpha	Classification repeated four times.
9	41	5—alpha	SPECAT or SHD designator repeated five times.
10	48	2—alpha	Language media format (LMG information). Leave blank unless specific LMF is required.
11	52	4—alpha	Content indicator code (CIC) normally "ZYUW". Other CICs may be used as prescribed in applicable directives.

Elements of the Joint Message Format (continued)

*12	58	alpha numeric up to 12	A unique sequence assigned by the originator for positive message identification.
*13	1	0 or 3–alpha	Book message information. If "YES" is used, the CIC field must contain "ZEXW" or "ZYQW".
14	5	variable to end of line	Message handling information.
15	15	variable	Start of From Plain Language Addressee (PLA) with office symbols, if available.
16	15	variable	Start of To PLA with office symbols, if available. If no ACTION address, Item 19 applies.
17	20	variable	PLA continuation line(s) applies.
18	15	3–alpha, type in "AIG" and number	Start of address indicating group information.
19	10	4–alpha, type in prosign "INFO"	Start of information line.
20	15	variable	PLA for INFO addresses.
21	15	Type in operating signal "ZEN"	Start of ZEN information.
22	19	variable	Start of PLA(s) to be delivered by other than electrical means.
23	11	Type in prosign "XMT."	Exempt Prosign.

Elements of the Joint Message Format (continued)

24	15	variable	Any exempted PLA when AIG(s) are used in the IO line.
25	1	variable	Start of classification line.
26	1	4—alpha	End of classification indicator.
27	1	variable	Start of text.

Notes:
*These entries must be made on all subsequent pages for proper handling.
**The first character to appear on the DD Form 173 will define the left margin (character position 1). In this case, page numbering information in the upper left hand corner of the form. Each line is limited to 69 characters, including positioning blanks, correction signs, and spaces.

simply as a DF. The DF is the most widely used format for correspondence in the U.S. Army: between Army staff agencies; between their organizational elements; between organizational elements of the same major command headquarters, installation, or unit; between a tenant activity and other organizational elements or units on the same installation; or between an agency of HQDA and a field unit or staff support agency. The DF is an informal means of communication and can be either typed or handwritten. Use it as much as possible in any case when no other form for a personnel action is prescribed, to originate an action, or to obtain comments, recommendations, and other information.

Each signed portion of a DF is referred to as a comment, and each comment should be numbered consecutively. Do not type a sequential comment on the bottom of the last page of a multipage DF. Use a separate page for comment. If there is enough room at the bottom of a one-page DF, a subsequent comment can be typed at the bottom of the same page. If there is not sufficient space, use a separate page for comment.

The examples provided are self-explanatory and demonstrate proper formatting for a Disposition Form.

MESSAGE FORMAT

DD Form 173, *Joint Message Form,* is used throughout the Department of Defense for the preparation of electronically transmitted messages. AR 105-31 discusses the preparation and dispatch of the general service message. The entries in the example Joint Message Form are keyed to the accompanying explanation of elements of the form. These items provide the correct format and data necessary for the proper preparation of the Joint Message Form.

JOINT MESSAGEFORM											SECURITY CLASSIFICATION UNCLASSIFIED
1 PAGE 2	DTG/RELEASER TIME			PRECEDENCE		CLASS	SPECAT	LMF	CIC	ORIG/MSG IDENT	
	3 DATE-TIME	4 MONTH	5 YR	6 ACT	7 INFO	8	9	10	11	12	
01 OF 02	261100Z	JUN	88	PP	RR	UUUU		AT	ZYUU	3291800Z	
BOOK 13	MESSAGE HANDLING INSTRUCTIONS: 14 THIS AREA IS FOR MESSAGE HANDLING INSTRUCTION ONLY.										

15 **FROM**: CDRUSACEEIA FT HUACHUCA AZ//CCC-TAD//

16 **TO**: CDRUSAIX SFRAN CA//AMXXXCDC/ AMCCCODL/ AMXXXADY/

17 AMXXSSD/ AMXXXRDD//

18 AIG 5410

20

19 INFO:AFCD KELLY AFB TX//DCXX//

21 22

ZEN CDRUSAEPG FT HUACHUCA AZ//STEEP-MT//

ZEN CDRUSACC FT HUACHUCA AZ//CC-OPS-OE//

24

23 XMT: CUSASSLNO WASH DC//CC-LNOW

COMUSKOREA SEOUL KOREA

25

UNCLAS

26

QQQ

27

SUBJ: DDFORM 173 MESSAGE FORMAT PREPARATION

THIS IS A SAMPLE MESSAGE INDICATING REQUIRED POSITIONING OF DATA.
FORM ALIGNMENT- CORRECT ALIGNMENT OF THE MESSAGE FORM IN THE
TYPEWRITER IS ESSENTIAL. ALIGN THE MESSAGE FORM SQUARELY, USING THE
BORDERLINES AS A HORIZONTAL AND VERTICAL GUIDE. TO SET THE FIRST TAB,
ALIGN THE FORM SO THAT THE FIRST CHARACTER POSITION WOULD BE PRINTED
JUST INSIDE THE EXTREME LEFT MARGIN OF THE "PAGE" BLOCK AND, FOR THE
HORIZONTAL ALIGNMENT, ADJUST THE FORM SO THAT A CHARACTER WOULD
PRINT WITHIN THE TWO HORIZONTAL REFERENCE MARKS AT THE UPPER LEFT
CORNER OF THE FORM. THIS IS THE REFERENCE POSITION FOR LINE SPACING
AND TAB POSITIONING FOR THE REST OF THE FORM. NOTE THAT ALL LINES MUST

DISTR:

DRAFTER TYPED NAME, TITLE, OFFICE SYMBOL, PHONE	SPECIAL INSTRUCTIONS
A. B. DOOR, COMM SPEC, CCC-TAD 6131, 4 JUN 88	
RELEASER — TYPED NAME, TITLE, OFFICE SYMBOL AND PHONE: F. T. SMITH, COL, USA, CCC-TAD, 6222	
SIGNATURE	SECURITY CLASSIFICATION: UNCLASSIFIED — DATE TIME GROUP

DD FORM 1 MAR 79 173/2 (OCR) — PREVIOUS EDITION IS OBSOLETE S/N 0102-LF-000-1735 — ☆U.S. GOVERNMENT PRINTING OFFICE: 1985-485-115

Joint Message Form DD 173, annotated format.

JOINT MESSAGEFORM						SECURITY CLASSIFICATION UNCLASSIFIED				
PAGE	DTG/RELEASER TIME			PRECEDENCE		CLASS	SPECAT	LMF	CIC	ORIG/MSG IDENT
	DATE-TIME	MONTH	YR	ACT	INFO					
02 of 02				PP	RR	UUUU				3291800Z
BOOK	MESSAGE HANDLING INSTRUCTIONS									

FROM:

TO:

BE DOUBLE SPACED; THAT ALL PROSIGNS BEGIN IN TAB POSITION 10 OR 11; ADDRESSEES IN TAB POSITION 15; CONTINUATION LINES IN TAB POSITION 20; AND START OF TEXT AT THE LEFT MOST MARGIN. NO LINE MAY EXCEED 69 CHARACTER POSITIONS INCLUDING POSITIONING BLANKS, CORRECTION SIGNS, AND SPACES.

REFER TO NUMBER CODE ON SUCCEEDING PAGE FOR EXPLANATION OF FIELD ENTRIES.

6
5
4
3
2
1
0

DISTR:

DRAFTER TYPED NAME, TITLE, OFFICE SYMBOL, PHONE	SPECIAL INSTRUCTIONS	
RELEASER TYPED NAME, TITLE, OFFICE SYMBOL AND PHONE		
SIGNATURE	SECURITY CLASSIFICATION UNCLASSIFIED	DATE TIME GROUP

DD FORM 1 MAR 79 173/2 *(OCR)* PREVIOUS EDITION IS OBSOLETE S/N 0102-LF-000-1736 ☆U.S. GOVERNMENT PRINTING OFFICE: 1985-485-135

Joint Message Form DD 173, annotated format **(continued).**

10

Special Purpose Formats

This chapter on special purpose formats presents examples and instructions on the composition and structure of specific items of standardized information. You may need some of the formats on very short notice, especially the ones that are hard to find and hard to memorize. Each of them, however, is very important in specific situations either because of the information it provides for combat service support operations or because of a need for accuracy in reporting or passing information to higher headquarters or adjacent units.

The first eight formats presented pertain to nuclear, biological, and chemical warfare (NBC). These message formats are designed to allow the logistician to report rapidly the effects of an NBC attack and to react to the information provided by NBC reports from other units or higher headquarters. The message forms are self-explanatory in their use, but they are also very detailed to ensure accurate communication of an NBC hazard, whether from friendly or hostile weapons. It is very important for the combat service support officer to remember that friendly NBC weapons will kill support soldiers just as dead as will enemy weapons.

DOWNWIND CHEMICAL HAZARD PREDICTION REPORT

The hazard from a chemical attack is not limited to the immediate area of the detonation. Winds can carry contaminants over great distances. To prevent casualties, quickly prepare and dispatch the downwind chemical hazard prediction report to warn all endangered units. Remember that the prediction of affected areas is only an approximation, and units receiving this report must react just as quickly as the troops who suffered the direct attack.

NUCLEAR STRIKE WARNING MESSAGE

This message goes to all friendly units that might be affected by the detonation of a friendly nuclear device. The report form is self-explanatory.

DOWNWIND CHEMICAL HAZARD PREDICTION

FRIENDLY CHEMICAL STRIKE WARNING MESSAGE

PRECEDENCE: ____________________
DATE/TIME (ZULU): ____________________
SECURITY: ____________________
FROM: ____________________
TO: ____________________
TYPE OF REPORT: DOWNWIND CHEMICAL HAZARD PREDICTION

ALPHA: ____________________
(Attack Serial Number)

*DELTA: ____________________
Date/Time the attack started (ZULU)

*ECHO: ____________________
Date/Time the attack ended (ZULU)

*FOXTROT: ____________________
Location of attack in UTM coordinates or name of place.

GOLF: ____________________
(Means of Delivery)

HOTEL: ____________________
(Agent Symbol)

INDIA: ____________________
(Number of Shells)

*PAPA: ____________________
UTM grid coordinates of expected contamination.

ZULU: PREVAILING SURFACE WINDS: dddsss
(ddd wind direction in degrees from which the wind is blowing; sss wind speed in KMPH)

Downwind chemical hazard prediction message format.

EFFECTIVE DOWNWIND MESSAGE

This message provides units the data to prepare a simplified fallout prediction. Prepare the effective downwind message for specific yields.

NBC-1 INITIAL REPORT

The NBC-1 report is the most widely used NBC message. Any unit that observes an NBC attack uses this report format to provide information to higher headquarters and adjacent units. All units should be familiar with the NBC-1 report and its functions. Prepare quickly and accurately after the observation of an NBC attack.

NBC-2 EVALUATED DATA REPORT

The NBC-2 report consolidates information from more than one

PRECEDENCE: ______
DATE/TIME: ______
SECURITY: ______
FROM: ______
TO: ______
TYPE OF REPORT: STRIKEWARN

ALPHA: ______
Code word indicating nuclear strike (target number)

*DELTA: ______
Date/Time of burst in local or ZULU time. Date/Time after which the strike will be cancelled in local or ZULU time.

*FOXTROT: ______
DGZ (UTM Grid coordinates)

HOTEL: ______
Type of burst: Air, Surface, or ADM

INDIA: ______
For all bursts (in hundreds of meters) four digits: MSD 1-Warned Protected, Negligible Risk. MSD 2-Warned Exposed, Negligible Risk. MSD 3-Unwarned Exposed, Negligible Risk.

YANKEE: ______
Azimuth of left then right radial lines (degrees or mils, state which) four digits each. (Measure clockwise from grid north to the left and then to the right radial lines).

ZULU: ______
Effective wind speed in kilometers, three digits. Downwind distance of Zone I in kilometers, three digits. Cloud radious in kilometers, two digits.

**ZULU INDIA: ______
Effective wind speed to the mearest kilometer per hour, three digits. Downwind distance of Zone I to the nearest tenth of a kilometer, four digits. Downwind distance of Zone II to the nearest tenth of a kilometer, four digits. Cloud radious to the nearest tenth of a kilometer, three digits.

* Must be encoded if broadcast prior to H-30 minutes. During exercises line FOXTROT will always be encoded.
** For friendly ADM, surface or subsurface bursts.

Nuclear strike warning message format.

NBC-1 initial report. It is usually prepared at division level but can be formulated at separate battalion or brigade level. Its function is to disseminate information on the extent of the NBC effects on the battlefield so that units can respond appropriately to prevent casualties.

NBC-3 EXPECTED CONTAMINATION REPORT

The NBC-2 report and current wind information are used to predict the downwind hazard area. This information is dispatched to appropriate locations in the form of an NBC-3 report. Units receiving this report should use it as a source of battlefield intelligence when considering courses of action.

NBC-4 RADIATION DOSE RATE REPORT

When any units detect NBC contamination through monitoring or

JOINT MESSAGEFORM						SECURITY CLASSIFICATION: CLASSIFICATION				
PAGE	DTG/RELEASER TIME			PRECEDENCE		CLASS	SPECAT	LMF	CIC	ORIG/MSG IDENT
	DATE TIME	MONTH	YR	ACT	INFO					
1 of 1	082200S	PP								

BOOK | MESSAGE HANDLING INSTRUCTIONS

FROM: CDR, _____ DIVARTY/CHEM SEC/

TO: (ALL MAJOR SUBORD HQS)

BT
CLASSIFICATION

SUBJECT; EFFECTIVE WIND MESSAGE

AREA OF WIND DATA: GATESVILLE, TX PK 1877

ZULU: (DTG OF WIND DATA)

ALPHA: DDDSSS (0-2 KT)

BRAVO: DDDSSS (2-5 KT)

CHARLIE: DDDSSS (5-30 KT)

DELTA: DDDSSS (30-100 KT)

ECHO: DDDSSS (100-300 KT)

FOXTROT: DDDSSS (300 KT - 1 MT)

* * * * * * *

BT
GPX

DDD = DOWNWIND DIRECTION IN DEGREES.

SSS = DOWNWIND SPEED IN KILOMETERS/HOURS

DISTR:

DRAFTER TYPED NAME, TITLE, OFFICE SYMBOL, PHONE: I.M.GASST, MAJ, CM, CML OFF

SPECIAL INSTRUCTIONS

RELEASER — TYPED NAME, TITLE, OFFICE SYMBOL AND PHONE: U.R. KNOTT, LTC, FA, S3

SIGNATURE: /S/ KNOTT

SECURITY CLASSIFICATION: CLASSIFICATION

DATE TIME GROUP

DD FORM 1 MAR 79 173/3 PREVIOUS EDITION IS OBSOLETE ☆U.S. GPO 1979—0-302-175

Effective downwind message format.

N B C -1

NUCLEAR, BIOLOGICAL, OR CHEMICAL INITIAL OBSERVER'S REPORT

PRECEDENCE: ____________________

DATE/TIME
(LOCAL OR ZULU): ____________________

OBSERVER LOCATION OR
REPORTING ACTIVITY: ____________________

TO: ____________________

TYPE OF REPORT:		NBC-1 (NUCLEAR)	NBC-1 (CHEMICAL)	NBC-1 (BIOLOGICAL)
ALFA	Strike serial number (Assigned by responsible CBRE).			
BRAVO	Position of observer (UTM or place, encoded).			
CHARLIE	Azimuth of attack from the observer (deg or mils).			
DELTA	Date/Time attack started (Local or Zulu).			
ECHO	Illumination time (sec) or time attack ended (DTG).			
FOXTROT	Location of attack (UTM or place, actual or estimated).			
GOLF	Means of delivery (if known).			
HOTEL	Type of burst (air, surface, unk), type of agent, or type of attack (Bio, Chem).			
INDIA	Type and number of shells, aircraft, etc (say which).			
JULIET	Flash to bang time (sec).			
KILO	Crater present or absent and dia if known (meters).			
LIMA	Cloud width at H+5 min (state deg or mils).			
MIKE	Cloud Angle at H+10 min (say top or bottom and deg or mils)			
SIERRA	DTG of reading or when contamination init detected (local or Zulu-say which)			
XRAY	Located area of contamination (UTM):			

REMARKS: The Type of Report and Items D, H, and either B and C or F must always be reported, other items are optional.

NBC-1 report: Initial observer's report format.

reconnaissance, they should report this information on the NBC-4 report. Higher headquarters plot and consolidate NBC-4 reports to identify the complete location and extent of hazard areas.

NBC-5 CONTAMINATED AREA REPORT

NBC-4 reports are analyzed and plotted on the situation map. The data derived provide details necessary to develop a contaminated area overlay. One of the means of transmitting this information to the units is the

N B C 2

EVALUATED DATA REPORT NUCLEAR-BIOLOGICAL-CHEMICAL ATTACK

PRECEDENCE: ____________________

DATE/TIME (LOCAL OR ZULU): ____________________

OBSERVER LOCATION OR REPORTING ACTIVITY: ____________________

TO: ____________________

TYPE OF REPORT:		NBC-2 (NUCLEAR)	NBC-2 (CHEMICAL)	NBC-2 (BIOLOGICAL)
ALFA	Strike serial number (assigned by area CBRE).			
DELTA	Date/Time attack started (Zulu).			
FOXTROT	Location of attack (UTM coord or place; actual or estimated, state which).			
GOLF	Means of delivery, if known.			
HOTEL	Type of burst (air, surface, unk), agent or type of attack (bio, chem, etc.).			
NOVEMBER	Estimated yield (KT).			

REMARKS: Used by CBRE/CBRS to transmit evaluated data on NBC attacks.

NBC-2 report: Evaluated data report format.

NBC-5 report. It is prepared from the contaminated area overlay and consists of a series of grid coordinates. The recipient plots the points indicated on his own map and thereby reproduces the contaminated area overlay.

NBC-6 NBC ATTACK SUMMARY

The NBC-6 report summarizes all data concerning an NBC attack, and it is prepared at battalion level. It is narrative and has no prescribed format. The only requirement for its content is that it be as detailed as possible.

PERSONNEL DAILY SUMMARY

The sample personnel daily summary format provided is only one variation of this report. The point of this report is to establish the known personnel strength despite the overall confusion of the situation. Commanders need accurate reporting of their unit strengths to enable them to compute and plan the use of their combat power.

N B C 3

NUCLEAR, BIOLOGICAL, OR CHEMICAL EXPECTED CONTAMINATION

PRECEDENCE: ____________________

DATE/TIME (LOCAL OR ZULU): ____________________

REPORTING ACTIVITY: ____________________

TO: ____________________

TYPE OF REPORT:		NBC-3 (NUCLEAR)	NBC-3 (CHEMICAL)	NBC-3 (BIOLOGICAL)
ALFA	Strike serial number.			
DELTA	Date/Time attack started (Local or Zulu, say which).			
FOXTROT	Location of attack (UTM coord or place), actual or estimated, say which.			
PAPA	Area of expected contamination (UTM coord).			
YANKEE	Azimuth of left then right radial lines (deg or mils, say which), 4 digits each.			
* ZULU	Effective wind speed (kph) 3 digits; downwind distance of Zone I (km), 2 digits; cloud radius (km), 2 digits. (sssdddrr).			

*NOTE: When the effective wind speed is less than 8 kph, only 3 digits will be reported. These figures will specify the downwind distance of Zone I.

NBC-3 report: Expected contamination report format.

PERIODIC LOGISTICS REPORT

The periodic logistics report format provided is not a required format. Instead, it is a suggested structure to aid logisticians in the preparation of this report. This report is a major tool for logisticians to inform their commanders, their supported commanders, their supported units, and their supporting units of the current combat service support situation. It is therefore an opportunity to actively influence the tactical decisions made by the supported commanders and, through those decisions, to directly influence the outcome of current operations.

Periodic logistics reports from higher, subordinate, and adjacent units also provide valuable information that logisticians can incorporate into their own operational planning and forecasting. This report is very important.

N B C 4

REPORT OF RADIATION DOSE RATE

PRECEDENCE: ____________________

DATE/TIME (LOCAL OR ZULU): ____________________

OBSERVER OR REPORTING ACTIVITY: ____________________

TO: ____________________

TYPE OF REPORT:		NBC-4 (NUCLEAR)
QUEBEC	Location of reading (UTM coord).	
ROMEO	Dose rate, rad/hr (this is not normalized to H+1). The words "INITIAL, INCREASING, PEAK, or DECREASING" may be added.	
SIERRA	Date/Time of reading. (Local or Zulu, say which).	

Report items QUEBEC, ROMEO, and SIERRA as often as necessary.

NBC-4 report: Radiation dose rate report format.

PERIODIC OPERATION REPORT

This report is most important to logisticians as a source of information. Although this format may be used within combat service support units, it is essential to the operating support unit to receive copies of the periodic operation report from their supported unit. From these reports, the supporting commander can identify immediate targets for his combat service support efforts.

PERIODIC PERSONNEL REPORT

Like that of the periodic operation report, the value of the periodic personnel report to logisticians is in the information it reveals. The troop strength and condition data are vital to the planning of support operations. Although the support unit may have its own internal periodic personnel report, the one provided to it by the supported unit is most important to mission planning.

N B C 5

NUCLEAR-BIOLOGICAL-CHEMICAL CONTAMINATED AREA REPORT

PRECEDENCE: ______

DATE/TIME (LOCAL OR ZULU): ______

OBSERVER LOCATION OR REPORTING ACTIVITY: ______

TO: ______

TYPE OF REPORT:		NBC-5 (NUCLEAR)	NBC-5 (CHEMICAL)	NBC-5 (BIOLOGICAL)
ALFA	Strike serial number(s) causing contamination (if known).	______	______	______
OSCAR	Reference date/time for estimated contours (when not H+1 hour).	______	______	______
SIERRA	Date/Time contamination initially detected (state local or Zulu)		______	______
TANGO	H+1 date/time, or the date/time of latest reconaisance or contamination in the area (chem or bio) State local or Zulu time.	______	______	______
UNIFORM	1000 rad/hr contour line (UTM coord), (Red).	______ ______ ______ ______		
VICTOR	300 rad/hr contour line (UTM coord), (Green).	______ ______ ______ ______		
WHISKEY	100 rad/hr contour line (UTM coord),(Blue).	______ ______ ______ ______		
X-RAY	30 rad/hr contour line (UTM coord), (Black); or area of toxic contamination (UTM coord), (Yellow).	______ ______ ______	______ ______	______ ______

NBC-5 report: Contaminated area report format.

OPERATIONAL SITUATION REPORT

The operational situation report is prepared by the operations officer (S3) of each unit, but all other staff sections and the supporting units provide input to it. This report is an overall snapshot of the condition of the supported unit and its attachments, the enemy capabilities and probable courses of action, and the general conditions of current operations. The supporting logistician not only provides input but also can glean a great deal of data to assist in the management, control, and planning of support operations. The commanders and staff officers of all combat service support units must closely study and evaluate carefully the operational situation report, whenever it is available.

HEADQUARTERS ____________
(unit)

Unit	Strength			Daily losses					Gains		Remarks
	Auth	Asg	Pers/dy	KIA	WIA	MIA	Nonbat admin	Total			
(a)	(b)	(c)	(d)	(e)	(f)	(g)	(h)	(i)	(j)	(k)–(w)	(x)

____________ G1 ____________ Time signed

Note. Figures that have not changed during the period need not be transmitted.

Explanation of columns:

a–Includes all assigned and attached units. b–Shows TOE authorized strength, to include assigned and attached units. c–Shows assigned strength, to include assigned and attached units. d–Indicates number of personnel present for duty. e–f–g–Self-explanatory. h–Shows total personnel lost because of nonbattle deaths, injuries, disease or for administrative reasons. i–Shows total of columns e through h. j–Shows replacements and returned to duty. k to w–To be used as desired. x–Any pertinent remark, including key personnel losses (by name, rank, position) or items of information necessary to explain unusual entries in previous columns; numbers of personnel known to be captured may be included.

Personnel daily summary report format.

Periodic Logistics Report Format

....
(Classification)

(Omit paragraphs and subparagraphs not applicable.)

Copy no ___ of ___ copies
Issuing headquarters
Place of issue (may be in code)
Date-time group

PERIODIC LOGISTIC REPORT NO _______

Period covered: (date and time to date and time)

References: Maps (series number, sheet(s), edition, scale)

Disposal instruction: (if any; e.g., DESTROY WITHIN 48 HOURS OF RECEIPT)

1. LOGISTIC SITUATION AT END OF PERIOD

2. SUPPLY

a. Supported strength

b. Status of supply

c. Local procurement

d. Miscellaneous

3. SERVICE

a. Transportation. For each pertinent item, outline briefly the progress of major movements and bottlenecks.

(1) Highway.

(a) Transportation vehicles and motive power classified by principle run or local area. For each type of vehicle or motive power, show total

....
(Classification)

Periodic Logistics Report Format (continued)

....
(Classification)
(Short title identification)

available, total operating, total deadline, and breakdown of deadlined equipment into categories of maintenance.

(b) Tonnage of supplies, numbers of vehicles, and number of persons transported, classified by principle run or local area.

(c) Terminal operations. Show, for each, tonnage of supplies, number of vehicles, and number of persons loading and unloading; terminal equipment available and working.

(2) Air. Similar to (1) above.

(3) Rail. Similar to (1) above.

(4) Water. Similar to (1) above.

(5) Pipeline.

(6) Supply movement. Tonnage of supplies received in area and evacuated from area. Classify by means of transportation.

(7) Personnel movement. Number of personnel received in area and evacuated from area. Classify by means of transportation.

b. Construction. List principal projects, showing percentage of completion and projected operational and completion date for each.

c. Installation. For the principal installations of each service not covered above, show workload on hand at start of period, received, completed, and on hand at end of period, classified to conform to the class of work performed. List installations opened and closed during the period (state, location, date, and time).

d. Miscellaneous. Real estate, laundry, bath, clothing exchange, decontamination, and impregnation/reimpregnation, as required.

4. MAINTENANCE

Show quantity of principal items or classes of equipment awaiting maintenance on hand at start of period, received, completed, and on hand

....
(Classification)

Periodic Logistics Report Format (continued)

. . . .
(Classification)
(Short title identification)

at end of period. Also show major items of equipment deadlined, by type and reason therefore, and items of equipment evacuated.

5. MISCELLANEOUS

a. Boundaries. Changes during the period and activities relative to anticipated changes.

b. Headquarters. Locations and activities relative to movements during the period and activities relative to anticipated changes.

c. Changes in assignment during period assigned; relieved. (Show date and time.)

d. Protection. Losses or damage to logistic activities due to enemy, subversive, or natural causes. State corrective action taken.

e. Plans and orders. Receipt and issue of basic combat service support plans or instructions. Attach a copy of each administrative/logistics order (or changes thereto) issued since the preceding report.

f. Other logistic matters. Logistic matters not otherwise covered, such as exploitation of civilian and enemy prisoner labor.

/s/. . . . .
Commander

Authentication:

Annexes:

Distribution:

. . . .
(Classification)

Periodic Operation Report Format

....
(Classification)

(Omit paragraphs and subparagraphs not applicable.)

Copy no ___ of ___ copies
Issuing headquarters
Place of issue (may be in code)
Date-time group

PERIODIC OPERATION REPORT NO _______

Period covered: (date and time to date and time)

References: Maps (series number, sheet(s), edition, scale)

Disposal instruction: (if any; e.g., DESTROY WITHIN 48 HOURS OF RECEIPT)

1. OWN SITUATION AT END OF PERIOD

2. INFORMATION OF ADJACENT UNITS AND SUPPORTING TROOPS

3. OWN OPERATIONS FOR THE PERIOD

4. COMBAT EFFICIENCY

5. RESULTS OF OPERATIONS

6. MISCELLANEOUS

....
(Classification)

Periodic Operation Report Format (continued)

....
(Classification)

/s/......................
Commander

Authentication:

Annexes:

Distribution:

....
(Classification)

Periodic Personnel Report Format

....
(Classification)

(Omit paragraphs and subparagraphs not applicable.)

Copy no ___ of ___ copies
Issuing headquarters
Place of issue (may be in code)
Date-time group

PERIODIC PERSONNEL REPORT NO _______

Period covered: (date and time to date and time)

References: Maps (series number, sheet(s), edition, scale)

Disposal instructions: (if any; e.g., DESTROY WITHIN 48 HOURS OF RECEIPT)

1. MAINTENANCE OF UNIT STRENGTHS

   a. Strengths

   b. Replacements

2. PERSONNEL MANAGEMENT

   a. Military personnel

   b. Civilian personnel

   c. Enemy prisoners of war and civilian internees/detainees

3. DEVELOPMENT AND MAINTENANCE OF MORALE

   a. Morale and personnel services

   b. Graves registration

....
(Classification)

Periodic Personnel Report Format (continued)

....
(Classification)

4. HEALTH SERVICES

a. Evacuation

b. Hospitalization

5. MAINTENANCE OF DISCIPLINE AND LAW AND ORDER

Military discipline, military justice, comments on straggling, and any unusual problems concerning law and order.

6. HEADQUARTERS MANAGEMENT

Discipline, standards of shelter throughout the area, and use by the headquarters of private and nonmilitary public buildings.

7. MISCELLANEOUS

Important engagements participated in and names of individuals distinguishing themselves in such engagements. Add (as an annex) photographs of personnel and important scenes or events bearing on personnel activities.

/s/......................
Commander

Authentication:

Annexes:

Distribution:

....
(Classification)

Operational Situation Report Format

....
(Classification)

(Omit paragraphs and subparagraphs not applicable.)

Copy no ___ of ___ copies
Issuing headquarters
Place of issue (may be in code)
Date-time group of signature
Message reference number

SITUATION REPORT NO _______

Period covered: (date and time to date and time)

References: Maps (series number, sheet(s), edition, scale)

1. ENEMY

a. Units in contact.

b. Enemy reserves that can affect local situation.

c. Brief description of enemy activity during period covered by report.

d. Brief estimate of enemy strength, materiel means, morale, and his probable knowledge of our situation.

e. Conclusions covering courses of action open to enemy.

2. OWN SITUATION

a. Location of forward elements.

b. Location of units, headquarters, and boundaries.

c. Location of adjacent units and supporting troops.

....
(Classification)

Operational Situation Report Format (continued)

....
(Classification)
(Short title identification)

d. Brief description and results of operations during period of report.

e. Noneffective units.

3. COMBAT SERVICE SUPPORT

General statement of the CSS situation, if other than normal, as it directly affects the tactical situation.

4. GENERAL

Information not covered elsewhere.

5. COMMANDER'S EVALUATION

To be completed when directed by higher authority.

Acknowledgment instructions.

/s/......................
Commander

Authentication:

Annexes:

Distribution:

....
(Classification)

11

Staff Duties and Responsibilities

Logisticians will often find themselves at a loss to determine the responsibilities of each staff position in the logistics chain. This chapter is a list of several logistic positions and their responsibilities. Because all staff officers, including the operations officer, operate as supporting elements, this chapter will discuss first the primary staff positions and then more specific logistic roles and positions.

CHIEF OF STAFF/EXECUTIVE OFFICER

The executive officer is responsible for the coordination of all staff actions. The alternate name for this position, chief of staff, describes the primary function of this position. Executive officers complete the following actions:

- Formulate and announce staff operating procedures.
- Ensure the commander and staff are informed on matters affecting the command.
- Represent the commander when authorized.
- Ensure the commander's decisions are implemented.
- Maintain master policy file.
- Ensure liaison is established and maintained.
- Require all staff officers, unless instructed otherwise by the commander, to inform the executive officer of recommendations or information they give directly to the commander or instructions they receive directly from the commander.

ASSISTANT CHIEF OF STAFF/G1/S1

The G1/S1 is the principal officer for matters concerning human resources and has these responsibilities:

- Preparation of administrative plans, orders, and estimates.
- Maintenance of unit strengths.

- Replacement policies and requirements.
- Soldier support services.
- Safety and accident prevention.
- Discipline, law, and order.
- Headquarters management.
- Administrative support for other personnel, such as enemy prisoners of war, augmentees, and so forth.

ASSISTANT CHIEF OF STAFF/G2/S2

The G2/S2 is the principal staff officer for military intelligence matters. The G2/S2 is responsible for these activities:

- Production of intelligence.
  - Recommending priority intelligence requirements and information requirements.
  - Identifying requirements for target acquisition, surveillance, and reconnaissance.
  - Requesting, receiving, and processing information from other intelligence elements. Processing information into intelligence.
  - Supervising and coordinating the command's intelligence collection/target acquisition activities.
  - Conducting intelligence preparation of the battlefield.
  - Disseminating information.
- Counterintelligence.
- Intelligence training.

ASSISTANT CHIEF OF STAFF/G3/S3

The G3/S3 is the principal staff officer for operations, organization, and training and has these responsibilities:

- Recommend priorities for critical resources for the command, such as ammunition basic loads, allocation of nuclear and chemical ammunition, required supply needs, need for unit replacements, and so forth.
- Maintain a current operations estimate of the situation.
- Prepare operational plans and orders.
- Develop and maintain the troop basis.
- Estimate numbers and type units to be organized and equipped.
- Assign, attach, and detach units, detachments, or teams.
- Receive units, detachments, or teams and orient, train, and reorganize them.
- Process the Army authorization documents system reports and submit modified or recommended changes to TOEs.
- Conduct training:
  - Identify training requirements based on combat and garrison missions and training status of the unit.
  - Ensure that training requirements for combat rest on conditions and standards of combat, not on administrative convenience.
  - Prepare and carry out training programs, directives, and orders, and plan and conduct field exercises.

– Determine requirements for and allocation of training aids and facilities, including ammunition for training.
– Organize and conduct schools.
– Plan and conduct training inspections and tests.
– Compile training records and reports.
– Maintain the unit readiness status of each unit in the command.
– Plan the budget for training and monitor the use of training funds.

• Exercise staff supervision over psychological operations (PSYOPS).

• Incorporate electronic warfare into operational plans.

• Identify the command's operational security (OPSEC) and OPSEC support needs.

ASSISTANT CHIEF OF STAFF/G4/S4

The G4/S4 is the principal staff officer for logistics and is responsible for these activities:

• Supply requirements, requisitions, procurement, storage, distribution, accountability, and security.

• Maintenance, including monitoring and analyzing status, determining requirements, and recommending maintenance priorities.

• Transportation.

• Services, including facilities and installations, real estate, real property, food service, fire protection, and personal services.

ASSISTANT CHIEF OF STAFF/G5/S5

The ACofS/G5/S5 is the principal staff officer for the commander in all matters pertaining to civilian effects on military operations and the political, economic, and social effects of military operations on civilian personnel in the area of operations.

DIVISION MATERIEL MANAGEMENT CENTER

Materiel management centers (MMC) exist at all levels of command from separate brigade upward. This chapter, however, will discuss only the division materiel management center (DMMC) because it is typical of all MMCs in its functions and vital to the efficient operation of the division.

A division materiel management center (DMMC) provides materiel management for weapons systems, controls maintenance priorities, and coordinates and controls supply functions to meet the operational needs of its division. The center extends its management influence through liaison with the supporting and supported units organic to the Division.

In its role of management support, a DMMC does the following things:

• Advises the division support command (DISCOM) commander and staff on management of supply and maintenance operations.

• Prepares or reviews and approves detailed plans and policies for the operation of distribution points, quick service supply operations, direct exchange operations, self-service supply center operations, central issue facility, and other supply and maintenance operations. Coordinates this approval with, and in accordance with guidance received from, the DISCOM commander.

• Establishes coordination channels with higher echelon materiel management centers and takes action required in relation to evacuation of materiel, provision of backup support, emergency requirements, and technical assistance.

• Provides continuous evaluation, in coordination with assigned combat service support units, of supply and maintenance workload/capabilities of supported units.

• Develops and monitors authorized stockage lists of supplies and equipment maintained by combat service support units. Appropriate management elements of the materiel management center are responsible for the authorized stockage lists within their assigned classes of supply.

• Assists combat service support units, upon request, in the discharge of their responsibilities as they relate to supply and maintenance operations.

• Prepares and distributes directives concerning materiel management procedures when authorized by the DISCOM Commander. Makes direct contact with support operators on such matters as receipts, material release orders, inventories, input data for reports, and preparation and submission of requests. Although DISCOM headquarters retains authority for command directives relating to operational matters, refers command and logistics directives relating to division operations external to the support command to the division G4. Implements all directives through the normal chain of command.

• Places requirements on the division movement control center (DMCC) for transportation to support materiel missions.

• Provides for the receipt and processing of requisitions from combat service support units' activities.

• Develops and controls operational readiness float lists for selected equipment stored and maintained in the combat service support units.

• Coordinates with combat service support units for processing equipment before issue.

• Performs stock control (automated and manual) for items managed (the accountable officers are in the DMMC).

• Provides quality control for physical inventory and reconciliations of stock records.

• Provides catalog and technical document reference services.

• Maintains, with automated data processing (ADP) support, the Army equipment status reporting data.

• Maintains automated records on Classes II, III (packaged), IV, and IX supplies.

• Assists the division G4 in developing plans for purchasing and contracting service relating to supplies and services.

• Provides maintenance management information for maintenance units.

• Coordinates with the division G4 on all matters pertaining to the internal supply and maintenance support for the division.

• Publishes technical directives and information for the division commander routinely.

Within the DMMC the following personnel actually coordinate and manage the combat service support efforts of the division.

Division Materiel Management Officer

The division materiel management officer (DMMO) plans, directs, and supervises all center operations. The DMMO implements DISCOM managerial policies and prescribes procedures and mission performance standards in concurrence with appropriate interpretation of higher echelon policies. It is the DMMO's responsibility to ensure the completion of required recurring reports concerning center operations and the logistic system status of the division. The DMMO coordinates the interface between the divisional and supporting nondivisional combat service support units and assists the supported units in using the services of the support units. The DMMO is a primary advisor to the DISCOM commander and through the DISCOM commander to the division commander on the logistic status of the division.

General Supply Officer

The general supply officer (GSO) supervises and controls the Class I, II, III, IV, VI, and VII management elements of the DMMC. In this capacity, the GSO exercises manual stock control over all the supply assets of the division in these classes, including water and Class VI free issue supplies. It is the GMO's responsibility to monitor division requirements in each commodity that he or she manages and determine appropriate basic load quantities. The GSO advises and coordinates with the divisional support units to receive, store, and distribute supplies to requesting units. In the case of controlled or scarce resources, the GSO advises the DMMO and the DISCOM commander on indicated allocation quantities to each unit and also develops contingency plans and load data to prevent critical shortages at times of great demand. The GSO is also responsible for the coordination of the turn-in of all major items of equipment.

Division Ammunition Officer

The division ammunition officer (DAO) serves as the chief of the Class V section of the DMMC. The DAO represents the DISCOM commander in all matters concerning ammunition and ammunition supply operations. This officer assists the G3 and the G4 in establishing required supply rates (RSRs) and checks the RSRs against the established controlled supply rates (CSRs) established by higher headquarters. The DAO's section provides ammunition expenditure data to the division for planning and management purposes. The DAO computes and develops basic load data for the division based on weapon density and supervises and directs the ammunition transfer points (ATPs) to maintain those basic load quantities while providing adequate support to the combat units.

Division Property Book Officer

The property book officer supervises and controls the property book and assets accounting section of division materiel management centers. This officer ensures that the authorized property of the division is accounted for and further ensures that all units are equipped in accordance with their assigned Table of Organization and Equipment. The property book officer manages the hand receipt accounts for the division's units, as well as procedures for requesting and turn-in of organization and installation property. The property book branch also processes reports of survey, statements of charges, and similar documents for the adjustment of accountable property.

Division Maintenance Management Officer

The division maintenance management officer supervises and controls the efforts of the maintenance management section of the DMMC. This section is the primary centralized management activity for the overall maintenance system within the division. This officer assists the units of the division in planning, reporting, compiling, and interpreting maintenance data to provide the basis for sound management decisions at every level of the command. The data analyzed and organized by his section include both organizational and direct support functions. The maintenance management officer therefore actually has staff supervision of the maintenance reporting system in the division. With his or her view of the maintenance status of the units, this officer identifies trends and problem areas and recommends support actions to correct systemic problems. It is his or her responsibility to monitor the readiness of critical weapons systems and critical equipment and to compile the reported materiel readiness analysis for the division. This officer assists all levels of command in the formulation of policies and procedures concerning maintenance operations and develops support concepts and plans for tactical operations. The division maintenance management officer coordinates maintenance support plans with both the supported and the supporting units and assists them in executing effective maintenance operations.

Division Class IX Officer

The division Class IX officer is the officer in charge of the DMMC Class IX section. It is this officer's responsibility to manage and control the automated Class IX system for the division. Like the maintenance management officer, the division class IX deals mostly with information from unit reports and automated stock status reports, using a continuous flow of raw data to appraise repair parts supply operations in the division. The Class IX section maintains liaison with all supporting agencies and units involved in providing repair parts and major assemblies to the units of the division.

The Class IX officer collects data to analyze trends and identify systemic problems within the Class IX system as well as isolating exceptional problems occurring within particular divisional units. The Class IX section acts as the central processing point for all repair parts requests from units within the division. These requests are received from the requesting units by the direct support units of the division who then batch them and carry them to the Class IX section. By receiving all requests and managing the automated supply system, the Class IX section has the required demand history to develop and maintain stock status data on all authorized stockage lists (ASLs) in the division and to monitor and supervise the establishment of stockage levels in individual unit prescribed load lists (PLLs). In addition, this section uses stock status reports, daily transaction registers, daily error and edit transaction listings, and supply management reports to monitor and adjust inventory quantity levels as appropriate for efficient and responsive repair parts support in the division.

OTHER LOGISTICS POSITIONS

Many other logistics positions in the combat service support system are not in the DMMC. An explanation of the duties and responsibilities of some of these positions follows:

Movement Control Officer

The movement control officer (MCO) is assigned to the DISCOM Headquarters. The MCO controls employment of motor transport assets for logistic operations within the division area and coordinates transportation policies with the division transportation officer. All transportation users in the division area forward requirements for transportation to the MCO. Requirements generated in the brigade support areas are usually consolidated by the forward area support coordinating officer (FASCO) or the support operations officer of the forward support battalions for submission to the MCO.

Division Transportation Officer

The division transportation officer (DTO) is a part of the division commander's staff. The DTO is responsible to the G3 for coordination of all transport requirements in support of tactical troop movement and works with the G4 on logistic and administrative transportation requirements. This officer is the communication/coordination link between the division and the corps support command movement control center (MCC). The DTO gives the movement control officer (MCO) broad policy guidance, basic plans and policies, and staff supervisory assistance in transportation matters concerning both air and surface transportation.

Support Operations Officer

The support operations officer is a primary staff officer in both forward support battalions and main support battalions of heavy divisions (infantry, armor, and mechanized infantry). It is his responsibility to provide staff supervision, management, and coordination of the combat service support mission of his multifunctional battalion. This supervision includes the allocation of support resources to supported units in accordance with command priorities. The support operations officer maintains liaison with supported units and analyzes mission performance and mission requirements by monitoring logistics reports and through direct coordination. This officer provides mission status reports to his battalion commander and through him to the supported unit commanders. It is also this officer's responsibility to coordinate with the DISCOM staff support requirements that are beyond the capability of his battalion. Higher or adjacent combat service support units must meet these requirements.

Forward Area Support Coordinating Officer

Forward support coordinating officers (FASCOs) are assigned to the DISCOM of light divisions (light infantry, airborne, air assault). There is one designated FASCO for each brigade whose primary responsibility is to coordinate combat service support efforts between the brigade executive officer and the DISCOM units located in the brigade support area (BSA). This officer maintains communications with the DISCOM headquarters and identifies problem areas requiring support beyond the capabilities of DISCOM units within the BSA. He or she monitors tactical operations of the brigade and ensures that DISCOM units are kept informed of possible mission effects while assisting the DISCOM headquarters in maintaining an accurate picture of the situation. As a result of this officer's mission analysis, he or she advises the DISCOM Headquarters of recommended changes and adjustments to the strength and composition of the forward DISCOM units supporting his or her brigade. In addition to other duties, the FASCO also coordinates the security activities of forward DISCOM elements within the BSA and advises and assists the brigade executive officer and the S4 in the selection of appropriate operational sites for the combat service support in the BSA.

Technical Supply Officer

Technical supply officers (TSOs) are assigned to every direct support or general support maintenance company having a Class IX supply activity. The TSO is responsible for the supervision of the Class IX activity and oversees the receipt, storage, and issue of repair parts and major assemblies, as well as direct exchange items. This officer also normally supervises the turn-in and identification of excess repair parts items from customer units. In nondivisional units, the TSO usually controls the repair parts supply system through an automated stock control system managed within an automatic data processing section organic to his unit. In divisional units, the TSO batches and delivers all requests to the Class IX section of the DMMC and receives material release orders (MROs) from DMMC to issue items to fill those requests. Direct coordination between the TSO and the DMMC is essential.

Materiel Officer

The position of materiel officer is in the maintenance battalions of light divisions (airborne, air assault, light infantry) and in nondivisional maintenance battalions. This officer's primary function is the management of the maintenance support mission and all support operations. The materiel officer allocates resources for all operations in accordance with command guidance and his or her own estimate of the situation. This officer plans and coordinates the organization of all operations with subordinate shop officers and acts as the primary operator of the direct support maintenance system.

Automation Management Officer

The automation management officer works in the division headquarters group under the supervision of the division G1. This officer acts as the primary advisor on all automatic data processing (ADP) matters affecting the command. It is his or her responsibility to provide staff supervision for the data processing unit within the division and to manage the Army standard data systems employed by the division.

The Division Surgeon

The division surgeon advises and assists the division commander in conserving the fighting strength of the division through preventive, curative, and restorative care and related services. He or she determines requirements for the requisition, storage, maintenance, and distribution of medical, dental, optic, and veterinary equipment and supplies. This officer recommends the unit assignment of all medical personnel coming into the division and coordinates the medical training requirements within the division. He or she oversees and coordinates treatment services, dental services, veterinary services, preventive medicine services, medical laboratory services, medical supply operations, medical civic action, casualty reporting from the medical units, assignment of medical units, and allocation of medical capabilities.

Veterinary Officer

The veterinary officer coordinates and works under the supervision of the command surgeon, advising the command surgeon on matters concerning the procurement, storage, and care of animals used by military units. The veterinarian is responsible for the inspection of all food items being delivered to the command and the inspection of food preparation and storage areas, including transport procedures. It is the responsibility of the veterinary service to ensure that an effective preventive medicine program is in effect to prevent the spread of communicable diseases from animals or food products.

Division Engineer

The division engineer commands the engineer battalion organic to the division, and the brigade engineer normally commands the engineer company attached to the individual brigade. In either case, they are the senior engineer officers within the command. It is their responsibility to determine the engineer support requirements and the Class IV requirements for the operations of the supported units. They plan and execute all activities supporting mobility of friendly forces, countermobility of enemy forces, survivability of friendly elements through the construction of fortifications, general engineering requirements, such as bridging, construction, and mine clearing operations, and topographical analysis. The division or brigade engineer prepares the engineer portion of all plans and orders, allocating appropriate resources to aid organic units in area damage control operations as they produce engineering requirements.

12

Weapons System Replacement Operations

The concept presented in this chapter is the most challenging function of the combat service support system and requires intense coordination among all levels of support. The weapons system replacement process incorporates every technique, uses all elements of data, and requires the professional use of every tactical and logistic tool available to the logistician for successful completion.

Weapon system replacement procedures provide combat ready assets to the combat commander instead of simply resupplying parts, pieces, and materials. A howitzer or a tank is, after all, just a piece of steel unless it is fueled, armed, manned, and equipped with all the accoutrements necessary for its use. Weapons systems replacement operations (WSRO) identifies each end item as an operating element instead of a stack of components. The following terms are keys to this concept.

• *Ready-for-issue weapon.* A weapon, such as a tank, howitzer, or armored personnel carrier, has been taken from its storage area or its source. It has been fueled and equipped with all of its basic issue items, but they are still packed in boxes on board. All components have been mounted (fire control, machine guns, radios), and ammunition has been loaded in the bulk issue pack.

• *Ready-to-fight weapon system.* A completely processed weapon with fuel, ammunition, all equipment properly mounted/stowed, all basic issue items ready for use, and the crew aboard. Completely processed also means that systems have been zeroed or synchronized and that the crew has been trained.

• *Link-up.* Process required to render a ready-for-issue weapon into a ready-to-fight weapon system.

The key to this concept is proper and complete coordination to enable all levels of support and the requesting unit to jointly manage weapons systems. Not only do the CSS units need to understand the requirements of producing ready-to-fight weapon systems, but also the battlefield reporting system has to be effectively used by all units to provide data on the status of all assets at all locations. To properly support the battlefield, the reporting system must also accurately reveal the strengths and weaknesses of all units so that combat power can be replaced or rebuilt to meet the most critical needs of the forces engaged.

Within each division, the actual procedures used to employ WSRO must be tailored to meet the individual needs of the units and the situation. The basic process, however, remains the same regardless of location or unit. The common factor is the requirement to assign at each level command a weapons systems manager (WSM) charged with weapon system management. This officer's mission is to increase the number of functional weapon systems in the battalions selected by operational necessity or command priorities.

Within the battalion task force, the battalion commander normally designates the battalion executive officer (XO) as the WSM for the battalion. The XO coordinates the efforts of the S1, the S4, and all other combat service supporters. He allocates weapons systems to the companies with the aid of both the S1 and the S4, using the information gathered from the current situation reports received from the companies. The data derived is divided into three areas: command information, logistical information, and personnel information. The command information goes immediately to the battalion commander. The vital information in the other two categories is analyzed in detail and passed to the division support command (DISCOM), the brigade S4, the brigade S1, and the division adjudant general (AG), as appropriate.

At brigade level, the commander normally assigns the brigade XO as the WSM. Because, however, brigades maintain a headquarters that influences combat power primarily through task organization, weapons systems are not directly allocated at the brigade level. Instead of allocating weapons systems, the brigade WSM puts his greatest WSRO effort into monitoring the weapon systems status of the subordinate battalions and ensuring that the data forwarded to higher levels is accurate and current.

The division level of WSRO allocates replacement weapons systems directly to battalions in accordance with command guidance and reported critical shortages. The DISCOM commander will assign an WSM to the DMMC as a permanent position. This officer must possess primary skills in both maintenance and supply operations. The division AG will designate an individual or individuals from the personnel management activity as responsible for coordinating and providing crew member or entire crew replacements. The WSM must maintain current status information on the weapons systems in the units, the availability of crews and crew replacements, and equipment available for issue or due-in. The sources of crew replacements and equipment are new replacements, repaired equipment, and personnel returning from medical units. The WSM monitors available weapons or crews within units caused either by crew survival or individual casualties. This is another source of equipment and personnel. No possible source of personnel or idle equipment should be wasted or ignored.

As indicated by the discussion so far, accurate and timely status information is essential to WSRO. The battalion WSM must identify and report the needs of his battalion to the brigade WSM very quickly. He, in turn, must report this information as rapidly as possible to the division WSM. The division WSM must then consolidate this report with the other supported unit reports and forward the division requirements back to the corps. To ease the rapid action required to provide adequate support, all status reports within WSRO will serve as requisitions for shortages. This automatic requisitioning must be applied to prevent duplication of effort and inefficient use of management time in repetitive reporting systems. Simultaneously, the establishment of a requisition for an end item should generate all required requests for ancillary equipment, basic issue items, ammunition, and fuel.

Personnel replacements and resupplied equipment arrive at the rear of the theater and are transported forward by the most expeditious method. On the way forward, the equipment is processed as rapidly as possible by corps support units. This processing includes the installation of fire control equipment, radios, machine guns, and the filling of fuel tanks to bring equipment up to a ready-for-issue status. At the DISCOM, the primary link-up occurs at the Class VII supply point. The crew is assigned to the equipment and completes its transformation into a ready-to-fight weapon system. The DISCOM must provide facilities for boresighting, zeroing, synchronization, and arming the weapon system. Complete ready-to-fight weapon systems are usually driven from the division support area (DSA) to the unit under their own power or by their own assigned prime mover.

It may be necessary for the weapon system to be prepared and moved forward with only a partial crew. This method should, however, be the exception, and only complete weapon systems should move forward of the DSA. The crew members available within the receiving battalion should be closely monitored by the WSM, and available crew members are moved to the DSA to prepare their equipment. This crew preparation must be done with equipment being repaired, as well as with resupplied equipment. Crew members who otherwise would not be effectively used in the unit may be moved to the DS support unit to rearm and prepare their own system immediately, while it is being repaired.

Within the DSA, the AG replacement detachment, the Class VII issue facility, and the maintenance activities should all be closely located to ease dependable and rapid coordination. The process of WSRO is continuous. The DMMC will be notified when assets are being delivered to the division by a specific corps unit. In accordance with local procedures, the DMMC notifies the Class VII supply activity, the maintenance activity and the replacement detachment. Simultaneously, the DMMC alerts the FASCO or the support operations officer of the appropriate brigade to allow for their planning. The WSM checks the reported status of the receiving unit to ensure that crew members are available. He advises the personnel manager of any known shortages. The personnel manager coordinates with the replacement detachment and has required replacements placed on standby, available for pickup by the receiving unit. The WSM, through the DISCOM, then notifies the FASCO or support operations officer to have crew members from the receiving unit report to the Class VII activity and to pick up replacement crewmembers from the replacement detachment. The unit crew members, the replacement crew members, and the equipment come together at the Class VII activity and link-up begins. The crew stows the basic issue items and loads ammunition. Then they boresight, zero, or synchronize the weapon as applicable. The Class VII activity notifies the DMMC property book section of the link-up for proper accountability. When link-up has been completed, the ready-to-fight weapon system is dispatched with receiving unit guides to proceed directly to its unit.

In summary, battle loss information is passed from battalion to brigade to DMMC and constitutes a request for replacement. The DMMC requests the replacement equipment from corps level and immediately identifies the quickest source of replacement. When a replacement system is obtained, whether from maintenance or from resupply, a crew is identified and moved to meet the equipment at the Class VII activity in the DSA. This crew can come from the unit or from the replacement detachment in the DSA, or both. The crew completes the stowage of basic issue items, loads the ammunition, completes all operational checks with assistance from the DS maintenance unit (as required), and boresights and zeros the weapon. The property book section makes applicable account entries, and the DMMC coordinates the movement of the weapon system forward. The ready-to-fight weapon system then moves forward to its receiving unit.

Weapons system replacement operations is the most difficult single support concept in combat service support. It requires the efforts of every element of the logistic system to complete the delivery of ready-to-fight weapons systems to the combat units effectively. In future combat situations, WSRO will be a vital part of success on the battlefield.

Appendix

Which Regulation?

This list of publications provides a quick reference for logisticians to find more information on specific subjects. It is not a complete listing of every regulation or field manual published by the U.S. Army, but it does reflect a good cross-section of the references logisticians in the field most often use. (Get out your microfiche reader, and see the latest quarterly edition of DA PAM 25-30 for the latest changes, revisions, and supersessions of any Army publications you may need, especially now that UPDATE publications are replacing and consolidating older publications. Your publication clerk should be able to help you find or order the publications you need.)

ARMY REGULATIONS

AR 10-5	*Organization and Functions—Department of the Army*
AR 11-12	*Logistic Priorities*
AR 30-1	*Army Food Service Program*
AR 30-7	*Operational Rations*
AR 30-12	*Inspection of Subsistence Supplies and Services*
AR 30-18	*Army Troop Issue Subsistence Activity Operating Procedures*
AR 40-13	*Medical Support Nuclear/Chemical Accidents and Incidents*
AR 40-61	*Medical Logistics Policies and Procedures*
AR 40-538	*Property Management During Patient Evacuation*
AR 40-905	*Veterinary Health Services*
AR 55-1	*CONEX/MILVAN Equipment Control, Utilization, and Reporting*
AR 55-29	*Military Convoy Operations in CONUS*
AR 55-113	*Movements of Units Within CONUS*
AR 58-1	*Management, Acquisition, and Use of Administrative Use Vehicles*
AR 59-11	*Army Use of Logistic Airlift*
AR 75-15	*Responsibilities and Procedures for Explosive Ordnance Disposal*
AR 115-10	*Meteorological Support for the U.S. Army*
AR 140-1	*Army Reserve Mission, Organization, and Training*
AR 140-15	*Maintenance of Equipment*
AR 190-13	*The Army Physical Security Program*
AR 220-1	*Unit Status Reporting*
AR 220-10	*Preparation of Overseas Movement of Units (POM)*
AR 220-15	*Journals and Journal Files*
AR 310-25	*Dictionary of U.S. Army Terms*

AR 310-50	*Authorized Abbreviations and Brevity Codes*
AR 340-1	*Records Management Program*
AR 340-15	*Preparing and Managing Correspondence*
AR 350-9	*Reserve Component Deployment Training with CONUS Commands*
AR 350-10	*Management of Individual Training Requirements and Resources*
AR 350-15	*The Army Physical Fitness Program*
AR 380-5	*Department of the Army Information Security Program Regulation*
AR 381-12	*Subversion and Espionage Directed Against the Army*
AR 381-26	*Army Foreign Materiel Exploitation Program*
AR 385-32	*Protective Clothing and Equipment*
AR 385-40	*Accident Reporting and Records*
AR 385-64	*Ammunition and Explosives Safety Standards*
AR 500-10	*Nonindustrial Facilities for Mobilization*
AR 500-60	*Disaster Relief*
AR 530-1	*Operations Security*
AR 600-38	*Meal Card Management System*
AR 612-2	*Preparation of Replacements for Overseas Movement (POR)*
AR 638-30	*Graves Registration and Functions in Support of Major Military Operations*
AR 680-1	*Unit Strength Accounting and Reporting*
AR 700-9	*Policies of the Army Logistics System*
AR 700-22	*Worldwide Ammunition Reporting System*
AR 700-23	*Supply of Health and Comfort Items*
AR 700-127, WC/1	*Integrated Logistic Support*
AR 700-135	*Mobile Field Laundry and Bath Operations*
AR 700-138	*Army Logistics Readiness and Sustainability*
AR 703-1	*Coal and Petroleum Products Supply and Management Activities*
AR 710-2	*Supply Policy Below the Wholesale Level*
AR 750-1	*Army Materiel Maintenance Policies*
AR 795-3	*Logistics Planning for the United States and the Federal Republic of Germany*

UPDATE REFERENCES

UPDATE 2-11	*Unit Supply Handbook*
UPDATE 3-10	*Maintenance Management Handbook*
UPDATE 5-12	*All Ranks Personnel Handbook*
UPDATE 6-12	*Officer Ranks Personnel Handbook*

DEPARTMENT OF THE ARMY PAMPHLETS

DA Pam 25-30	*Consolidated Index of Army Publications and Blank Forms*

DA Pam 310–35	*Index of International Standardization Agreements*

FIELD MANUALS

FM 3–3	*NBC Contamination Avoidance*
FM 3–5	*NBC Decontamination*
FM 3–100	*NBC Operations*
FM 5–20	*Camouflage*
FM 5–100	*Engineer Combat Operations*
FM 6–20	*Fire Support in the AirLand Battle*
FM 7–10	*The Infantry Rifle Company (Infantry, Airborne, Air Assault, Ranger)*
FM 7–20	*The Infantry Battalion (Infantry, Airborne, and Air Assault)*
FM 7–30	*Infantry, Airborne, and Air Assault Brigade Operations*
FM 8–15	*Medical Support in Divisions, Separate Brigades, and the Armored Cavalry Regiment*
FM 8–35	*Evacuation of Sick and Wounded*
FM 8–55	*Planning for Health Service Support*
FM 9–13	*Ammunition Handbook*
FM 10–14	*Unit Supply Operations*
FM 10–14–2	*Guide for the Battalion S4*
FM 10–23	*Army Food Service Operations*
FM 10–24	*Ration Distribution Operations*
FM 10–52	*Field Water Supply*
FM 10–63	*Handling of Deceased Personnel in Theaters of Operation*
FM 10–63–1	*Graves Registration Handbook*
FM 10–69	*Petroleum Supply Point Operations and Equipment*
FM 10–71	*Petroleum Tank Vehicle Operations*
FM 10–280	*Mobile Field Laundry, Clothing Exchange, and Bath Operation*
FM 11–50	*Combat Communications Within the Division (How to Fight)*
FM 11–92	*Combat Communications Within the Corps (How to Fight)*
FM 12–15	*Wartime Casualty Reporting*
FM 17–95	*Cavalry Operations*
FM 19–1	*Military Police Support for the AirLand Battle*
FM 19–4	*Military Police, Team, Squad, Platoon Combat Operations*
FM 19–10	*Military Police Law and Order Operations*
FM 19–30	*Physical Security*
FM 20–22	*Vehicle Recovery Operations*
FM 21–10	*Field Hygiene and Sanitation*
FM 21–20	*Physical Fitness Training*
FM 21–31	*Topographic Symbols*

FM 21–75	*Combat Skills of the Soldier*
FM 22–9	*Soldier Performance in Continuous Operations*
FM 24–1	*Combat Communications*
FM 25–1	*Training*
FM 25–2	*Unit Training Management*
FM 27–10	*The Law of Land Warfare*
FM 29–2	*Organizational Maintenance Operations*
FM 29–12	*Division Maintenance Operations*
FM 29–52	*Supply and Service Operations in Separate Brigades and the Armored Cavalry Regiment*
FM 33–1	*Psychological Operations*
FM 34–10	*Division Intelligence and Electronic Warfare Operations*
FM 38–725–1	*Direct Support System (DSS) Commanders Handbook*
FM 41–10	*Civil Affairs Operations*
FM 43–11	*Intermediate Maintenance Operations (Direct Support)*
FM 44–1	*U.S. Army Air Defense Artillery Employment*
FM 44–1-2	*Air Defense Artillery Reference Handbook*
FM 44–3	*Air Defense Artillery Employment: Chaparral/Vulcan/Stinger*
FM 44–90	*Hawk Battalion Operations*
FM 54–23	*Materiel Management Center, Corps Support Command*
FM 54–40	*Area Support Group*
FM 55–2	*Division Transportation Operations*
FM 55–10	*Movement Control in a Theater of Operations*
FM 55–12	*Movement of Units in Air Force Aircraft*
FM 55–15	*Transportation Reference Data*
FM 55–40	*Army Combat Service Support Air Transport Operations*
FM 55–65	*Preparation for Unit Movement Overseas by Surface Transportation*
FM 63–1	*Combat Service Support Operations in a Separate Brigade*
FM 63–2	*Combat Service Support—Division (How to Support)*
FM 63–2–2	*Combat Service Support Operations: Armored, Mechanized, and Motorized Divisions*
FM 63–3	*Combat Service Support Operations—Corps (How to Support)*
FM 63–20	*Forward Support Battalion*
FM 63–21	*Main Support Battalion, Armored, Mechanized, and Motorized Divisions (SPT Main)*
FM 71–1	*The Tank and Mechanized Infantry Company Team (How to Fight)*
FM 71–2	*The Tank and Mechanized Battalion Task Force (How to Fight)*
FM 71–3	*Armored and Mechanized Infantry Brigade*

FM 71–100	*Armored and Mechanized Division Operations (How to Fight)*
FM 90–3	*Desert Operations (How to Fight)*
FM 90–10	*Military Operations in Urbanized Terrain (MOUT) (How to Fight)*
FM 90–13	*River Crossing Operations (How to Fight)*
FM 90–14	*Rear Battle*
FM 100–1	*The Army*
FM 100–5	*Operations*
FM 100–10	*Combat Service Support*
FM 100–15 (Test)	*Larger Unit Operations*
FM 100–20	*Low Intensity Conflict*
FM 100–26	*The Air-Ground Operations System*
FM 101–5	*Staff Organization and Operations*
FM 101–5–1	*Operational Terms and Symbols*
FM 101–10–1/1	*Staff Officers' Field Manual: Organizational, Technical, and Logistical Data (Volume 1)*
FM 101–10–½	*Staff Officers' Field Manual: Organizational, Technical, and Logistical Data Planning Factors (Volume 2)*
FM 101–10–2	*Staff Officers' Field Manual: Organizational, Technical, and Logistical Data, Extracts of Nondivisional Tables of Organization and Equipment*
FM 101–31–1	*Staff Officers' Field Manual: Nuclear Weapons Employment Doctrine and Procedures*

TRAINING CIRCULARS

TC24–18	*Communications in a "Come-as-You-Are" War*
TC34–50	*Reconnaissance and Surveillance Handbook*
TC25–1	*Unit Training Land Requirements*
TC25–5	*Unit Learning Centers*

ADDITIONAL IMPORTANT REFERENCES

AAP–4	*NATO Standardization Agreements and Allied Publications*
AAP–6	*NATO Glossary of Terms and Definitions for Military Use*

INTERNATIONAL STANDARDIZATION AGREEMENTS

STANAG 2002	*Marking of Contaminated or Dangerous Land Areas, Complete Equipment, Supplies and Stores (ABCA STANAG 124)*
STANAG 2003	*Patrol Reports by Army Forces (ABCA STANAG GR)*
STANAG 2008	*Bombing, Shelling, Mortaring, and Location Reports*
STANAG 2010	*Bridge Classification Markings*
STANAG 2019	*Military Symbols (ABCA/QSTAG 508)*
STANAG 2020	*Operational Situation Reports*

STANAG 2021 *Computation of Bridge, Raft, and Vehicle Classification*
STANAG 2025 *Basic Military Road Traffic Regulations*
STANAG 2029 *Method of Describing Ground Locations, Areas, and Boundaries*
STANAG 2033 *Interrogation of Prisoners of War (PW)*
STANAG 2034 *Ammunition Supply Procedures (ABCA/QSTAF 516)*
STANAG 2035 *Marking of Headquarters and Dumps*
STANAG 2036 *Land Minefield Laying, Marking, Recording, and Reporting Procedures (ABCA/QSTAF 518)*
STANAG 2041 *Operation Orders, Tables, and Graphs for Road Movement*
STANAG 2044 *Procedures for Dealing with Prisoners of War (PW)*
STANAG 2047 *Emergency Alarms of Hazard or Attack (NBC and Air Attack Only)*
STANAG 2067 *Straggler Control*
STANAG 2070 *Emergency War Burial Procedures*
STANAG 2079 *Rear Area Security and Rear Area Damage Control*
STANAG 2082 *Relief of Combat Troops*
STANAG 2083 *Commanders Guide on Radiation Exposure*
STANAG 2084 *Handling and Reporting of Captured Enemy Equipment and Documents*
STANAG 2101 *Principles and Procedures for Establishing Liaison*
STANAG 2103 *Reporting Nuclear Detonations, Radioactive Fallout, Biological and Chemical Attacks, and Predicting Associated Hazards*
STANAG 2104 *Friendly Nuclear Strike Warning to Armed Forces Operating on Land*
STANAG 2113 *Destruction of Military Technical Equipment*
STANAG 2129 *Recognition and Identification of Forces on the Battlefield*
STANAG 2133 *Vulnerability Assessment of Chemical and Biological Hazards*
STANAG 2135 *Procedures for Requesting and Providing Logistics Assistance*
STANAG 2136 *Minimum Standards of Water Potability*
STANAG 2143 *Explosive Ordnance Reconnaissance/Explosive Ordnance Disposal (EOR/EOD)*
STANAG 2144 *Call for Fire Procedures*
STANAG 2150 *NATO Standards for Proficiency for NBC Defense*
STANAG 2154 *Regulations for Military Motor Vehicle Movement by Road*
STANAG 2155 *Road Movement Documents*
STANAG 2156 *Surface Transportation Request and Reply to Surface Transportation Request*
STANAG 2165 *Forecast Movement Requirements—Rail, Road, and Inland Waterways*

STANAG 2174	*Military Routes and Route/Road Networks*
STANAG 2868	*Land Force Tactical Doctrine (ATP-35)*
STANAG 3204	*Aeromedical Evacuation*
STANAG 3345	*Data/Forms for Planning Air Movements*
STANAG 3427	*Colors for the Identification of Airdropped Supplies*
STANAG 3428	*Exchange of Information on Aerial Delivery Systems*
STANAG 3463	*Planning Procedures for Tactical Air Transport Operations for Fixed-Wing Aircraft*
STANAG 3466	*Responsibilities of Air Transport Units and User Units in the Loading and Unloading of Transport Aircraft in Tactical Air Transport Operations*
STANAG 3570	*Drop Zones and Extraction Zones—Criteria and Markings*
STANAG 3597	*Helicopter Tactical and Nonpermanent Landing Sites*
STANAG 3628	*Helicopter Tactical Refueling*

Glossary

Selected Acronyms and Abbreviations

ACR	armored cavalry regiment
ACCB	air cavalry combat brigade
ADP	automated data processing
AG	adjutant general
AME	airspace management element
AMTF	airmobile task force
APC	armored personnel carrier
ARAAV	armored reconnaissance airborne assault vehicle
ARTEP	Army Readiness Training Evaluation Program
ASL	authorized stockage list
ASP	ammunition supply point
ATP	ammunition transfer point
BAI	battlefield air interdiction
BAS	battalion aid station
BBL	barrels
BSA	brigade support area
CB	citizens band
CEOI	communications electronics operating instructions
CFL	coordinated fire line
CIC	content indicator code
COMINT	communication intelligence
COSCOM	corps support command
CP	command post
CSR	controlled supply rate
CSS	combat service support
CTOC	corps tactical operations center
DAO	division ammunition officer
DF	disposition form
DISCOM	division support command
DMCC	division movement control center
DMMC	division materiel management center
DMMO	division materiel management officer
DOS	day of supply
DSA	division support area
DS	direct support
DTO	division transportation officer

EDRE	emergency deployment readiness exercise
ELINT	electronic intelligence
EW	electronic warfare
EXTAL	extra time allowance
FARP	forward area rearm/refuel point
FASCO	forward area support coordinator
FAST	forward area support team
FCL	final coordination line
FEBA	forward edge of the battle area
FFA	free fire area
FIST	fire support team
FLOT	forward line of own troops
FM	frequency modulation
FPF	final protective fire
FPL	final protective line
FRAGO	fragmentary order
FSB	forward support battalion
FSCL	fire support coordination line
FSCOORD	fire support coordinator
FSE	fire support element
FSOP	field standing operating procedures
FTX	field training exercise
GMT	Greenwich mean time
GRREG	graves registration
GSO	general supply officer
GSR	general support reinforcing
HET	heavy equipment transporter
KMIH	kilometers in the hour
KPH	kilometers per hour
LC	line of contact
LD	line of departure
LMF	language media format
LOC	lines of communication
LP	listening post
LTON	long ton
MBA	main battle area
MCC	movement control center
MCO	movement control officer
MEDSOM	medical supply, optical, and maintenance unit
MIH	miles in the hour
MMC	materiel management center
MOPP	mission-oriented protective posture
MOS	military occupational specialty
MOUT	military operations on urbanized terrain
MRO	materiel release order
MSB	main support battalion
MSD	minimum safe distance
MSR	main supply route

NBC	nuclear, biological, and chemical warfare
OP	observation post
OPSEC	operational security
OPORD	operations order
PDF	primary direction of fire
PL	phase line
PLA	plain language addressee
PLL	prescribed load list
PMCS	preventative maintenance checks and services
POL	petroleum, oils, and lubricants
PP	passage point
PSYOPS	psychological operations
R	reinforcing
RACO	rear area combat operations
RDF	radio direction finding
RFA	restrictive fire area
RFL	restrictive fire line
ROMADS	radio operators and drivers
RP	release point
RSR	required supply rate
SALUTE	size, activity, location, unit/uniform, time, equipment
SCORES	Scenario-Oriented Recurring Evaluation System
SEAD	suppression of enemy air defense
SHD	special handling designator
SIGINT	signal intelligence
SIGSEC	signal security
SLAR	side-looking airborne radar
SOP	standing operating procedures
SP	strongpoint; startpoint
SPECAT	special category
SQT	skill qualification test
STON	short ton
TACC	tactical air control center
TACE	tactical air coordination element
TACP	tactical air control party
TACS	tactical air control system
TDIS	time distance
TELINT	telemetry intelligence
TOC	tactical operations center
TOE	Table of Organization and Equipment
TOT	time on target
TRP	target reference point
TSO	technical supply officer
VPKM	vehicles per kilometer
VPM	vehicles per mile
WSM	weapon systems manager
WSRO	weapon systems replacement operations
XO	executive officer

Index